Endorsements

Cricket and Conquest is simply the finest book ev
It should sit alongside the works of CLR James an
every cricket lover. For the first time, Odendaal, Red   ... tell the complete
and unvarnished story of South African cricket: black and white and people called coloured,
male and female. They have left no archive unexamined and no story unscrutinised in their
quest for the truth. This book is not only a major work of scholarship, it is a work of
passion: for cricket, for social justice and for a history that includes all those who ever
swung a bat or bowled a ball.
**Prof Tony Collins, former Director of the International Centre for Sports History and
Culture at De Montfort University, author of** *A Social History of English Rugby Union* **and
three times winner of the Lord Aberdare Literary Prize for Sports History book of the year.**

Cricket and Conquest bowls over prevailing histories, de-colonising existing narratives of
the game in a manner that does not seek to consolidate an innings, but opens up the field
of study. A book that covers a broad canvas, but when there are master craftsmen at the
wicket, refusing to get bogged down, throwing all that came before into a spin, you read,
with boyhood anticipation and wonder, knowing that what was will never be the same.
As the title implies, the Gatling gun came with the cricket bat. Did those subalterns who
picked up a bat confront or collaborate with conquest? The writers' approach to this issue,
by showing the interconnectedness of white and black cricket, by turning boundaries inside
out, makes for fascinating reading.
Prof Ashwin Desai, University of Johannesburg and author of *A Reverse Sweep: A story of
South African Cricket since Apartheid* **(forthcoming).**

Some books scream out to be written, but often they remain undone because of the difficulty of the task. Here is something immensely important and satisfying - the story of South
African cricket, told at last with both eyes open. It is an expiation of a long and shameful
story: how the game which prides itself on fair play collaborated with cruelty, not just for
a while but for decade after decade. And persuaded itself that most of this history did not
exist. It's beautifully done as well.
Matthew Engel, Editor of Wisden, 1993–2000, 2003–2007.

Magnificent. A grand narrative, superb in its design and execution, busting the myth that
South Africa's cricket history was merely a white man's story. Set against a background of
imperial greed and military savagery in the high days of the British Empire it reveals how,
after promising beginnings, black cricketers were excluded from the game at the same time
as the hopes and dreams of their people for full citizenry were progressively dashed. This
book is one the authors lived to write. Revisionist history at its best.
Dr Bernard Whimpress, author of *Passport to Nowhere: Aborigines in Australian Cricket
1850–1913* **and co-author of** *The History of Australian Cricket.*

Cricket and Conquest will set new standards in sports scholarship around the world. The authors have broken new ground at every turn of the project. Breaking down the uniform singular narrative of cricket's initiation in South Africa as part of the colonial mission and introducing resistance and indigenous subversion into the mix from the earliest days, this book should encourage researchers from across the world to look at their own established cricket narratives in an entirely new light.

Dr Boria Majumdar, author of *Twenty-Two Yards to Freedom: A social history of Indian Cricket* and co-author, with Sachin Tendulkar, of the bestselling *Playing it My Way: My Autobiography*.

Against a backdrop which is sexist and increasingly racist, the local black populations and women of diverse heritages are in this story active participants in the early globalisation of the (white) 'gentleman's' game. The book and the series when completed will provide a comprehensive and intersectional history of the game in South Africa. A painstakingly constructed and detailed story which gives new life to CLR James's famous statement 'what do they know of cricket who only cricket know'.

Rhoda Reddock, Professor of Gender, Social Change and Development, the University of the West Indies, St. Augustine Campus, Trinidad and Tobago.

André Odendaal has reserved his place among the greatest chroniclers of our national story. Here in *Cricket and Conquest*, he and his fellows make visible the 'invisible lineages' of our history through a masterful blending of history, biography, politics, and sport. Required reading for our times – and a work that will last.

Prof. Xolela Mangcu, University of Cape Town. Sociologist, public intellectual and author of *Biko: A Biography*.

André Odendaal is a master at uncovering neglected histories and he and his co-authors have gone beyond the boundary of previous excellence to produce what must be the definitive history of South African cricket. Reminiscent of CLR James's classic work, *Cricket and Conquest* explores the paradox of a game that accompanied colonial conquest being appropriated and turned into a site of struggle by the colonised. It is as much about the struggle against racial and colonial injustice as it is about cricket.

Elinor Sisulu, social activist, cricket lover and author of *Walter and Albertina Sisulu: In Our Lifetime*.

Destined to become an essential classic. Beautifully written and meticulously researched. The profound episodic stories of inclusion and exclusion are told with an admirable and engaging lightness of touch.

Paul Yule, Filmmaker, including *Not Cricket* 1 and 2 on *The Basil D'Oliveira Conspiracy* (BBC, 2004) and *The Captain and the Bookmaker* (BBC, 2008) about Hansie Cronje.

The ancestors come alive in *Cricket and Conquest*. The creativity, resilience and human agency of cricketers facing unspeakable prejudice and deeply institutionalised, deliberately created barriers is beautifully researched and narrated here.

Chris Nenzani, President Cricket South Africa

A magnificent piece of work that traverses the full history of our game. Meticulous research gives us a breathtaking panorama of our rich and diverse past.

Haroon Lorgat, CEO Cricket South Africa

CRICKET AND CONQUEST

The History of South African Cricket Retold

Volume 1, 1795–1914

by

André Odendaal, Krish Reddy,
Christopher Merrett and Jonty Winch

Published by BestRed, an imprint of HSRC Press
Private Bag X9182, Cape Town, 8000, South Africa
www.bestred.co.za

First published 2016

ISBN (soft cover) 978-1-928246-13-8

The views expressed in this publication are those of the authors. They do not necessarily reflect the views or policies of the Human Sciences Research Council (the Council) or indicate that the Council endorses the views of the authors. In quoting from this publication, readers are advised to attribute the source of the information to the individual author concerned and not to the Council.

This book is number 1 in the *African Lives* series. With its byline of *Memory Matters*, this is an independent initiative to provide a platform for voices and narratives about the past that encourage reflection on South Africa's present and future. The series editor is Professor André Odendaal.

The publishers have no responsibility for the continued existence or accuracy of URLs for external or third-party Internet websites referred to in this book and do not guarantee that any content on such websites is, or will remain, accurate or appropriate.

Copy-edited by Russell Martin
Typeset by Firelight Studio
Cover design by Dreamfuel
Printed by [name of printer, city, country]

Distributed in Africa by Blue Weaver
Tel: +27 (021) 701 4477; Fax Local: (021) 701 7302; Fax International: 0927865242139
www.blueweaver.co.za

Distributed in Europe and the United Kingdom by Eurospan Distribution Services (EDS)
Tel: +44 (0) 17 6760 4972; Fax: +44 (0) 17 6760 1640
www.eurospanbookstore.com

Distributed in North America by River North Editions, from IPG
Call toll-free: (800) 888 4741; Fax: +1 (312) 337 5985
www.ipgbook.com

Let them and me rest in obscurity and peace, let my tomb remain uninscribed and my memory in oblivion, till other men and other times can do justice to my character. When my country takes her place amongst the nations of the world, then and not until then, let my epitaph be written.

– Robert Emmet, Irish freedom fighter,
facing a death sentence in a British court, 1803

Contents

Acknowledgements

A research and writing enterprise on this scale could never have happened without support from many people and institutions. The first to thank is Cricket South Africa (CSA), which has given assistance in various ways since the adoption of the Transformation Charter way back in December 1998. 'Recording the full history of South African cricket' from then on became a key part of the priorities of CSA. It gave this history project official status without once interfering with its editorial content or independence. Field workers from the provinces consistently endorsed the idea at CSA planning conferences. Our thanks to them, the Transformation Monitoring Committee and all the presidents, board members and CEOs who backed us. Percy Sonn, Ray Mali, Mtutuzeli Nyoka, Norman Arendse, A.K. Khan, Chris Nenzani, Ali Bacher, Gerald Majola and Haroon Lorgat all gave support from on high. Regardless of what happened in later CSA ructions, Gerald and Ray, together with the late Khaya Majola, helped André Odendaal to get access to the most intimate stories and material relating to the experience of African cricketers, which greatly helped in the writing of his book *The Story of an African Game*, an important step in the compilation of this broad overall history of South African cricket. Norman Arendse has believed more than most in the necessity of validating the historical experiences that this work engages with. In the last phase, Maxwell Jordaan as responsible manager was quietly affirming and supportive of the project co-ordinator and the vision. We owe him a great deal. Krish Reddy likewise wishes to thank Ali Bacher for the recognition and respect he accorded him.

One of the most rewarding aspects of the process was the emergence of a network of historically minded writers, academics and activists from the non-racial tradition concerned with preserving memory and producing knowledge in the history-related projects of CSA and its affiliates. We admire the work done by, and have benefited from working with the likes of, Prof. Ashwin Desai, SABC commentator Aslam Khota, BBC correspondent Mogamad Ali, the bibliophile from 'Fietas' Yusuf Garda, Dr William Pick, senior writer on the *Cape Times* Dougie Oakes, Prof. Goolam Vahed, Dr Mtutuzeli Nyoka, filmmaker Junaid Ahmed, Judge Chris Nicholson, university lecturer and hard-working cricket administrator Mike Hickson, Prof. Vishnu Padayachee, Dr Lewis Manthatha, author John Young, the late community sports scribe Lennie Kleintjies, cricket and radio's Hussein Manack, former journalist Chris Day, and businessperson and entrepreneur Monwabisi Mfobo.[1] Their work, as well as that of the very few mainstream cricket journalists from the non-racial tradition – like former SACB first-class cricketer Michael Doman, Iqbal Khan and Zaahier

Adams – has helped give shape to our attempts to create new alternative narratives of cricket's past in South Africa. More recent entrants to cricket writing and commentating, such as Khanyiso Tshwaku of Times Media, Lerato Maleketu of CSA, Sixolele Sotyelelwa of SABC, Lungani Zama of the Independent Group, Mahlatse Maphahele of New Age, Sbu Mjelekiso of Times Media, Thando Gcamane and Mluleki Ntsabo (also SABC) and ex-cricketers turned TV pundits, Makhaya Ntini, Victor Mpitsang and Monde Zondeki, are also building the platform for a differently envisioned past and future.

Many others active in cricket currently gave support and helped collect material. They will be thanked in the volumes specific to the topic. For this first volume, Ahmed Jinnah, Rihan Richards and Eugene Jacobs helped us unlock valuable resources on early Kimberley cricket. In Durban, the friendliness of Faeez Jaffer, Cassim and Sabira Docrat, A.K. Khan, Pete de Wet and his team at Kingsmead made the visit to the KZNCU Archives an experience to savour. André Odendaal's colleagues at Western Province allowed him space to continue with his historical work, including through a clause in his CEO's contract and permission for him to take a sabbatical at the University of Kentucky in 2011, where this writing process was reignited in a significant way. He trusts that the legacy projects he started at WPCA as part of marketing the brand and its values, as well as the results he contributed to during his time (including ten memorable Cape Cobras trophies), convey a reciprocal respect. Norman Arendse, Solomon Makosana, Sadick Emeran, Mohammed Ebrahim, Beresford Williams, Shaun Christiansen, Cyril O'Connor, John Bester, Nabeal Dien and the executives, management and staff all helped. Ameena Smith's professionalism and Carol van Vuuren's wonderful support over ten years probably made this all possible in the end. Despite the cross-currents and vagaries of the system, the CSA cricket family have given this project tremendous support, and we trust it will have a positive long-term impact on South African cricket.

This volume rests on solid research in nineteenth- and early twentieth-century newspapers from various parts of southern Africa and overseas. Both André Odendaal and Jonty Winch discovered extensive sources on cricket in the course of their PhD and book research, and these form the basis of much of the work on black cricketers and the early English tours and playing mentalities in Cricket and Conquest. The newspapers were obtained through institutions such as the British Newspaper Library, the National Libraries in Cape Town and Pretoria, the Johannesburg Municipal Library, the Africana Library in Kimberley, and the Cory Library in Grahamstown. Besides marking the launch of the modern political struggle, the beginnings of an independent black press from the 1880s were particularly important in saving for posterity important aspects of the history of cricket in South Africa. John Tengo Jabavu, the brilliant 23-year-old founding editor of *Imvo Zabantsundu* (Native Opinion) in 1884, wrote about cricket in his first set of editorial notes and covered it for 30 years thereafter, broadening in the process the Xhosa language by finding words to describe this new game. Jabavu was an African James Lillywhite. A range of other alternative newspapers emerged in the following decades to record the progress of the players on the other side of the line. Among the most important through the decades, besides *Imvo*, were *Isigidimi samaXhosa*, *Izwi Labantu*, *The APO*, *Umteteli wa Bantu*, *The Sun*, the *Cape Standard*, *The Leader*, *Golden City Post*, *The Indicator* and the *Cape Herald*.

Among mainstream colonial newspapers, the *Diamond Fields Advertiser*, *Eastern Province Herald*, *Cape Times*, *Cape Argus* and *The Star* proved to be particularly useful. The late Mr Les Moult, co-author of the history of Cape Town Cricket Club, read decades of cricket reports in nineteenth-century Cape Town newspapers and, then, at the onset of dementia in his old age, he kindly gave André Odendaal his 21 notebooks of research. Jonty Winch has used these to provide some of the early cricket history detailed below.

As Jonty has noted, reporters in the late nineteenth century were considered ideal secretaries for sporting committees. Editors such as Jabavu and leading sports writers such as Charles Finlason, Harry Cadwallader and E.J.L. Platnauer helped build a solid record of South African cricket at that time. We pay tribute to the generations of players, newspaper reporters, officials and record-keepers who created the alternative archives (including personal scrapbooks, organisational minutes, photographs, scorecards and oral testimonies) upon which large sections of this series are based. Many of them were invisible to the ruling classes but left their mark in reports and reminiscences from the 1860s onwards.

The newspaper sources and collections of memorabilia and material were complemented by work in state and university archives and private collections in Britain and South Africa. We thank Rosemary and Jean Wilke and the Roedean archivist, Diana McGurk, for access to valuable archival material on early girls' cricket at Roedean in Johannesburg. Similarly, the minute book of the Durban and District Indian Cricket Union housed in the Krish Reddy Collection in the KZNCU Archives at Kingsmead, which was found in a basement of the pavilion at the old Curries Fountain sports ground, provided valuable insights into the organisational sophistication of the early black cricketers. Krish has a list of people the length of an arm he wishes to thank, with sincere gratitude, for help with valuable information over the years, but as this applies essentially to the post-1914 period, their names will be inserted in subsequent volumes where the impact of their contributions is mostly seen. Nazim Abdul Gani and Omar

Deoparsad of the Inter-Library Loan section of the University Library, University of Natal, Pietermaritzburg, helped Christopher Merrett acquire monographs and periodical articles essential to the research for this book, while Andrea Jones of Gloucestershire County Library Service, Chris Coley of Cheltenham and the staff of the Hampshire Local Studies Collection at the County Library, Winchester, helped him locate material on C.B. Llewellyn, which was not available in South Africa. Prof. Bruce Murray created the chance for Jonty to consult the minutes of the South African Cricket Association, which are housed in the William Cullen Library, University of the Witwatersrand. The secretary of the Western Province Cricket Club kindly allowed him time to research their minutes and records, which date back to 1876. At the Bodleian Library of Commonwealth and African Studies at Rhodes House, Oxford, the archivist, Lucy McCann, kindly arranged access to the papers of Cecil John Rhodes. In addition, a number of days were spent at the MCC Library at Lord's, where Neil Robinson was helpful in obtaining information. Further assistance was provided by the Cricket Library at The Oval and the Rugby Football Union Library at Twickenham. Dr Terry Rogers, the archivist at Marlborough College, made available records that were of importance in establishing an understanding of William Milton. Research in this regard was followed up through use being made of records located at the National Archives, Zimbabwe, where Ian Johnstone was of assistance. Krish acknowledges gratefully the assistance given to him by the staff of the Durban Documentation Centre in Derby Street; the Documentation Centre at the University of Durban-Westville; the Newspaper Department of the Durban Municipal Library; the Legal Deposit (Newspapers) at the Natal Society Library in Pietermaritzburg; and the Killie Campbell Africana Library in Durban. Isaac Ntabankulu helped us trace material dating from 1814 at UCT's Special Collections. Bernice Nagel and Annelize Rowan at the Kimberley Africana Research Library went out of their way to help source valuable newspaper material and photographs. Vida Allen, Sephai Mngqolo and Eugene Mogatsi of the nearby McGregor Museum were also most welcoming. At the Africana Museum in Johannesburg, Dudu Madonsela and Kenneth Hlungwane assisted us to digitise the Cricket South Africa Collection and rare old photographs.

Forty years after starting out on their writing missions, the authors have written or co-written over 20 books between them. This long build-up of research and writing prepared the ground for *Cricket and Conquest* and its three companion volumes in *The History of South African Cricket Retold*. All four authors therefore wish to thank once again all the individuals and institutions we have acknowledged in our previous writings. It is not possible to write without the support of friends, family and communities of librarians, archivists, journalists, publishers, sponsors and supporters, and we acknowledge those who created the platform for us. While the four volumes in this series will provide a whole new structure and framework for analysis of the general history of South African cricket, substantial parts of the text have been drawn, often directly, from the predecessor works that opened the way. This applies particularly to Jonty Winch's 2013 PhD on Sir William Milton and his book on *England's Youngest Captain* (2003), as well as André Odendaal's *The Story of an African Game* (2003) and *The Founders* (2013), and Bruce Murray and Christopher Merrett's *Caught Behind* (2004). We acknowledge all the publishers of our preceding books and articles. And we trust that this block-by-block building process and the literary architecture that has emerged enhance the value, revelatory detail and stylistic freshness of both the old and new works.

Apart from the writers, two people have contributed enormously to making the contents of this book as professional and accurate as possible. John Young, who received the John Kannemeyer Award for Biography from the Independent Publishers' Association of South Africa in 2016, has shared cricket history interests with André for 20 years and worked temporarily with him as researcher and editor in 2015 and 2016. His knowledge of cricket and language has benefited this work hugely. Similarly, internationally respected statistician Robin Isherwood helped us far beyond the call of duty. Hours-long proofreading sessions by Skype with Robin sitting in his beloved Lancashire instilled discipline, which even a stone-wall opener from 1890 would have appreciated. His contributions to South African cricket over the years have been immense, but he dictates that acknowledgement should go only up to a point. Thank you, Robin. His long-standing colleague Andrew Samson, who will be co-author of volume 4, which deals with later statistics, provided the SACA international and domestic stats used in this book. The inputs and audits of these two have been indispensable, especially since *Cricket and Conquest* is setting out to reconstitute what we believe are the still incomplete and racially skewed records of South African cricket, of which they have been among the primary custodians. Like conservation architects in a high-tech age, our goal is to re-engineer the foundations of a skewed cricket archaeology, but Robin and Andrew have never pretended to be anything other than the superb statisticians they are.

Michael Owen-Smith, who knows the playing history of SACA intimately, wrote the narrative part of chapter 38 as a guest contributor. The authors initially felt that their expertise did not lie in this area and we thank Michael for compensating in this respect. Archie Henderson did valuable proofreading. Ivor Markman helped with early research on the eastern Cape. Douglas Booth made useful comments on an early draft of the women's chapter. Vince van der Bijl and

Neale Emslie lent us old books. In memory of Clem Druker (an administrator and friend with a deep sense of cricket history), June Druker gave André a special bound copy of Luckin's history, which became a bedside companion. Thulani Zideba helped with translations. Laura Bekker of Rustenburg Girls' High, Dr Sheila Brock and Ted Doman passed on valuable photographs and, between them, David Larsen of Africa Media On-line, Alice Mann, Angus Mackinnon and Ra-ees Saiet digitised in an impressive way thousands of rare images.

Christopher Merrett's first publication on the history of sport appeared in 1983, but it was John Laband who set him on his way as a sports historian by asking him to contribute to *Pietermaritzburg 1838–1988: A new portrait of an African city* (1988, edited by Laband and Rob Haswell). Subsequently he benefited from the support and encouragement of friends in the Australian Society for Sports History, most notably Douglas Booth. In South Africa he owes a debt to Christopher Saunders, who has always shown an interest in his research and writing and who is an inspiring model as a productive academic. Thanks are also due to Martin Prozesky, Bruce Murray and André Odendaal for their interest. He wants to express the considerable debt he owes to comrades and colleagues in Aurora CC and the Maritzburg District Cricket Union, who welcomed him into non-racial cricket nearly 40 years ago and provided him with such rich and challenging hands-on experience. He says, 'Although ideologically divergent, Rajen Moodley and Mike Hickson (president and vice-president of the MDCU) were enormous influences on me. In Aurora, Roy Bunwarie (long-time president) and Malcolm McKenzie consciously and unconsciously assisted me in shaping many of my ideas about sport and society and helped in the construction of this book. Thank you, too, to all those cricketers in non-racial sport in Pietermaritzburg who made those experiences of the 1980s so rewarding – and for their confidence in me as umpire and administrator – Baby and Bully Haffajee, Amos Cassimjee, Farouk Ally, Mike Hart, Vis Naidoo, Tommy Nair, Viddy Naidoo, Krish Pillay and Neville Richardson spring to mind, but there were countless others.'

England-based Jonty Winch has gained from working in London alongside a group of historians with a common interest in early South African cricket history, notably Richard Parry, Dale Slater, Bernard Hall (grandson of A.B. Tancred) and Geoff Levett. At Stellenbosch, Professors Albert Grundlingh and Bill Nasson provided encouragement and invaluable criticism, while pointing to relevant reading material. Jonty and the above-mentioned London group have been involved in two volumes running parallel to our work, namely B. Murray and G. Vahed (eds), *Empire and Cricket: The South African experience 1884–1914* (2009) and B. Murray and R. Parry (eds), *Cricket and Society in South Africa: Union to isolation, 1910–1971* (forthcoming). These studies, with a flexibility to focus on eclectic themes, complement in many ways the work in *The History of South African Cricket Retold*. Although the two history projects are separate and perhaps differ fundamentally in perspective at times, there has been a cooperative relationship between them. We want especially to thank Richard Parry for sharing material on Kimberley, among other topics, and Dean Allen, author of the attractive *Empire, War and Cricket: Logan of Matjiesfontein* (2015), who has allowed us to use some of his rare photographs.

The University of Missouri (St Louis) and the University of Kentucky in Lexington provided the project co-ordinator, André Odendaal, with opportunities to research and write during sabbaticals in the US in 2004 and 2011 respectively. His first big stint of writing on this volume happened in the unlikely surroundings of a snowy St Louis. Prof. Joel Glassman and Prof. Chuck Korr, a sports historian and friend, made the visit possible. Welcoming colleagues and students in the Center for International Studies, the History Department and Pierre Laclede Honors College made it a pleasure. The second time round, Prof. Mark Kornbluh invited him to spend a semester writing and teaching in Lexington. The kindness of Mark, Dr Mimi Behar and the staff and students in the History Department at UKY renewed his faith in common decency at a time of CSA and political coups and conspiracies of Shakespearean dimensions at home.

Tony Tabatznik's extreme generosity made it possible for André to write full-time in the final stages. He is also grateful for collegial support on history issues over the past ten years from friends such as the late Jakes Gerwel, Peter Hain, Ashwin Desai, Peter Alegi, Ramachandra Guha, Tony Collins, Bob Edgar, Luyanda ka Msumza, Albie Sachs, Susan Rabinowitz, Christopher Saunders, Christopher Merrett, Ahmed Kathrada, Barbara Hogan, Neeshan Balton, Yusuf Garda, Busani Ngcaweni, Lyndon Bouha, Yolisa Tshongolo, Archie Henderson, Rashid Omar, Nolubabalo Tongo, Geraldine Frieselaar, Mariki Viktor, Xolela Mangcu, Mwelela Cele, Olusegun Morakinyo, Khwezi ka Mpumlwana, Kurt Dewhurst, Marsha McDowell, Peter Limb, Kuthala Priscilla Nopoto, Seelan Naidoo, Sibongiseni Mkize, James Early, June Bam, Andrew Bank, Colin Bundy, Albert Grundlingh, Cornelius Thomas, Jo-Ann Duggan, Anthony Bateman, Jeremy Hill, Brian Willan, Erika Oosthuizen, Martin Plaut, Gordon Metz, Lawson Naidoo, Adam Asmal, Derek Pringle, Mike Atherton, Lerato Malekutu, Paul Yule, Peter Oborne, Sandra Shell, Philani Nongongo, Somine van der Merwe and Denver Webb. The elders who initiated André into things he did not know about cricket and his country, and his extended 'families' in Queenstown, at Queensland CC in Lenasia, United CC in Cape Town, UWC and Robben Island, have been thanked elsewhere, but he is grateful to all those who have helped shape his writing and life.

Jeremy Wightman of HSRC Press and BestRed, accompanied by Greg Houston, took five minutes to decide to publish this book and the full four volumes of *The History of South African Cricket Retold*. We thank him for recognising the importance of our project and for the energy with which the BestRed team of Charlotte Imani, Mthunzi Nxawe, Samantha Hoaeane and Vernon Joshua set about producing the book. Russell Martin copyedited the manuscript with his usual elegance. Abie Collins and Alberico Vollmer of Dreamfuel have designed all four covers for the series.

Finally, families and partners share the pain. Jonty is grateful to his wife, Norma, and sons, Matthew and Jamie, for their help and interest. Krish thanks his dear wife, Praba, for her constant encouragement in all the work that he has done. Her forbearance in affording him the opportunity to spend so much time on his various research projects is sincerely appreciated. Christopher concludes, 'Above all, extra special thanks go to my wife Christine, who has brought meaning, purpose and happiness to my life and whose practical and moral support has enabled me to finish this book.' André thanks Zohra Ebrahim for the companionship and love of 25 years and the sacrifices she has made from the time he set out to ensure *The History of South African Cricket Retold* became a reality way back in December 1998, and all the others at home – Thenjiwe Perhe and Rehana, Adam, Nadia and Mary Odendaal – for putting up with it all.

About the authors

André Odendaal, the lead writer and project co-ordinator of this book and the three accompanying volumes, is an honorary professor in history and heritage studies at the University of the Western Cape. After graduating with a PhD in history from Cambridge University, he taught at UWC and was founding director of both the Mayibuye Centre for History and Culture in South Africa at UWC and the Robben Island Museum, the first heritage institution of the new South African democracy. After this, he took over for ten years as CEO at the historic Newlands Cricket Ground and the successful Cape Cobras professional team and Western Province. He played first-class cricket for Boland (SACU), Transvaal and Western Province (SACB), as well as Cambridge University in England. Odendaal was the only provincial cricketer designated 'white' to join the non-racial SACOS during the apartheid years, taking a stand with a small group of like-minded players. He was an anti-apartheid activist in the UDF, NECC, NSC and ANC and chaired the UCBSA's Transformation Monitoring Committee from 1998 to 2002. In that year he received the President's Award for Sport (Silver Class) for his contribution to sport. André has written ten books on the history of the liberation struggle and the social history of sport in South Africa, including *Vukani Bantu!* (1984), *The Story of an African Game* (2003) and *The Founders* (2012). He is currently also writer and research co-ordinator for the Albie Sachs Trust on Constitutionalism and the Rule of Law.

Krish Reddy has painstakingly recovered much of the lost statistical records of black and non-racial cricket in Natal and South Africa, details of which were published regularly in the *Mutual and Federal South African Cricket Annual* from 1996 to 2004. In 1986 he compiled a history of the Natal Cricket Board as part of their 25th anniversary celebrations. He is the author of *The Other Side: A miscellany of black cricket in Natal*, published in 1999, and also the co-author with Ashwin Desai, Vishnu Padayachee and Goolam Vahed of *Blacks in Whites: A century of cricket struggles in KwaZulu-Natal*, published in 2002. The UK-based Association of Cricket Statisticians and Historians chose him as their Statistician of the Year in 2007 for his research on the scores of 223 first-class matches in non-racial cricket in South Africa during the period 1971–1991. In December 2009 he was awarded the ICC Volunteers' Medal 'in recognition of outstanding service to cricket'. After several years of close involvement with the non-racial Natal Cricket Board, Krish served a three-year term on the executive of the KwaZulu-Natal Cricket Union after unity in 1991. He was also a provincial selector for ten consecutive seasons from 1996/7 to 2005/6. A retired school principal, Krish is a patron of the KwaZulu-Natal Cricket Union.

Christopher Merrett was born in Britain, grew up in the Bahamas and has lived in South Africa since 1975. He has a BA (Hons) degree in geography, Master's degrees in library science and geography, and a PhD in history – from the universities of Oxford, Sheffield, Natal and Cape Town. Christopher worked for 30 years in libraries, becoming university librarian at the University of Natal (Pietermaritzburg campus) in 1996. After serving as director of administration on the same campus from 2002 to 2007, he switched careers and spent seven years in the newsroom of *The Witness*. His writing has concentrated on the history and politics of South African sport; human rights issues; and the local history of Pietermaritzburg. He has written or co-authored five books including *A Culture of Censorship: Secrecy and intellectual repression in South Africa* (1994) and *Caught Behind: Race and politics in Springbok cricket* (with Bruce Murray, 2004). A member of the path-breaking Aurora Cricket Club from 1979, he umpired nearly 100 league and inter-district matches, and two SACB first-class matches in 1982. He was also secretary of the Maritzburg District Cricket Union for five years and contributed to the protests against rebel teams who defied the sports boycott of South Africa. During the State of Emergency of the late 1980s, he was a member of the Pietermaritzburg Detainees Support Committee and was charged with two others under the Foreign Funding Act.

Jonty Winch grew up in Zimbabwe and has worked in education, journalism and photography in southern Africa and Britain. He received a Master of Arts degree with distinction from De Montfort University's International Centre for Sports History and Culture and was then awarded his PhD from the University of Stellenbosch. He has written six books including *Cricket's Rich Heritage: A history of Rhodesian and Zimbabwean cricket 1890–1982* (1983); *Cricket in Southern Africa: Two hundred years of achievements and records* (1997); and *England's Youngest Captain: The life and times of Monty Bowden and two South African journalists* (2003). He has also produced articles for accredited international academic journals, winning the British Society of Sports History's 'Best Article in *Sport in History*' in 2008. His recent writings on the development of imperial games in nineteenth-century South Africa and the former Rhodesia have considerably improved our understanding of the connections between sport and politics at that time. Jonty's interest in sport has also included his involvement in the administration of cricket, rugby and canoeing at the University of the Witwatersrand; serving on provincial committees; playing rugby for Varese in Italy's Serie B, and coaching numerous school and university teams on sports tours to various African countries and overseas.

Visual material sources

The first number indicates Insert, the second number is the Page number within the insert and the final number is for the Image on the page, left-to-right, top-to-bottom, or clockwise starting top left. Example: one of four images placed in the bottom left corner on the second page of the first insert would be [Insert]1: ([page]2.[image]3). One of two images (bottom) on page 3 of the second insert would be: 2(3.2). Sources are listed for the first time in the order in which the images appear in the inserts.

INSERT ONE (following page 22)
D. Frith, *Pageant of cricket*: 1(1.1)
Library of Parliament: 1(1.2), artist J. C. Frederici.
Lady Anne Barnard, *South Africa a century ago*: 1(1.3).
wikipedia: 1(1.4): https://nl.wikipedia.org/wiki/Huibert_Gerard_Nahuys_van_Burgst;
geni.com: 1(2.1): www.geni.com/people/Brig-Gen-Henry-Clavering/6000000018388602472.
UCT Libraries: 1(2.2), BC923C1; 1(3.2)
A. Odendaal, K. Reddy and A. Samson, *The Blue Book, A history of Western Province cricket, 1890-2011*: 1(2.3)
N. Worden, E. Van Heyningen, V. Bickford-Smith, *Cape Town, The making of a city*: 1(2.4)
Western Cape Archives and Records Service: 1(2.4) original; 1(3.1) M455; 1(3.3) M2/76; 1(5.3) AG13389
B. Maclennan, *A proper degree of terror*: 1(4.1); 1(4.4)
Souvenir, the Commemoration of the 1820 Settlers of Albany: 1(4.2)
Ivor Markman, www.stgeorgespark.nmmu.ac.za: 1(4.3); 1(4.5); 1(5.1)
National Library of South Africa: 1 (5.2); 1 (6.1)
S.E.K. Mqhayi, *U So-Gqumahashe*: 1(6.2)
R. Guha, *The Picador book of cricket*: 1(6.3)
R.H.W. Shepherd, *Lovedale South Africa, The story of a century*: 1(7.1)
Lovedale Missionary Institution, South Africa: Fifty views from photographs: 1(7.2)
J.A. Mangan (ed.), *Pleasure, profit and proselytism: British culture at home and abroad*: 1(7.3)
Nelson Mandela Bay Municipality Africana Library: 1(8.1)
W.M. Luckin, *The history of South African cricket*: 1(8.2); 1(8.3)

INSERT TWO (following page 152)
W.M. Luckin, *The history of South African cricket*: 2(1.1); 2(1.3); 2(3.2); 2(8.1)
Sussex County Cricket Club Museum: 2(1.2)
Western Cape Archives and Records Service: 2(1.4) AG12502; 2(4.3) AG419
National Library of South Africa: 2(2.1) *The South African Illustrated News*, 17 January 1885; 2(4.4) A.920.JAB
L. Moult and P. Hartman, *Playing the game*: 2(3.1) *Cape Argus*, 3 February 1876
Cory Library, Rhodes University: 2(4.1); 2(4.2); 2(6.1); 2(7.1)
André Odendaal Collection: 2(5.1)
T.D. Mweli Skota (ed.), *The African yearly register*: 2(5.2)
Imvo Zabantsundu: 2(5.3)
Museum Africa, Johannesburg: 2(8.2)

INSERT THREE (following page 268)
Cape Argus: 3(1.4); 3(1.5)
National Library of South Africa: 3(1.1); 3(7.2); 3(8.1) APO Album
W.M. Luckin, *The history of South African cricket*: 3(1.2); 3(1.3); 3(2.3); 3(4.1); 3(4.3); 3(5.1)
Wikipedia: 3(2.1), West Indies cricket team 1906
B. Murray and G. Vahed (eds), *Empire and cricket*: 3(3.2); 3(3.3)
D. Allen, *Empire, war & cricket*: 3(6.2); 3(7.1) National Library of South Africa; 3(7.3) Public Collection, Anglo-Boer War Museum, Bloemfontein
Western Cape Archives and Records Service: 3(3.1) J1167
Western Province Cricket Association Archives: 3(4.2); 3(4.3); 3(4.4)
Museum Africa, Johannesburg: 3(4.1)

The Star, reproduced in *The Barnett Collection: A Pictorial History of Early Johannesburg*, vol. 1: 3(5.2)
O. Schreiner, *Trooper Peter Halkett of Mashonaland*: 3(5.2)
André Odendaal Collection: 3(6.1)
M. Plaut, *Promise and Despair. The first struggle for a non-racial South Africa*: 3(8.2

INSERT FOUR (following page 298)
Lovedale Missionary Institution, South Africa: Fifty views from photographs: 4(1.1); 4(1.2)
National Library of South Africa: 4(2.1) *Afrikanerland*, Christmas no. 1893
A century of South African sport, TopSport: 4(2.2)
André Odendaal Collection: 4(2.3) Colleen Roberts' papers, Oenone Gradwell scrapbook; 4(5.1) photographs from a British periodical published during the South African War given to the author by Robert Edgar and Leteane Monatse; 4(7.1) and 4(7.2) mounted original photographs given to the author by Robert Edgar and Leteane Monatse
Cricket South Africa Collection, Museum Africa, Johannesburg: 4(3.1); 4(4.1); 4(4.2) PH 2016-19, photos by Horace W. Nicholls
D. Allen, *Empire, war & cricket*: 4(3.2)
Western Cape Archives and Records Service: 4(6.1) AG13656; 4(8.1) L1344
Ivor Markman, www.stgeorgespark.nmmu.ac.za: 4(6.2)
Rustenburg Girls High School Archive: 4(8.2)

INSERT FIVE (following page 342)
National Library of South Africa: 5(1.1)
B. Willan, *Sol Plaatje, Selected writings*: 5(2.1)
Ahmed Jinnah portfolio: 5(2.2)
KZNCU Archives: Reddy Collection: 5(2.3); 5(6.1) and 5(8.1) and 5(8.3) Rama Thumbadoo original photograph
W.M. Luckin, *The history of South African cricket*: 5(3.1); 5(3.2); 5(4.1) photograph The Bewer Studio
A century of South African sport, TopSport: 5(3.2)
Cricket South Africa Collection, Museum Africa, Johannesburg: 5(8.2)
UCT Libraries: 5(8.3)

INSERT 6 (following page 388)
W.M. Luckin, *The history of South African cricket*: 6(1.1); 6(1.3); 6(2.1); 6(3.1); 6(3.3); 6(4.4); 6(5.1); 6(6.1); 6(8.1); 6(8.2); 6(8.3); 6(8.4); 6(8.5); 6(8.7); 6(8.8)
D. Allen, *Empire, war & cricket*: 6(1.2)
Kimberley Africana Research Library, McAnda Collection: 6 (2.1)
Cory Library, Rhodes University: 6(2.2); 6(2.4)
André Odendaal Collection: 6(3.2) Ottomans Centenary Brochure
National Library of South Africa: 6(4.1) *The Graphic*, 17 March 1906
KZNCU Archives: Reddy Collection: 6(4.3); 6(4.5)
Museum Africa, Johannesburg: 6(5.2); 6(6.2) *African world and Cape-Cairo express*, 23 June 1904; 6(6.3); 6(6.4); 6(7.1)
B. Murray and G. Vahed (eds), *Empire and cricket*: 6(5.3)
C. Greyvenstein, *The Fighters, a pictorial history of SA boxing from 1881*: 6(1.2)
T.D. Mweli Skota (ed.), *The African yearly register*: 6(7.3)
Missouri Historical Society, St Louis, USA: 6(7.4)
The National Archives, ref copy 1/442: 6(7.5)
Gauteng Cricket Board: 6(8.6)

Abbreviations

ANC	African National Congress
APO	African Political Organisation
BNCU	Border Native Cricket Union
BSAC	British South Africa Company
CMR	Cape Mounted Rifles
CSA	Cricket South Africa
DDICU	Durban and District Indian Cricket Union
DFCCU	Diamond Fields Colonial Cricket Union
EP	Eastern Province
EPCCU	Eastern Province Coloured Cricket Union
GW	Griqualand West
GWCCU	Griqualand West Colonial Cricket Union
GWCCU	Griqualand West Coloured Cricket Union
GWCRFU	Griqualand West Colonial Rugby Football Union
ICC	International Cricket Council
KWT	King William's Town
KZNCU	KwaZulu-Natal Cricket Union
MCC	Marylebone Cricket Club
MDCU	Maritzburg District Cricket Union
MDICU	Maritzburg District Indian Cricket Union
MLA	Member of the Legislative Assembly
MPL	Member of the Provincial Legislature
NECC	National Education Crisis Committee
NSC	National Sports Congress
PECC	Port Elizabeth Cricket Club
SABC	South African Broadcasting Corporation
SABCB	South African Bantu Cricket Board
SACA	South African Cricket Association
SACB	South African Cricket Board
SACBOC	South African Cricket Board of Control
SACCB	South African Coloured Cricket Board
SACOS	South African Council on Sport
SACRFB	South African Coloured Rugby Football Board
SACS	South African College School
SACU	South African Cricket Union
SAICCB	South African Independent Coloured Cricket Board
SAICU	South African Indian Cricket Union
SANNC	South African Native National Congress (later ANC)
SARFB	South African Rugby Football Board
SARWCA	South Africa and Rhodesia Women's Cricket Association
SAWCA	South African Women's Cricket Association
SWD	South Western Districts
TCCU	Transvaal Coloured Cricket Union
UCBSA	United Cricket Board of South Africa
UDF	United Democratic Front
WASP	White Anglo-Saxon Protestant
WP	Western Province
WPCCU	Western Province Coloured Cricket Union
WPCU	Western Province Cricket Union
ZAR	South African Republic

Quoted material reflects the terminology and associated ideologies held by the speaker(s) during the period covered by this work. Although the authors were uncomfortable using terms which are considered racist, offensive and demeaning, the decision to retain the usage of such language in quoted material was made in the interest of historical accuracy, and because these quotes serve as irrefutable evidence of the attitudes and violence often contained in language. To diminish their potency might create space for the continuation of the types of historical silences and denial which this work seeks to combat.

Introduction

Cricket has a vast literature covering an almost infinite variety of subjects, but one of the biggest gaps in knowledge that still exists relates to the history of cricket in South Africa. Only a very partial narrative has been told of the game in the country since its start more than two centuries ago. There are great chunks of the history that even acknowledged authorities like the bible of cricket, *Wisden Cricketers' Almanack*, have not recorded. And the repression of these subjugated cricket memories came about not as an accident of history, but as a direct consequence of it.

Cricket and Conquest is the first in a series of four volumes, written under the subtitle of *The History of South African Cricket Retold*, which aim to provide for the first time an inclusive general history of South African cricket covering the 221 years since the game was first played here.

The series has five main goals. Firstly, it attempts to put in place new paradigms for understanding cricket's past (and present) in South Africa. Secondly, it tries to go beyond existing colonial and apartheid narratives by integrating, from the beginning, at every stage and in every area, the experiences of hitherto excluded black cricketers in the country.

Next to deep-seated race and class discrimination, ingrained sexism has been at the core of the 'traditions' and 'culture' of cricket since the start. Thirdly, therefore, this project also tries to take out of a gender ghetto, and insert into the mainstream of cricket history, the hitherto invisible role played by women in the socially constructed 'gentlemen's game' – so exclusionary that the sexuality of those who sought to play it was questioned and turned into a source of ridicule.

Fourthly, given the depth of past exclusions and the fact that statistics are integral to the culture and romance of cricket, *Cricket and Conquest* and the companion volumes start the process of reconstituting the entire statistical history of South African cricket.

The fifth and final goal is to provide for the first time standardised organisational histories for each of the 11 national South African cricket boards that have existed to date: the SACA, SACCB, SAICCB, SABCB, SAICU, SACBOC, SARWCA, SACU, SACB, SAWCA and the UCBSA, renamed Cricket South Africa (CSA) in 2006. Most of these national bodies are scarcely known, not to mention their having a place in the current history of cricket.

The challenges of meeting these goals are substantial, given the length and depth of cricket's history in southern Africa and the shortcomings in the conventional, long-established narratives of the past. Indeed, this series – decades in the making – seeks to retell the history of an entire sport in South Africa from day one in 1795 to the present.

i. A new paradigm for understanding the past

The founding myths of cricket in southern Africa have been passed down uncritically for generations in South Africa and in England, where they were largely shaped. The game has one of the largest literatures of any sport, and histories of cricket have tended to reflect in complacent and nostalgic ways the Victorian ideas and accompanying colonial, patriarchal and racist values in which it was drenched for generations.

The notion of cricket as a British and gentlemen's game that has somehow been neutral, 'above politics' and marked by 'fair play', is still widely held without much critical reflection in cricket circles. In this version, cricket was an innocent pastime played under sunny skies on the African veld in the spirit of fair play by quirky Englishmen and the few locals who understood its peculiarities and the delightfully eccentric nature of English culture.[1] The fact that cricket's much trumpeted 'traditional culture' at different stages featured only white men in colonial contexts in Africa, Asia and the Caribbean is often politely and conveniently glossed over, concealing the discriminatory history of the game and further reproducing, in different times and different contexts, the exclusions that lay at cricket's core in the past.

Cricket and Conquest tells a different story. It demonstrates how cricket arrived in Africa as part of the baggage of invading British military forces and how it accompanied them every step of the way through the subcontinent in a hundred-year process of systematic and violent conquest. The inherent violence that underpinned cricket's growth in southern Africa also shaped its character. The mindsets behind British and settler militarism directly shaped attitudes that became entrenched in the game in southern Africa. Its 'culture' became infused with notions of racism, narrow masculinity, social Darwinism and imperial superiority.

It was impossible for the archetypal British game, with its close military associations, to remain innocent against the long background of conquest and dispossession in southern Africa. Indeed, cricket would become tightly woven into the fabric of imperialism and colonial power. (See, for example, chapters 9, 24, 28, 29 and Epilogue.)

A recent study has underlined that 'cricketing characters and events had a significant impact on political, social and ideological developments' in South Africa and cricket played a 'central role' in the unfolding historical processes in the subcontinent in the late nineteenth and early twentieth centuries.[2] In other words, the development of cricket closely followed broader political and social developments. This has applied throughout South African cricket's two-century-long history, and all four volumes will emphasise the point.

Cricket cannot be separated from the social and political milieu in which it is played. As Brailsford put it, 'Ever since human beings began to live in organised communities, politics and play have been irresistibly entangled.'[3] Stoddart argued in a similar vein that 'Cricket everywhere is a product of its environment, whether in subtle or in spectacular form. It is contoured by the social and cultural needs and inclinations of its players and supporters, and to read cricket is to read life.'[4] Harold Wesso noted that all 'geographical space', including that used for the playing and administration of cricket, 'is socially produced'.[5]

Cricket's origins lie in agrarian eighteenth-century England and in a 'sentimental ruralism'.[6] Later, the cause of sport was appropriated by the mid-Victorian bourgeoisie to establish its hegemony and envelop the upper working classes with notions of respectability.[7] Urban life needed standardisation and regulation, and in these circumstances muscular Christianity thrived and athleticism was bound up with bodily health, duty and godliness.[8] Cricket was cloaked in ethics of the highest order in which the game became the epitome of manners and an ordered society. This was in part a function of its complex rules.[9] The rituals embodying the relationships between teams and players, and in particular with the umpire, became a symbol of high moral purpose, self-discipline, a balanced approach to life and social responsibility. In the colonies, cricket came to symbolise Empire and British superiority, as we shall see in the chapters below.

The socio-political dimensions of cricket and sport in general are impossible to deny. Thus, starting with *Cricket and Conquest*, the aim of this series is to debunk and replace tired but entrenched colonial (and racially exclusive) founding narratives of cricket in the country with ones that are broader, more inclusive and consciously post-colonial, locating cricket developments in their political, economic and social contexts.

ii. Black South Africans are among pioneers of cricket in the world

This is the first general history of South African cricket to include and analyse in substantial detail the experiences and cultures of black and women cricketers from the beginnings of the game. It shows incontestably that an emergent, enfranchised black middle class in southern Africa, educated at mission stations that dotted the landscape of the eastern Cape like little English villages, were among the pioneers of the game in South Africa and the broader colonial world in the nineteenth century, playing at a much earlier time and on a scale and at a level not yet appreciated (chapters 3, 4).

Introduced to the game in the 1850s, more than 150 years ago – long before a city like Johannesburg was even founded – they were among the earliest to play competitive sport in the subcontinent. The multi-team Native Inter-Town Tournaments in the early 1880s, started shortly after the first such competition by British colonists (and before white rugby players followed suit), were proof of this (chapters 11, 15). The combined eastern Cape Native Inter-Town team selected in 1887 was perhaps the first representative regional or provincial sports team in South Africa. These Inter-Town cricketers took on and beat white sides, hired the best facilities in the Cape Colony to play on, and had their activities widely reported in the press. Some of them excelled against top colonial cricketers. They also planned to tour overseas and sought matches against touring teams coming to the country from 1888 onwards (chapters 12, 21).

Unique African-rooted cricket cultures also developed among the Muslim descendants of slaves and the ethnically mixed communities in Cape Town (chapters 1, 2, 22, 25, 26) and in the growing cosmopolitan environments in Kimberley, Johannesburg and Durban (chapters 14, 25, 37) from the early nineteenth century onwards. A third series of inter-town tournaments – the precursors of later provincial or inter-colonial cricket – emerged around the fulcrum of Cape Town and Kimberley. The quality of the play here was shown by the thousands of spectators who came to watch at Newlands in 1890, the national team selected after the 1891 tournament, and the performances by a 'Malay' team against the English professionals on the second English tour in 1892. One batsman, L. Samsodien, hit the highest score in 21 matches against the tourists and the vastly experienced English professionals compared the star fast bowler, H. 'Krom' Hendricks, to Fred 'The Demon' Spofforth, the sensational Australian who stood out in the early era of test cricket with his devastating pace, 'aquiline nose and "Mephistophelian cast of countenance"' (chapters 22, 25, 26).

The experiences of the eastern Cape Africans were comparable in certain ways with the Parsis from Bombay, who were pioneers of cricket among the colonised people in India. Both communities acted as middlemen of sorts between the colonisers and the conquered native people, and developed strong cricket traditions. While the Parsis set up clubs earlier than the Africans, the latter played in inter-racial matches against British colonists earlier than the Indians. The southern Africans in addition preceded by some way the descendants of slaves and indentured workers on the islands of the Caribbean in setting up clubs and competitions (chapter 8).

By 1890, several different cricket traditions, each located within a specific context and social milieu, became evident in southern Africa. At various times, particular individuals and cricket communities had different views of themselves and different visions for South Africa's common future. Exploring cricket's complex origins thus also helps illuminate changing notions of identity in South Africa over the past 200 years, contributing to better understanding of current debates and struggles (see, for example, chapters 20–26). There were no fixed binaries, and cricketers had overlapping identities, which created the possibility at one stage of the colonised people being accepted into the colonial cricket mainstream. One of the goals of the book is to explore the complexities and contradictions which went with the growth of the game in this country.

Part III shows that in the decade before 1894, as South Africa readied itself for and entered test cricket, a door opened. A multi-ethnic cricket community sharing many similarities and interacting in significant ways emerged in the Cape Colony, making possible the emergence of an inclusive South African cricket set-up based on the small but energetic Cape liberal tradition (rooted in a pre-diamonds and gold era), which included an emerging, enfranchised, cricket-loving black middle class in Cape Town, Kimberley and the eastern Cape.

But in Part IV we see how Cecil John Rhodes and his influential cricket-loving cabals in sport and politics, linked to rapacious imperialist interests and hard-line 'native policy', closed the door on black cricketers. They introduced legislation which would set the pattern for the future in politics, and in a very public way established the formal colour bar in sport through the patently unfair exclusion of H. 'Krom' Hendricks from the first South African cricket tour abroad in 1894 – and by vindictively rebuffing his attempts to play 'official' cricket for a decade after that.

By the 1890s, it can be argued, black cricketers in southern Africa were among the global trend-setters in the game. Besides showing their prowess against top-level cricketers, and now blocked from becoming part of the cricket mainstream, they started provincial bodies and well-organised and well-publicised 'inter-colonial' (or inter-provincial) competitions similar to SACA's Currie Cup (1890), England's County Championship (formalised in 1890) and the new Sheffield Shield in Australia (1892/3). Their copycat Barnato tournaments were started less than a decade after the launch of these three landmark domestic competitions (see chapters 34 and 35 below).

The colonised black players also launched one of the earliest national controlling cricket bodies in the world. The South African Coloured Cricket Board (SACCB) emerged from the decade and a half of active organising and growth described below to become only the third permanently established representative national association worldwide. Founded in 1903, the SACCB would precede by two years the Australian Cricket Board and by a quarter of a century or more the West Indian, Indian, New Zealand and Pakistan cricket boards representative of the great Asian and Caribbean traditions of cricket (chapter 33).

These points are made not to exaggerate the past, but to explain clearly from the outset of this four-volume study that black cricketers were active participants in the unfolding history of the game in South Africa from the start. In fact, looking back in retrospect, their early vision had a defining long-term impact on South African cricket. The new SACCB declared in clause 25 of its founding constitution in 1903 that 'this Board does not recognise any distinction amongst the various sporting peoples of South Africa, whether by Creed, Nationality or otherwise'.[10] The SACCB formed by excluded black cricketers in the first decade of the twentieth century thus became the first repository of a vision of unity in cricket across class and colour divides that would be finally realised when democracy arrived in the last decade of that century.

The cricketing dramas that unfolded in the nineteenth and early twentieth centuries are part of a truly remarkable story. A whole new set of cricket characters, known up to now by only a select few working in the basements of archives, will emerge in the multi-coloured tapestries created here to take their rightful places in history.

iii. Correcting cricket's flawed colonial records
As indicated, black cricketers wished from the start to be part of the cricket mainstream in southern Africa, but the trend in colonial cricket and society was to exclude and segregate them politically, economically and socially. By the mid-1890s, as a consequence of the discovery of the richest diamond and gold deposits in the world, the powerful Cecil John Rhodes and his circle of cricketing imperialists began the process of marginalising them in cricket and society (chapters 27, 28, 29). In the course of the next hundred years the cricketers on the edges were simply written out of history and extinguished from cricket records by the colonial ruling classes in England and South Africa and their media and social institutions. And these exclusions came to be seen as 'natural' because statistics are 'neutral' and 'don't lie'.

The mammoth 848-page general *History of South African Cricket* (1915), edited by Maurice Luckin, which claimed to give 'the full scores of all important matches since 1876', included only one scorecard of a black cricket team. Luckin had just stepped down as secretary of the South African Cricket Association at the time of publication in 1915. His book not only provided the basis for the drawing up of South African first-class records, but after 100 years it continues to be accepted uncritically as a standard reference work for cricket in South Africa for the pre-1915 period.

Although Luckin covered five Champion Bat tournaments and one 'extraneous' tournament for white cricketers (1876–91), he was completely silent about six parallel 'Native' Inter-Town tournaments and two 'extraneous' tournaments which took place between 1884 and 1898, as well as seven 'Malay' Inter-Town tournaments and an 'extraneous' tournament held between 1890 and 1898.

Similarly, when Luckin detailed the scores of the first inter-provincial or inter-regional competitions from 1890 onwards, he covered only the whites-only Currie Cup tournaments but failed completely to include the parallel provincial tournaments for the Barnato Memorial Trophy, even though these were well reported in the main colonial newspapers, sometimes in adjoining columns on the same page as the Currie Cup matches.[11]

This book therefore provides the first-ever integrated statistical overview of the 22 known Inter-Town tournaments in the Cape Colony from their beginnings in 1876 up to the onset of the first regional (later provincial) tournaments in the 1890s. It also covers the advent of the era of provincial cricket from the 1890s to 1914, including both the Currie Cup (for white cricketers) and the Barnato Memorial Trophy (for the cricketers excluded by the colonial establishment) (see chapter 35).

After more than a century and a quarter, working from almost a zero base, we attempt to restore to the record here around 400 of the early black Inter-Town players and over 50 black Inter-Town matches for which we have statistics. They finally become 'real' cricketers and part of the permanent narrative of the game. We also add a further 160 known black provincial players and 17 known pre-1914 inter-provincial scorecards to this reconstituted record. Thus, from one decontextualised scorecard involving 18 black players in Luckin, we jump in this book to some 500 representative cricketers and 70 top-level pre-1914 matches. The cricketers become recognisable as rounded, living, breathing players with their own peculiar traits, ambitions and trajectories in life.

Cricket and Conquest thus begins the process of reconstituting the entire statistical history of South African cricket. In the three volumes that follow, some 3,000 additional provincial cricketers who participated in over 1,000 matches in more than 100 official tournaments of the various national cricket controlling bodies are added to this list. The result will be the creation of a completely new integrated body of statistics for South African cricket for the 140-year period from the beginnings of representative matches and multi-team competitions in 1876 through to 2016.

After an exhaustive search spanning decades, we can now confidently put an end to many of the unacceptable exclusions that have for so long blighted cricket and its records. The cricket DNA samples tested here prove undeniably that the indigenous people were part of the record in a fundamental way from the beginning. Although their exploits have never appeared in *Wisden* or any other of cricket's 'bibles', they can now without exaggeration be classified among the pioneers of cricket and organised sport in South Africa.

Cricket and Conquest, at the same time, broadens and deepens existing knowledge of the early years of establishment white colonial cricket. For example, it corrects and supersedes in detail and understanding old histories of the earliest known matches and the founding of the first clubs. The comparative account of how the growth of the game in South Africa paralleled international developments, and the descriptions of the beginnings of white Inter-Town, provincial and international cricket, also add significantly to what has been known to date (chapters 1, 10, 16–20 and 24). More importantly, a PhD-level biography by one of the authors also enables us to give rare insights into the backgrounds, personal lives, views, networks and approaches of many of those who led and fundamentally shaped the direction of South African cricket in the late nineteenth century, providing a solid platform for the vigorous revisionist narratives articulated here.

Although the early tournaments were designated as racially separate throughout the period from 1876 to 1898, players and teams from different communities and ethnicities interacted, shared venues and column inches in the same newspapers, and influenced and sometimes socialised with and played against each other (for example, chapters 12, 22, 25–6). The intersection between different cricket worlds is something that standard histories of cricket (including Luckin and *Wisden*) have ignored or failed to understand, resulting in the simple deduction in later years that black South Africans did not play or simply had no record or tradition worth noting in 'Western games'.

Cricket, we believe, needs to confront the fact that *Wisden*, its later South African counterpart, the *Cricket Annual*, and the mainstream literature remained 'all-white' for a century when it came to covering South Africa. In a sport that prides itself on its statistics and the integrity and correctness of its authorities, these 'bibles' almost completely ignored (and remained complacently ignorant of) the many activities and deep subcultures of cricket outside the colonial and apartheid elite social circles in South Africa. This included representative cricket matches that were reported in the mainstream press over decades, at times in depth.

Wisden and its derivative satellite projects were in reality active vehicles for promoting and reproducing colonial mindsets and exclusionary cultures in cricket. Far from being the source of authority in this period, their nineteenth- and twentieth-century records are in fact deeply flawed with regard to colonial South Africa and, most likely, other countries such as India and the West Indies. This polite 'whitening' of the record – in cricket and more broadly – which accompanied the violent conquest of African people and the theft of their land in the nineteenth century, amounted to a form of social and intellectual genocide.

Cricket histories in England and in South Africa came to resemble the much reviled school textbooks of the apartheid era, which somehow managed to omit Mandela, Sobukwe and Biko, the ANC, PAC and Sharpeville, from accounts of the political history of the country. No blood was 'spilled on these pages', one reviewer noted. They were 'history as negation'. In relation to the subject, they were what the black hole is to matter: 'a kind of anti-knowledge'.[12] This kind of history completely excluded black people as active agents in society; it became part of the broader pattern of colonial and apartheid control.

What does this mean for the integrity of South African and global cricket's current records and complacent cultures? *Cricket and Conquest* means to challenge and pose fundamental questions about the overall integrity of cricket's official records. Knowing about the gross exclusions of the past and the mindsets that underpinned them, do we then just carry on as normal? We will raise these matters again in the remaining volumes of *The History of South African Cricket Retold*.

Fortunately, memory is resilient, and repression and a cold distancing of 'the Other' did not extinguish an archive waiting to be rediscovered. The brand-new body of statistics created in this four-volume history should help in a meaningful way to correct the record and thereby contribute to redressing long-standing injustices. The new records will hopefully also help undermine destructive and deeply ingrained colonial and apartheid mindsets, which have for nearly a century and a half fortified a reactionary, racially exclusive cricket 'culture' and 'traditions' used as self-righteous excuses to exclude and discriminate against people in real life – right up to the present day.

iv. Women in a 'gentlemen's game'

The struggles of the twentieth century for fairness in South African sport were centred largely on race. The exclusion of black cricketers was seen as the primary issue. But racism in cricket went hand in hand with another aspect of deep-seated institutionalised discrimination – sexism. For over a century the same power relations and socially constructed conventions that made cricket a white imperial game also reinforced patriarchal control over the female body, on and off the field, to the extent that the femininity of women was questioned if they played cricket. The depth of the prejudices women have faced is well illustrated by the remark made by W.G. Grace when he dismissed as 'neither ladies nor cricketers' some players who appeared before large crowds as aspirant professionals.[13]

This new four-book narrative will include the first comprehensive history of women's cricket in South Africa, giving details and statistics of numerous tournaments and cricket weeks as well as the entry of South Africa into international women's cricket. *Cricket and Conquest*, the first volume, traces early attitudes to the involvement of women in cricket and shows how – by playing, and sometimes through explicit argument – women players challenged and inverted entrenched notions of cricket as the 'gentlemen's game' (chapters 30, 31).

The moves in the past decade to bring women and men cricketers together purely as cricketers under the single umbrella of the International Cricket Council is a step of deep historical significance. As part of its transformative thrust, this book seeks to develop understandings of the past which will help speed up the integration of women on an equal basis in a still deeply sexist cricket environment and society at large.[14]

v. Organisational histories: Constructing a new family tree

The whites-only South African Cricket Association (SACA), which oversaw the participation of its SACA South African team in international cricket between 1889 and 1970, is often incorrectly assumed to have been the only cricket controlling body in South Africa during the colonial and apartheid years. But South Africa SACA was only one of nine such national bodies operating in accordance with the chessboard designs of colonial and apartheid thinking before cricketers were united for the first time in 1991, as South Africa made the transition to democracy. The others were the South African Coloured Cricket Board (SACCB, founded in 1903), the South African Independent Coloured Cricket Board (SAAICB, 1926), the South African Bantu (later African) Cricket Board (SABCB, 1932), the South African Indian Cricket Union (SAICU, 1940), the South African Cricket Board of Control (SACBOC, 1947), the South Africa and Rhodesia Women's Cricket Association (SARWCA, 1952), the South African Cricket Union (SACU, 1977) and the South African Cricket Board (1977).[15]

It is only in the last 25 (out of 221) years that all South African cricketers have played under one controlling body, namely the United Cricket Board of

South Africa, founded on 29 June 1991, which changed its name to Cricket South Africa in 2006.

The fifth and final goal of this book and series, then, is to provide standardised organisational histories for each of the 11 'national' cricket controlling bodies or South African cricket boards that have existed to date (see chapters 23, 34, 35 for the start of this process). Each of the 11 organised their own club leagues and provincial tournaments. Each selected South African teams. Half of these have had no formal written history – until now.

vi. The scope of this series

The three volumes to follow *Cricket and Conquest* are:

- *Divided Country, Volume 2, 1914–1950s,* which examines the era of deepening segregation and apartheid from around the time South Africa came into being as a single country to the 1950s when seven different South African cricket boards divided on ethno-religious and gender lines existed concurrently. It will provide organisational histories for each of the seven 'South Africas' for the first time.

- *Batting for Freedom, Volume 3, 1950s to 2016,* which chronicles the slow disintegration of the colonial and apartheid order and the dramatic roller-coaster quest for change, unity and fundamental transformation in cricket in the six decades between the mid-1950s through the advent of democracy to the present.

- *Correcting the Record, Volume 4, Statistics 1876–2016,* which rounds off the attempt to put in place a new body of cricket statistics for the past 140 years of South African cricket. In particular, it will include the full scorecards of the hitherto unpublished 223 three-day matches played by SACBOC and SACB, which were retroactively declared first-class by the United Cricket Board and the International Cricket Council in 1996, as well as bringing women fully into the statistical canon of South African cricket. In addition, more than 100 hitherto unpublished team photographs will insert many of these previously excluded players visually into the cricket record as identifiable people and cricketers for the first time.

These volumes 2–4 will be published by our current publisher in stages over the next two years. Given close global linkages in cricket past and present, it is hoped also that international publishing partners will be found.

The highlighted details, organisational developments, interconnections and path-breaking roles played by black and women cricketers in the overall evolution of the game over the past 221 years make this a completely *new* general history of South African cricket.

The fact that *Cricket and Conquest* will be completed in time for the 25th anniversary of Cricket South Africa and cricket unity underlines our wish that the new series will contribute in some way to making the sport genuinely inclusive and actively intolerant of the inherited brand of class snobbishness, racism, sexism and social discrimination that has for so long been integral to its culture. Ongoing exclusions that are an imprint of the deep past described here somehow remain naturalised in cricket, and this must change.

We trust that this series will lead to the history of South African cricket (and sport in general) being talked about in decisively different ways in the future. The product of decades of needle-in-a-haystack research, it will hopefully assist South African cricket to go forward open-eyed into the future, with greater self-knowledge and confidence in its multiple identities.

It is a sobering thought: cricketers in South Africa have been formally united behind a vision of equality for only 25 of the 221 years since the game arrived on African shores.

Robert Emmet, the Irish freedom fighter, said while facing the death sentence in the court of an occupying power, 'let my tomb remain uninscribed and my memory in oblivion, till other men and other times can do justice to my character. When my country takes her place amongst the nations of the world, then and not until then, let my epitaph be written.'[16]

Humbled by the responsibility we have been given in the South African context during a moment such as that envisaged above, we doff our hats to the ancestors, the cricketing Emmets of Africa – women and men, black, white, pink and purple. We trust we have at last appropriately inscribed their names onto the parchment scrolls of history and that there is now a greater wholeness to the record of the origins of cricket in southern Africa than before. We hope too that this history, filled with a poignancy beyond imagining, affirms a dignity that past systems and times denied so many of these pioneers.

André Odendaal, Krish Reddy, Christopher Merrett, Jonty Winch
23 May 2016

Six PRINTS of MANLY RECREATION, as practised in PUBLIC PLACES in and about LONDON.

CRICKET. Played by the Gentlemen's Club, White Conduit House, Islington.

'None but gentlemen ever to play'. The first known cricketer in South Africa, Charles Anguish, had a direct line to the heart of the British cricket establishment in the 1790s. Brother of the Duchess of Leeds and educated at Eton, he played for the historic White Conduit CC (precursor of the MCC), as well as for Middlesex, Surrey and the MCC from 1789 onwards. His teammates included famous cricketers such as the Earl of Winchilsea, the Duke of Richmond and 'Silver Billy' Beldam. Anguish committed suicide soon after arriving in Cape Town in 1797. This painting of the Gentlemen's Club, White Conduit House, in Islington, London, is from 1784.

Cricket came by warship to the southern tip of Africa. The first British invasion under General Elphinstone in 1795.

Above left: Lady Anne Barnard, high-society friend of Charles Anguish, who described their outing together to the base of Table Mountain in 1797. Reprinted from Lady Anne Barnard, *South Africa a Century Ago*. **Above right:** The first account of cricket at the Cape was given by a Dutchman who didn't want to be there and who didn't know what the game was about. The Dutch lawyer, Dr Huibert G. Nahuys van Burgst, became a gentleman-prisoner of the British in April 1806 and wrote about games of cricket played in the area now known as Green Point Common.

Above: Brigadier General Henry Mordaunt Clavering captained the 'Officers of the Colony' in the first cricket match for which a news report survives.

Below: 'On the level ground by the seas at the Lion's Tail'. The first games of cricket were played at today's Green Point Common in 1806 (left of the lighthouse). Two cricket clubs are based there today still. It is the second oldest ground in continuous use in the world, outside England. This image dates from 1832.

SUPPLEMENT to the CAPE TOWN GAZETTE of the 2d January, 1808, No. 103.

A grand Match at *CRICKET* will be played, for One Thousand Dollars a fide, on Tuesday the 5th of January 1808. on the Camp Ground, between the Officers of the Artillery Mefs, having Colonel Austin of the 60th Regt. and the Officers of the Colony, with General Clavering, ☞ Wickets to be pitched at 10 o'Clock.

The first known news report of a cricket match played in South Africa.

CRICKET.

THIS Morning will be played at Green Point, a Grand Match at CRICKET: The Gentlemen of the Ordnance Department, and the Officers of the 87th Regiment, playing the Officers of the remainder of the Army, for One Thousand Rds. a fide.

Wickets to be pitched at ½ paft 9 precifely.

TABLE MOUNTAIN FROM THE PARADE.

Above: The 'Indians', the name given to British officers on leave from India, watching cricket on the Parade Ground next to the colonial fort on the beachfront in Cape Town. Cricket was played on the Parade until the 1880s.

Far left: A newspaper advert about cricket at naval headquarters at Simonstown in 1814.

Left: 'Round-a-bush' military camp (1807), today's Rondebosch Common, where British soldiers were first encamped and played. It later became home to more than ten cricket pitches and cricketers played there for decades before the forced removals under the Group Areas of the 1960s and 1970s.

Military sketch of the ground near Rondebosch with the encampment, November 1807.

'Moral Bob' Godlonton, 1820 settler and newspaper editor, reported on a cricket match in 1844. He detested liberals and missionaries and preached war and the confiscation of Xhosa land. His son, Benjamin D'Urban Godlonton, was to play in the Champion Bat tournament, the earliest competitive cricket in South Africa.

Sir John Graham cleared the Xhosa from the Zuurveld, had a town named after him, and his grandsons became prominent in cricket in the Cape Colony. Graham said, 'shooting every man who can be found ... is detestable work ... we are forced to hunt them like wild beasts'; but 'a proper degree of terror' was necessary to achieve British aims.

NOTICE.

A MEETING will be held at Sidbury on THURSDAY, 11TH MAY, At 12 o'clock, for the purpose of establishing a **CRICKET CLUB.** All Lovers of this Noble Game, in the neighborhood, are requested to attend.

Announcement of the first known cricket club in South Africa in the *Grahamstown Journal*, 4 May 1843.

Grahamstown in 1848.

PORT ELIZABETH
CRICKET CLUB!

THIS Club having been formed afresh, the Members, and all those who may be desirous of joining, are hereby requested to attend a Meeting to be held at the COMMERCIAL HOTEL **ON THURSDAY EVENING NEXT,** 27th instant, at 8.30 p.m. sharp! for the purpose of forming Rules, Regulations, and for General Business connected with THE FORMATION AND CONTINUANCE OF THE CLUB.
BY ORDER.

Eastern Province Herald, 25 January 1859.

CRICKET.

THE Admirers of this truely noble Pasttime are requested to assemble at the Ground on MONDAY Next, at 2 o'Clock, to enjoy a Friendly Game and to adopt some plan for the formation of a Club.

Eastern Province Herald, 4 February 1847.

CRICKET.

THE Unmarried Cricketers of Port Elizabeth are anxious to play a friendly game with the Married. The Undersigned will be happy to make the necessary arrangements if applied to.
P. SCALLAN
J. MURRELL.

Eastern Province Herald, 6 November 1847.

CRICKET

ON SATURDAY NEXT a grand Match will be played on the HILL. THE MILITARY vs. THE CIVILIANS.

Eastern Province Herald, 24 November 1857.

Above and left: Fathers and sons. British conquest brought radical change and disruption to the lives of the indigenous people. A number of Xhosa chiefs were imprisoned on Robben Island on trumped-up charges in the 1860s (above). Many of their sons were sent to be given a British education at Zonnebloem College in Cape Town, across the bay from where their fathers were held. Cricket quickly became their favourite sport. By the early 1860s, Zonnebloem had two teams, which included Nathaniel Umhalla, grandson of Ndlambe (front, second from right), who also studied in England. Umhalla would go on to become a pioneering player and administrator.

Queenstown  Free Press.

"BRITANNIA RESTS HER LIBERTY ON THE BASIS OF A "FREE PRESS.""

VOL XIII]   QUEENSTOWN, CAPE OF GOOD HOPE, NOVEMBER 4, 1870   No. 68

GRAND CRICKET MATCH

Last Wednesday the Cricket match between eleven of the town bats, and a like number of the students of St. Marks, and other Mission Stations, caused a great deal of excitement. Ever since the challenge was accepted by the Queenstown Club, the game has been looked forward to with no little interest, not only by the lovers of cricket, but by the townsfolk generally. It was a novelty in these parts for our swarthy brethren to pit themselves against Englishmen in a game of skill—especially cricket in which Englishmen take credit for being the most proficient in the world, and it therefore did not surprise us to see such a throng of ladies, gentlemen, children and natives, as were never on our cricket ground before, turn out on this occasion to witness the sport. Early in the morning the ground was decorated with bunting, tents and refreshment booths were erected, and the playing space marked off with small flags. The weather upon the whole was charming. It was a little too windy in the forenoon; and once it seemed as though it would be very hot, but light fleecy clouds played before the sun all day and tempered his rays. The Queenstown Club won the toss and sent their swarthy opponents to the wickets about eleven o'clock. Their play on the whole was creditable; and the last wicket fell for a score of 46—Our men then went in; and it seemed as though they were going to stay in all day. Two wickets fell pretty quickly; but it was a couple of hours and more before the third came to grief; and when they finished their innings with a score of 220 it was past four o'clock. Some of the bowling on the side of the natives was very good, it was that swift round-hand which we certainly think much fairer, and shewing greater skill than the pitching of the ball practised by our own men, but it was irregular, and we were certainly surprised at the number of catches which the natives allowed to slip through

their fingers This large score left the native batsmen 175 runs behind, so that to win the game was now an impossibility. It was enough to dishearten bolder spirits than they have; and we did not wonder that they were long in going to the wickets again But at last they made bold to play the unequal game; and well did they struggle in this second innings to maintain their reputation. There was not sufficient time to finish; but when the stumps were drawn for seven wickets down, they had made the respectable score of 112 runs. Their play this innings was excellent; and we fancy if they had had the good luck to put the Queenstown men first to the wickets, and thus have found out the stuff their opponents were made of they might have come off in the contest much better than they did. The return match will be played next January at St. Marks, we expect the African cricketers will then give a better account of themselves. From what we heard it appears to us they undertook this game without sufficient preparation. They live considerable distances apart, and it is several months since they all played together. However good players they may be, the want of united practising must mar sadly against their efficiency in a match. Some of the best native cricketers we also heard were not able to come on this occasion; if they have such men, by all means let them be present at the return match.

One of the most pleasing features of the game to our minds was the nice spirit in which it was carried on by both sides. There was no temper shown, no impatience, no complaints on the part of any one; every one behaved himself as a gentleman.

Among the talk upon this unusual event we were surprised to hear some intelligent men, at least they call themselves such, shake their heads at it, and speak as though they thought the Europeans were demeaning themselves in playing such a game. We cannot see it, and must attribute such feelings to that abominable prejudice which could raise impassable barriers between one race and another. Occasional friendly games like that on Wednesday would, we are sure, promote kindly feelings between Kaffirs and English, and from all we saw and heard of these native players we certainly think there was nothing derogatory in Englishmen playing with them. They are far removed from the raw Kaffirs, in fact they are men who as far as book learning goes, are far better educated than many of their opponents. Several of them have been to England, and others have lived in Capetown; and at present we believe they are engaged in teaching at various mission stations. The following is the score :—

Nathaniel Cyril Umhalla. This top-order batsman's cricket career stretched from the 1860s to the 1890s.

ALL QUEENSTOWN ELEVEN.
FIRST INNINGS.

W M Fleischer, b. Benikazi	41
A P Dowdle, b David	3
Dan Spengler, b Benikazi	4
P H Dowdle, run out	60
J Brown, run out	1
G Biok, c Snookie, b Toisa	18
F S P Stow, c Toisa, b Benigazi	20
A Watkins, b Banigazi	6
M Morum, c Gawe, b Benigazi	16
W J Nettelton, b Benigazi	1
G Webster, not out	2
Byes 33 ; Leg Byes 3 ; Wides 11..	52
Total	**224**

ST. MARKS ELEVEN.
FIRST INNINGS.

G Nxitanama, c Back	4
S Gawe, c Dowdle	0
G Baliwie, b Fleischer	0
N Umhalla, c Back	12
A David, b Fleischer	2
J Benigazi b Dowdle	3
S Snooke, c Webster	12
H Xexo, c Dowdle	6
A Kuxe, c Dowdle	6
A Toisa, not out	1
S Darala, b Dowdle	0
Byes, 3 ; Wides, I	4
	46
Less 1 short run	

SECOND INNINGS.

G Nxitanama, b Dowdle	18
S Gawe, not out	0
G Baliwie, not out	0
N Umhalla, run out	16
A David, run out	15
J Benigazi, b Fleischer	17
S Snooke, b Stow	9
H Xexo, b Stow	7
A Kuxe, not out	7
A Toisa, c Stow	3
S Darala, not out	1
Byes, &c.	26
	112

An 1870 report (above) of one of the earliest matches between colonisers and colonised in the world – preceding similar matches in India (below). The report noted that, following the recent law changes, African players were using the more modern 'round hand' (over-arm) bowling technique.

General view of the match

Above: Architecture of Empire. The students prepare for a day of festivities and sports on the Queen's birthday at Lovedale College, which was established in 1841. Lovedale was the nursery for a deep indigenous cricket tradition, one of the oldest in the Empire.

Creating model Victorians in the colonies: Lovedale students in their dining hall (middle) and at drill (bottom).

Above: Colonial-Born vs Home-Born became a popular sporting event among white colonists in the mid-1800s. The group of Port Elizabeth footballers pictured here in 1862 very likely also played cricket, as their clothing and the Pretoria photograph below suggest.

Right: A 'Veterans' team in Kimberley, 1878. Back row: [X] Vivian, J.P. Ablett, Major T. Maxwell, C.E. Nind, M.B. Beevor, W.F. Sheasby. Middle row: William Ling, A.F. Tancred, H.B. Roper. Front row: Patrick Sim, W.T. Graham, G.S. Chandler.

Bottom: Pretoria cricket and football team, 1878. Julius Jeppe, who played a major role in the development of Johannesburg, is standing back left.

PART ONE

WAR GAME, 1795–1870s

Who built Thebes of the Seven Gates?
In the books stand the names of kings.
Did they then drag up the rock slabs?
And Babylon, so often destroyed,
Who kept rebuilding it?
In which houses did the builders live
In gold-glittering Lima?
Where did the bricklayers go
The evening the Great Wall of China was finished?

Great Rome is full of triumphal arches.
Over whom did the Caesars triumph?
Were there only palaces for the inhabitants of much-sung Byzantium?

Even in legendary Atlantis
Didn't the drowning shout for their slaves
As the ocean engulfed it?
The young Alexander conquered India.
He alone?
Caesar beat the Gauls.
Without even a cook?
Philip of Spain wept when his fleet went down.
Did no one weep besides?
Frederick the Great won the Seven Years War.
Who won it with him?

A victory on every page.
Who cooked the victory feast?
A great man every ten years.

Who paid the costs?

So many reports,
So many questions.

– Bertolt Brecht, 'Questions of a worker reading history'

1

Cricket comes by boat to Africa

With the English officers at the Cape I was on the best of
friendly terms. With a number of them serving in the artillery
and light dragoons I twice a week played a game of ball-
casting, called cricket by the English, on the level ground by
the sea at the Lion's Tail. Round about twelve o'clock we
started our sport, sometimes with more than thirty persons.
A small cart carrying food and wine followed us and in a
jovial spirit we usually had our midday meal out in the open.

– Huibert Nahuys van Burgst, 1806[1]

Cricket came by warship to the southern tip of Africa. The symphony of willow
caressing leather does not immediately conjure up images of war. But the first
bats and balls arrived under sail, stashed in naval holds in the company of trum-
pets, drums, rifles, bayonets, cannons and trunks containing a few private items,
like perfumed letters and slivers of lace.

Britain initially occupied the Cape, which had been ruled by the Dutch for
143 years, in June 1795. The purpose was to ensure that the 'Gibraltar of the
Indian Ocean' did not fall into the hands of the revolutionary French with
whom Britain was at war in Europe. It was an easy invasion by a fleet of eight
vessels. They included three 74-gun warships, the *Monarch*, *Arrogant* and *Victorious*, commanded by Admiral Elphinstone, a veteran of the American War of
Independence and later the campaign against Napoleon.[2] After a brief battle at
Muizenberg, 1,200 infantrymen and 200 artillerymen marched across to Table
Bay, took Cape Town and raised the Union Jack over the Castle, whose distinctive ramparts still remain a prominent part of the city centre today, more than
200 years later.[3]

The ease with which the British took over the colony reflected not only on
the weak patchwork defences of the local militia, but also the good fortune the

soldiers experienced in simply getting to the Cape in reasonable health. In his epic book, *Frontiers*, Noël Mostert has described the early journeys from Europe to the Cape and to India as 'probably the most terrible self-imposed ordeal within the European experience'. The trip took months and 'was a dreadful prospect for everyone who confronted it, especially in its early days, but its basic character never really changed until well into the nineteenth century'. There was a lack of fresh food, provisions rotted, conditions were unhygienic, people were packed together, sickness 'was general' and storms caused disruption – 'broken timbers and gears, leaks, tumbled goods and shifted cargo, injuries' – and they also put out of commission the edge-of-ship lavatories or 'heads', adding to the smelly dankness on board. One had to expect the worst, Mostert concludes. 'Every man, or woman, who mounted the gangplank of an East Indiaman did so almost as though it were a scaffold. Everyone who stepped on the decks of those cramped and unwieldy vehicles had to do so on the assumption that it was a potential sentence of death.'[4]

The first known cricketer to arrive at the Cape survived the uncomfortable, unhygienic journey about which there were no 'safe assumptions about personal survival, or arrival', only to commit suicide soon after landing in 1797. He was the unfortunately named Charles Anguish, one of the officials appointed to run the new administration. Younger brother of the Duchess of Leeds, his privileged status in British society probably explained both his unusual cricket pedigree and why he was appointed to the military position of comptroller of customs at the Cape. Born in Bloomsbury in London, he went to Eton College and was among the wealthy young men who played for the White Conduit Club – 'precursor' of the MCC – at Islington in the 1780s, together with the influential Earl of Winchilsea. In the White Conduit Club, 'there was no social mix, indeed the rules of the club stated "none but gentlemen ever to play"'.[5]

Lord's and the MCC soon afterwards replaced the White Conduit Fields and Club as the premier venue and team in London – and the MCC's first match in 1787 was against his club, with Anguish participating. He became a member of the MCC, playing from the age of 20 in 1789 until 1795. He also turned out for Surrey in 1791 and Middlesex in 1794. Altogether he appeared in 40 'major' matches, 32 of them deemed 'first-class'. Many were at Lord's, and Anguish played alongside some of the leading names of the time: the Earl of Winchilsea, Charles Lennox (the 4th Duke of Richmond) and 'Silver Billy' Beldam. His name is one of those which appear in the important-sounding 'list of cricketers who took part in matches designated first-class by *Cricket Archive* between 1787 and 1825'.[6]

In September 1791, Anguish starred in an away win by 'the Gentlemen of the Mary-le-bone Club' against Nottingham in front of a crowd of over 10,000 people. Batting at no. six, he top-scored with 47 (more than double the next batsman) in a ten-wicket win. Lord Winchilsea took six wickets for the MCC in the match. The report noted, 'the extraordinary skilfulness displayed by the Mary-le-bone in all the various parts of the game was unequalled, and justly excited the astonishment of the beholders [on the Upper Meadow at Nottingham], by their superior agility'.[7] This report does not quite square with Cricket Archives statistics and other assessments that Anguish did not bowl and was a tail-end batsman with a top score of 29 in 59 innings in 32 matches at an average of 6.79.

Did Charles Anguish play at the Cape after his arrival in 1797? We do not know because there are no extant reports of cricket during the first years of the British occupation. We cannot even hazard an educated guess; although some have not surprisingly speculated that he 'might have swung a cricket bat after being appointed', Anguish had by 25 May of the same year died an untimely death at the age of 28.[8] The observant Lady Anne Barnard described him as 'a good-humoured, easy-tempered young man' who loved the Cape and 'promised fair to contribute to the pleasures of our society'. She put his demise down to 'bodily malady only' and perhaps 'some medical prescriptions' he had been taking.[9] However, the *Gentleman's Magazine* gave him a less flattering obituary: 'he was a young man of abilities, and of a good temper, but with so odd a cast of manners that he was perpetually on the brink of a quarrel, even with those who knew his intentions were quite harmless, and could make every allowance for his peculiarities.'[10] In his timeline of the history and spread of the game throughout the world, Rowland Bowen notes, 'Tradition that cricket was played' at the Cape between 1795 and 1797, and it seems highly likely that some of Charles Anguish's fellow officials or military officers, operating within his privileged circle, were familiar with the game and relaxed in some way with bat and ball. Everywhere the British landed, they played cricket.[11]

Having dislodged the Dutch, the British occupiers remained temporarily until 1802, when the Cape was returned to the Dutch under the Treaty of Amiens, and they then retook the Cape a few days after the New Year celebrations in 1806. This time the invading fleet was much bigger. As one historian graphically put it, 'Sentries on Signal Hill saw the horizon begin to fill with sails and by afternoon the enemy fleet, awesome in its magnitude, had moved into Table Bay.' The invasion force, headed by the 64-gun man-o'-war *Diomede*, consisted of more than 60 ships and several thousand soldiers. It turned out to be one of the biggest sea-based invasions in the history of the British Empire until D-Day in 1944.[12]

Colonel John Graham, a Scottish aristocrat, whose grandson decades later played in the first-ever representative cricket tournament in southern Africa, was part of the landing party of Argyll and Sutherland Highlanders at modern-day Melkbosstrand. He described the chaos and clamour of the moment:

> The boats unavoidably got into such a crowd that many of the turning boats could make no use of their oars. We were not half a common shot from the beach or sand hills. One of the boats of the Charlotte had been unable to push to windward of the rock, she touched it, instantly turned bottom up, and down went 36 of our brave fellows, cheering as they sank. Only three bodies were thrown up on shore, or ever seen again.[13]

The 1806 invasion started a century and a half of colonial rule administered from Whitehall in London. As one historian has noted, the British added 'a new element ... to an already complex mix of people at the Cape', and 'Motivated by imperialism, deceit, greed, prejudice and humanitarianism, the colony's new rulers would play a leading role in constructing one of the world's most troubled societies'.[14] Cricket and its spread through southern Africa were extremely closely linked to the process of military and political conquest in the nineteenth and early twentieth centuries. Starting off as a garrison game, it was at first confined to barracks, only gradually spreading to involve civilians and school-children, among both the indigenous people and arriving settlers from Europe.

Cricket was played on a regular basis almost immediately after the intimidating, if not accident-free, entry of the British fleet. The first evidence is from the accounts of Dr Huibert Nahuys van Burgst, a highly qualified Dutch lawyer who was later knighted.[15] Nahuys van Burgst was detained by the British while on a 'confidential government mission to Batavia' (Indonesia) on behalf of the Cape's former colonial masters. When a Danish ship on which he was a passenger sailed into Table Bay on 24 April 1806, the British flew Dutch flags 'from all the forts and bastions of Cape Town' and wore Dutch-blue uniforms over their red tunics to entice the boat into landing. Only when they were 'a few cable lengths from the land' did those on board realise the British were in charge. Nahuys van Burgst stayed in Cape Town for more than two months. Housed in the same quarters as the English surgeon and chief officer, who combined 'French courtesy with English sincerity', the baron-to-be not surprisingly seems to have enjoyed his time at the Cape. Thanks to him, we have a sense of how the game started in southern Africa:

> With the English officers at the Cape I was on the best of friendly terms. With a number of them serving in the artillery and light dragoons I twice a week

played a game of ball-casting, called cricket by the English, on the level ground
by the sea at the Lion's Tail. Round about twelve o'clock we started our sport,
sometimes with more than thirty persons. A small cart carrying food and
wine followed us and in a jovial spirit we usually had our midday meal out
in the open.[16]

The level ground by the sea at the Lion's Tail where the first matches were played
is today's Green Point Common. This is the reason why the maverick Rowland
Bowen, in his pioneering account of cricket history, has described the Green
Point Common as 'probably the oldest surviving cricket ground but one outside
the British Isles'.[17]

Bertolt Brecht, the German poet and playwright who empathised with the
underclasses in society, wrote: 'A victory on every page/Who cooked the victory
feast?' It takes little imagination to deduce that local slaves or free black people
were probably involved in conveying the food and wine in the carts at these early
games on Green Point Common, and in preparing the meal for the players, or
simply watching. In this way, black people were from the start no doubt involved
in various ways with the new game of cricket. Even if indirectly. Brecht would
have wondered, did they not also help fetch the balls for the well-fed officers
when it was their time to field in the afternoon sun?

Nahuys van Burgst's chronicled match is nearly two years earlier than what
was for long accepted as the very first report of cricket at the Cape, namely the
announcement of a contest in 1808 between two teams of British military officers
on the Green Point Common, with the artillery once again involved. A notice
in the *Cape Town Gazette and African Advertiser* of 2 January 1808 declared,
'A grand match at cricket will be played for 1,000 dollars a side on Tuesday,
January 5, 1808, between the officers of the artillery mess, having Colonel Austen
of the 60th regiment, and the officers of the Colony, with General Clavering. The
wickets are to be pitched at 10 o'clock.'[18]

Who were the two principals in this early match on the local scene, the
notice of which has for so long been endlessly rehashed without any context?
Lieutenant Colonel Thomas Austen was commander of the 4th battalion of the
60th Regiment, which had been sent to the Cape after a long tour in Jamaica
and Martinique, while the 47-year-old Brigadier General Henry Mordaunt
Clavering belonged to a distinguished aristocratic and military line and married
Lady Augusta Campbell, daughter of the fifth Duke of Argyll. His grandfather Sir James was also a field marshal and his father, Lieutenant General John
Clavering, led the attack on Guadeloupe in 1759 and became commander-in-
chief in India in 1774. One of his sons, Captain Douglas Clavering, was an Arctic

explorer who was working his way up the ranks when he disappeared off Sierra Leone in 1827. Douglas was then commanding the *Redwing*, whose task it was to bring to an end trading in slaves, which Britain had declared illegal in 1807.[19]

On the very day of the match Colonel Austen was plunged into a scandal that must have rocked the local army. He was relieved of his command of the 4th 'Foot' on 5 January for 'various neglects of duty, highly prejudicial to the service'. The point was made that his conduct was 'highly unbecoming of an Officer and a Gentleman'. The first charge was that he allowed his quartermaster, one Marriot, who had been court-martialled and found guilty of 'peculation', to leave the colony without first getting him to pay back the 500 rixdollars he had embezzled. Moreover, Austen was accused of failing to properly oversee the regiment's clothing, rations and fuel and charged with selling 'canteens to the Serjeants' and appropriating for himself wood meant for non-commissioned officers and privates while 'the regiment was encamped at 'Roundabush'. 'Roundabush' was a corruption of the Dutch name Rondebosch, where several thousand troops were stationed at what was called the Camp Ground, on the spot where Rondebosch Common is today.[20]

Three months later Thomas Austen went back to the Caribbean with his regiment – this time to Barbados – and stewed in his disgrace for more than two years before being court-martialled on five counts in 1810. In a surprising twist to the story, Austen was found not guilty on all charges and his accuser, Lieutenant Colonel Lomax, instead lost his commission and was dismissed (but later accepted back at half-pay). The court deemed Lomax's charges to be 'both frivolous and vexatious' and 'carried out to gratify private resentment'. The court, having honourably acquitted the accused, ordered that its ruling 'shall be read at the head of every corps, and entered into the regimental orderly books', but this must have been scant compensation for the poor colonel who had had his career and reputation blemished.[21]

Sport in South Africa today is often embroiled in front-page controversies. We can safely say that off-field dramas attached themselves to cricket from the very beginning.

In the same year that the unfortunate Colonel Austen was being court-martialled in far-away Barbados, the *Cape Town Gazette and African Advertiser* again carried a cricket announcement. This time the match being advertised was between the 'Ordnance Department and the Officers of the 87th Regiment' against the 'Officers of the rest of the Army' on 13 January 1810. It, too, was played for a stake of one thousand dollars.[22]

Gambling on cricket was a common practice in England and, as we shall see later, it happened regularly throughout the nineteenth century in southern Africa and other parts of the colonial world as well. We can deduce from descriptions of the horse races in Cape Town after the formation of the African Turf Club in 1797 that there were no bookmakers in this early period. Each bet was 'a matter of separate arrangement between two parties. One would offer the odds, and if anyone muttered the magic word "Done", it was a bet and neither party could cry off unless with the consent of the other.'[23]

As in cricket, military officers were prominent in entering their horses and gambling on them, and it was noted that 'The Malays also were very much addicted'. The social hierarchies then in operation could be seen in the fashions and the transport (and parked positions) of the spectators. There was a 'regular gradation from the well-appointed English carriage to that curious piece of antiquity, the ancient Dutch – the gig, the light wagon cart, and the long heavy wagon with its eight horses in hand, hired for the day and stuffed with black damsels arrayed in their brightest colours.' Confirming the involvement of the local black population, including women, in the social activities of the British at the Cape, the famous traveller William Burchell noted in 1810 that 'Malays and negroes' mingled with whites, all crowding and elbowing, eager to get a sight of the momentous contest.[24] The different forms of entertainment also overlapped. On 21 October 1814 a 'Grand Match of Cricket' was played on the Simonstown racecourse between 'twenty-two gentlemen of the navy for a Subscription Purse'. After this, 'various music and truly British Amusements' were organised including: 'Sack Races – Foot Races – A Pig to be run for, with its tail skinned and greased – Bobbing for Oranges – Smoaking [sic] for Tobacco – Eatin' rolls and treacle – Also, a Handicap Race, by Horses bona fide the Property of Naval Officers, [and] a grand Jingling Match will conclude the whole.' Lt Garrett of the Royal Navy was 'Clerk of the Course' and 'Sporting Characters' were referred to the 'South African Club House' for further details, indicating that some rudimentary structures for sport were beginning to appear at the Cape.[25]

A distinguishing aspect of colonial cricket in the first decades of the nineteenth century that jumps to the fore is the leading role played by class-conscious 'gentlemen' officers, who brought pomp and pageantry to the play, and would give the game an elite character in Africa. Imperial nations, whose status is inevitably based on force, reify their military. This was as true of Britain in the nineteenth century as it is of America today. The image of the officer and gentleman became a central part of cricket's self-image as it spread through southern Africa.

Although the connection is tenuous, it is also worth noting that this early cricket also marked the beginning of the globalisation of the game. An intimate connection developed via the military between cricket in Cape Town and the colonial project in India and other colonies. Besides Colonel Austen's subsequent posting to Barbados, where the British were similarly introducing the game, troops being transported in East Indiamen, vessels to and from India, regularly played at the Cape. Chapter 2 also describes how the so-called 'Indians' – officers, troops and officials who served in India and came to rest and recuperate at the Cape – later directly influenced the development of local cricket.

The British population in Cape Town was at first very small. When the British arrived for a second time in 1806, the total number of people was around 17,000, with slaves in the majority, followed by around 7,000 'Europeans'. Colonists of Dutch and German extraction still made up 90 per cent of the last category in 1820. So there was no immediate large-scale take-up of the game by the locals. At first it was really the military playing among themselves who participated.

During the course of the nineteenth century, tens of thousands of British soldiers came to be stationed in South Africa. Their influence was strongest in Cape Town, the seat of British power in the Cape Colony. But cricket spread throughout modern-day South Africa as the British military presence expanded in the 1820s to 1850s, firstly into Xhosaland (today's Eastern Cape), then Zululand (KwaZulu-Natal) and finally to the central interior. Rather than spreading out systematically overland from Cape Town, to Swellendam, Oudtshoorn and so on, cricket followed the seaward movements of the soldiers and officials, making big jumps along the east coast to Port Elizabeth, and later to Durban, and from these ports into their hinterlands. In those wagon-and-cart days, inland travel and communication were difficult: the first (short) railway line in southern Africa was opened only in 1860 and the telegraph line and telephone were to come later.

The *Diamond Fields Advertiser*, reviewing the early history of cricket in 1889, explained:

> The game was played in the interval between native wars, when garrison elevens taught colonists the fine old English game. At Cape Town and Grahamstown and on the border, many exciting games have been played between town and garrison and the veteran cricketers in the Colony today will tell you that they learned their cricket in these matches … The development of cricket since must be credited a great deal to colonists who have been coached in the large schools of England and to English visitors. Considering the population of the Colony an extraordinary interest is taken in the game and it is not confined to towns.[26]

As British settlers put down permanent roots and the population grew in those decades, the game spread beyond the military into schools and clubs.

As we shall see, the indigenous people, who for ages had enjoyed different forms of recreation, were quick to learn and imitate the new ruling classes. 'Throughout pre-colonial Africa … dances and games were long performed with a seriousness akin to sport in modern industrial societies', and 'for purposes not altogether different: the striving for status, the assertion of identity, the maintenance of power in one form or another, and the indoctrination of the youth into the culture of their elders'.[27] Now a new form of organised leisure was being introduced to them.

As the nineteenth century proceeded, cricket came to be defined in strongly ideological terms as a 'gentleman's game', but women, too, were involved in it from the beginning. Lady Anne Barnard's closeness to the ill-fated MCC, Middlesex and Surrey player Charles Anguish was a case in point. They went on an outing to 'Paradise' together. This was a government cottage on the slopes of Table Mountain near present-day Newlands, which the governor, Lord Macartney, 'has given us to be rural in', she explained.[28] Women endured the same long boat journeys as the men, acted in general support roles and were an integral part of the social activities that accompanied the 'pitching' of wickets. This book will for the first time try to do justice to their experiences in cricket.

2

First port of call

Cape Town, 1795 onwards

Skirmishing round their serried ranks on every patch of green
[were] crowds of small boys of all colours playing cricket.

– *Cape Monthly Magazine*, 1873[1]

Ben Maclennan has painted a graphic picture of the 'brutal, corrupt, and extraor-
dinarily inefficient' British army at the time that Britain took over the Cape.
Officers' commissions were purchased or gained through personal influence.
Ordinary soldiers often joined up to escape unemployment or were entrapped by
'recruiting sergeants' working for payment per head, or 'hustled straight from jail
into a red jacket'. The cat-o'-nine tails was still 'regarded as the universal panacea
for errant rank-and-file'.

> The day-to-day management of the army was equally irrational. Each colonel
> of a regiment ran it according to his own notions – drill varied from unit to
> unit – or neglected it altogether. Junior officers had little to do with the day-to-
> day running of the regiment, a task which was generally delegated to the
> more experienced non-commissioned officers. They were expected to attend
> a few parades, to be sure, but much of their time was spent at the theatre,
> or clubs where they could – and did – indulge in gambling, dining and vast
> bouts of drinking.[2]

Although they would take some time to filter through to the Cape, the
changes brought about in the British Army after 1795, when Frederick, Duke
of York, assumed command, were quite fundamental. In the course of the next
decade military training colleges were opened, logistics and relations between
officers and troops were improved and systematised, and the idea of a 'thinking
fighting man' was developed. Moreover, 'Physical fitness, rather than the ability

to consume excessive amounts of alcohol, was held up as the hallmark of a good soldier, and to this end officers were urged to show every encouragement to their men to take part in "cricket, hand or foot ball, leap frog, quoits, vaulting, running foot races etc.," and in short at all manly and healthy exercises.'[3]

A cricket history of 1851 noted that 'Our soldiers, by order of the House Guards, are provided with cricket grounds adjoining their barracks' and, for the sailors and soldiers going abroad, 'Her Majesty's ships have bats and balls to astonish cockroaches at sea, the crabs and turtles ashore'.[4]

The number of British troops in Cape Town reached a peak of 4,000 soon after the occupation of 1806. Many officers lived in private residences in the town centre and headquarters were at the impressive Castle on the foreshore. The parade ground alongside it was where drill and recreation merged – and where the locals of all hues would observe and imitate the troops. Until today the Castle and Parade have remained central features of the city. As with Fort William in Kolkata, the Esplanade in Mumbai and St Ann's Garrison in Bridgetown, Barbados, with its 30-acre Garrison Savannah, these symbolic features of colonialism – the fort and the parade ground – were situated at virtually the same spot where ships from Europe landed. One cricket historian has noted that the British liked to keep the water at their backs and their guns facing the 'hordes likely to emerge from the interior'.[5]

Besides the Castle and the earliest playground at Green Point, facilities for the British military were also subsequently set up in Rondebosch – home base of the unfortunate Colonel Austen – Wynberg and Simonstown, all areas which featured in the subsequent growth of cricket in Cape Town.

It is no accident that the name of the linking street that passes the famous Newlands Cricket Ground today is Campground Road. The army camp ground with its tented population became a major early cricket venue (and an aerial photograph taken more than a hundred years later, in the 1940s, shows more than ten cricket pitches on it). In the 1810s, the soldiers moved to a permanent military base at Wynberg because of its better location. The navy soon moved its headquarters from Table Bay to Simonstown, giving that village the distinctive character it has retained for two centuries.

The cricket matches of the British military became regular fixtures after 1806 and were 'important events in the social life of the young Colony'.[6] Details of cricket in the first few decades of British rule are virtually nonexistent in the available literature. The *Cape Town Gazette and African Advertiser*, in which some of the earliest evidence of cricket appeared, was not a reliable reporter, being an official government publication 'largely confined to official notices and advertisements'. Focused primary research is needed in the archives of the various British military regiments in order to uncover sources that tell us more than what amateur sport history enthusiasts have so far been able to find.

A coherent picture of cricket in Cape Town and the Cape Colony only starts emerging in the 1840s, but, according to the cricket historian N.S. Curnow, 'it is likely that the game continued to be played at Cape Town throughout the intervening period [from 1810]'.[7] 'From being a backwater of the VOC empire', Cape Town was by the 1840s becoming 'the flourishing capital of an expanding British colony'.[8] Britain 'increasingly felt the need to make over her new possession "in her own image", to adjust the alien laws, customs and institutions to the realities of British rule'. The aim was 'not merely a nationalistic urge' but to build an improved form of government. Although the British did not wish to alienate Dutch-speaking subjects who had first settled at the Cape from 1652, steps were taken to 'encourage or compel the use of the English language in most spheres of public life'.[9]

By the 1830s change was becoming evident. Slavery was abolished in 1834 and 5,550 freed slaves were added to the population of 4,000 free blacks. Increasingly this part of the population came to be described as 'Malay' or 'coloured', with the first term further categorising the person as a follower of Islam. The free people proved receptive to the new British games. As they acquired greater economic, social and political mobility after emancipation and with the onset of colour-blind 'responsible government' in 1852, they also became more free to play. The 'European' section similarly diversified and grew to more than half of the town's total population of just over 20,000 by 1840. There was now some kind of base for the growth of the game in the town, at a time when British military numbers had fallen from a peak of around 4,000 to 2,000 in the 1820s, as their presence was demanded elsewhere in the expanding colony.

One section of the colonial population that played an important part 'in the construction of "British" society' in the town was the so-called 'Indians'. They were British officers, troops and administrators who were serving or had served in India and had come to the Cape to rest or recuperate. Rather than tackling the extra leg or legs home to England (which could take 100 days each way), they stopped over in Cape Town with its healthy climate to spend their leave. The 'Indians' were often from aristocratic backgrounds, were well connected and close to the governor. They were 'chiefly observed at the race course', but they did help construct deliberate English protocols in the town and set the tone for others to follow.[10]

CIVILIANS HELP GROW CRICKET IN CAPE TOWN, 1840s and 1850s

In the 1840s, cricket started moving beyond the military barracks into the civilian population. The Wynberg area, about fifteen kilometres from the Castle and the town centre, was prominent in this forward move. One of the main fields and the first cricket club in Cape Town emerged there. The recuperating 'Indians' were involved in various ways. They had a significant presence in the village which sprang up next to the Wynberg camp. (Both the village and the military base still exist, with Waterloo Street, which divides them, a reminder of their distant origins.) According to a local historian, Les Moult, the 'Indians' cared for and maintained 'one field that had been kept in fairly good trim' in Cape Town. This was Higgs Field, not far from the military camp, situated off Main Road in today's suburb of Plumstead.[11] The first century in South Africa was reputedly scored there when a batsman named Taylor hit 110 at the 'Wynberg ground' in January 1842 for Civilians vs the Military. Taylor carried his bat and was still not out when his team were dismissed for 186.[12] If this is true, it was an extremely rare event, as the writer has not found evidence of another such high individual score until 40 years later.

Shortly after this, in 1844, the first cricket club in Cape Town was formed in Wynberg, the Wynberg Cricket Club. In October 1844 it hosted a match between 'Cape Town' and 'The Colony', presumably at the Higgs Field. In 1845 a match between 'Indians' and Civilians was reported. The owner of the land (after whom the field was named) died that year, but Mrs Higgs continued to allow cricket to be played there. Meanwhile, Simonstown, where the British naval base was situated, took on 'The World' in 1846, and we are told that Civilians vs the Military became a regular fixture, 'sometimes played at Green Point'.

The formation of the Diocesan College, commonly known as Bishops, in Rondebosch in 1849, as well as the first reference to a match in 1854 between 'Hottentots and Africander [sic]' in the Cape Colony, opened up other new fronts.[13] A former Bishops pupil recalled how the game became organised at the school:

> The college, then as now, was noted for its cricket. Football was not played in the Cape in the fifties, so that cricket held the field, more or less all year round. We practised without nets or matting. We simply picked out the best piece of turf we could find and played on that, and often had to shift the wickets before the game was over. In bowling you had to keep the hand below the shoulder, or you would be no-balled, and putting on a break was almost unknown. However, the unevenness of the ground answered the same purpose, for you could never tell which way the ball would go after it pitched, or whether it

would rise or shoot. In these circumstances the wicketkeeper's lot was not always a happy one; nor was the batsmen's, for we had neither gloves nor pads. Many more players were caught out then than now. The reason for this was that our fields were dotted all over with molehills, so that no ball would travel far if hit on the ground. The only way, therefore, to score more than one or two for a hit was to raise the ball.[14]

Playing on unprepared grass surfaces was the norm in Cape Town until the late 1870s, when the first matting was laid. Given these conditions, scores were generally very low. Twenty was regarded as a 'capital' individual score, while teams seldom reached 100. 'Extras' was often the top score and long stop was, therefore, a key position. When E.A. Judge made 45 for Bishops in 1859, it was regarded as a 'huge' score.

The Cape Town Cricket Club, catering for 'all who seek healthful and vigorous exercise', came into existence on 28 December 1857. It used the *Cape Argus* to advertise itself, drew up a constitution with 17 rules and elected a president, treasurer, secretary and committee to run the club. None of these members had titles indicating that they were in the military. Many players were apparently 'clerks in mercantile firms'. It was decided that Wednesdays and Saturdays would be 'Field Days'. Rule 9 outlined procedures for matches: 'two members would be appointed to choose sides, then each side would elect its own captain, who would have entire control of the game'.[15]

Most of the six reported games of the new club in its first season were played 'on the property of Mrs Higgs', which was by now well established, with others taking place in Green Point. Cape Town CC (55 and 51) lost to the existing Wynberg CC (63 and 59) by 16 runs. It also played an 'eleven of the Old Cricket Club' at Green Point. The other matches involved either random selections – 'youthful versus aged' – or military teams, including the 68th Regiment; a combined team of the officers of the flagship HMS *Boscawen* and the navy vessel HMS *Castor*; and troops of the Royal Artillery passing through Table Bay on the way to India on the transport vessel *Leopold I*.

Surprisingly, given the fact that the two countries played each other for the first time only two decades ago in 1991, this report confirms that southern African cricket's links with India were frequent in the early days and are as old as the game here.

THE GAME BECOMES A FASHIONABLE FORM OF RECREATION AT THE CAPE, 1860s

In the 1860s cricket became increasingly popular in Cape Town. Several factors were responsible for this. The growth of schools cricket broadened the base, a new governor – Sir Philip Wodehouse – arrived who became an active patron of the game, a prestigious annual Mother Country vs Home-Born challenge match was started, and a new club was launched which would come to see itself as 'the MCC of the Cape Colony'.

The arrival of the Canon George Ogilvie, as new headmaster at Bishops in 1861, gave local cricket a fillip. 'A stern disciplinarian' and himself a cricketer 'of very considerable merit', Ogilvie was described by the Bishop of Cape Town as a 'strong, manly Christian'. His first project as headmaster was to build much-needed new buildings and then oversee 'the clearing of the new cricket field'. He captained the Bishops team for many years and also introduced the 'carrying code of football' (or rugby) to South Africa. Cricket and rugby were at the core of the educational project as Bishops developed into an elite school of the colonial establishment.[16]

Meanwhile, Zonnebloem College, another Anglican church school, introduced cricket in the same year that Ogilvie arrived. What was particularly noteworthy about Zonnebloem was that the pupils were the sons and daughters of Xhosa, Tswana, Sotho and other chiefs. Wodehouse's predecessor as governor, Sir George Grey, personally oversaw its establishment in the late 1850s. It was based first at the residence of the local bishop at Bishop's Court, before moving to Zonnebloem, the location of modern-day Walmer Estate on the edge of District Six. The governor's aim was to forcefully integrate the Xhosa into the colonial economy and acculturate or 'civilise' them. He saw the school as an important pilot project. We are told that 'whereas parsimony was the usual practice at Zonnebloem, expenditure on cricket equipment featured in the accounts as a regular and rather extravagant outlay'.[17] The story of these young 'princes' and how they enthusiastically took to cricket is described in detail elsewhere, but by 1864, the year in which overarm bowling was legalised in England, the school had two teams. The first team played its first away match in Rondebosch in August 1864, followed by a match in Wynberg in February 1865. They also played cricket on the 'Braak' or town square in Stellenbosch during a school outing to that village.[18] In 1866 Zonnebloem beat the Reformed Club, comprising mainly soldiers, in a game at the Fort Knokke Ground in Papendorp (today's Woodstock) near their school.[19] These pupils were among the pioneers of the game in this country. Among them was Nathaniel Umhalla, later a journalist and political activist and founder member of the early South African Native Congress, who had a parallel career as a batsman, captain and cricket administrator which stretched over 30 years. (References to Africans playing cricket in other regions go back even earlier, to 1857 and 1859, as we shall see below.)

Another important educational institution, the South African College (SAC), then situated in the town and offering both schooling and undergraduate courses, also became known for its cricketing prowess in the 1860s. In the first recorded contest against Bishops in 1869, the SAC won. At first the boys literally played in the municipal paddock, sharing the space with the governor's cows. Only when Sir Hercules Robinson become governor in the 1880s did he 'willingly give up all his rights, and the paddock was given over to the College'.[20] Both the University of Cape Town and the South African College School (SACS) emerged from this College, leading to the inter-school contests that continue to this day.

According to the historian A.F. Hattersley, cricket's 'promotion as a fashionable form of recreation' by the governor, Sir Philip Wodehouse, was another reason for its growth in the 1860s. In 1862, the first of his eight years as governor, the first of the Mother Country vs Colonial-Born contests took place at Rondebosch Camp Ground under his auspices. Three church ministers and a colonel played in the match, which the colonials won by six wickets, thanks to good performances by Adrian van der Bijl and Charlie van Renen, who was described as the *facile princeps* of local cricketers. They took 14 of the wickets to fall and both scored runs: 23 and a top score of 30 respectively. These annual matches, attended by high society and accompanied by military bands and fanfare, remained popular until early in the twentieth century, when 'this famous fixture had to be abandoned owing to the sheer inability to raise a Mother Country team capable of extending the Colonial-Born players'.[21]

The Civil Service Club, founded in 1861, deepened the British nature of local cricket. According to one history, the club's membership was 'confined to the civil service, diplomatic service, army and navy, and learned professions, with merchants only as honorary members. The Civil Service Club expressed implicitly the British aristocratic contempt for trade.' (On the other hand, merchants dominated the City Club, formed much later in the in 1870s, which also had some 'anglicised Dutch' as members.)[22]

Despite their reduced numbers in the 1860s, British military units continued to be prominent in Cape Town cricket, probably providing the core of the Home Country teams in the annual matches against the Colonial-Born. In 1863, for example, the Wynberg Club played the 10th Regiment and in 1867 Colonial-Born played the Garrison in a variation of the big annual match. The Garrison was one of the three or four strongest local teams going into the 1870s, and in that decade the 86th and HMS *Rattlesnake* also 'put very fair elevens into the field'. Captain C.H. Jackson of the 86th was for many years 'quite the mainstay' of the Home Country team.[23]

Perhaps the biggest impetus for the future of the game was the formation in 1864 of the Western Province Cricket Club (WPCC) to better coordinate the local game. It was started two years after the Home-Born vs Colonial-Born games began; it serviced the same elite social base and its home ground became the long-standing Higgs Field venue in Wynberg, now renamed Southey's Field. This is confirmed by the claim that the WPCC was founded by 'certain players from Cape Town Cricket Club, Rondebosch Cricket Club and Wynberg Cricket Club'.[24] The pioneering Wynberg Club, started in 1844 and still active in 1863, now disappeared from the historical record, and its star batsman, Charlie van Renen, who made the 'sensational score' of 85 not out in 1863, began playing for WPCC.[25] In the course of time, the WPCC, or the 'Club', as it was known, became the headquarters and centre of cricket in Cape Town. It came to assume for itself the title of the 'MCC of the Cape Colony' and operated in a fashion after that body. It was also described by the club historian as the South African counterpart of the famous Hambledon Club to which 'many of the best cricketers belonged [and] in its heyday took on All England'.[26] By 1871 the WPCC had 93 members. It provides an intriguing window on the cultural life of the colonial elite at the Cape. An editorial in the *Cape Argus* went as far as to suggest that the club 'should be called the "Institution"'.[27]

In October 1864 the *Cape Argus* reported on a match of the new club, played between members living in Wynberg and Cape Town, on the one side, and those from Claremont, Rondebosch and the Diocesan College, on the other. Officers, clergymen and educationists were prominent members, reflecting the social composition of both the club and the game in those early years. 'For many years the matches at Southey's Field were the occasion of very fashionable gatherings. A military band – granted free in those days – was generally in attendance, and the Governor, Admiral, General and other distinguished people were very often present.'[28]

The local 'Cape royalty' – wealthy, anglicised Dutch-speaking landowners – also became an integral part of the club, as the names of Van Renen, Van der Bijl, Cloete, Versfeld, Overbeek and Muller indicate. By the 1850s, many families from Dutch-speaking backgrounds in the Western Cape had become 'closely identified with British ways of life, culture and traditions'.[29] They produced some fine cricketers and were regarded as part of the cream of Cape colonial society. For example, Adrian van der Bijl, who starred in the first Home-Born vs Colonial-Born game, was sent to England to be educated at the prestigious Marlborough College, before transferring to Merchiston Castle School in Edinburgh, where he captained his new school against Royal High in the first-ever inter-school rugby match in 1858.[30] Four years later Adrian was scoring runs and taking wickets in the first fixture of the Colonial-Born cricketers against their Home-Born opponents, starting a particular cricket tradition at the Cape among Afrikaners of European ancestry who became anglicised and embraced British culture and its class system. His son would play for South Africa and become president of the later Western Province Cricket Union. His grandson would participate in the famous ten-day timeless test in 1939, study at Oxford and become headmaster of Diocesan College Preparatory School. More than a hundred years later, in the 1970s and 1980s, a fourth generation, Bishops-educated great-grandson would go on to become one of the best bowlers in the country and play for Middlesex at Lord's. England had by then, in a sense, become 'home' through cricket for the Van der Bijls.

The long-established Southey's Field (also referred to as the Cape Lord's) was the idyllic venue for the new club's matches. Sheep kept the grass low and creases were marked with a knife. The field came to be regarded as 'one of the most popular resorts in the neighbourhood of Cape Town'. A leader article in the *Cape Times* recalled the enjoyment of being there 'when the sun was warm and the wind soft and low, and in the carriages, on horseback, or on foot the feminine grace and the masculine strength of the suburbs thronged that pleasant ground, listening to the strains of the band (refreshed by tickey beer) and witnessing the manly contest at the wicket between naval and military heroes or the more notable civilian clubs'.[31]

CRICKET IN CAPE TOWN GROWS 'AS NATURALLY AS WITHIN THE PRECINCTS OF YORK AND CANTERBURY', 1870s

'Cricket everywhere!' wrote one new arrival at the Cape in the early 1870s. On sailing into Table Bay, he had been delighted to see 'our beloved game going on half way up "the Devil's Peak"': 'behind Zonnebloem, on a ledge scooped as it were from the mountain's side, we have beheld stalwart young Kafirs bowling and hitting with freedom and skill'. His pleasure did not end there: 'Fort Knokke must have been named prophetically ... for there elevens, military and civilian, receive and distribute thumps to one another's shins' and, not far away, there are 'the cricketing glories of the Parade'. He also mentioned that 'as naturally as within the precincts of York or Canterbury, cricket grows beneath the shadow of St George's Cathedral' whilst 'breezy Green Point Common, one of the finest natural grounds on earth, at times swarms with cricketers'.[32]

To compensate for the few clubs and representative sides in existence at the time, many matches were played with scratch sides such as Town vs Suburbs, Married vs Single, A to J vs K to Z, and Ugly vs Handsome. Nevertheless, clubs were starting up all over: one began in Stellenbosch in the same year as WPCC, in 1864; a new Claremont CC, 'certainly very little junior, if at all' to the WPCC, was up and running by 1868; Bishops beat both the WPCC and the Garrison in 1870; and, Civilians beat the Civil Service in 1873. Clubs like Diggers and Villagers were started, and those in neighbouring country towns 'began to come into prominence'.

Recent research has revealed that the strength of Stellenbosch and country cricket over the next few decades was on par with the best in the city, and, moreover, many of the top players were Dutch-speakers. Cricket in Stellenbosch had from the earliest years been 'the most popular sport in the town ... there were no special fields or facilities and any open area would be used for matches'.[33] In 1871, the Stellenbosch and District team entertained the Western Province CC when it made its first venture into the country districts. Stellenbosch became the focal point of a flourishing cricket culture that penetrated deep into the countryside, to villages such as Eerste River, Somerset West, Paarl, Wellington, Ceres, Worcester, Robertson, Swellendam and Riversdale. Blessed with space, good weather and a healthy, outdoor life, athletic young farmers and townsmen developed an instinctive fondness for the English game. A report of a match played on Easter Monday, 1876, stated: 'This noble game is becoming exceedingly popular in the Worcester district ... The village-green swarmed with spectators of every sex, age and colour assembled to witness the much talked of cricket match between a Worcester XI and employees on the extension [railway] line.'[34]

The president of the Stellenbosch cricket club was Jan Hendrik Hofmeyr (known as 'Onze Jan'), who was to start the Afrikaner Bond in the 1880s as a political organisation representing the interests of the Dutch-speaking colonists. He came to love cricket while studying at the South African College. The cricket tradition he represented was one where Afrikaners sought access to the game on the basis of cooperation with the English, rather than assimilating into the imperial project, like the Van der Bijls and Van Renens. This meant building unity between local whites and accepting a broad definition of what constituted an Afrikaner: 'anyone who, having settled in this country, wishes to remain here to help to promote our common interests and to live with the inhabitants as members of one family'.

If Afrikaners made their presence felt early in cricket at the Cape, the black communities did not stand back either at this time. Muslim descendants of slaves (generally, but not always correctly, called 'Malays') and 'coloured' people had for a long time been part of the local cricket scene, and early newspapers refer to their involvement in cricket every week throughout the summers. The *Norsemen* passengers were well beaten when they stopped over in 1871 to play a coloured XI at Southey's Field. In 1873 reference was made to the 'cricketing glories of the

Parade'. Her Majesty's servants would fire 'blank cartridge in the mornings at the Masonic Hotel, and round shot at one another in the shape of cricket balls in the evenings'. And, said the writer, 'skirmishing round their serried ranks on every patch of green [were] crowds of small boys of all colours playing cricket'.[35] The Parade provided much enjoyment, but the authorities were conscious of mounting opposition to the games being played. Complaints were voiced, such as that of 'Vally', who wrote to the *Cape Times* a few years later: 'I have no wish to interfere with certain "darkeys" who play what they call "cricket" on the Parade every afternoon; but I would be glad if some arrangement could be made whereby passers-by – and especially ladies – would be protected. No matter how many or who passes, they stop for no-one ...'[36] This is how colonised people throughout the world were inducted into the new British game. In his history of Indian cricket, Mihir Bose quotes an early observer, who noted how

> Parsee boys began with a mock and farcical imitation of European soldiers and officers playing at Fort George, Bombay, their chimney-pot hats serving as wickets and their umbrellas as bats in hitting elliptical balls stuffed with old rags and sewn by veritable unskilled cobblers. Some enthusiastic boys at first only gleefully watched from a distance at Fort George, and then hunted after and returned the balls from the field to the players. For such gratis services rendered heartily and joyfully the officers sometimes called them to handle the bat, which was done with extreme pleasure and delight. Thus were learned the initiatory practical cricket lessons by the Parsees.[37]

In 1876 a Cape newspaper reported that 'our Malay population has its knights of the willow also and some are very dexterous ... we should be glad to hear of a match being arranged between Christian and Malay'.[38] The racially mixed Zonnebloem College team remained part of the Cape Town cricket scene for decades as well. In 1910 the mayor recalled a time when the college had the best team in the whole Peninsula.

In 1875 Cape Town was the biggest settlement in southern Africa and the seat of the colonial government with a municipal population of 33,000. Cricket was well established by this time. Indeed, the faint outlines of five distinct African-based cricket cultures, all emanating from the game's protocols laid down by the British military and imperial establishment, were already evident in the town and its environs by then. Each could be traced to distinct historical origins and locations.

One was an Eastern or Asian-African stream represented by the Muslim descendants of slaves from Asia, who had been in touch with the British from the day of their landing; another, emanated from force-fed, church-educated and

Christianised sons of African chiefs, mainly Xhosa-speaking; a third comprised an assimilated, class-conscious Dutch-speaking colonial elite; a fourth represented Dutch-speakers defining themselves as Afrikaners, who sought to play the game while retaining their identity and specific interests; and, finally, there was an emerging tradition of play amongst the Christianised descendants of the original indigenous Khoisan people of the area as well as immigrants from Europe and elsewhere. Their distinct identity as 'coloured' cricketers would only appear later when they were refused entry to the mainstream cricket fraternity by colonial whites, whose religion, culture, languages and habits they otherwise largely shared.

These interlinked cricket cultures provided a solid base for the formalised leagues and organisational coordination that were to follow in the 1880s and 1890s and, more immediately, for the first official Cape Town team, which would be selected in 1876.[39]

3

Second port of call

The eastern Cape, 1810s onwards

> The only way of getting rid of them is by depriving them
> of the means of subsistence and continually harassing
> them ... taking from them the few cattle which they
> conceal in the woods with great address, and shooting
> every man who can be found. This is detestable work
> ... we are forced to hunt them like wild beasts.
>
> – Colonel John Graham, 1812[1]

Before the British took over the Cape Colony in 1806, it consisted of four large districts covering hundreds of square kilometres. These were the Cape district (around Cape Town), Stellenbosch, Swellendam and Graaff-Reinet. The eastern boundaries of the colony stretched nominally to the Great Fish River around 900 kilometres away from Cape Town, although land on either side of this river remained contested by both colonist and Xhosa.

Within six years of the British arriving, they intervened militarily to drive the Xhosa forcibly out of the area to the west of the Fish. Colonel John Graham, who had been part of the British landing party in Cape Town in 1806, headed the military clear-out under instructions from the hardline governor, Sir John Cradock. When Graham attacked the strongholds of chiefs Chungwa and Ndlambe, his orders were to 'stay ... so long as a kaffir remains alive'.[2] An estimated 20,000 Xhosa, shocked by the indiscriminate killings, of women and children as well, who were traditionally left unmolested in war, were driven back across the Fish River through a 'proper degree of terror' in what Noël Mostert called the 'first great "removal" in South African history'. In 1812, the new towns of Cradock and Graham's Town, where the headquarters of the Cape Regiment was located, came into being in this new frontier area. A string of 20 military posts and forts were built to maintain the Fish River as the permanent colonial boundary. Some, like Fort Hare (Alice), Fort Beaufort and Fort Wiltshire (Victoria East), would later develop into towns.[3] The British soon succeeded in establishing undisputed authority over the colonial border. The foundation for future relations between black and white was established. What historians have described as a fluid, 'open' frontier closed.[4] In Mostert's words, one 'historical cycle' ended – the westward expansion of the Xhosa – and another began.[5]

It was in the conquered areas that 4,000 new British settlers were located in 1820. They were mostly from London, Bristol and East Anglia and they jumped at the chance of free land and a free passage in the depression that followed the Napoleonic Wars. The new settlers disembarked in Algoa Bay (later Port Elizabeth) – some reportedly carrying their cricket bats – and were settled in the newly created Albany district around Grahamstown. Villages such as Port Alfred, Bathurst and Salem sprang up. The new fields of British settlement became strong cricket-playing areas.

The harsh dry conditions in Albany were not what the settlers expected. They were warned, 'When you go out to plough, never leave your guns at home.'[6] They soon became as hardily colonial as the unsympathetic soil they were trying to cultivate. The British settlers brought the white population in the Cape Colony up to 47,000 and, although in a minority, they started making a big impact on colonial life. 'Within a few years of the start of the British Government's settler scheme, part of the colonial landscape had been overlaid with social and physical features of English life, such as newspapers, debating societies, horse racing and village green matches. Even the buildings began to change, with the square-built architecture of Georgian Britain moving into the towns.'[7] As with early Cape Town, no reports have been found specifically relating to cricket in the eastern Cape in the 1820s and 1830s, although it is likely that it was played and that there are archival sources that researchers still need to unlock.

The first recorded club in South Africa was formed in the heart of '1820 Settler country', at Sidbury, near Grahamstown, on 11 May 1843. A notice of a meeting 'for the purpose of establishing a cricket club' was put in the *Grahamstown Journal*. It appeared on the front page, with the plea that 'All lovers of this Noble Game, in the neighbourhood, are requested to attend'. The club is still in existence today.[8] By January 1844 there was also a Grahamstown Cricket Club in place. A notice in the *Cape Frontier Times* called members to the residence of the secretary, E.T. Taylor, to elect a 'Managing Committee'. He 'particularly requested' a full attendance. The local newspaper proudly commented:

> It is with much satisfaction that we notice the formation of a club amongst us. This game is of English origin, and it is played by no nation except the English, who have introduced it into all the countries where they have spread their race. And we hope that this, our national game, will be carried on in all these regions of Southern Africa with as much pride and spirit as it is cultivated in the Fatherland.[9]

The news of the new club was welcomed by 'A Lover of the Game' in the letter columns, who said cricketers in Port Elizabeth were keen to play against it: 'I was glad to hear a suggestion thrown out that the Port Elizabeth cricketers would be happy to try their strength against the Metropolitans, during the Easter week, upon Quagga's Flat – a proposition that I have no doubt will be readily responded to by the players of Graham's Town.'[10]

Grahamstown became a municipality in 1837 and its 'status and dignity' were enhanced when it was made the British military headquarters after the fierce sixth border war with the Xhosa in 1835: 'Regular regiments of the line were stationed on the place so that, what with the appearance of numerous red coats and the enlivening music of the bands, Grahamstown seemed almost to be a different place. Not an insignificant consideration was the large amount of British taxpayers' money which was put into circulation.'[11] This town in the disputed territory had grown to include 700 houses and 3,000 people by 1834, making it the second largest in the colony after Cape Town. Visitors commented on its very British atmosphere.

But despite the outward signs of a few solid houses and the balls of the military and government officials, it was a rough place. Some streets were in an 'execrable' state scarred by dongas, jackals ate the offal left alongside the butcher shops, and harsh military punishments were carried out in public. Soldiers were given 'forty save one' lashes with a cat-o'-nine tails on their bare backs while tied hand and foot to a big wooden triangular stake planted in front of the Drostdy building. Other transgressors were publicly drummed out of the army after the 'buttons, facings and other ornaments' of their uniforms were ripped off. The drum and fife band then played the 'Rogue's March' as they were marched off the parade ground with 'some parting kicks from men stationed there for that purpose'.[12] The military flavour of the town was inescapable: 'perpetual bugle calls, parade-ground drills and galloping cavalry platoons underlined the lurking tensions in the area'.[13]

On 23 July 1844, the settlers in nearby Salem (meaning peace, as in the Arabic *Salaam*) celebrated the 'day of arrival' some 25 years before. Robert Godlonton recorded that at the celebrations, 'The youth and young men, and some even of riper age who had not lost their relish for the sports of their youth, were quickly engaged in the manly exercise of cricket.'[14] Why would the game have taken place in mid-winter? Guy Butler suggests in *Love Feast* that it may have been linked to a harvest festival at the local church. Later, Queen Victoria's birthday on 24 May was another popular occasion for cricket matches involving the mission schools and clubs in the region. The award of commonage land to the Salem party on 13 December 1836 may have contributed to the growth of the game there as well. The names of the early settler families – Gush, Emslie, Long, Wilmot, Pringle, Hobson, Purdon – still feature in provincial teams and in the matches between Salem and its old rivals in the Pineapple Tournaments for which the area is famous.

Only two months after the formation of the first club in Sidbury, a second was founded in nearby Port Elizabeth, 90 kilometres away, where the settlers had landed. PE, as it became known colloquially, was fast becoming a thriving seaport, exporting wool and other agricultural goods to Britain, and it would grow into an economic hub for the whole eastern Cape and, indeed, for the Cape, at one time outstripping Cape Town in importance. In July 1843 local enthusiasts got together to form the Port Elizabeth Cricket Club (PECC). In December that year, a newspaper correspondent noted that 'Some spirited and successful attempts have been made to introduce the truly old English game of cricket amongst our towns people'. He added that 'Already some well contested matches have been played'. The scorecard for one of these on New Year's Day in 1844 between the Married and Single Members of the PECC, was included.

Although Ivor Markman has established that the original PECC did not survive long, regular games continued to be held in the port city. For example, in 1845 the bachelors of the Port Elizabeth Club beat the Married Gentlemen in a game which 'commenced with spirit and continued interesting both to players and spectators'. In 1847 'the admirers of this truly noble pastime' were called to assemble 'at the Ground for a friendly game 'and to adopt some plan for the formation of a club'. The Port Elizabeth Union Cricket Club emerged, and it later developed rules and regulations and informed members that they should meet for practice every Monday afternoon at four o'clock, and for a 'Field Day' on the first Monday of each month after lunch. In 1848 there was a friendly for 'the Port Elizabeth Juveniles as are willing to partake of the truly noble pastime'. In 1852 and again in 1856 attempts were again made to revive clubs, and in 1857 a 'grand match' was played on 'the Hill' between The Military and The Civilians.

Finally, in 1859 the modern-day Port Elizabeth Cricket Club (PECC) was formed afresh, putting cricket permanently on an organised basis. The *Eastern*

Province Herald commented that it was gratified 'to find none of that rigmarole characteristic of amusement clubs formed but to fail'. The new club had an entrance fee of ten shillings and a five-person Committee of Management. It ordered 'plant' (equipment) – which came from Cape Town on board the steamboat *Zulu* – started soliciting local businesses for support, and was given two acres of land by the municipality for a dedicated field. The founding meeting took place at the Commercial Hotel on 27 January 1859. Forty members were enlisted and the *Herald* said 'it would indeed be discreditable to our prestige as descendants of "The Sons of Merrie England" were it now to languish for want of support and attendance'.

A second club, the Knickerbockers (later, Union CC), was formed in 1867. It was a breakaway from the PECC and, like the PECC, was based in St George's Park, which became the permanent home of cricket in the town. The first inter-club contest of the traditional rivals was held in a carnival atmosphere: 'The band of the 86th Regiment, by kind permission of the Colonel and Officers, was on the ground and played some capital selections.'

Two years later, in 1869, black Africans, who were not permitted by colonial custom into the whites-only sporting scene, formed a club as well. Reference to this is made in a newspaper report on Peter Rwexu, who became the 'father of cricket' and a prominent community leader in Port Elizabeth.[15] Another report attributes to Rwexu and Messrs Ngcoza and Mqikela the forming of the Fear Not Cricket Club in 1872. Whether the two reports refer to the same event is not known. But Fear Not CC became a feature of the Port Elizabeth sports scene and 22 years later, Rwexu, who was a wicketkeeper, was still playing with his son and the sons of his two co-founders.

In 1876 the South End Cricket Club was formed in the racially mixed area with the same name near the harbour. South End became a vibrant cosmopolitan community, much like District Six in Cape Town and Fordsburg in Johannesburg, before it was destroyed in the apartheid era. The South End CC, reported to be an amalgamation between two already existing clubs, survived right through to the 1970s, when it was consolidated with other clubs under a new name.[16]

Here is proof that black people have been playing cricket from the earliest days in the province. By the 1870s some among them had been born and 'resided all their lifetime in Port Elizabeth'. They lived mainly in the town, in three municipal locations set aside for Africans, namely Strangers, Coopers Kloof and Reservoir. They had built good houses and several churches and schools for themselves. This first generation of urbanised Africans were national pioneers in more ways than one. The first black temperance and benefit societies in the colony were formed in Port Elizabeth in the 1870s and, in the next decade, the first proto-national political organisation, Imbumba Yama Nyama, also called the South African Aborigines' Association, had its base there. In 1884 Peter Rwexu's wife was one of the founders of a croquet club for African women in the port city. The first organised rugby for black people started here too a few years later. These 'school people' were linked in many different ways, through church, club, school and workplace, just as the white cricketers formed part of a specific community.

Before the discovery of gold and diamonds, the economy of the Cape Colony rested on the wool industry. A railway line connecting Port Elizabeth and neighbouring Uitenhage with the wool-producing areas of Cradock and Graaff-Reinet was opened in 1880. Together with merchandise along the line of rail came people and ideas, as well as organised voluntary associations and activities, including cricket teams and matches. Cricket was being played in Graaff-Reinet by the 1850s and the well-known Standard CC of Cradock was formed in 1864. Sporting connections developed between these towns and Port Elizabeth. The *Graaff-Reinet Herald* of 19 July 1854 stated:

> What with Dissolving Views, the Races and now two Cricket Clubs, we are going ahead surprisingly well. To be sure there is very little business doing right now and this melancholy fact doubtless accounts for a loss of gaiety. But, be that as it may, we have the satisfaction of announcing that on Monday July 31, a grand match will be played between our local clubs. The challenge, given by The Tradesmen was cordially accepted by The Gentlemen, with the proviso that the match should be for bats and balls and not for money. Most find this an agreeably English custom. The number of spectators is expected to be quite considerable, as the match has excited a good deal of interest throughout town. Both parties feel quite confident of winning.[17]

XHOSALAND BECOMES 'THE BORDER'

Meanwhile, from the 1840s onwards, the British and their colonial proxies forcibly extended the boundaries of the Cape Colony, from the area around Grahamstown further inland and eastwards. As the process of military conquest intensified and Africans were dispossessed of more territory, cricket rapidly followed. Both before and after formal conquest and the annexation of new areas of Xhosaland, missionaries, traders, administrators and soldiers moved in and introduced the game. The conquered inhabitants proved remarkably receptive, giving rise to a cricketing culture that is one of the oldest and most unique in the world, as we shall see.

In 1847, after the War of the Axe, the Xhosa were forced to forfeit more of their land and the boundaries of the Cape Colony moved further eastwards to incorporate the new Victoria East district, with new towns such as Alice and Fort Beaufort arising. The area from the Keiskamma River (the boundary of Victoria East) to the Kei River in the east became for a short time the separate colony of British Kaffraria, with King William's Town as its capital.

Within a year or two of the war ending, cricket was being played by the soldiers and officials in the town. In a match in 1853, the *Grahamstown Journal* noted that most of the spectators were local African people. Political and economic integration was leading to social integration of sorts as well. In 1855 a newspaper reported that a race meeting in that town was 'enlivened' on the fourth day by 'Kaffir races on horseback and on foot'.

For the next three decades King William's Town remained the military headquarters on the frontier for the regiments responsible for subjugating the Xhosa people and steadily extending the boundaries of the Cape Colony. The Cape Mounted Rifles and the Cape Infantry were among the regiments stationed here. The first club in the town was the Union Cricket Club, followed by Alberts and the Kaffrarians, but it was the soldiers stationed in that town who ensured that this was one of the strongest cricket centres in South Africa up to the 1880s – King William's Town won the first-ever inter-town tournament in 1876, as we shall see.[18]

Following the next frontier war, which ended in 1853, the boundary shifted yet again – to the Kei River – and the new district of Queenstown was established in territory from which the Thembu had been chased out. The new towns of Cathcart, Queenstown and Bolotwa were started, and the land of the Thembu was parcelled out to English and Dutch-speaking colonists who had fought for the government in the war. 'Any attempt to establish a European community was naturally fraught with danger', said a town historian, but 'the pioneers were armed with strong religious faith, as well as with carbines'.[19] Once again there were soon reports of cricket being played in these areas. The earliest one came from the Bishop of Grahamstown in September 1860. Inspecting the inland Anglican mission schools, he noted the enthusiasm for the game among black pupils at St Mark's mission, some 50 kilometres from Queenstown:

> Before chapel there was a hearty game of cricket going on, with somewhat defective instruments it is true, but with great earnestness and considerable skill. A bat and ball kindly sent to the St Mark's boys by two young ladies in England, were much valued, and they had made a second bat for themselves, but for the wickets they used stones, as the ground was too hard for any wickets made by them. Sometimes the English word 'out' but more generally the Kaffir 'ufile' ('He is dead') proclaimed the fall of an adversary.[20]

More informally, in 1862, John Shedden Dobie, a traveller from Natal who had come to buy sheep, met a farmer one-day's ride from Queenstown – 'a good-looking fellow, but decidedly like all I have seen, having a deuced seedy appearance, boots all worn out on the sole!' – who had been 'amusing himself by playing cricket with Kaffirs'.[21] In 1865 the locals officially formed a club in Queenstown, tying their 'mounts to ... the horserails which stood in the street', before electing the local civil commissioner as first president.[22]

East London became the third major cricket centre to emerge in the part of Xhosaland that the colonists called the 'Border' region of the eastern Cape. The region, and the development of cricket, were shaped profoundly by an ever-changing border, as black people were pushed this way and that and finally dispossessed of their land and incorporated into the colony. Started as a military outpost in 1847 during the War of the Axe, East London remained a small settlement until the 1870s, isolated on the extremity of the Cape Colony. Between 1853 and 1863 the colonial civilian population rose from a meagre 124 people to only 366. However, once it was decided to build a railway line stretching to Queenstown and Aliwal North (and, eventually, Johannesburg), East London grew steadily as a port and an important regional commercial centre. The establishment of a municipality in 1873 was a signal of this new growth.[23] Five years later, the first newspaper, the *East London Advertiser*, appeared and the first known cricket club, Buffalos – named after the river that divides the town and runs into the sea – was started.[24] And within five years of that, the people dispossessed of their land by the formation of this town followed with their own clubs, the most important – Gaika CC – named after the former chief living in this area, Ngqika.

The Xhosa had suffered nine wars of dispossession and lost much of their land in the 100 years between the 1780s and 1880s. In that time, cricket had expanded as the frontier moved inexorably eastward. It was in this crucible of war and conquest that one of the hardiest and most African-rooted cricket cultures in South Africa emerged. Never was the Oxford historian Cecil Headlam's aphorism more appropriate than here: 'First the hunter, the missionary and the mercenary; next the soldier and the politician, and then the cricketer – that is the history of British colonialism.'[25]

4

The beginnings of a unique African cricket tradition

Hail Great Britain
You come with a bottle in the one hand and a Bible in the other;
You come with a preacher assisted by a soldier;
You come with gunpowder and bullets;
You come with cannons and guns-which-bend-like-knees.
Please forgive me o God, but whom should we obey?

– S.E.K. Mqhayi[1]

Sometimes the English word 'out' but more generally the Kaffir 'ufile'
('He is dead') proclaimed the fall of an adversary.

– Bishop of Grahamstown, 1860[2]

British missionaries began setting up schools in the lands of the Xhosa long before the colonial boundary reached the people in the aftermath of the different wars. Chiefs, cautiously seeking to understand European ideas and keen to make use of the missionaries as intermediaries, gave them permission to live among the Xhosa and helped them identify sites where they could settle. Eventually more than a hundred mission stations, laid out like little English villages, were spread across the landscape of the region.

A whole range of schools for African children with strong cricket traditions sprang up throughout the eastern Cape. The first was the famous missionary institution, Lovedale College, on the outskirts of Alice, a town which grew up around the army garrison at Fort Hare. Set up by the Presbyterians in 1841, Lovedale's classes were racially mixed at first. Many cricketers and sportsmen emerged from the school in subsequent decades, including Percy Ross Frames, later chairman of De Beers Consolidated Mines and first president of the South African Rugby Board. In 1853, the Methodists started Healdtown College, 30 kilometres away from Lovedale, near Fort Beaufort. The Anglican Church built St Matthew's College in the Keiskammahoek valley, the same distance in the other direction. The valleys, stretching beneath the mountains from Fort Beaufort, Alice, Middledrift, Pirie, Burnshill and Mount Coke through to King William's Town, became known as the 'black cricket belt of the Border', and until well into the twentieth century they produced more than half of all black matriculants in South Africa. A distinct tradition of intellectual thought, politics and sport, which was to shape the path of twentieth-century South Africa, emerged from these few schools. They were the nurseries for the unique cricket cultures for which the region is still known today. This long and proud tradition, one of the oldest in the old colonial world, has been completely ignored in early histories of South African cricket.[3]

Meanwhile, St Andrew's College, like Bishops in Cape Town, was established by the Anglican Church in 1855 in Grahamstown. (St Andrew's was for white children only; the Anglicans also started the so-called Kafir Institution in the same town in 1860.) Other new elite schools for white boys were the Grey Institute in Port Elizabeth, established in 1856, and Dale College, which came into being in King William's Town in 1877. At all of these schools, both black and white, the children were educated in the British way. They became cricket nurseries comparable to schools anywhere else in the British Empire. To better understand the deeper history of South African cricket, we need to elaborate a little more on the uniqueness of the eastern Cape mission schools for African children.

At these European oases with white-washed buildings and clusters of exotic trees, students were given a basic Western education and taught Christian doctrine in combination with British cultural values. They were also instructed in agriculture and trades and were encouraged to wear European clothes and build square houses. They were expected to forgo local customs such as initiation, polygamy and *lobola*, the transfer of cattle on marriage, which the missionaries regarded as 'uncivilised'. Cultural conversion, therefore, had to accompany the acceptance of the Christian religion. This threatened the whole fabric of Xhosa society, because it undermined traditional relations and authorities.[4] As one missionary put it: 'The moment a Caffre becomes a convert, he comes into direct opposition to the institutions of his country. Circumstances occur almost every day in which he cannot obey his chief, or yield to the abominable customs in which very much of the chief's influence consists ... The pure gospel of the Son of God cannot prevail in Caffraria while Caffre institutions remain.'[5]

Recreation became a matter of supreme importance at the mission schools because many of the amusements of tribal Africans were deemed 'incompatible

45

with Christian purity of life' and had to be abandoned by those embracing the new religious ideas. Provision was, therefore, made for 'healthy exercise and the profitable employment of leisure'.[6] Drill became a regular feature on timetables and sports like cricket and football were introduced.

Reports from Lovedale showed very well the connection between religion, education, culture and sport at the time. In 1870 festivities were held to celebrate the founding of one of the earliest African Sunday school unions. After a day and a half of church services and festivities, the nearly 700 young people involved 'broke up into parties for various sports, among which the English game of cricket attracted many of the elder boys and young men'.[7] On the Queen's birthday in 1877, all the pupils at Lovedale, in a way typical of other schools, had a day of sports in the fields.[8] Forty years after the formation of Lovedale, going into the 1880s, this cricket tradition had become firmly rooted. A missionary newspaper reported that there were five clubs around Lovedale at that time and also teams in the adjacent rural villages of Ntselamanzi and Gqumahashe. The thousand pupils who passed through the institution in the 1870s were to provide a solid foundation for the future spread of cricket.

The earliest testimony of cricket at these new colonial schools in the eastern Cape was the report already quoted from St Mark's Mission near Queenstown by the Bishop of Grahamstown in September 1860. St Mark's, which had around 50 outposts and 30 schools, some up to 80 miles from its main location, also features in some fascinating later reports.

In 1869, old boys of Zonnebloem College in Cape Town held a reunion at St Mark's at which 'several games of cricket' were played and there was an athletics meeting that included a 'ball throwing contest'. The following year the black St Mark's team challenged the white Queenstown club. The *Queenstown Free Press* has left us with an account of the match, played in November 1870. This match and the report on it are made even more remarkable by the common assumption that existed among whites during the apartheid era that black people had never played cricket.

The whole of Queenstown turned out to see the unusual combination from St Mark's take on the town team. The *Queenstown Free Press* reported:

> It was a novelty in these parts for our swarthy brethren to put themselves against Englishmen in a game of skill – especially cricket in which Englishmen take credit for being the most proficient in the world, and it therefore did not surprise us to see such a throng of ladies, gentlemen, children and natives as were never on our cricket ground before, turn out on this occasion to witness the sport.[9]

Early in the morning of the match, the ground was 'decorated with bunting', tents were put up and 'refreshment booths were created'. The playing space was marked off with flags. The weather 'upon the whole was charming', and play started at 11 o'clock.

This is the earliest detailed match report and scorecard involving African people found so far, and it deserves to go into this record. The St Mark's line-up, in batting order, that day (as recorded by the *Free Press*) was G. Nxitanama, S. Gawe, G. Baliwie, N. Umhalla, A. David, J. Benikazi, S. Snooke, H. Xhoxho, A. Kusse, A. Toise and S. Darala. Queenstown won the toss and sent their 'swarthy opponents' in to bat. The *Free Press* reported that 'Their play on the whole was creditable'. St Mark's managed 46, which in those days was sometimes enough to win by an innings. Nathaniel Umhalla, batting at no. four, was joint top scorer with 12. Queenstown soon dominated. They knocked up an unusually high 220 before being all out. The newspaper observed, 'Some of the bowling on the side of the natives was very good, and it was that swift round hand which we certainly think much fairer, and showing greater skill than the pitching of the ball practised by our men'. However, it continued, the bowling was 'irregular' and too many catches were dropped. Extras was second top score, including 11 wides and 38 byes. This was perhaps explained by the fact that the visitors, who lived a 'considerable distance apart', had not been able to prepare or play together for several months. The best Queenstown batsmen were Dowdle (60) and Fleischer (41). Former Zonnebloem student J. Benikazi stood out as a bowler, taking six of the Queenstown wickets. With winning impossible, the Africans now 'made bold to play the unequal game; and well did they struggle'. When play ended the total was a respectable 112 for seven: Umhalla 16, Benikazi 17 and Nxitanama 18, were responsible, helped by 25 extras.

The Queenstown people were clearly impressed. Moreover, the spirit on both sides was good: 'There was no temper shown, no impatience, no complaints on the part of anyone; everyone behaved himself as a gentleman'.[10] Not everyone approved though. The *Free Press* noted:

Among the talk upon this unusual event we were surprised to hear some intelligent men, at least they call themselves such, shake their heads at it, and speak as though they thought the European were demeaning themselves in playing such a game. We cannot see it, and must attribute such feelings to the abominable prejudice which would raise impassable barriers between one race and another. Occasionally friendly games like that on Wednesday would, we are sure, promote kindly feelings between Kafirs and English, and from all we saw and heard of those native players we certainly think there was nothing derogatory in Englishmen playing with them.[11]

Far from being inferior, argued the *Free Press,* the African players were in many respects more sophisticated than their white opponents. Not only did they have cultured bowling styles, and not only were they 'far removed from the raw Kafirs', they were also better educated and more well travelled than the local cricketers: 'In fact, they are men, who as far as book learning goes, are far better educated than many of their opponents. Several of them have been to England, and others have lived in Cape Town.'[12] Here the newspaper was referring to the former students at Zonnebloem, some of whom had been sent to study in Britain at St Augustine's College in Canterbury. They included the all-rounder J. Beni-kazi, who took six wickets, Arthur Toise, H. Xhoxho and top-order batsman Nathaniel Umhalla, who got double figures in both innings and was described as the most 'enlightened native' on the Anglican missions.[13]

The Queenstown match in 1870 predates by seven years the first such contest between local people and the British in India, namely the Parsis vs the Bombay Gymkhana in 1877.[14] These pioneer games in India are recorded in Ramachan-dra Guha's majestic study of Indian cricket, *A Corner of a Foreign Field.* (The games in which Umhalla and his fellow students played for Zonnebloem in Cape Town in 1865 predated the Indian game by 12 years.)

How did it come about that Africans were playing colonial white clubs so early when all over the Empire the club, the last retreat for colonial whites, was maintained as an exclusive place where the indigenous people could cook, clean, serve and prepare the wicket, but not play. In the Indian case, the British agreed to the game because Sir Cowasji Jehangir, described as a wealthy 'Parsi potentate', paid for 'the furnishings' of the white gymkhana's pavilion, 'although he knew this would not buy him membership.' In the African cases, the facilitator was no doubt a well-placed church minister – not inconceivably, even the Bishop of Grahamstown himself, under whose direct authority St Mark's fell. Cricket was at the core of the mission project and the Anglican Church was no doubt market-ing its exceptional Zonnebloem students, with their aristocratic background, whose education had resulted from an initiative of the Cape governor himself.

The historic Queenstown match was regarded as such a success that a return fixture was agreed upon straight away. The match took place a few weeks later in January 1871. This match was very closely contested with the result in the balance right up until the end. The St Mark's 'Native Eleven' scored 46 and 98, to which Queenstown replied with 92 and 37 for six before bad light stopped play. Sixteen runs to go. Four wickets to take. Both teams would have seen themselves as favourites to win had the weather not intervened, but, given the state of the game and conditions at the time, the 'claim of the swarthy brethren' would probably have had the most merit.[15]

M.W. Luckin's standard colonial-era *History of Cricket in South Africa* notes that in 1871 'Natal' travelled down to the Cape Colony to play Queenstown in one of the first cross-territorial matches on record.[16] This is further corroborative evidence that the quality of the local cricket, and therefore the achievements of the St Mark's team, should not be underestimated. There is a further report of St Mark's playing the Bolotwa Mission a few years later. St Mark's and Bolotwa are today hardly recognisable dots on a map, but these echoes of the game in the nineteenth century indicate the area was something of a stronghold; in 1892, the white Bolotwa team played in an inter-town tournament in East London and just lost to the hosts.

In any event, the cold fact of history is that cricket at certain black mission schools predated the game at top white schools in the eastern Cape, such as St Andrew's, Grey High, Dale College, Selborne College and Queen's College, which are assumed to have been the school nurseries for the region. St Andrew's, for example, was founded later than Lovedale, and the first record of cricket there is from 1877 when two masters 'organised the school-club, and made cricket a serious undertaking'[17] – and all this was happening before cities like Johannesburg even existed.

By the 1870s the number of graduates from the mission schools in the eastern Cape had swelled to the extent that they became a distinct stratum of colonial society. The 'new Africans' self-consciously sought to develop the same skills and lifestyles as white colonists. They started pushing for involvement in the evolving Cape colonial society, economically, politically and socially. They began to qualify as teachers, ministers, law agents, clerks, interpreters, blacksmiths, telegraph operators and printers. Others farmed, producing goods for the market rather than for subsistence purposes. To advance and encourage these activities, they formed the first modern church, temperance, mutual aid, farmers', teachers' and cultural associations.

In their quest for a place in the economic and social order of the colony, the new mission-educated intellectuals by the late 1870s also started to demand political rights for qualified black people in line with Christian and British liberal values which emphasised equality. Growing in numbers and chastened by government behaviour in the ninth war of dispossession in 1877–8, they started 'shooting with the pen', writing to the newspapers, petitioning parliament and mobilising organisationally to fight for black rights. In the next decade, the young graduates from places like Lovedale, Healdtown and St Matthew's would form new organisations and newspapers, using the weapons of deputations, mass meetings, petitions, protests and other forms of constitutional struggle that became familiar later.

The political system in operation at the Cape in that time provided some outlet for these aspirations, as the Cape constitution of 1853 made no colour distinction but maintained a qualified, non-racial franchise. It was based on mid-Victorian liberalism, which emphasised the importance of free wage labour, secure individual property rights within a free market and a system of political representation. The young intellectuals were hopeful that the Cape system would lead to progress and the eventual acceptance of Africans as full citizens, and they therefore started registering as voters in increasing numbers. They held that this constitutional system could be a model for the future, particularly as most of their fellow colonists virulently opposed social and political equality, and there were no meaningful political rights for indigenous people in any other territory in southern Africa, British- or Afrikaner-ruled.

This Cape model of political inclusivity, which allowed for black people to vote and stand for parliament, as well as the intense process of African political mobilisation that occurred in the 1880s, was unusual for the colonial world. Historians have claimed that 'If anything, the Cape was in advance of, or at least equal to, most of Europe where the franchise was concerned'.[18] The Reform Acts of 1867 and 1883 were the starting point for democratising the political system in Britain, and it was not until 1890 that a working-class candidate went to parliament. Other European states, such as Belgium, Norway, Sweden, Finland and Italy, only started opening up their systems between 1894 and 1913.

The new cricket-loving African intellectuals wanted nothing less than eventually to be assimilated fully into the Cape Colony as British or colonial citizens. By 1884 they were talking about sending their own representatives to parliament and they were influencing the election outcomes in several eastern Cape constituencies. As a unique group of mission-educated and enfranchised Africans, they came to occupy a special position in Cape and South African politics.[19] The renowned author J.M. Coetzee observed that colonialism meant 'the end of Xhosa military power, but it was by no means the end of the Xhosa':

> With the hold of tradition broken, individual Xhosa were released to sink or swim in the colonial economy. Many sank, some swam ... From [the missionary institutions] for advanced education began to emerge a new Xhosa elite, 'Christian, articulate, model Victorian gentlemen in their conservatism, respectability and sobriety' ... Westernised by force ... [they] were to provide

black South Africans with political leaders for the new age they were entering, including most of the founding fathers of the African National Congress.[20]

Sport was to be integral to this whole process of assimilation and mobilisation as the aspiring middle class of Western-educated and Christianised Africans responded to new opportunities and opened up the way for the future. It was one of many aspects of British culture that they enthusiastically adopted to promote their goals of participation in the new colonial society. Cricket, in particular, was taken very seriously. This was because the Victorians regarded it as embodying a perfect system of ethics and morals. Like the main character in the novel *Tom Brown's School Days*, they accepted that 'it's more than a game. It's an institution' – it cultivated manly qualities of discipline, team work, unselfishness, reliance on others, skill, 'gentleness and firmness and I know not what other rare qualities'.[21]

The new black spokespersons were intent on using sport as an instrument of improvement and assimilation. By enthusiastically playing the most gentlemanly and Victorian of games, they intended to demonstrate their ability to adapt to European culture and behave like gentlemen – and, by extension, to show their fitness to be accepted as fellow citizens. Through sport the representatives of this emerging class could pay homage to the ideas of 'civilisation', 'progress', Christianity and Empire that were so precious to the British Victorians, and they could call for imperial concepts of 'fair play' to be respected. Cricket would become a vehicle for asserting their own self-conscious class position and showing the ruling classes that indigenous people could do as well as any other citizen if given a chance.[22]

In short, with Africans now living within the same boundaries as their conquerors from Britain and other parts of Europe, and now operating within a common economy and society, they realised that the only way forward was for them to play the coloniser at his own game.

5

Berthing in Port Natal, 1840s onwards

> A cricket match is said to have come off at the Camp,
> with not a little spirit. So much for sportive activity; and
> anything is almost better than sloth, for 'Satan finds some
> mischief still for idle hands to do'. And, while officers
> have been taking a little exercise with bats, wickets and
> balls, instead of bullets, rockets and bombshells, some
> activity has been evinced in raising a Native Militia.
>
> – *Natal Witness*, 24 March 1848[1]

After taking over the Cape Colony, with its major towns of Cape Town and
Port Elizabeth, the British skipped along the east coast by sea to eThekwini
(Durban) and eMgungundlovu (Pietermaritzburg) in Zululand. Thus modern
KwaZulu-Natal became the third regional growth point for cricket in southern
Africa. Once again a deeply enduring cricket tradition developed. The mainly
English-speaking white population so proudly identified itself as English in this
province that it was still often referred to in the late twentieth century as the 'last
outpost of the British Empire'.

Britain annexed Port Natal and started the town of Durban in 1843 in a
place the original occupiers of the land, the Zulu, called Thekwini. The Dutch
Voortrekkers, trying to escape from British control, had moved overland out of
the Cape Colony and asserted control over Zululand after defeating Dingane at
Ncome in 1838. They then set up the short-lived Republic of Natalia (1838–43),
claiming as its territory the land from the Mzimkhulu River in the south to the
Thukela in the north and from the Drakensberg Khahlamba mountains to the
coast, a vast area. However, the British were afraid that the port would fall into
the hands of another European power, and intervened. In 1845 the former Zulu
lands became a separately administered district of the Cape until 1856, when
the territory became the Colony of Natal with limited self-government. Once

again the Boers trekked away beyond British boundaries into the interior. British settlers followed in their wake, taking over their farms in Natal. The Zulu were pushed back into reserves and governed according to a system of indirect rule, known as the Shepstone system, that would later become a model for apartheid.

Cricket soon took root in the port town of Durban and in the capital of Natal, Pietermaritzburg, situated on the escarpment some 80 kilometres inland. The first known games took place here in 1847 and 1848. In March 1848, the *Natal Witness* noted that the soldiers of the 45th Foot Regiment (later known as the 2nd Battalion Sherwood Foresters), commanded by Colonel Edmond French, played the game at their camp, Fort Napier, in Pietermaritzburg. The editor, D.D. Buchanan, was a strict teetotaller and was unhappy about the social impact the game was having on the new town. First he complained about the drinking and then about children missing Sunday school to play cricket, saying their behaviour compared poorly with that of their servants, 'the off-spring of Ham'.

> A cricket match is said to have come off at the Camp, with not a little spirit. So much for sportive activity; and anything is almost better than sloth, for 'Satan finds some mischief still for idle hands to do'. And, while officers have been taking a little exercise with bats, wickets and balls, instead of bullets, rockets and bombshells, some activity has been evinced in raising a Native Militia.[2]

A few months later, Buchanan complained again, saying that outside the military camp, there was 'not a solitary English child who will have to thank his parents that ever he was a Sunday scholar in Pietermaritzburg in 1847':

> are [the heads of families] contented that idleness and mischief fill up the sacred hours of white children, while the offspring of Ham is being instructed in the grandest truths that ever enlightened or elevated human nature? – that while our servants' children are 'remembering the Sabbath Day to keep it holy', their masters' sons are gambling with money and marbles, or defying public decency with the bat and the ball.[3]

Despite these complaints, cricket became popular among the civilians of Pietermaritzburg. They founded the first club in Natal in 1851. This was West End CC, which practised on vacant land in Church Street. It was reported that the West End club 'intend to practise the old English game regularly, so that they may prepare themselves for friendly contests'. On New Year's Day in 1852, in a festival atmosphere generated by 'numerous groups of spectators', West End played a second club, East End, on the Market Square. A third team, Olympic CC, was set up in 1852 and the Pietermaritzburg CC was established in 1859.[4]

The 'sons of Ham' were not only diligent in attending Sunday school. As in the eastern Cape, they also started playing cricket at a very early stage, but for various reasons never on the scale of those in the colony to the south. The earliest reference is from the Anglican mission at Ekukhanyeni, some 14 kilometres from Pietermaritzburg, which was headed by the controversial Bishop John Colenso. A fiery critic of Natal colonial policy, Colenso built a boarding school for the sons of Zulu chiefs 'who would conduct themselves as any young nobleman at Eton and Harrow'. This was even before Sir George Grey embarked on his experiment at Zonnebloem in Cape Town with the sons of Xhosa and Sotho chiefs. Colenso noted in 1857 that the young Zulu 'would make excellent cricketers and even now pitch and catch a light ball, as if they have been used to it all their lives'.[5] Ekukhanyeni was started in February 1856 and by the following year observers were commenting on the fielding skills of the Zulu pupils: 'they rarely fail to strike down the wicket from a distance' – a skill attributed to their familiarity with 'flinging assegais'.[6]

This experiment did not last long, however. Ekukhanyeni was closed after only four years, and the main cricket schools in Pietermaritzburg became the white Maritzburg College (1863), Hilton College (1872) and Michaelhouse (1896); Durban High School was founded in 1866. In a mission field dominated by American, Norwegian and German societies that did not actively encourage cricket and in a relatively unintegrated society, few Zulu people took to cricket. The only exceptions were at the Methodist mission stations like Edendale near Pietermaritzburg. Up to the 1890s, government policy (unlike that in the Cape Colony) was not to assimilate the Zulu. Instead, colonial control was based on a system of indirect rule and segregation which left old social conventions and practices intact. Africans were governed indirectly through the chieftaincy and customary practices. A layer of British judicial and administrative machinery was placed on top of existing pre-colonial African institutions. This system 'utilised the existing distribution of power in Zulu society to achieve control and the extraction of surplus'.[7]

Meanwhile, cricket was taking off on the coast as well. On the Queen's birthday in 1858, a side representing Durban was involved in a 'spirited match' with a team from nearby Verulam, both part of what was then known as the County of Victoria. This was soon followed by a contest between Married and Single.

The first inter-town match between 'eleven of the Maritzburg Club and eleven gentlemen of Durban' took place in Durban on 2 May 1860 after a challenge from Pietermaritzburg. There was no organised cricket in Durban at that stage, so a meeting was called at Deer's London Hotel where 'eleven players were elected as Champions for Durban'. They included two future Natal prime ministers, Harry Escombe and Henry Binns, as well as the son of an ex-Bishops crick-eter from Cape Town, Theophilus Shepstone, who was the secretary for Native Affairs. The *Natal Mercury* reported:

> Yesterday the stores and other places of business closed about noon, and the town turned out en masse to witness the fight. The cricket ground was on the grassy flat near the gardens, and through the kindness of the military authorities several marquees had been erected. Refreshment stalls were also provided by private speculators and the scene with its horsemen, flags and wagons was a very gay and inspiring one. Wickets were pitched at about half-past ten o'clock and the playing continued with much spirit until half-past four ... The great crowd of by-standers seemed to take a keen interest in the progress of the game, and the final result was hailed with loud cheers.[8]

The *Natal Star* concurred that 'the scene presented was gay and animated in the extreme' and that 'the game was as nobly contested as it was possible to be'. Finally, 'a sumptuous dinner at Wood's Hotel crowned the day's proceedings, in which victors and vanquished vied with each other in the exhibition of those nobler virtues of the heart which do honour to our race whether under success or defeat'.[9] Though some of their players had not practised 'for months past' – and against the initial betting odds – Durban (42 and 53 for three) comfortably beat Pietermaritzburg (34 and 52). This event was apparently not repeated for many years, not least because the travelling time for the challengers to the coast was then three days by ox-wagon 'omnibus'. The match was revived in 1888 and thereafter held annually.

At this stage Durban and Pietermaritzburg were the only colonial towns in the Natal. The inland capital was slightly bigger, with a population of just under 5,000 in 1862: 3,118 whites, 1,795 Africans and 78 'coolies, or browns'. During the 1860s, thousands of indentured labourers from India were imported to work on Natal's sugar plantations, and this part of the population were to make a big impact on the economic, political and social life of the colony, including cricket, in succeeding decades.

Local Maritzburg matches in 1860 involved Married vs Single sides and Pietermaritzburg CC vs the Garrison. In 1862 a Durban match involved Brick-layers vs Town. During the 1860s cricket started being recorded in emerging small towns and rural areas of the colony at Richmond, Pinetown, Ladysmith and York – and later in Alfred County and Newcastle. By the 1870s club cricket was well established in both Durban and Pietermaritzburg and a club was estab-lished at Umzinto in 1871. Occasional tours took place and in 1871 Natal played at Queenstown in the eastern Cape in one of the first cross-territorial matches on record. But the game would only get a widespread presence in the rural areas – for instance, at Ixopo, Port Shepstone, Greytown, Verulam and Dargle – in the next decade. Properly organised leagues date only from 1894, with the winners contesting the inter-town Dunne Cup.

Matches between scratch sides remained the norm in the 1870s: for instance, Public Schools and Universities of Great Britain vs Colonists on 25–26 October 1870 in Pietermaritzburg, and United Kingdom Born vs The World in February 1878. J.J. Sewell top-scored with 31 in this match with an innings 'spoken of as one of the finest displays of scientific batting ever seen in the city'. Sewell had played at Lord's with W.G. Grace at the bearded doctor's second appearance there in 1864. His son, C.O.H. 'Skilly' Sewell, played for South Africa as a 19-year-old in 1894, captained the Gloucestershire county team and became a military captain in the Gloucestershire Battalion. The strong British influence was unmistakable and the scribes of early Natal cricket regularly refer to military figures who played a part in the development of the game in the colony.

In the late 1870s, the British military advance in southern Africa reached one of its most spectacular and defining moments. Following the subjugation of the Xhosa in the eastern Cape after nine wars, the *amasoja ebomvu* (red soldiers) looked to the north and levelled their aim at the Zulu, as well as others. Diamonds had been discovered and Britain wanted the whole of southern Africa under its control. Zulu independence posed an obstacle to that goal. Sir Bartle Frere, the governor of the Cape and British high commissioner for South Africa, now set out to find a pretext for war with the Zulu so that 'he could solve the native question once and for all' and create his confederation of South African territories, including a tame Zulu entity run as a 'subject ally', like an Indian princely state, by a British representative. Lord Chelmsford, raised to the peerage after his campaign in the eastern Cape, set up his headquarters in Pietermaritzburg to plan for what he expected to be an easy win. With fatal complacency, the British decided to surround the Zulu kingdom and advance on King Cetshwayo's *ikhanda* or seat of power at oNdini in widely dispersed but 'convergent columns', with the British infantry as the main assault force. Chelmsford lumbered into Zululand, having bought over 30,000 oxen, mules and horses and over 1,500 wagons and carts to transport his army's mountain of supplies. The British forces invaded Zululand on 11 January 1879. Not for one moment did Chelmsford think that once on the march he would need to cover his bases in case of a first attack. But that is what happened. 'Go! And toss them into Maritzburg,' exhorted a Zulu battlefield leader, Sikizane kaNomageji, as he sent off a section of the 27,000-strong Zulu army to mount their surprise attack on the British camp at Isandlwana. The toll was devastating: 1,210 British troops and 67 officers, including the two colonels in charge, succumbed, in addition to 1,000 of the attackers.[10] In one description of the carnage, we are left with a graphic image of the bloody intersection between cricket and war in southern Africa in the nineteenth century. Strewn across the veld amidst the more than 2,000 bodies were supplies and objects of every kind, including 'camp beds, boots, bellow sponges, books, photographs, papers and even cricket pads'.[11]

The victors also carried off more than 1,000 Martini-Henry rifles and 250,000 rounds of ammunition and then attacked a British post at Rorke's Drift. A small force held off the Zulu attackers in a rearguard fight, leading to the award of 11 Victoria Crosses for gallantry, the most ever awarded in one battle. Inevitably the global superpower would have its way. To rescue British imperial prestige following this course of events, Frere had to modify his easy plans for a quiescent Zulu statelet in his planned confederation. The Zulu kingdom now had to be totally destroyed. A total of 2,400 British soldiers and over 7,000 of their horses died in the effort. For every British soldier, three Zulu combatants perished. At the end of it all, oNdini went up in flames, the king was exiled and the Zulu lost their independence.[12]

As the description indicates, many cricketers took part in these colonial wars. Besides the British soldiers, at least one local club cricketer died in this conflict as well. James Sivewright, president of the Western Province Cricket Club, became the only non-combatant to win the South African Medal with three clasps in the war. An expert in telegraphy, Sivewright spent much of 1879 constructing communications for the invading army.[13]

Luckin in his *History of South African Cricket* notes, 'In the 'eighties and 'nineties Maritzburg was a veritable cricket paradise. The Military, the Civil Service and the ordinary civilian … were cricket mad … and there were few days in summer that did not witness some match or other on the picturesque Oval.'[14] The writer could have added that the creation of this strong base for cricket in the colony's capital came at a high price for both the Zulu people and the British.

6

Cricket reaches the interior Highveld

The Boer Republics, 1850s onwards

The 13th Light Infantry, the 21st Royal Scots Fusiliers,
some companies of the 80th and 94th Irish were
stationed in Pretoria, and matches, as well as athletic
competitions, between the military and the civil population
were frequent, and always keenly contested.

– Julius Jeppe, recalling the late 1870s[1]

When the Dutch-speaking Voortrekkers moved from the coastal plains over the mountainous escarpment onto the Highveld, they hoped to get away from British rule. But the British pursued them. In 1848, after the Battle of Boomplaats, Sir Harry Smith annexed the area between the Orange and Vaal Rivers on behalf of the colonial power and called it Trans-Orangia. The new settlement of Bloemfontein became the capital and cricket was played almost immediately. In 1850 the 45th Regiment stationed there 'issued, with the permission of their Colonel, a challenge to the residents there to play any eleven that might be put up by them'.[2]

Soon afterwards Britain agreed to the independence of the Boers both south and north of the Vaal. In the north, the South African Republic (ZAR) came into existence in 1852 with Potchefstroom initially as the capital, and Trans-Orangia became the Orange Free State Republic in 1854. The new OFS, situated geographically in the middle, also took an ideological middle position with regard to the British. English-speakers were welcomed and several reached high office; English was also 'commonly spoken in town and business life'. Cricket took off here far earlier than in the ZAR to the north.[3] By January 1855 there was an English-language newspaper, *The Friend*, and a cricket club in Bloemfontein. A notice in the newspaper that month announced: 'It is hereby notified that a meeting of the Bloemfontein Cricket Club will be held at the Rifle Club

Room on Monday, 5th inst., for the purpose of framing rules and regulations for the same. Members are requested to attend.'[4] The notice was signed by Nathaniel Barlow, member of a family who were prominent for many years in both local cricket and the affairs of the newspaper. Barlow incidentally died 'from a chill' contracted while watching the first English cricketing tourists 34 years later.

The fragile roots of the game in the interior, and its arrogantly English flavour, are well demonstrated by this quote from Luckin's *History of South African Cricket*:

> As the [British] inhabitants of Bloemfontein in 1855 did not total a hundred souls the formation of the cricket club by these early British settlers in a spot which [the Cape governor] Sir George Grey regarded later as 'remote wilderness', proved how deeply ingrained the sporting element was in the lives of those pioneers. During the intervals of peace when they were left unmolested by the Basutho these gentlemen found time to have a friendly game.[5]

Between 1866 and 1868 Mother Country vs Colonial-Born matches were played in the town. The Mother Country 'just succeeded in winning the rubber'. Several clubs were formed together with scratch teams such as Banks and Farmers. Meanwhile, the game was active in Winburg, Boshof and Smithfield in the 1860s. In Smithfield, a match was abandoned in 1866 owing to 'the only three balls left from last year's practice successively coming to grief'. In the 1870s, cricket was introduced to the new schools of St Andrew's and Grey College in Bloemfontein and it also spread to towns like Hopetown, Fauresmith and Kroonstad. Under the headmastership of the Rev. Douglas McKenzie, St Andrew's College was the initial nursery of Free State cricket, but in the twentieth century Grey would rise to prominence as the alma mater of modern stars like Kepler Wessels, Hansie Cronje, Nicky Boje and Boeta Dippenaar.[6]

CRICKET IN THE ZAR IN THE DAYS BEFORE GOLD

The first cricket club in the ZAR was established in 1863 at Potchefstroom, the first capital of the Republic, although the game had been played casually there from 1861. In 1870 cricket was introduced to Pretoria, the new capital, and played informally on the Market Square where, according to some accounts, there was ill-tempered competition for space with the Boers encamped for the quarterly celebration of *nachtmaal*. Pretoria and Potchefstroom were playing each other from 1874 although individual double-digit scores were rare. This was not surprising as the outfield was untended and grass on the pitch was removed with spades, tramped down by black labourers and watered overnight from a *sloot*.

The following lengthy account by Julius Jeppe, son of a German immigrant, who became a successful businessman and later vice-president of the Wanderers CC in Johannesburg, gives an excellent picture of the earliest ambience of the cricket and social life of the new white, and chauvinistically male, ruling classes in Pretoria in the 1860s and 1870s:

The game was not introduced into Pretoria until 1870, and even then was only played in the most primitive fashion. I well remember how about a score of barelegged youngsters pushed, dragged, and rolled the trunk of a willow tree through the rank vegetation of Pretoria's main street to the village carpenter's shop, and with what interest we watched day after day the cunning way in which he fashioned two bats out of that trunk. In the meantime an old Hottentot, clever with his needle, was commissioned to manufacture a ball, we supplying him with the corks of bottles, sail twine, and a slab of raw hide, and we were a proud lot indeed when with this material we pitched our first wicket on the Market Square, opposite the 'Raadzaal' (Parliament House). 'Tip and Run' was the only game then played, but serious practice was never indulged in. However, we got quite clever at placing balls, and played regularly every afternoon throughout the year – that was unless the Market Square, in the middle of which stood the old Dutch Reformed Church, was occupied by Boers coming into Church, and especially at Nachtmaal time every quarter, when from Friday to Tuesday the square was crowded with wagons and tents; it is true we always tried to pitch our wicket on some unoccupied piece of ground, but we were invariably interrupted by young Boers, who took great delight in preventing our play. This, of course, led to reprisals on our part, and we used to sally forth at night with sharp knives, cut down the tent ropes, and let the tent descend gently upon the sleeping occupants; or we would dam-up one of the four furrows running round the square, and so flood the whole of it, which generally resulted in a pitched battle between town and country, in which the former usually came off second best.

... A year or so after this the first imported bats and balls made their appearance, with the arrival of R. Winstanley, who, a finished cricketer himself, soon licked us into shape. This Winstanley would have been considered a great cricketer anywhere had he been less indolent; he was a first-class bat, but always refused to make runs; his underhand 'googlies' – 'twisters,' as we then called them – breaking both ways, would even today puzzle many good bats.

Fortunately for us in Pretoria, he loved the game and was a good coach, and it was due to him that in 1874 we were able to accept our first challenge from Potchefstroom.

The excitement produced by that challenge in the 'Village of Roses', as Pretoria was called, was enormous; it even induced the Poet Laureate of the Transvaal, Albert Brodrick, to produce the following lines:

THE MATCH

In the midst of bills and worries, and all our countless cares
Of winding up of companies, in which we have taken shares,
A door is opened unto us, and pleasure lifts the latch;
Eleven bold Pretorians have gone to make a match.
No match that leads to Hymen, so ladies don't presume
To try a 'catch', for Cricket takes our 'boys' to Potchefstroom
From school, from farm, and pulpit, and from the crowded store;
They've gone to add to salted 'bays' one little 'Laurel' more!

Oh! may the sun of victory shine on their bats and stumps,
Oh! may the team of Potchefstroom be left in doleful dumps.
They say that betting now is 10 to 8 against 'our lot,'
It strikes me (being prejudiced) 'others will get it hot!'
Although we know that Ludorf bowls with fiery force and skill,
And Thomson is supposed to be a very bitter pill;
And Botha's (2), and many more, in fact a very host –
Yet listen half a minute and hear Pretoria boast.

There's Richard Coeur de Lion, indicative of scores,
And Noble, Rex, and Cartwright, whose every name ensures
A 'battery' that almost makes their foemen 'go to grass,'
Grace in their eye, their stroke a sort of coup de grace;
Marais, who studied 'fielding,' and then the jovial Hans,
And Rufus and brave Charlemagne, the rival Predikants!
With such a noble list I ask: How can Pretoria fail,
Unless fatigue upon the road their energies assail?
If they should win, of course they'll have the honours that they earn;
If they should lose, they'll have three cheers, and hopes for the 'Return.'

It took quite a week to make the necessary arrangements for the three days' journey by mule wagon to the old capital and to procure the necessary sashes and ribbons of blue, red and white with which to adorn our persons for the great event. President Burgers was then lying seriously ill in Landdrost Goetz's house in Potchefstroom, and as we approached Potchefstroom our fear that this might interfere with the contest increased; however, on arrival, we were met by the entire population of Potchefstroom, headed by the Landdrost, Attorney-General Buchanan and his charming wife, with the cheering news that the President was better, and that the pitch was ready 'schoffeld' for the morrow's contest. The members of our team were billeted with the different reigning families of Potchefstroom, and nothing could exceed the magnificent ... hospitality extended to us, which, however, did not deter them from giving us a most disheartening beating.

Winning the toss, they elected to bat first, and in spite of our champion bowler, Winstanley, made 101, to which F. Ludorf, not out, contributed 50. Our first innings only produced 37, and our second innings closed equally disastrously for 36.

Potchefstroom's performance was considered quite a creditable one, as double figures were but rarely reached in any one innings, this being chiefly due to the condition of the pitch and the field, matting and rollers being quite unknown, and the only preparation made was that the grass was removed by means of spades, and the furrows which abounded in all Transvaal towns, and the next morning half a dozen niggers were set on to tramp down the surface. The field received no attention, and as a rule the grass stood feet high all over it.

Sweet revenge, however, came to us the next day, when the customary 'Handsome v. Ugly' match took place, for a panel of Potchefstroom ladies had placed in the first-mentioned team all Pretoria's representatives (with the single exception of the writer, who has not yet recovered from the shock), and, filled with pride at their selection, the 'Beauties' gave the 'Beasts' a sound thrashing, and our revenge was complete.

After our success in the 'Handsome v. Ugly' match, it was but natural that we should promptly challenge Potchefstroom to a return match to be played in August at Pretoria.

On that occasion, Pretoria went 'mafficking' for a week, all business being practically suspended, and even the Volksraad, which was sitting at the time, repeatedly adjourned, so that the members might watch this funny game played with a stick and a ball.

The old members from the backveldt took great interest in the game although they couldn't understand it; yet they certainly encouraged it until one unfortunate afternoon, when the President's secretary, Jim Noble, a mighty slogger, put a ball through a window of the Volksraad Chamber, and nearly knocked the Speaker off his perch. Then and there the members rose in their mighty wrath and for the next couple of hours seriously discussed the closing of the Market Square to cricket.

Fortunately, President Burgers and Attorney-General Buchanan, both lovers of the game, interceded for us and persuaded the indignant 'Landvaders' to overlook this grave insult to their dignity. Potchefstroom again won the match, this time by 127 runs. Next year, however, in October 1875, we managed to beat them in their own city, and thereafter these annual picnics continued with varied luck for many consecutive years.

A junior cricket club was started in Pretoria in 1875, the number of members being limited to eleven.

We obtained President Burgers' permission to call ourselves 'The President's Eleven,' and to be a member of that club was considered by the 'jeunesse dorée' of Pretoria a very high distinction. Election was by ballot, and whenever a vacancy occurred, great excitement prevailed throughout the town until it was filled.

The first match between this and the Pretoria Club was played towards the end of 1875, again in front of the Raadzaal, the stoep of which was turned into a grand stand, and a band, consisting of a cornet, an English concertina, and a guitar, played by the brothers Denny and Arthur Smithers, and a certain Miller, was in attendance.

At one time it looked as if we were going to beat the senior club, especially when that safe bat, our schoolmaster, Frank Rex, a descendant of kings, was seen standing with his bat poised in the air and allowed a fast one from our captain, Fritz Stiemens, to take his middle stump. Rex was supposed to be under the mesmeric influence of the burly bowler Johnson, who having quarrelled with Rex at the commencement of the match, must have cast his spell upon him when he saw the ball coming straight for the wicket; however they just managed to beat us.

I believe that during this period Potchefstroom also played various matches against Free State teams, but no records of these seem to have been kept.

The advent of the British troops with the annexation of the Transvaal by Shepstone in 1877 naturally gave a great impetus to cricket and all other sports in Pretoria.

The 13th Light Infantry, the 21st Royal Scots Fusiliers, some companies of the 80th and 94th Irish were stationed in Pretoria, and matches, as well as athletic competitions, between the military and the civil population were frequent, and always keenly contested.

Most of the regiments were camped where the present Police Barracks now stand, and soon after the arrival of the troops a good cricket and football field and a running track were laid out ... on the level wet ground of the camp, and there are still many Pretorians who remember with pleasure and gratitude the generous hospitality always extended to the local residents by the officers of the different regiments.

Colonel Sir Owen Lanyon, who took over the Administratorship from Sir Theophilus Shepstone in 1879, and Godfrey Lagden (now Sir Godfrey Lagden), his secretary, did much for cricket, especially the latter, who was one of the safest and best bats Pretoria ever possessed. During these years of the military occupation cricket naturally improved enormously.

It was Lieut. Waddy, of the 13th Light Infantry, and Stanhope, of the same regiment, who finished the work of teaching us cricket, which was so ably begun by men like the Rev. Roberts (now Archdeacon Roberts), who came to Pretoria with Bishop Bousfield, and who was a splendid left-hand bowler, a great bat, a very keen cricketer, as well as a splendid Rugby three-quarter.

Thanks to him, George Irving Davis, Arthur Smithers (a great slogger), and Jacob Swart, who, having learnt his cricket at Home, was head and shoulders above his contemporaries, the town generally held its own against the military at cricket, as well as at athletics. The giant in athletics was Henry Nourse. I remember on one occasion, when we were playing a cricket match against the military at their camp, Nourse, on returning from lunch, made a clean jump over a buck-wagon. This naturally rather astonished the Tommies, and the officers, always keen on competitions, were soon busy getting up a sports meeting, at which they hoped to take our friend Henry down a peg or two. A sporting manager of a local bank, however, who was a strong believer in Nourse's prowess, netted a handsome sum by backing Nourse to win more than half of the events on the programme. Of these were eleven, and Nourse won six – namely, the High Jump, Long Jump, Hurdles (then 440 yards), Putting the Shot, the 100 Yards and the 440 Yards. Considering that in addition to the Pretoria population, over 3,000 troops were stationed in camp at that time, it was a performance which few men could have achieved. Personally, I have always considered Nourse the best all-round man South Africa ever produced.

The last match against the military was played about the second week in December, 1880.

Sir Owen Laynon was sitting in the refreshment tent after Pretoria had finished its innings, talking to the Rev. Roberts, when an orderly brought a despatch. He read it, and then said to Roberts: 'There is serious news. War has begun; the troops and the Boers are fighting at Potchefstroom.' The match, however, was finished, the military winning.

After the retrocession of the Transvaal nearly all the old cricketers left in the great exodus, many of them for Kimberley.

We in Pretoria thought it would be a fitting farewell to them if on their way to Kimberley they played for the last time for Pretoria, and a week's tournament began at Potchefstroom on the 18th August, 1881.

We proceeded there by ox-wagon, taking five days for the journey. The first three days were devoted to cricket, and the rest of the week to football. We were beaten by three wickets at cricket, but took it out of them at football, and, moreover, had the time of our young lives.

Then came the sad parting. Swart, Davis, Arthur Smithers, Hastie, and others proceeded to Kimberley, the rest of us returning in our ox-wagon to Pretoria. On that journey we were overtaken by a snowstorm, and for three days were unwelcome guests at the store and homestead of a gentleman who hailed from 'somewhere' in Europe ...[7]

This lengthy contemporary narrative captures well the unconventional origins of the game, and the social contexts in which it was first played, in the interior of the African subcontinent. However, while cricket on the Highveld goes back to the early 1860s, it was only after gold was discovered on the Witwatersrand and Johannesburg was founded in 1886 that this area became a major force in cricket, as it began to develop into the economic hub and most populous city in southern Africa.

7

The New Rush

*Diamonds, dust and cricket in the new territory
of Griqualand West, 1870 onwards*

> We have often heard of the industrious city – the metropolis
> of Great Britain. The crowding of its streets, and the noise of
> the machinery and workmen. But I question if the noise there
> has been anything approaching what I heard at New Rush.
>
> – Rev. Gwayi Tyamzashe, 1874[1]

Cricket's steady journey into the interior of southern Africa, from the coastline
to the Highveld regions of Bloemfontein, Potchefstroom and Pretoria, snaked
sharply south-westwards in the 1870s to a 'scrubby area of semi-desert where
6,000 acres of land was the minimum required to run a small herd of cattle'.
This dry patch of land came to be known as Griqualand West. It is today part
of the Northern Cape province. The detour was for a good reason: the richest
diamond deposits in the world were discovered there. Suddenly it became 'the
richest prize in Africa'.[2]

After the news broke of the first diamond found at Hopetown in 1867,
fortune-seekers from throughout the world flocked there. By 1870 there were
10,000 diggers in the area, mostly on the banks of the Vaal River, where towns
like Hebron (today, Windsorton) and Barkly West sprang up. Then in 1871 the
jackpot was discovered on Colesberg Kopje on the farm of the De Beer family. The
kopje, or hill, was 'the top of an ancient pipe of diamondiferous lava'. Men started
digging greedily for the spectacular wealth that it contained, until the hilltop in
the veld became the subterranean Big Hole, which is so famous today. A tent town
of 20,000 inhabitants shot up around the New Rush, as it was called. It soon
grew into a wild, rumbustious city of Kimberley, where huge fortunes were made.

Britain moved quickly to secure the area and declared it the separate Crown Colony of Griqualand West in 1871. With British control assured, it became part of the Cape Colony in 1880.[3] By the end of that decade, the so-called Diamond City had become the most influential centre for sport in southern Africa.

The conditions on the diamond fields were initially very rough. People lived in makeshift canvas-and-wood dwellings or in wagons. 'There were no sanitary services and deaths from fever were frequent, even after the opening of an elementary hospital in 1872.'[4] Water was scarce, dirty and expensive, and it took a month or more for supplies from Port Elizabeth and Cape Town to reach the area.

There were fortune-seekers from every part of southern Africa and indeed the world, who worked hard and played hard. People were bound together in new ways. The Rev. Gwayi Tyamzashe from Peelton near King William's Town, who arrived in 1872 with the purpose of setting up a new congregation of Presbyterians for the Free Church of Scotland, commented disapprovingly on how this polyglot mixture of cultures and people expressed itself:

> The evenings resounded with the noise of the concert, the circus and all sorts of dances from one end of the camp to the other. The life then of both coloured and whites was so rough I thought this place was only good for those who were resolved to sell their souls for silver, gold and precious stones, or for those who were determined to sell their souls for the pleasures of a time.[5]

Amid this mayhem and rush for wealth, cricket made its appearance. The first recorded match in the new diamond diggings took place at the small town of Hebron on the banks of the Vaal River. On 27 December 1870, the Old Colonists (98 all out) defeated the Natalians (51 and 36) by an innings and 11 runs. The first club in the area was the Paragon CC, based at nearby Klipdrift, which had its own ground, built by convict labour, by 1872. When a Klipdrift XI played Grahamstown Club in August the following year, a 'Thespian band was in attendance to liven the proceedings'.

The first game in Kimberley was played on 23 March 1872, when the Natalians defeated the Port Elizabethans by nine wickets. In June, New Rush took on Du Toit's Pan at Colesberg Kopje, site of the great find, and in October the Vine Hotel took on Mrs Hopkins' Boarders at the Great Western Hotel.

By 1873, Richards, Glanville & Co., located on Main Street, like other shops was advertising 'Cane handle bats, stumps, gauntlets, and leg guards'; and the first cricket ground had been built 'below the Market Square, New Rush' (around present-day Roper Street). This ground was built by the Union Diggers Cricket Club. There was another 'to the immediate west of the old De Beers Mine', which became home to the Kimberley Cricket Club.[6] As could be expected, the conditions for cricket were at first not optimal. At New Rush in 1872, a correspondent complained:

> Cricket is a fine healthy game, and a pleasant one when played at under a clear cloudless sky and upon a well laid out and well kept cricket ground – but cricket as it was last Saturday, in driving clouds of dust; dust as hot as brick dust from a burning kiln, … [followed by] heavy showers of rain that turned the dust into red mud, is certainly not pleasant'.[7]

According to the correspondent, the players looked like diggers clocking off from work at the end of the match; one could hardly 'distinguish one face from another', although the players had been 'as neat as pins when they pitched their wickets'.[8] At the other ground, the 'cocoanut mat' used in 1874, 'very narrow, was stretched along a cart track – by courtesy called a road – which diagonally traversed the open ground. The pitch was to some extent levelled and smoothed by dragging the matting up and down.'[9] The ground was eventually fenced in, 'thus stopping the scotch carts with loads of maiden blue'.

As Kimberley became a settled, prosperous town and as the numbers increased, so the cricket facilities and standards improved. 'Daily afternoon practice' was started and matches were played on public holidays and most Saturday afternoons in summer. But, as in other regions, teams were generally raised in pick-up fashion from Kimberley and Du Toit's Pan in the name of the Kimberley Cricket Club. The small pool of 30 or so players would be pitted against one another, whether as Natal vs Cape, Married vs Single, or Home-Born vs Coloni-al-Born.[10] In the last-mentioned contests in 1875/6, the first of two matches was tied before Home-Born ran away with the second, thanks to an unusual century from Dr Dixon. 'The year 1877 may be set down as the period in which the game became fairly popular; young Kimberley was beginning to demonstrate to the Homeborn men that they were also able to do something with the bat and ball.'[11]

The driving force behind the Kimberley CC was the Sussex-born digger and newspaper proprietor, William Ling – 'the father of Kimberley cricket' and 'the W.G. of the place'. He 'assumed complete control … being captain, secretary, committee, groundsman, player, and most certainly treasurer of a unique order for he collected a few subscriptions from those who cared to pay and made up whatever was short from his own pocket'. On the field, he owed his comparison with Grace to 'cricketing ability, flowing beard and all, sound scientific bat, good lob bowler, and always the captain of the side'.[12]

Ling was no liberal, leading a vigilante force who wanted a curfew which ensured Africans were out of town at night (in order, he argued, to curb diamond smuggling), so there was no thought at this stage that his club would have any black members. However, educated black professionals from the cricket-loving eastern Cape schools and skilled artisans from Cape Town, the earliest home of the game in Africa, were among those making their way to the Diamond Fields in numbers, and the first cricket played by the black inhabitants in Kimberley probably stemmed from attempts by the 'respectable' section of the community to curb the social excesses noted by the Lovedale-educated Tyamzashe. By 1874 he commented that things were improving and, 'During the short period of two years there has been a wonderful change regarding the moral condition of the Diamond Fields.'[13] Evidence indicates that as early as 1876 a True Templar lodge consisting of 40 'natives' was 'actively engaged in reclaiming the victims of drink', organising processions and 'various games and amusements with the full support of the sober element of the white population'. No doubt, cricket was part of this effort, given the influx from the eastern Cape and its role in the colonial 'civilising' mission.[14] The chances are high that Tyamzashe was involved – it is interesting to note that he was one of the few Africans who owned diamond claims, seeking his fortune like many others.

The churches and temperance bodies were soon followed by musical groups, mutual improvement societies and social clubs. As early as April 1878 the Kimberley African Amateur Minstrels gave a performance in the town, 'the earliest African musicians to perform as a group'.[15] With their unique qualifications and ethnically diverse composition, the emerging black middle class of 'school people' and artisans generally occupied the most sought-after and best-paid jobs available to black residents. Among the early settlers who later became well-known Kimberley citizens were the Wesleyan lay preacher Johannes Kozani from Grahamstown, the ex-Lovedalian Jonas Msikinya, and Joseph Moss, who became president of the Griqualand West Colonial Cricket Union. They were part of a cosmopolitan social environment that was new to southern Africa and, as on the mission stations of the eastern Cape, the ideas of 'progress' and 'civilisation' remained important lodestars for them.

The emerging middle class soon developed a 'network of regular activities and involvement'[16] in which music and sport played an important part. As David Coplan explains, 'Music became a bond of interest and association and a means of expressing social aspiration.'[17] It came to feature at almost every social occasion. Cricket was likewise to become enmeshed in the social activities of this emerging black middle class. Schooled in this unusual cosmopolitan environment, they learned to network across accepted barriers and would go on to be pioneers of the game on a national level in the 1880s and 1890s.

8

Southern Africa and the spread of cricket across the world

> Cricket and rugby find a ready home in the East as in
> England much more so than on the Continent. There
> boys take to them like ducks to water and the qualities
> cultivated by them, loyalty, courage, esprit de corps
> and honour are not western but belong to the race.

> – A missionary quoted in J.A. Mangan, *Imperial Origins*[1]

By the beginning of the 1870s, just over 60 years after the British had planted the Union Jack in Cape Town, the game of cricket had spread with British military expansion from the southern tip of the African continent 1,500 kilometres inland: first to the modern day coastal regions of the eastern Cape (1810s–1820s) and KwaZulu-Natal (1840s), then to the Highveld of the interior – the Free State (1850s), followed by the South African Republic (1860s) and the hastily created mineral-rich territory of Griqualand West (1870s).

It is striking how many similarities there were in the development of cricket in the different areas in those first decades. The first-hand accounts all tell more or less the same story: the key role of the British military garrisons; the very British protocols and social pomp that went with it; the rudimentary facilities available; the gambling for stakes; the involvement of high-level political and society figures; the strong masculine culture associated with it; and the beginnings of white, exclusive, male, by-invitation-only 'gentleman' clubs; the impact of church schools and missionaries; the involvement of black South Africans from the very beginning; and the complete absence of women as players.

There are three common assumptions about the early development of cricket in South Africa. One is that it spread inland from the coast: there is considerable truth in this, but it was in fact a more complex process, as we have seen.

The second long-held notion is that cricket was exclusively a white game. This was not the case. Black people in southern Africa were among the pioneers of cricket – not only in South Africa, but elsewhere in the world, as we shall see. Another assumption, looking back, is that South Africa naturally took its place alongside England and Australia as a test-playing nation on a competitive footing in the 1890s.

In this chapter, we will compare the growth of cricket in other countries with South Africa to see what other similarities and differences there were during this period. We will see that things were not as straightforward as many assume: for example, the game in South Africa was at first poorly organised, unlike in countries like the United States and Canada, which are now regarded as minnows in world cricket.

The reference to pick-up teams of Port Elizabethans and Natalians playing on the Diamond Fields in the beginning of the 1870s is an indication of how the game had become established in various parts of southern Africa, and how these different regions were slowly developing specific identities and starting to interact with each other. Meanwhile, what was happening in the different states and colonies on the subcontinent was also part of a broader international pattern. By the 1870s, cricket was making progress in varying degrees in other former and current British colonies in Asia, the Americas and Australasia. It was taking root in Canada, the United States of America, Barbados, Jamaica, Trinidad and smaller British-ruled islands of the Caribbean, as well as in India, Ceylon (Sri Lanka), Australia and New Zealand on the other side of the Pacific Ocean. This parallel spread of cricket from Britain to other parts of the world between the 1790s and 1870 laid the foundation for the organised international cricket of the modern era and was related in various ways to unfolding developments in southern Africa.

US AND CANADA

Surprisingly, given the subsequent virtual disappearance of the game there, the United States of America was an early growth point outside Britain. The US had through armed struggle claimed its independence from Britain in 1776, but the colonial game flourished there in the early 1800s, becoming 'America's first modern team sport'. In 1809 there was a club in Boston, and in the 1830s the game took root in New York City and Philadelphia on the mid-east coast, which to this day remains one of the main centres for cricket in the US.

The St George's CC was founded in Manhattan in 1838 and played against 'eleven Long Islanders' in Brooklyn for a stake of $500. The game was enthusiastically covered in the media. Inter-city matches were introduced in the 1840s.

Cricket also accompanied the great movement to the West. For example, Chicago played Milwaukee in 1853 and the game spread to places like Cincinnati, St Louis and California on the opposite side of the continent. There were three clubs in San Francisco in 1855. Movement also happened to the southern states below Philadelphia, and northwards to the New England colonies. In 1859 there were six clubs in Baltimore and one in New Orleans.

Americans, in fact, claim to have been the first to play international cricket. From 1840 onwards, clubs from Toronto and New York, later adding Montreal and Philadelphia to the mix, met regularly in what was described as the annual 'international contest between Canada and the United States'. These contests apparently 'generated considerable excitement (and gambling) on both sides of the border'. In 1856 annual all-star games were started between 'eleven Englishmen and eighteen Americans'. Three years later, tremendous interest was generated by the visit of an England cricket team, captained by George Parr. This was the first cricket tour from England. Large crowds watched, but the English easily defeated their American and Canadian opponents. By this time several national meetings had been called to form a controlling body for cricket in the United States. They were not successful, partly because New York and Philadelphia would not relinquish their dominant positions, and because a request for East vs West competitions was ignored.

According to the historian George Kirsch, there were an estimated 10,000 players and 500 clubs in 22 states by 1860. However, the growth of the game was dramatically arrested by the outbreak of the American Civil War in the next year. Baseball, which 'was naturalised in nearly every state of the Union' by off-duty soldiers during the war, quickly became the national game. Its meteoric rise, the Puritan-influenced 'prevailing attitude that exercise and sport did not mix with education' and the growth of what has been called 'American exceptionalism' after the Civil War, all combined to deal cricket a blow, which was to be fatal in the long term.[2] It remained a relatively healthy minority game until World War I, with regular visits from English teams, but thereafter it virtually disappeared.

Cricket in Canada followed the American trend. Starting in the 1830s, it was on par with the US by the 1860s. Successive governors-general promoted the game and the British model was adopted in schools. In the 1850s there were 37 teams in Ontario alone. However, it subsequently followed the same slow decline as the neighbouring US, partly because of the game's ideological attachment to Empire and its inability to make adaptations to local demands, including the length of games. Lacrosse and baseball became the popular sports in Canada.[3]

CARIBBEAN ISLANDS (WEST INDIES)

The place in the Americas where cricket became permanently established was on British-controlled islands in the Caribbean, most notably Barbados, British Guiana, Trinidad and Jamaica. The experiences here were also closer to those of South Africa than America and Canada. Contributing to this were the climate, the particular forms of slavery and colonialism, the relatively underdeveloped economies, the educational system and the racially ordered nature of the societies, where white minorities rigidly governed subjugated majority black populations, contributed to this.

As J.A. Mangan has pointed out, 'Caribbean cricket is analysed most profitably through the specific components'. Conditions and historical experiences differed significantly from one island to another. Any history of West Indian cricket must start with Barbados. With British colonial rule unbroken for more than three centuries, it has the third oldest parliament in the Americas and came to be known as 'little England'. Small wonder then that it has one of the deepest traditions of cricket in the world. Only 21 miles long and 14 miles wide, the island's population has never exceeded 300,000, yet it has produced an array of cricket's greats, from Walcott, Weekes and Worrell to Sobers, Greenidge, Haynes, Marshall and Garner. The population in the late 1800s was 188,000 – most were black, with a white population of 15,000 and a small percentage of creole people called 'brownskins'.

The first club in Barbados, St Ann's Garrison Cricket Club, was in existence by 1806 – the same year the British permanently occupied the Cape and the first cricket match reported there. As in South Africa, the British military garrison and regiments were the early practitioners, and the club was based at Bridgetown's version of the Cape Town Castle. Cricket notices and reports were put out in the newspapers 'alongside references to the sale of slaves and the fluctuations of sugar markets'.[4] By 1849 there were two civilian clubs in Bridgetown in the vicinity of the Garrison: City and St Michael's. Their games were watched by 'highly respectable ladies and gentlemen' and 'evinced great spirit and extreme goodwill'. Plantation owners specially prepared the field and provided tents and refreshments. The governors and other senior officials regularly attended. When Queen Victoria's son Prince Alfred visited the island in 1861, he went to the Garrison for a game of cricket with the officers. The 'Gallant 49th' Regiment also played against the elite Codrington College, and probably also the Lodge School. In 1866 the first inter-island match was played between Barbados and Demerara (now Guyana) on the Garrison ground, but only a few of these inter-island contests were organised before the 1890s, when formal competition started.

Sugar dominated the Barbadian economy for centuries, and it was the sugar planting aristocracy who controlled cricket. As in South Africa, the British and local whites created a segregated cricket environment. The first clubs and representative sides were for whites only. The same situation applied in Jamaica, where the only clubs formed before 1870 were the Vere and Clarendon CC and Jago CC, started in the same year as the Cape Town CC in 1857, and the Kingston CC (1863). The first two were clubs of the planters and the last represented their 'mercantile allies' in the city. The patron of Kingston Club was the Jamaican governor, Edward Eyre. 'Baked hard in the Australian outback', according to Niall Ferguson, Eyre was to achieve notoriety two years later when he forcefully put down a rebellion. No examples of black people playing in this pre-1870 period are mentioned in the most important West Indian cricket histories. Black South Africans were, therefore, participating in cricket at least a decade before their counterparts in the Caribbean, where cricket in the schools apparently only got going in the 1870s. The first black clubs in the islands came later too, in the 1890s.[5]

INDIA

From the perspective of the twenty-first century, perhaps the most important early British export of cricket happened on the opposite side of the world from the Americas – in India. This huge subcontinent was the 'jewel in the Crown' of the British Empire. Its gigantic population and economic potential have made it the financial jewel in the crown of world cricket today as well.

The developing game of cricket in southern Africa had various links with India from the earliest stages, and the two shared some common colonial characteristics. Chapter 2 provides evidence that British officers who had served and likely played in India were involved in organising some of the earliest games in Cape Town. British troop carriers en route to and from India regularly stopped over to play while restocking in Table Bay, and the 'Indians' who came to Cape Town to rest and recuperate helped give the town a particular British character.

In southern Africa, three regions initially contributed most to the growth of cricket – Cape Town, the eastern Cape and Kimberley. In India it was three great seaside cities – Calcutta, Madras and Bombay – which provided the foundations for the game. The vast interior of the subcontinent remained a threatening place for the colonists. Unlike in South Africa, no great experiment in assimilation took place outside the cities; no 1820 settlers; no century of large-scale close proximity with independent indigenous populations, with concomitant periods of conflict and cooperation.

The first club was Calcutta Club on the east coast, started in 1792 and reputed to be the second oldest in the world after the MCC. British merchants landed here before the British army, which soon built Fort William and its great *maidan* or parade, which became the playground of the city right next to where Eden Gardens stands today. Here games were organised before the cricketers 'showed their ability in another way' at dinners and dances at the club. Men in teams reflecting the early commercial nature of the city – like Old Etonians vs an XI comprising 'lesser members of the East India Company' in 1804 – played and gambled on the games. Then came Madras further to the south, on the same coastline on the Bay of Bengal. Cricket in Bombay started later. In 1825 several grand matches involving the military or 'Queen's Royals' from 'the famed counties of Hampshire, Sussex and Kent' were held every Thursday once exercise was 'revived' with the onset of the cold weather from November.

By the end of the nineteenth century Bombay was the cricket capital of the vast Indian subcontinent. The reason for this was that, unlike Calcutta where strict segregation was maintained between the British and indigenous Bengalis, 'an intermediary stepped in to convert cricket from a diversion of the British in India to the Indian's national game'.[6] These were the Parsis, forming a community of some 100,000 people in Bombay, who had come from Persia more than a thousand years before. Though they adopted Gujarati as their language, they maintained their customs and religion – Zoroastrianism – and were known for their trading and commercial activities, 'professions viewed with disdain by the high-born Hindu'. Commerce brought them into close contact with the English and they soon developed into local intermediaries both on an economic and social level. Much like the descendants of slaves in Cape Town and the mission-educated African school people in the eastern Cape, the Parsis soon started emulating the British in cricket and by the 1840s had a flourishing cricket culture. The surnames of the international cricketers that the Parsis later produced – Merchant, Carpenter and Engineer – reflected their deep commercial traditions.

Recent histories by Ramachandra Guha, Mihir Bose and others – among the best written on the game anywhere – have done justice to the experience of Indian cricketers (as opposed to the exploits of the colonial element) and have detailed the enthusiasm and skills of the Parsis at the game. The first Parsi club was Orientals, started in 1848, seven years after the founding of Lovedale College in Africa, followed two years later by the Zoroastrians CC, which still exists today. Guha sums up the progress that followed:

> At least thirty Parsi clubs were formed in the 1850s and 1860s, named for Roman gods and British statesmen: Jupiter, Mars, Gladstone and Ripon, for example … Sorabji Shapoorji Bengalee, C.I.E., endowed a prize for the best Parsi club. His grant generously allowed for a band to be in attendance during matches, for tents to be pitched for the convenience of the players and for food

to be provided for them and for spectators as well. These Parsi prize matches, held annually between 1868 and 1877, enormously consolidated the Parsi interest in cricket.[7]

The record shows that this indigenous cricket tradition in one part of India became formalised two decades earlier than in southern Africa. Parsi cricket differed from Africa in one important respect: there were wealthy patrons, including the famous Tata and Wadia families, who could fund its growth. Africans were ahead of the Parsis in one respect by 1870, though. They had started playing matches against British colonists in Cape Town and the eastern Cape, while the first contests between colonisers and local people still lay several seasons into the future in Bombay.

Meanwhile, the Hindu community in Bombay started its first clubs in the 1860s, namely the Bombay Union Cricket Club (1861) and the Hindu Cricket Club (1866). Hindu children were taught about the game at Elphinstone High School. From these origins emerged the famous gymkhanas or clubs for the different communal groups on the famous public spaces or *maidans* in the southern part of Bombay. Numberless locals converged on them over the years to create a unique tradition and to make cricket the most popular game by far in the country.

As at Zonnebloem College in Cape Town, British soldiers, administrators and missionaries also taught the game to the princely classes in India, and it was they who were responsible for taking it to more far-flung areas. Maharajas and nawabs provided patronage of various kinds and eventually imported British professionals to coach locals. Cricket with its class connotations appealed to the Indian princes, who could play it but still maintain a social distance.

Richard Cashman has noted that one of the reasons why cricket became popular in western and southern India was that it was amenable to Hindu social customs, including Jain beliefs such as *ahimsa* (non-injury of life). Indians generally did not take to blood sports involving bodily contact (like rugby and, to a lesser extent, soccer), but no such reservations existed with regard to cricket.[8]

SRI LANKA

On the island of Ceylon (modern-day Sri Lanka), lying off the tip of the Indian subcontinent, cricket 'became greatly enjoyed and elegantly played' from an early time. The first all-white, all-British club was the Colombo Cricket Club, formed in 1838. The manner of its formation was typical of what often happened in South Africa as well: a notice was placed in the local newspaper advertising the founding meeting in a local library, and games soon followed. As in South

Africa, missionaries spearheaded English-language education among the colonised people (as part of government attempts to curb traditional Buddhist influences) and were an important element in the transmission of cricket to the local
population. The missionaries introduced the game at the Colombo Academy
(now Royal College) in the same year as the founding of the Colombo CC, 1838.
As it spread to other institutions such as St Joseph's College, St John's College,
St Thomas's College, Wesleyan College and Trinity College in Kandy, a new,
young, Western-educated anglicised Ceylonese elite took up cricket in numbers.
Cricket was at first played informally at the schools, and by the boys at 'sectional
clubs' playing outside the school on Colombo's Esplanade and Banack Square.
In the late 1870s the first inter-college contests were set in motion. A missionary
noted in the early 1900s, 'Cricket and rugby find a ready home in the East as
in England much more so than on the Continent. There boys take to them like
ducks to water and the qualities cultivated by them, loyalty, courage, *esprit de
corps* and honour are not western but belong to the race.'[9]

AUSTRALASIA

The other two colonies that developed into bastions of Empire were New
Zealand and Australia, where European settlers defeated the indigenous Maori
and Aboriginal people and turned them into marginalised minorities in their own
land. Cricket became especially strong in Australia. *The Oxford Companion to
Australian Sport* gives an admirably condensed version of the origins of the game
in that country, showing how strong the similarities are with other colonies,
including South Africa:

> Cricket was played in Sydney from 1803, but reports of the game were
> infrequent until 1826, when the Australian Cricket Club was formed. Many
> more clubs were formed in New South Wales and in other colonies in the
> 1830s. Most of them were organised around public houses, and gambling
> was a focal point. Many of these clubs did not survive long, the most notable
> exception being the Melbourne Cricket Club, founded in 1838, which became
> the most powerful Australian club, even organising national tours in the late
> nineteenth century. Visiting regiments contributed to the growth of cricket and
> contests between civilian and military teams were frequent and popular. Inter-
> colonial matches did much to enhance the popularity of cricket and to create a
> network of associations. The first match was between Tasmania and Victoria at
> Launceston in 1851, though it was not until 1856, when the New South Wales
> side defeated Victoria at the Melbourne Cricket Ground, that inter-colonials
> became an annual fixture.[10]

The early start with competitive cricket and international tours is what particularly distinguishes Australian from South African cricket. The first English teams visited in 1861/2 and 1863/4 and the first Australian tour to England was – by a strange anomaly – an Aboriginal team in 1868, a full decade before any other Australian teams followed. This prepared the stage for the great rivalry between England and Australia as the premier cricket nations in the world during the colonial period, which began during the last quarter of the nineteenth century.

In New Zealand rugby rather than cricket became the national game in the new colony. The first cricket clubs were formed in the 1840s and the first inter-provincial match took places between Auckland and Wellington in 1860. In 1863/4 an English team stopped over during their tour to Australia, a tradition which persisted thereafter and gave New Zealand its main form of international contact. According to John Arlott, the game here 'progressed in minor key; fine players have been produced, but never in sufficient abundance to make any real impact'.[11]

* * * * *

Looking back at the spread of cricket across the world, we see that the game in South Africa was at first less well-organised than countries like the United States and Canada, which are no longer regarded as major cricket-playing nations. Unlike in North America, there were by the 1870s relatively few clubs in South Africa. There were also no coordinated activities within regions; no official leagues or competitions; no meaningful contacts between the different southern African colonies and republics; no formal links with other countries; and no regional and national associations. Standards were low and there was little continuity. Cricket had spread to every part of southern Africa, but it was still being played in a fairly undeveloped and uncoordinated way.

On the other hand, though lagging behind in certain respects, cricket in pre-1870 southern Africa was not so different from anywhere else in the world. It was a social pastime, played mainly by the British military and the new colonial civilian and administrative elite, although the native communities were also beginning to adopt it. There were also many other similarities with other colonies: the early garrison character of the game typified by the playing fields next to the forts in Bridgetown, Cape Town, Bombay, Calcutta and Galle; the similar racial hierarchies accompanying slavery, colonialism and the 'civilising mission' in West Indies, India and Sri Lanka; the ways in which specific communities – the school people in the eastern Cape, the Cape Muslims and the Parsis in Bombay – served as intermediaries in spreading the game more broadly to the colonised populations; the gambling for stakes in South Africa, Canada, the US and Australia; the climate and rugged white racist identities in Australia and South Africa; and the generally similar British schooling systems in all these places, except the US.

Overall, cricket had spread spectacularly from one country to many in the first 70 years of the nineteenth century. The game had become part of the architecture of Empire, creating the foundations for future growth and competition on an international level. The first test match between England and Australia in Melbourne in 1877 was a marker of what was to come. A new era was at hand for cricket, both globally and in southern Africa.

PART TWO

AFRICA'S FIRST COMPETITIONS, 1876–1890

9

Cricket, war and change

For South Africa the twentieth century might be said to have
been born in the 1870s, and it is from this point that it becomes
difficult to avoid referring to South Africa as a single entity.

– Noël Mostert, *Frontiers*[1]

A convergence of forces put cricket in southern Africa on a new path in the
last quarter of the nineteenth century. The first was the rise of modern sports
in Britain as a result of industrialisation and urbanisation. The second was the
discovery of the richest diamond and gold deposits in the world, which fundamentally reshaped the future of southern Africa and the lives of the people living
there. Both stimuli also speeded up the development of cricket and its integration
across a vast area of over one million square miles, five times the size of Britain,
where the game had originated.

GROWTH OF SPORT IN ENGLAND

The industrial revolution in England led to a big increase in the number of people
living in towns. The urban population grew from 50 per cent of the national
total in 1852 to 70 per cent in 1901. In the expanding urban environments,
working hours increased and became more tightly regulated, necessitating new
ways of enjoying recreation. Sports more suited to these crowded, confined,
regulated spaces emerged, such as rugby, soccer, athletics, golf and tennis. The
ancient game of cricket had to adapt. Before industrialisation, cricket could be
played after a successful harvest with little regard for time constraints. It adapted
to the times and, by the 1870s, was becoming recognisable as the sport we
know today. Gentlemen amateurs had taken over control, banishing the 'overt
betting and "selling" of matches by well-known players'; facilities improved;
and technical skills became more advanced in the aftermath of legalised overarm
bowling in 1864.[2]

Sport became progressively more organised and popular as the century proceeded. The expansion of railways increased mobility and allowed competitions to take place between teams from different areas. The growth of income allowed more working-class people to spend some of their wages on leisure and as spectators of games. Health, living standards and life expectancy improved. Legislation and trade union lobbying led to the recognition of the 'free Saturday afternoon' as a 'time off' for sport. The national school system expanded, and 'muscular Christians took team games to the urban working class in an effort to evangelise through sport'.[3]

Rules for different games, which had previously varied from place to place, were now standardised. Clubs became the basis of organised sport – Birmingham, with a population of 400,000, had 224 clubs by 1880 for cricket alone. The formation of national sporting associations followed. Local authorities and entrepreneurs started investing in facilities and events. Increased mobility and better facilities also led to bigger crowds. Commercialised spectator sport for the mass market became one of the economic success stories of late Victorian England.

The expansion of Britain's Empire and the rise of strong European and American nation-states in turn led to the beginnings of international sporting contests. These powerful countries both cooperated with and competed against each other, as can be seen in the 'New Imperialism' of the late nineteenth century, when European powers carved up Africa and allocated to themselves agreed spheres of influence on the continent. Britain, the undisputed global superpower, which could boast that the sun never set on its Empire, became the world leader in sport and in spreading games and organising international competitions in this new phase of economic globalisation and competition.

Cricket was in the forefront of the broader social and sporting revolution taking place in the last decades of the nineteenth century. In 1873, an unofficial county championship competition was started, with nine counties playing 31 matches between them. It became the main competition in England. Shortly after this, following privately organised All-England tours to North America in 1872 and Australia in 1873, the first official test match was played between James Lillywhite's England team and Australia in Melbourne in March 1877. The following year Australia reciprocated with a tour to England, heralding the onset of regular rivalry between international representative sides. A charismatic medical doctor, W.G. Grace, emerged as the first of the modern-era superstars of the game. He became a personification of the Victorian era, some say the second most famous personality of the period after the Queen herself.

Other sports such as golf, tennis, rugby, soccer and athletics were becoming organised at more or less the same time. The Open Championship in golf teed off in 1860, and England tackled Scotland in the first-ever rugby international in Edinburgh in 1871. The first Wimbledon tennis championships were held in 1877, a few months after the first cricket test. These early international events were followed by the first modern Olympic Games in 1896.

Sport as we know it today was starting to take shape, and the colonials at the bottom tip of Africa, located halfway on the sea journey between England and Australia, took note of these developments. The new trends soon blew over to southern Africa. From 1875 to 1885 a number of the new sporting codes became established here. The first rugby, football, athletics, cycling, horse racing, golf and tennis clubs were formed and competitions were started. Sport became much more organised. Southern Africa increasingly became part of new global arrangements – in cricket, as well as economically and politically.

DIAMONDS AND GOLD TRANSFORM SOUTHERN AFRICA

In the same way that the industrial revolution in Britain revolutionised sport in the 'Mother Country', the discovery of diamonds in the late 1860s in southern Africa – and the fabulous quantities of gold that were about to reveal themselves – set in motion a dramatic economic and industrial revolution that had a massive impact on the subcontinent. Tens of thousands of fortune-seekers from different parts of Africa and the world flooded into the interior Highveld regions. From the bare veld arose two settlements that would become the economic centres of a rapidly changing regional economy.

Initial tent and shanty towns turned into cities with advanced infrastructure, bustling with life and initiative, bringing together a breathtakingly rich mix of cultures and influences. Traditionally-minded people from different backgrounds complained of a new kind of environment where 'Mammon was king'. Sport, music and other forms of culture began to flourish, including cricket. Britain, which had hitherto not shown an inclination to extend herself too much in southern Africa, because of the high cost of the wars in the eastern Cape and elsewhere, now became interested in bringing the whole subcontinent under its control in a confederation that could ensure its control of the fabulous new mineral resources. It started intervening militarily and adapting administratively to speed up the conquest of the various independent territories, both African- and Boer-led. Colonial governments began to impose taxes on Africans aimed at forcing them to leave their land and subsistence lifestyle and become part of the rapidly expanding labour market. People from throughout the subcontinent streamed to the diamond and gold mines in search of money and the guns necessary to hold onto their land and independence. Among those attracted to the new centres of growth were cricket-loving mission-educated Africans from the eastern

Cape and artisans from Cape Town, who came to occupy the most sought-after positions open to black people. They would become political, community and cricket leaders in the new cosmopolitan mining environments.

After the discovery of gold on the Witwatersrand in 1886, the South African Republic underwent a convulsion. The mining town of Johannesburg grew in leaps and bounds on the bare veld, and within ten years it was bigger than Cape Town, with a population of over 100,000.[4] Railways were built to transport people and the heavy equipment needed for mining from the coast. Soon these new conglomerations of humanity were linked to all the major port cities of South Africa and from there, by ship, to the wider world. The whole of the subcontinent became much more interconnected, physically and politically. The various colonies, states and independent African societies in the region formed a complex puzzle until 1910, when they were finally amalgamated into the single geo-political entity that South Africans inhabit today. However, as Noël Mostert has noted, 'For South Africa the twentieth century might be said to have been born in the 1870s, and it is from this point that it becomes difficult to avoid referring to South Africa as a single entity.'

SCORECARD OF BRITAIN'S COLONIAL WARS, 1868–1902

Modern-day South Africa was built on the back of this minerals-led economic surge and a wholesale process of violent conquest and incorporation in the subcontinent that followed. Britain and its proxies set out to pacify, reorganise and unify southern Africa and succeeded within a few decades in doing so. All this was in the service of the new mining economy under the British flag, which required for its efficient operation political stability, geographical unity and a cheap, controlled labour force. Previously independent societies were steamrolled into submission, generally with the aid of British troops. African territories fell one by one. The pattern of settlement, and of identity and state formation in the interior of southern Africa, which had been extremely fluid and undefined up to the 1860s, became fixed.

The detailed scorecard of this process of conquest – shorn of the human drama, violence and pain accompanying it – was as follows:

In **1868** Britain annexed Basutoland after Moshoeshoe sought British protection from Orange Free State designs on his territory.

In **1871** Britain annexed Griqualand West soon after diamonds were discovered there, sidelining Tlhaping, Griqua and other claimants. Reflecting the gung-ho culture of the times, the foremost cricket personality on the diamond fields,

William Ling (sometimes called the W.G. Grace of Kimberley), raised an armed vigilante force to impose 'discipline' in the town.[5]

In **1873–4**, fearing the relative autonomy and prosperity of a chiefdom living in the foothills of the Drakensberg, British Natal defeated the Hlubi in the so-called Langalibalele Rebellion.

In **1877** Britain annexed the South African Republic and renamed it the Transvaal, partly because the Boer Republic was threatened with bankruptcy and was having difficulty subduing African chiefdoms in its territory.

In **1877–8** the Xhosa were finally subjugated militarily in the ninth Cape–Xhosa war. Nkosi Sandile was killed by colonial forces, shot through the side by a Snider bullet. The incorporation of the Transkeian territories of Fingoland, Griqualand East, Thembuland, Gcalekaland and Bomvanaland into the Cape Colony's Transkei region quickly followed.[6] Nathaniel Umhalla, the Zonnebloem and St Mark's cricketer, was charged with treason for refusing to turn against his people, while the Cape Mounted Rifles, which had in its ranks the best player in the colony at the time, Lieutenant R.B. Stewart, was at the centre of the operations that led to nearly 4,000 Xhosa and Thembu deaths.[7]

In **1878** British forces quelled an uprising of Griqua, Tlhaping and Khoisan protesting against their loss of land in Griqualand West.

In **1878–9** Cape Colony forces put down the 'Moorosi Rebellion' of the Phuti in Basutoland, killed the chief and opened his lands to white settlement.

In **1879** the British invaded Zululand. The Zulu shocked the invaders at the Battle of Isandlwana, where cricket pads were found among the detritus and 2,000 dead bodies strewn across the battlefield. But the British returned to defeat the Zulu at the Battle of Ulundi. King Cetshwayo was sent into exile. Further north, British and Swazi forces in the same year also subjugated Chief Sekhukhune, who had up to then resolutely preserved Pedi independence. He was taken prisoner and 'led captive' into Pretoria.

In **1880–1** the Gun War broke out in Basutoland as the Cape set out to assert control over the Basotho, who had enjoyed relative autonomy until then. However, Lerotholi defeated the Cape forces at Kalabani before Britain brokered a truce between its two possessions. The war also created divisions within the Sotho. Paramount Chief Letsie's sons and other chiefs ignored his agreement to hand over arms, using them to fight instead.

In **1881** the Transvaal Boers defeated the surprised British at the Battle of Majuba and reclaimed their independence. The British first-class cricketer Edward Wilkinson was one of the casualties at 'Scheins Hoogte'.[8] In the same year, the South African Republic was restored, but its independence was limited.

In 1883–4, civil war broke out in Zululand between Cetshwayo's successor, Dinuzulu (who called on Boer forces to help him), and the British-appointed chief Zibhebhu kaMpitha.

In April 1884 Germany claimed Walvis Bay and subsequently proclaimed a protectorate over South West Africa (taking more than two decades to subdue with extreme force the area today known as Namibia). In the same year the Orange Free State took advantage of a succession battle in Moroka's Territory (Thaba Nchu) to alienate parts of Rolong lands. The son of the *kgosi* was one of those who had studied at Zonnebloem and was sent to England with the cricket-loving Nathaniel Umhalla.

In 1884–5 the Warren expedition annexed the Tswana-inhabited areas south of the Molopo River as British Bechuanaland (part of today's North West Province and Northern Cape). The areas north of the Molopo (modern-day Botswana) were proclaimed the Bechuanaland Protectorate. This put an end to the short-lived Boer Republics of Goshen and Stellaland, which Britain feared could link up with the Germans. Meshach Pelem, who would many years later donate a cup named after himself for an important cricket competition, was one of the black loyalists on the expedition.

In 1886 the Boers took over parts of Zululand, previously ruled by Zibhebhu, the enemy of Dinuzulu, and called it the New Republic. In 1887 Britain annexed the remaining parts of Zululand.

In 1888 Cecil John Rhodes formed the British South Africa Company (BSAC) to further his expansionist ambitions. Its so-called Pioneer Column entered what was to become Rhodesia (Zimbabwe) and established Salisbury (later Harare). The youngest-ever England cricket captain was a celebrity participant. In 1893 the BSAC went to war with the Ndebele. One of the administrators in charge of this newly conquered country and many of its officials were deeply involved in playing cricket and organising the game in the subcontinent, as we shall see.

In 1894 Mpondoland (an independent 'treaty-state' for 50 years) became the last territory along the south-east coast to lose its independence, when it was annexed by the Cape as part of the Transkei.

In 1895 the South African Republic annexed Swaziland, and British Bechuanaland was incorporated into the Cape Colony.

In 1896 Rhodes's friend Dr Jameson led a party which unsuccessfully attempted a coup in the South African Republic. Touring England players visited him in jail and played cards with him and his fellow conspirators.[9]

In 1896–7 the Langeberg Rebellion of the Tlhaping in British Bechuanaland was put down.

In 1897 Natal annexed Zululand.

In **1898** the South African Republic subjugated the Venda.

In **October 1899**, with its eyes on control of the goldfields themselves, Britain precipitated the South African War against the South African Republic, pitting one set of European colonisers against another. The Orange Free State was soon drawn into the war. It has been described as Britain's 'most important conflict between Waterloo in 1815 and World War I in 1914'.[10] A bitter victory, reached at a greater cost than expected, was achieved by the British in May 1902. Two test players, John Ferris of Australia and Frank Milligan of England, and ten other first-class cricketers were among those who lost their lives for the Empire.[11] Another first-class cricketer, Pieter de Villiers, fought on the enemy side, was captured wearing cricket whites (albeit the worse for wear), and sent as a prisoner of war to Ceylon.[12]

And so, year by year, the dominoes fell, enabling Britain to consolidate various fragmented political entities into a single Union of South Africa by 1910. Precolonial entities collapsed one after the other in the wake of the mineral discoveries and lost their independence.[13] Many submitted 'voluntarily' to their pacification, but this process can be fully understood only against the background of a century of conflict and the systematic use of force.[14] Annexation merely legalised a gradual process of expanding British rule. Those who refused to bend the knee were conquered militarily. A spokesperson in the liberation struggle years, later to become president of South Africa, explained:

> South Africa was conquered by force and is today ruled by force. At moments when White autocracy feels itself threatened, it does not hesitate to use the gun. When the gun is not in use legal and administrative terror, fear, social and economic pressures, complacency and confusion generated by propaganda and 'education', are the devices brought into play in an attempt to harness the people's opposition. Behind these devices hovers force. Whether in reserve or in actual employment, force is ever present and this has been so since the White man came to Africa.[15]

He continued:

> The British brought new dimensions to the whole process of conquest in the nineteenth century. They modernised the petrified and outdated Boer economy and subjugated the indigenous workers and peasants in a much more systematic, sophisticated and brutally exploitative manner.

> In the end it was the British armies which defeated the African people, the British which drove us off our lands, broke up the natural economy and social system of the indigenous people. It was they who imposed the taxes on the

African peasants and ... laid down labour laws which govern the black workers in South Africa today.[16]

As this book will show, cricket went along as part of the baggage of the conquering military columns. Throughout the nineteenth century it was in the middle of the maelstrom generated by this process of violent, systematic conquest and the appropriation of more than a million square kilometres of territory across southern Africa. Its growth and character were indeed shaped by this historical storm.

* * * * *

While this process of conquest was unfolding in southern Africa, the European countries met at Bismarck's villa in Berlin in 1884 to carve up the continent. Secure in their own understanding of themselves as the ultimate arbiters of geography and power, European leaders drew lines across maps, cutting through households and history, to divide the whole of Africa into specific regions where each power 'had the right to "pursue" the legal ownership of land, free from interference by any other'.[17] Except for two countries that remained independent – namely Liberia and Ethiopia – Africa was now painted red (Britain), blue (France), green (Portugal) and so on.

By 1902, southern Africa was producing a quarter of the world's gold and a new town called Johannesburg, barely 15 years old, was a key part of the global economy. The world market came to be 'controlled from London'. In keeping with the concept of sovereignty-based New Imperialism, Britain consolidated various territories into one South Africa so as to become part of 'a configuration of states which in their internal developments were expected to complement the economy of Great Britain'.[18] Rapidly modernising sport became part of this new phase of globalisation. As Immanuel Wallerstein has noted, 'with the emergence of the modern world system organized culture began its career as a potent weapon of the elite classes'.[19]

The opening up of southern Africa stimulated cricket, leading to greater organisation and integration internally, and the development of international contacts, which in turn led to tours by visiting teams. The mindsets that accompanied British and colonial militarism also had a direct impact on the culture of the growing game of cricket in southern Africa. Cricket became infused with notions of racism, a narrow masculinity, social Darwinism and imperialist superiority. It was impossible for the archetypal British game, with its close military associations, to remain innocent against the background sketched here. Indeed, it would become even more tightly woven into the fabric of an oppressive imperialism and colonial power as the last quarter of the nineteenth century unfolded.

10

Champion Bat ushers in new era

The launch of inter-town tournaments, 1875/6 onwards

> Port Elizabeth has felt honoured in her guests, and
> notwithstanding her own discomfiture in the tented
> field, is genuinely glad to think that the 'Canterbury
> week' of 1876 – the first we trust of a long series – has
> been, so far as was practicable, a signal success.

> – *Eastern Province Herald*, 18 January 1876

The growth of the game in Britain and its colonies, and the events that occurred in southern Africa from the middle of the 1870s onwards, propelled cricket onto a formally organised level. Cricket started taking on its popular, modern, competitive form, both internationally and in South Africa. Previously unconnected areas began to be laced together slowly into a national framework, and tentative preparations began for southern Africa's entry into the slowly unfolding British imperial network of international competition.

A challenge issued in 1875 by the mayor of Port Elizabeth to other towns in the Cape Colony inaugurated a new stage in cricket's development. It led to the organisation of the first inter-town tournament between representative teams from the main towns in the colony early in the New Year in 1876. This was the first formal multi-team cricket competition in southern Africa, linking different regions and extending beyond participants from one or two towns. A start was made in the slow process of building organised competitions and the broad integration of cricket enthusiasts in different centres.

The local *Eastern Province Herald* gave some idea of the thinking of the organisers of the new tournament when it compared it to the 'Canterbury week' in England and said it hoped this would be the first of a 'long series'. The Canterbury Cricket Week was the oldest cricket festival in England. Organised by the Kent County Cricket Club, it was started in 1842 and was held at the St Lawrence Ground 'with its tents and famous lime tree, unchanging in a changing world'. Besides the matches involving Kent CCC, 'several other events and ceremonies', including a Ladies' Day, made it a social event to remember. It is still going more than 170 years later.[1]

The municipality of Port Elizabeth hosted the first Inter-Town Tournament and also presented the Champion Bat as the prize for the winning team. Four centres accepted invitations, namely Cape Town, Port Elizabeth, Grahamstown and King William's Town. 'Some fear was at one time entertained that at the last minute the expected visitors would not arrive', but when the ship *Zulu* appeared in the bay with the 'King' team from East London, and Cape Town followed soon afterwards, the stage was set. 'The ground was ... in splendid shape; fences had been erected to prevent any crowding of the players; refreshment booths were there ..., separate tents were provided for the use of the respective teams, ample accommodation for lady visitors was ensured, and care was taken that the scorers should not be subjected to any inconvenience.'[2] Right down to the copy-cat accommodation for 'the ladies', this was clearly a very 'English' event. The 'redoubtable kaffrarians' from King William's Town were the first winners, heading the table with three wins: they beat Grahamstown by six wickets, Port Elizabeth by three and Cape Town by four. The *Eastern Province Herald* generously conceded, 'Their physique, pluck, athletic training and fine discipline bore down all opposition'. The hosts propped up the table with three losses.[3]

That first tournament involved five matches. Although double innings contests, they all were completed in one day. The century was passed only once in 20 innings when King William's Town scored 102/4 to beat Grahamstown. Of 16 completed innings in which all ten wickets fell, the average score was a paltry 65, the lowest 22 and the highest 99.

In the very first match Calderwood of Grahamstown won the toss and went into bat with his partner against the hosts – it took 12 four-ball overs to reach four runs in that first innings before 'the first life was taken'. Three batsmen reached double figures, but thereafter no batsman in the next three completed innings scored more than eight; the feats of Hashim Amla and A.B. de Villiers still lay far into the future.

The highest individual tournament score was 37 by W. Heugh for King William's Town (vs Port Elizabeth). In some innings extras formed significant (or even ludicrous) percentages of the total runs, suggesting either appalling pitches or incompetent wicketkeeping, or both. Wicketkeepers did not use pads in those days (a practice introduced only in 1906). The highest extras figure was 42 per cent in Port Elizabeth's first innings against Cape Town, but there were four other innings in which extras made up more than a third of the runs. Bowling figures were inversely impressive. The leading wicket-takers, both with 22 victims, were Melck of Cape Town (average 3.3 in two matches) and Phillips of King William's Town (average 5.2 in three matches), although the best performance of 8/32 was recorded by A. Edkins of Grahamstown in the match against King William's Town.

The close involvement of the military in cricket at the time is reflected in the fact that the winners' attack revolved around a 'good pair of soldier bowlers', Phillips and Gillman of the 32nd Regiment, who took 29 wickets between them. An 'extraneous match' on the final day pitting Civilians against the Military Past and Present brought the tournament to a close and underlined the prominence of the military. It replaced the scheduled Cape Town vs Grahamstown match, probably because the outcome would have made no difference to the final standings; these kinds of contests were 'a favourite in those warlike times'.[4] They were clearly meant to deepen colonial solidarity in the process of military conquest, which was then entering a particularly expansive phase. The ninth war of dispossession in the eastern Cape was imminent, and in the next quarter of a century Britain would complete the forceful subjugation of the entire area known today as South Africa and Zimbabwe.

There were four British regiments in southern Africa in the late 1870s, and most of the troops were stationed in King William's Town, with the others mainly at the capital in Cape Town. The town also hosted the headquarters of the 1,200-strong Cape Mounted Rifles, who were frontier police recruited and paid for by the Cape government. Those in the ranks were paid £100 a year, which was an attractive income even though the men had to pay for their own horses, and also see to their own keep. The CMR was the main fighting force on the frontier and its men were said to be 'much more efficacious' than the ordinary British soldiers. Most of the recruits were from England, and not only were they all mounted, but most of 'the men themselves come from a much higher class than that from which our soldiers are enlisted'.[5]

The scorecards of the first tournament reflected the snobbery of the English class system. The two bowling stars already mentioned had only their surnames given in the scorecards, indicating that they were ordinary troops, while their teammates who were officers had their ranks included, like the opening batsman, Lieutenant Fownes, and Lieutenant Gallwey. Civilians, it seems, were accorded the respect of having their initials included.

The participants were rooted in the colonial experience, and some would go on to make their mark in cricket and society. Sir John James Graham was the grandson of Captain John Graham, who had set the stage for the 1820 Settlers to occupy 'empty' land by clearing 20,000 Ndlambe and Gqunukhwebe Xhosa out of the area west of the Fish River through 'a proper degree of terror' in the 1810s. Described as the 15th Laird of Fintry, he played in 1876 for the team of the town named after his grandfather. John James's Grahamstown teammate William Hopley, later became a judge and the first president of the South African Cricket Association. His younger brother, Sir Thomas Lynedoch Graham, who studied at Cambridge University and became Attorney General of the Cape, also later played a bit part in a defining moment in South African cricket history as a member of the Western Province Cricket Club in Cape Town, as we shall see.[6]

The *Eastern Province Herald* described the tournament as 'a gathering such as Port Elizabeth has never seen before' and judged it a big success:

> It is no light thing for men of business to travel hundreds of miles to engage in friendly contest. The result of the manly competition ... cannot be otherwise than distinctly healthy, not alone by encouraging out-door exercise and its attendant advantages, but by bringing together the champions of scattered localities, teaching them to appreciate and learn something from the world beyond their immediate circle, and thus by rubbing away angles, undermining prejudices, to pave the way for that cosmopolitan tendency of mind which disgusts men with petty localism and leads them to see the untold benefits derivable from union.[7]

The Champion Bat tournament was held five times in 15 years, subsequently expanding to include other towns in the colony, including Kimberley. The Diamond City had been invited to the first tournament, but it only made its debut third time round in 1884. It decided to snub the first tournament for reasons which had to do with its location, its rumbustious Wild West start as a settlement and the character of William Ling, the larger-than-life leader of early Kimberley cricket.

Ling and his colleagues decided against going to Port Elizabeth. They gave as their reason the distance of 743 kilometres, which would 'probably have taken them more than two weeks by ox-wagon and, where roads existed, by coach'. However, Richard Parry, the foremost historian of Kimberley cricket, is not convinced. He contends it was mainly for political reasons that they stayed away. Ling challenged British authority over the diamond fields and was brought to trial in 1875 for 'riot' when he led an armed vigilante force of 50 men who 'sought to release a digger convicted of firearms offences'.

Ling began his defence with an impassioned objection to the jurisdiction of the court arguing that Griqualand West should be part of the independent Afrikaner republic of the Orange Free State to the east and not British at all. This treasonous view had widespread digger support in the midst of the labyrinthine network of claims and counter-claims to the Diamond Fields by the British, various Griqua chiefs, the Orange Free State Republic, and the indigenous black population.[8]

In the process of mobilising his armed Diggers' Protection Association, which also sought to prevent 'our black servants from being on the streets at night', the local cricket ground was 'put to use for drills' by the bearded, charismatic cricketer.

Instead of going to Port Elizabeth for the Champion Bat tournament, Kimberley cocked a snook at the colonial establishment and travelled to the Free State capital 117 kilometres away to play against Bloemfontein and the small settlements of Barkly West and Caledon instead. According to Parry, 'The political significance of the visit was not lost on Ling and his team, who were presented to President Brand of the OFS and gave him three rousing cheers.'

After the historic first Inter-Town Tournament in 1876, the War of Ngcayecibi of 1877–8 broke out, once again unsettling the 'frontier'. King William's Town, home of the first champions, became the centre of the war effort. General Thesiger, later Lord Chelmsford, who was in charge of 4,000 troops (mostly local black allies), was headquartered in the town, which was 'teeming with refugees' since 'every farm within a radius of seven miles to the north and east had been burnt out'.[9] This was the last of the nine major outbreaks of armed hostilities in the so-called Hundred Years War and, as Mostert has noted, it marked 'the final military fall and subjugation of the ... principal houses of the Xhosa nation'.[10] As usual, much blood was shed in the advancement of British power. In one Xhosa attack described by Tim Couzens:

> The artillery shells and rockets failed to stop this charge, as brave as Major General Pickett's at Gettysburg. But then the infantrymen, concealed in the rifle pits, revealed themselves and sent a volley into the Xhosa that mowed them down like grass. Muzzle-loaders were no match for the new Martini-Henrys. The late last flower of Gcaleka warriordom, after 20 minutes, wilted. They were pursued by Carrington's horse, the mounted police and the Mfengu.[11]

Close on 4,000 Xhosa died in the war as well as 193 combatants on the side of the British forces. In a footnote to the conflict, one of the cricketers referred to in previous chapters, Nathaniel Umhalla, who played for Zonnebloem College in the early 1860s and for St Mark's Mission in 1870, was arrested and charged with treason in the aftermath of the war. This son of a chief, who had studied in England, was found not guilty; he would remain at the forefront of cricket's remarkable development in King William's Town, despite losing his government job.

It took four years before the second Champion Bat tournament was held in the 1879/80 season. King William's Town, bruised from the experience of war, was the venue. The second tournament was limited to eastern Cape teams. Kimberley once again decided against playing and, much to the chagrin of the organisers, Cape Town also chose not to participate. Queenstown, started as a colonial settlement on conquered Thembu lands 27 years earlier with a six-sided fortress at its centre, stepped into the breach and agreed to send a team.

The hosts won for the second time in a row, beating Port Elizabeth in a play-off, after losing an early match. A crowd of some 2,000 was in attendance on the opening day and the standards seemed to be much better than at the inaugural event. The scores were higher and all the matches went into a second day. The first individual century was scored and totals of 100 runs were recorded in ten innings, the highest being 222 by King William's Town (vs Port Elizabeth) and 217 by Grahamstown (vs King William's Town). The average for the 23 innings in which all ten wickets fell improved from 65 in 1876 to 107, the lowest being 47 (by Queenstown vs King William's Town). Extras played a more modest role, and this time there was no innings where over a third of the runs came from that source.

King William's Town's second successive win came once again on the back of outstanding performances by military men, this time officers with British public school backgrounds from the Cape Mounted Rifles. Lieutenant Robert B. Stewart scored 105 in the decisive final match against Port Elizabeth, as well as two of four half-centuries. An ex-Wellington College pupil from the West Country, he arrived in South Africa with something of a cricket pedigree: he 'certainly was the most renowned South African cricketer of his day'. Strong on the off-side, his signature shot was the late cut, which he executed with perfect timing and he was 'worth his place in any side for fielding'.

Stewart's teammate, Lieutenant Lyndhurst Winslow, who took 27 wickets, had an even more impressive pedigree. He played five matches for Sussex in 1875 before leaving for South Africa the following year. Among his teammates, therefore, was James Lillywhite, who had become England's first test captain in 1877. Indeed, five of that first England touring party had played for Sussex at one stage. Described as an 'attacking right-hand batsman', Winslow scored 124 on debut against Gloucester at Hove.[12] He was the father of Charles Winslow, who won gold medals in tennis at the 1912 Stockholm Olympics, and grandfather of

Paul Winslow, who played cricket for South Africa in the 1950s. Owen Dunell, ex-Eton and Oxford University, was the third top-class player next to Stewart and Winslow to debut in the Inter-Town Tournament in 1880. He became a mainstay of the Port Elizabeth side and eventually the first player to captain South Africa at cricket.

As in 1876, one did not have to look hard for the colonial pedigrees of players in the succeeding Inter-Town tournaments. Altogether some 60 of the 209 cricketers who participated shared family names with those on the list of 1820 Settlers, though not all were necessarily related.[13] Benjamin D'Urban Godlonton, the Port Elizabeth opening bowler, was the highest wicket-taker in 1880, capturing two more than Winslow. Named after the land-grabbing Cape governor Sir Benjamin D'Urban, Godlonton was the son of an 1820 Settler, Robert Godlonton, whose report on cricket in Salem in 1844 was noted in chapter 3. After arriving at the Cape with a printing press in 1820, Godlonton Senior (also known as 'Moral Bob') became the leading newspaper editor and vociferous political spokesman of hardline racial attitudes on the frontier. He viewed Africans as irredeemable thieves and 'the most barbarous savages, sunk into the lowest abyss of moral degradation'. His motto towards the indigenous people was 'destroy ... the nest, [and] we shall not be liable to the incursions of the brood'.[14] The definitive history of the area and time concludes that it was through Grahamstown and Godlonton 'that white South Africa first became powerfully vocal in defence of itself, and of its outlook, and its attitudes towards the country's indigenous people'.[15] Most of the soldiers and young colonists participating in the tented Inter-Town tournaments would most likely have shared the stark views about black and white conveyed by Godlonton's newspapers: 'These antagonistic powers ["civilisation" and "barbarism"] are now brought into collision, and are engaged in deadly feud; it is a conflict of light and darkness – of truth and error – of order and confusion.'[16] While Godlonton's opponents saw him as a rumour-monger, gun-runner and war-profiteer, his supporters described him as an 'unflinching champion' of the settlers against 'the cruel calumny' of unsympathetic officials, liberals and missionaries alike.[17]

Owen Dunell led the charge when Port Elizabeth unseated the King William's Town double champions to win the third Champion Bat tournament at home in 1884, the year that Godlonton Senior died. Dunell made a top score of 78 not out and came second behind Lieutenant Stewart in aggregate and average with 185 runs at an average of 46. Stewart scored three of the seven half-centuries during the week, for an average of over 50.

The hosts won all three of their matches, and Kimberley, who entered for the first time, were the wooden spoonists. The debutants could not come to grips with the different conditions in the windy city of Port Elizabeth, where matting wickets were laid over soft turf, rather than the packed earth with pace and bounce with which they were familiar in dry Kimberley. They managed, though, to beat Grahamstown and Uitenhage – peeved by their exclusion from the cricket week – in friendlies played before the tournament. The omnipresent William Ling (born in the 1820s) was in the team, but making his swansong. Kimberley was by now connected by rail to the coast and was becoming a rich new growth point for the game. After the tournament, a new era was at hand for its cricket.

Cape Town, making a much anticipated return to the tournament, came second. They made both the highest score (225 vs King William's Town) and the lowest, when they came unstuck and were 35 all out against Port Elizabeth. One of the debutants from Cape Town was a young one-eyed, left-handed all-rounder, Charlie Vintcent. He was second in the tournament bowling averages with 26 wickets at an average of 7.0. A. Geard of Port Elizabeth took the most wickets (35). Like Stewart and Dunell, the 'footloose' Vintcent, son of a Mossel Bay businessman and later a politician, who was educated at Charterhouse in England, was to become one of the stand-out players in southern Africa. All-rounder Charles Finlason of Kimberley was third best in the averages. Finlason was one of the trio of Kimberley players who would go on to achieve prominence in the future. The others were Irvine Grimmer, the first high-arm off-spinner of note in the country, whose wicked turn was to bamboozle the best, and the young opening batsman A.B. Tancred, who made an immediate impact in Kimberley after finishing his schooling in Grahamstown.

From the venues and results up to that point, it is clear that Port Elizabeth and King William's Town could claim to be the strongest cricket centres in southern Africa in the late 1870s and early 1880s. King had won two of the first three tournaments and been the hosts once. PE had hosted two of the three and won when the frontiersmen from 'the Border' were not the victors.

Details of the remaining Champion Bat tournaments will follow in later chapters, but if one looks in overview at the five tournaments spread over the period 1876–1891, they involved 27 matches and were generally characterised by very low scoring, yielding just three centuries, though there were 19 half-centuries. Given the long breaks between them, there was understandably little player continuity from series to series. Only Stewart of King William's Town batted consistently (over the second and third tournaments of 1880 and 1884), scoring 488 runs in 11 innings at an average of just over 54, with a century and five half-centuries and just one dismissal within single figures. The bowling figures were often impressive, but it is difficult to assess the bowling standards in view of the low scores and the fact that the records of bowlers are in any case incomplete – full bowling analysis was not always provided in those early days of four-ball overs.

The Champion Bat tournament was launched three years after the unofficial county cricket championship in England, and one year before the first-ever test match between England and Australia. No doubt these unfolding developments, and the fact that several of the organisers and participants in the Champion Bat competitions had direct experience of the British game, influenced South Africans to move into a more organised mode as well.

The Champion Bat competition was followed by similar 'Native' and 'Malay' Inter-Town tournaments. Altogether, these socially distinct cricket communities staged no less than 22 Inter-Town tournaments at an average of one a year between 1876 and 1898, as we shall see.

There were clear overlaps between the towns involved in the three different competitions: teams from Port Elizabeth and Kimberley featured in all three. Cape Town, Grahamstown, King William's Town, Queenstown and Uitenhage had teams in two of the competitions, while East London and teams from outside the Cape Colony – Johannesburg, Bechuanaland (Botswana) and Natal, still either small and on the peripheries of an undeveloped subcontinental transport network – appeared in only one.

The scope and cross-community nature of these earliest forms of inter-regional competition have not been fully recognised or properly detailed before. They paved the way for the inter-colonial tournaments, starting in the 1890s, which became the bedrock of organised cricket in South Africa in the twentieth century. The Currie Cup and the Barnato Memorial Trophy emerged directly from them and then gradually superseded the Inter-Town tournaments as the highest levels of domestic competition in southern Africa.

Remarkably, given South Africa's subsequent history, indigenous people were in the forefront during the new era of organised competitive sport in the subcontinent. Already at this early stage they were interacting with the white cricketers, occasionally sharing municipal and club facilities with them, achieving relatively high standards of play and generally making clear their desire to be fully part of the evolving game in southern Africa. The intensive organisation of the early 1880s, some 'capital' performances and several acclaimed victories over their white counterparts, described below, would underline the point.

11

'Native' champions

A second inter-town tournament, 1884/5 onwards

> Our countrymen have gone on the even tenor of their way
> without noticing their critics ... the natives do not only mean to
> persevere in playing at cricket, but are resolved to proceed from
> conquering to conquest so far as the cricket world is concerned.

> – *Imvo Zabantsundu*, 3 November 1884

Black cricketers in the Cape Colony were excluded from the whites-only Champion Bat competition. Few colonists would have given a thought in 1876 to the idea that the indigenous people should or could become part of this new social institution in the life of the British and settler establishment. However, not to be outdone, the emerging mission-educated indigenous middle class launched a separate Native Inter-Town Tournament based on the Cape Colony's premier competition, in the 1884/5 season.[1] The 'Native' version of the premier competition was organised in the same month that white cricketers held only their third tournament – and a year before the first inter-town tournament for white rugby players was organised.

The new event reflected the relative strength of cricket in the eastern Cape at the time and showed interesting parallels with the Champion Bat tournaments. Just like its counterpart, the 'Native' tournament was launched by eastern Cape cricketers and it also involved four towns. Moreover, it took place over the same Christmas and New Year holiday period and was played on the same top fields in the host towns. The venue of the first tournament demonstrated the aspirations of the black cricketers. This was the Grahamstown municipal oval, 'City Lords', which was the home ground of the local white team which had played in the first two Champion Bat tournaments. Costing a pound and a penny per day to rent, matting included, the ground a few years later hosted a match during the first international tour to South Africa, when it was described in these flattering terms: 'The "Lords" is one of the prettiest, if not *the* prettiest, cricket grounds in the colony, situated about a mile and a half from the town, and from it a grand view is obtained of the hills that surround the Cathedral City.'[2]

The African cricketers were not just after the view. They sought equality as cricketers and citizens in the Cape Colony, and the new 'Native' tournament boldly underlined the fact that they were among the pioneers of organised sport in South Africa. Numerous African clubs had been formed in the region by the early 1880s. This was part of the broader political and economic mobilisation of the mission-educated school people in that decade. Alongside a host of political, educational, religious and social bodies, a whole array of cricket clubs made their appearance. These included Try Again Cricket Club from Grahamstown; Fear Not CC and Kreli Star from Port Elizabeth; Good Hope CC from Uitenhage; and Gaika CC and Nxaruni CC from East London. Kreli (Sarhili) and Gaika (Ngqika) were proudly named after chiefs in the days of independence.

At the educational centres, life was equally busy. *Isigidimi samaXhosa* reported that the Oriental CC of the workers beat the Occidental CC of the students at the 'Kaffir Institution' in Grahamstown. Healdtown College beat the Fort Beaufort CC. And no fewer than five clubs existed around neighbouring Alice, where Lovedale College was based, including Fight Again CC (Ntsela-manzi) and Never Give Up CC (Gqumahashe). True to its name, Never Give Up is still in existence today, older for example than Wanderers in Johannesburg.

In May 1883 East London's Gaika CC played Champion CC from King William's Town in the first reported inter-town match for black cricketers. Two pioneering black newspapers, *Isigidimi samaXhosa* and *Imvo Zabantsundu*, started covering these matches and encouraged teams from different towns to meet, just as their white counterparts were doing. *Isigidimi* also attempted to foster the game by placing news of a century by 'Dr Grace' against Australia,[3] and giving advice on how cricketers could best protect their bats in hot climates, where they broke easily. The suggested remedy was *'uyifake kunye namafuta embizeni, uyibilise ke yonke lonto kunye'* (You put it together with fat [oil] into a pot and bring everything to a boil together).[4] *Isigidimi* noted that the educated and Christianised school people *'tina mpi imnyama igqobokileyo'*, had left behind the old tribal ways, but had not yet adopted the new, namely the pursuits of cricket, lawn tennis, croquet, hunting and dancing of the English. It encour-aged them to do so.[5]

The brilliant 23-year-old editor of *Isigidimi*, John Tengo Jabavu, had taken on the job at the paper with the aim of 'educating the people to their rights under the Queen's sway', but he soon found himself frustrated by the paternalistic control of the missionaries at Lovedale. So he set up his own newspaper with the help of his black and white political allies. The first issue of *Imvo Zabantsundu* (*Native Opinion*) appeared on Monday, 3 November 1884. Its appearance was a landmark occasion in the political history of South Africa, heralding the birth of an independent black press, a major step forward in the struggle by the colonised for a voice within the colonial system. Jabavu and his weekly King William's Town-based newspaper made an immediate impact as a vehicle for promoting the goals and publicising the activities of the new African intellectuals. Within a short time, he could state without fear of contradiction that as the standard bearer of 'Native Opinion' his newspaper was now a power in the land.[6]

Imvo soon revealed just how popular cricket was among eastern Cape Africans. In the very first edition, Jabavu devoted his editorial notes to the game:

> To our Colonial English contemporaries, the playing of the game of cricket by natives would seem to be regarded as a strange phenomenum [*sic*]; and already all sorts of guesses are indulged in as to the probable motives of the sons of Ham in taking to this English time-honoured pastime. 'Mimicry', 'travesty of civilization' and expletives of a like character have been hinted as the possible causes, but our countrymen have gone on the even tenor of their way without noticing their critics ... the natives do not only mean to persevere in playing at cricket, but are resolved to proceed from conquering to conquest so far as the cricket world is concerned.[7]

In the letters column of the first issue of *Imvo*, 'Umtandi-we-Cricket' (A lover of cricket) from Port Elizabeth suggested that 'the leading native clubs in the colony', such as those at Grahamstown, East London, Port Elizabeth, Queenstown, St Matthew's Keiskamma Hoek and Lovedale, should arrange a tournament in King William's Town in the 'New Year's vacation'.[8] Jabavu enthusiastically supported this idea and said thought should also be given to a 'native eleven, consisting of those who distinguished themselves in the proposed tournament being equipped for a cricket campaign to England'.[9]

Less than two months later, the first Native Inter-Town Tournament kicked off, with Grahamstown finally chosen as the venue. East London (Gaika CC), King William's Town (Champion CC), Grahamstown (Fear Not CC) and Port Elizabeth (Ethiopian CC) sent sides to play at the postcard-pretty City Lords ground.[10] Captained by Nathaniel Umhalla, the appropriately named Champion CC from King William's Town emerged as winners. They beat East London by an innings, Grahamstown by three wickets, and Port Elizabeth by six wickets. It was the first contest between teams from the two towns, and Champion CC were thrilled to beat the Port Elizabeth cricketers with their big reputations. Fast bowler Austin Ngcumbe was the star of the winning team, twice taking ten wickets, followed by nine in another match. For the next decade he would be one of the stars in the region. As in the white tournaments, the scores were very low, with the bowlers completely dominating the bat. The available scorecards show that in nine completed innings, the totals were under 50 in five cases and just over 50 in the other four.[11] The *Cape Mercury* commented that 'the play of the four teams is much alike', with their fielding 'much superior' to their batting.[12]

The winners from King William's Town must have been elated by the win, but they had some logistical problems getting home safely. They had their horse impounded and damages of £5 10s 6d were demanded for its return. A local white attorney intervened on the team's behalf. Mr Wright, 'as if emulating [the generous hospitality of] the dark citizens, added to our score of good luck by exerting himself successfully without charge for the recourse of our stallion.'[13] When the team got back home, special celebrations were held at the Victoria Grounds. The local women led by Mary Ann Bovana, sister of the club secretary, and Elizabeth Kwankwa, were prominent in the proceedings. Captain Nathaniel Umhalla spoke of the fine hospitality provided by Grahamstown and after that Austin Ngcumbe, unable to speak from the emotion, was presented with *intonga*, a trophy, or in a literal sense a stick, for his man-of-the-tournament exploits.[14]

After losing to King William's Town at the first Inter-Town tournament in 1884/5, the Port Elizabeth Africans turned the tables on their main opponents at home in the 1885/6 tournament, winning by two wickets in a low-scoring encounter in which only five batsmen reached double figures.[15] In *Imvo*'s report on '*Umdlalo we bola eBayi*', the tournament was described as a big success, thanks to the lively organising committee. There were only three teams, with East London missing from the year before. The matches were played at the Union CC ground in the city's St George's Park precinct (a large facility which confusingly also includes the St George's Park cricket ground, headquarters of the PECC, as well as tennis, bowls, a cemetery, a water reservoir, a duckpond, several playing areas for children and a large conservatory). Union, it was noted, had 'a Pavilion that is big enough to accommodate all the spectators'. Frank Makwena 'took to every corner of the streets to put up posters about the match and even outside the hotels, where he received financial assistance from white people'. The mood was good and the pavilion full – but with black people only, as there was 'an English tournament' at the main PECC St George's ground next door. Vendors sold food, 'Ginger Beer as well as Hope Beer'. The entrance fee of 6d was used to cover the fee for hiring the venue and players' lunches.

In attendance were a number of important churchmen and leaders of two newly formed political organisations to protect black people's interests, Imbumbumba Yama Nyama and the Native Educational Association. They included Rev. Samuel Nsiko and Rev. Daniel Mangas from the host city, Rev. W.P Momoti from Graaff-Reinet, Rev W.B. Rubusana from Peelton as well as leaders from Rabula in Keiskamma Hoek and Grahamstown. The poet, cleric and writer Isaac Wauchope, doing justice to his praise name, Silwangubo ('He who fights with the blanket [protecting his fist]'), delivered traditional praises. On the one hand, he warned Port Elizabeth were stepping on coals disguised as ash in taking on the defending champions and, on the other, he answered the challenge by saying PE need not fear a King without a king.

The pavilion had three rooms, each with a defined purpose during the tournament. The first was the changing room for the visitors and the middle one was the eating area for the players. PE's Mr Cricket, Peter Rwexu, was said to have 'made a lot of meat and ginger beer for the teams'. The last room belonged to a Mr Bairstow, who hired it from Union CC so that he could sell liquor. 'He displayed all his bottles of alcohol but did not sell a single one of them. He thereafter took all his beverages and packed them away'. The school people were strong supporters of the temperance movement and, particularly with all the churchmen and political leaders present, Mr Bairstow was unlikely to do good business there.

There were five bulls who fought in this contest of the ball (*Inkunzi ebezi silwa kule Bhola*) at the third tournament in three years, in 1886/7. Queenstown sent a team for the first time and East London were back in action. The participants were now no longer the club champions from each town, but combined town teams. *Qonce*, as King William's Town is known in isiXhosa, once again turned the tables on *iBhayi* (Port Elizabeth) to regain the champions tag before their home crowd. In the deciding match, the bowling figures balanced themselves out, with Bali getting amongst the wickets for the hosts and Qoqo for PE, but William Seti provided the batting stability (19 and 27 run out) to carry the hosts through to a 36-run win. Butler with six wickets and second top score of 22 played his part as well.[16] Seti won the bat presented by Colonel Bayly for the best average (24),[17] but the biggest impact was made by the duo from third-placed Grahamstown, H. May and T. Gule. They hit the highest tournament scores of 45 and 43 respectively, and took over 50 wickets between them. Debutants Queenstown lost all four of their matches, but opening bowler Lutu fought valiantly in a losing cause. Several bowlers took more than 20 wickets, underlining their dominance over batsmen in a way which was reminiscent of the first counterpart tournament for the Champion Bat. The comparative stats were: highest team score 141 (Native Inter-Town Tournament) vs 99 (Champion Bat); highest individual innings 45 vs 37; lowest team score 11 vs 22; and the average for 27 completed innings, 51 vs 64.

Another feature of the tournament was the presence of players from coloured communities. Butler – who was good enough to be selected for the combined tournament team – and Fisher of King William's Town were members of the local coloured club, Try Again CC.[18] The presence of names like May, Kinner and Draai in the three other teams indicates this might have been the intention rather than the exception. The definition of 'Native' here was therefore broader than just indigenous black Africans, to use the terminology of present-day South Africa.

Given that both sets of cricketers lived in close proximity to each other and shared common aims of integration into colonial society, this inclusive approach made sense. Regular matches were played between African and coloured teams, and there were some mixed clubs as well. In Port Elizabeth, for example, on Christmas Day in 1883 the Fear Not took on a local Muslim or 'Malay' team, Star of the East. The latter won. The report noted that the victory was achieved because the opponents came with *'nabafundisi bawo'* (with their 'ministers' or imams). Early in 1884, Fear Not turned the tables in the return game, winning by the big margin of seven wickets. This time they had their lucky charm 'Mpinda' with them. Bill Swartbooi starred 'and his crippled father even cried because of his superb performance'.[19] In preparation for the first Native Inter-Town Tournament the same year, Champion CC from King William's Town played a hotly contested warm-up match against Try Again before going on to win in Grahamstown.[20] Graaff-Reinet, with its mixed, Afrikaans-speaking population, had the integrated Star of Venice club, for which W.P. Momoti turned out as a middle-order batsman. One of the founders of the first African political organisation, Imbumba Yama Nyama, in 1884 and a spectator at the Inter-Town tournaments in the season that followed, he was a trail-blazer in more ways than one.[21]

PIONEERS OF CRICKET IN SOUTH AFRICA

In summary, there were six telling lessons and comparative perspectives to be learned from the early Native Inter-Town cricket tournaments. Firstly, the first three Native and Champion Bat tournaments had the same geographical base, the same host towns, some shared venues, virtually the same participating centres (especially when Kimberley later joined the Native tournament), and the same winners, with King William's Town winning twice and Port Elizabeth the other time in both cases. Cricket was not something happening in a vacuum but part of a wider social context. A correspondent in *Imvo* noted in 1888 that 'It is admitted by all that King and Port Elizabeth have the most powerful Native elevens in the Eastern Province and up to the present day no fair conclusions have been tried between these two rivals'.[22] It is telling that these two towns also initially provided the champion teams in the first three corresponding white tournaments.[23]

Secondly, the organisation of the first African Inter-Town tournament in 1884/5 was a remarkable achievement if one considers the fact that white cricketers were holding only their third Inter-Town tournament in nearby Port Elizabeth in the same month.[24] By January 1887 the Africans had organised three tournaments in three seasons, catching up with the numbers of Champion Bat tournaments held at three- or four-year intervals by their white counterparts.

Thirdly, the African cricketers were ahead of other sports of the white colonial establishment. When they launched the Native Inter-Town tournament in December 1884, white rugby players had not yet organised any similar competitions – the first inter-town rugby tournament would only happen in 1885, also in Grahamstown.[25] (The quick adaptation to British games applied in tennis, too. The 'first known' tennis tournament was held in 1881, and by the time a South African, E.L. Williams, reached the Wimbledon men's doubles final with an English partner three years later in 1884,[26] black players in various parts of the eastern Cape had formed men's and women's tennis and croquet clubs as well.)[27]

Fourthly, African cricketers started challenging white teams to matches and showed that in the circumstances their standards were by and large comparable to those of their counterparts. They hoped that this engagement would be the beginning of an evolutionary process of increased involvement for black citizens in colonial cricket and social life.

Fifthly, at the end of the 1886/7 competition, the Africans selected a team comprising the best players in the tournament for the first time to play a team of local *amaNgesi* ('the English'). Effectively, a combined Eastern Cape Province side, this was the first representative regional team to be selected in southern Africa, pointing the way towards the later provincial system.

Finally, the African cricketers developed their own cricket press. Starting in the missionary sheets and then in their own independent newspapers, they were to generate a regular body of reporters and a steady flow of information from 1880 onwards, which significantly strengthened organisation and promoted interest in the game. In this respect, John Tengo Jabavu, editor of *Imvo*, became the James Lillywhite Senior of African cricket. As we will see, his newspaper printed thousands of cricket reports from Cape Town to Johannesburg to Bulawayo, as well as every nook and dorp in the eastern Cape, in the nearly four decades between 1884 and his death in 1921, when his sons D.D.T. and A.M. 'Mac' Jabavu continued with the task. (*James Lillywhite's Cricketers' Annual* covered English cricket between 1872 and 1900, and the first captain of England in official tests in 1877 was the publisher's cousin, James Lillywhite Junior.)[28] Jabavu, himself president of a local cricket club,[29] who later donated a trophy named after himself for the inter-town competitions, became the heartbeat of the cricket news distribution network. Cricketers and officials wrote to *Imvo*, sending in reports from the grass roots. The paper reported on games and plans and made suggestions, including the idea to send the best players from the Native Inter-Town Tournament to tour overseas. The innovative editor from King William's Town and his family were part of a tradition which was in more ways than one way comparable to their cricket cousins in Sussex.

The first Native Inter-Town tournaments revealed that there was a high level of organisation and a profound aptitude for and understanding of cricket by the indigenous black population in the very formative years of sport in South Africa. For decades to come, such inter-town tournaments would become commonplace. In sum, it is undeniable that African cricketers were among the pioneers of modern sport in South Africa. This fact flies directly in the face of racist assumptions formed during the colonial and apartheid years that cricket and rugby are really not part of the 'culture' of black people in South Africa, and that they never took to 'European' games, thus excusing the rigid discrimination and exclusion in the twentieth century that stemmed from these attitudes.[30]

12

Abantu namaNgesi

'The people and the English' – Cricket, colour and citizenship in the 1880s

Those who play together will not object to work
together, and the manly fellows who donned the
flannels last week will have a heartier feeling of respect
for their dusky conquerors than they had before.

– *Imvo Zabantsundu*, 9 March 1885

The first Native Inter-Town tournaments and the advent of competitive play marked the 'arrival' of African cricket. They also opened up a window period of a decade or so in which players, teams and personalities from the white cricket establishment and black cricketers engaged with each other in all three of the major sports playing regions – the eastern Cape, Kimberley and Cape Town – raising the hopes and possibility that cricket in southern Africa could eventually end up becoming integrated.

The church-educated mission people were grounded in the English public school ethos and adopted both the game and its ideology with intense enthusiasm. Cricket for them became an instrument of improvement and assimilation – a way to demonstrate their ability to adopt and absorb European culture, behave like 'gentlemen' and win acceptance as citizens. Their enthusiasm for cricket underlined the point that they subscribed to the ideas of 'civilisation', 'progress', Christianity and Empire that so defined being British, but on terms also articulated by themselves as Africans.[1] Through education and new patterns and activities, including their engagement with cricket, the school people sought to construct for themselves a modern identity which would enable them to participate fully in the political, cultural and economic life of the Cape Colony. In short, they aimed to become full citizens.

Unusually for the colonial world at the time, black citizens of the Cape Colony were actually allowed the vote on a common voters' roll in the Cape (until 1936) if they had certain educational and property qualifications. This encouraged them to become politically active within the system, and by the end of the 1880s there were around 10,000 registered black voters in the eastern Cape. In at least six constituencies they held the decisive vote. They sent out a clear message that white businessmen who wanted their business and white politicians who wanted their vote needed to show sympathy with their goals of advancement.

It was these young people, driven by African notions of *ubuntu*, Christian teachings of equality and British liberal values of individual freedom, who started forming independent political organisations and newspapers to express African opinion within colonial debates. Growing in numbers, the new intellectuals began writing to newspapers, petitioning parliament and mobilising organisationally to fight for black rights. Living as they now did within a common economy and common boundaries, the way forward for Africans was to 'shoot with the pen' – to fight by constitutional means for a greater role for themselves within the new colonial society.

The formation in 1880 of the Native Educational Association and in 1882 of Imbumba Yama Nyama (the South African Aborigines' Association) in the eastern Cape heralded the start of formal 'struggle' politics. Imbumba, which urged Africans to be 'inseparably united', was a direct response to the formation of the Afrikaner Bond, which marked the beginning of organised Afrikaner nationalism in the Colony. Throughout the eastern Cape fledgling political organisations sprang up, designated as Native Vigilance Associations or *Iiliso Lomzi*, the Eyes of the Nation.

The process of political mobilisation took a big step forward when J.T. Jabavu launched *Imvo Zabantsundu* in 1884. Now, with their own 'national' newspaper, the new intellectuals could keep in step with the political situation, articulate their grievances, and link up the struggles in different areas to establish their claim to be full citizens of the colony. They also wanted to become full citizens in cricket as well, and used their connections and influence in a focused way to pursue this goal, not least on the sports field. During the 1880s and 1890s, hundreds upon hundreds of cricket reports appeared in *Imvo*, even during the winter. These were printed under the title *Ibala labadlali* (Sports Field or Patch of the Players). By 1887 Jabavu had appointed a 'sporting editor'.[2] The big merchant house of Dyer and Dyer soon began placing advertisements directed specifically at African cricketers and clubs in the newspaper. In addition to tweed jackets and *impahla yabafundisi – iminqwazi ne kolala, i makentoshi, njalo njalo* (clothes of priests – hats and collars, mackintoshes, etc. etc.), cricket kit of every variety, as well as tennis racquets and nets, was offered. There were special discounts for clubs, who were encouraged to send for price lists before making purchases.[3]

FIRST CHAMPIONS TEST THEIR METTLE

After the excitement of the inaugural 1884 'Native' tournament over the New Year in Grahamstown, there was a flurry of further activity in its immediate aftermath. African cricketers who had participated challenged their white counterparts, and several challenge matches followed against white clubs in King William's Town, Cradock and Port Elizabeth during the second half of the season.

The new inter-town winners, Champion CC of King William's Town, took aim at Albert CC, 'the leading European Club in this town'. At least three of the Alberts players – Schermbrucker, Byrne and Tully – had just participated in the white Inter-Town Tournament in Port Elizabeth. E.J. Byrne had played in all three Champion Bat tournaments so far, captaining the town's top club team to victory in the first two. E.P. Schermbrucker was the best batsman in the team after the legendary Captain Robert Stewart, ending sixth in the batting averages at the recent 1884 tournament, with a top score of 43 against Port Elizabeth. He was said to have 'rivaled Stewart in run-getting of late' and had a 'sound defence and good punishing strokes', though he was not a stylist.[4]

The historic clash on the town's main sports field in March 1885, the Victoria Grounds, was 'a clear [first innings] victory for the players of colour', according to the local *Cape Mercury* newspaper. The King William's Town African eleven bundled out the white team for 55 runs and passed this total with only three wickets down, before being all out for 89. The bowling of the Rev. John Gawler and Austin Ngcumbe was outstanding. The *Mercury* commented that they sent down several maidens before Alberts got their first run, and 'the bowling of the two seemed to surprise the Albert batters, and it took them all their time to guard their wickets'.[5]

The newspaper reported that the dismissals of the local star, Schermbrucker, for three and one, triggered great excitement among the African players. This was not only because he was a good batsman; he was also the son of Frederick Schermbrucker, a former cabinet minister and commander of the Frontier Armed and Mounted Police troops, who had been involved in the killing of King Sandile of the Ngqika in the nearby Pirie Bush in the recent frontier war of 1877–8. Standing around the grave of Sandile, Schermbrucker was reported to have said that his death should be a warning to the Ngqika: this was what happened to 'the man who lifts up arms against his Queen'; 'instead of being lords and masters in the country they once owned', they 'will now be servants'. As a result Schermbrucker Senior was highly unpopular with the local black voters and Jabavu's newspaper; working in combination, they opposed him in local elections.[6] The palpable excitement after the fall of Schermbrucker Junior's particular wicket surely conveyed more than just a cricket message to the establishment. To complicate the drama even more, Nathaniel Umhalla, the cricket-loving son of a chief, who had been charged with treason after the 1877–8 war, was playing in the team against Schermbrucker Junior. Further, some of Umhalla's teammates might have been British auxiliaries during the hostilities, either on the battlefield or off it, because the school people were expected to show their loyalty during periods of crisis.[7]

But to return to the match: Alberts scored 104 in their second innings, and by the time Champion went in again, it was already a quarter to six. When the second wicket fell, it was dark and 'impossible for the batsmen to see properly', according to the *Mercury*. Nevertheless, play continued until stumps were drawn at 51 for seven, the unfinished game having swung back in favour of the white team by this time.

In those days of four-ball overs, Austin Ngcumbe's final figures were four for 28 off 53 balls and seven for 47 off 100 balls. He was well backed up by Gawler, who took six wickets altogether. Gawler was the grandson of the legendary Xhosa warrior-'prophet' Makhanda kaNxele, or Makana, who drowned while trying to escape from Robben Island in 1819. A teacher at St Matthew's (who had adopted or been given a colonial magistrate's name – like Nelson Mandela many years later), he was elected first president of the pioneering Native Educational Association in 1879.

Commenting on other aspects of the game, the *Mercury* said that 'the fielding of the Natives was sound, and their throwing is excellent, but their batting in most cases wanted defensive power'. Tshatshu (21) and Gawler (17) were the best batsmen and, *Imvo* commented tongue-in-cheek, they did better against 'the balls of those eminent local cricketers Schermbrucker and Leary' than vice versa. The paper, moreover, reported that the Africans gained the victory 'in the face of disadvantage'. 'It was against the rules of cricket to allow players from clubs other than Alberts to bowl, nor was it fair to the Natives to change one of the Umpires without consulting the Champions.'[8]

The *Mercury* said the match was significant 'to all those who take an intelligent interest in the progress of the country'. Evoking images of peace only a few years after the final war of dispossession, the newspaper said the game reminded one of an 'old song':

And men learn't wisdom from the past,
In friendship joined their hands;
Hung the sword in the hall;
The spear on the wall,
And ploughed the willing lands.

The newspaper concluded, 'those who play together will not object to work together, and the manly fellows who donned the flannels last week will have a heartier feeling of respect for their dusky conquerors than they had before.'[9]

Jabavu republished this extract from its counterpart with approval in *Imvo*, leaving out this significant rider by the *Mercury*: 'But we should be sorry for their victory, if it were the means of puffing them up with conceit, by which we do not mean that they ought not to be filled with some honest pride that the first cricket match of any note that has taken place between the two races should result in an unmistakeable win for the Africans.'[10] But the delighted *Imvo* editor added that such cricket matches were 'calculated to make the Europeans and Natives have more mutual trust and confidence than all the coercive and repressive legislation in the world'.[11]

There was sufficient needle in the match, including the complaints about Alberts using players from other clubs and about the bias of their umpires, for the local white club to ask for a return game a few weeks later. This time, Alberts had the better of the contest, winning easily on the first innings. Both the son of the commander whose unit members had helped kill the Ngqika king and the former treason trialist on the other side fared much better than they had done in the first encounter. Schermbrucker hit an undefeated century this time, to take Alberts to a daunting 210 – no other batsman reached 20 – and Umhalla top-scored with a rearguard 46 in the follow-on innings to help Champion CC comfortably save the day. After Alberts bundled Champion out for 48, the African batsmen showed what they were made of in the follow-on, hitting 146 for four in the hour and a half before stumps.[12]

The King players had lived through a memorable few months to put African cricket on the map.

PORT ELIZABETH ALSO CHALLENGE THEIR COUNTERPARTS

The Port Elizabeth team followed the example of their King colleagues by taking on and beating the white Cradock town club early in 1885. The Africans also won the return match, scoring 71 and 69 against the single-innings 45 of the country town. *Imvo* exclaimed, 'Bravo, Africans, Bravissimo' in its columns.[13] Commenting on the win despite a lack of experience and facilities, Jabavu declared: 'It is enough to say that the contest shows that the native is a rough diamond that needs to be polished to exhibit the same qualities that are to be found in the civilised being, and that he is not to be dismissed as a mere "schepsel", as it has been the habit of the pioneers to do so hereto.'[14]

A few weeks later, the Port Elizabeth Africans decided to take on Goliath, challenging the local Port Elizabeth Cricket Club (PECC) to a match. PECC, formed in 1859, was one of the oldest clubs in southern Africa, and Port Elizabeth were the reigning holders of the Champion Bat, the main white competition in South Africa at that stage. The 'native team' was a combined town team, drawn from all the clubs. As usual, most of the players were community leaders, prominent in church, education and political affairs. The local newspaper listed their employment details 'to show that those who engage in the ennobling time-honoured game of cricket have either worked or are working their way up the social ladder by hard, honest labour'.[15] It consisted of Frank Makwena (captain), H. Pezisa, George Ross, Moses Foley, J. Morley, J. Mdana, T. Klaas, B. Christian, B. Swartbooy, A Mabope and Paul Xiniwe. Ross and Foley were African-Americans who had settled in Port Elizabeth and become integrated into the activities of the aspiring local black middle class. They were members of Imbumba and founders of an unusual economic cooperative called the African and American Working Men's Union, which sought to uplift black people economically and used as a rallying cry the slogan 'Africa for the Africans'.

After beating the Cradock team, Port Elizabeth's African team must have been buoyant going into the match against PECC. However, they were annihilated, replying to the PECC's 180 with a measly 13 and 11 for three. Godlonton – top wicket-taker in the 1880 Champion Bat tournament – and Ogden were the bowlers who wreaked the havoc, claiming four and six wickets each in the miserable first innings. Ogden also top-scored with 48 and the stalwart Peter Heugh, the only man to play from inception in 1876 to end in 1891 in the Champion Bat tournaments, hit 47. Bob Christian (four wickets) and H. Pezisa (three) were the most successful African bowlers.[16] This was clearly meant as a shock-and-awe exhibition: virtually the full team of the reigning Champion Bat champions playing against the Africans. No less than eight of the PECC players were Inter-Town Tournament players, of which three appeared in three or more of the prestige four-yearly events.

Imvo lamented:

'Dirty' indeed was the licking received by a team of the Port Elizabeth Natives from the local European Club. We trust the return match will soon come off and leave the fair fame of Native cricketers vindicated. The explanation given by the defeated team is that they had challenged the second eleven of the Port Elizabeth Club, but to their utter surprise they found themselves in the field pitted against the eminent cricketers who beat the Colonial Clubs at the late Tournament in Port Elizabeth. On the sight of these illustrious knights of the willow they lost heart.[17]

The newspaper added that 'the thrashing administered to the local Albert Club by the Natives the other day' apparently had a lot to do with the turnout of the top players.[18]

FIRST REPRESENTATIVE REGIONAL TEAM TAKES TO THE FIELD

At the third Native Inter-Town Tournament in King two seasons later, a combined tournament team was selected to play against a local white team. It was composed of five players from King William's Town and three each from Port Elizabeth and third-placed Grahamstown. William Seti, who won the bat presented by Colonel Bayly for the best average (24),[19] opened the batting with his King teammate J. Sidayiya. The middle order were Stephen Boyce and the well-known community leader Paul Xiniwe (both PE) as well as W. Nombewu from Grahamstown. Nombewu's teammates H. May and T. Gule, who had hit the highest tournament scores of 45 and 43 respectively and had taken over 50 wickets between them, came next in the order, followed by Butler from King, another all-rounder. Austin Ngcumbe, the most devastating bowler at the inaugural tournament, was still an automatic choice, and his townsman E.B. Soga and K. Bopi of Port Elizabeth rounded off the attack. Qoqo, Lutu and D. Soga, the main bowlers for Queenstown and East London, who had shouldered the load in losing causes, taking over 50 wickets between them, must have considered themselves unlucky to miss out. There was no shortage of bowlers, as in the white tournaments. Good batsmen and the absence of big scores remained the feature of this early cricket – not one 50 was scored in the entire tournament.

In the match between the combined Eastern Cape province tournament team and 'the English' from King William's Town, the latter won comfortably by nine wickets, thanks to an eight wicket haul in the first innings by the Champion Bat tournament star and former Sussex player, Lyndhurst Winslow. Only William Seti, top of the averages in the tournament, with 33, was able to withstand the attack before being bowled by Winslow. All-rounder E.B. Soga managed 22 in the second innings as the Africans gave way with 75 and 95 all out in reply to the 135 all out and 35/1 of *amaNgesi*.[20]

SEEKING A PLACE IN THE SYSTEM

It is remarkable, looking back from the vantage point of today, that top white clubs in two of the four towns in the Cape Colony which participated in the Champion Bat tournaments, and a number of the Champion Bat participants played against their black counterparts in the mid-1880s. Moreover, the standards of black and white cricketers were often on par in many aspects. Austin Ngcumbe's 11 wickets against Alberts surely qualified him to play at the highest level.

These inter-race matches were in line with paternalistic colonial practices which allowed the odd encounter to take place across the colour line on special occasions, such as Christmas, New Year or Empire Day. Using their muscle as voters and, therefore, as full citizens who could influence local elections, black cricketers applied to use the grounds of municipalities and white clubs from time to time, and were allowed to do so. This included some of the main venues in the strongest cricket towns, namely Victoria Grounds in King William's Town, City Lords in Grahamstown and St George's Park (at the Union CC ground), which were used as venues in the corresponding white Inter-Town tournaments as well.

The cricket contests across the colour line were in a real sense microcosms of the battle of ideas raging on the 'frontier' which would determine the future direction of the colony and the country. Schermbrucker Junior and Benjamin D'Urban Godlonton represented (through their fathers) the harsh anti-native element in colonial politics that wanted to see 'the kaffir put in his place', as it was crudely put at the time. The black players, on the other hand, were part of and often led the emerging political struggle for a society that they hoped would become more inclusive. If the King William's Town and Cradock matches presaged what was to come, it was a sign that Africans could hold their own in any company, given a chance. But if the Port Elizabeth contest was an indicator, a hard future awaited them.

Newspaper reports from the mid-1880s show that African teams in the eastern Cape regularly played – and beat – white teams. There would be many more such examples during the course of the next decade, in other areas too, especially in cosmopolitan Kimberley and Cape Town, where top-class players and similarly strong cricket cultures emerged in black communities.

The Champion fixture against Alberts became a regular one, and they also played against the Cape Infantry and the well-known local sporting school, Dale College.[21] In 1887 Champion beat Dale, which was described as an invaluable cricket nursery,[22] and Lovedale College gave them the same medicine in 1891. These victories were not unusual: newspapers reported on similar successes by teams in Alice, Queenstown and St Mark's around this time.[23]

In a warm-up game for the 1892/3 Native Inter-Town Tournament, King William's Town narrowly lost to the Cape Mounted Rifles, who had pushed a CMR XXII into the field for two games against the English tourists in the previous season and lost badly. The Africans fell one run short of the soldiers' 119, '*kodwa singati baqatwa yi Umpire yecala lama CMR*', but it seems they were cheated by the umpire from the CMR.[24] The idea of indigenous players beating a team from the dominant classes did not sit well with colonists. By defeating the 'Europeans', the King black players were inverting the basic message of colonialism – that the dispossessed were weaker and should be subservient. Mihir Bose has commented on similar circumstances in India in the encounters between the British and the Parsis in Bombay, which were known to lead to 'displays of feeling'. The British objected to Parsi umpires, although they were agreeable to the Parsis appointing their own white umpires – otherwise, this would have meant 'an Indian, a subject race, giving decisions on an Englishman, the master race'.[25]

This was cricket with an epic dimension.

13

The MCC of the Cape Colony

Stiff upper lips and prejudice in the 'classic and perennially fragrant metropolis'

A poor, niggery, yellow-faced, half-bred sort of
place, with an ugly Dutch flavor about it.

– Anthony Trollope, 1877[1]

Cape Town was the main seat of British power in southern Africa for most of the nineteenth century. It had the longest cricket tradition and the expectation was that it would do well in the Champion Bat tournaments. But it failed to win the first tournament in 1876, withdrew from the second tournament in 1880, took part only reluctantly in the third in 1884, and was absent again from the fourth in 1887, before finally hosting and winning the fifth and final one in 1890. What was the explanation for this roller-coaster behaviour in the first representative cricket competition on the continent?

The main problem was the peculiar structure of local cricket and the peculiar attitudes and outlook that prevailed and that became institutionalised in the 1880s at the Western Province Cricket Club (WPCC), which regarded itself as the 'MCC of the Cape Colony'. Started in 1864, the WPCC ran the local game as the fiefdom of the local British elite. Its concerns were primarily about 'Home' and narrow class interests, rather than developing cricket in the city, the surrounding rural areas and the Cape Colony as a whole. It became known as an enclave of institutionalised snobbery and imperial jingoism, particularly after the former England rugby player William 'Joey' Milton took over as secretary and treasurer in 1877.

A recent biography of Milton has carefully unpacked how this situation arose. Firstly, in the style of the MCC, the Western Province CC arrogated to itself the role of leading cricket in the city and chose its opposition through an arrangement whereby local clubs forwarded requests for matches. Milton and 'The Club' designed the fixture list to suit themselves, and in the process the WPCC distanced itself from the rest of the town and from the country districts. The programme for 1880/1 showed that the club's matches all took place within the southern suburbs and that it did a minimal amount of travelling, while also offering the attraction of the 91st Regiment Band at all its fixtures.

WPCC played at the old Southey's Field location in Wynberg, about 15 kilometres from the centre of Cape Town. Town clubs found it difficult to break into the elite group that resided in the southern suburbs. While better cricketers cherished the hope of being able to play and beat the WPCC, this could not be taken for granted. In September 1886, 'Longstop' wrote in the *Cape Times* that 'no one doubts Western Province CC is the leading club of the province but this does not entitle them to ignore applications for fixtures from the secretaries of local clubs. I myself know of three clubs who have been thus treated.' The writer added, 'the Western Province CC fixture is the most important of the season', but this caused real frustration: 'secretaries of other clubs allow fixtures to stand over until dates are settled with the Western Province CC'.[2]

The situation relating to Stellenbosch and surrounding towns was even more discouraging. Stellenbosch was primarily a Dutch-speaking club. It was also a virtual factory for fast bowlers going into the 1880s and it regularly beat town teams, including the WPCC. Its leader was the prominent Cape politician J.H. Hofmeyr, editor of the *Zuid-Afrikaan* newspaper and first head of the Afrikaner Bond, whose love for the game developed when he went to school at the South African College. His club had a number of stars, particularly fast bowlers. When given a game in 1877, they easily beat WPCC by nine wickets with Lammi Neethling (6/13 and 5/6) and Ernst 'Baba' Schröder (4/31 and 4/17) dominating the visitors' batsmen.[3] Milton, however, continued to keep the Afrikaner clubs at arm's length. His refusal to cater satisfactorily for the country districts effectively meant a refusal to support the Afrikaners in their efforts to play the game. Hofmeyr, on the other hand, sought to build unity between local whites. Though he specifically represented Afrikaner interests, his definition of Afrikaner was very broad: 'anyone who, having settled in this country, wishes to remain here to help to promote our common interests and to live with the inhabitants as members of one family'.[4]

Charles Neumann Thomas, who had played in the first match involving the WPCC in 1864 and was chairman in 1877 and 1881/2, admitted that 'the opinion is often expressed and more than one communication has found a piece in [the press] that the Western Province CC is not a representative one, and that it does little or nothing for the promotion of good cricket'. While he did not dispute the allegation, he said it was the club's desire to provide the required leadership and 'prove itself worthy of the name which was given it many years ago when it was the only cricket club in the neighbourhood of Cape Town'.⁵ Letters flowed in the press. One to the *Cape Times* called for a 'Cricket Association' and 'complained that cricket is simply ruled by about four members who live in Wynberg'.⁶ The *Cape Argus* published a letter that stated, 'No club should call itself the "Western Province" unless it represents every club in the province.'⁷

The jingoism of Milton and the club assumed English superiority in all matters and would not accommodate itself to reaching out to fellow colonists, whether poor, Afrikaner or black. This attitude also meant that, unlike in rugby, where they were well represented in the local leadership, Afrikaners did not become accepted into the cricket establishment in the Western Cape, a situation that helped shape the future direction of cricket. Just like the colonists living in Canada and the US, Afrikaners did not make cricket their game because of its overt imperial protocols and loyalties. They started participating in large numbers only in the 1960s, and especially after cricket unity and the advent of democracy in the 1990s.

The extent to which the WPCC dominated local cricket can be seen from the fact that the Home-Born and Colonial-Born fixtures, started at the time of Governor Wodehouse in 1862 and the highlight of the season in Cape Town and elsewhere, became closed shop contests, restricted to the members of WPCC only. Under pressure from other clubs, the WPCC agreed to allow players from them to participate in 1883, but 'The Club' (a name that did not need to qualify itself in the normal way) still chose the teams.

The WPCC also got special treatment in the press. The *Cape Times* was an enthusiastic mouthpiece for imperialism, and popularised both cricket and this establishment institution in ways none of the other local newspapers did. The founding editor, Frederick York St Leger, lived in Tennant Road in Wynberg, in the same suburb in which the club operated and Milton lived.

The WPCC could also commandeer the finest players from abroad arriving at Cape Town. A constitutional provision allowed them temporary club membership and the WPCC claimed first pick of any number of top-class players coming to visit or passing through the Cape. On the same principle, when the Club did on one occasion agree to a fixture at Worcester, it quickly destroyed any goodwill by collecting the Stellenbosch speedster E.L. Schröder en route and thereafter using him to full advantage in destroying the host team – he returned a match analysis of ten for ten. The action was not dissimilar to 'gentlemen' calling upon professionals to bowl out the opposition in English cricket. Sir Derek Birley noted in his classic social history of English cricket that representatives of the Mother Country thought 'it was an inversion of the natural order of things if they did not win' and that it was 'not entirely necessary always to behave well towards colonials'.[8]

As an ex-Marlborough schoolboy, Milton was deeply conscious of the ethics and values of cricket. Yet his and his colleagues' sense of 'fair play' was shaped by prevailing assumptions of the moral and physical superiority of white Anglo-Saxons reinforced through the argument that 'social distances were considered an important and integral part of maintaining order'.[9] The WPCC lived, almost exactly, up to Jan Morris's description of 'the club' for the British in the colonies:

> The club, in the highly class conscious nineteenth century British society, was based on the notion of hierarchy and exclusion. In the African and Asian colonies of Britain this notion of exclusivity, going far beyond the sports field, was taken to even greater extremes. Here the club served as a symbol, not only of social status, but also of political domination. It was developed as an enclave of power and privilege in an alien setting. Its members were patently different from the unadmitted millions. Not only in colour and status, but also in place. More than anywhere else, it was the place where the imperialists celebrated their Britishness, authority and imperial lifestyle.[10]

Using the example of India, Guha has written:

> Places such as the Calcutta Cricket Club and the Madras Cricket Club provided English food and English entertainments ... cricket was collective, longer lasting and rather more ceremonial [than the other games]. The slow stateliness of the walk to the wicket, the interruptions between balls and overs, the graceful clothes that the players wore, the greenness of the grass, the understated gaiety of the lunch and tea intervals – all these made cricket an extended escape from India, from its chatter, its dirt, its smells and its peoples.[11]

The WPCC across the Indian Ocean in Cape Town completely fitted this bill.

Similarly, it has been said that 'the sportsmanship of cricket and the nature of cricket as a sport of the Empire helped to persuade the white English that they could be trusted to exercise authority over other races in a reasonable and selfless manner'.[12] Once again Milton's personality, style and actions fitted into this mould. During his tenure as secretary and treasurer from 1877 to 1896, the WPCC became an exemplar par excellence of a class-bound mindset and a template – a 'culture' – of rigid imperialism and racism for cricket in Cape Town during a formative period of the game in southern Africa. When present-day conservatives or cricket romantics talk about the 'traditional culture of the game', they are often echoing aspects of this early British cricket culture.

Milton played rugby for England as half-back in 1874 and 1875. After reaching the top in sport through the small public school network of the time, he failed to find similar career satisfaction as a civil servant in London. An opportunity arose when his father's cousin, the famous Victorian novelist Anthony Trollope, decided to visit the Cape, partly as a public awareness campaign to promote Britain's southern African empire. Milton accepted the invitation to join Trollope. They were welcomed by the high commissioner, Sir Bartle Frere, who personally organised Trollope's itinerary. The year before, Frere had overseen the military takeover of the independent South African Republic, and he was driving plans for a broad confederation which would bring southern Africa under British rule; the discovery of diamonds had focused minds and renewed British appetites for taking over the subcontinent.

Trollope's first impressions of the Cape were contemptuous: 'it seems like a poor, niggery, yellow-faced, half-bred sort of place, with an ugly Dutch flavor about it'. Africans he described as 'much more of a Savage than the ordinary negro' encountered elsewhere,[13] and held out little hope for their future. If Milton's subsequent actions are anything to go by, he shared the family view about the colony and its inhabitants.

Welcomed at the very highest level, Milton was playing cricket for the Western Province CC within two days of his arrival in late 1877, and a few months later he was elected secretary and treasurer of the club. Soon he was also settled into a job in the civil service as officiating clerk to the Executive Council (effectively the cabinet of the Cape Colony).[14]

In the first few years, Milton played a large part in getting rugby accepted at the Cape, which is a story all of its own. But his first interest was cricket. He served as an administrator and treasurer of the WPCC for 18 years from 1877, and he captained the club for 11 seasons from 1885 onwards as a hard-hitting batsman, useful bowler and more than capable wicketkeeper.[15] For nearly 20 years he ruled the cricket roost in Cape Town, supported by various influential chairmen and all the while rising in influence and social status. He became close to Cecil John Rhodes and ended up as permanent head (from April 1894) of the Prime Minister's Department. Milton's career was one of those that best exemplify the close connections between cricket, colonialism and conquest in the nineteenth century.

This dyed-in-the-wool imperialist and his Western Province CC colleagues opposed suggestions that cricket's administration be shared with other clubs, believing that their duty was to set an example that other clubs should follow. He was similarly dismissive of attempts to spread the game outside his tight Cape Town circles – hence the reluctance to participate in the Champion Bat tournaments.

King William's Town's defeat of Cape Town in the first Champion Bat tournament in 1876 had been a blow to the prestige of the 'metropolis'. When the eastern Cape decided to renew cricket links with the other towns after the wars of the late 1870s by staging a second Champion Bat tournament, the Western Province CC and its leaders were not interested. In January 1880, the mayor of King William's Town sent a telegram to his counterpart in Cape Town: 'Rumour current here that there is some difficulty in Cape Town in arranging for cricket team to come to tournament ... Please use your influence to remove any obstacles to team starting, otherwise the whole tournament may be a failure.' Cape Town's attitude was shown by a response at a subsequent council meeting: 'If necessary the receipt of the telegram can be acknowledged with the best compliments of the season. The fact is, now the war is over, they do not know what to do with themselves up there.'[16]

Cape Town did not attend the 1880 tournament and the absence of 'a metropolitan team at King William's Town was the theme of much regret, expression given to it both individually and also in the speeches made'.[17] In 1884 there was renewed pressure for Cape Town to take part at Port Elizabeth. Milton and the influential James Sivewright, president of the club and later a cabinet minister, were quick to declare that they were unavailable. Despite the absence of several key players, Cape Town nevertheless did send a weakened team. They introduced a great talent in a one-eyed teenager, Charlie Vintcent, who inspired easy victories over Kimberley and King William's Town. However, the Capetonians stumbled in the deciding match for the second tournament in a row, this time against Port Elizabeth.

Again in 1887 Cape Town was absent from the Champion Bat tournament. Part of the reason was that the WPCC planned a marquee cricket day that clashed with the tournament dates. It was the opening of its new ground in Newlands, with the annual glamour match between Home-Born and Colonial-Born. The reports and scores of the two events appeared side by side in the *Cape Times*, and the newspaper commented, 'The Newlands ground is certainly an improvement on Colonel Southey's old field at Wynberg, being larger, as level as a table, and commanding a pretty view.'[18]

The Cape Town cricketers did finally entertain a tour from Kimberley by the 'Stray Klips' (a play on the Afrikaans slang word for 'diamonds') in January 1887; the WPCC lost heavily to them by 105 runs. A composite team, Cape Town Wanderers (for which Milton again made himself unavailable), was in turn sent to Kimberley in 1888. The Cape Town combination lost two of the three games by an innings. There was good reason to believe that Cape Town was falling behind other centres and that standards there were not what they should be. In a letter published in the *Daily Independent*, 'A Disgusted Cape Town Man' stated: 'It does not seem to have struck anyone, how singular it is that Kimberley cricketers should have success in beating Cape Town. That Kimberley with its three clubs should be able to pick an eleven strong enough to beat Cape Town with its twenty-odd clubs and the military thrown in.'[19]

The class distinctions which prevailed in English cricket were also very much apparent in Cape Town and they revealed themselves in a way that was embarrassing for the Mother City during the tour to Kimberley. It was reported that the all-rounder, Private Edward Beech of the Garrison Club, the first player in southern Africa to score two centuries in the same match, was forced to travel separately from the team in third class. Once there, this member of the Royal Scots Band was 'studiously and contemptuously ignored by those who had sought his aid to wrest the honours of the willow from Kimberley'.[20] This led to the Cape Town players being mocked for their off-field snobbishness as well.

Guha has written about how the Bombay Gymkhana, the elitist establishment institution serving the 7,000 whites in a city of 650,000 people, 'kept out all Indians, but also whites of uncertain pedigree, such as the petty tradesman and the soldier without commission'.[21] This apparently applied to the WPCC as well. The Pirates Cricket Club tried to make Private Beech's stay as pleasant as possible but, said a correspondent in *The Lantern*: 'Because that good cricketer happens to be a mere private his co-workers have considered it infra-dig and derogatory to the sublime positions they claim on the social pedestal to have any intercourse with him away from the cricket field.'[22] An 'Old Cricketer' added: 'Poor Private Beech has not even the consolation of knowing that his services as a cricketer can guard him against the daily affront and humiliation of social avoidance as if he were a machine, instead of a sentient being, with feelings and faculties quite as refined as those of any other wanderer from the classic and perennially fragrant metropolis.'[23] Beech was no slouch at the game. He soon afterwards went to live in Kimberley and scored a century for Griqualand West in the 1890/1 season.

The dig at the cricket establishment in Cape Town by the letter writers might have been amusing had the impact of the exclusionary and racist nature of the Cape Town cricket establishment of the 1880s and 1890s not been so enduring and damaging to South African cricket in the long term. Although out of step with the integrative aims of both Afrikaner and black cricketers on their doorsteps in Cape Town, as well as the trend towards creating a broad South African cricket identity through the Inter-Town tournaments, the preoccupation of the

WPCC notables with class and race difference had become set in stone by the time the club reached its 25th anniversary in 1889. Milton and the WPCC took the lead role in imposing segregated sport in Cape Town in the 1890s.

Indeed, the 'MCC of the Cape Colony' and its long-standing secretary and treasurer would become the fathers of apartheid in cricket. As with the famous clubs in India, which stayed mostly all-white until independence in 1947, the venerable WPCC club would remain a bastion of unreconstructed WASP values, excluding Afrikaners, Jews and black people as members until deep into the twentieth century. Their power stemmed not from their popularity in an expanding game but from their close connections with the imperial establishment in the Cape, including the empire-builder and mining magnate, Cecil John Rhodes.

14

The balance shifts from the military to the money

The rise of Kimberley and the birth of Johannesburg

A vital means of putting the town on the map and reassuring
potential investors that the combination of stability and growth
was available in the arid hinterland of the northern Cape.

– Richard Parry, *Cricket Lore*

Old William Ling had his moments. The digger, who had started a newspaper, also headed an armed vigilante group and singlehandedly ran Kimberley cricket for 15 years. As a player, he opened the bowling with his underarm lobs at the age of 58 in 1884 and took two quick wickets to make the eventual Champion Bat champions, Port Elizabeth, three down for ten. But this was only a last flicker. Kimberley lost by four wickets, and after that first-ever trip to the coast, Ling passed away within five years without playing representative cricket again.

After the 1884 Inter-Town Tournament, Kimberley cricket consciously reinvented itself. The old guard was shifted aside, several new clubs were formed, steady sources of financial support were found and facilities were improved. Within three years, W.S. Woodthorpe, the Kimberley captain in their first two Champion Bat tournaments, could say, 'In 1884 cricket had been played in a very primitive way on grounds not to be compared with the level and billiard table like surfaces currently available.' He credited the 'kind, munificent and sportsmanlike way' the community had supported cricket for this upswing, which saw Kimberley going from wooden spoonists in 1884/5 to champions at the next tournament three years later in 1887/8.

Charles Finlason, 'the life and soul of Diamond Fields cricket',[1] became the motivating force on and off the field as Kimberley strove to become a leading cricket centre. Finlason started the Eclectics CC and a second club, Pirates, was formed by members who similarly peeled away from the Kimberley CC, for long the only club and central organising hub. The Glover brothers, George and Ernest, whose father started the well-known Glover's Athletic Bar, were prominent at Pirates. Competition at the local level now intensified. Kimberley could boast that it had three good grounds with pavilions whereas Cape Town had only one.

The real reason for the rapid growth of cricket in Kimberley lay deeper below the surface, though; it had to do with controlling the production and sale of diamonds. Kimberley was in the early 1880s undergoing a transition from a chaotic tent town where thousands of diggers (including some registered black claimants) were competing for wealth to a settled city where only three people controlled the industry. They were Cecil John Rhodes, Barney Barnato and Alfred Beit. As historians have noted, 'the ideological value of cricket was soon recognised by the successful entrepreneurs who sought to control the diamond industry'.[2] 'New Rush' metamorphosed into the home of monopoly capitalism in southern Africa. This was to have enormous political and social consequences for South Africa and remains substantially unchanged to this day. Sport, money and political control came together in Kimberley in a new way, which had a permanent impact on sport. Richard Parry, whose work has directly shaped this chapter, explains:

> Cricket performed a significant shaping role in the search for social control in Kimberley and it did so on a number of levels. It functioned as a source of recreation for a small but important section of the population which at times engendered considerable interest. It also provided a means of rooting peculiarly British values into a late nineteenth century society which, in practical terms, was British in name only, but, more importantly it served as a vital means of putting the town on the map and reassuring potential investors that the combination of stability and growth was available in the arid hinterland of the northern Cape.[3]

Unlike Cape Town, which remained ambiguous about and unsuccessful in the Inter-Town tournaments, Kimberley deliberately used their dismal last-place performances in the 1884 Champion Bat contest as a motivation to overhaul the game in the city.

CHALLENGING AND BEATING ALL-COMERS

If Cape Town's colonial cricket leadership represented crusted metropolitan mind-sets, burgeoning Kimberley, a new experiment in every sense, was a place with fresher attitudes and optimism about the future. When Milton in Cape Town ignored an invitation to send a team to a tournament at the Diamond Fields in

Easter 1886, Finlason explained: 'It was partly from want of chips [but also] because several of [Cape Town's] best men have an idea that on matting in a different light, with grey or brown ground, they would fail to "come off".'[4]

The sporty newspaperman loved a challenge, and tremendous excitement was generated when he arranged a two-week tour of the Cape by Kimberley's Stray Klips in January 1887. The players were largely from Eclectics, the club that Finlason had founded in Kimberley, with fixtures arranged through Milton. The focal point was the game against the Western Province CC at Southey's Field, where 'the carriage enclosure was full and the fair sex turned up in great force, many of them wearing the Eclectic colours'. Kimberley's irrepressible cricketers had not only 'captured the hearts of the Cape Town ladies' but won the battle by 105 runs in a low-scoring match. Irvine Grimmer, another of the big characters in Kimberley cricket and an off-spinner who was prepared to flight the ball, was hit for 45 runs in the home side's first innings of 59, but wickets tumbled – he took eight – and then another nine in the second innings to give him the extraordinary match analysis of 17 for 83.[5] The Stray Klips tour reinforced Finlason's oft-stated view that cricket was making greater progress in Kimberley than it was at the Cape.[6] Kimberley went on to organise and win the 'Extraneous' Tournament that they hosted in April 1887, and then the fourth Champion Bat tournament at Grahamstown in December of the same year.

The 'Extraneous' Inter-Town Tournament seemed to be a serious attempt by Kimberley and Port Elizabeth to broaden competitive cricket beyond the base of the existing Champion Bat tournament, because it involved Natal and Bechuanaland. All but four of the 22 players at some stage participated in the Champion Bat tournaments, indicating that the 1884 champions and the soon-to-be 1888 champions put fully representative teams into the field. The other two territories had previously not been involved, although cricket was popular in Natal. They were outside the Cape Colony ambit covering the Champion Bat tournament, hence 'extraneous' in the title. Bechuanaland was probably invited as outflow of the armed Warren Expedition, which had in 1885 set out from Kimberley to annex Tswana territory in what became the Bechuanaland Protectorate. This was partly because the British did not want the road to the north, which Cecil John Rhodes was greedily eyeing, to be cut off. Prominent cricketing personalities were involved in the expedition, including Meshach Pelem, and it is also probably the reason why the brilliant Charlie Vintcent found himself playing for Bechuanaland in the 1887 tournament.

Natal lost by nine wickets to Kimberley and by an innings and 108 runs to Port Elizabeth, beating only Bechuanaland (by an innings). In 18 completed innings, 300 was reached once (by Port Elizabeth vs Natal) and five times teams failed to reach

100, the lowest innings being Port Elizabeth's 37 (vs Kimberley). There were ten half-centuries and a highest score of 97 by J. Jackson of Port Elizabeth (vs Natal). Grimmer of Kimberley was again the star. He and A. Rose-Innes of Port Elizabeth took 23 wickets apiece. Charles Finlason provided great support with 21 wickets.

Kimberley emphatically won again when they went down to Grahamstown for the Champion Bat tournament. They dominated in devastating fashion, beating both Grahamstown and King William's Town by an innings before accounting for Port Elizabeth by 187 runs. Charlie Vintcent, who had since established a business in Kimberley, and Grimmer captured 55 wickets between them in three matches. Kimberley had every right to claim that they were the best team in the Cape Colony.

In 22 completed innings in the six matches in the Champion Bat tournament, 200 was passed three times (twice by Kimberley and once by Port Elizabeth), 100 on only five other occasions, and the average dropped to 102. Innings totals of 50 or less were recorded three times, the lowest being 20 by King William's Town (a total of only 57 in the match with a highest score of nine vs Kimberley). Only three half-centuries were scored, the highest being 97 by E.H. Buckland of Grahamstown (vs Port Elizabeth) while Dunell scored 88* (vs King William's Town). Bowling records are incomplete, but Charlie Vintcent and Irvine Grimmer, both of Kimberley, took 30 and 25 wickets respectively (in successive matches against King William's Town and Port Elizabeth they removed all 39 batsmen to fall to bowlers); Barber of Grahamstown bisected them with 26 wickets and the best innings return of nine wickets (vs Port Elizabeth). Owen Dunell, who excelled in this tournament, was a former Eton and Oxford University player, who was to captain the first 'national' team when South Africa entered the test arena the following season.

Soon after returning from Grahamstown, Kimberley faced and overcame its fourth big cricket challenge in two years, a tour from Cape Town by a team called the Cape Town Wanderers. The authorities there had finally decided to accept an invitation to visit the Diamond Fields in April 1888. 'The Owl', writing in the *Wynberg Times*, commented: 'I do hope our representative cricketers will be able to visit Kimberley at Easter and take down some of the conceit of the boys there.'[7]

Cape Town Wanderers were humbled, losing two of their three matches by an innings. Kimberley's batsmen were in imperious form; the runs flowed and there were large scores, while the top Cape spearheads, 'Gobo' Ashley and Nicolaas 'Nico' Theunissen, were bowled into the ground in the course of capturing 37 of the 40 wickets taken on the tour. The tourists' batting was disappointing except for an unbeaten 123 from Captain Robert Spurway, which helped set up a victory over Eclectic CC.

After five years of growth and hard work, the establishment team of colonial Kimberley was without doubt the strongest in southern Africa by 1888. Another five years of top-class performances lay ahead before Kimberley's golden age came to an end around 1893.

THE OTHER UNKNOWN KIMBERLEY

Meanwhile, in the background, while Charles Finlason and his merry men were grabbing the headlines, black cricketers were following the same trend. In the New Year of 1888, only three years after the white Kimberley cricketers had first linked up with the eastern Cape during the 1884/5 Champion Bat tournament, their African counterparts made their first tour to Port Elizabeth – indeed, it was at the very same time that Finlason and company were busy participating for the second time in (and winning) the Champion Bat in nearby Grahamstown.

The Kimberley visitors were described as being 'charming, decent and civil gentlemen', young men who were liked in every respect. The highly respected Peter Rwexu, described as a 'renowned PE citizen', welcomed the team. He was regarded as 'the best choice for such duties' and 'the crowd applauded him'. Bob Christian put the Kimberley side up at his home and Mrs Naniwe Wauchope supplied the bedding for the visitors. The 'countless others' who contributed were also thanked.[8]

The match was played at the white Union CC grounds. It cost a sixpenny to sit on the pavilion. The wind was howling through the trees on St George's Park, giving substance to PE's nickname of the Windy City. But this did not disturb the proceedings. The black community of PE and the surrounding areas 'fully supported the game'. Moreover, 'For the first time in the history of matches in the area married men brought their wives and single men brought their partners.' The reporter, 'Nkosi', said this needed to be applauded, 'as it is a symbol of change in our communities'.[9]

Kimberley stumbled in their first visit to the lion's den in *eBhayi*. The 'PE Native Team' won comfortably by 118 runs, but the tour opened the way for regular contacts between coast and interior in the same way it had done for the white players. That first team also demonstrated the diversity that was a feature of the Kimberley sports scene from the start: Hermanus, Michaels, Coutriers, Ciliwe, Macumela, Haupt, Mabeta, Ngesi (captain), Josephs, Kaba and Pu were the players involved.[10]

Kimberley participated regularly from 1890/1 onwards in the official Native Inter-Town tournaments held in the eastern Cape. The captain that season was John Sepuru. The two main Africans clubs in Kimberley, whose founding dates are unknown, were the Duke of Wellington CC (known simply as 'Duke') and the Eccentrics CC. In the decades that followed, the local derby between them became a big social occasion for a distinctive middle class on the diamond fields and cricket became part of a whole range of social activities.[11]

This was not all. There was a significant level of ethnic intermingling in Kimberley and so-called Malay cricketers were also playing cricket to a high standard by the late 1880s. In 1887 the strongest 'Malay' club, Red Crescents, undertook a tour to Cape Town, following the example of the white Stray Klips who had toured earlier that year. In 1889 the Universal CC played a 'scratch XI' of white cricketers, following the same pattern of challenge matches seen in the eastern Cape.[12] The local 'Malay' cricketers came strongly to the fore from 1890 onwards when a third inter-town cricket competition with a wider, cross-regional reach than its predecessors got going. The 'Malay' tournaments were to showcase, more than anywhere else and in a very public way, the real talent and sophistication that black cricketers possessed at the time. They made history by being the nurseries for the very first black national team and also the first non-racial provincial cricket body in the country.

Moreover, the champion white cricketers were well aware of the parallel processes taking part in local cricket and, as in the eastern Cape, several of them were happy to 'patronise' the black cricketers. The father of the well-known Kimberley all-rounder George Glover, who eventually played for South Africa, presented the Glover Trophy for the Malay Inter-Town tournaments, and helped organise one of them, while his sons were involved in a number of the challenge matches that were organised.

The richness and vitality of this cricket legacy in Kimberley is still largely unacknowledged. By the beginning of the 1890s Kimberley had become a 'supremely British place', and cricket an integral part of the project to make the subcontinent British.[13] Cricketers, both black and white, seized the opportunities that came with this. Socially they promulgated the values of the game, economically they benefited from the spectacular wealth of the new mining oligarchs – witness the Barnato Memorial Trophy and the bestowal of favoured jobs – and politically there were chances to assert themselves locally and lead in the formation of national associations and plans for sport across the subcontinent.

The rise of Kimberley as a cricket power between 1884 and 1887 and its dominance between 1887 and 1892 also showed the broadening network of cooperation in South Africa. Initially, Port Elizabeth made sense as a kind of half-way house venue for the Champion Bat tournaments between Cape Town and the growing eastern Cape towns. Now the centre of the game itself was starting to shift inland to the new hub of the colonial economy in southern Africa, connected to the coast by a brand-new railway network.

15

Subjugated memories

Reconstituting the statistics of the inter-town tournaments, 1876–1898

> Their lives stretched back into the invisible centuries and all
> that had come down from those differently coloured ages were
> legends and rich traditions, unwritten and therefore remembered.
> They were remembered because they were lived ...
> It was in the books that he first learnt of his invisibility. He searched
> for himself and his people in all the history books he read and
> discovered to his youthful astonishment that he didn't exist.
> ... Those who worked with him in those years saw him
> as a simple man. Actually, they didn't see him at all.
>
> – Ben Okri, *Astonishing the Gods* (1995)[1]

The Inter-Town tournaments from 1876 onwards provided the platforms and personnel to launch the modern game in South Africa. Like spring buds on a bare branch, subsequent inter-provincial tournaments, national organisations and the first international tours emanated from them. As we have seen in chapters 10 to 14, a diverse range of cricketers and communities were involved, including particular black cricket communities with distinct cultures and star players, who were among the pioneers of organised sport in South Africa.

There were altogether 22 of these path-breaking Inter-Town tournaments. Maurice Luckin's *History of South African Cricket* (1915), which formed the basis for drawing up South Africa's official records, covered only the five Champion Bat tournaments and one extraneous tournament for white cricketers (1876–91). He was completely silent about the six parallel Native Inter-Town tournaments and two extraneous tournaments which took place between 1884 and 1898, as well as the seven Malay Inter-Town tournaments (Glover Cup) and one extraneous tournament held between 1890 and 1898, even though they were reported in newspapers like *Imvo Zabantsundu*, the *Diamond Fields Advertiser*, the *Cape Times*, the *Cape Mercury* and the *Eastern Province Herald*.

The fifth white two-day Champion Bat inter-town contests were later given first-class status and the players classified as provincial even though they merely represented a club team from one city.[2] On the other hand, black inter-town or black provincial cricketers who played in similar two-day inter-town and provincial matches, and in a selected provincial and a national tournament team, are neither recognised as first-class nor have had their scores even recorded officially to date. The reasons for these omissions in the statistical record in the last quarter of the nineteenth century and their implications for cricket up to the present time have been discussed fully in the Introduction to this volume.

As part of the task of reconstituting the statistical history of South African cricket from the very beginnings of the game, this chapter therefore provides the first-ever integrated statistical overview of the 22 known Inter-Town tournaments in the Cape Colony from their beginnings in 1876 up to the onset of the first regional (later provincial) tournaments in the 1890s. We restore to the record around 400 of the early black Inter-Town players and over 50 Inter-Town matches for which we have statistics. The names listed below finally become part of the permanent history of the game. In chapter 35 we similarly add 160 known black provincial players and 17 known inter-provincial scorecards to this reconstituted record.

This means that from the one decontextualised match scorecard and 18 black cricketers mentioned in Luckin's century-old standard history, *Cricket and Conquest* unveils a statistical canvas showing details of 70 previously ignored top-level pre-1914 matches and some 550 representative cricketers, with many more to come in the succeeding volumes in this series. Altogether, a staggering 3,000 additional provincial cricketers who participated in around 1,000 official matches in well over 100 tournaments and competitions of the various national boards that existed before unity in 1991 will be added to the list, bringing for the first time some kind of wholeness to the existing, fragmented, incomplete and racially exclusive records of pre-1991 South African cricket.

In keeping with the inclusive approach of this study, this chapter also offers more than has existed to date for the establishment white Inter-Town cricketers between 1876 and 1891. The overall Champion Bat statistics are summarised here for the first time, and all 209 participants are listed for the first time as well, giving readers a sense of the size of the early gene pool of players that prepared the way for eventual Currie Cup and international cricket, and the continuities or ruptures evident from their time to the onset of these higher forms of competition. Although the early Inter-Town tournaments were racially designated throughout the 1876 to 1898 period, players and teams from differ- ent communities and ethnicities interacted, shared venues and column inches in the same newspapers, and influenced and sometimes actually played against one another. There was regular contact between the white and black Inter-Town cricketers from the mid-1880s onwards and, significantly, 'coloured' players (who sometimes referred to themselves as 'Africanders' or 'Afrikanders' in those days)[3] participated regularly in the Native Inter-Town Tournament, and African and coloured Christian cricketers played in the so-called Malay (synonymous with Muslim) tournaments.

The 'whitening' of the record – in cricket and more broadly – which accom- panied the violent conquest of the African people and the theft of their land in the nineteenth century, is part of what, without seeking to exaggerate, we have called a form of social and intellectual genocide. The question that Cricket South Africa and international authorities now need to deal with is this: should certain inter-town and provincial matches played by black cricketers also be included in official and first-class records? And if the answer is no, how then do cricket authorities and scribes keep talking about cricket's great traditions and 'fair play' when they continue to reinforce colonial exclusions and colonialism's deliber- ately partial records? The reactionary mentalities and injuries of the past simply have to be confronted.

* * * * *

This chapter may not be the most readable section in this book because it is statistical (and readers who wish to follow only the narrative sections can skip seamlessly over it), but it is among the most important. Not all the statistics in this chapter are complete. Many gaps still exist. There are some tournaments that we know took place, but for which no match statistics have yet been found. For a number of other tournaments there are only partial details of matches played. Where the record is incomplete, this is indicated in the hope that future research- ers will be able to fill the remaining gaps. In cases where information is missing, *[No details available]* will be indicated in square brackets. [X] indicates a missing initial, while [x] in lower case indicates missing bowling or batting figures. For example, [X] Abdol 6/16 or ... [X] Buhlungu 8/[x]. The original sources for the statistics are also indicated in the footnotes, so that the never-ending process of statistical verification and recovery can continue independently of the authors. This is not the end of the process of re-creating the record, but hopefully just a solid start.

15.1 WINNERS OF THE INTER-TOWN TOURNAMENTS, 1875/76–1897/98[4]

ET = Extraneous Tournament
* Cape Town played as Western Province
** Numbering because two Malay I-TTs were held in the same season

Season	White I-TT (Champion Bat)	Native I-TT (Jabavu Cup from 1897/98)	Malay I-TT (Glover Cup from 1890/91)
1875/76	King William's Town (in PE)		
1879/80	King William's Town (in KWT)		
1884/85	Port Elizabeth (in PE)	King William's Town (in Gtn)	
1885/86	–	Port Elizabeth (in PE)	
1886/87	Kimberley (ET in Kby)	King William's Town (in KWT)	
1887/88	Kimberley (in Gtn)	–	
1889/90	–	–	Cape Town (in CT)
1890/91	Cape Town* (in CT)	Port Elizabeth (in PE)	Kimberley (in Uitenhage) i** Kimberley (in Kby) ii**
1891/92	*Replaced by Currie Cup*	–	Cape Town (in Kby)
1892/93		Uitenhage (in KWT)	Cape Town (in CT) No winner (ET in CT)
1893/94		–	–
1894/95		–	–
1895/96		King William's Town (ET in KWT)	Cape Town* (in CT)
1896/97		Uitenhage (ET in PE/Uit)	–
1897/98		Port Elizabeth (in KWT)	Kimberley (in CT)
1898/99		*Both tournaments now replaced by Barnato Memorial Trophy tournament as the premier event*	

15.2 LIST OF PLAYERS IN INTER-TOWN TOURNAMENTS, 1875/76–1897/98

15.2.1 WHITE INTER-TOWN TOURNAMENTS, 1875/76–1897/98 (CHAMPION BAT)

Note: *ET = Extraneous Tournament in Kimberley in 1886/87*

Player	Team(s)	Tournaments/Seasons
Ashley, WH	WP	1890/91
Bailey, A	Port Elizabeth	1875/76
Bailey, HP	Port Elizabeth	1875/76
Barber, SH	Grahamstown	1887/88
Barnes, G	Queenstown	1879/80
Bayly, SJH	King William's Town	1887/88
Beech, E	GW	1890/91

Benton, E	King William's Town	1884/85, 1887/88
Bestall, C	Queenstown	1879/80
Blaine, A	King William's Town	1875/76
Boyes, CE	King William's Town	1887/88
Brady, J	Queenstown	1879/80
Britton, AH	Port Elizabeth	1886/87 (ET), 1887/88
Britton, CE	Port Elizabeth/EP	1886/87 (ET), 1887/88, 1890/91
Brown, C	Queenstown	1879/80
Brown, H	King William's Town	1875/76
Buckland, EH	Grahamstown	1887/88
Budler, E	Port Elizabeth	1884/85
Bulgin, J	Queenstown	1879/80
Burleigh, JL	GW	1890/91
Byrne, EJ	King William's Town	1875/76, 1879/80, 1884/85
Cadle, A	EP	1890/91
Caldecottt, AE	Kimberley	1884/85
Calderwood, T	Grahamstown	1875/76, 1879/80
Carpenter, F	Port Elizabeth	1879/80
Carpenter, GR	Port Elizabeth/EP	1890/91
Castens, HH	WP	1890/91
Catton, WJ	Grahamstown/EP	1887/88, 1890/91
Childe, [X]	Cape Town	1875/76
Cloete, H	Cape Town	1884/85
Clough, T	Grahamstown	1875/76, 1879/80
Coghlan, JC	Kimberley/GW	1887/88, 1890/91
Cooper, AE	GW	1890/91
Copeland, WF	EP	1890/91
Couper, JR	King William's Town	1879/80
Cox, AE	WP	1890/91
Crawford, FF	Natal	1886/87 (ET)
Cronin, CE	Queenstown	1879/80
Cunningham, JP	Natal	1886/87 (ET)
Curteis, [X], Lt	Cape Town	1875/76
Dalgety, EH	King William's Town	1879/80, 1884/85
Dannett, [X]	Bechuanaland	1886/87 (ET)
Davey, DC	Natal	1886/87 (ET)
Davies, HL	King William's Town	1887/88
Deane, J	WP	1890/91
Degacher, [X], Capt	Cape Town	1875/76
Dell, A	Queenstown	1879/80
Dell, S	Grahamstown	1875/76
De Villiers, JS	EP	1890/91
De Villiers, PH	Kimberley/WP	1886/87 (ET), 1887/88, 1890/91
Dexter, W	King William's Town	1879/80

Dick, RJ	King William's Town	1879/80
Dixon, TJ	Kimberley	1886/87 (ET)
Dold, HO	Grahamstown	1887/88
Dold, LB	Grahamstown	1887/88
Dold, S	Port Elizabeth	1886/87 (ET)
Donoghue, [X]	King William's Town	1875/76
Dunell, OR	Port Elizabeth	1879/80, 1884/85, 1887/88
Dyason, CE	Port Elizabeth	1886/87 (ET)
Edkins, A	Grahamstown	1875/76
Edkins, S	Kimberley	1884/85
Edwards, WW	Natal	1886/87 (ET)
Ehlert, J	Kimberley	1886/87 (ET)
Eliot, AEA	Kimberley	1887/88
Elliott, CG	Port Elizabeth	1887/88
Elliott, GJ	Port Elizabeth	1886/87 (ET)
Ellis, JD	King William's Town	1875/76
Finlason, CE	Kimberley/GW	1884/85, 1886/87 (ET), 1887/88, 1890/91
Fitzpatrick, GT	WP	1890/91
Fletcher, F	Grahamstown	1875/76
Ford, H	Cape Town	1875/76
Forde, J	Cape Town	1884/85
Fownes, [X], Lt	King William's Town	1875/76
Fuller, [X], Dr	Kimberley	1886/87 (ET)
Gallwey, WJ	Natal	1886/87 (ET)
Gallwey, [X], Lt	King William's Town	1875/76
Geard, A	Port Elizabeth	1884/85
Geard, [X]	Bechuanaland	1886/87 (ET)
Giddy, HR	King William's Town	1884/85
Giddy, LL	King William's Town/EP	1887/88, 1890/91
Giddy, S	Cape Town	1884/85
Giesen, A	Port Elizabeth	1875/76
Giesen, H	Port Elizabeth/Queenstown	1875/76, 1879/80
Giesen, HR	Port Elizabeth	1884/85
Gillman, [X]	King William's Town	1875/76
Gingell, [X]	Port Elizabeth	1886/87 (ET)
Glass, W	Grahamstown	1879/80
Glover, C	GW	1890/91
Glover, GK	GW	1890/91
Godlonton, BD	Port Elizabeth	1879/80
Goldsmith, SJ	Port Elizabeth	1887/88
Graham, J	Grahamstown	1875/76
Green, L	Grahamstown	1875/76
Grimmer, IR	Kimberley	1886/87 (ET), 1887/88
Hearne, F	WP	1890/91

Hendry, J	Natal	1886/87 (ET)
Heugh, P	Port Elizabeth/EP	1875/76, 1879/80, 1884/85, 1886/87 (ET), 1890/91
Heugh, W	King William's Town	1875/76
Hickley, CS	WP	1890/91
Hill, A	Kimberley	1886/87 (ET)
Hime, M	Natal	1886/87 (ET)
Hopgood, [X]	Grahamstown	1879/80
Hopley, WM	Grahamstown	1879/80
Howe, RRB	Kimberley	1884/85
Jackson, A	Port Elizabeth	1879/80
Jackson, J	Port Elizabeth	1886/87 (ET)
Jennings, M	King William's Town	1884/85
Jones, A	Cape Town	1875/76
Keane, R	King William's Town	1884/85
Kelly, W	Port Elizabeth	1879/80
Kempis, GA	Natal	1886/87 (ET)
Klinck, FG	Kimberley	1886/87 (ET), 1887/88
Lamb, J	Grahamstown	1887/88
Lambert, A	King William's Town	1879/80
Lawrence, A	Grahamstown	1879/80
Leach, AG	Grahamstown	1887/88
Levy, F	Kimberley	1884/85
Ling, E	Kimberley	1884/85
Ling, W	Kimberley	1884/85
Lloyd, LO	Grahamstown	1879/80, 1887/88
Lochner, [X]	Bechuanaland	1886/87 (ET)
Longden, A	Grahamstown	1875/76
Lovell, GHS	GW	1890/91
Lucy, [X]	Bechuanaland	1886/87
Lyons, J	Port Elizabeth	1887/88
Mackenzie, JG	Port Elizabeth	1875/76
Mahoney, [X]	King William's Town	1879/80
Mann, [X]	Bechuanaland	1886/87 (ET)
McCallum, [X]	Bechuanaland	1886/87 (ET)
McKeating, F	Port Elizabeth/EP	1886/87 (ET), 1887/88, 1890/91
Melck, [X]	Cape Town	1875/76
Middleton, J	WP	1890/91
Mills, J	Cape Town	1875/76
Milton, WH	WP	1890/91
Molteno, J	Cape Town	1884/85
Moxey, E	King William's Town	1884/85
Murray, [X]	Grahamstown	1879/80
Nash, C	King William's Town	1887/88

Newsome, [X]	Port Elizabeth	1879/80
Nicholls, EC	Port Elizabeth	1875/76
Nicholson, R	Natal	1886/87 (ET)
Noble, J	Kimberley	1884/85, 1886/87 (ET)
Nunn, [X]	Bechuanaland	1886/87 (ET)
Ogden, E	Port Elizabeth	1886/87 (ET)
Parkin, DC	EP	1890/91
Parkin, E	Port Elizabeth	1875/76
Parkin, H	Port Elizabeth	1879/80, 1887/88
Pattison, [X]	Grahamstown	1879/80
Perring, CC	Kimberley	1886/87 (ET), 1887/88
Phillips, H	Port Elizabeth	1879/80
Phillips, [X]	King William's Town	1875/76
Philpott, E	Grahamstown	1875/76
Porter, A	King William's Town	1887/88
Porter, N	King William's Town	1887/88
Proudfoot, DG	Port Elizabeth/EP	1884/85, 1890/91
Redwood, CL	Natal	1886/87 (ET)
Reid, [X]	Bechuanaland	1886/87 (ET)
Rennie, [X]	Bechuanaland	1886/87 (ET)
Renny-Tailyour, E	Port Elizabeth	1875/76, 1879/80, 1884/85
Reynolds, G	Grahamstown	1875/76
Richards, AR	WP	1890/91
Richards, WHM	Cape Town	1884/85
Ridgeway, J	Queenstown	1879/80
Robb, F	Cape Town	1884/85
Roberts, R	Grahamstown	1875/76
Robertson, TW	King William's Town	1875/76
Robinson, S	Natal	1886/87 (ET)
Rose-Innes, A	Port Elizabeth	1886/87 (ET), 1887/8
Rutherfoord, CSE	GW	1890/91
Saunders, OE	King William's Town	1879/80
Schermbrucker, EP	King William's Town	1879/80, 1884/85, 1887/88
Seccull, AW	Grahamstown	1887/88
Sheehan, J	King William's Town	1879/80, 1884/85
Singleton, J	Port Elizabeth	1879/80, 1884/85
Smith, FW	Kimberley	1884/85, 1886/87 (ET), 1887/88
Smith, H	Port Elizabeth	1875/76
Smith, H	King William's Town	1875/76, 1887/88
Smith, HM	Port Elizabeth	1887/88
Solomon, R	Grahamstown	1879/80
Solomon, W	Cape Town	1884/85
Southey, C	King William's Town	1887/88
Spring, [X], Lt	Cape Town	1875/76

Steele, H	Cape Town	1875/76
Stevens, RW	Port Elizabeth	1884/85
Stewart, RB	King William's Town	1879/80, 1884/85
Steytler, ES	Cape Town/WP	1884/85, 1890/91
Stradling, EJ	Cape Town	1884/85
Stratford, J	Grahamstown	1887/88
Tancred, AB	Kimberley/GW	1884/85, 1886/87 (ET), 1887/88, 1890/91
Tanner, HW	Natal	1886/87 (ET)
Tarleton, [X], Dr	Natal	1886/87 (ET)
Thompson, W	Queenstown	1879/80
Tully, W	King William's Town	1884/85
Turberville, FS	EP	1890/91
Van Breda, P	Cape Town	1875/76
Van der Bijl, VAW	WP	1890/91
Van Reenen, H	Cape Town	1875/76
Van Reenen, JB	Cape Town	1884/85
Vaughan, CR	Cape Town	1884/85
Vigne, JT	Kimberley	1887/88
Vintcent, CH	Cape Town, Bechuanaland, Kby	1884/85, 1886/87 (ET), 1887/88
Vintcent, J	Bechuanaland	1886/87 (ET)
Walker, [X]	Bechuanaland	1886/87 (ET)
Walker, C	Grahamstown	1879/80
Wallace, F	Grahamstown	1887/88
Walshe, AWP	GW	1890/91
Weakley, G	Queenstown	1879/80
Webb, H	Kimberley	1884/85
Webster, HH	Port Elizabeth	1884/85, 1886/87 (ET), 1887/88
Wheatley, WB	Port Elizabeth	1875/76
Williams, HP	Port Elizabeth	1875/76
Wimble, BS	Port Elizabeth/EP	1884/85, 1886/87 (ET), 1887/88, 1890/91
Winslow, L	King William's Town	1879/80, 1884/85, 1887/88
Wishart, [X]	Bechuanaland	1886/87 (ET)
Woodthorpe, WS	Kimberley	1884/85, 1886/87 (ET), 1887/88

15.2.2 NATIVE INTER-TOWN TOURNAMENTS, 1884/85–1897/98 (JABAVU CUP FROM 1897/98)

Note: ET = *Extraneous Tournaments in 1895/96 and 1896/97 in King William's Town and Port Elizabeth/Uitenhage respectively*
PE2nds = *Port Elizabeth second XI*

Player	Team(s)	Tournaments/Seasons
Abrams, R	Queenstown	1897/98
Adons, J	Grahamstown	1886/87
Baart, S	East London	1892/93, 1897/98

Baba, [X]	Champion CC (KWT)	1895/96 (ET)
Badisi, [X]	Grahamstown	1884/85
Balfour, B	Port Elizabeth	1886/87
Bali, C	King William's Town	1885/86, 1886/87, 1890/91, 1892/93
Barnabas, J	King William's Town	1884/85, 1885/86, 1890/91, 1892/93
Barnabas, [X]	Grahamstown	1884/85
Bassie, FJ	King William's Town	1895/96 (ET), 1896/97 (ET), 1897/98
Bomela, C	Grahamstown	1885/86, 1886/87
Booi, C	King William's Town	1897/98
Bopi, CN	King William's Town	1890/91, 1892/93, 1895/96 (ET), 1896/97 (ET), 1897/98
Bopi, K	Port Elizabeth	1884/85, 1885/86, 1886/87
Bovana, N	King William's Town	1884/85, 1885/86
Bovana, W	King William's Town	1885/86
Boyce, Stephen	Port Elizabeth	1885/86, 1886/87, 1890/91
Buhlungu, B	King William's Town	1895/96 (ET)
Bulcha, H	King William's Town	1897/98
Busakwe, S	Port Elizabeth	1895/96 (ET), 1896/97 (ET), 1897/98
Butler, [X]	King William's Town	1886/87
Calver, A	Grahamstown	1885/86
Chake, [X]	Uitenhage	1892/93
Christian, RZ 'Bob'	Port Elizabeth	1884/85, 1885/86, 1886/87, 1890/91
Dalaza, P	Port Elizabeth	1897/98
Dalaza, T	Port Elizabeth	1897/98
Dalaza, V	Port Elizabeth	1896/97 (ET)
Dalaza, [X]	Port Elizabeth	1895/96 (ET)
Danga, [X]	Grahamstown	1884/85 capt
Dlamini, [X]	Uitenhage	1892/93
Dlepu, [X]	Grahamstown	1884/85
Dlepu, [X]	Uitenhage	1892/93
Dolly, [X]	Uitenhage	1896/97 (ET)
Draai, [X]	East London	1886/87
Dyantyi, [X]	Queenstown	1886/87
Faku, J	Grahamstown	1885/86, 1886/87
Fisher, [X]	King William's Town	1886/87
Fobe, N	Queenstown	1897/98
Fobe, W	Queenstown	1897/98
Foley, MD	Port Elizabeth	1884/85, 1885/86, 1890/91, 1892/93, 1896/97 (ET)
Foley, [X]	King William's Town	1885/86
Frielander, L	Grahamstown	1885/86
Ganya, W	King William's Town	1884/85, 1885/86, 1886/87
Gawler, J, Rev.	Port Elizabeth	1890/91
Genge, [X]	Champion CC (KWT)	1895/96 (ET)

Gula, T	Kimberley	1890/91, 1892/93
Gule, T	Grahamstown	1885/86, 1886/87
Hanns, [X]	Queenstown	1892/93
Haya, R	Port Elizabeth	1897/98
Haya, RZ	King William's Town	1890/91, 1892/93, 1895/96 (ET), 1896/97 (ET), 1897/98
Hlati, D	Port Elizabeth	1884/85, 1886/87, 1890/91
Hlati, [X]	Grahamstown	1884/85
Holmes, [X]	East London	1886/87
Isaac, [X]	Uitenhage	1896/97 (ET)
Jacob, [X]	East London	1886/87
Jacobs, [X]	Uitenhage	1892/93
Jafer, [X]	Uitenhage	1896/97 (ET)
Jewis, M	Grahamstown	1885/86
Julius, [X]	Port Elizabeth 2nds	1896/97 (ET)
Kadi, DJ	Port Elizabeth	1890/91, 1896/97 (ET)
Katyana, [X]	Uitenhage	1892/93
Kinner, [X]	Queenstown	1886/87
Klaas, T	Port Elizabeth	1885/86
Kolele, [X]	Frontier CC (KWT)	1895/96 (ET)
Kriel, [X]	Uitenhage	1896/97 (ET)
Kulati, [X]	Port Elizabeth	1895/96 (ET)
Kunene, E	East London	1892/93, 1897/98
Landule, R	King William's Town	1884/85
Landule, [X]	East London/KWT	1884/85, 1886/87, 1890/91
Latola, [X]	Uitenhage	1892/93, 1896/97 (ET)
Legalagala, [X]	Queenstown	1886/87
Lutu, [X]	Queenstown	1886/87
Lutu, [X]	Uitenhage	1892/93
Mabelana, N	Port Elizabeth	1896/97 (ET), 1897/98
Mabope, AX	Port Elizabeth	1884/85, 1885/86
Macumela, [X]	Grahamstown	1884/85
Macumela, [X]	Uitenhage	1892/93, 1896/97 (ET)
Magaba, EP, Rev.	Kimberley	1892/93
Magabela, S	King William's Town	1895/96 (ET), 1896/97 (ET), 1897/98
Magoda, G	Queenstown	1892/93, 1897/98
Makambi, [X]	East London	1892/93
Makeke, T	King William's Town	1897/98
Makeke, [X]	East London	1892/93
Makonjwa, [X]	Frontier CC (KWT)	1895/96 (ET)
Makwena, F	Port Elizabeth	1885/86
Malgas, [X]	East London	1884/85 capt
Malo, [X],	King William's Town	1884/85
Maloni, T	Port Elizabeth	1895/96 (ET), 1896/97 (ET), 1897/98

utenant (later Captain) Robert Stewart of the pe Mounted Rifles, 'the most renowned South rican cricketer of his day', scored the first atury and averaged over 50 in the white inter- wn tournaments for the Champion Bat held ween 1875/6 and 1890/1.

The county cricketer from Sussex in England, Lieutenant Lyndhurst Winslow, made his Champion Bat debut for King William's Town in 1879/80.

T. Calderwood, captain of Grahamstown in the first two Champion Bat tournaments in 1875/6 and 1879/80.

affrarian Rifle Volunteers, c.1877. Colonel F.W. Schermbrucker (standing left) commanded the black colonial militia which killed King andile. He became an MP and sponsor of cricket, and his son played in the inter-town tournaments and some historic matches against lack cricketers in King William's Town in the mid-1880s. The close connections between cricket and colonial conquest can also be seen y the names of others in this photo, like William Warren, Kei Road farmer; T.R.M. Cole, King William's Town magistrate; Mr Bryne (*sic*), ing William's Town attorney; George Broster, King William's Town messenger of the court; James Sansom, Komgha farmer; and T.H. iddy, King William's Town attorney. Warren was the surname of the first Border Cricket Union president and Byrne the captain of King Villiam's Town in the first two white inter-town tournaments.

The third white Champion Bat tournament, 1884/5. The winning Port Elizabeth team posing here with Cape Town: 1 W.H.M. Richards (CT), 2 P. Heugh (PE), 3 C.H. Vintcent (CT), 4 C.N. Thomas (CT, umpire), 5 D.G. Proudfoot (PE), 6 J. Singleton (PE), 7 C.R. Vaughan (CT), 8 S. Giddy (CT), 9 O.R. Dunell (PE, captain), 10 J. Molteno (CT), 11 R.W. Stevens (PE), 12 H. Cloete (CT), 13 E. Budler (PE), 15 G. Cloete (CT), 16 J. Forde (CT), 17 E. Renny-Tailyour (PE), 18 A. Geard (PE), 19 E.J. Stradling (CT), 20 H.H. Webster (PE professional), 21 B.S. Wimble (PE), 22 J.B. van Reenen (CT), 23 H.R. Giesen (PE), 24 F. Robb (CT).

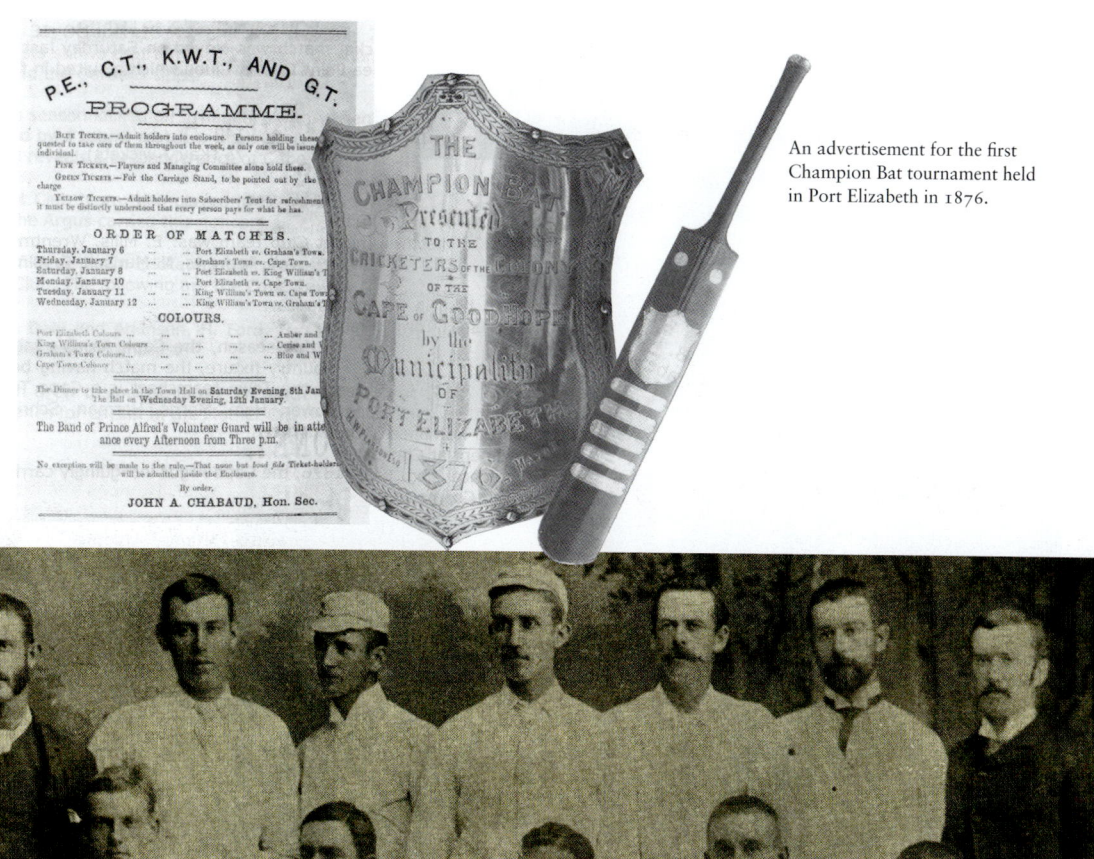

An advertisement for the first Champion Bat tournament held in Port Elizabeth in 1876.

berley, winners of the fourth Champion Bat tournament in Grahamstown, 1887/8, posing with the trophy. Back row: A. Hill, Elliott, F.G. Klinck, I.R. Grimmer, C.C. Perring, C.E. Finlason, C. Coghlan. Middle row: P.H. de Villiers, C.H. Vintcent, . Woodthorpe (captain), A.B. Tancred, J.T. Vigne. Front row: F.W. Smith, J. Coghlan.

Left: Cricket was popular everywhere in 'the black cricket belt of the Border' by the late 19th century.

Active cricketer since the 1860s, Nathaniel Umhalla captained the winning team, King William's Town, in the first Native Inter-Town Tournament in Grahamstown in 1884/5 and top-scored with 46 in one of the challenge matches against the local white Albert CC team that season.

Below: City Lords ground, Grahamstown, picturesque venue of the first Native Inter-Town Tournament in 1884.

Left: An African James Lillywhite Senior. Pioneering newspaper editor John Tengo Jabavu (standing), a key promoter of early African cricket, pictured here as part of a 'Native Voters Delegation' with Elijah Makiwane (left) and the Rev. Isaac Wauchope, a guest and praise singer at the 1885/6 Native Inter-Town Tournament.

Kingstown
15th Nov. 1892

To the Mayor & Councillors
Kingwilliamstown

Hon Gentlemen

On receipt of the Town Clerk's letter informing us that our application for the Victoria ground for our cricket tournament arranged to commence from the 26th Decr to the 4th Jany '93 has not been entertained by the Council on account of "all the space being taken up by the various local clubs". We interviewed several of the prominent cricketers in town and they invariably stated that those days are vacant, that they are arranging to go up and play up country during the holidays: and in fact that even if they had fixtures for that time they would waive them in order to allow us space our tournament space. Therefore gentlemen under these circumstances we beg you to reconsider your decision and grant us the ground for our tournament for which we have already invited teams, and incurred expense. I am not at all anticipating any difficulty as the ground was granted us on a previous occasion.

Hoping to speedily get a favourable reply,
I remain &c Gentlemen
Your humble & obedient servant
Paul Xiniwe
&c &c &c

Top left: Letter from Paul Xiniwe, political activist, entrepreneur and veteran inter-town cricketer, asking the King William's Town Council to reconsider its decision to deny the cricket organisers use of the main municipal Victoria Cricket Ground for the 1892/3 inter-town tournament.

Top right: Paul Xiniwe.

Bottom right: Newspaper advertisements in isiXhosa aimed at cricketers, 1889.

Imvo Zabantsundu.
(NATIVE OPINION)

Authorised Medium for the Publication of Government Notices addressed to Natives throughout the Colony and the Territories.

[IXABISO 3d.]   KING WILLIAMS TOWN, NGOLWESI-NE, OCTOBER 17, 1889.   [No. 247.]

IXESHA LE BHOLA, 1889.

DYER no DYER,

John J. Irvine & Co.,
KINGWILLIAMSTOWN.

Members of the Gold and Blue football teams, which would later be consolidated, pose for a series photograph of a formal game at the college in 1894 (next page).

The first South African team vs Major Warton's English team, at Port Elizabeth, March 1889.
Nine of the eleven players were graduates of the inter-town tournaments, going back to 1879/80.
Back row: Albert Rose-Innes, A.B. Tancred, Charles Finlason, Charlie Vintcent, Fred Smith.
Middle row: C.R. Deare (umpire), Philip Hutchinson, Owen Dunell, William Milton.
Front row: A.E. 'Okey' Ochse, Robert Stewart, Gustav Kempis.

FIRST ENGLISH CRICKET TEAM IN SOUTH AFRICA, 1888·9.

J. BRIGGS.	M. READ.	SIMPSON. (CAPTAIN)	H. WOOD.	A. J. FOTHERGILL.
B.A.F. GRIEVE.	M.P. BOWDEN.	R. GARDNER-WARTON.	C.A. SMITH. (CAPTAIN)	E. McMASTER.
	HON. C.J. COVENTRY.	R. ABEL.	F. HEARNE.	

Mapikela, [X]	Queenstown	1886/87, 1892/93
Maqanda, H	Grahamstown	1886/87
Maqoma, D	Port Elizabeth/PE2nds	1895/96 (ET), 1896/97 (ET)
Matayo, J	Kimberley	1890/91, 1892/93
Matayo, W	Kimberley	1890/91, 1892/93
Matross, [X]	East London	1892/93
May, H	Grahamstown	1885/86, 1886/87
Mbedu, [X]	Uitenhage	1892/93, 1896/97 (ET)
Mbusi, [X]	East London	1884/85
Mcanyangwa, C	East London	1892/93
Mcanyangwa, H	East London	1892/93
Mcanyangwa, [X]	East London	1886/87, 1892/93
Mcanyangwa, [X]	King William's Town	1890/91, 1892/93
Mcilongo, [X]	Port Elizabeth 2nds	1896/97 (ET)
Mdana, S	East London	1886/87
Mdana, [X]	Grahamstown	1884/85
Mdana, [X]	Port Elizabeth	1884/85
Mdunyelwa, H	Grahamstown	1886/87
Menze, J	King William's Town	1892/93, 1895/96 (ET), 1896/97 (ET), 1897/98
Menze, W	Port Elizabeth	1897/98
Menze, [X]	King William's Town	1892/93
Mfamana, [X]	Grahamstown	1884/85
Mgudlandlu, [X]	Port Elizabeth	1895/96 (ET)
Mhlabi, [X]	Kimberley	1892/93
Mhlati, S	Kimberley	1890/91
Mjokozeli, [X]	East London	1892/93
Mjuza, [X]	Queenstown	1886/87
Mkapa, T	East London	1897/98
Mkefa, [X]	Queenstown	1886/87
Mlilwana, Robert B	Queenstown	1886/87
Mlungwana, A	Queenstown	1897/98
Mnxitama, [X]	East London	1884/85
Mokuena, [X]	Kimberley	1892/93
Mona, [X]	Port Elizabeth	1895/96 (ET)
Mondel, [X]	Kimberley	1892/93
Mondel, [X]	Uitenhage	1892/93
Morley, J	Port Elizabeth	1884/85, 1885/86
Morley, K	East London	1897/98
Mpahlele, C	Queenstown	1892/93, 1897/98
Mpahlele, [X]	Queenstown	1892/93
Mpaki, [X]	Queenstown	1892/93
Mphu, [X]	Frontier CC (KWT)	1895/96 (ET)
Msengana, J	Queenstown	1892/93, 1897/98
Mtsamana, [X]	East London	1886/87

Mtshatshisa, W	Port Elizabeth/PE2nds	1896/97 (ET), 1897/98
Mtshete, [X]	Port Elizabeth 2nds	1896/97 (ET)
Mtule, A	Kimberley	1890/91
Mtule, [X]	Port Elizabeth	1886/87
Mtuyedwa, [X]	Queenstown	1892/93
Muleka, [X]	East London	1892/93
Mzimase, [X]	Kimberley	1892/93
Mzini, [X]	Kimberley	1892/93
Nano, SC	Kimberley	1890/91
Ngcotoza, [X]	Port Elizabeth 2nds	1896/97 (ET)
Ngcoza, E	Port Elizabeth	1885/86, 1890/91, 1896/97 (ET)
Ngcoza, [X]	Kimberley	1892/93
Ngcumbe, A	King William's Town	1884/85, 1885/86, 1886/87, 1890/91, 1892/93, 1895/96 (ET)
Ngece, [X]	Queenstown	1886/87
Ngeni, [X]	Port Elizabeth	1895/96 (ET)
Ngesi, E	Grahamstown	1885/86
Ngesi, Enoch	Kimberley	1890/91
Ngqaka, [X]	East London	1892/93
Ngqina, [X]	Port Elizabeth	1886/87
Ngxoweni, [X]	King William's Town	1892/93
Nikani, J	Port Elizabeth 2nds	1896/97 (ET)
Nini, S	King William's Town	1885/86, 1886/87
Nini, X	Champion CC (KWT)	1895/96 (ET)
Nkole, H	Queenstown	1897/98
Nkole, [X]	King William's Town	1884/85
Nobatana, E	East London	1897/98
Nobatana, [X]	King William's Town	1892/93
Nogwina, T	Port Elizabeth	1897/98
Nombewu, W	Grahamstown	1884/85, 1886/87
Nomo, [X]	Port Elizabeth 2nds	1896/97 (ET)
Nongalaza, [X]	Queenstown	1886/87
Nozwane, [X]	King William's Town	1884/85
Nqini, T	East London	1897/98
Nqini, [X]	East London	1892/93
Ntinge, F	East London	1897/98
Ntshona, [X]	Frontier CC (KWT)	1895/96 (ET)
Nukuna, Richard	Queenstown	1886/87, 1892/93
Oliver, [X]	Port Elizabeth 2nds	1896/97 (ET)
Payi, E	KWT/Frontier CC	1892/93, 1895/96 (ET)
Peters, H	Grahamstown	1885/86, 1886/87
Petros, [X]	Uitenhage	1892/93
Pezisa, H	Port Elizabeth	1884/85 capt
Phu, [X]	Port Elizabeth	1895/96 (ET)

Qondani, [X]	King William's Town	1884/85
Qoqo, W	East London	1897/98
Qoqo, [X]	Port Elizabeth	1886/87
Rashe, J	East London	1897/98
Rhabula, [X]	Queenstown	1892/93
Ross, A	Port Elizabeth	1895/96 (ET), 1896/97 (ET), 1897/98
Ross, George A	Port Elizabeth	1884/85, 1885/86, 1890/91
Rune, D	King William's Town	1892/93, 1895/96 (ET), 1896/97 (ET), 1897/98
Rune, D	Port Elizabeth	1892/93, 1895/96 (ET), 1897/98
Rune, N	Port Elizabeth	1896/97 (ET)
Rune, S	King William's Town	1892/93
Rune, [X]	King William's Town	1892/93
Sebe, T	East London	1892/93
Sepuru, J	Kimberley	1890/91 capt, 1892/93
Seti, William N	KWT/Champion CC	1884/85, 1885/86, 1886/87, 1890/91, 1892/93, 1895/96 (ET)
Shelton, [X]	Kimberley	1892/93
Sidayiya, J	KWT/Frontier CC	1884/85, 1885/86, 1886/87, 1890/91, 1895/96 (ET)
Sinuka, BG	Port Elizabeth	1890/91
Sinzani, [X]	Uitenhage	1896/97 (ET)
Siwundla, [X]	East London	1884/85, 1886/87
Siyeka, [X]	East London	1886/87
Siyo, W	King William's Town	1896/97 (ET)
Small, J	Kimberley	1890/91
Soga, D	East London	1884/85, 1886/87
Soga, EB	King William's Town	1884/85, 1885/86, 1886/87
Soga, J	King William's Town	1884/85, 1885/86, 1886/87
Soga, R	East London	1884/85
Solani, [X]	East London	1884/85
Stenge, R	Grahamstown	1885/86
Swartboy, B	Port Elizabeth	1884/85, 1885/86
Thoba, H	Kimberley	1890/91
Thomas, D	King William's Town	1884/85, 1886/87
Thomas, [X]	East London	1884/85, 1886/87
Thomas, [X]	Port Elizabeth/PE2nds	1895/96 (ET), 1896/97 (ET)
Thomas, Z	Port Elizabeth	1890/91
Thu, [X]	Uitenhage	1892/93, 1896/97 (ET)
Tisana, [X]	Uitenhage	1892/93, 1896/97 (ET)
Toise, ED	King William's Town	1895/96 (ET), 1896/97 (ET), 1897/98
Toise, W	King William's Town	1895/96 (ET), 1896/97 (ET)
Tshaki, [X]	Uitenhage	1892/93
Tshatshu, [X]	King William's Town	1884/85
Tshazibana, [X]	King William's Town	1895/96 (ET)

Tshona, [X]	Port Elizabeth	1886/87
Tu [X]	Uitenhage	1892/93
Tywayi, W	Grahamstown	1884/85
Umhalla, NC	King William's Town	1884/85 capt
Umvalo, [X]	King William's Town	1884/85, 1886/87
Vaaiboom, A	Port Elizabeth	1890/91
Vane, SC	Kimberley	1890/91
Vena, J	Port Elizabeth	1896/97 (ET)
Vena, [X]	King William's Town	1892/93
Vyoli, B	Kimberley	1890/91
Wilson, [X]	East London	1886/87
Xelo, J	King William's Town	1884/85, 1886/87
Xinishe, [X]	Queenstown	1892/93
Xiniwe, P	PE/King William's Town	1884/85, 1886/87, 1890/91, 1892/93, 1895/96 (ET), 1896/97 (ET), 1897/98
Yobo, [X]	Port Elizabeth	1895/96 (ET), 1897/98
Yutu, C	Port Elizabeth 2nds	1896/97 (ET)
Zondani, N 'senior'	King William's Town	1885/86, 1886/87, 1890/91, 1892/93, 1895/96 (ET), 1897/98
Zondani, T 'junior'	KWT/Champion CC	1890/91, 1892/93, 1895/96 (ET), 1897/98
Zondani, [X]	King William's Town	1886/87
Zuma, [X]	East London	1886/87
Zwaartbooi, [X]	East London	1892/93

15.2.3 MALAY INTER-TOWN TOURNAMENTS, 1889/90–1897/98 (GLOVER CUP FROM APRIL 1891)

Notes:

CTU & CU was a joint Cape Town Union and Claremont Union team that played against a combined Port Elizabeth and Johannesburg team (PE & Jhb) at the end of the 1889/90 tournament.

1890/91 (i) and (ii) indicate one or the other of the two inter-town tournaments held that season.

A second tournament was held directly after the Glover Cup was completed in Cape Town in January 1893: this is recorded as (ET), Extraneous Tournament. This was to give Claremont a chance to play against the visiting teams that had competed in the Glover Cup against Cape Town.

South African Glover Cup XI, also known as the South African Malay team: A combined tournament team (here SAGC XI) was selected after the tournaments in 1890/91 and 1891/92. Several players specifically resisted being called 'Malays'.

Player	Team(s)	Tournaments/Seasons
Abdol, J	Kimberley	1895/96
Abdol, [X]	Claremont/Cape Town	1889/90, 1890/91 (i)
Abdol, [X]	Johannesburg	1889/90
Abdullah, M	Kimberley	1892/93, 1892/93 (ET)
Abrahams, E	Cape Town	1895/96
Abrahams, H	Claremont/CTU & CU	1889/90

Abrahams, J	Johannesburg	1895/96
Abrahams, W	Claremont/CTU & CU/Cape Town	1889/90, 1890/91 (i)
Abrams, E	Cape Town/Kimberley/SAGC XI	1890/91 (ii), 1891/92, 1892/93, 1892/93 (ET)
Abrams, M	Cape Town	1890/91 (ii)
Abrams, R	Cape Town	1890/91 (ii)
Achmat, A	Johannesburg/PE & Jhb	1889/90, 1892/93, 1892/93 (ET), 1895/96
Achmat, [X]	Cape Town	1895/96
Adams, A	Kimberley	1890/91 (ii)
Adams, B	Cape Town	1895/96
Adams, E	Claremont/CTU & CU	1889/90, 1890/91 (i), 1892/93 (ET)
Adams, E	Claremont	1892/93 (ET) (Two E Adams in same team)
Adams, E	Cape Town	1895/96
Adams, J	Port Elizabeth/SAGC XI	1890/91 (ii)
Adams, M	Kimberley/SAGC XI	1891/92
Adams, [X]	Cape Town	1890/91 (i)
Adderjance, H[5]	Claremont	1889/90
Aderjance, [X]	Claremont	1889/90
Aderyanse, H	Cape Town	1890/91 (i)
Aderyanse, L	Cape Town	1890/91 (i)
Aijahn, [X]	Cape Town	1889/90
Ajoep, [X]	Port Elizabeth/PE & Jhb	1889/90 capt
Allei, [X]	Claremont	1889/90
Amaar, T	Cape Town	1890/91 (ii)
Andrianse, N	Cape Town	1890/91 (i)
Appollis, B	Johannesburg	1895/96
Appollis, M	Johannesburg	1892/93, 1892/93 (ET),
Ariefdien, E[6]	CTU & CU/Cape Town/SAGC XI	1889/90, 1890/91 (ii), 1891/92, 1892/93, 1895/96
Armar, T	Cape Town	1889/90
Astrie, H	Port Elizabeth	1889/90
Badierdien, A	Port Elizabeth	1889/90
Bergman, C	Johannesburg	1892/93, 1892/93 (ET)
Boyce, D	Port Elizabeth	1890/91 (i)
Burness, J	Port Elizabeth	1890/91 (i)
Butler, B	Johannesburg	1892/93, 1892/93 (ET)
Cupido, W	Johannesburg	1892/93, 1892/93 (ET)
Davids, [X]	Claremont	1892/93 (ET)
Dent, M	Johannesburg	1892/93, 1892/93 (ET)
Dick, [X]	Kimberley	1890/91 (ii)
Dientjie, [X]	Claremont	1892/93 (ET)
Dollie, A	Johannesburg	1892/93, 1892/93 (ET)
Dolly, F	Port Elizabeth	1890/91 (i)
Du Toit, K	Cape Town/SAGC XI	1890/91 (ii), 1891/92, 1892/93, 1895/96
Eachmat, [X]	Johannesburg	1889/90
Ebriem, E	Claremont	1892/93 (ET)

Eshaak, L	Cape Town	1889/90 capt
Esmieh, M	Cape Town	1889/90
Flooks, J	Kimberley	1897/98
Fortuin, P	Kimberley	1892/93, 1892/93 (ET)
Fredricks, A	PE & Jhb	1889/90
Fredricks, G	Port Elizabeth/PE & Jhb	1889/90, 1890/91 (i)
Fredricks, L	Port Elizabeth/PE & Jhb	1889/90, 1890/91 (i)
Fredricks, L	Claremont	1892/93 (ET)
Galer, A	Cape Town	1890/91 (ii)
Gamat, AG	Cape Town	1892/93
Gasant, M	Johannesburg	1892/93, 1892/93 (ET)
Gatardien, [X]	Johannesburg	1892/93, 1892/93 (ET)
Gihier, A	Cape Town/CTU and CU	1889/90
Goliath, J	Kimberley	1892/93, 1892/93 (ET)
Grendon, R[7]	Kimberley/SAGC XI	1890/91 (i), 1890/91 (ii), 1891/92, 1892/93, 1892/93 (ET), 1895/96, 1897/98
Hajup, [X]	Port Elizabeth	1890/91 (i)
Hendricks, A	Port Elizabeth	1889/90
Hendricks, A	Johannesburg/PE & Jhb	1889/90
Hendricks, A	Cape Town	1895/96
Hendricks, A	Kimberley/SAGC XI	1890/91 (ii), 1891/92, 1892/93, 1892/93 (ET)
Hendricks, B	Kimberley	1892/93, 1892/93 (ET)
Hendricks, H 'Krom'	Cape Town	1891/92, 1892/93
Hendricks, J	Cape Town/CTU & CU	1889/90
Hendricks, J	Kimberley	1895/96
Hendricks, K	Cape Town	1895/96
Hendricks, M	Kimberley	1895/96
Hendricks, Omar	Johannesburg	1889/90
Hendricks, T	Kimberley	1895/96, 1897/98
Hendrik, [X]	Kimberley	1890/91 (i)
Irjaan, A	Cape Town	1889/90
Isaacs, E	Kimberley	1892/93, 1892/93 (ET)
Ishaak, D	Cape Town	1889/90
Ismael, MS	Cape Town/CTU and CU	1889/90, 1890/91 (ii), 1892/93
Jabaar, M	Johannesburg	1889/90, 1892/93, 1892/93 (ET)
Jabaar, M	Kimberley	1897/98 capt
Jabaar, T	Kimberley	1897/98
Jackson, A	Port Elizabeth	1890/91 (ii)
Jackson, O	Port Elizabeth	1890/91 (ii)
Jacobs, J	Claremont	1892/93 (ET)
Jacoef, G	Cape Town	1889/90
Jaijer, A	Cape Town	1889/90
Jamieldien, [X]	Cape Town	1895/96
Jamieldien, [X]	Kimberley	1890/91 (i)
Josephs, C	Johannesburg	1892/93, 1892/93 (ET)

Kamallie, G	Kimberley	1890/91 (i), 1890/91 (ii)
Kamies, J	Kimberley	1890/91 (ii)
Karrimdien, G[8]	Port Elizabeth	1889/90
Kashiem, G	Port Elizabeth	1889/90
Kasseim, E	Port Elizabeth	1889/90
Kassiem, MG	Cape Town	1891/92
Laban, D	Claremont	1889/90
Lamberts, [X]	Johannesburg	1895/96
Lamrah, M	Cape Town/CTU and CU	1889/90
Lanerto, C	Johannesburg	1892/93, 1892/93 (ET)
Laran, A	Johannesburg	1889/90
Leach, C[9]	Cape Town	1892/93, 1895/96
Lennit, J	Johannesburg	1895/96
Le Roux, A	Cape Town	1890/91 (ii), 1892/93
Loster, S	Cape Town	1890/91 (i), 1892/93
Madatt, M	Port Elizabeth	1890/91 (ii)
Madatt, S	Port Elizabeth	1890/91 (ii)
Magiet, S	Cape Town	1892/93
Magmoet, [X]	Johannesburg	1895/96
Majiet, A	Kimberley	1890/91 (ii)
Majiet, A	Johannesburg	1895/96
Mallick, K	Port Elizabeth	1890/91 (ii)
Mallick, S	Port Elizabeth	1890/91 (i)
Mannor, S[10]	Claremont/Cape Town and CTU/CU	1889/90, 1890/91 (i), 1892/93 (ET), 1895/96
Marks, C	Port Elizabeth	1890/91 (i)
Marlie, N	Claremont	1892/93 (ET)
Martin, J	Kimberley	1895/96
Martin, S	Kimberley	1897/98
Martin, T	Kimberley/SAGC XI	1891/92
Martin, T	Johannesburg	1895/96
Mogamat, A	Kimberley	1891/92
Morest, J	Cape Town	1890/91 (ii)
Naderdien, [X]	Port Elizabeth	1890/91 (ii)
Nasierdien, [X]	Port Elizabeth	1890/91 (ii)
Nurjart, M	Kimberley	1897/98
Oxallic, M	Cape Town	1889/90
Palmer, J	Johannesburg	1889/90
Palmer, J	Kimberley/SAGC XI	1890/91 (ii), 1892/93, 1892/93 (ET)
Paule, M	Johannesburg	1889/90
Petersen, J	Cape Town	1892/93
Rasin, E	Port Elizabeth	1889/90
Regal, M	Kimberley	1895/96
Richards, F	Johannesburg	1892/93, 1892/93 (ET)
Rose, W	Port Elizabeth	1890/91 (i)
Ryloen, K	Port Elizabeth	1890/91 (ii)

Saban, A	Port Elizabeth	1890/91 (ii)
Saban, D	Cape Town	1889/90, 1890/91 (i)
Saban, H	Cape Town	1889/90, 1890/91 (i)
Sahadien, [X]	Claremont	1892/93 (ET)
Sakiem, E	Port Elizabeth	1889/90
Sakim, A	Port Elizabeth	1890/91 (i)
Salam, H	Claremont	1889/90
Salie, M	Johannesburg	1889/90
Salie, M	Johannesburg	1895/96
Salie, M	Kimberley/SAGC XI	1890/91 (ii), 1892/93, 1892/93 (ET)
Salie, N	Kimberley	1895/96
Salie, S	Cape Town	1889/90
Samar, A	Port Elizabeth	1889/90, 1890/91 (i)
Sampson, T	Kimberley	1895/96
Samsodien, A	Cape Town	1892/93
Samsodien, A	Johannesburg	1895/96
Samsodien, L	Cape Town/CTU & CU/SAGC XI	1889/90, 1890/91 (ii), 1891/92, 1895/96
Samsodien, M	Cape Town	1889/90
Samsodien, R	Cape Town/SAGC XI	1889/90, 1890/91 (ii), 1891/92
Samsodien, R	Claremont	1892/93 (ET)
Samsodien, S	Cape Town	1889/90
Samuel, G	Kimberley	1895/96
Satarr, L	Port Elizabeth	1890/91 (ii)
Savall, [X]	Johannesburg	1889/90
Schippers, J	Kimberley	1897/98
Schroeder, M	Kimberley	1897/98
Seldon, A	Kimberley	1895/96
Seyeifi, E	Port Elizabeth	1889/90
Sheldon, J[11]	Kimberley	1890/91 (ii), 1891/92, 1892/93, 1892/93 (ET)
Shelton, [X]	Cape Town	1890/91 (i)
Slamang, M	Cape Town	1895/96
Souk, A	Port Elizabeth	1890/91 (ii)
Souk, M	Port Elizabeth	1890/91 (ii)
Stemmet, E	Claremont	1889/90, 1892/93 (ET)
Stephanus, J	Cape Town	1890/91 (ii)
Stephanus, M	Cape Town	1890/91 (ii)
Stokes, [X]	Johannesburg	1889/90, 1892/93
Tape, G	Cape Town	1890/91 (i)
Tape, [X]	Johannesburg	1889/90
Thomas, K	Port Elizabeth	1890/91 (ii)
Van der Schyff, B	Claremont/CTU & CU Cape Town	1889/90, 1890/91 (i), 1897/98
Vogt, J	Kimberley/SAGC XI	1890/91 (i), 1890/91 (ii), 1891/92
Williams, L	Johannesburg	1895/96
Williams, M	Kimberley	1892/93, 1892/93 (ET)

15.3   SUMMARISED SCORECARDS OF THE INTER-TOWN TOURNAMENTS, 1875/76–1897/98

1875/76

1st CHAMPION BAT TOURNAMENT, 6–12 JANUARY 1876, PORT ELIZABETH[12]
Participating teams: Cape Town, Grahamstown, King William's Town, Port Elizabeth
Winners: King William's Town.

Grahamstown beat Port Elizabeth by 47 runs, 6 January 1876
Grahamstown 54 (T Clough 12; E Renny-Tailyour 5/32, HP Bailey 4/16) and 47 (J Graham 8; JG Mackenzie 4/7, HP Bailey 4/10)
PE 32 (H Giesen 8; A Edkins 5/11, T Clough 5/11) and 22 (P Heugh 7; T Clough 5/5, A Edkins 4/11)

King William's Town beat Grahamstown by 6 wickets, 7 January 1876
Grahamstown 90 (A Edkins 28; W Heugh 7/34) and 69 (J Graham 19; A Blaine 3/14)
KWT 59 (A Blaine 13; A Edkins 8/32) and 102 for 4 ([X] Gillman 35*; A Edkins 2/49)

King William's Town beat Port Elizabeth by 3 wickets, 8 January 1876
PE 61 (HP Bailey 12; [X] Phillips 4/24, [X] Gillman 4/26) and 55 (HP Bayley 18; [X] Phillips 5/21, W Heugh 3/14)
KWT 84 (W Heugh 37; JG Mackenzie 4/15) and 42 for 7 ([X] Gillman 16*; JG Mackenzie 2/12)

Cape Town beat Port Elizabeth by 3 wickets, 10 January 1876
PE 67 (P Heugh 11; [X] Melck 5/16, H van Reenen 5/23) and 89 (E Renny-Tailyour 26, HP Bayley 18; [X] Melck 7/24)
Cape Town 89 (Lt Curteis 22; H Giesen 6/35) and 69 for 7 (H van Reenen 22; HP Bailey 2/6)

King William's Town beat Cape Town by 4 wickets, 11 January 1876
Cape Town 99 (Lt Curteis 30*; [X] Phillips 4/28) and 37 (H van Reenen 9; W Heugh 6/17)
KWT 80 (Lt Fownes 24; [X] Melck 6/19) and 59 for 6 ([X] Donoghue 12; [X] Melck 4/13)

Cape Town versus Grahamstown, 12 January 1876 (not played)
Replaced by Civilians vs Military 'extraneous match'.

Extraneous Match. Civilians beat Military by 88 runs on the first innings, 12 January 1876, Port Elizabeth
Civilians 133 (H Giesen 33, P van Breda 27, H van Reenen 15, Extras 25; H Bailey 6/32, [X] Phillips 1/27)
Military 45 (Lt Curteis 11, [X] Williams 7; E Renny-Tailyour 7/12, H van Reenen 1/20) and 37/4 (Lt Fownes 14*; E Renny-Tailyour 2/18, H Blaine 2/10)

1879/80

2nd CHAMPION BAT TOURNAMENT, 14–22 JANUARY 1880, KING WILLIAM'S TOWN[13]
Participating teams: Grahamstown, King William's Town, Port Elizabeth, Queenstown
Winners: King William's Town.

King William's Town beat Port Elizabeth by 5 wickets, 14–15 January 1880
PE 96 (A Jackson 37; RJ Dick 5/37) and 97 (OR Dunell 29; L Winslow 6/41)
KWT 155 (RB Stewart 52; BD Godlonton 6/47) and 40 for 5 (L Winslow 12*; J Singleton 3/12)

Queenstown beat Grahamstown by 9 wickets, 14–15 January 1880
Grahamstown 64 (LO Lloyd 17; G Barnes 4/[x]) and 66 ([X] Hopgood 21; G Barnes 6/[x])
Queenstown 98 (H Giesen 30; A Lawrence 4/[x]) and 34 for 1 (H Giesen 19)

Port Elizabeth beat Queenstown by 167 runs, 16–17 January 1880
PE 107 (E Renny-Tailyour 29; J Ridgeway 6/33) and 182 (E Renny-Tailyour 57, OR Dunell 47; J Ridgeway 3/38)
Queenstown 56 (C Bestall 8; J Singleton 6/19) and 66 (C Bestall 25; J Singleton 7/20)

Grahamstown beat King William's Town by an innings and 10 runs, 16–17 January 1880
KWT 94 (J Sheehan 28; R Solomon 4/[x], T Clough 4/[x]) and 113 (EH Dalgety 33*, T Clough 5/[x])
Grahamstown 217 ([X] Pattison 40, C Walker 39*; L Winslow 7/[x])

Port Elizabeth beat Grahamstown by 6 runs, 19–20 January 1880
PE 120 (H Parkin 19*; C Walker 4/34) and 100 (E Renny-Tailyour 36*; WM Hopley 5/38)
Grahamstown 86 (A Lawrence 13*; BD Godlonton 6/29) and 128 (T Calderwood 55; BD Godlonton 4/44)

King William's Town beat Queenstown by an innings and 15 runs, 19–20 January 1880
KWT 153 (RB Stewart 67; J Bulgin 5/[x])
Queenstown 47 (J Ridgeway 9, A Dell 9; L Winslow 9/[x]) and 91 (H Giesen 22; JR Couper 3/[x])

King William's Town beat Port Elizabeth by an innings and 110 runs, 21–22 January 1880
Port Elizabeth 50 (H Phillips 13; RJ Dick 5/[x], RB Stewart 5/[x]) and 62 (H Phillips 22; L Winslow 3/[x])
KWT 222 (RB Stewart 105, L Winslow 36; BD Godlonton 8/[x])

1884/85

3rd CHAMPION BAT TOURNAMENT, 22 DECEMBER 1884 – 1 JANUARY 1885, PORT ELIZABETH[14]
Participating teams: Cape Town, Kimberley, King William's Town, Port Elizabeth
Winners: Port Elizabeth.

Port Elizabeth beat King William's Town by 9 wickets, 22–23 December 1884
PE 216 (OR Dunell 78*, HH Webster 36; M Jennings 4/81) and 41/1 (P Heugh 23*)
KWT 131 (EP Schermbrucker 43, L Winslow 29; A Geard 5/30) and 124 (RB Stewart 66*; A Geard, 9/46)

Cape Town beat Kimberley by an innings and 71 runs, 23 December 1884
Cape Town 183 (JB van Reenen 40, J Molteno 31; CE Finlason 8/61)
Kimberley 64 (S Edkins 22; F Robb 4/4, CH Vintcent 4/25) and 48 (CE Finlason 19; CH Vintcent 6/22)

Port Elizabeth beat Kimberley by 4 wickets, 26–27 December 1884
Kimberley 75 (FW Smith 19; A Geard 6/30) and 163 (AB Tancred 33; A Geard 5/52)
PE 165 (RW Stevens 39, E Budler 34; CE Finlason 8/45) and 74/6 (P Heugh 23; AB Tancred 2/9)

Cape Town beat King William's Town by 179 runs, 27 and 29 December 1884
Cape Town 176 (EJ Stradling 55*, CH Vintcent 36; E Benton 5/69) and 225 (CR Vaughan 68, ES Steytler 41; E Benton 6/61)
KWT 125 (RB Stewart 61; CH Vintcent 4/32) and 97 (R Keane 44; CH Vintcent 4/32)

King William's Town beat Kimberley by an innings and 33 runs, 30–31 December 1884
KWT 170 (RB Stewart 69, EP Schermbrucker 42; AB Tancred 6/68)
Kimberley 52 (WS Woodthorpe 19*; E Benton 5/23) and 85 (WS Woodthorpe 32; E Benton 4/36, L Winslow 4/45)

Port Elizabeth beat Cape Town by 4 wickets, 31 December 1884 – 1 January 1885
Cape Town 35 ES Steytler 9; A Geard 6/6) and 186 (WHM Richards 46, EJ Stradling 30; HH Webster 5/51)
PE 203 (OR Dunell 71, H Giesen 47; CH Vintcent 4/64) and 21/6 (S Giddy 4/8)

* * * * *

1st NATIVE INTER-TOWN TOURNAMENT, DECEMBER 1884 – JANUARY 1885, GRAHAMSTOWN[15]
Participating teams: East London, Grahamstown, King William's Town, Port Elizabeth
Winners: King William's Town.

King William's Town (Champion CC) beat East London (Gaika CC) by an innings and 13 runs
KWT 38 ([X] Nkole 13, A Ngcumbe 11; D Soga 5/[x], [X] Malgas 3/[x])
EL 15 (A Ngcumbe 7/[x], N Bovana 3/[x]) and 10 (N Bovana 5/[x], A Ngcumbe 4/[x], J Sidayiya 1/[x])

King William's Town (Champion CC) beat Grahamstown (Fear Not CC) by 3 wickets
Grahamstown 33 ([X] Mfamana 12, [X] Dlepu 6; A Ngcumbe 7/[x], N Bovana 3/[x]) and 53 ([X] Macumela 18, [X] Dlepu 11; N Bovana 7/[x], A Ngcumbe 2/[x], WN Seti 1/[x])
KWT 50 (N Bovana 12, A Ngcumbe 10*, NC Umhalla 6; [X] Danga 4/[x], [X] Badisi 3/[x]) and 37/7 (J Sidayiya 20, [X] Danga 5/[x])

King William's Town (Champion CC) beat Port Elizabeth (Ethiopian CC) by 6 wickets
PE 27 (K Bopi 6, J Morley 5, GA Ross 5; A Ngcumbe 7/[x], N Bovana 3/[x]) and 59 (GA Ross 39, RZ Christian 8; A Ngcumbe 8/[x], N Bovana 2/[x])
KWT 67 (NC Umhalla 18, A Ngcumbe 15, [X] Nozwane 15*; GA Ross 6/[x], B Swartboy 2/[x]) and 20/4 (H Pezisa 3/[x], GA Ross 1/[x])

1885/86

2nd NATIVE INTER-TOWN TOURNAMENT, DECEMBER 1885 – JANUARY 1886, PORT ELIZABETH[16]
Participating teams: Grahamstown, King William's Town, Port Elizabeth
Winners: Port Elizabeth.

Port Elizabeth beat Grahamstown by 9 runs
PE 51 (E Ngcoza 10, MD Foley 10; L Frielander 5/[x], H May 4/[x]) and 29 (L Frielander 3/[x], H May 3/[x], T Gule 3/[x])
Grahamstown 45 (T Gule 23; F Makwena 6/[x], GA Ross 3/[x]) and 26 (F Makwena 7/[x], GA Ross 3/[x])

Port Elizabeth beat King William's Town by 2 wickets
KWT 30 (J Soga 10; MD Foley 8/[x]) and 54 (N Zondani 11, W Ganya 9; F Makwena 5/[x], K Bopi 3/[x])
PE 52 (F Makwena 17, MD Foley 9, GA Ross 9, C Bali 4/[x], A Ngcumbe 3/[x]) and 33/8 (A Mabope 11, S Boyce 5; C Bali 3/[x], A Ngcumbe 2/[x], W Bovana 2/[x])

1886/87

3rd NATIVE INTER-TOWN TOURNAMENT, 27 DECEMBER 1886 – 6 JANUARY 1887, KING WILLIAM'S TOWN[17]
Participating teams: East London, Grahamstown, King William's Town, Port Elizabeth, Queenstown
Winners: King William's Town.

King William's Town beat Queenstown by 10 wickets
KWT 77 (WN Seti 19*, W Ganya 15, [X] Zondani 11; [X] Lutu 6/[x], [X] Nongalaza 3/[x]) and 3 for 0
Queenstown 35 ([X] Kinner 8; A Ngcumbe 5/[x], [X] Butler 5/[x]) and 43 ([X] Ngece 16; A Ngcumbe 3/[x], J Sidayiya 2/[x], [X] Zondani 2/[x], EB Soga 2/[x])

Grahamstown beat East London by an innings and 105 runs
Grahamstown 131 (T Gule 43, H May 22, H Mdunyelwa 18; [X] Thomas 3/[x], D Soga 3/[x], S Mdana 2/[x])
EL 11 ([X] Draai, 3; H May 4/[x], T Gule 4/[x]) and 15 ([X] Siyeka 8; H May 6/[x], T Gule 3/[x])

East London beat Queenstown by 5 wickets
EL 63 ([X] Mcanyangwa 32; [X] Lutu 3/[x], [X] Mapikela 2/[x], [X] Nongalaza 2/[x]) and 20/5 (D Soga 10*; [X] Lutu 3/[x])
Queenstown 21 ([X] Legalagala 6; D Soga 5/[x]) and 61 ([X] Mapikela 10; D Soga 5/[x])

King William's Town beat Port Elizabeth by 36 runs
KWT 40 (WN Seti 19; [X] Qoqo 6/[x], K Bopi 3/[x]) and 79 (WN Seti 27, [X] Butler 22; [X] Qoqo 4/[x], RZ Christian 3/[x])
PE 34 ([X] Balfour 7; [X] Butler 5/[x]) and 49 (P Xiniwe 11, [X] Tshona 10; C Bali 4/[x], J Sidayiya 3/[x])

Grahamstown beat Queenstown by an innings and 60 runs
Grahamstown 141 (H May 45, T Gule 20; [X] Lutu 5/[x], [X] Nongalaza 3/[x])
Queenstown 30 ([X] Legalagala 8, T Gule 4/[x], H May 4/[x]) and 51 ([X] Legalagala 26; H May 6/[x], T Gule 2/[x])

Port Elizabeth beat East London by 16 runs
PE 44 (S Boyce 21; D Soga 6/[x], [X] Landule 3/[x]) and 55 (P Xiniwe 23; D Soga 6/[x], [X] Landule 2/[x])
EL 43 ([X] Mcanyangwa 10, [X] Jacob 10; [X] Qoqo 6/[x], K Bopi 4/[x]) and 40 ([X] Holmes 23; [X] Qoqo 4/[x], K Bopi 3/[x])

King William's Town beat Grahamstown by an innings and 1 run
KWT 54 (S Nini 11*, J Xelo 10; T Gule 5/[x], H May 4/[x])
Grahamstown 18 (J Faku 4; [X] Zondani 4/[x], C Bali 4/[x], D Thomas 2/[x]) and 35 (H Maqanda 13; C Bali 4/[x], [X] Butler 3/[x])

Port Elizabeth beat Grahamstown by 25 runs
PE 105 (S Boyce 32, RZ Christian 15, B Balfour 13; T Gule 4/[x], H May 4/[x]) and 17 (K Bopi 7; H Peters 5/[x], H May 3/[x])
Grahamstown 63 (W Nombewu 25, [x] 18; K Bopi 5/[x], [X] Qoqo 4/[x]) and 34 ([X] Qoqo 6/[x], K Bopi 3/[x])

Combined Eastern Cape Inter-Town XI lost to 'English XI' (amaNgesi) by 9 wickets
Combined Eastern Cape Inter-Town XI 75 (WN Seti 33, H May 14; L Winslow 8/[x]) and 95 (EB Soga 22, J Sidayiya 13; [X] Simpson 3/[x], [X] Davies 3 [x])
'English XI' 135 (C Boyce 30*, CW Tully 26, L Winslow 21; EB Soga 4/[x], T Gule 4/[x], A Ngcumbe 1/[x], [X] Butler 1/[x] and 36/1 (H Smith 23; T Gule 1/[x])

* * * * *

EXTRANEOUS WHITE INTER-TOWN TOURNAMENT, 11–22 APRIL 1887, KIMBERLEY[18]
Participating teams: Bechuanaland, Kimberley, Natal, Port Elizabeth
Winners: Kimberley.

Kimberley beat Port Elizabeth by an innings and 37 runs, 11–12 April 1887
PE 37 (IR Grimmer 7/20, CE Finlason 3/17) and 70 (F McKeating 35; CE Finlason 4/33, IR Grimmer 2/25, CC Perring 2/8)
Kimberley 144 (IR Grimmer 50, FW Smith 26, PH de Villiers 20; S Dold 3/46, A Rose-Innes 5/64)

Natal beat Bechuanaland by an innings and 17 runs, 12–13 April 1887
Ntl 255 (FF Crawford 90, DC Davey 82; [X] Geard 2/39, [X] Mann 2/14)
Bechuanaland 61 (R Nicholson 5/35, M Hime 4/22) and 177 (J Vintcent 57, [X] Rennie 22, [X] Reid 20; M Hime 6/88, R Nicholson 2/56)

Port Elizabeth beat Bechuanaland by 4 wickets, 14–15 April 1887
Bechuanaland 55 (A Rose-Innes 4/22, S Dold 4/28) and 160 ([X] McCallum 57, [X] Walker 28; A Rose-Innes 6/41, S Dold 4/71)
PE 127 (F McKeating 43, CE Britton 30; [X] Wishart 5/17, CH Vintcent 1/28) and 89/6 (CE Britton 31; [X] Wishart 4/23)

Kimberley beat Natal by 9 wickets, 17–18 April 1887
Ntl 109 (WW Edwards 49; CE Finlason 4/31, IR Grimmer 3/55) and 64 (FF Crawford 23; IR Grimmer 5/25, CE Finlason 3/11)
Kimberley 105 (FG Klinck 26, CE Finlason 23; Dr [X] Tarleton 4/38) and 70/1 (AB Tancred 45*)

Port Elizabeth beat Natal by an innings and 108 runs, 19–20 April 1887
Ntl 123 (R Nicholson 33, WW Edwards 29; A Rose-Innes 4/37, BS Wimble 2/13, HH Webster 2/18, S Dold 2/47) and 136 (Dr [X] Tarleton 56*, M Hime 28; A Rose-Innes 4/33, BS Wimble 4/35)
PE 367 (J Jackson 97, BS Wimble 83*, AH Britton 37, E Ogden 36; J Hendry 4/58, Dr [X] Tarleton 2/45, WW Edwards 2/48)

Kimberley beat Bechuanaland by 7 wickets, 21–22 April 1887
Bechuanaland 175 ([X] McCullum 37, CH Vintcent 46, [X] Rennie 25; CE Finlason 3/46, IR Grimmer 2/60, CC Perring 2/26, AB Tancred 2/21) and 143 (CH Vintcent 35, J Vintcent 35*; [X] McCullum 29; CE Finlason 4/53, IR Grimmer 4/58)
Kimberley 203 (AB Tancred 56, WS Woodthorpe 36, TJ Dixon 31; [X] Lochner 3/18, [X] Dannett 3/41) and 119/3 (TJ Dixon 67*, FW Smith 27*; [X] Lochner 2/13)

1887/88

4th CHAMPION BAT TOURNAMENT, 26 DECEMBER 1887 – 3 JANUARY 1888, GRAHAMSTOWN[19]
Participating teams: Grahamstown, Kimberley, King William's Town, Port Elizabeth
Winners: Kimberley.

Port Elizabeth beat King William's Town by 170 runs, 26–27 December 1887
PE 129 (HH Webster 39, F McKeating 31; HL Davies 6/36) and 203 (OR Dunell 88*, AH Britton 44; C Nash 6/65)
KWT 67 (SJH Bayly 23; A Rose-Innes 6/46) and 95 (LL Giddy 20; BS Wimble 6/12)

Kimberley beat Grahamstown by an innings and 141 runs, 26–28 December 1887
Grahamstown 30 (SH Barber 11; IR Grimmer 5/[x]) and 65 (AG Leach 17; CH Vintcent 5/[x])
Kimberley 236 (AB Tancred 54, IR Grimmer 37; HO Dold 2/[x], AW Seccull 2/[x])

Kimberley beat King William's Town by an innings and 75 runs, 28–29 December 1887
KWT 37 (N Porter 9; IR Grimmer 6/18, CH Vintcent 4/13) and 20 (LL Giddy 7; CH Vintcent 6/10, IR Grimmer 4/9)
Kimberley 132 (FG Klinck 36, CE Finlason 36; L Winslow 4/[x])

Grahamstown beat Port Elizabeth by 98 runs, 28–29 December 1887
Grahamstown 162 (EH Buckland 97; A Rose-Innes 5/[x]) and 86 (AW Seccull 24; SH Barber 9/[x])
PE 98 (F McKeating 35; SH Barber 6/[x]) and 52 (OR Dunell 18; SH Barber 9/[x])

Kimberley beat Port Elizabeth by 187 runs, 29–31 December 1887
Kimberley 135 (PH de Villiers 28; H Parkin 3/[x], BS Wimble 3/[x]) and 208 (AB Tancred 48, WS Woodthorpe 40; AH Britton 3/[x])
PE 96 (OR Dunell 25; CH Vintcent 7/[x]) and 60 (OR Dunell 15; IR Grimmer 5/[x])

King William's Town beat Grahamstown by 8 runs, 2–3 January 1888
KWT 62 (LL Giddy 22; SH Barber 5/[x]) and 116 (SJH Bayly 55; SH Barber 4/[x])
Grahamstown 96 (EH Buckland 47; L Winslow 4/[x]) and 74 (LO Lloyd 24; L Winslow 3/[x], HL Davies 3/[x])

1888/89

No official Inter-Town tournaments in this season

1889/90

1st MALAY INTER-TOWN TOURNAMENT, 13–27 JANUARY 1890, CAPE TOWN[20]

Participating teams: Cape Town, Claremont, Johannesburg, Port Elizabeth
Winners: Cape Town.

Port Elizabeth beat Cape Town by 3 wickets, 13–14 January 1890
Cape Town 83 (L Samsodien 29; [X] Ajoep 6/20, L Fredericks 4/35) and 52 (L Samsodien 10; [X] Ajoep 5/20, L Fredericks 2/20, G Fredericks 3/11)
PE 57 (L Fredericks 18; G Jakoef, 5/19, [X] Aijahn 3/18, L Samsodien 2/8) and 80/7 (H Astril 25*, L Fredericks 22; G Jakoef 2/42, L Samsodien 2/12)

Claremont beat Johannesburg by 2 wickets, 14–15 January 1890
Johannesburg 64 (J Palmer 18, A Hendricks 13; E Adams 5/28, [X] Abdol 2/22, H Abrahams 3/13) and 102 (A Laran 22, [X] Eachmat 33; W Abrahams 5/26, E Adams 2/34)
Claremont 21 (B van der Schyff 9*, S Manor 5; [X] Eachmat 4/9 A Hendricks 4/11) and 150/8 (H Abrahams 50*, E Adams 46; [X] Eachmat 4/68, A Hendricks 2/56)

Claremont drew with Port Elizabeth, 20 January 1890
Claremont 71 (W Abrahams 42; L Fredericks 5/19, [X] Ajoep 4/30) and 124 (E Adams 83, S Mannor 13; [X] Ajoep 3/45, L Fredericks 4/29)
PE 41 (G Fredericks 16, H Astrie 8; [X] Abdol 7/14, E Adams 3/25) and 42/6 (E Kasseim 16; E Adams 1/5, E Stemmet 4/21)

Cape Town beat Johannesburg by 2 runs, 21 January 1890
Cape Town 50 (E Ariefdien 16; A Achmat 4/23, A Hendricks 2/24) and 86 (L Samsodien 28; A Hendricks 5/25, M Salie 4/29)
Johannesburg 111 ([X] Abdol 29, M Salie 18, [X] Tape 17; E Ariefdien 5/27, G Jacoef 3/51, S Samsodien 2/22) and 23 ([X] Stokes 10; E Ariefdien 5/6, L Samsodien 5/16)

Cape Town and Claremont beat Port Elizabeth and Johannesburg on the first innings by 36 runs, 27 January 1890
Cape Town and Claremont 126 (B van der Schyff 30, E Adams 27, W Abrahams 18; A Achmat 4/24, L Fredericks 2/24, [X] Ajoep 2/30, A Hendricks 2/39) and 94/7 (H Abrahams 34, L Samsodien 30; G Fredericks 6/15)
Port Elizabeth and Johannesburg 90 (L Fredericks 39, G Fredericks 13; E Ariefdien 9/28, J Hendricks 1/18)

1890/91

5th CHAMPION BAT TOURNAMENT, 26 DECEMBER 1890 – 23 JANUARY 1891, CAPE TOWN[21]

Participating teams: Eastern Province, Griqualand West, Western Province
Winners: Western Province.

Western Province beat Eastern Province by and innings and 145 runs, 26–27 December 1890
EP 160 (DC Parkin 63*, BS Wimble 37; JS de Villiers 5/50, VAW van der Bijl 2/40) and 104 (BS Wimble 37, DG Proudfoot 26; WH Ashley 4/21; WH Milton 4/29)
WP 409 (HH Castens 165, CS Hickley 45, AE Cox 56; DG Proudfoot 3/64, DC Parkin 3/113)

Eastern Province beat Griqualand West by 20 runs, 29–30 December 1890
EP 150 (LL Giddy 42, DC Parkin 25, BS Wimble 20; GK Glover 3/48, AE Cooper 3/31, CE Finlason 2/20) and 150 (CE Britton 35, F McKeating 34, FS Turberville 22; GK Glover 4/37, CE Finlason 4/37)
GW 208 (E Beech 111, AWP Walshe 24; BS Wimble 5/77, DC Parkin 4/69) and 72 (DC Parkin 6/25, BS Wimble 4/47)

Western Province beat Griqualand West by 83 runs, 1–3 January 1891
WP 111 (AE Cox 24; AE Cooper 4/37, AWP Walshe 5/18) and 236 (F Hearne 55, AE Cox 48, PH de Villiers 51; GK Glover 4/60, CE Finlason 3/50)
GW 139 (CE Finlason 46, AB Tancred 20; VAW van der Bijl 6/56, J Middleton 3/43) and 125 (GHS Lovell 26, C Glover 23; VAW van der Bijl 3/36, PH de Villiers 3/41, WH Ashley 2/22)

* * * * *

4th NATIVE INTER-TOWN TOURNAMENT, [XX] DECEMBER 1890 – 3 JANUARY 1891, PORT ELIZABETH[22]

Participating teams: King William's Town, Port Elizabeth, Kimberley [Rest unknown – only the 'final match of the series' reported]
Winners: Port Elizabeth.

Port Elizabeth beat King William's Town by 20 runs, 3 January 1891
PE 46 (RZ Christian 15, Z Thomas 11, CN Bopi 8/[x], C Bali 3/[x]) and 59 (DJ Kadi 19, Z Thomas 14, CN Bopi 4/[x], C Bali 2/[x], A Ngcumbe 2/[x])

KWT 61 (J Sadayiya 13, P Xiniwe 9*, E Ngcoza 6/[x], GA Ross 3/[x]) and 24 (N Zondani 7*, MD Foley 5/[x], E Ngcoza 3/[x])

* * * * *

2nd MALAY INTER-TOWN TOURNAMENT, 2–10 JANUARY 1891, UITENHAGE[23]
Participating teams: Cape Town, Kimberley, Port Elizabeth, Uitenhage
Winners: Kimberley.

Cape Town beat Port Elizabeth by 16 runs, 2 January 1891
CT 35 (G Fredricks 6/12, W Rose 3/9) and 43 ([X] Hajup 5/18, W Rose 3/3)
PE 41 (J Burness 15, C Marks 10; [X] Abdol 6/16) and 21 (B van der Schyff 6/5, W Abrahams 3/3)

Kimberley beat Uitenhage by an innings and 77 runs, 4 January 1891
KBY 128
Uitenhage 24 and 27

Kimberley beat Port Elizabeth by 3 wickets, 6 January 1891
PE 49 and 60
KBY 62 and 48/7

Cape Town beat Uitenhage by 106 runs, 7 January 1891
CT 102 and 77
Uitenhage 34 and 39

Cape Town declared winners against Kimberley, who 'refused to play the match out', 8 January 1891
KBY 61 ([X] Jamiedien 19, R Grendon 11) and 97
CT 54 ([X] Adams 15, [X] Shelton 11, N Andrianse 9)

Final match: Port Elizabeth vs Uitenhage, 10 January 1891
[Details unknown]

* * * * *

3rd MALAY INTER-TOWN TOURNAMENT (1st FOR GLOVER CUP), 30 MARCH – 9 APRIL 1891, KIMBERLEY[24]
Participating teams: Cape Town, Kimberley, Port Elizabeth
Winners: Kimberley.

Kimberley beat Port Elizabeth by an innings and 80 runs
PE 28 (M Souk 14; A Hendricks 6/9, R Grendon, 4/19) and 63 (K Thomas 25, A Souk 13; A Hendricks 7/33, R Grendon 3/30)
Kimberley 171/4 dec (R Grendon 80*, J Vogt 52; M Madatt 2/81)

Cape Town beat Port Elizabeth by an innings and 62 runs
PE 50 (J Adams 19; E Ariefdien 10/18) and 63 (J Adams 21, A Souk 19; E Ariefdien 4/20, R Abrams 3/10)
Cape Town 175/6 dec (E Abrams 91, E Ariefdien 54; M Souk 6/15, [X] Nasierdien 3/38)

Final: Kimberley beat Cape Town by 7 wickets
Kimberley 191 (R Grendon 111, M Salie 34, A Hendricks 12; E Ariefdien 7/65, L Samsodien 2/22) and 78/3 (M Salie 35*, J Sheldon 21, R Grendon 12; E Ariefdien 2/34, J Stephanus 1/22)
Cape Town 104 (R Samsodien 34, E Abrams 25; A Hendricks 7/38) and 160 (E Abrams 70*, E Ariefdien 22, L Samsodien 16, J Morest 16; R Grendon 3/45, A Hendricks 3/62, A Adams 2/18)

South African Glover Cup XI drew with Kimberley 'Europeans', 9 April 1891, Eclectic Ground, Kimberley
South African Glover Cup XI 97 (R Grendon 30, E Abrams 17, A Hendricks 17, E Arifdien 15*; IR Grimmer 7/39, H Ford 2/29) and 217/7 (R Grendon 92, L Samsodien 45, E Abrams 24, J Vogt 24, E Ariefdien 21*; H Ford 4/29, IR Grimmer 2/57, F Glover 1/44)
Kimberley 'Europeans' 197/6 dec (A Bennitte 69, F Glover 61, RCD Snedden 40*; A Hendricks 4/72, E Ariefdien 1/47, R Grendon 1/47)

1891/92

4th MALAY INTER-TOWN TOURNAMENT FOR GLOVER CUP, 28–30 DECEMBER 1891, KIMBERLEY[25]
Participating teams: Cape Town, Kimberley (Red Crescent CC)
Winners: Cape Town.

Cape Town beat Kimberley by 9 wickets, 28–29 December 1891, Pirates Ground
Kimberley 41 (M Adams 11, R Grendon 8, E Ariefdien 6/13, H Hendricks 4/24) and 91 (R Grendon 24, J Vogt 17, E Abrams 13, A Mogamat 10; H Hendricks 6/39, L Samsodien 2/13, MG Kassiem 1/23)

Cape Town 106 (E Ariefdien 26, A Samsodien 16, R Samsodien 14, MG Kassiem 11; E Abrams 4/22, J Sheldon 3/15, M Adams 2/25, R Grendon 1/12) and 28/1(C Leach 11, E Ariefdien 8*; M Adams 1/16)

SA Glover Cup XI drew with S Powell's Team, 30 December 1891, Eclectic Ground, Kimberley
Combined Glover Cup XI 260 (R Grendon 187, K du Toit 28, R Samsodien 27*; F Bryant 8/87, C Glover 1/63)
S Powell's Team 123/6 (RCS Snedden 40, C Glover 34, E Glover 30; T Martin, 2/34, E Abrams 1/15, M Adams 1/20, R Grendon 2/47)

1892/93

5th NATIVE INTER-TOWN TOURNAMENT, 26 DECEMBER 1892 TO 3 JANUARY 1893, VICTORIA GROUNDS, KING WILLIAM'S TOWN[26]
Participating teams: East London, Kimberley, King William's Town, Queenstown, Uitenhage
Winners: Uitenhage.

King William's Town beat East London by 8 wickets, 26 December 1892
KWT 95 (P Xiniwe 29, A Ngcumbe 14, [X] Nqini 3/[x], [X] Muleka 2/[x]) and 18/2
EL 43 (H Mcanyangwa [x]*, A Ngcumbe 4/[x], CN Bopi 3/[x]) and 69 ([X] Matross 19, [X] Muleka 13, [X] Ngqaka 11*, A Ngcumbe 7/[x])

Kimberley beat Queenstown by 4 wickets, 27 December 1892
Queenstown 43 ([X] Shelton 5/[x], T Gula 2/[x]) and [x] ([X] Mpaki 10; [X] Mondel 4/[x], [X] Ngcoza 4/[x])
Kimberley 50 ([X] Mondel 19, J Msengana 6/[x]) and 28 for 6 ([X] Mapikela 2/[x])

Uitenhage beat East London by [x], 28 December 1892
Uitenhage 96 ([X] Macumela 34, [X] Latola 27; [X] Mcanyangwa 5/[x], [X] Makambi 2/[x]) and 61/9 ([X] Tisana 27*, [X] Macumela 20, [X] Matross 4/[x], [X] Mcanyangwa 3/[x])
EL 32 ([X] Zwaartbooi 11, [X] Dlamini 4/[x], [X] Latola 3/[x]) and 136 (H Mcanyangwa 45, [X] Matross 24, [X] Lutu 3/[x], [X] Latola 2/[x], [X] Dlamini 2/[x])

King William's Town beat Queenstown by 7 wickets, 28 December 1892
Queenstown 42 ([X] Rhabula 11, CN Bopi 3/[x]) and 33 ([X] Xinishe 7*, A Ngcumbe 6/[x], CN Bopi 2/[x])
KWT 71 (CN Bopi 15, [X] Nobatana 11, C Mphahlele 3/[x], J Msengana 2/[x]) and 11/3 ([X] Mpaki 2/[x])

Uitenhage beat Kimberley by 6 wickets, 29 December 1892
Kimberley 10 ([X] Dlamini 6/[x], [X] Macumela 2/[x]) and 63 ([X] Mzini 21, [X] Shelton 8, [X] Dlamini 7/[x])
Uitenhage 63 ([X] Mondel 17, [X] Katyana 13*, [X] Tisana 12, [X] Ngcoza 4/[x], [X] Shelton 4/[x], and 11/4 ([X] Mzini 2/[x])

East London beat Queenstown by [x], 30 December 1892
Queenstown 63 and 43
EL 61 and 41/[x]

Uitenhage beat King William's Town by 8 runs, 31 December 1892
Uitenhage 55 and 87
KWT 74 ([X] Rune 27, [X] Ngxoweni 22, [X] Dlamini 2/[x]) and 60 (RZ Haya 10*, J Barnabas 12, A Ngcumbe 11, [X] Dlamini 2/[x])

Kimberley beat East London by 1 run, 1 January 1893
Kimberley 90 ([X] Mondel 23, [X] Mzini 15, [J or W] Matayo 10) and 50 ([J or W] Matayo 14, [X] Mhlabi 12)
EL 73 ([X] Matross 20, H Mcanyangwa 17, [X] Muleka 17) and 66

Uitenhage beat Queenstown, 2 January 1893
Match forfeited

King William's Town beat Kimberley by 94 runs, 2–3 January 1893
KWT 95 (P Xiniwe 18, J Barnabas 15*, T Gula 5/[x], [X] Ngcoza 2/[x]) and 81/4 dec ([X] Nobatana 24, P Xiniwe 23, N Zondani 13*)
Kimberley 51 (W Matayo 19, CN Bopi 7/[x], [X] Menze 2/[x]) and 31 ([X] Rune 5/[x], CN Bopi 4/[x])

* * * * *

5th MALAY INTER-TOWN TOURNAMENT FOR GLOVER CUP, 28 DECEMBER 1892 – 6 JANUARY 1892/93, CAPE TOWN CC GROUND, NEWLANDS, CAPE TOWN[27]
Participating teams: Cape Town, Johannesburg, Kimberley
Winners: Cape Town.

Cape Town beat Kimberley by 8 wickets, 28–29 December 1892, Cape Town CC Ground
Kimberley 33 (Armien Hendricks 10*; H 'Krom' Hendricks 5/8, E Ariefden 5/18) and 81 (Armien Hendricks 22; H 'Krom' Hendricks 6/36, E Ariefden 4/42)
Cape Town 59 (J Sheldon 9/25) and 59/2 (H 'Krom' Hendricks 24, S Magiet 17*)

Kimberley beat Johannesburg by an innings and 123 runs, 2–3 January 1893, Cape Town CC Ground
Kby 256 (E Abrams 137, J Sheldon 54, B Hendricks 32; B Butler 3/[x], C Bergman 2/[x])
Jhb 96 (W Cupido, [X] Stokes 19; M Williams 5/[x]) and 37 (M Williams 3/[x], R Grendon 7/x])

Cape Town beat Johannesburg by 112 runs, 5–6 January 1893, Cape Town CC Ground
CT 153 (K du Toit 38, C Leach 27, E Ariefdien 17, J Petersen 29*; C Bergman 3/[x], B Butler 2/[x], M Jabaar 2/[x], M Appollis 2/[x]) and 100 (C Bergman 4/[x])
Jhb 81 (M Dent 24, H Hendricks 5/[x], E Ariefdien 5/[x]) and 60 (H Hendricks 7/[x] and E Ariefdien 2/[x])

* * * * *

EXTRANEOUS MALAY INTER-TOWN TOURNAMENT, 9, 11 AND 16 JANUARY 1893, WESTERN PROVINCE CC GROUND, NEWLANDS, CAPE TOWN[28]
Participating teams: Claremont, Kimberley, Johannesburg
Winner: Unknown.

Kimberley beat Claremont by an innings and 31 runs, 9 January 1893, WPCC Newlands
Kimberley 151 (H Sheldon 45, E Abrams 52; E Adams 4/[x])
Claremont 40 ([X] Sahadien 11*; B Hendricks 7/[x], R Grendon 3/[x] and 70 (R Samsodien 19; JSheldon 3/[x])

Claremont vs Johannesburg, 11 or 16 January, 1893
[Details unknown]

1893/94

No official Inter-Town Tournaments in this season

1894/95

No official Inter-Town Tournaments in this season

1895/96

6th MALAY INTER-TOWN TOURNAMENT FOR GLOVER CUP, 4–9 JANUARY 1896, CAPE TOWN CC GROUND, NEWLANDS, CAPE TOWN[29]
Participating teams: Western Province/Cape Town), Johannesburg, Kimberley
Winners: Western Province/Cape Town.

Cape Town beat Johannesburg by an innings and 76 runs, 4–5 January 1896, Cape Town CC Ground, Newlands, Cape Town
Cape Town 241 (E Abrahams 46, A Hendricks 45, J Abrahams 3/38; E Adams 38, J Abrahams 2/35, T Martin 2/48)
Johannesburg 53 (A Samsodien 18, J Lennit 11; K du Toit 7/23, [X] Jamieldien 3/21) and 112 (M Salie 49, J Abrahams 29, T Martin 10; K du Toit 3/2, [X] Jamieldien 1/26)

Kimberley vs Johannesburg, 6–7 January 1898, Cape Town CC Ground, Newlands, Cape Town
[Details unknown]

Western Province beat Kimberley by an innings and 190 runs, 8–9 January 1896, Cape Town CC Ground, Newlands, Cape Town
WP 301 ([X] Achmat 73, A Hendricks 59, L Samsodien 37, K Hendricks 32, K du Toit 32; A Seldon 4/103, J Abdol 3/30)
Kby 32 ([X] Jamieldien 5/11, K du Toit 5/18) and 79 (A Hendricks 6/21, B Adams 3/11)

* * * * *

EXTRANEOUS NATIVE INTER-TOWN TOURNAMENT, 3–6 April 1896, VICTORIA GROUNDS, KING WILLIAM'S TOWN[30]
[No official Inter-Town tournaments in this season]
Participating teams: Port Elizabeth, King William's Town, Champion CC, Frontier CC
Winners: King William's Town.

Port Elizabeth beat Champion CC on the first innings, 3 April 1896
PE 147 (S Busakwe 42, A Ross 33, [X] Thomas 21, T Maloni 19; [X] Toise 4/[x], A Ngcumbe 2/[x], [X] Zondani 2/[x])
Champion CC 25 (W Toise 8; T Maloni 4/[x], [X] Kulati 3/[x]) and 68/2 (A Ngcumbe 33*, D Rune 21, ED Toise 12)

Port Elizabeth beat Frontier CC on the first innings, 4 April 1896
Frontier CC 75 (P Xiniwe 18, [X] Makonjwa 13, CN Bopi 13*; [X] Phu 4/[x], and 50/6 dec (P Xiniwe 23*, [X] Makonjwa 10; [X] Kulati 2/[x], S Busakwe 2/[x])
PE 85 ([X] Dalaza 30, T Maloni 19, [X] Thomas 15; S Magabela 4/[x], [X] Tshazibana 4/[x]) and 25/7 ([X] Dalaza 7; [X] Tshazibana 3/[x], S Magabela 2/[x])

King William's Town beat Port Elizabeth by 100 runs, 6 April 1896
KWT 52 (P Xiniwe 10, CN Bopi 10*, T Maloni 5/[x]) and 112 ([X] Tshazibana 57, FJ Bassie 24, P Xiniwe 12*; T Maloni 6/[x], [X] Kulati 2/[x])
PE 38 ([X] Ngeni 9; RZ Haya 4/[x], [X] Tshazibana 3/[x]) and 26 (T Maloni 7, [X] Tshazibana 4/[x], S Magabela 3/[x])

1896/97

EXTRANEOUS NATIVE INTER-TOWN TOURNAMENT, 1–[X] JANUARY 1897, PORT ELIZABETH/UITENHAGE[31] [No official Inter-Town Tournaments in this season]
Participating teams: Port Elizabeth, King William's Town, Uitenhage, Port Elizabeth 2nds
Winners: Uitenhage.

King William's Town beat Port Elizabeth by 33 runs
KWT 139 (W Mtshutshisa 59, W Toise 14, RZ Haya 13, CN Bopi 11; E Ngcoza 3/[x], MD Foley 3/[x], T Maloni 2/[x], A Ross 1/[x]) and 69 (FJ Bassie 23*, CN Bopi 14, ED Toise 13, E Ngcoza 5/[x], MD Foley 3/[x])
PE 87 (A Ross 32, DJ Kadi 16; S Magabela 3/[x], RZ Haya 2[x]) and 88 (CN Bopi 4/[x], S Magabela 3/[x])

King William's Town beat Port Elizabeth 2nds on first innings
PE 20 ([X] Mcilongo 8; D Rune 6/[x], CN Bopi 2/[x])
KWT 78 (D Rune 31, W Toise 19; W Mtshatshisa 4/[x], C Yutu 4/[x])

Uitenhage beat King William's Town on first innings
KWT 65 (D Rune 24, P Xiniwe 15, FJ Bassie 14; [X] Latola 3/[x], [X] Macumela 3/[x], [X] Mbedu 3/[x]) and 89 (FJ Bassie 36, RZ Haya 17*, D Rune 14; [X] Mbedu 4/[x], [X] Dlamini 3/[x], [X] Latola 2/[x])
Uitenhage 101 ([X] Macumela 20, [X] Dolly 23, [X] Jafer 9; CN Bopi 3/[x], W Siyo 2/[x], S Magabela 2/[x]) and 51/8 ([X] Tisana 16*, [X] Macumela 15*, W Toise 6/[x])

1897/98

6th NATIVE INTER-TOWN TOURNAMENT (1st for JABAVU CUP), 27 DECEMBER 1897 – [X] JANUARY 1898, KING WILLIAM'S TOWN[32]
Participating teams: East London, King William's Town, Port Elizabeth, Queenstown
Winners: Port Elizabeth.

King William's Town beat East London by 99 runs, 27 December 1897
KWT 144 (FJ Bassie 40, S Magabela 28, ED Toise 13; E Kunene 5/[x], T Nqini 3/[x]) and 111 (ED Toise 41, J Menze 14, FJ Bassie 13; E Kunene 4/[x], W Qoqo 3/[x])
EL 96 (T Nqini 25*, W Qoqo 20, E Nobatana 13; S Magabela 5/[x], CN Bopi 3/[x]) and 60 (E Kunene 33*, S Baart 9; S Magabela 5/[x], CN Bopi 4/[x])

Port Elizabeth beat Queenstown by an innings and 68 runs, 28 December 1897
PE 146 (D Rune 41, N Mabelana 29, S Busakwe 26; C Mpahlele 3/[x], J Msengana 2/[x])
Queenstown 33 (A Mlungwana 12; R Haya 4/[x], T Maloni [Maloney] 3/[x]) and 45 (N Fobe 10, A Mlungwana 10; R Haya 4/[x], D Rune 3/[x], T Maloni 2/[x])

Queenstown beat East London by 82 runs, 29 December 1897
Queenstown 72 (A Mlungwana 28, C Mpahlele 9; E Kunene 6/[x], T Nqini 2/[x]) and 143 (W Fobe 30; R Abrams 29*, H Nkole 15; E Kunene 4/[x], T Nqini 2/[x]))
EL 61 (T Mkapa 20*, E Nobatana 13; J Msengana 4/[x], C Mpahlele 4/[x]) and 72 (W Qoqo 45, J Rashe 8; C Mpahlele 4/[x], J Msengana 2/[x])

Port Elizabeth beat East London by 5 wickets, 30–31 December 1897
EL 91 (S Baart, 43, W Qoqo 13; W Menze 7/[x]) and 88 (K Morley 22, F Ntinge 15, W Qoqo 20*; R Haya 4/[x], [X] Yobo 3/[x])
PE 146 (T Maloni 38, W Mtshatshisa 34; W Qoqo 3/[x], E Kunene 3/[x]) and 42/5 (T Dalaza 15*; W Qoqo 2/[x], E Kunene 2/[x])

King William's Town beat Queenstown by an innings and 9 runs, 31 December 1897
Queenstown 64 (A Mlungwana 37, G Magoda 18; S Magabela 5/[x], D Rune 2/[x]) and 97 (W Fobe 23; J Menze 6/[x], S Magabela 2/[x])
KWT 170 (FJ Bassie 82*, J Menze 11, CN Bopi 33; J Msengana 4/[x], W Fobe 2/[x])

Port Elizabeth beat King William's Town by 98 runs
PE 123 (D Rune 40, P Dalaza 25, T Nogwina 14; S Magabela 3/[x], H Bulcha 2/[x]) and 124 (N Mabelana 27, S Busakwe 18; H Bulcha 3/[x], S Magabela 3/[x], CN Bopi 2/[x])
KWT 97 (FJ Bassie 36, P Xiniwe 10*; A Ross 3/[x], D Rune 2/[x]) and 52 (T Makeke 11; A Ross 6/[x], T Nogwina 2/[x])

* * * * *

7th MALAY INTER-TOWN TOURNAMENT FOR GLOVER CUP, [X] December 1897 – [X] JANUARY 1898, 'THE NEWLANDSGROUND', Cape Town[33]
Participating teams: Cape Town, Kimberley [other participants unknown]
Winners: Kimberley.

Kimberley beat Cape Town by an innings and 80 runs, [X] January, 1898, 'the Newlands Ground', Cape Town
[Details unknown]

Postscript: The Native and Malay Inter-Town Tournaments were replaced as the premier domestic competition for black cricketers by the Barnato Memorial Trophy provincial tournaments from 1898/99. But the African tournaments contested between the major centres continued for several decades after 1897/98, remaining a feature of African cricket into the 1930s and beyond.

15.4   STATISTICAL OVERVIEW OF THE INTER-TOWN TOURNAMENTS, 1875/76–1898/99

15.4.1 WHITE INTER-TOWN TOURNAMENTS FOR THE CHAMPION BAT, 1875/76–1890/91

BATTING RECORDS
Three centuries were scored in 33 games.

HIGHEST INDIVIDUAL SCORES
1.   HH Castens 165, Western Province vs Eastern Province, 1890/91
2.   E Beech 111, Griqualand West vs Eastern Province, 1890/91
3.   RB Stewart 105, King William's Town vs Port Elizabeth, 1879/80
4.   J Jackson 97, Port Elizabeth vs Natal, 1886/87 (ET)
5.   EH Buckland 97, Grahamstown vs Port Elizabeth, 1887/88
6.   FF Crawford 90, Natal vs Bechuanaland, 1886/87 (ET)

HIGHEST TEAM TOTALS
1.   409, Western Province vs Eastern Province, 1890/91
2.   367, Port Elizabeth vs Natal, 1886/87 (ET)
3.   255, Natal vs Bechuanaland, 1886/87 (ET)
4.   236, Kimberley vs Grahamstown, 1887/88
5.   236, Western Province vs Griqualand West, 1890/91

HIGHEST TOTAL BY EACH TEAM
Bechuanaland 177, vs Natal, 1886/87 (ET)
Cape Town/WP 409, vs Eastern Province, 1890/91
Grahamstown 217, vs King William's Town, 1879/80
Kimberley/GW 236, vs Grahamstown, 1887/88
King William's Town 222, vs Port Elizabeth, 1879/80
Port Elizabeth/EP 367, vs Natal, 1886/87 (ET)
Natal 255, vs Bechuanaland, 1886/87 (ET)
Queenstown 98, vs Grahamstown, 1879/80

LOWEST TOTAL BY EACH TEAM
Bechuanaland 55, vs Port Elizabeth, 1886/87 (ET)
Cape Town/WP 35, vs Port Elizabeth, 1884/85
Grahamstown 30, vs Kimberley, 1887/88
Kimberley/GW 48, Cape Town, 1884/85
King William's Town 20, vs Kimberley, 1887/88
Port Elizabeth/EP 22, vs Grahamstown 1875/76
Natal 64, vs Kimberley, 1886/87 (ET)
Queenstown 47, vs King William's Town, 1879/80

BOWLING RECORDS
10 or more wickets were taken in a match 20 times in 33 games.

BEST BOWLING IN A MATCH
1.   14/76 (9/46 and 5/30), A Geard, Port Elizabeth vs King William's Town, 1884/85
2.   13/39 (6/19 and 7/20), J Singleton, Port Elizabeth vs Queenstown, 1879/80
3.   12/40 (5/16 and 7/24), [X] Melck, Cape Town vs Port Elizabeth, 1875/76
4.   11/82 (6/30 and 5/52), A Geard, Port Elizabeth vs Kimberley, 1884/85
5.   11/130 (5/69 and 6/61), E Benton, King William's Town vs Cape Town, 1884/85
6.   10/23 (4/13 and 6/10), CH Vintcent, Kimberley vs King William's Town, 1887/88*
7.   10/27 (6/18 and 4/9), IR Grimmer, Kimberley vs King William's Town, 1887/88*
8.   10/32 (6/19 and 4/13), [X] Melck, Cape Town vs King William's Town, 1875/76
9.   10/47 (4/25 and 6/22), CH Vintcent, Cape Town vs Kimberley, 1884/85
10.   10/63 (4/22 and 6/41), A Rose-Innes, Port Elizabeth vs Bechuanaland, 1886/87 (ET)
11.   10/73 (6/29 and 4/44), BD Godlonton, Port Elizabeth vs Grahamstown, 1879/80
12.   10/74 (8/45 and 2/29), CE Finlason, Kimberley vs Port Elizabeth, 1884/85

Note:
SH Barber took 6/[x] and 9/[x] for Grahamstown vs Port Elizabeth in totals of 98 and 52, 1887/88
A Rose-Innes took 5/[x] and 8/[x] for Port Elizabeth vs Grahamstown, 1887/88
CH Vintcent took 7/[x] and 4[x] for Kimberley vs Port Elizabeth, 1887/88
G Barnes took 4/[x] and 6/[x] for Queenstown vs Grahamstown in totals of 64 and 66, 1879/80

Also note*: The figures achieved by Vintcent and Grimmer were in the same match: their combined analysis was 20/50.
King William's Town was bowled out for 37 and 20.

BEST BOWLING IN AN INNINGS
1.   9/46, A Geard, Port Elizabeth vs King William's Town, 1884/85
2.   8/32, A Edkins, Grahamstown vs King William's Town, 1875/76
3.   8/45, CE Finlason, Kimberley vs Port Elizabeth, 1884/85
4.   8/61, CE Finlason, Kimberley vs Cape Town, 1884/85
5.   7/20, J Singleton, Port Elizabeth vs Queenstown, 1879/80
6.   7/20, IR Grimmer, Kimberley vs Port Elizabeth, 1884/85
7.   7/24, [X] Melck, Cape Town vs Port Elizabeth, 1875/76
8.   7/34, W Heugh, King William's Town vs Grahamstown, 1875/76
9.   6/6, A Geard, Port Elizabeth vs Cape Town, 1884/85
10.   6/12, BS Wimble, Port Elizabeth vs King William's Town, 1887/88
11.   6/17, W Heugh, King William's Town vs Cape Town, 1875/76
12.   6/18, IR Grimmer, Kimberley vs King William's Town, 1887/88*

Note:
L Winslow took 9/[x] for King William's Town vs Queenstown in a total of 47, 1879/80
SH Barber took 9/[x] for Grahamstown vs Port Elizabeth in a total of 52, 1887/88
BD Godlonton took 8/[x] for Port Elizabeth vs King William's Town in a total of 222, 1879/80
L Winslow took 8/[x] for King William's Town vs Queenstown in a total of 47, 1879/80
A Rose-Innes took 8/[x] for Port Elizabeth vs Grahamstown in a total of 86, 1887/88
CH Vintcent took 7/[x] for Kimberley vs Port Elizabeth in a total of 96, 1887/88
L Winslow took 7/[x] for King William's Town vs Grahamstown in a total of 217, 1879/80.

TEAM RECORDS

TEAM	PLAYED	WON	LOST
Bech/land	3	0	3
CT/WP	7	5	2
Gtn	8	3	5
KWT	13	8	5
Kby/GW	11	6	5
Natal	3	1	2
PE/EP	18	9	9
Qtn	3	1	2

Note: In one 'Extraneous Match', Civilians beat Military.

15.4.2 NATIVE INTER-TOWN TOURNAMENTS, (LATER) JABAVU CUP, 1884/85–1897/98

BATTING RECORDS
Twelve scores of 40 or more were scored in 30 games.

HIGHEST INDIVIDUAL SCORES
1. FJ Bassie 82*, King William's Town vs Queenstown, 1897/98
2. W Mtshutshisa 59, King William's Town vs Port Elizabeth, 1896/97 (ET)
3. [X] Tshazibana 57, King William's Town vs Port Elizbaeth, 1895/96 (ET)
4. H May 45, Grahamstown vs Queenstown, 1886/87
5. H Mcanyangwa 45, East London vs Uitenhage, 1892/93
6. W Qoqo 45, East London vs Queenstown, 1897/98
7. T Gule 43, Grahamstown vs East London, 1886/87
8. S Baart 43, East London vs Port Elizabeth, 1897/98*
9. D Rune 41, Port Elizabeth vs Queenstown, 1897/98
10. EP Toise 41, King William's Town vs East London, 1897/98
11. FJ Bassie 40, King William's Town vs East London, 1897/98
12. D Rune 40, Port Elizabeth vs King Williams' Town, 1897/98

Note*: Baart's 43 was scored in a total of 91.

HIGHEST TEAM TOTALS
1. 170, King William's Town vs Queenstown, 1897/98
2. 146, Port Elizabeth vs Queenstown, 1897/98; 146, Port Elizabeth vs East London, 1897/98
3. 144, King William's Town vs East London, 1897/98*
4. 143, Queenstown vs East London, 1897/98

Note*: King William's Town scored 111 in the second innings, proving conclusively that the pitches in 1897/98 must have been far better than at any previous tournaments. The tournament was named the Jabavu Cup in that year.

HIGHEST TOTAL BY EACH TEAM
East London 136, vs Uitenhage, 1892/93
Grahamstown 141, vs Queenstown, 1886/87
Kimberley 90, vs East London, 1892/93
King William's Town 170, vs Queenstown, 1897/98
Port Elizabeth 146, vs Queenstown, 1897/98; 146, vs East London 1897/98
Queenstown 143, vs East London, 1897/98
Uitenhage 101, vs King William's Town, 1896/97

LOWEST TOTAL BY EACH TEAM
East London 10, vs King William's Town, 1884/85
Grahamstown 18, vs King William's Town, 1886/87
Kimberley 10, vs Uitenhage, 1892/93
King William's Town 24, vs Port Elizabeth 1890/91
Port Elizabeth 17, vs Grahamstown, 1886/87
Queenstown 21, vs East London, 1886/87
Uitenhage 63, vs Kimberley, 1892/93

BOWLING RECORDS
10 or more wickets were taken in a match at least 16 times. (Records are not complete.)

BEST BOWLING IN A MATCH
1. 15/[x] (7/[x] in a total of 27 and 8/[x] in a total of 59), A Ngcumbe, King William's Town vs Port Elizabeth, 1884/85
2. 13/[x] (6/[x] in a total of 10 and 7/[x] in a total of 63), [X] Dlamini, Uitenhage vs Kimberley, 1892/93
3. 13/[x] (6/[x] in a total of 45 and 7/[x] in a total of 26), F Makwena, Port Elizabeth vs Grahamstown, 1885/86
4. 12/[x] (6/[x] in a total of 44 and 6/[x] in a total of 55), D Soga, East London vs Port Elizabeth, 1886/87
5. 12/[x] (8/[x] in a total of 46 and 4/[x] in a total of 59), C Bopi, King William's Town vs Port Elizabeth, 1890/91
6. 11/[x] (7[x] in a total of 15 and 4/[x] in a total of 10), A Ngcumbe, King William's Town vs East London, 1884/85
7. 11/[x] (4/[x] in a total of 43 and 7/[x] in a total of 60), A Ngcumbe, King William's Town vs East London, 1892/93
8. 11/[x] (7[x] in a total of 51 and 4/[x] in a total of 31), A Ngcumbe, King William's Town vs Kimberley, 1892/93
9. 11/[x] (5/x] in a total of 52 and 6/[x] in a total of 112, T Maleni, Port Elizabeth vs King William's Town, 1895/96 (ET)

BEST BOWLING IN AN INNINGS
1. 8/[x] in a total of 30, MD Foley, Port Elizabeth vs King William's Town, 1885/86
2. 8/[x] in a total of 59, A Ngcumbe, King William's Town vs Port Elizabeth, 1884/85
3. 8/[x] in a total of 46, C Bopi, King William's Town vs Port Elizabeth, 1890/91
4. 7/[x] in a total of 15, A Ngcumbe, King William's Town vs East London, 1884/85
5. 7/[x] in a total of 27, A Ngcumbe, King William's Town vs Port Elizabeth, 1884/85
6. 7/[x] in a total of 33, A Ngcumbe, King William's Town vs Grahamstown, 1884/85
7. 7/[x] in a total of 51, [X] Bopi, King William's Town vs Kimberley, 1892/93
8. 7/[x] in a total of 91, W Menze, Port Elizabeth vs East London, 1897/98
9. 7/[x] in a total of 63, [X] Dlamini, Uitenhage vs Kimberley, 1892/93
10. 7/[x] in a total of 26, F Makewna, Port Elizabeth vs Grahamstown, 1885/86

TEAM RECORDS*

TEAM	PLAYED	WON	LOST
East London	11	3	8
Grahamstown	6	2	4
Kimberley	4	2	2
King William's Town	16	12	4
Port Elizabeth	11	8	3
Queenstown	10	1	9
Uitenhage	4	3	1

Note*: Two unofficial 'Extraneous Tournaments' were played which included club teams: these tournaments have been included in the statistics, but only the Inter-Town matches and not the extra 'club' matches within the tournaments.

15.4.3 MALAY INTER-TOWN TOURNAMENTS (LATER, GLOVER CUP), 1889/90–1892/93

Note: Two tournaments were held in 1891. The first was held in January and is recorded as 1890/91 (Jan), the second (March–April) is given here as 1890/91 (March).

BATTING RECORDS
Two centuries and eleven half-centuries were scored in 23 recorded games.

HIGHEST INDIVIDUAL SCORES
1. E Abrams 137, Kimberley vs Johannesburg, 1892/93
2. R Grendon 111, Kimberley vs Cape Town, 1890/91 (March)
3. E Abrams 91, Cape Town vs Port Elizabeth, 1890/91 (March)
4. E Adams 83, Claremont vs Port Elizabeth, 1889/90
5. R Grendon 80*, Kimberley vs Port Elizabeth, 1890/91 (March)
6. [X] Achmat 73, Western Province vs Kimberley, 1895/96
7. E Abrams 70*, Cape Town vs Kimberley, 1890/91 (March)
8. A Hendricks 59, Western Province vs Kimberley, 1895/96
9. E Ariefdien 54, Cape Town vs Port Elizabeth, 1890/91 (March)
10. H Sheldon 54, Kimberley vs Johannesburg, 1892/93

11. J Vogt 52, Kimberley vs Port Elizabeth, 1890/91 (March)
12. E Abrams 52, Kimberley vs Claremont, 1892/93 (ET)
13. H Abrahams 50*, Claremont vs Johannesburg, 1889/90

HIGHEST TEAM TOTALS
1. 301, Western Province vs Kimberley, 1895/96
2. 256, Kimberley vs Johannesburg, 1892/93
3. 241, Cape Town vs Johannesburg, 1895/96
4. 191, Kimberley vs Cape Town, 1890/91 (March)
5. 175/6 dec, Cape Town vs Port Elizabeth, 1890/91 (March)
6. 171/4 dec, Kimberley vs Port Elizabeth, 1890/91 (March)
7. 160, Cape Town vs Kimberley, 1890/91 (March)
8. 154, Cape Town vs Johannesburg, 1892/93

HIGHEST TOTAL BY EACH TEAM
Claremont, 150/8 vs Johannesburg, 1889/90
Western Province, 301 vs Kimberley, 1895/96
Johannesburg, 112 vs Cape Town, 1895/96
Kimberley/GW, 256 vs Johannesburg, 1892/93
Port Elizabeth, 80/7 vs Cape Town, 1889/90
Uitenhage, 39 vs Cape Town, 1890/91 (Jan)

LOWEST TOTAL BY EACH TEAM
Claremont, 21 vs Johannesburg, 1889/90
Cape Town, 35 vs Port Elizabeth 1890/91
Johannesburg, 23 vs Cape Town, 1889/90
Kimberley/GW, 32 vs Western Province, 1895/96
Port Elizabeth, 21 vs Cape Town, 1890/91 (Jan)
Uitenhage, 24 vs Kimberley, 1890/91 (Jan)

BOWLING RECORDS
10 or more wickets were taken in a match at least ten times.

BEST BOWLING IN A MATCH
1. 14/38 (10/18 and 4/20), E Ariefdien, Cape Town vs Port Elizabeth, 1890/91 (March)*
2. 13/42 (6/9 and 7/33), A Hendricks, Kimberley vs Port Elizabeth, 1890/91 (March)
3. 12/88 (5/[x] in a total of 81 and 7/[x] in a total of 60), H 'Krom' Hendricks, Cape Town vs Johannesburg, 1892/93
4. 11/40 (6/20 and 5/20), [X] Ajoep, Port Elizabeth vs Cape Town, 1889/90
5. 11/44 (5/8 and 6/36), H 'Krom' Hendricks, Cape Town vs Kimberley, 1892/93
6. 10/25 (7/23 and 3/2, K du Toit, Cape Town vs Johannesburg, 1895/96
7. 10/33 (5/27 and 5/6), E Afriefdien, Cape Town vs Johannesburg, 1889/90
8. 10/63 (4/24 and 6/39), H Hendricks, Cape Town vs Kimberley, 1891/92
9. 10/100 (7/38 and 3/62), A Hendricks, Kimberley vs Cape Town, 1890/91 (March)
10. 9/48 (5/19 and 4/29), L Fredricks, Port Elizabeth vs Claremont, 1889/90
11. 9/60 (5/18 and 4/24), E Ariefdien, Cape Town vs Kimberley, 1892/93
12. 9/99 (7/65 and 2/34), E Ariefdien, Cape Town vs Kimberley, 1890/91 (March)

Note*: Ariefdien also scored 54 in this match. Port Elizabeth were bowled out for 50 and 63.

BEST BOWLING IN AN INNINGS
1. 10/18, E Ariefden, Cape Town vs Port Elizabeth, 1890/91 (March)
2. 9/25, J Sheldon, Kimberley vs Cape Town, 1892/93
3. 9/28, E Ariefdien, CT/Claremont vs PE/Johannesburg, 1889/90
4. 7/14, [X] Abdol, Claremont vs Port Elizabeth, 1889/90
5. 7/23, K du Toit, Cape Town vs Johannesburg, 1897/98
6. 7/33, A Hendricks, Kimberley vs Port Elizabeth, 1890/91 (March)
7. 7/38, A Hendricks, Kimberley vs Cape Town, 1890/91 (March)
8. 7/65, E Ariefdien, Cape Town vs Kimberley, 1890/91 (March)
9. 6/5, B van der Schyff, Cape Town vs Port Elizabeth, 1890/91 (Jan)
10. 6/9, A Hendricks, Kimberley vs Port Elizabeth, 1890/91 (March)
11. 6/12, G Fredricks, Port Elizabeth vs Cape Town, 1890/91 (Jan)
12. 6/13, E Ariefdien, Cape Town vs Kimberley, 1891/92

13. 6/15, G Fredricks, PE/JHB vs Cape Town/Claremont, 1890/91
14. 6/15, M Souk, Port Elizbaeth vs Cape Town, 1890/91 (March)
15. 6/16, [X] Abdol, Cape Town vs Port Elizabeth, 1890/91 (Jan)
16. 6/20, [X] Ajoep, Port Elizabeth vs Cape Town, 1889/90
17. 6/21, A Hendricks, Western Province vs Kimberley, 1895/96

Note: H 'Krom' Hendricks took 7/[x] (in a total of 60), Cape Town vs Johannesburg, 1892/3
[X] Hendricks took 7/[x] (in a total of 40), Kimberley vs Claremont, 1892/93 (ET)
R Grendon took 7/[x] (in a total of 96), Kimberley vs Johannesburg, 1892/93

TEAM RECORDS

In January 1893 a tournament was arranged to take place after the completion of the Glover Cup (Dec–Jan 1892/93). This was to give Claremont, who had not played in the Glover competition, a chance to play against all the visiting teams: statistics from this match are marked as ET (Extraneous Tournament) and the results are included in the list below.

TEAM	PLAYED	WON	LOST	DRAWN	RESULT UNKNOWN
Claremont	4	1	1	1	1
Cape Town/WP	13	10	2	0	1
Johannesburg	7	0	5	0	2
Kimberley/GW	14	6	7	0	1
Port Elizabeth	9	3	5	1	0
Uitenhage	3	0	2	0	1

Note: A combined Cape Town Union/Claremont team beat a combined Port Elizabeth/Johannesburg team on the first innings in 1889/90: individual statistics have been included from this match, but not from the matches played by combined Malay–Glover tournament teams playing against non-Glover Cup teams, for example 'Kimberley Europeans' or S Powell's Team. The latter matches represent a form of representative contest rather than being part of the tournament.

PART THREE

THE DOORS OPEN: THE FIRST INTERNATIONAL TOUR AND VISIONS OF AN INCLUSIVE FUTURE, 1888–1894

16

'Time for South Africa to send Home something besides gold, diamonds and millionaires'

From inter-town to international cricket

Merchants in Australia think nothing of giving £10 or
£20 each to send home a good eleven, and have their
appointments still open for them when they come back.
[Yet] Cape Town could not send a team to Port Elizabeth.

– Cape Times, 13 September 1880

Cricket in southern Africa grew between 1876 and the end of the 1880s and in the process became much more interconnected. The Inter-Town tournaments provided a benchmark of this progress. They were also a mirror of the different cricket cultures emerging in the various regions that had been conquered and colonised by the British. Each region had particular characteristics shaped by its specific context and historical experiences. By the late 1880s they were increasingly working together. The next step was to connect with 'Home' and plan the first tour to the subcontinent by a British team.

For many white colonials, playing the game of cricket in the colonies was a kind of identification with 'Home'. They also showed a continuing interest in the progress of the game in England. Players arriving in southern Africa as soldiers, civil servants and settlers brought the latest cricket news, ideas and techniques. The Home-Born versus Mother Country matches, which were so popular in every area, stressed this relationship of learning and mutual connection.

From early on, colonial newspapers reported on the first overseas tours by British or colonial teams, still very much a rarity until the 1880s. The new Ashes series between England and Australia, starting in 1877, set the tone for modern international contests. As the game spread in southern Africa, local cricket followers naturally made comparisons and started discussing the possibility of joining this growing international trend. Owen Dunell, for instance, the star for Port Elizabeth in the Inter-Town tournaments, had 'extensive knowledge of English cricket', he himself noting in 1887: 'I have seen all the great wicket-keepers, both English and Australian, of the last sixteen or seventeen years.'[1] In other words, since at least 1872 he had watched from close up as international cricket got under way, and he was ready to contribute to the planning and play when it arrived on South African shores.

In the late 1870s and early 1880s, Cape Town newspapers carried reports on the success that Australia had achieved in cricket and questioned why the Cape could not attain similar status. The *Cape Times* expressed its frustration when it said, 'Merchants in Australia think nothing of giving £10 or £20 each to send home a good eleven, and have their appointments still open for them when they come back. [Yet] Cape Town could not send a team to Port Elizabeth.'[2] In 1881, the *Cape Argus* wrote pessimistically that 'it will be a long time before [cricket in] South Africa will attain to the pitch of perfection already reached by some of the sister colonies in the Australian group'. A few months later, the same newspaper pointed to the financial success experienced by Australian touring teams and stressed that 'it is time the Colony did something to show that it is not dead to sports and manly pastimes'.[3]

Many top cricketers from 'Home' had played in South Africa during visits or stints in the civil service and military. For example, players with experience of the English first-class game who turned out for clubs in Cape Town from 1877 onwards included Lieutenant William Davidson (MCC and Northants), Lieutenant Lyndhurst Winslow (Sussex, who subsequently starred in the Inter-Town tournaments) and Major Frank Crawford (Kent and MCC). In the 1880s Sir Edward Wallington, an Oxford Blue, was given a game when his ship docked at Cape Town en route to Australia. The former Essex cricketer Major Robert Gardner Warton also played regularly with William Milton for the Western Province Cricket Club after 1883, and their partnership would later influence local cricket in important ways.

All this meant that people in the Cape Colony were kept informed of international developments, which, in turn, stimulated the aspiration to connect with the growing world of cricket. It was natural that the colonial elites would seek to link up with metropolitan developments, particularly in the last quarter of the nineteenth century as international sport started to gather pace.

It was reported as early as 1883 that a team from the Cape Colony was planning a tour to England. The following year the newspaper editor John Tengo Jabavu suggested in *Imvo Zabantsundu* that a team of black cricketers from the eastern Cape should be sent to England. Africans had just launched the first Native Inter-Town Tournament, and he was now looking beyond this. Jabavu believed a tour to Britain would show 'the tone that British values gave to the society of Africans'.[4] He added that it would also be an unusual attraction – if matches between pipe-smokers and non-smokers could be popular in England, think how much more interest a team from the African continent would generate. At the same time the missionary newspaper *Isigidimi samaXhosa* was introducing W.G. Grace to Xhosa audiences. It carried news of his century against Australia in an article headed '*Eze bola*' (About the ball or games).[5]

Jabavu's proposal for an overseas tour was made a full decade before any South African team actually toured England, showing how far ahead of the time black cricketers were in their thinking. The plans for going to England were not as fanciful as they may have seemed. The first Australian touring side to Britain in 1868 was a team of native Australians from the now-extinct Werrunbrook people from Victoria. The Aborigines had a tough five months' schedule, playing no fewer than 47 matches, some watched by up to 7,000 people.[6] Though well treated, they 'remained a novelty' and were 'gawped at' by the Victorians:

> The more educated justified their curiosity as scientific and wondered about their relative status in the Darwinian hierarchy and the family of races. The *Sheffield Telegraph* reported that the Aboriginal team turned out to be 'a really fine body of men, of superior type for Australians, and in "build" and physique not only far removed from the low, Negro type of the genus homo, but able to "take their own part" with well-developed Europeans'.[7]

Jabavu's suggestion of a tour in 1884 was not realised, but it made clear that cricket was a popular game which was thriving in the eastern Cape in the early 1880s when modern-day sports were still in their infancy in southern Africa, and African sports people clearly intended to be part of cricket's development both locally and internationally.

Charles Alcock, the Surrey CCC secretary and point man for those wishing to tour England, wrote in *Cricket: A Weekly Record of the Game*, 'It may not be long after all before Kaffreland is able to send us as fine a specimen of native cricket as that excellent all-round player, the Australian Aboriginal, Mullagh, who made such a capital show here in 1868.'[8] The enthusiasm of Jabavu, Alcock and others was not shared by William Milton, the tart imperialist, who withheld his support even for the Inter-Town tournaments. He said: 'The idea of sending a team to England capable of holding its own with a first-class English eleven is ... a seeming impossibility, and a great impossibility it is, I fear, likely to remain, until a greater interest is taken in the development of cricket in South Africa by those who possess the power of giving some practical proofs of that interest.' He argued that cricket had potential at the Cape but lack of opportunity was causing the game to languish in comparison with the progress in other colonies. He put the problem down to inadequate facilities, claiming the ground at Wynberg was 'little better than the hard road and not quite so good as a Namaqualand saltpan'.[9] This was to be one of the reasons why he and the WPCC later initiated the idea of constructing the Newlands grounds as a grand venue for international tours.

Nevertheless, interest remained in competing against teams from England and Australia, and from the mid-1880s onwards this enthusiasm was fuelled by sportswriters in South Africa, most notably Harry Cadwallader – formerly a reporter for the *Sussex Daily News* – and Charles Finlason, an erudite commentator on the game and the Kimberley *Daily Independent*'s 'Gossip'. Cadwallader, who arrived at the Cape in 1885, was soon a controversial and active critic of Milton's cricket administration. His first article to create widespread interest concerned the arrival of the Australian cricket team at Table Bay in October 1886. The visitors had communicated with the Cape court of the Indian and Colonial Exhibition in London in the hope of extending their stay at the Cape in order to play cricket. The communication was ignored, and the Australians were only able to leave the boat briefly before moving on to New Zealand. Cadwallader was incensed by this missed opportunity and, in an article for the *Whitehall Review*, he lamented the inability of Cape cricketers to 'organise something', noting that 'the leading club of the Colony, the Western Province Cricket Club, should have taken some measure to accord a hearty welcome to a team of cricketers whose play is universally noted; it was certainly their place to move in the matter'. Cadwallader went on to praise the Cape Press Cricketers Club – for which he was the opening batsman – for 'coming forward at the eleventh hour and presenting the Australian team with a framed testimonial of the esteem in which the visiting cricketers were held in the Cape Colony'.[10] His actions served as an early indication that he was an ambitious, even fanatical supporter of the game, one who would enliven the local cricket scene. Unfortunately for him, his report was misleading: the Australian cricketers were in fact met by Milton and members of the WPCC soon after nine o'clock on the day after their arrival. They were escorted around the Houses of Parliament, Library and Museum before returning to the vessel at noon. It emerged that Milton was not to blame for the breakdown in communication; the message had simply not been passed on by the officials in London, who had also told the Australians that 'they would find no cricket worth paying attention to at the Cape'.[11]

Meeting the Australian touring side stimulated interest at the Cape, but did not hasten the process of establishing international links. Poor communications, financial constraints, the relative strengths of the teams involved, the difficulty of taking time away from work and fears over professionalism were some of the issues faced in planning early sporting tours. These cricket tour discussions were taking place at the same time that rugby officials at the Cape, many with dual cricket roles, were similarly planning a tour to England. In 1886 Rowland Hill, the Rugby Football Union secretary and crusty advocate of amateurism, vetoed the idea because of his fear of professionalism.[12] Again, in early 1888, an English rugby team was due to stop over in Cape en route to Australasia, but the Western Province Rugby Football Union suddenly abandoned the idea because 'the English sporting' papers conclusively prove that the English football team which touched at Cape Town is not an amateur team.'[13] For class-conscious amateurs like Hill, it was taboo to pay people to play and he did not trust the entrepreneurs involved in these early sports tours. But the demand for cricket and rugby tours in either direction grew all the same, fuelled by the press, with *The Empire* stating, 'It is time for South Africa to send Home something besides gold, diamonds and millionaires.'[14]

In his desire to make the English public aware of developments at the Cape, Cadwallader began inserting details of local cricket matches in overseas journals such as *Sporting Life* and *Cricket: A Weekly Record of the Game*. His efforts prompted the New Brighton Cricket Club to contact the Cape premier, Sir Gordon Sprigg, in early 1888 in the hope that their team would be welcome at the Cape. Sprigg's involvement in the matter gave it some prominence, but Cadwallader was more interested in attracting the Australians, who were visiting England again. He pointed out that two of their players, '[Jack] Blackham and [Sammy] Jones, were both here *en route* home in October 1886 and expressed much regret at their not being able to meet our representatives'.[15] Cadwallader was provocative in suggesting: 'If our Kimberley friends could only be induced to stir in the matter the thing would go through undoubtedly and colonial cricket would be more benefited by such a visit than the sanguine imagine.'[16] It was not as if the Diamond Fields had been inactive: a local businessman was said to have offered to underwrite the expenses of a touring team and that Henri Bettelheim, a cricket professional, had left for England armed with a guarantee of £2,000 to entice the Australians to play in Kimberley.

There were also plans for a Cape Colony team to visit England in 1889. In continuing to play one side off against the other, Cadwallader mischievously informed readers of the jingoistic Cape weekly *The Lantern* that Cape Town was doing nothing to promote a tour. The *Daily Independent* in its 'Gossip' column by Charles Finlason reacted by urging Milton to become involved, only to discover that he had dispatched letters to Melbourne and London.[17] On enquiring what Milton planned to do next, Finlason was informed by the *Cape Argus* that 'it may ease "Gossip's" mind to hear that the matter is being attended to by the Western Province CC through the medium of that urbane and model secretary, C.W. Alcock of the Surrey CC'.[18]

In England, the Australian manager, Charles Beal, was more concerned with the form of his inexperienced team.[19] When he eventually turned his attention to South Africa, he forwarded a terse reply in mid-August: 'Thousand: you pay expenses, travelling and hotels'.

Milton met with his WPCC committee before advising Kimberley that the project 'will come to about £1,500 for at least six matches. We consider it expensive. Please let us know your views and what you would guarantee. Port Elizabeth guarantees nothing beyond gate-money.'[20] The Kimberley cricket authorities were not prepared to contribute more than a third, a decision that would have some bearing on the meeting that J.H. Hofmeyr, then president of the Leeuwenhof Cricket Club in Cape Town, chaired in late August. Milton delivered the opening address, spelling out developments that had taken place in 1886 and then outlining what had transpired in recent weeks. He reminded the gathering that 'considerable regret was expressed' that no offer was made to induce the Australians to stay for a cricket tour in 1886. Accordingly, he had negotiated a month's tour and, when the Australians had forwarded their terms – which were duly communicated to Kimberley and Port Elizabeth – it was calculated that Cape Town would be called on to contribute up to two-thirds of the estimated cost of £1,500.[21]

However, by early 1888 the time was ripe and serious plans were being made to organise a tour. The fact that the fourth white Inter-Town Tournament was being held that season, and that the WPCC was in the process of building a major new ground at Newlands, indicated the readiness of colonial cricketers for such a venture. The lead was taken by William Milton, secretary of the WPCC, and another prominent member, the Essex cricketer and Sandhurst-trained military officer, Major Robert Warton, who had been posted to Cape Town in 1883 as a member of the General Staff in South Africa. Cementing ties with the Mother Country was their preferred option. Having gone some way towards discouraging his audience from inviting the Australians, Milton together with Warton, who was in England at the time, offered an alternative arrangement – a tour of an English team of amateurs and professionals to the Cape assembled by Warton himself.

Both Warton and Milton were members of a committee set up to oversee the acquisition and building of the Newlands ground, and the plans for the tour can be traced to this period of cooperation between the two men at their club, the Lord's-away-from-Home in Cape Town. By the time Warton returned to England in 1888, the tour plan had been hatched. He set about putting together a team to tour South Africa, liaising closely with Milton, who, in turn, was the South African contact person dealing with various interested local parties.

Milton let Warton know that 'Kimberley and Cape Town had each offered 75 per cent of the gate money, while Port Elizabeth offered the whole amount taken there'. A local advocate proposed that Warton's team 'be not entertained but that a further effort be made to arrange more advantageous terms with the Australians', but he received little support. Most people favoured the Milton–Warton plan, and it was agreed that 'the committee of the Western Province CC be empowered in their discretion either finally to accept or reject the proposals of Major Warton's team'. In the end £100 was guaranteed, with the Western Province Rugby Football Union and J.H. Hofmeyr making notable contributions.[22]

Milton had received the go-ahead, but the next few months would prove difficult. The financial implications were not as straightforward as he had outlined, yet there were compelling reasons to proceed. For Milton, the tour 'would do much to unite a white community in a distant clime'. And the *Diamond Fields Advertiser* stated that South African cricketers had learned everything they could from each other; now it was time to take the next step and open international contacts. It was time for Major Warton to 'give the final push to the course of instruction which was begun by his brother officers when the colony was still in its infancy'.

17

First international team arrives in Africa

Newlands Cricket Ground was a picture to be remembered
with its surrounding mass of pines, overtopped by the
great table mountain on one side, the new stand covered
with red cloth standing out prominently against the green
background. The picturesque effect given on our own
grounds being enhanced by the bright and varied colours of
many Malay women in their holiday attire. I suppose some
4,000 were present to witness the first struggle between
an English eleven and the pick of the local talent.

– Aubrey Smith, 1888[1]

The first cricket touring team from abroad finally sailed into Cape Town harbour
on Friday, 14 December 1888. The newspapers reported that the townsfolk of
Cape Town spent all of the previous day waiting for the mail steamer to bring
Major Warton's side but, to their great disappointment it was late, and they were
unable to see it enter Table Bay. No one was more frustrated than Harry Cadwallader, the enthusiastic reporter of the *Diamond Fields Advertiser*. He intended to
steal a march on Cape Town's welcoming party by arranging to be transported
out to the steamer once it was in sight. When the sun disappeared from view, he
decided to remain at the offices of the local port authorities, waiting for some
news. Eventually it came, shortly after two o'clock in the morning. Cadwallader
immediately scrambled into a hired boat and made his way out to the ship. The
English cricketers awoke early that morning, eagerly anticipating the spectacular
view of the Cape that confronts ships from more than 150 kilometres out to
sea. There were shouts of delight when the players caught their first glimpse of

Table Mountain. Everyone was on deck by the time Cadwallader was allowed to climb aboard.

The boat entered the dock at mid-morning. 'We found a large crowd awaiting us,' recalled Warton, 'a large percentage being Kaffirs and Malays.'[2] After introductions to the reception party of local dignitaries, the team were driven to their hotels in waggonettes drawn by white horses.

Soon after settling into their hotel, the English management entered into a 'council of war' with Milton and his assistant, Thomas Lynedoch Graham – grandson of Captain John Graham, who had chased the Xhosa over the Fish River in the 1810s, and brother of the Grahamstown batsman who had played in the first Inter-Town Tournament in 1876 . Final arrangements were amicably agreed to, most notably the confirmation of matches to be played in Johannesburg.

Over the next few days some demanding practice sessions were held at Claremont and Newlands in order to knock the players into shape as quickly as possible. They had a week to acclimatise before playing their first match. Two aspects of South African cricket to which they had to become accustomed were the light and the matting pitches. The weather was also very hot and reports referred to the side experiencing a few sweltering days when the temperature was 105 degrees in the shade. Nevertheless, Aubrey Smith, the captain, was impressed with the facilities, particularly as he had been told before sailing that his team would be playing on the 'hard, high road'.[3]

Wherever the English players went, they created interest. On their first evening in Cape Town, they were taken to a large church bazaar which was being held to raise funds towards an organ. Their arrival was immediately announced and two of the players were pressed into service – Arthur Skinner for a recitation and Aubrey Smith for a rendering of the song 'Enniscorthy'.

Towards the end of the week, some players were driven round the densely wooded suburbs on the other side of Table Mountain. Others were taken to see one of the best of the old 'Dutch farms', Groot Constantia. It belonged to Mr Alan Cloete, 'who entertained them for the greater part of the day, showing them some splendid vineyards which have fortunately escaped the Phylloxera and other diseases; the house being a beautiful old Dutch habitation at least 120 years old and arranged with all the care and thought shown by the old Dutchmen of that time'.[4]

A highlight of the first week was a public dinner for 120 people at which the governor of the Cape Colony and high commissioner for South Africa, Sir Hercules Robinson, was present. The chair was occupied by Sir Thomas Upington, who had served as prime minister of the Cape for two years before resigning and was described as a peerless parliamentarian. Other guests included Sir J.H.

de Villiers (the chief justice), Sir David Tennant (speaker of the House of Assembly), Sir Thomas Scanlen (a former prime minister) and J.H. Hofmeyr (parliamentary leader of the Afrikaner Bond and president of the newly formed Cape Town Cricket Club).

No visitors to South Africa had ever received a welcome of the magnitude accorded to Warton's team, and prominent local figures sought political mileage from events associated with the tour. At the dinner, speakers focused on the use of cricket to realise the values of British elite culture through northern expansion into the African hinterland. Upington and Warton were prominent in exchanging wildly applauded comments. 'Some years ago,' Upington told guests,

> when I was first elected to political life in this country, if anyone spoke of the British flag being hoisted at the Zambezi, he was looked upon as a lunatic. However, things have changed lately and I sincerely hope before Sir Hercules Robinson's period of office in this Colony has terminated, that what is at the present moment known as 'the sphere of influence' will be known as the British Protectorate up to the Zambezi. And I shall be inclined to go further ... I see no reason why we should not cross the Zambezi ... (Hear, hear, loud and prolonged cheers – loud applause).

Major Warton also enthusiastically supported these expansionist imperial ideas, but when it came to his turn to speak, Aubrey Smith chose his words carefully. 'Such visits', he said,

> do more than anything else to promote the interests of cricket and to further the feeling of sport which every British man has within himself. And they do more than that. They make one feel, as subjects of Her Majesty, that there is a link between the mother country and the colonies, far thicker than anyone realises at home. When they come to a colony, Englishmen find brothers and cousins extending to them the right hand of welcome and they feel then that in reality they are Englishmen one and all.[5]

Throughout the demanding tour, Smith was suitably diplomatic, possessing the oratorical skills to more than hold his own at the customary receptions and shows of imperial solidarity.

The public dinner was indeed a grand function, which served to put into perspective the significance of the tour. There were a number of other festivities, including a great smoking concert, which some 600 people attended and at which the cricketers presented the first half of the programme. Major Warton recalled, 'It was a Christy Minstrel show with the Boss (Smith) as Bones and

Monty Bowden as Tambo. It was no end of a success, four or five encores being obtained. Bowden's song, *To be there*, and the Boss's stump speech and song, *The man that struck O'Hara*, going down with great effect.'[6]

* * * * *

For the English team, Major Robert Warton and William Milton had assembled a mixed-strength group appropriate to the standard of play in South Africa, but the South Africans wanted the strongest possible team to ensure good gates and see 'what really good cricket is'. Five players – Bobby Abel, Maurice Read, Johnny Briggs, Harry Wood and George Ulyett – had been selected for England in various tests against Australia during 1888.[7] Another, George Lohmann, was a late withdrawal but there were two other leading cricketers in Aubrey Smith and Monty Bowden, who had represented Gentlemen against the Players and Australians during the recently completed English season. The core was provided by a group of Surrey stars, the professionals Abel, Read and Briggs, and the wicketkeeper batsman, Bowden, who, though an amateur, demanded the same as the professionals, £100 plus travel expenses. The captain, Aubrey Smith, who later became a famous Hollywood actor, was also paid a generous sum. Smith had toured Australia and, though still young at 25, was regarded as an excellent captain.

Amateurs were supposedly men of means who played purely for the enjoyment of it, but under the table they were often paid as handsomely as the professionals. Warton did, however, include a few of the archetypal British amateur gentlemen 'who could afford the tour'. The Earl of Coventry, an ex-MCC president, 'arranged his son's selection' apparently 'as a boost to the lad's confidence'. The 21-year-old Charles Coventry 'was at a loose end because he had been unable to pass the examination necessary to gain a commission in the army'. Another amateur was J.A.P. 'Emile' McMaster, whose test match on tour was his only first-class match. Educated at Eton, he 'quite naturally was made a member of the MCC before he was an adult'. He was chosen as a batsman although his top score was 14 in a club game in London. In the test he was out second ball for a duck and it was reported also that 'McMaster, most unluckily, missed an easy catch at mid-wicket'. 'We chose McMaster', the captain later explained, 'because he was such a damn good after-dinner speaker.'[8]

The British class system was very much in evidence during the tour, and in South Africa it would be overlaid by a paternalistic superiority towards the colonials, which upset some people. A strict adherence to class distinctions between 'amateur' and 'professional' in England was maintained on tours abroad. The amateurs had superior travel and accommodation arranged for them, often staying at different hotels. In Cape Town, the amateurs were booked into the International Hotel and the professionals into less salubrious quarters at the George.

Warton requested that the separation be maintained on the tour in accordance with the prevailing practice, and the members of the WPCC were not going to argue; this was, after all, the same treatment Private Beech had received during the recent Cape Town Wanderers tour to Kimberley. When the English reached Kimberley, one journalist was horrified to discover that at a dinner at the Kimberley Club 'the really capable portion of the [English] team, the professionals, were not present nor we believe, even invited'.[9]

The tour started with two matches in Cape Town over Christmas. The first was against a Western Province XXII and the second against a Combined XV of the Cape Colony, the first representative local white team drawn from the best players from the Inter-Town tournaments. The opening day of the first match was an enormous success. The weather was beautiful and an excellent matting pitch was laid in the centre of a good grass ground. A temporary grandstand, capable of holding 400 persons, was erected from 'which an uninterrupted view of the matches may be secured'. Hundreds of people arrived by train every ten minutes at Newlands station and, according to one report, 'a very large percentage of the crowd were ladies'.[10]

'Newlands Cricket Ground was a picture to be remembered,' wrote Aubrey Smith,

> with its surrounding mass of pines, overtopped by the great table mountain on one side, the new stand covered with red cloth standing out prominently against the green background. The picturesque effect given on our own grounds being enhanced by the bright and varied colours of many Malay women in their holiday attire. I suppose some 4,000 were present to witness the first struggle between an English eleven and the pick of the local talent.[11]

The Western Province XXII won the toss and elected to bat. A great cheer went up for the touring side, who walked onto the field at midday. They were neatly turned out in kit which reflected the touring colours of chocolate and yellow. On the field, the players wore chocolate caps or white broad-brimmed hats. Some also made use of Union Jack badges, and ties that were chocolate in colour with yellow stripes. They were a proud team, determined to live up to reputations that had been built through the generous coverage that South African papers accorded English cricket.

The local batsmen followed. Dick Richards took first strike, facing the opening four balls from Johnny Briggs. Five-ball overs were not employed in South Africa until the 1891/2 season. The first four overs were maidens. Local players and supporters were startled that the English wicketkeeper, Monty Bowden of Surrey, stood up to the opening bowler (and took eight stumpings in the match) and also that he did not require a 'back-stop'. This was very new to South Africa, though not completely without precedent. In January 1887 Fred Smith had shocked onlookers when he dispensed with his long-stop in a match between WPCC and Stray Klips.

The colonials, despite a jittery performance in the field, dismissed their opponents for 135 and 123 to win by 17 runs. Excuses were offered, not least of which was the energy-sapping heat and the fact that the English had suffered from the festivities of the previous few days. Warton referred to the 'the unceasing hospitality of the residents who will not realise that we are here on cricket intent. Club vies with club in hospitality, acquaintance with acquaintance. We have invitations sufficient to fill up a month at Cape Town instead of a fortnight'.[12] Johnny Briggs adopted a more generous viewpoint in *Athletic News*: 'I am sorry to say we lost, and would very likely lose again if we had to play the same twenty-two as they are a very good lot. Two of their bowlers are very good, especially Ashley who bowls left arm, about medium, and comes back a little.'[13]

Off the field, the festivities continued. Christmas Eve featured a smoking concert at the Exhibition Building, where Aubrey Smith was again called upon to perform *The man that struck O'Hara* and Monty Bowden rendered *Kissing* in a 'suitably impassioned manner'.[14] Reference was also made of Captain Baden-Powell (later, of Boy Scout fame) producing a musical sketch, *Public entertainers*.

The next day involved a drive of 20 miles ('Good for the liver,' as Read remarked) to Simon's Bay, where Admiral Wells and the officers of HMS *Raleigh* entertained the team royally to Christmas lunch. The players were transported to the venue in two waggonettes each with four horses. The tourists appreciated the drive. For the first ten miles as far as Wynberg, the road was shaded by avenues of magnificent oaks or tall pines. There were also oleanders and plumbago in full bloom with huge magnolias appearing at intervals. Later on, the landscape changed but the scenery was no less eye-catching. 'After Muizenberg,' said Major Warton, 'the road passed along the foot of mountains rising sheer out of the sea. The white sands round Fish Hoek Bay have all the appearance of snow, suitable for Christmas, were not the fancy dispelled by the intense heat of the sun.'[15] The jolly tars and marines cheered wildly as the players stepped on board. 'We were shortly taken down to the main deck,' continued Major Warton, 'which was one mass of decoration, raised by the clever hands of the tars. At intervals of a yard all round the deck on both sides stood men with plates of cake, biscuits, and cold plum pudding, offering them with Christmas wishes as we passed along in single file.' A sumptuous feast was greatly enjoyed, and in the early afternoon the players were given a guided tour of the ship.[16]

In the second match in Cape Town, watched by 6,000 spectators, the tourists again stared defeat in the face against a Cape Colony XV captained by Owen Dunell from Port Elizabeth, with 12 other Inter-Town Tournament stalwarts in it. This was the first-ever team chosen to represent the Colony. Two of the Inter-Town stars featured in the climactic ending, the two Charleses, Finlason and Vintcent. The home team needed 12 runs to win with five wickets standing. Briggs bowled Finlason. It was a critical moment. Smith came back for Fothergill and with his third ball bowled Vintcent (24). The initiative suddenly lay with the English. Briggs, through subtle variation of pace and length, outwitted another two batsmen, and when last man, the Rev. Arthur Porter from King William's Town, ran himself out, the match ended amid a happy delirium of excitement. A cloud of hats flew up in honour of the Englishmen who had snatched the match out of the fire and won by 11 runs. In no time, the players were mobbed in a spirit of non-partisan enthusiasm.[17]

This historic encounter between 'Home' and a representative team of one of its African colonies – in physical, political and cultural terms, as much as cricket-wise – heralded a new phase in the growth and development of cricket on the subcontinent.

For colonial society in Cape Town, the cricket games provided a venue for continuing a memorable two weeks of socialising. It was important to be seen in the company of one or other of the famous cricketers. At every opportunity, the English players were prevailed upon to discuss aspects of the game with supporters whose enthusiasm rather outweighed their knowledge. 'It was a new, less discerning audience to that which they were accustomed,' commented one journalist.[18]

The *Daily Independent* also noted, 'A fair amount of betting has been and is being indulged in. As each man has his own views and there are no bodies at present to fix the odds, no real idea can be arrived at as to the state of the betting.' Examples were frequently quoted and the same newspaper recorded, 'Versus Cape Town XXII, bets were given at £10 to £3 on Warton. Against the Colonial XV at Cape Town, £50 to £30 on Warton and £10 to £15 on Warton.' Many strenuously opposed the introduction of the betting element into cricket. That even players had wagers on the results gave rise to the suggestion that they 'cared more for what they had on the result than for the cricket itself'.[19]

The interest over the week was unparalleled in Cape Town cricket. Two thrilling encounters gave the tour a wonderful start and raised the level of interest in the game to new heights.

18

Journey that inscribed Empire and cricket onto the landscape of a subcontinent

> Whether the Imperial Federationist is quite capable of producing
> a federal programme or not, we [are not sure. However,] we
> cannot but think that ... the best of all field games would have
> a more unifying effect than any number of formal conferences
> ... Cricket may yet prove a grand political healer.
>
> – *Cape Times*, 2 January 1889

The English tour of 1888/9 was a considerable undertaking, not least because there were no national or provincial cricket administrations in place. It was William Milton of the WPCC who liaised with the centres involved, structured the itinerary, headed selection committees, controlled the financial arrangements, and arranged for the Cape government to give the touring team the run of the railways at an almost nominal rate.

The English tour proved expensive and complicated. Warton, for example, drew up contracts to pay his professionals £100 plus expenses, only to discover that the leading amateurs, Monty Bowden and Aubrey Smith, required similar packages in addition to their superior accommodation and travelling arrangements. Bickering on both sides over finance placed the tour in jeopardy, a situation compounded when Warton suddenly announced that he had decided to adhere to his original demand for 'three-quarters of the gate money, over and above the guarantee of £1,800 minimum already made'. It was not until early November 1888 when additional matches were confirmed that the guarantee was declared sufficient without the need for a percentage of the gate money. Milton promptly contacted the various centres, stating:

This we take to mean that [Warton] withdraws his request for three-fourths of the gate. This is the result, I think, of a letter I wrote to him on the 17th October. I had previously pointed out that, with Johannesburg and Graaff-Reinet, the guarantee list amounted to £2,250, and if Natal came in £400 or £500 more might be expected. I am glad he has withdrawn his demand, as it was creating a bad impression in some quarters.[1]

The tour itself was a remarkable venture in which the visitors travelled great distances by boat, train, coach or cart with hardly a break.[2] 'The visit was very largely due to Milton's energy and enthusiasm. Practically unaided he made all the arrangements in connection with the tour. But for him that first visit might very well have been deferred for several years with the inevitable consequence that the development of South African cricket would have been correspondingly delayed.'[3]

The tour itinerary was not finalised until the team's arrival in Cape Town. At one stage it was expected to exclude Johannesburg and Natal, but as the interest rose, the guarantees rolled in and Milton negotiated a special travel discount on the railways from the Cape government which enabled it to proceed successfully. A survey of the fixtures and travel arrangements provides a fascinating glimpse into the South African cricketing infrastructure and the vast practical hurdles that had to be overcome to spread the game in those days. The team embarked on an epic three-month journey, feted at every stop.[4] Only the 'Model Republic' – the Orange Free State – did not host a fixture; the wealthy Sam Barratt, who had built a cricket oval on his farm, led the opposition against a match because it would be 'crippling the resources and there was no enclosed ground'.[5] His negative stance was criticised by the Bloemfontein *Friend* and attention was drawn to an article in the *Cape Town Weekly* that commented that cricket had an important role in bringing the different territories of southern Africa together: it could do more than 'the Imperial Federationist' and 'any number of formal conferences' in acting as 'a grand political healer'.[6]

Following the first two matches and the hectic fortnight of social engagements in Cape Town, the English team went by boat to Port Elizabeth in the *Roslin Castle*, which at that stage held the record of 18 days and 21 hours for the trip from England. Imperial identity was reinforced at Port Elizabeth where 'flags hung in profusion from the galleries with the Union Jack conspicuous because it was supported by two cricket bats ... on the stage there was a large and excellent photograph of W.G. Grace set amongst ferns and other green plants.'[7] The match against a Port Elizabeth XXII started on New Year's Day and 'all business in the town had closed by the start of play on the second day'. Then the team made its way south again – to Oudtshoorn, going by boat to Mossel Bay and then travelling for two and a half hours in the dark and rain in six Cape carts 'not provided with lights' to Great Brak River. They planned to reach George that night but were warned it would be dangerous so the players 'selected their chairs and corners' in the local hotel before setting off again at four in the morning. After three hours they reached George, 'where a good wash, an excellent breakfast and a brief rest were thoroughly welcomed', before setting out for the crossing of the 'thick-wooded' Outeniqua Mountains up Montagu Pass. The English were overwhelmed by the mountainous landscape: 'The trees were chiefly iron-wood with "sugar bushes" in full flower and the hills aflame with gladioli.' After being drenched again by rain, they found shelter at a 'quaint little Dutch shanty called the North Station Hotel', where they changed clothes and where there was also 'a general scramble for ducks, fowls and whisky'. In the delightful travel descriptions of the journey, we are told:

> North of the Outeniqua Range, the touring party found the roads heavy from the rains – but whiled away the time by 'stalking hawks and inspecting ostriches from a wise distance'. About a mile from the Oliphants River [they were met] by horsemen – 'genuine Dutch Boers' – who brought the news that the river was in flood and they would be unable to cross as there was no bridge.[8]

Undeterred, Major Warton decided to press on: 'Our jarveys [or drivers] were reliable and, preceded by a couple of horsemen, in we plunged.' At one stage the water was above the floorboards and 'we clutched our coats ready to strip and jump'. But they made it across, to the welcoming cheers of the Oudtshoorn reception committee. The huge effort involved in the journey to play a South Western Districts XXII was made largely because of the old boys' network. Jack van Reenen, a star in Cape Town cricket for many years, had become civil commissioner in Oudtshoorn and he had the necessary contacts with Milton to ensure that this remote country area got a fixture.

After the match, the English were given a smoking concert that went on until after midnight. Then at sunrise a 'great number of coaches and carts' accompanied them for a memorable picnic at the Cango Caves, before they made their way north over the Zwartberg Pass on a road well tended by convict labour. Warton described the descent on a 'zigzag road which we saw traversing to and fro, to a great depth, almost sheer below us. As our coach and six horses swerved round the sharp turns there was a general tendency to sit tight and hold on to anything – many preferring pedestrian exercise for the greater part of the way down'. Travelling until late at night, the tourists took a short nap at Prince Albert, before tackling the last 30 miles through 'some thirty miles of bleak desert' to the railway siding at Prince Albert Road Station. 'It was jolt, jolt, jolt at a miserable pace, for our horses were done up, three going very lame.' The poor animals had covered 360 miles on 'primitive roads' in eight and a half days. Warton noted they had been 'flogged to death'. It was with relief that the team finally boarded the train for the 16-hour trip to Kimberley.[9]

On 14 January the visitors were back on the field, surprised to find a field 'innocent of a blade of grass', but 'hard as asphalt, and as level as a billiard table'. Kimberley, eager to challenge Cape Town and Port Elizabeth for supremacy in South African cricket, had been preparing for the encounter for weeks. 'The pavilion was decorated with flowers while small flags were placed on every post and pillar.' The crowd of over 4,000 was the biggest ever seen at a match in the city.

In 1889 the railway line from Cape Town ended in Kimberley, so the tourists had to tackle the next stage to Johannesburg in 'American-built stage-coaches that rocked and jolted their way to the goldfields'. The manager was once again very descriptive about the journey:

> Those who visited the Colonial Exhibition will remember Buffalo Bill's coach. Let them picture twelve individuals jammed inside – three on a seat, with shoulders overlapping, with shin bones and seats in contact; eight men including two drivers, outside, and some 6,000 lbs of baggage on top. Let them imagine that coach being drawn by twelve horses at a gallop [changed every ten miles], over a rough road on a piping hot day. Let them picture all this and they will have some faint conception of the pleasures our festive cricketers derived from their journey from Kimberley to Johannesburg.[10]

The 300 mile trip took 60 hours, with brief overnight stops in Bloemhof and Klerksdorp. The road was busy – 100 coaches were noted in one day – and hostelries along the way provided meals of roast leg of lamb or tripe with coffee for 2s 6d to 3s. At one stage the coach got stuck in mud and all the passengers had to disembark. Sing-songs did little to stave off the discomfort and the heat.

Johannesburg was only three years old at that time. Everywhere there was frenetic activity and new buildings going up: 'Vast amounts of brick and mortar lay besides barricades and scaffolding on the verges of every road.' Where once there had been a few wagons, tents and shacks in what was known as Ferreira's Camp was now a sea of corrugated iron that overflowed beyond Commissioner and Jeppe streets. Except for the tall head-gear of the mine shafts, there were none of the steeples, spires and chimney stacks generally associated with towns and cities. One of the cricket correspondents described the new settlement with outright disapproval: 'The smells of Johannesburg are as numerous as its flies and

fleas ... There are no sanitary arrangements whatsoever, and the greatest careless-
ness is displayed by the inhabitants.'[11] Nevertheless, there was a smell of money
in the air and two of the party stayed behind after the tour in search of fortune.
The players were given generous presents, including a gold nugget with diamonds
in it, and tips on what Stock Exchange portfolios to invest in. Some apparently
made money from these. They were put up at the Rand Club and played at a new
cricket ground on the site of the current Johannesburg railway station. This was
the soon-to-be-famous Wanderers, built in record time for their visit.

The Wanderers owes it origins to the ex-Kimberley cricketer Jacob Swart,
who arrived in Johannesburg in August 1888. Within three weeks he had called
a meeting to form a club and build a ground to host the forthcoming English
visitors. The pavilion was still half completed but the brand new ground fenced
with galvanised iron was in excellent condition for the match. 'The excitement
almost paralysed the town' and almost 3,000 people attended daily, paying up
to three guineas for the week of cricket against a Johannesburg XXII and a
Transvaal XV. The latter team, branded the 'Republicans' in the press, included
players from Pretoria, Potchefstroom and Barberton, the centres which had
participated with Johannesburg in an inter-town tournament the year before. The
visitors expected to meet 'two and twenty Dutchmen' in the match, but the team
was composed entirely of 'Englishmen', including Lyndhurst Winslow, who had
helped King William's Town win the Champion Bat in 1880. The English team
were enchanted with Johannesburg, which Warton described as 'one of the most
extraordinary towns now thriving on the world's surface'.[12]

From Johannesburg they went to Pietermaritzburg, splitting up into two
groups and following different paths so that the manager and others could make
a detour to the Majuba battlefield, where Britain had suffered a rare military
defeat at the hands of the Boers in 1881. Warton hoped the going would be
easier for his group, but the road 'was absolutely the very worst of any we had
travelled yet – up and down steep hills, literally strewn with large boulders, and
over which we were bumped mercilessly, till our joints and every joint in our
bodies ached again'. The last 30 miles before Newcastle took eight hours. It took
another long journey before the exhausted tourists finally reached the head of
the railway line under construction from Durban into the interior. They slept at
Ladysmith, an hour and a half down the line, before going on to Pietermaritzburg for matches against a local XXII and 'the best fifteen representatives of the
Natal Colony'. Then it was on to the coast for a game against a Durban XVIII.
It was played in Albert Park in hot humid weather, and the outfield was so heavy
that the ball could not go far.

After Durban the destination was Port Elizabeth, via East London, King William's Town, Grahamstown and Graaff-Reinet, for the first test or 'representative' game. A relaxing 20-hour trip by sea to East London was followed by two matches against the Cape Mounted Rifles in King William's Town, a short distance inland. The matches were made possible by the CMR commanding officer, Colonel Bayley, who agreed to pick up the costs for the game and a week's entertainment in the town. Fillis's Circus was one of the attractions.

After easily beating the soldiers, the English took the day-long journey on the 'post-cart' to Grahamstown. On the way, Warton explained, 'we soon found ourselves potting storks, cranes and wild turkeys by the roadside with revolvers ... The Vale abounds with baboons; we heard them barking on the hilltop, but did not have the luck to get a shot at any.'[13] The post-cart entered town accompanied by a huge cavalcade of horsemen and a large crowd awaited them at the hotel. The match was played at the City Lords ground, which impressed the tourists. After another party that lasted into the small hours of the morning, the tourists embarked on the 300-mile train trip to Graaff-Reinet via Port Elizabeth. Warton was struck by the little town. The pitch for the game against a Midlands XXII was lightning-fast, prepared with a mixture of 'antheap, cinder and cement'. Back in Port Elizabeth an Eastern Province XV was dispensed with and then the first-ever test match followed on 12 and 13 March. The tourists rounded off the tour by going back to Kimberley by train for a needle return match against the local team before ending up back in Cape Town for the second test and their boat voyage home.

All in all, it had been an epic journey of 15,975 miles in 146 days, covering large parts of modern-day South Africa. The return trip from England pushed the mileage by boat up to 13,003 miles; train and coach or cart transport amounted to 2,218 and 754 miles respectively. It was a busy journey. Only five days were described as 'off-days'; 41 days were spent on board ship and 25 travelling by coach, cart or rail. On top of this there were four practice days, '14 Sundays', and 57 days performing out on the field.[14]

In the present age of globalisation, internet and air travel, it is difficult to imagine the physical constraints that hampered economic and social development in that time, but this journey does so in a graphic way. It also gives us a sense of the times. Britain controlled a quarter of the world's surface in the 1880s and the feted players reflected the confidence of the Empire. With Rhodes and others they shared the excitement and possibilities of expansion and new territories. Almost without exception, they were treated like conquering heroes and readily assumed the mantle of bearers of the 'civilising mission'. Their tour started a long tradition of visits by English cricketers to South Africa, to enjoy both South African summers and deep social relationships with sections of the white minority. This tradition remained intact well into the next century.

In many ways the 14 cricketers and their 6,000 pounds of luggage imprinted the game – and the particular character with which they imbued it – very firmly on the colonial landscape. At the same time the historic tour effectively united the disparate southern African cricket regions (at a time when South Africa was not yet a single country) and also brought the subcontinent into the mainstream of international cricket. It very much followed the precedents already set in England, Australia, Canada and America. Like these, those in charge in South Africa had strong connections with the colonial and British establishment. Like them too, the tour was organised as a private venture. It was dominated by 'amateurs', but included paid professionals to do the work and generate spectator interest. Thirdly, a prominent local MCC-type club acted as the sponsor. This was common in the days before national boards – for example, in Australia the Melbourne Cricket Club organised tours until the Australian Cricket Board was formed. And finally, it was as much a private-sector venture, based on a new market, as an imperial and national cricketing enterprise.

19

The first South African team and test matches

An excellent spirit prevailed.

- Daily Independent, 23 March 1889

Prior to the tour, Warton had been confident that the local opposition would easily be dispensed with. He noted that the professionals, who carried the lion's share of the hard work, felt the tour would be far less challenging than visiting Australia. However, the tourists lost four of the first six matches, albeit against heavily stacked XVs, XVIIIs and XXIIs, and suddenly found themselves scrabbling to regain respectability. First they lost against Western Province, then narrowly scraped in against the Cape Colony, before losing also to Port Elizabeth. Two matches at Kimberley, current holders of the Champion Bat competition, followed. These were bitter contests in the course of which the tourists were outplayed. When a Kimberley XVIII and then a Cape Colony XV achieved victories, the tourists faced a crisis situation.

These home wins confirmed the important role the Inter-Town tournaments had played since 1876 in providing a platform for representative cricket. Both the Cape Colony XVs included 13 players who had proved themselves in the tournaments. The star performer since 1880, Captain Robert Stewart of the Cape Mounted Rifles in King William's Town, and eight others also found themselves in the first test team. No less than 35 of the 41 home players in those three teams were ex-Inter Town participants. The English subsequently presented the new Currie Cup to Kimberley for being the best performers against them at a time when they were the reigning Champion Bat holders. The continuity with the past was clear: the tour was not a new start on a clean slate for cricket in the subcontinent, but the next step in a continuing effort built over a decade.

The Western Province Cricket Club (WPCC), which until then 'had in the fullest sense acted as the MCC of the Cape Colony' and organised the tour, selected the combined sides – Western Province and Cape Colony – for the first tour games. These were the first broadly representative teams in southern Africa after the combined eastern Cape African Inter-Town XI which had been selected in 1887. Milton at the WPCC was clearly in charge of the tour plans and liaised with both local clubs and the major colonial centres such as Kimberley, King William's Town and Port Elizabeth to include players from those areas in the Cape Colony team. Kimberley had a special welcoming committee drawn from the Eclectics, Kimberley and Pirates clubs, which worked for weeks to prepare for the English and get the best local team in the field. Holders of the Champion Bat and victors over all the major centres in the previous year, Kimberley did their best to outdo the arrangements in Cape Town and live up to its champion status. There was also much to celebrate on the field of play, where the tourists were beaten in both matches. Kimberley fielded 18 and then 15 players, but there were some fine individual achievements and, in successive matches, Charlie Vintcent's 87 and Fred Klinck's 81 were scored against an English attack that was desperate to succeed.

After four defeats in six matches, the *Sunday Times* in London complained about the tourists' calamitous record and quoted W.G. Grace as saying, 'it is the heat of the sun and the accidents that are accountable for the poor displays … The sun must have been very hot.'[1] 'Referee', writing in the *Empire,* was blunt in his condemnation: 'Never in the history of cricket touring', he said, 'has an English team made so miserable a start. When we send men out to play cricket we want them to win, for if they cannot win our name goes down.'[2] But the tide turned when the tourists came from behind to win in Johannesburg. Thereafter, the team never lost another match.

In the new city of Johannesburg, just three years old when the tourists arrived, cricket had been played from the start, but there was not yet an overarching organising body. A syndicate, which included the former Sussex and King William's Town Inter-Town tournament player, Captain Lyndhurst Winslow, was formed to provide the guarantee for the tour. This set in motion the beginning of organised cricket there: the new ground of the Wanderers club was hastily built and a Transvaal XV, dubbed the 'Republicans', was selected from players from Johannesburg, Potchefstroom, Barberton and Pretoria. These four towns had taken part in an inter-town tournament in the previous 1887/8 season, which Johannesburg won, and so there was a benchmark for measuring local talent.[3]

Pietermaritzburg and Durban were the established cricket centres in Natal in 1889. Their relative importance at the time can be gauged from the fact that two games were played in the inland capital and only one on the coast, although the

Durban XVIII surprisingly held the English to a draw. Five matches followed in the eastern Cape, where sides were unable to cope with the bowling of Smith and Briggs, the latter claiming 27 wickets for 23 runs in one match against the Cape Mounted Rifles XXII at King William's Town. The Grahamstown XXII recorded eleven 'ducks' in their second innings; and against the Midland Districts XXII at Graaff-Reinet, the first 16 overs were maidens, with seven wickets falling to Smith and Briggs before a run was posted. The local batting was poor and, with Smith bent on smashing all opposition, the tour record was improved. All in all, they played 19, lost 4, drew 2 and won 13, including the two 'representative' games as they were called (only much later were they recognised as official tests).

When it came to selecting the first 'representative' side for the notional country called 'South Africa' in the two 11-a-side matches in Port Elizabeth and Cape Town in March 1889, they were chosen by the hosts and in each case a local player captained the team. It was not altogether surprising that in the first test at Port Elizabeth, Aubrey Smith of Charterhouse and Cambridge should be opposed by a South African captain who was a product of Eton and Oxford, namely Owen Dunell, a Port Elizabeth-born businessman, who had been a solid performer and regular captain of PE in the Inter-Town tournaments since making his debut in 1880. Besides his Eton and Oxford appearances, Dunell had extensive knowledge of English cricket going back to the early 1870s;[4] that he also covered the tour as a newspaper correspondent seemed to confirm his professional interest in the game.

The captain and the local committee carefully chose players from the different regions that had played for the South African team against the tourists. Kimberley, current holders of the Champion Bat, had four players. A.B. Tancred was a top-order batsman, forced to open because of 'nerves', and soon entrenched himself as South Africa's top batting star, being regularly described as the 'Colonial W.G.'. Charlie Vintcent was an opening bowler and outstanding athlete, who had been at Charterhouse together with Aubrey Smith. The English thought him to be 'good enough for Surrey'.[5] He was South Africa's most outstanding all-round sportsman, a fine cricketer and footballer, and the fastest man over 100 yards, an athletic prowess that was all the more remarkable in that he had lost his right eye as a boy of 11. The remarkable player-journalist, Charles Finlason, who had taken six for 25 against the English in one innings, was included as an all-rounder. In the Kimberley match, he claimed the wicket of the English skipper, Aubrey Smith, first ball and, according to newspaper reports, bowled 'exceedingly well [and] sent down all kinds of balls, now a fast one and then a tempting round-arm lob with a good break on it'.[6] The fourth 'digger' was the wicketkeeper Fred Smith. All four of the Kimberley caps had participated in the

Inter-Town tournaments since 1884, when Kimberley made its debut in the tournament. The first three had all starred in these. Smith must have been a skilled wicketkeeper because, although he appeared in the batting scorecards from time to time, he never once reached 30 in his three tournaments.

The tour organiser, William Milton, a hard-hitting batsman, whose arrival usually signalled the scattering of fielders in the direction of the boundary, was the only Western Province player in the first representative team. He had hit a match-winning 36 and 40 to take the Western Province XXII to victory against the tourists in Cape Town. Nico Theunissen from Victoria College (later Stellenbosch University), a fast bowler who had caused consternation amongst the English in the same match by injuring batsmen and claiming 11 wickets, declined an invitation and was replaced by a local boy, Bert Rose-Innes. Theunissen claimed 34 wickets for 314 runs (average 9.23) and recorded five wickets in an innings five times out of a possible six in the three matches that he played against the tourists. Finlason believed that the absence of Theunissen's 'considerable pace, and great knee-shaking, rib-roasting, finger-mangling bump' made the English favourites for the test.[7] Without Theunissen, he said, the betting should be two or three to one on the English team, whereas with him he would have put short odds on a home-team win. That Theunissen did not play could be attributed to the Afrikaner community's lack of interest in the match at Port Elizabeth. The Stellenbosch fast bowler was refused time off from lectures because his professor thought '*sulke speelitjies*' (such little games) were a waste of time.[8]

Outside the three main cricketing centres of the Cape Colony, two players from Natal were selected and one each from the Transvaal and Orange Free State, although the OFS had not played the tourists. The OFS representative was 19-year-old Arthur Edward 'Okey' Ochse. There was criticism in some newspapers about his selection, but although young and untried he had scored 80-odd in a match against Kimberley.[9] The Natal representatives were the English-born Philip Hutchinson, who was 'considered the best batsman in the Colony and had few superiors as a bowler', and Gustav Kempis, an accurate left-handed medium-pace bowler who 'could break either way with equal facility'. Kempis died (of a fever on Chiloane Island, Mozambique) a year later at the age of 24, shortly after 'migrating into the interior'.[10] William Newby of Transvaal was selected but was unable to play, and Lieutenant Robert Stewart took his place. By far the best batsman of the Inter-Town Tournament era, Stewart, originally the reserve, was drafted into the team at the eleventh hour to general approval; many people thought his inclusion actually strengthened the side. It was only when the match started and it was discovered that the veteran was handicapped by an injured leg that his selection was queried.

Dunell's team included seven colonial-born players (himself, A.B. Tancred, Charlie Vintcent, Okey Ochse, Fred Smith, Bert Rose-Innes and Gustav Kempis) and four brought up in the 'Mother Country' (Lieutenant Robert Stewart, Charles Finlason, Philip Hutchinson and William Milton). However, even the colonial-born players were closely linked to Britain, in one way or another. Dunell and Vintcent had studied there. 'Okey' Ochse was originally – and incorrectly – recognised as the first Afrikaner to play test cricket, but his father was English-speaking and a close acquaintance of Rhodes, while his mother was the daughter of a Brighton vicar.

Thus the first South African team had no Afrikaners in it and the cricket euphoria that swept the country tended to be restricted to the white English-speaking communities as a result of the programme designed by Milton. His biographer points a finger at him for overlooking the relatively large Afrikaner community that made up teams in the districts surrounding Cape Town and his long reign as the local tsar of cricket, maintaining that it had a negative impact on the subsequent development of the game, by contributing to the focus by Afrikaners on rugby. While matches depended on the provision of guarantees, the districts were essentially within the domain of the WPCC. Those key Afrikaners involved in the tour – Jack van Reenen, Pieter de Villiers and Nico Theunissen – were past and present members of the WPCC. Other names, such as Van der Spuy, Schuurman, Van Niekerk, Morkel, Swart, Lodewyks and Steinhobel, did feature in sides that opposed the English team, but they were a very small percentage of the Afrikaners who played the game.[11]

The first South African team represented various parts of the fragmented southern African political map. The first 'national' team – albeit English-speaking and white – came into being before there was a nation, a significant but perhaps understated development at the time, in that the majority of the cricket-playing population expected unification in due course under the British flag.

There was plenty of pre-match hype, with some writers promoting the argument that if South Africa won the match or made even a fair show, it would rank with Australia. The representative matches were not designated as official 'tests' until a later date, although a leading cricket historian wrote in *The Cricketer Annual* of 1930–1 that 'the term "Tests" was, at the time, applied to them'. Certainly, the South Africans approached the matches with national fervour and pride. The players were smartly turned out in 'greenish-bronze' caps that had been specially purchased for the occasion. The wife of the South African captain had embroidered the letters 'SA' in yellow on the front of each cap.[12] This was another sign of the growing integration of the southern African region, economically and otherwise. For the British, South Africa was a concept in the process of becoming a reality – and they had the political, economic and military power to ensure it happened, as history would show.

The first test match began at noon on Tuesday, 12 March 1889 under a clear Port Elizabeth sky on the Port Elizabeth Cricket Club ground within St George's Park, right next door to the Union CC ground where the 1885/6 Native Inter-Town Tournament had taken place. The weather was warm although a light north-western wind kept the players cool. The ground was ringed with tents and resplendent with flags and bunting. There was a large crowd. Some people had come to the city for the agricultural show but most were enthusiastic supporters who had travelled from outposts around the country to watch the historic encounter.

Dunell won the toss for South Africa and decided to bat first on the green matting wicket. The Englishmen received a tremendous ovation when they took the field, as did the South African opening pair, Tancred and Rose-Innes, wearing their hand-embroidered caps. Briggs had the distinction of sending down the first over; it was a maiden played by Rose-Innes. Although the wicket held no terrors for the batsmen, the bowlers quickly gained the ascendancy. The first nine overs of four balls each were maidens. Two wickets fell during this time, those of Rose-Innes and Hutchinson, who was bowled first ball.

The first scoring shot ever for South Africa was an on-drive for two by Tancred off Fothergill, 20 minutes after the start of play. The Kimberley pair of Tancred and Vintcent scratched their way to ten before the latter lunged forward to a ball from Briggs and edged a catch to slip. It was the first of three successive catches by Abel. He also snapped up the nervous-looking Ochse (who twice survived appeals by Harry Wood for stumpings) for four and Milton off Fothergill for one. Dunell joined Tancred at 17 for five and they set about repairing the damage. The batsmen held firm, and lunch was taken at 52 for five (Tancred 24, Dunell 14). After the break, Briggs was brought back, with Smith continuing to operate at the other end. It was the English captain who posed the greatest problem, and he took all five of the remaining wickets. The South Africans were all out for 84 (Smith five for 19 and Briggs four for 39). Dunell, who remained unbeaten on 26, was given a well-deserved reception by the home crowd on his return to the pavilion.

Abel and Ulyett opened for the English against the bowling of Kempis and Finlason. When Abel whipped Kempis's second ball to the leg boundary, the tourists were on their way. South Africa's meagre total was not expected to create any problems, and so it came as a surprise when Kempis bowled Ulyett with a splendid delivery. Moments later, he struck again when Maurice Read mishit and skied the ball upwards, Dunell taking the catch at slip. England were 14 for two, and the South Africans were back in the game. Abel, who scored an invaluable

46 to put his side ahead, was out at 87 for eight and South Africa seemed to stand a chance. With the English score on 103 for nine, the last man, Fothergill, arrived at the wicket with one intention – to hit out at everything. He and his partner, Basil Grieve, enjoyed the luck 'that fortune sometimes confers' on a last-wicket stand, particularly as Rose-Innes beat both batsmen frequently. But a missed stumping and a last wicket partnership of 45 took England to 148 and a priceless 68 run lead. Rose-Innes took five wickets, a fine debut for the young bowler, and Kempis was consistent, only being withdrawn from the attack after bowling 31 consecutive overs.

The deficit proved dispiriting for the South Africans. In addition to injuries to Stewart and Finlason, Smith had hurt his thumb while wicketkeeping and Milton was complaining of the effects of sunstroke and seasickness from the voyage round the coast.[13] South Africa began their second innings the following morning with a strong north-west wind blowing. They were given a better start. Tancred and Rose-Innes put together 21 before the latter was given out after some deliberation by the umpire. But their 129 all out was too little. Fothergill of Somerset claimed four for 19 off 18.1 overs.

The English required 66 runs to win. Grieve and Abel saw them home to victory by eight wickets, shortly before half past three on the second day. It was an important victory for the visitors, who realised that more 11-a-side matches should have been organised. 'With twenty-two or eighteen in the field the batsmen get disheartened,' said Abel, 'and the Colonists themselves cannot test the real strength of their bowlers. Put a bad man on with eleven scouting and he will be knocked all over the place; but when there are additional men to field he may take wickets and then people believe he is a good bowler.'[14]

Although they were well beaten, the South Africans were very proud to have played in the inaugural match between the two countries. Finlason wrote, 'From several quarters comes the suggestion that the eleven men who first represented South Africa should be each presented with a small gold medal with an appropriate inscription engraved thereon. Such a memento would be much prized by the South African players for when they become old fossils they will always be able to show with pride the little piece of gold which proves that they once attained the greatest honour that could be paid to a cricketer in South Africa. I commend this suggestion to the consideration of Mr Dunell and the Port Elizabeth Committee.'[15]

Dunell was said to be largely instrumental in the success of the inaugural test. 'As captain of the team and especially as a member of the entertaining committee,' said Finlason, 'he was most successful. He spared no pains to make the visitors comfortable and was lavish in his hospitality. The entertainments were so numerous and so well managed that if any visiting cricketer failed to enjoy himself it was his own fault.'[16]

As the match ended sooner than anticipated, it was decided to play an exhibition game on the Friday to entertain the many visitors to Port Elizabeth. The professionals were asked to play; Briggs, Abel, Ulyett and Hearne represented the married men and Read took the field for the bachelors. A large crowd applauded rapturously as Milton plundered the bowling to score 62, with local hero Dunell providing an unbeaten 59. The Married Men scored 225, to which the Single Men could only reply with 113 for five.

Afterwards a smoking concert for around 450 people was given in the Drill Hall as a farewell function for the tourists. Numerous speeches, songs and recitations took place, with Monty Bowden and several other English cricketers contributing to the programme. A report of the evening noted, 'An excellent spirit prevailed.'[17] At the event, the Lancashire supporters of Port Elizabeth gave Johnny Briggs a handsome gold medal as a souvenir of his visit and a local resident donated a well-filled purse. Surrey supporters presented Bobby Abel with a gold medal and purse, while the Yorkshiremen made a similar award to George Ulyett. Filled purses were also handed to Fothergill and Hearne.

This was a fitting conclusion to South Africa's first-ever test match. It was a very relaxed touring team that left for Kimberley by train amid cheers from a huge crowd which had assembled on the platform. They had developed into a formidable combination. 'We are very strong now and could play against any county team,' remarked Abel, 'so I should say the betting at any time would be in favour of us.'[18]

END OF AN HISTORIC VISIT

Milton had earlier requested that 'the towns where the matches are played should choose the [South African] teams, as I believe is the case with representative matches in England'. As expected, the WPCC selected Milton as captain for the second test and brought in local stars Theunissen, 'Gobo' Ashley and Dick Richards at the expense of Finlason, Kempis and Stewart.

Aubrey Smith was unable to get to Cape Town in time for the second representative match at Newlands. He was said to be suffering from 'a fever that mystified doctors', but there were feelings that he might not have been keen to play. Monty Bowden took over as captain. This led to some interesting cricket trivia: Smith was the only player to captain England on his sole appearance in test cricket, and his replacement, Emile McMaster, made his test debut in his only first-class match. Bowden, who was 23 years 144 days old on the opening day of the match, remains England's youngest-ever test captain.

England won the toss and the 4,000 crowd saw England again dispose of South Africa by an innings and 202 runs in an emphatic victory. England scored 292, thanks to Bobby Abel's 120 in 226 minutes. Ashley was outstanding, capturing seven for 95 off 43.1 overs. After this, South Africa were bowled out for 47 in an hour and a half, and they could only muster 43 in the follow-on. In the course of the home side's capitulation, Briggs teased and tormented the mesmerised South Africans to claim 15 wickets for 28 runs – the most wickets by one bowler in a day (not even two sessions!) of test cricket. A.B. Tancred established a record that could never be taken away from him. Keeping up an end while his teammates floundered, he became the first batsman in test cricket to bat through an innings. Another test record was established in that his score remains the lowest – 26 not out – by a batsman carrying his bat through a completed innings. Major Warton thought it bewildering that men who had scored half-centuries against the tourists in earlier matches should suddenly find Briggs impossible to encounter.[19] The crowd gave the Surrey professional a tremendous ovation.

The massive win – still the largest margin of victory by an innings in test matches between the two countries – served as an indication of the disparity that existed in the standard of play between the two sides, placing doubts on South Africa's ability to stand alongside England and Australia as a cricket-playing nation. It reinforced the jingoistic British notion of South Africa as 'minors' rather than emphasising its readiness to compete on equal terms, as Finlason and others had hoped to prove.

After play ended, spectators assembled at the grandstand where Thomas Fuller (later Sir Thomas), a parliamentarian and former editor of the *Cape Argus*, spoke of the great impact that the tour had made. 'Today has seen the close of a passage in South African history which will never be forgotten,' he said.[20] Lady Robinson, wife of the governor of the Cape Colony and high commissioner for South Africa, then made a number of presentations. A.B. Tancred and Nico Theunissen were given the awards, donated by the Union Steamship Company, for the best batsman and bowler in matches against the tourists. In addition, a watch was promised to Ashley for his fine bowling. Each of the professionals received purses containing £20. These were collected partly by public subscription and partly by drawing upon the funds of the WPCC. Thomas Fuller noted that the purses were 'given not as an honorarium, or for services rendered, but as a mark of esteem and admiration, not only for the brilliant exposition of cricket the professionals had displayed, but for their social qualities and gentlemanly behaviour'.[21] After Major Warton had briefly responded and given thanks to Lady Robinson, proceedings ended with three cheers. A luncheon and more speeches followed.

More will be said about the tour in the next few chapters, but it was a visit that had commenced and cemented imperial friendships. After a special train had conveyed the party to the docks, a large concourse of spectators assembled to bid farewell to the English team. The warning bell had to sound several times for those not 'Homeward bound' to leave the ship and, amid hearty cheering, the *Garth Castle* steamed away for England.

20

'Home', 'new chums' and the assertion of South African cricket identities

> In South Africa the people are very much republicans and
> nobody much respects anybody. It is the generally accepted
> belief that everybody is as good as his neighbour in theory,
> and a good deal better in practice; and the aristocrat or
> the famous Englishman who comes into the country finds
> himself treated on terms of equality by every Tom, Dick
> and Harry he meets, in a way that benumbs him.
>
> – Charles Finlason, *A Nobody in Mashonaland*[1]

The first international tour galvanised cricketers in the disparate regions of southern Africa and brought them into the kind of close working relationships needed to take cricket into the modern era. For the first time there was an organising centre: from his base in Newlands in Cape Town, William Milton acted as the cog of what would become a national enterprise. At the same time, the idea of representative regional teams was established. Each region was pushed to create unified selection and organisational structures beyond those already in place for the Inter-Town tournaments and the odd internal tour. Out of this, the regions developed the structures and necessary consensus to choose a representative South African cricket team, pointing to the way forward administratively and politically for the broader society as well. In the mindset and language of the British and their allies in the subcontinent, the concept of 'South Africa' as one political entity under British rule was being constructed as something inevitable and concrete, even though it would take another 21 years and a long and costly war before it became formalised politically.

Cricket also developed the profile and public awareness necessary to make it a modern 'national' sport. Newspapers and specialist reporters covered the tour, spreading the narrative of an integrated, organised sport at home and in England, and prompting politicians in different regions to unite behind the notion of a new kind of national relationship with the imperial motherland. Through the contests South African cricket could measure itself against 'Home' and develop the confidence to participate internationally. The four early defeats inflicted on the tourists excited local supporters. The game's entrepreneurs were immediately encouraged to explore further opportunities to arrange matches at an international level, while local enthusiasts were galvanised into establishing cricket administrations. Cricket became a national game in an organised sense for the first time. But would it incorporate all cricketers into its future development and structures?

Although the test match results strengthened the jingoistic imperial lobby, which categorised local cricketers as 'minors' in a paternalistic relationship with 'Home', many different identities emerged at the time, and not all South African cricketers shared the feeling of imperial reverence and colonial subservience. The person who best gave expression to this was the Kimberley bowler Charles Finlason, who played in the first-ever test in Port Elizabeth. He was also the cricket correspondent for the Kimberley *Daily Independent*. He had an agile and perceptive understanding of cricket which showed in his reports, where he demonstrated a style conspicuously ahead of its time. His comments in his column, 'The Day's Gossip', were unashamedly partisan and provoked considerable controversy, attracting a large readership. He was not afraid to be critical of the English, going against the tide by predicting their downfall and mocking the overt respect accorded to them. Nor was he bothered by having to compete on the field against the players he deprecated in print. He believed that Kimberley was superior to any other centre in the colony and could be compared favourably with most English counties – and that South African cricket was every bit as good as, if not better than, that played in Australia.

Finlason pressed for an early psychological advantage over the first English tourists when he directed his attack at Warton. He was scathing about the English manager, who had claimed somewhat arrogantly in an interview that the touring side wanted to play against odds because the professionals 'did not anticipate hard work on the tour ... as had been the case in Australia'.[2] The success of Australian cricket had helped forge a national identity in that country that was envied by other colonies. 'Affection for the "Old Country" was tinged with a sharply democratic "Jack's as good as his master" attitude.'[3] Finlason adopted a similar stance with a view to putting heart into those colonial players who 'deemed it presumptuous to hope to make five runs or to take a single wicket'.

Finlason did not share the view that matches played against Warton's team were simply learning experiences for South African cricketers. He was of the opinion that it was vital to gain as many victories as possible against the tourists in order to prove a point. He predicted that the English would be beaten and wrote with undisguised glee when proved correct.

Finlason did not lose sight of the fact that there were some fine players in Warton's team. He often referred to their records overseas to give greater credibility to his argument that the South African cricketers were as strong as their Australian counterparts. For Finlason, beating the Mother Country 'was a rite of passage for settler communities, an indicator perhaps of eventual fitness for dominion status'.

When the English team captain proclaimed, 'We are able to accept defeat because we are Englishmen and every Englishman knows how to accept defeat,'[4] Finlason responded that, contrary to their self-image, the English did not like losing. He became impatient with their excuses: 'Hospitality too profuse, travelling too hard, light too puzzling, odds so great ... the latest excuse has been made by Mr Bowden in the *Potchefstroom Budget* where he attributes the defeats of his team partly "to the inferior grounds". What will they come up with next?'[5] He also made fun of English stereotypes about Africa. 'It seems that they were told dreadful stories in London about Kimberley and Johannesburg bowie-knife rowdies. Some members of the team I am told were looking out for lions between Beaufort and Kimberley. Had they made the journey twenty years ago they might have been more successful.'[6]

Finlason went on to strike at the very heart of the public school ideal by accusing Smith and his English team of infringing the spirit of 'fair play' through controversial on-field antics 'that no colonial man would care to try'.[7] 'Whatever the merit of these accusations, 'they stemmed in part from the breakdown of class in the colonial context, following the Australian model.'[8] Finlason, an independent spirit, detested a system which had not only created an 'elite' but cultivated a network that assisted its members to penetrate top positions in the professions. He liked Africa because – in the words of Lord Kimberley – 'nobody stays a gentleman for long'.[9] As Finlason later wrote: 'In South Africa the people are very much republicans and nobody much respects anybody. It is the generally accepted belief that everybody is as good as his neighbour in theory, and a good deal better in practice; and the aristocrat or the famous Englishman who comes into the country finds himself treated on terms of equality by every Tom, Dick and Harry he meets, in a way that benumbs him.'[10]

Finlason often wrote of his dislike for the 'new chum'. He told readers, 'The newly imported young man fresh from "Home" succeeds somehow in being particularly offensive to "old chums" and men born in the country. They go about with an air of pity for men and things Colonial and are always making comparisons between the colony and home very much against the former. They are usually dressed in new clothes for they bring out a big outfit, having heard there are "no tailors that can fit you, by Jove", in the unhappy land which is to supply them with a fortune without their working for it. They are "standoffish" to colonials and show that they think it "demmed cheek" for a fellow to speak to them without an introduction.'[11]

It was Finlason's comments about the English behaviour on the field of play that caused the greatest controversy. As one of South Africa's leading players, his articles naturally demanded attention. He made interesting observations, such as that the English fielding was different in style from that in vogue in the colony. He noted, for example, 'They field with an elan that is rarely shown by a Colonial team. Sometimes almost every man on the field appeals with a shout and when an attempt is made at stumping a man, a number of the fieldsmen give a little spring into the air. Every ball too, is watched with an intense keenness which sometimes embarrasses a Colonial batsman who is not used to that sort of thing at all. The manner in which they appeal, again, is novel to us. The words, "How's that?" are shouted out so as to be heard a half a mile away.'[12]

Never one to sidestep the unpalatable aspects of an issue, Finlason was prepared to comment on aspects of play that other reporters chose to ignore. He wrote:

> I think too that now and again there is a tendency to rush an umpire. An umpire indeed, has to have a firm will, great presence of mind and fine judgement when he is umpiring with the Englishmen in the field. Sometimes an appeal is made with an almost irresistible air of confidence, and the trick of throwing up the ball as if there could be no manner of doubt has been more than once resorted to in the matches played. I am not sure now whether Rose-Innes was run out in the second innings of the All Colony match played at the metropolis, and if he were not out as many say, the trick played was quite new to the Colonial public. Rose-Innes was just on the crease or thereabouts when Wood put down the wicket, threw up the ball and shouted "Out!" The fieldsmen with one accord rushed off the field, and I doubt whether the umpire ever gave a decision. I hear that this is an old professional trick, often resorted to by pro's in England. It is a trick, however, that no Colonial man would care to try.[13]

An outcry followed Finlason's observation. He had openly accused the English of infringing the spirit of the game, even of cheating, and his report was considered by many to be in poor taste. The *Port Elizabeth Advertiser* supported Finlason's outspoken claims,[14] but most of those who knew he was right balked at the idea of supporting him. Eventually matters came to a head during the week of cricket in Kimberley. Finlason's opponents broached the subject of his writing at the after-match banquet. When a local businessman, D.J. Haarhof, was asked to propose the toast to 'the Press', he said: 'I am sure we are not all satisfied with the manner in which one of the 'papers in Kimberley has referred to the English cricket team and their play. I know that the finger of scorn has been placed at Kimberley men because of remarks which appeared in the *Daily Independent* of Kimberley.' A section of the audience – which included the English cricketers – applauded loudly, with shouts of 'Quite right!' Haarhof continued, 'the 'paper I have alluded to should not be regarded in any way as reflecting the feeling or spirit of the people of Kimberley.'

Finlason was undeterred and stood his ground against the critics and the jingoism underlying the tour:

> I have reason to know that ... nearly every Colonial-born man in Kimberley is on my side, and of the Home-born men who have not for the nonce become violent and unreasonable partisans of the Home-born cricketers. All the feeling that has been aroused is chiefly due to that so much to be deplored Home-born and Colonial-born feeling. Nothing that the Colony has can equal anything that the Old Country has; nothing that a Colonial-born man can do can equal what a Home-born man can do. Such are the unfortunate opinions which are held by many men who owe every farthing they have in the world to the Colony they milk systematically in and out of season.[15]

It was strongly suspected that the touring side had put pressure on local administrators to silence Finlason. It was no secret that Aubrey Smith and Finlason had little time for each other. 'It is a fact', said the editor of the *Diamond Fields Advertiser*, 'that such was the discontent felt among the members of the English team, from the gentlemanly captain downwards, at the ungracious dissertations which found place in a Kimberley newspaper that they were seriously considering the advisability of returning to Kimberley if such a line of writing were persisted in or unless some amends were made for the same.'[16]

The storm dominated the national press for several days and there was much emotive comment. Throughout the drama, the *Daily Independent* refused to place restrictions on Finlason's writing. Indeed, the publicity was good for business. As the most informed cricket correspondent in the colony, Finlason's comments were sought after and reproduced by other newspapers on a daily basis. Finlason did not alter his stance: he remained as sensitive as ever to any assumptions of superiority on the part of the tourists and continued to express his delight that their cricket record had been severely dented.

This controversy also prefigured the split that would occur in the mid-1890s in Cape politics between those motivated mainly by South African interests, including many Cape liberals (who ended up siding with the Afrikaner Bond), and the jingoistic British imperialist camp headed by Cecil John Rhodes and his allies (which included the tour organiser and South African captain, William Milton).

The tour brought to light many of the problems that had been simmering for a number of years. They were not restricted to the case of conflicting views between whites over whether or not they should be supporting the colony against the country some still regarded as 'Home'. At the same time, black players in the different regions, Christian and Muslim, drawing on liberal and 'fair play' principles, were also seeking a role in colonial cricket. There was also a great rivalry between centres stemming to a large extent from 'the impact of mineral discoveries, the boom-and-bust cycles of speculation and depression and notably the switch in focus from diamonds to gold'.[17] The English captain claimed that wherever his side went, they were urged 'to thrash Kimberley'. Johannesburg in turn was described as 'an abode of fleas, flies and favours' which had difficulty raising a cricket side; and nobody much liked the 'Metropolis' (Cape Town) for the air of superiority it always projected on matters related to cricket.[18] It was all these conflicting tensions, rivalries, claims and demands that made up a unique pattern in the early development of South African cricket.

21

'Gentlemen, we beg you to reconsider your decision'

The position of African cricketers by the 1890s

> We have already invited teams and incurred expenses
> – of course not anticipating any difficulty as the
> ground was granted us on a previous occasion.
>
> – Paul Xiniwe, 1892

The emerging black sportsmen and enfranchised activists in the eastern Cape, who used cricket as an instrument for 'improvement' and assimilation in colonial society, also became increasingly vocal by the 1890s. Well organised, as the Native Inter-Town tournaments showed, they wished to be recognised as part of the local cricket constituency.

When the tour plans were being finalised by Milton and Warton in late 1888, black cricketers were at exactly the same time exploring the idea of a second, equally exciting venture – in the opposite direction, to England. The idea of sending a combined side chosen from the best players at the Inter-Town Tournament on a tour of England, first mooted by the newspaper editor John Tengo Jabavu in 1884, came up for discussion in earnest again in 1888. A 'number of gentlemen from England' were apparently enquiring about the prospect. They wished to ascertain whether there was the enthusiasm and ability to make viable a 'tour through Great Britain' during the following English season starting in April. The conditions for selecting players were demanding:

1st Good character, total abstainers and generally intelligent;
2nd Smart and athletic, good figure, with no deformity;
3rd Must be willing to practise incessantly the next six months;

4th All candidates required to prove their proficiency before being chosen, and to pass a committee of experts.[1]

Tours of 'natives' from the colonies fitted into a longstanding curiosity with the exotic and a long tradition of exhibiting 'savages' and human freaks in the metropolis. Influenced by the pseudo-science of social Darwinism, the British in the nineteenth century hierarchically classified and compared people from the colonies with themselves. Sarah Baartman, a Khoikhoi woman, was displayed naked as a freak 'African Venus', and 'primitive' people were included in circuses. In similar vein, during the first cricket tour from Australia in 1868 the Aboriginal members were made to throw boomerangs during the intervals.[2] Entrepreneurs in southern Africa were seemingly trying to cash in on this market, although not necessarily in such a crude fashion.

African cricket players showed an interest in using such opportunities to their advantage. *Imvo Zabantsundu* said, 'There can be no question that the project will commend itself to the Native athletes, just as it has completely fascinated us. We trust that the various Kafir clubs will lose no time in arranging for an undertaking that is fraught with momentous issues for the native races of this country.'[3]

Once again, the idea was tied to broader developments in the game internationally. The Parsi community in Bombay in India, which had at least 30 cricket clubs by the end of the 1860s, sent a team to tour England in 1886; and a second tour followed in 1888, no doubt feeding into the proposal of a South African 'native' tour. The Parsi tourists in 1888 performed well: Dr M.E. Pavri, the 'W.G. Grace of the Parsis', took 170 wickets at measly cost.[4] Local fans in South Africa were confident that an African team would also do well in England. 'N[ative] Cricketer' noted that Bobby Abel, the English test player and Surrey professional, was about to go to India to coach among the Parsis. He said he had no doubt that 'the Natives of this country, with proper coaching, would thoroughly efface the best records of our friends in India'.[5] Other letters to the editor of *Imvo* supported the plan and made suggestions about how to implement it. The idea was for a so-called 'Anglo-African' team to be selected after a tournament featuring the best players. But in the end, the tour, like the 1884 suggestion from Jabavu, did not materialise, and it took six more years before the first (all-white) touring team left South African shores in 1894.

News of the growth of cricket among Africans reached the first tourists, and the English team actually expected to play against a black team in South Africa. At the farewell luncheon given by Sir Donald Currie for the cricketers aboard the *Garth Castle*, prior to its departure, one of the speakers, the assistant agent general of the Castle Company, provided some background information on cricket at the Cape, and pointed out, 'No sport has taken such deep root among the black people of South Africa as cricket.'[6] Currie himself delivered a speech in which he dwelt upon the mystique of the African continent and warned the cricketers of 'the great running powers of the Kafir tribes'.[7] Both Currie and the English were certainly under the impression that they would be up against black players in the course of their tour.

In the eyes of the growing black middle class, the tourists, as representatives of Great Britain, were imbued with qualities and values that reflected the Africans' aspirations and worldview. Given the discrimination and often harsh realities of life they faced at the Cape, they idealised British values, even if there was a mismatch between the high-sounding Christian liberal principles espoused by the British and the actual experience of black people. Despite the obvious contradictions, they glorified things British (the ideal) as against things colonial (the reality). The romanticisation of Queen Victoria as the great protector of her subject people's rights was part of an approach to hold the imperial rulers in London and Cape Town to standards supposedly inherent in British rule in the face of the deteriorating conditions in which the colonised found themselves. Generally, the African and coloured voters in the Cape Colony supported parliamentary candidates who were liberal-minded or pro-British in their approach, because they saw them as a lesser evil and a bulwark against those colonial hardliners who opposed political rights for blacks.

A large percentage of the big crowd that greeted the tourists at the Cape Town docks were from the black communities. Major Warton saw Africans and Cape Muslims ('Malays') playing and commented on the large number of 'Malay' spectators at Newlands with their conspicuously colourful dress.[8] Two of the players had 'dusky' women acquaintances sitting with them in the pavilion when the first match of the tour started. A *Potchefstroom Budget* reporter was shocked to see two English cricketers sitting with black companions 'in sight of some thousands of spectators' at Newlands. He proffered the view that 'the professionals in question were quite unconscious of any impropriety'.[9]

When the tourists reached King William's Town to play against the Cape Mounted Rifles, fully 2,000 people were in attendance. The black spectators, in an obvious political commentary, cheered on the tourists against the badly outclassed local white side. In the report on the match, *Imvo* noted, 'It is singular that the sympathies of the Native spectators were with the English.'[10] The English captain, Aubrey Smith, expressed his feelings on this issue in an after-dinner speech when the tourists were in Port Elizabeth:

Our visit, from all that I can see, is calculated to have so great an effect on the cricket of the Cape, not only amongst the white population, but even amongst the black. I noticed while driving through the suburbs of Cape Town that every spare patch of ground was used by the blacks to pitch wickets – or paraffin cans in some cases – in order to play cricket. I think it is not only here but wherever you go in the colonies you will find it is cricket which binds men together in the cause of sport and I hope it will always be so.[11]

While Smith's liberal words would have been welcomed by black cricketers, the British tourists essentially regarded themselves as superior to the exotic Others they encountered, even if they were sometimes prepared to offer recognition in a paternalistic way. Major Warton commented on 'Messrs Kaffer' who 'smoked their pipes and chattered as they sat beside their huts' while their women worked in the fields,[12] and Aubrey Smith himself recalled the 'nigger' skits they had performed on tour. The Afrikaners were similarly ranked lower down the ladder, as the accounts of 'genuine Dutch Boers' in the visitors' travel descriptions testify.[13]

When England inflicted the huge innings and 202-run defeat on South Africa in the second and final match of the 1888/9 tour, *Imvo* conveyed the feeling of 'Native Opinion' on the tour: 'In sporting circles the sensation of the week has been the uplifting of the curtain over the ridiculous mouse, the South African team. People were led to believe that the South African eleven which played Major Warton's team would do wonders as it was composed of such well-known cricketers of South African fame.'[14] This response could be read as a metaphor for developments beyond cricket as well. The cricket result showed the superiority of imperial ideas and government over the flawed and negatively experienced colonial model. Many school people supported the idea of direct rule from London in a Crown Colony, as had been the case in Bechuanaland since 1885, instead of Responsible Government, which left them largely in the hands of colonial whites. Secondly, the defeat challenged the whole notion of the superiority of colonial whites and cricketers. If qualified black cricketers were given the chance, they felt, South Africa would have a better team. Black players, if given the same opportunities as whites, could do just as well.

The cricketing personality Paul Xiniwe was involved in an interesting spin-off from the debate about black players touring England and participating within the structures of cricket in southern Africa. He actually took part in a tour of England three years later in 1891–2 – but as part of the first African choir to go abroad. Shortly after playing in the 1890/1 Native Inter-Town Tournament in Port Elizabeth for the competitive King William's Town side, Xiniwe was on a boat headed for England for a year-long tour with the pioneering African Native Choir. The choir took part with over 28,000 visitors and singers in the final event of the Jubilee celebrations for Queen Victoria at the Crystal Palace. The choir's participation earned its members an invitation to perform for the Queen at her summer palace of Osborne on the Isle of Wight. Xiniwe introduced the choir to the monarch. A glittering audience was present: 'ladies in silken gowns, soldiers in uniform, Scots in green and yellow kilts, Indians wearing turbans, a West African boy in a scarlet tunic and twenty or thirty Englishmen in black frock coats and trousers.'[15] After the royal command performance, Xiniwe and the choir spent five months on the road, touring the north of England, Scotland and Ireland before returning to London for the summer where they sang at many high-society events 'almost every afternoon or early evening … at the great houses around London'.[16]

In the first half of their performances, clothed in 'tribal' dress, the choir sang African folksongs. In the second, the choristers wore their 'Christian clothes' and performed in English. This was a complex interplay of identity and ritual, which challenged stereotypes and allowed for the creation of multiple meanings. British journalists, having deemed Africans 'so undeveloped as to be thought scarcely worthy of association with music', expressed surprise at the quality of their singing. One critic put an isiXhosa solo on a par with Rossini's *Cujus animam*, saying that it was 'difficult to accept it as a specimen of native music at all'.[17]

David Coplan, the historian of African music in South Africa, has commented on how the skill of the choristers and their 'sartorial code-switching' confused British audiences and commentators, who '(then as now) had serious difficulty deciding whether they preferred their visiting Africans "civilised" or "uncivilised"'. Coplan notes that the British onlookers were 'explicitly disturbed by the multi-layered ambiguous cultural politics ingeniously expressed by this mixing of dress codes', while 'the performers themselves, of course, took nothing but easy confidence and pride in their sartorial code-switching'.[18]

This skill and self-confident identity, the code-switching and the mixed reactions that Paul Xiniwe and his fellow choristers received, mirrored what was happening in cricket at the time. It was no coincidence that the versatile young choir leader, a one-time 'Sporting Editor' of *Imvo*, who was soon to open the first black-owned hotel in the colony, was also a top-order batsman who played in seven of the Native Inter-Town tournaments held between 1884 and 1998. Together with his colleagues in cricket, education, religion, politics, the economy and social life, Xiniwe's demand was for the evolutionary incorporation of qualified African individuals into the new colonial structures. And they were in a hurry to show their fitness to be regarded as citizens of the colony in the fullest sense.

How determined they were to be treated equally was demonstrated during the preparations for the Native Inter-Town Tournament in 1892/3. Xiniwe – recently returned from England – was in the forefront. When the King William's Town council refused the tournament organisers access to the local municipal Victoria Ground, the home of local white cricketers, he and his fellow administrators challenged the decision and won. King were the tournament hosts that season, and the local organising committee wrote to the town council 'with the object of ascertaining whether it will be pleased to allow us to hire the [Victoria] municipal Cricket Ground, at as moderate a sum as possible for at least ten days during the Tournament'.[19] The town clerk took six weeks to reply, and the answer was negative, on account of 'all the space being taken up by the various local clubs'. Paul Xiniwe, 'for the sec', appealed directly to the mayor and town council:

> We interviewed several of the prominent cricketers in town and they invariably stated that those days are vacant, that they are arranging to go up and play up country during the holidays; and in fact that even if they had fixtures for that time they would waive them in order to allow us our tournament space. Therefore gentlemen under these circumstances we beg you to reconsider your decision and grant us the ground for our tournament to which we have already invited teams and incurred expenses – of course not anticipating any difficulty as the ground was granted us on a previous occasion.[20]

Xiniwe got his way. Permission was granted for the tournament to proceed at the Victoria Ground, and he invited the mayor to 'preside over our concert', which was a special fundraiser for the tournament held in the town hall.[21] These kinds of 'every day struggles over leisure space and the meaning of free time' were crucial avenues for contesting, negotiating and shaping ruling-class efforts to control the lives of the colonised.[22]

Black cricketers were matching step by step what was happening in the white establishment fold – and they were fighting actively to become part of mainstream cricket.

22

'The most gorgeous of Eastern spectacles'

A third inter-town tournament launched, January 1890

> The visage presented to the visitors at Newlands yesterday, could hardly have been rivalled by the most gorgeous of Eastern spectacles, whilst the beautiful background of trees and the lofty mountain rising beyond toned down the daring blaze of colour, the whole forming a picture which must have printed itself indelibly upon the retina of all who made the journey to the ground. The whole of the Malay population appeared to have deserted Cape Town for the sylvan pastures ...
>
> – *Cape Times*, 14 January 1890

First the imperialists and 'Home chums'. Then rugged white South African republican views and African demands for incorporation. Now, within a season of the English tour, it was the turn of Muslim and Christian coloured cricketers in Cape Town to assert themselves and initiate new tournaments.

Following the white Champion Bat tournament and the Native Inter-Town Tournament, a new 'Malay' Inter-Town Tournament was launched in Cape Town in the 1889/90 season. The two home sub-union teams from Claremont and the city-based Cape Town Union took on Kimberley and Johannesburg, which was then only a five-year-old settlement. The City of Gold already had close connections with the Mother City. One writer observed: 'Anyone watching the departure of the mainline night trains will have seen how largely the Malays have availed themselves of the opportunity of going to Johannesburg to make their fortunes, just as a few years ago they went to Kimberley.'[1] The local Muslim community in Cape Town, which adopted the British games very early, was at the heart of organising the tournament.

Islam had been brought to the Cape by political prisoners and slaves in the seventeenth and eighteenth centuries and had grown as a religion for those excluded from the mainstream of Cape society. The Cape Muslims, or 'Malays' as they were generically and incorrectly labelled, formed their own community schools and institutions and practised their distinct codes of behaviour based on the Koran. Islam – regarded not only as a religion but as a way of life – provided a strong rallying point. In the words of Achmat Davids, the Cape Muslims were 'an unintegrated community in the nineteenth century'.[2] The values of Christianity and the British Empire taught in church mission schools to the school people in the eastern Cape and to Christianised 'coloureds' in the western Cape obviously did not have the same pull or acculturating influence for these descendants of political prisoners and slaves. Their religion was traditionally for those excluded from colonial society, and they tended to be inward-focused, adapting to the broader politics and social life on their own terms, in this way giving them a distinctive character and meaning. The fact that they were responsible for the first written Afrikaans – in Arabic script – underlined this point, as did the name they gave to the first black cricket club in Cape Town in 1882, Ottomans CC, named after what a club brochure described as the 'great Ottoman Empire', whose ruler was the guardian of the holy places of Mecca and Medina.

By the mid-1880s this distinct community constituted a third of the population of Cape Town, and its members were important participants in the local economy with their skills as artisans. The total city population in 1891 was 67,000, which jumped to 171,000 by 1904. There were also many coloured voters, both Islam and Christian; the figure for the colony as a whole stood at 14,836 in 1904. They formed 35 per cent of the electorate in District Six in Cape Town and well over 20 per cent in Paarl, Stellenbosch and Namaqualand.[3] They therefore had influence in Cape Town and the neighbouring areas.

The Cape Muslims became passionate rugby and cricket followers at an early stage. They adopted the new games on their own terms, giving them a distinctive character and meaning. Teams were community-based, often coming from one street or family or from the *Jamaahs*, organised groups that met for religious purposes, whose activities spread out into the social sphere as well. For example, people would gather for the *Mouled Jamaahs* to celebrate the birth of the prophet Mohammed. Here groups would vie with one other in 'producing recitations in melodious tones' in praise of the prophet. First, one group would present (*toekan*) and then others would reply (*jawap*). These were often great social occasions, lasting well into the night. From these communal activities there emerged formal sports clubs and choirs, which were predominantly (but not exclusively) Muslim.[4] A local Muslim sports historian has explained, 'As most of the leading administrators were also the Imams of the congregation, they felt it was better to organise separately as they were mostly against the drinking habits of the other groups, especially over the festive season.[5]

The names of some of the earliest clubs in Cape Town – Ottomans CC in cricket and Arabian College and Hamediahs in rugby – indicated their links with the cohesive and well-established Muslim community in Cape Town. Ottomans was founded in 1882 by Abdullah Gamat, known as 'Boeta Plaat'. The club had one address for over sixty years – 23 Pentz Street in the Bo-Kaap – and 'only about four sets of officials' in its first century of existence. For those who took on the responsibility of administration, it was a lifetime's job, part of a commitment to religion and community as a way of life.[6]

In Chapter 2 we have noted how cricket had become well established in the black communities of Cape Town by the 1870s. By the mid-1880s there were many active clubs for African and coloured cricketers and they played all over the city: Green Point Common, the Early Morning Market, Woodstock, the Campground at Rondebosch, Mowbray, Wynberg, Simonstown and elsewhere.

> Regularly active teams included Africans, Blue Bells, Alberts, Good Hope, Rising Star, Primrose, Union, Victoria, Star of Africa and Ormonde. These were not just popular with the players. Alberts 1sts and 2nds played their Union equivalents over the New Year and the pitch for the first team game was completely ringed with spectators ... Other local clubs like Docks, Simonstown and Woodstock had both coloured and white players, and mission schools such as Zonnebloem of course fielded black and white players.[7]

In 1887 a 'detachment of Malay cricketers' was part of the procession that proceeded through Cape Town to celebrate the fiftieth-anniversary Jubilee of Queen Victoria's reign, marching in happy formation with the 'Volunteer Artillery, Friendly Societies, bakers, painters, and coach builders', as well as Hadjis and Khalifa performers.[8]

The English manager, Major Warton, vividly described the enthusiasm for the game in the black communities of Cape Town during the 1889/90 tour. 'On our way home we saw as quaint a sight as cricketers ever saw at Mowbray. Two or three cricket matches by Malays and Kaffirs, and hundreds of Malay women in the many coloured costumes were there to do honour to their friends.'[9] This growth in the game provided the basis for the first 'Malay' Inter-Town Tournament in January 1890. It was played in front of large crowds of several thousand people and brought to the fore the well-developed cricket culture in Cape Town.[10] There were two Cape Town teams representing the central Cape Town Union and the suburban Claremont Union, as well as the visiting Port Elizabeth and Johannesburg teams. Kimberley for some reason did not participate, despite the good standard of cricket in that city and despite the fact that a Kimberley XI toured the Cape in the same season, winning at Robertson, Worcester, Paarl, Wellington and Cape Town, where they beat a North Staffordshire regiment team.[11]

As in the eastern Cape, where the African players used the Victoria Grounds in King William's Town, the City Lords ground in Grahamstown and the Union CC field in St George's Park in Port Elizabeth as Inter-Town venues, the local cricketers in Cape Town got to play on the elite venue in the city, the newly built Newlands. Matches were played over three weeks, every Monday and Tuesday, when the field was not being used by white cricketers.

The *Cape Times* described the opening day and the exotic flavour of the cricket in a vivid way:

> From an early hour, the road from Cape Town was alive with a string of vehicles, heavily weighted with Malays, who evidently intended to make a day of it and from the brake with four horses and the more modest pair drawing the comfortable Cape cart down to the humble everyday business car, every conveyance was pressed in the service. The trains, too, were well-freighted, and before noon, at least 2,000 must have entered and were dispersed into groups around it, the numerous baskets showing that there was no fear of a famine, whilst later on, one hospitable dame entertained her friends to what may be representing the Malay four o'clock tea.
>
> After the luncheon hour, the band of the East York attended, and music was added to the picturesque scene, to which further attraction was lent by the arrival of many of the elite of the white population, who massed themselves upon the pavilion stand, the quiet refined costumes of the ladies throwing into greater relief the wealth of colour in the other portions of the ground. At the conclusion of the second innings of Cape Town, many indulged in the promenade of the ground, and inspected the rich if bizarre toilets, whilst the henna-deepened dark eyes shot many a glance of appreciation or covert mirth at those who made the circuit. Many and daring were the combinations of colour indulged in, but there were not wanting dresses which might teach a lesson in harmonious blending and a rich combination of claret and brown, relieved by lace and enriched with embroidery, was conspicuous, whilst a superb lilac with white satin bodice and pearl embroidery harmonized admirably with the

almost perfect profile of a tall beauty, and a deep purple shot with white also arrested the attention.[12]

The first match started with Cape Town winning the toss and deciding to bat against Port Elizabeth. The no. three batsman, L. Samsodien, whose name would feature prominently in the next few years, top-scored with 29. The opening bowlers, Ajoep and L. Fredericks, took six and four wickets respectively to restrict the home team to 83 in their first innings. With the home quickie Jakoef leading from the front with 5/19, PE fell for 57, 26 short. A home victory was on the cards. But in the logic-defying way that cricket works, PE shot out Cape Town for 52 (Samsodien top-scored with 10) thanks to another five wickets from Ajoep and three wickets from G. Fredericks. Two middle-order twenties by L. Fredericks and H. Astril took the visitors to the 79 runs required for victory.

L. Samsodien took two wickets in each innings and also made the best score of the match. He followed this up with another twenty (28) and 5/16 to help his team to a narrow win against Johannesburg. In his third match, he joint top-scored with 30 when the two home sides, Claremont and Cape Town Union, combined to beat the up-country best of Port Elizabeth and Johannesburg. His one innings was described as 'well-made'. This all-rounder had signalled that he was a player to be watched.

Other individual highlights were the bowling performances of Samsodien's teammate E. Ariefdien, who took the most wickets – 19/61 – including 9/28 in an innings in the final match. E. Adams of Claremont scored the most runs (156) thanks to his 83 against Port Elizabeth, which was also the highest score by far. L. Fredericks of Port Elizabeth took 17 wickets, and his 39 in the final game won him a bat for the highest score by a visitor. Claremont were unbeaten in their two games and Johannesburg lost both of theirs, while the other two teams each won one and lost one.

The tournament climax was the match between a combined Cape Town and Claremont team and a combined Port Elizabeth and Johannesburg team, which the Capetonians won by 36 runs on the first innings. The combined local team, selected several months before the white Western Province Cricket Union was formed and almost a full year before the first white Western Province team played in the Champion Bat tournament, was therefore the first provincial cricket team selected to represent Western Province.[13] This is one of the many facts that escaped the early historian Luckin in what he claimed was a comprehensive history of South African cricket.

The *Cape Times* reported that, judging by the gate receipts, over 5,000 spectators attended the first day. The person who conveyed this information was none other than Thomas Lynedoch Graham, the secretary of the WPCC. WPCC had made the ground available and collected all the income for itself. From what can be ascertained, all the matches were umpired by a Mr Simpson and Frank Hearne, the WPCC's star English professional, who played for both England and South Africa in test matches. White businessmen presented bats as prizes. Graham wrote to the *Cape Times* praising the conduct of the spectators as admirable and saying there was not a single incident of rowdiness. He also praised the sportsmanship and the play. The pavilion was apparently set aside for white spectators, and it seems that the tournament organisers had to set up separate toilets for their spectators.

The tournament was run by a local organising committee. The main figure was the leader of the Cape Town Union, Abdol Burns, the cab-driver son of a Scotsman and a local woman, 'whose influence among the Cape Muslims was tremendous'.[14] Articulate in English and well read, Burns emerged as a local spokesman in the late 1860s, when he spoke out at a protest meeting against the flogging clauses in a proposed Masters and Servants Bill. He became prominent in electoral politics as well. The *Cape Argus* recalled later that 'no political meeting, especially at election time was complete without a speech by Abdol Burns, and his speeches contained more solid sense than those of many persons better placed in life'. Like his African counterparts in the eastern Cape, he supported the liberal parliamentarian Saul Solomon – and Burns's strength was that he 'intelligently blended his community's religious sentiments with the strategies of political action and agitation, at the same time seeking a constitutional solution to the problem'.[15]

Burns's involvement in organising the tournament as leader of the Cape Town Union also had broader social significance – for the local community and for Cape Town sport and society. The *Cape Times* touched on this in a condescending and racist editorial after the tournament, which noted that the 'fortunes of the olive-complexioned cricketers' were followed 'with no small degree of interest' by the 'European' population. According to the paper, they were an integral part of the service economy at the Cape – as masons, laundresses, drivers, 'handicraftsmen' and general factotums – and the future educational and cricket progress of the younger generation, who had taken to the game in a serious way 'in the last few years', would be watched with interest. Although aliens from 'mysterious Asia, with their dark tendency to the arts of magic and their Asiatic fatalism', they were 'capable of a higher degree of civilisation than the simpler African races, of that there can be no doubt'.

Finally:

However we may have lamented the spread of the Asiatic influence in Cape Town, we have always had a saving cause for the Malays. They have not come here to try their own fortunes against the Europeans; but their fathers were brought here against their will as slaves for the convenience and comfort of our predecessors, and they have the same right to regard this country as their home. Of all the people benefited by emancipation, they have proved themselves most worthy. We have had no Hayti [sic] in Cape Town by reason of the presence of Malays in our midst. As far as members of an alien race can amalgamate with a European community they have become an integral part of the population of Cape Town.[16]

All the reports commented on the unusualness and colour of the occasion. Indeed, one of the games was started more than an hour late because of a wedding in Claremont 'at which several of each team were present'. A new self-confident identity was being brightly painted on the broad cricket canvas.

The historic Cape Town tournament again provides irrefutable evidence of two trends: firstly, contrary to long-held beliefs, black players were as enthusiastic, skilled and forward-looking as their white cricket counterparts from the beginning and, secondly, at this early stage there was considerable cross-community contact. Segregation was far from being fixed as the final solution in colonial politics. By the 1890s black sports people, and some liberal-minded whites, were hoping for greater recognition of and involvement by black players in the wider cricket environment. The new Malay Inter-Town tournaments would be one of the platforms used to bring across this message, particularly when Abdol Burns and his colleagues persuaded cosmopolitan Kimberley to enter the fray the following season.

23

The formation of the South African Cricket Association, April 1890

It is necessary that a representative institution of cricketers be formed.

– John Piton, 1890

By the 1890s, there was a fluidity in the development of cricket in southern Africa. Various cricket identities and cultures in-the-making were bumping up against one another, as the last three chapters have shown.

In April 1890, just over a year after the English tour and a few months after the first Malay Inter-Town Tournament, a meeting was called with the aim of forming a national cricket body. The different communities of black cricketers clearly aspired to be part of the evolving cricket dispensation, and they already showed a high level of organisation through their tournaments as well as an impressive level of skill in the matches they were given against white teams. A number of 'friends of the natives' in mainstream colonial white cricket, representing the minority tradition of Cape liberalism in politics, were not averse to black citizens getting greater access. But would the imperialist-minded cricket establishment agree? Developments after the first English tour would provide the answer. The tour had stimulated local cricket and underlined the need for a single controlling body for the various territories in southern Africa. Although subject to different governments, two of them independent republics and two British colonies, local cricketers had been brought, as a result of the English tour, into an increasingly integrated and unified network. At the same time, it had become evident that within each region there were specific cricket identities, all shaped by particular historical experiences and contexts. That the time was ripe for unity was also brought home by the fact that local rugby players had set up the South African Rugby Football Board in 1889.

The first known calls for a national cricket body occurred in 1888 because of dissatisfaction in Cape Town with the way in which Major Warton's cricket tour was organised. 'C.E.J.' wrote a letter to the *Cape Times* in August of that year calling for a 'South African Cricketer's Congress' or 'Representative Union'. The Kimberley journalists Charles Finlason and Harry Cadwallader expressed their support. When in late November 1888 the *Cape Times* stated that 'a proposal is already taking shape in Cape Town for the formation of a South African or rather Cape Colony Cricket Association',[1] Finlason backed the idea. 'The *Cape Times* strongly protests against the Western Province Cricket Club taking all arrangements absolutely into their own hands without reference to the cricketers belonging to any other club ... an attempt is being made to form a sort of association something after the style of the MCC.'[2] The article attracted the interest of Harry Cadwallader, who said that he had 'for a long time been impressed with the necessity for such an Association'. He contacted the sports editor of the *Cape Times*, saying that he thought he could be of assistance as he was 'not unacquainted with the working of institutions of the kind in England and other of the colonies'.[3] Cadwallader provided a number of ideas for consideration. These were published in the *Diamond Fields Advertiser* and later became the basis for the draft constitution of the South African Cricket Association.

After Transvaal issued a challenge to Kimberley in January 1890 for a match over Easter to compete for the Currie Cup, which had been presented to Kimberley by the English cricketers, Cadwallader revived the idea to form a national body despite the vast distances and poor communications in the country. In February 1890 he told a meeting of Kimberley cricketers that there was considerable sympathy countrywide for his proposals. He added that he had hoped a movement in the direction intimated would follow but admitted that there had been no sign of it. This disappointed him, and he urged some action be taken to form a national body to consider 'English and Australian teams willing if not anxious to call at the Cape'. 'If nothing is done,' he said, 'there is a real danger of a fiasco developing similar to that which took place in 1887–8 when two English touring sides toured Australia.'[4]

Cadwallader moved a resolution which he hoped would meet with the unanimous approval of Kimberley cricketers: 'That this meeting of Kimberley cricketers approves of the suggestion to establish a Cricket Association for South Africa on the basis of the rough draft presented by the mover who be authorised to act as Hon. Secretary *pro tem* to communicate with other clubs on the matter and recommends that a meeting of cricketers and delegates be held at the forthcoming Easter Tournament.'[5] The motion was carried unanimously.

The Transvaal team arrived in town on 2 April 1890 for the challenge match against Kimberley for the new Currie Cup amid countrywide excitement. In a see-saw game that swung this way and that, Transvaal won thanks to a brilliant 126 not out by Monty Bowden, the Surrey and England wicketkeeper-batsman, who had stayed behind in Johannesburg to pursue his fortune on the stock exchange after the 1888/9 tour.

On 9 April 1890, two days after the conclusion of the first Currie Cup match, an inaugural congress of delegates met to decide upon the rules for the proposed South African Cricket Association (SACA). The delegates, who met at Glover's Athletic Bar in Kimberley, were William Hopley (Western Province), the South African caps Bertie Rose-Innes (Port Elizabeth) and Charlie Finlason (then based in Klerksdorp), the Pretoria star John Piton, the Kimberley off-spinner Irvine Grimmer and his co-delegate A. Bennitte, F.T. Clarkson from Natal and the indomitable Harry Cadwallader. Five of the players in the recent match had been appointed as delegates, but Monty Bowden (Wanderers) and Charlie Vintcent (Nondescripts) failed to arrive. They had other things on their minds, preferring to have a night out with their cricket-playing friends to say farewell to Aubrey Smith and Dr Spranger Harrison, who were leaving for Cape Town on that night's train. A Mr Nixon from the Orange Free State was another who failed to arrive.

William Hopley was elected the first chairman. He was an advocate who became a High Court judge in 1892. He also had impeccable old-school-tie credentials – St Andrew's College, Diocesan College and Cambridge University – and a strong cricket background. He had played at Cambridge, participated in the Inter-Town Tournament in 1880 as a top-order batsman for Grahamstown, and was one of the founder members of the Eclectic Cricket Club in Kimberley.[6]

The formal side of the founding meeting proceeded smoothly. Cadwallader had informed all the major centres of the gathering and provided his 'rough draft' of the rules and objectives to be considered by the delegates. John Piton moved that 'in the opinion of the Congress, it is necessary that a representative institution of cricketers be formed'. The motion was accepted unanimously. The rules and objectives were considered next. After some discussion, they were passed with minor amendments. Hopley then proposed Cadwallader as honorary secretary and he was duly elected. The fact that he was relocating to Cape Town was not seen as a problem, it being agreed that the place of residence need not be obligatory. Cape Town was seen as 'a suitable place for the correspondence about South Africa and abroad'. Cadwallader was also appointed temporary treasurer.[7]

The first three issues tackled by the new SACA showed where their priorities lay. These were to authorise the second Currie Cup tournament in 1891, discuss the distribution of English professional coaches wintering in South Africa, and plan further international cricket tours.

The most controversial issue was the invitation by the newly formed Wanderers Club of Johannesburg for the Australian team to visit South Africa after their 1890 tour of England. A Mr Francis, who was returning home to Australia, had agreed to act on behalf of the Wanderers and promote the tour. It was proposed to offer a guarantee of £3,000 for a two-month visit. But when the time came for SACA to discuss the issue, 'no details of the tour could be provided as the Wanderers representative, Bowden, was unable to attend because of a pressing engagement' (partying with his fellow cricketers).[8] This had serious repercussions for the planned tour – and the course of relations with Australia. The Wanderers officials negotiating with their Australian counterparts required the support of the national body. When William Hopley asked for information about the proposed tour, there was no response. This posed a problem because Hopley, a close associate of the overbearing William Milton, knew that the WPCC had received offers from Johnny Briggs and George Lohmann to bring out English teams for the new season. He warned the meeting: 'Unless something was decided at once, South Africa might fall between two stools and be unable to obtain either team.'[9] SACA therefore decided to go with the Western Province plan for a second English team instead of the Australians.

Finally, there was a governing body for cricket in the whole of southern Africa.

24

Cricket and the Imperial mission

The rise of Johannesburg and the first Currie Cup

> Before many years are out, we may expect to see
> the image of Queen Victoria stamped on the gold
> with which King Solomon overlaid his ivory throne
> and wreathed the cedar pillars of his temple.
>
> – *Cape Argus*, 24 November 1889

The formation of SACA in Kimberley on 9 April 1890 put South African cricket on an organised footing. The Currie Cup competition, which started with the match between the holders, Kimberley, and the challengers, Transvaal, in the same town during the same week likewise initiated a new era on the playing field.

The Sir Donald Currie Challenge Cup was presented to Kimberley a few days before the first English team left Cape Town in March 1889. It had been donated to the tourists by Currie, owner of the Union-Castle Mail Steamship Company, for handing over to the side that played 'the best all-round cricket' against them. A committee of English players and Major Warton decided 'without hesitation' that Kimberley deserved to be the recipients.

The presentation ceremony took place at a dinner held aboard the *Garth Castle*, to which 95 people were invited. Five members of the Cape parliament attended, including Colonel Frederick Schermbrucker of King William's Town, the frontier military commander and father of the Champion Bat cricketer. 'We will endeavour to keep it as long as we can,' said A.B. Tancred on receiving the Currie Cup, 'although I know that there are many towns keen to take it from us.' 'You bet,' called out a voice amid laughter.

Some of the members of the first English touring team stayed behind after the tour, including the captain, Aubrey Smith, his replacement as captain in the second test match, Monty Bowden, Charles Coventry and Emile McMaster (who moved to Natal). The first two remained actively involved in local cricket and played in the first Currie Cup match 12 months later. The Johannesburg *Diggers News* announced on 6 April 1889: 'Mr C. Aubrey Smith, who captained Major Warton's eleven, and the demon wicket-keeper, Mr M.P. Bowden, have pitched their tent on the Rand and will play for the All-Comers today against a team of Port Elizabeth men on the Rand.'[1] These two cricketers established the new business of Smith & Bowden, at 26 Royal Chambers in Marshall's Township and registered as members of the Johannesburg stock exchange. The economic boom of 1888–9 saw the exchange rapidly expanding with over 900 members and a further 300 brokers and speculators clamouring for admission. The new partners were well pleased with their early progress. Success came relatively easily, which might not have surprised the two gentlemen cricketers used to a lifestyle that had never been over-demanding. Their names, of course, were a marketing asset and they relied heavily on help from their well-to-do friends at the Wanderers Club. By the end of their first winter, *Cricket: A Weekly Record of the Game* was able to report that the partners in the firm of Smith & Bowden 'are flourishing in their new home'.[2] Charles Finlason noted, 'The two did exceedingly well at first; both possessed of the most pleasing and cordial manners and made friends with everybody unconsciously and without effort.'[3]

Tall and handsome, the cricketers cut something of a dash and were in demand socially. Smith was drawn into the theatre, elected to the influential Wanderers committee and mixed with the older, more affluent members of the club. He was also elected captain of the Wanderers team. Bowden socialised with the younger set and was friends with Louis Vintcent, who had made a name for himself as a rugby player in the Western Province, captaining Villagers and, after moving north, scoring Transvaal's first-ever try during the inaugural inter-provincial tournament at Kimberley in 1889.

Smith became seriously ill just before the 1889/90 season and was unable to play cricket until December – a premature obituary of him appeared in the newspapers at the time, which only added to his fame. Smith was found in 'a very weakened state, semi-conscious, not having eaten properly for weeks, with only a bottle of Van der Hum and a large but nearly empty tin of Huntley and Palmer's biscuits for company'. Friends were called and nursed him back to health.[4] Smith was lucky. The climate of Johannesburg was healthy but the conditions under which people lived were such that 'camp fever' was rife. The disease was actually typhoid, with the outbreak so serious that the district surgeon told a Sanitary Board meeting, 'Johannesburg is second only to the Panama Canal as regards the death toll.'[5]

Smith's illness seemed to herald a change in his fortunes and those of Bowden, and the difficult summer in Johannesburg made things worse. A severe drought set in. Violent dust storms and windswept grounds affected local enthusiasm for cricket. The food supply to the Rand began to dwindle. The headline 'The Famine' appeared in daily newspapers and a deputation was sent to Pretoria to discuss the situation with President Kruger.[6] Then in November, heavy rains arrived, resulting in widespread flooding. The Wanderers grounds were largely washed away although the completed clubhouse stood firm. 'It was a splendid sight, despite the fashionable chalet-like features being executed in galvanised iron. Cattle still grazed on unprepared ground in the vicinity but Victorian opulence had unmistakably been imposed on the dismal scene.'[7]

Finally, in December the partnership of Smith & Bowden, like so many other businesses, was forced to close as a result of a dramatic financial crash. They were left in debt to cricket friends like Bertie Mosenthal.[8] Smith attributed the closure of the business to bad luck. The untimely 'boom burst', he explained, coincided with months of intense heat, followed by a time of famine, and then both he and Bowden became ill.[9] However, others had a different story to tell. The Comtesse de Brémont, an American who was an old friend of Oscar Wilde's mother, commented on the two cricketers in her novel, *The Gentleman Digger*, and made little effort to disguise the identities of the characters she described. There were references to a 'tall, slender chap, the captain of the cricket team,' with the question being asked, 'So then he is a stockbroker?' 'Well, yes and no,' came the reply. 'When the team first came to the Rand we set him and another cricketer up in brokering. They prospered for a few months but were not smart enough to go ahead on their own legs. You must know that it is necessary for shareholders to keep each other a little in the dark about the firms they buy and sell through. That necessitated a change of broker every few weeks. So the cricketers could not always count on their friends, and were not keen enough to know how to work the job. Achilles is only good for athletics, or acting, and the other is nearly as bad. Well, the concern of Bo and A will not hold out many days. Poor boys, I'm sorry – but they'll get a fresh chance in Matabeleland if they take it.'[10]

Smith and Bowden were only two of the many top-class cricketers who were drawn to Johannesburg in search of career opportunities after the first English tour. Others included the inter-town stalwarts Charlie Vintcent, Bentley Wimble and W. 'Billy' Heugh; Charles Finlason, the mover and shaker from Kimberley; and John A.E. Hickson, who had represented Middlesex in England. 'There was practically only one big club, the Wanderers', captained by Aubrey Smith, according to Luckin's *History*, and it 'much outclassed the rest'. In addition to Wanderers matches, there were also contests such as Stock Exchange vs All-Comers, Old Kimberleyites vs All-Comers, and the ubiquitous Home-Born vs Colonial-Born.[11]

After a match in January 1890, Aubrey Smith called a meeting in the hall which formed part of the Wanderers pavilion to decide whether a team from the Transvaal should be sent to Kimberley to compete for the first Currie Cup 'Challenge'. At the time, there was no properly constituted governing body in existence for Transvaal cricket: the Transvaal Cricket Union would only be established after a series of meetings with centres such as Potchefstroom, Barberton, Krugersdorp and Pretoria at the Goldfield Hotel in October 1891. The decision whether to play an inter-provincial match was left to the players and officials from the two sides that gathered that day. Smith chaired the meeting, which quickly and unanimously agreed that a team should challenge Kimberley. He was also made captain. A committee, which included Bowden, Godfrey Cripps, John Piton and the former Champion Bat players Billy Heugh, Charlie Vintcent and Fred Smith, was formed to make all the necessary arrangements.

Several preparatory matches were organised, some in the form of trials and others as fundraisers, such as the match against Mr Brough's Theatrical Company on 5 February. (The Currie Cup venture cost the team £265, against which they received £74 as their share of the gate in Kimberley). The final Transvaal squad of 14 included 11 players from Johannesburg, together with Dr Tom Dixon from Potchefstroom, who had produced the highest batting average at the Transvaal inter-town tournament in 1887, John Piton from Pretoria and the controversial Charles Finlason, then living more than 160 kilometres away in Klerksdorp.[12]

Before the Transvaal team departed, a smoking concert was held at the Wanderers to bid farewell to Aubrey Smith, who was leaving town. The team was given a rousing send-off early the following morning. The match had attracted enormous interest, being the main topic of conversation in the sporting world for two months. The Transvaal players arrived in Kimberley on Wednesday, 2 April 1890, and practised hard at the Eclectic Ground on the Thursday and Friday. Heavy showers that day, followed by a hot sun on the Saturday morning of the match, affected the pitch.

Kimberley chose to bat first on winning the toss. They were all out for 98 in an hour and 40 minutes. The *Diamond Fields Advertiser* reported, 'The feeling was general amongst those on the ground that they might bid goodbye to all chance of winning the match; bets of five to one and even ten to one were freely laid on Johannesburg.'[13] However, Kimberley pulled back to dismiss Transvaal for 117. In their second innings, Kimberley reached 235, thanks to a century from the South African opener, A.B. Tancred. Transvaal began their second innings at three o'clock, chasing 217 to win the match. Four down for less than 100, Transvaal seemed to be in trouble in their second innings, but Bowden was in brilliant form and his stroke play delighted the crowd. He ended up with a match-winning 126, and shared an unfinished fifth-wicket partnership that realised 126 with Charlie Vintcent, who plundered 60. At a quarter past five on the second afternoon, an imperious drive to the ropes won the match, and the Currie Cup, for the delighted Transvaal players, who raced onto the field. A historic victory, so unlikely at one stage, had been achieved by a margin of six wickets.

In scenes of unrestrained joy, Bowden was seized by his teammates and carried around the ground. It had been a sterling battle, and Kimberley's defeat was the major sporting story in newspapers throughout the country. 'The interest displayed in the match', commented the *Diamond Fields Advertiser*, 'was evidenced by the large number of telegrams which were sent away to all the large centres at the close of each innings.'[14]

The diaries of the leading socialites and sports people in Kimberley were very full at this time. Following the match played between 5 and 7 April, the new SACA was formed on Wednesday, 9 April, at Glover's Athletic Bar. The next night, 10 April, Transvaal collected the Currie Cup at a function at the Craven Hotel. After the mayor of Kimberley, Thomas Goodwin, handed over the cup, it was filled with champagne and then passed around. Bowden said: 'I have never before played in such an exciting contest. At the conclusion of Kimberley's first innings, I telegraphed Johannesburg to say that I thought Transvaal was sure to win, but at the conclusion of the Transvaal innings I had to wire just the reverse. There is no game so uncertain as cricket and the result of the match has proved that.'[15]

CRICKET AND CONQUEST: THE PIONEER COLUMN AND THE CURRIE CUP

Amidst this great cricket excitement, another historic event was taking shape in Kimberley. For weeks the town was abuzz with the presence of a force of 200 men called the Pioneer Column. This was set up by Cecil John Rhodes to embark on a vanguard expedition to 'open up' what we now know as Zimbabwe and secure the mineral resources that were believed to be perhaps bigger than those to the south.

In the late 1880s, Rhodes had bought up all the mines in Kimberley and amalgamated them into De Beers Consolidated Mines, which became the mightiest diamond company in the world. In 1890 he also became prime minister of the Cape Colony. Positioned at the centre of the nexus of economic and political power, Rhodes now also planned to expand the influence of Britain, the Cape and his own interests by annexing further African territories. The most influential man on the continent, empowered by a Royal Charter, sought to acquire more land to build a great federation in southern Africa as the first stage in the development of Britain's Cape-to-Cairo imperial domain.

Rhodes now set out to conquer and create for himself a country. The 200-strong Pioneer Column was recruited from various trades and professions. Its members were promised that they would be free to set up their own businesses and form the basis of a new community in the territory to be acquired to the north. The venture gathered rapid support, particularly among men who found themselves destitute as a result of the collapse of the Rand share market. The expedition leader was Frederick Courteney Selous, who as a 19-year-old in 1871 had sailed to South Africa and set himself up as an ivory hunter and trader, roaming around the territory of modern-day Botswana and Zimbabwe, then remote places little known to the British. Selous was in Kimberley until Sunday, 13 April 1890, and local citizens jostled with one another to catch a glimpse of one of the most heroic figures of the period. His men were gathering at the same time as the cricketers were in town. The Central Hotel, where the cricketers stayed, was also where the Pioneer Column was headquartered, and the social festivities surrounding the cricketers and the pioneer columnists overlapped. Several of the cricketers were persuaded to join the column.

Brian Willan has commented that Kimberley was a 'supremely British place' in the 1890s. Nowhere was this imperial link more closely shown than at Kimberley at this juncture. The Pioneer Column's activities and the first Currie Cup match became intertwined events, emphasising how much cricket was part of the imperial mission in southern Africa.

Numerous accounts of the land frequently referred to as 'Zambesia' were current at the time, often filled with fanciful, even mythical, significance. Prominence was given to reports made by the German explorer Karl Mauch, who wrote after his first visit to the Great Zimbabwe ruins in 1871: 'I do not think that I am far wrong if I suppose that the ruin on the hill is a copy of Solomon's Temple on Mount Moriah, and the building in the plain is a copy of the palace where the Queen of Sheba lived during her visit to Solomon.'[16] Great interest developed in the fabulous treasures and lost cities that were thought to exist in the area. Rider Haggard built these themes into his adventure stories, and his novel *King Solomon's Mines* (1885) became a spectacular Victorian bestseller. English readers were enthralled by the journey that Sir Henry Curtis and the intrepid hunter Allan Quatermain made into the northern interior. It was there that they overthrew the cruel Twala and claimed the legendary riches of King Solomon's Mines. Many adventurers of the time hoped to stumble across chambers of subterranean wealth such as Haggard had imagined. 'Before many years are out,' said an article in the *Cape Argus*, 'we may expect to see the image of

Queen Victoria stamped on the gold with which King Solomon overlaid his ivory throne and wreathed the cedar pillars of his temple.'[17]

It was not surprising, then, that the star of the first Currie Cup match, Monty Bowden, discovered that his two friends at the Wanderers, Louis Vintcent and Bentley Wimble, were interested in joining the Chartered Company's planned expedition to Mashonaland. Vintcent's father, the member of parliament for George, tried to dissuade his son from taking part by offering him a good position in his business house at Oudtshoorn. It was to no avail. 'Louis's imagination had been taken captive by the glowing stories he had heard of the new land of promise and nothing would satisfy him but a shy at Mashonaland.'[18]

Prior to the departure of the Pioneer Column, the Cape governor, Sir Henry Loch, made an official visit to Kimberley. A banquet was held in his honour at the town hall on Thursday, 17 April. Monty Bowden featured high on the published list of dignitaries attending the banquet, his name appearing alongside those of Cecil John Rhodes, Sir Thomas Upington, Sir John Willoughby (second-in-command of the Pioneer Police), Admiral Wells, the Rev. John Moffat and Sir Sidney Shippard (administrator of Bechuanaland) – figures deeply involved in the expedition to Mashonaland.

On 20 April, local cricketers staged a 'farewell' match in honour of their comrades accompanying the column. Besides Vintcent, Wimble and Bowden, the Kimberley cricketer Arthur Stanford also signed up. Bowden was invited to captain All-Comers against the combined Eclectic and Pirates cricket clubs. Up against them were the best Kimberley could offer, although the fixture was not allowed to become an intensely serious affair. It was meant to take everyone's mind off the expedition as reality began to take hold and some columnists began to have serious reservations: it was rumoured that the life of a Pioneer 'was a long way from being as rosy as had been painted'.[19] On Saturday 3 May, the *Daily Independent* reported, 'The force will have a very powerful cricket team … It would be sad if the Currie Cup found its way to Vryburg or Elibe or some town on the Zambezi.'[20]

Meanwhile, when local enthusiasts in Johannesburg began preparations for a celebration of the Pioneer Column, they discovered that the cup had not been brought from Kimberley. Investigations into its whereabouts led to a bizarre story that featured in most of the leading newspapers. During their time in Kimberley, Bowden and some of the Transvalers had stayed at the Central Hotel. With the players enjoying the good life, their debts mounted and eventually the management became concerned about payment. Bowden, as the group's spokesman, was asked for some form of surety. He obliged by handing over the one item of value that he possessed – the Currie Cup – to the bemused manageress, Mrs

Creagh. The *Natal Mercury* broke the news in dramatic fashion, claiming that the cricketers

> who had possession [of the cup] were, like many other Randites, 'stumped'. The landlady of the house in which they lodged, not being able to obtain her money, took possession of the object of ambition of every cricketer and town in South Africa. Now the question arises – 'What will she do with it?' Will a Natal or Cape team have to challenge the landlady and will she be prepared to do battle in Johannesburg? The subject is a serious one.[21]

There was no elected provincial cricket administration in the Transvaal to claim the cup but it eventually found its way to Johannesburg with Bertie Mosenthal. The details of the manner in which he obtained it were not published. A likely explanation was that Rhodes's Chartered Company picked up the tab for the cricketers' sojourn at the Central Hotel. They could not risk adverse publicity about members of the Pioneer Corps leaving behind unpaid debts.

These wonderfully vivid portraits of cricket in the early 1890s demonstrate how 'English' South African cricket was at the time, and how snugly it fitted into the colonial life and politics of Kimberley, the staging post for late-nineteenth-century British expansion. It is no surprise that both the national cricket and rugby associations were started in that city and that the first president of the South African Rugby Board was Percy Ross Frames, one-time chairman of De Beers Consolidated Mines.[22] The formation of SACA was an intrinsic part of the consolidation and expansion of the British Empire. Not only did Rhodes employ several top cricketers and officials in De Beers and acted as a patron and sponsor of SACA, but the white cricket establishments in Cape Town, Kimberley and Johannesburg, the driving forces behind the new body, were all closely linked to Rhodes and were ardent supporters of what he liked to call the 'Imperial factor'.

Even before the Pioneer Column, Warton, who had organised the first cricket tour, was rewarded by Rhodes by being appointed as the British South Africa Company's commissioner. He became one of the first Englishmen to cross the Zambezi in the course of leading three expeditions into a vast land that would be brought under the sphere of British influence. His job was to set up telegraph stations that would eventually link that territory to the Cape. Moreover, one of the cricketers on the first tour, the captain, Monty Bowden, went along with the Pioneer Column, whilst the incompetent amateur, the Hon. Charles Coventry (picked for the first English team because of his father's influence), received a commission in the Bechuanaland Border Police and would play an important role in the Jameson Raid.

Even more tellingly, William Milton, cricket's strongman in Cape Town, joint organiser of the first tour and secretary to Rhodes, would later have two spells as administrator of the new colony of Rhodesia. Others to hold the post included Dr Leander Starr Jameson and Joseph Vintcent, brother of the South African cricketer.

Cricket's big new steps – the formation of SACA and the first Currie Cup match – became entwined with Rhodes's imperial project and the launch of his plans to annex the land north of the Limpopo River. Milton was standing next to Rhodes when the 'prime minister read the telegram' which reported the Column's safe arrival at Fort Salisbury. He then handed the telegram to Milton 'with the characteristic remark, "My young men have got the country."'[23]

Rather than following the robust, fiercely independent colonial direction articulated by Charles Finlason or the inclusive, liberal approach favoured by black cricketers, the developing South African cricket establishment became almost indistinguishable from the political projects of Britain and the arch-imperialist, Rhodes, particularly after he became prime minister of the Cape Colony in 1890. From the perspective of today, Rhodes and the colonial cricket establishment – supremely confident in their imperial identities and intoxicated by the exercise of unbridled power and the process of conquest — were about to take the game firmly in the wrong direction.

25

'What man's accomplish'd ye can do'

Selecting a second South African team, April 1891

To you Abantu:
What Man's Accomplish'd Ye Can Do

1

Put forth – Abantu – all the pow'rs
Wherewith by Nature you're endow'd
The ignorance that round you tow'rs
Encircling you in a black shroud
Dispel! There is no time for sleep,
Or conversations that are in vain –
No time to squat about and weep
O'er privileges, and disdain
Facilities within your grasp.
Awake! – This age demands not cries
'Gainst wrong, but veritable deeds.

> – Robert Grendon, poet and member of the first
> South African 'Malay' team[1]

The era of inter-town competitive cricket, which started in January 1876 and in which cricketers from all communities played – albeit separately, through the Champion Bat, 'Native' and Glover Cup tournaments – reached its highpoint and perhaps its deepest level of convergence in the 1890/1 season. For the first time, all three cricket communities held their inter-town tournaments during the same season and at the same time – over the Christmas and New Year holidays. The whites played in Cape Town, the Africans in Port Elizabeth and the Malays in Uitenhage. The three tournaments delivered three different winners: Port Elizabeth won the African tournament, Cape Town/Western Province won the Champion Bat, and Kimberley came out on top in the Malay tournament. Developments at these 1890/1 tournaments showed the state of flux that cricket was in and the concern among all the cricket communities to take their organisations and playing standards to a new level.

After four Champion Bat competitions in which purely town teams had played, the fifth and final one expanded participation from towns to regions – namely Western Province (the winners, who were coached by the Kent and English professional Frank Hearne), Eastern Province and Griqualand West. This move presaged major changes in the organisation of cricket in southern Africa. This fifth tournament was in effect a bridge to an expanded, multi-team Currie Cup competition, which would become the premier tournament for white first-class cricket for the next hundred years. To emphasise the point, this last Champion Bat tournament was retrospectively declared first-class, although the matches were of only two days' duration and the club involved, WPCC, assumed the mantle of a province.

Similarly, the Malay cricketers upped the ante, not only by organising a second tournament in the same season, held in Kimberley over Easter, but by going on to choose the first black national team afterwards. They were clearly following the trend towards representative teams on a regional or larger scale. The decision by those excluded from SACA to put their own national team in the field happened within a year of SACA being formed, and only 25 months after the selection of the first all-white South African test team.

The second Malay tournament was due to be held in Uitenhage in January 1891 and the fifth and final Champion Bat tournament at the same time in Cape Town. So the two sets of Kimberley players came up with a logical, though, surprising solution for optimising their preparations: two matches between the two town sides that could serve as preparation for both and provide funds which they would share.

The white town side won the first match by five wickets and the high-scoring second one by 40 runs (Kimberley whites 301 for seven and Kimberley Malays 261 all out). The former were captained by Charles Finlason, who had played for South Africa during the first tour. George Glover, who was to be capped later, scored two fifties. Three stars emerged for the Malay team, the wicketkeeper, Palmer; the captain, Armien Hendricks, who put together three innings of 31, 65 and 95; and Robert Grendon from the Excelsior club, who took 7/75 in one spell with his 'medium-paced leg breaks' and who cut and glided impressively as an opening batsman, though he did not put big totals on the scoreboard.

Kimberley promptly won their tournament in Uitenhage, dethroning the Cape Town team to become champions. Grendon destroyed Uitenhage with a match analysis of 14/24. Their white counterparts were not as successful, losing both games in Cape Town.

The cooperation between the two town teams continued and reached new levels when they returned from their tournaments. Not only did the Eclectics CC (including the internationals Tancred and Finlason) play two more games against the Malay team, which the whites again won – once easily and the other time by 27 runs – but J.K. Glover, father of the two town cricketers George and Ernest, presented a Challenge Cup along the lines of the Currie Cup to the black cricketers and helped them organise a second Inter-Town tournament that season. There was an entrepreneurial aspect to this support. Glover owned the Glover's Athletic Bar in Kimberley – where the founding meeting of SACA took place in 1890 – and he helped organise the event with a commercial object in view.

After again taking five wickets against the white cricketers in the run-up to the third tournament in March 1891, Robert Grendon was once more in brilliant form, steering the home side to victory with innings of 80 not out against Port Elizabeth and a 'Nelson' hundred (111 scored out of 163) in the final against Cape Town. Kimberley won their second tournament of the season to become first holders of the Glover Cup. Armien Hendricks was also in devastating form with the ball, but the leading wicket-taker from Cape Town in 1890, E. Ariefdien of Western Province, put everyone in the shade with a stupendous performance against Port Elizabeth. After taking all ten wickets for 18 runs in nine overs in their first innings, he opened the batting and made 54 (higher than the PE total of 50). Opening the bowling in the second innings, he took a hat-trick off his first three balls.[2] As it followed his nine wickets in an innings in the first tournament, Ariefdien surely has to join the likes of Nathaniel Umhalla, Austin Ngcumbe and Robert Grendon in South African cricket's early Hall of Fame. That Grendon scored his 111 against Ariefdien while the Cape kingpin knocked over seven wickets around him attests to his exceptional skill. This was the first century scored to date in the Malay or Native Inter-Town tournaments, and it should be compared with the three centuries scored in the 15 years from 1876 to 1891 in the Champion Bat tournaments.

Richard Parry, whose well-researched account of the 1891/2 season in Kimberley provides the basis for this section, also describes the off-field activities:

> The [one] evening was spent at a Khalifa performance at the Glover's family club – Pirates – complete with a performance by the Pirates band in the interval. And a banquet was held the following night at Glover's Athletic Rooms hosted by former Port Elizabeth and Cape Town residents and attended by the three team captains ([Armien] Hendricks, L. Samsodien from Cape Town

and M. Souk and J. Adams from Port Elizabeth). Abdol Burns, the Cape Town Union president, presented the Glover Cup to Hendricks.[3]

The crowning moment of the tournament was the announcement of the first national team of black cricketers. It was dubbed the 'South African Malay' team by the press, much to the irritation of some of the players who were neither Malay nor Muslim. It would have been more correct to call it the South African Glover Cup XI. The team comprised two players from Port Elizabeth, four from Cape Town and five from Kimberley, and was captained by the consistent performer from the host city, Armien Hendricks. The brand-new South African team played against a select white Kimberley team, which included cricketers like the star spinner Irvine Grimmer, in April 1891 at the Eclectic Cricket Club ground off Park Road. The team in batting order, with detailed scores, was:

South African Glover Cup XI 97 (R Grendon 30, E Abrams17, A Hendricks 17, L Samsodien 9, E Ariefdien 15*, J Adams 0, J Vogt 0, K du Toit 0, M Salie 0, M Madatt 4, J Palmer 3, extras 2; IR Grimmer 7/39, L Heitsman 0/8, E Glover 1/23, H Ford 2/29, F Glover 0/4) and 217/7 (A Hendricks 7, R Grendon 92, E Abrams 24, L Samsodien 45, E Ariefdien 21*, J Adams 0, J Vogt 24, K du Toit 0, extras 4; IR Grimmer 2/57, F Glover 1/44, L Heitsman 0/13, H Ford 4/29, G Smith 0/16, E Glover 0/15, A Bennitte 0/25)

Kimberley 'Europeans' 197 for 6 dec (A Bennitte 69, L Heitsman 1, F Maxwell 9, JC Coghlan 8, F Glover 61, RCD Snedden 40*, G Smith 3, extras 6; E Ariefdien 1/47, A Hendricks 4/72, R Grendon 1/47, E Abrams 0/17, Madatt 0/8, Vogt 0/11)[4]

The South African Glover Cup team batted first and totalled 97 runs. The 'fine bat' Robert Grendon, also described as 'brilliant at point' in the field, top-scored with 30. Grimmer, who had established himself as one of the leading players in southern Africa, took seven wickets for 39 runs in 16 overs. Grimmer had a long list of match-winning performances behind his name. In 1887, when Kimberley won the Champion Bat, he and the one-eyed Charlie Vintcent bowled unchanged through five out of six innings and took 55 wickets between them. When the Stray Klips (drawn from several clubs) toured Cape Town in the same year, he took 16 for 83 against William Milton and his top-dog WPCC Club team. In December 1889 he was selected for the first combined Cape Colony team, and he was regarded as a test-standard player despite missing national selection. His figures for Kimberley XVIII against the tourists were 36/15/49/2. On the next 1891/2 English tour he could boast of figures of 46.3/16/75/4 against the tourists.

Clearly, the Glover Cup batsmen were in good company when they succumbed to the devastating spinner in their first innings.

Grimmer, who became assistant general manager of De Beers Consolidated Mines, was described as the first top 'break bowler' in South Africa. J.A. Noble recalled that his off-spin 'marked an era in South African cricket ... At first no one could make a show against these balls, which came in like lightning from the pitch with an almost incredible turn and twist on them ... he was the first to demonstrate the possibility of making the ball turn on our hard grounds.'[5]

In reply to the South African Malay team's first innings of 97, the Kimberley Invitation side – described as 'Europeans' in the newspaper reports – replied with 197/6 declared. The skipper and 'triton', Armien Hendricks, was the most successful bowler for the national team, with four wickets for 72 runs in 25 overs. When the Glover Cup XI went in to bat again, they found a way to counter the Kimberley bowling and hit a healthy 217 for seven before time ran out and the Invitation side were declared the winners on the first innings. The local star Robert Grendon this time scored a superb 92. Grendon's innings was described as 'a brilliant exposition of well-timed hitting, his cutting being particularly clean and hard'. He was well backed up by L. Samsodien, the Cape Town captain, who scored 45 runs.

The South African team had shown that black cricketers could more than hold their own, if given the opportunities. They had solid bowlers and batsmen, and the local newspaper reported, 'In one department – fielding – the Malays altogether eclipsed their opponents; not only did they cover the ground very fast, but their pickings up and returns to wicket, from long or near, was first-class.'[6]

At the fourth Inter-Town Tournament for the Glover Cup held in Kimberley in December 1891, a combined tournament team was once again selected and Robert Grendon was once again the star. The *Cape Times* reported that after Cape Town had convincingly beaten Kimberley by nine wickets to hold the Glover Cup aloft for the first time, the combined side 'met a fairly strong Kimberley [white] team and but for the want of time would have scored the first victory over the European team'. Batting first, 'Grendon was magnificent', knocking up 110 out of 149 for seven before he and the reliable Samsodien put together a partnership that extended the score to 260. Grendon, hitting with 'considerable power and precision', ended up with 187. The Kimberley whites were 123 for six when stumps were drawn.[7]

Robert Grendon was a remarkable figure who left his mark both on and off the sports field. Born in 1867 in present-day Namibia, he was sent to Zonnebloem College in Cape Town to be educated. From there he went to Kimberley to teach at the Beaconsfield Public School. He established himself as a leading public figure in the town, becoming, inter alia, first president of the South African

Coloured Rugby Football Board and an executive member of the South African League in politics. He later taught at the famous Ohlange Institute in Natal, a school founded by John Dube, based on the model of Booker T. Washington's 'self-help' schools in America. Gandhi's Phoenix settlement was close by. Known as Mafukuzela – the one who fights against obstacles – Dube became first president of the South African Native National Congress (later, the African National Congress) in 1912 and Grendon became editor of the SANNC's newspaper, *Abantu Batho*. He was also a poet and is regarded by literary scholars as an important figure in South African literature. After his radicalism and writings got him in trouble with the authorities, he moved to Swaziland, where he became personal tutor to the young prince Sobhuza, who later ruled as King Sobhuza for many decades.[8] At last this Renaissance African intellectual and talented batsman, leg-spinner and point fielder finds himself in an official history of South African cricket.

26

Demon Spofforth of Africa

*The assertion of inclusive identities and the first
taste of international cricket for black players,
March 1892*

On behalf of the Mohammedan community of Cape Town
we hereby sincerely thank the English cricket team for their
kindness in consenting to play the Mohammedan team and
we also congratulate our players for the fair stand they
made against the professionals, considering the drawbacks
they have as regards practice grounds etc. We hope that
the local cricket teams will, in future, show a similar
kindness in allowing us a better field to practise on.

– *Cape Times*, 28 March 1892

An interesting aspect of both the Kimberley team in the 1891 tournament and
the national team was that despite their carrying the name 'Malay', both were
open to people other than Muslims. The Kimberley team included five coloured
Christians, five Muslims and an African player selected from all the local clubs.
Some of the foremost players, including the Cape Town fast bowler H. 'Krom'
Hendricks and Robert Grendon, fell into a category which could not even
vaguely be called 'Malay'. Neither was Malay nor Muslim. Hendricks clarified
that he had a Dutch father and his mother came from St Helena. Grendon, raised
in today's Namibia, had an Irish father and a Damara mother. He later explained
that the perennially used term 'Malay' was wholly inappropriate: 'I notice it has
been selected as an appellation for teams composed of coloured cricketers ... when
used of Christians it has no signification whatsoever.'[1] As a politicised intellectual
he foresaw, moreover, that being stereotyped as 'Malay' could create barriers for

'non-Europeans' in their struggle to be recognised as British citizens, fit in every respect to participate in colonial life.

Hendricks's and Grendon's explanations about their origins once again show the fluid notions of identity and ethnicity operating in southern Africa in the early 1890s, especially in the cosmopolitan environments of the port city of Cape Town and the Diamond City of migrant fortune-seekers. There were numerous Muslim, African and coloured sides in Kimberley, and they regularly played against one another. The closeness of these players to the developments taking place in the white cricket establishment was by this stage uncannily intimate. The two town teams regularly played and ate together. The white clubs opened their facilities to their counterparts. The Glovers, doyens of the Pirates CC, presented what could be termed the Malay Currie Cup and they helped organise the April 1891 Inter-Town Tournament. Irvine Grimmer and William Hopley from the Eclectics CC, on whose ground the Malay team played, were delegates at the founding meeting of the new whites-only SACA when it was held in Glover's Athletic Bar, the venue for the tournament banquet as well. Hopley, in fact, was the incumbent SACA chair in April 1891. The cricketers were all part of a small but distinct and interconnected social milieu, and it seemed logical that this cooperation should deepen in the future.

As we have seen, Kimberley had a well-developed cricket culture by 1891. There was a sizeable black community (of 8,000 Africans and 1,500 coloured people) which spawned and supported a range of clubs and societies in the town. Cricketers of different backgrounds and beliefs played together and dreamed about the future together. For them, the next big step forward in terms of organised cricket was to form a provincial body, the Griqualand West Coloured Cricket Union (GWCCU), along the same lines as the white counterpart Griqualand West Cricket Union. This had happened by 1894. In keeping with the cosmopolitan environment, the new GWCCU represented black cricketers of different backgrounds, including Africans, who formed a strong component of the emerging black middle class in that city. It was described at the time as the 'largest coloured cricket union in South Africa'.[2] There were about ten cricket clubs affiliated to it, including Good Hope, Oddfellows, Primrose, Red Crescent, Standard, United, Duke of Wellington CC (known simply as Duke) and the Eccentrics CC.[3] The last two were African clubs, and each ran several teams. The local derby was a big social occasion and was often held as the main entertainment on Christmas Day.

Indicative of the growing integration that was taking place at all levels in cricket, one of the local clubs, Universals CC, went on a tour to Cape Town in 1892, beating Worcester, Robertson, Wellington and Paarl en route. There was a buoyancy in cricket ranks, which was well demonstrated by the hero's welcome that the Glover Cup champions from Cape Town Union received when they returned home in January 1892. A crowd of 3,000 was waiting when the president, Abdol Burns, and his contingent arrived back at the Cape Town station.[4]

Many of the people involved in Kimberley cricket were also part of the formation of the alternative Griqualand West rugby body in 1894. Significantly, it was decided to use the word 'Colonial' rather than the more conventional 'Coloured' in the organisation's title. This is the first recorded instance of a non-racial approach to sport in South Africa. It was specifically noted in the isiXhosa columns of *Imvo Zabantsundu* in 1894 that the rugby union did not discriminate on the basis of '*bala, luhlanga, lulwimi, nalunqulo*' (colour, nationality, language and religion).[5]

The secretary of both the new provincial cricket and rugby boards was the 25-year-old Isaiah Bud M'belle, described as 'a man of immense ability and wide-ranging talent'.[6] He was typical of the new generation of educated African intellectuals and sports leaders. Educated at Healdtown, he taught before becoming the first African to pass the qualifying examination for the Cape civil service. A speaker of no fewer than six languages, he was appointed as 'Interpreter in Native Languages' to the Northern Circuit of the Supreme Court in Kimberley. His salary of £25 per month reputedly made him the highest-paid African government employee in the colony.[7] He later became secretary-general of the ANC. Bud M'belle's sister married Sol Plaatje, who would achieve fame as a journalist, writer and political figure. Their marriage across conventional ethnic lines (Tswana and Hlubi), which caused unhappiness in family circles, was yet another example of how the younger generation of western-educated, urbanised and Christianised intellectuals were crossing old boundaries and shaping new directions.[8]

Cricket was the most popular game among Kimberley Africans, according to Brian Willan: 'Anybody who was anybody sought to become involved in running the club even if they did not actually play the game.' That is how Bud M'belle's brother-in-law, Sol Plaatje, became joint secretary of Eccentrics CC in 1895. The president was a post office employee, Boyce Skota, 'a very religious and real upright Christian gentleman', whose son Mweli Skota later became secretary-general of the ANC. Skota's vice-president was the Basutoland-born Patrick Lenkoane, described as 'one of the leading citizens among his people'. The captain was T.J. Binase, and the local Methodist and Anglican ministers were both honorary officials. H.C. Msikinya, vice-president of one of the local clubs, left to study at Lincoln College in America later in the decade and ended up playing American football for Lincoln.[9]

The 1880s and 1890s generations of school people were pioneers in so many different ways. The deliberate attempts of Kimberley sports people to play without regard to 'colour, nationality, language and religion', combined with the deep and distinctive traditions of sport that took root in the black communities of the eastern Cape and Cape Town, would provide the foundations for the later non-racial sports struggle in the second half of the twentieth century. Their inclusive vision would be fulfilled when cricket unity was realised in 1991, and it remains the core goal of the governing body, Cricket South Africa, today.

BLACK PLAYERS SEEK INTERNATIONAL COMPETITION

Having started their own inter-town tournaments, having played regularly against white teams without disgracing themselves and having selected their first national team and set up the first regional and provincial cricket bodies, black cricketers wanted to play against international teams as well. There was by now a recognition in both white and black cricket circles that the requests for more playing opportunities were not unreasonable and that the standard was sufficiently high for them to compete with local white sides and the international touring teams. But those supporting the increased incorporation of black cricketers into the cricket system were a minority within the white establishment.

Circumstances conspired to give black cricketers in Cape Town a shot at playing against the visitors at the end of the second English tour to South Africa by W.W. Read's team in March 1892. With the final test in Cape Town on the road to an early finish – it ended after one hour on the third day on 22 March – the local cricketers requested a match against the visitors. The Cape Town Union, reigning Glover Cup champions after winning the fourth Malay Inter-Town Tournament in Kimberley two months earlier, were keen to pit their skills against top-class competition. Such challenges were not unknown. For example, after the first-ever test in Port Elizabeth in 1889, the tourists and South African cricketers broke up into two teams for a friendly between 'married' and 'single', which was agreed to by the English because it would serve as a fundraiser for their professionals.

'On the conclusion of the Test ... a match was commenced by the professionals for their own benefit, against a picked team of eighteen Malay cricketers of the district.' The contest took place at Newlands on 22–23 March 1892 and, according to the *Cape Times*, it 'caused great interest among the Mohammedan community, who showed their appreciation of the great honour accorded them by attending the match in large numbers, as did many Europeans who were wishful of contributing to the benefit'.[10]

The Cape Town Union team, including many stars of the four Inter-Town tournaments since 1890, batted first. None of the first six batsmen reached double figures, although the newspaper noted that E. Adams (who made the highest individual score and run total in the first tournament in 1890) 'showed excellent form and style' before being run out. Then the experienced L. Samsodien, who had captained Cape Town in Kimberley the year before, joined with H. van der Schyff, another veteran from 1890, and 'a wonderful stand was made'. Samsodien took ten off one over from J.T. Hearne, the Middlesex all-rounder, with some elegant drives before being out for 'a grandly hit' 55 with the score on 92. His partner ended with 19 and then the Union team's innings subsided quickly to 113 all out.[11]

When William Chatterton from Derbyshire (who was also a footballer for Derby City) and Vic Barton of Hampshire opened the batting for the English, the Union's openers, Adams and Ariefdien, sent down five maidens before the first runs were scored. Ariefdien had stood out above everyone else at Newlands in 1890 and Kimberley in 1891 with his spectacular nine and ten wickets-in-an-innings bowling feats. Like a modern-day South American football star or Pakistani cricketer, he was simply Ariefdien in the scorecards, even though other players often had their initials included. He struck first, getting Chatterton caught with the score on only 16 after nine overs.

'Krom' Hendricks was an excellent foil to the bowling of Ariefdien and made a lasting impression on his opponents. Chatterton recalled later that he had 'played at home against Richardson, Lockwood and Mold, and against the greatest of Australian genius, Spofforth and Turner'. Yet the very ablest bowler he had ever met he believed to be 'not Spofforth, but a South African black, Hendricks'. He added: 'The memory of this man's pace from the pitch, his quick swing away, alternating with a fine break, stirred a cold and critical nature to enthusiasm.'[12]

After Chatterton's dismissal, a few sharp missed chances enabled the Middlesex pro J.T. Hearne (with an uninhibited 67) and his partner Barton (31) to relieve the pressure and take the English to a commanding position. Resuming on 57 for one overnight, they took the total past 100 before losing their second wicket. The captain, George Hearne of Kent, one of three Hearne brothers who played in the Newlands test, added 21 to take the internationals to 176 all out.

In the second innings, the Capetonians went into their shells, with only Mannor reaching double figures. Samsodien was caught off the left-arm medium-pace bowler Frederick Martin for nine just as he was building his innings. Martin, who took a sensational 12/102 in his test debut at The Oval in 1890, and Leicestershire's Arthur Dick Pougher (11 for 24 in 22.1 overs) bowled throughout to dismiss them for 70 in 44.1 overs. Pougher was to take five wickets for no runs against the Australians in 1896 when the MCC bowled them out for 18.

The locals lost by ten wickets, but there were some notable performances by the Cape Town cricketers. Armien Hendricks took four wickets for 50 runs in 25 overs. Fellow opener H. 'Krom' Hendricks, with whom he is often confused, took only one wicket, but he conceded just 29 runs in 23 tight overs. Complementing the praises of Chatterton, W.W. Read, the English tour captain, advised, 'If you send a team [to England], send Hendricks; he will be a drawcard and is to my mind the Spofforth of South Africa.'[13] F.R. Spofforth, known as 'The Demon', was the first great Australian fast bowler to wreak havoc against English teams.[14] The vastly experienced George Hearne, who played 252 times for Kent between 1875 and 1895, confirmed that the parallel was not exaggerated: 'A Malay named Hendricks was very fast indeed. In our last match against the Malays, the wicket was very bad and we didn't like facing the man at all. I was captain during the match and everyone began to ask me to let somebody else go in his place … The balls flew over our heads in all directions.'[15] The Surrey wicket-keeper Henry Wood, a survivor from Major Warton's first tour, who had just scored an unbeaten 134 in the test at Newlands, had to retire hurt after a 'bumping ball' hit him on the finger. The Surrey and England great George Lohmann and the South African test batsman C.H. Mills, who were presumably spectators, confirmed that Hendricks 'was by far the finest fast-bowler in South Africa'.

It was not only the bowlers from the Bo-Kaap and Claremont who starred. The top-order batsman Samsodien's 55 was the highest score against the English in their 21 matches on the tour. A regular run-maker in the Inter-Town tournaments, he had scored 45 in the previous season in the historic game for the South Africa Malay team against a strong white Kimberley invitation side, sharing a big partnership with Robert Grendon.

Samsodien's fifty was one of only two by South Africans on the tour. Charles Fichardt from the Orange Free State, who was selected for the test, was the only other batsman to reach the mark against the English. And in the 20 official matches, only four others managed forties – Castens, Halliwell, Routledge and Tancred, who also all represented South Africa. Only eleven others got to 30. The statistics tell the story. Fifty was a significantly big score at that time – there had also been only two half-centuries against the 1888/9 English tourists – and L. Samsodien was in select company. The Cape Times reported that he 'showed himself no mean batsman and set about scoring in fine fashion, cracking the bowlers for threes and fours with the utmost contempt, and to the great glee of the spectators'.

Following this game, the local sportsmen articulated what the game meant to them in a letter to the press:

On behalf of the Mohammedan community of Cape Town we hereby sincerely thank the English cricket team for their kindness in consenting to play the Mohammedan team and we also congratulate our players for the fair stand they made against the professionals, considering the drawbacks they have as regards practice grounds etc. We hope that the local cricket teams will, in future, show a similar kindness in allowing us a better field to practice on.[16]

Black cricketers – including Africans and 'coloured' Christians (like 'Krom' Hendricks) – were unabashedly seeking more opportunities and proving that they were capable of dealing with the best from the colony and abroad. The *Cape Times* assessment of the local team was that it 'gave more trouble and showed better form than some teams of odds and ends the Englishmen have recently met'.[17] This had been showed over and over again since Austin Ngcumbe made the Alberts stars in King William's Town jump with his pace and 11 wickets in 1885, through to Robert Grendon's scores of 92 and 187 against Kimberley establishment teams, including Irvine Grimmer, the season before.

The best black inter-town players were clearly up to the standard required to be competitive. Their performances against top white players in the eastern Cape, Kimberley and Cape Town over the years had shown this. Give us a chance: that is all they asked.

PART FOUR

THE DOORS CLOSE: INSTITUTIONALISING CRICKET AS A SPORT FOR 'EUROPEANS' AND MEN ONLY, 1894 ONWARDS

27

Fateful decision

*Rhodes and Milton exclude 'Krom' Hendricks from
the first South African tour to Britain, 1894*

> If he wants to go on the same footing as the others,
> I would not have him at any price. As baggage-man they
> might take him and play him in one or two of the matches
> when the conditions suited him. To take him as an equal
> would, from a South African point of view, be impolitic,
> not to say intolerable, and I would not have him on those
> terms if he were a better bowler than Lohmann.

– A.B. Tancred, South African opening batsman, 1894[1]

> Then, Sir, as to your remark that I 'might be taken home
> as baggage-man' I would beg to state that if chosen
> I would not think of going in that capacity.

– H. 'Krom' Hendricks, 'the best fast bowler in the country', 1894

In November 1892, the young South African Cricket Association (SACA) agreed
to send a national team to England for the first time in 1894. The question arose:
would black cricketers, who were increasingly showing their prowess on the
fields, be allowed to play for the officially recognised South Africa? The litmus
test was 'Krom' Hendricks, the fiery 'extra-fast' bowler, who had impressed the
English in Cape Town in March 1892. His name was among the nominations
sent in to the selectors by the major centres.

Hendricks immediately took the opportunity to demonstrate his skills. In
late December 1892 he played in a warm-up game for the Cape Town team

preparing for the fifth Malay Inter-Town Tournament against a 'European XI' drawn largely from the top Western Province Cricket Union (WPCU) league side, Cape Town Cricket Club, which had incidentally turned down his application to become a member. The tournament team batted first and scored 114. E. Ariefdien, the outstanding fast bowler and opening batsman, who had set several Inter-Town records already, top-scored with 34. Hendricks (5 for 47) and Ariefdien (4 for 42) then bowled unchanged in a fiery display that had leading white cricketers like Louis Smuts, J.B. Munnik, John Heynemann and the provincial player Arthur Seccull in all sorts of trouble. It was left to the professional Charles Mills from Surrey, who had played for South Africa the previous season, to fight a lone battle in a losing cause. Mills scored 61 out of his side's total of 101 before Hendricks and Ariefdien wrapped up the game.[2]

Two days later, with the largest attendance that had been seen at a cricket match in the Western Province that season, the fast-bowling duo scythed through the Kimberley batting line-up in the opening game of the Inter-Town Tournament for the Glover Cup played at the Cape Town CC ground, where the Newlands rugby stadium and the South African Sports Science Institute stand today. The talented batsman-poet Robert Grendon (0 and 6) made no impression as Kimberley (33 and 81) went down by eight wickets to the Capetonians (59 and 59/2). Only the national captain of the South African Malay team, Armien Hendricks, with 10* and 22 was able to withstand the pace onslaught. Hendricks took five for 8 and six for 36, and Ariefdien five for 18 and four for 42. Hendricks celebrated New Year 1893 by accounting for Johannesburg with his speed and stamina. His match analysis was 12 for 88.[3]

Watching all three performances was Harry Cadwallader, first secretary of SACA. The comments by the English professionals that Hendricks was the 'Demon Spofforth' of South Africa and that he would impress English audiences were confirmed in front of him. Cadwallader, a long-time proponent of an overseas tour, had been mandated by SACA to make the arrangements. He began to communicate officially with Charles Alcock, secretary of the Surrey CC and the Football Association and founder of *Cricket: A Weekly Record of the Game*, who was responsible for arranging the fixture lists of teams visiting England. By the end of 1893 the plans were well advanced. Cadwallader asked the major centres in South Africa to submit nominations to the national selection committee. They were also asked to choose the side they believed would be best equipped to represent South Africa on an overseas tour.

In the months leading up to the final selection, there was much discussion on the composition of the team, and whether a player of colour should be included. Early newspaper reports indicated that Hendricks was virtually certain of selection. On 11 January 1894 Reuters carried a message which was published in newspapers throughout the country: 'With regard to the proposed cricketing team for England, the Transvaal papers strongly advocate the inclusion of Hendricks, the Malay fast bowler, in the team.'[4] Those in favour of Hendricks being chosen were able to point out that he was easily the fastest bowler in the country. The only player who came close to him in terms of pace was Natal's Peter Madden, who had been labelled a 'chucker' and was not considered for the tour. Cadwallader himself used W.W. Read's 'Spofforth' comparison to justify Hendricks's inclusion.[5]

The rights of black citizens were constitutionally guaranteed in the Cape Colony, but how would the Cape Town establishment react to this suggested departure from social custom, particularly William Milton, the cricket president, and Cecil John Rhodes, the prime minister? They shared offices and, as it turned out, the decision would eventually lie with them.

Rhodes had helped the WPCU with fundraising for the tour, chairing a public meeting at the Commercial Exchange for that purpose. He had spoken positively in favour of it, saying he hoped to see the team include representatives not only from the Cape Colony but also from neighbouring states: Transvaal, Orange Free State, Natal, Bechuanaland and – to shouts of 'Hear, hear!' – from the Chartered territories, today's Zimbabwe. He warned the organisers against favouritism and urged them to 'take the best team wherever they might happen to be residing'.[6]

Did this apply to 'Krom' Hendricks as well? The answer was not long in coming.

CRICKET, CORRUPTION AND CAPE POLITICS

The issue of Hendricks's inclusion in the national cricket team became enmeshed with developments at the highest levels of Cape politics in two ways. Firstly, various cricket personalities were involved in the political machinations which led to the fall of the Cape government in 1892, and the political dramas and the realignment that followed had a direct bearing on the selection issue. Secondly, many leading Cape politicians held positions in local cricket clubs, and neither the Cape Town cricket nor the political establishment was enamoured of the idea of his going to England, particularly as it would clash with the segregatory legislation that Rhodes's government was busy passing.

Rhodes had come to power in 1890 with significant support from the Afrikaner Bond, whose leader was Jan Hendrik Hofmeyr. That the alliance with the Bond was crucial to the survival of Rhodes's government became clear when the government fell because of a scandal involving James Sivewright, the commissioner for Crown lands and public works and a leading Western Province cricket official. Sivewright had taken the railway line into the Transvaal and was knighted as a consequence.[7] But, according to Rhodes's biographer, he was a crook who abused several public positions. He became head of the Johannesburg Water Company and sold it water rights, which he had earlier acquired for himself, 'for a handsome profit'. As manager also of the Johannesburg Gas Company, he reputedly signed a contract in 1890 'in exchange for a healthy bribe'.[8] But the deal that had the biggest repercussion was the contract he granted James Logan, sponsor of the Western Province Currie Cup team and later of the 1901 South Africa tour to England, to supply refreshments on the entire Cape railway network for 18 years, without inviting tenders and for a ridiculously low payment.[9] When the liberal cabinet ministers John X. Merriman, J.W. Sauer and James Rose-Innes resigned in protest, Rhodes's government fell. But Rhodes was successfully able to manipulate the indecisiveness of his opponents and resumed power with a reconstructed cabinet and with the continuing support of the Afrikaner Bond.

At the time Merriman lamented to a correspondent the 'Rhodes-Hofmeyr way of doing business – the lobbying, the intrigue and utterly cynical disregard of anything approaching moral principle in the conduct of public affairs'.[10] With ties to the liberal lobby broken, Rhodes came out strongly against the liberal 'native policy' that had been one of the hallmarks of Cape politics. He was responsible for introducing into parliament in 1892 the Franchise and Ballot Bill, which placed restrictions on the right of Africans to the vote. The debate in parliament on the Bill was 'long and strenuous', but thanks to cooperation between Rhodes and Hofmeyr, it was finally passed. Hofmeyr's remarks during the debate summarised the feeling of most white colonists on the subject:

> the Bill would be the precursor of a better understanding between the two great European races, and that then they could talk of a United South Africa in its best sense. The English colonist and the Dutch colonist ... were equally faithful in their allegiance to the Crown ... There was only one other matter, which created a little suspicion in the minds of the Dutch Africanders. They feared that some Englishmen in the Colony were not clear upon the line of demarcation between barbarism and civilisation, as existed in India, in Natal, and other countries where the line of demarcation was drawn between the coloured barbarian and the civilised European.[11]

As the elections of 1894 approached, another such test case faced Rhodes. A Muslim imam from Cape Town, Ahmed Effendi, planned to stand for parliament. His supporters, many no doubt connected with the strong local cricket culture, hoped that local coloured voters would return him by 'plumping' their vote; each voter had four votes, and if they all gave them all to one candidate, the chances were good he would get in. Effendi's candidature became a test case for the colonial establishment, which wanted to prevent him from getting elected. Rhodes argued in favour of an amendment to abolish 'plumping', claiming it was 'illogical' for Cape Town to vote cumulatively. He aligned himself with the position that 'The Malays and people of that class were ... invading the town, and occupying the streets not occupied by them in times gone by'.[12] A regulation was quickly passed putting an end to plumping and to Effendi's chance of being elected.

In February 1894, Rhodes returned to Cape Town to 'a hero's welcome' after militarily suppressing what was called the Matabele Rebellion and adding the Ndebele stronghold to the Empire. At the same time he and William Milton, who was setting up the new Prime Minister's Department, were finalising Rhodes's 'Native Bill for Africa'. This was the Glen Grey Act, one of the foundations of apartheid legislation, which Rhodes succeeded in passing later that year. 'Conceived by Rhodes' and 'drafted by Milton', it was to be the solution for future 'native policy' in southern Africa. Not unlinked to the attacks on Hendricks and the emerging black middle class, the Act was meant to force Africans off their land and into the labour market and restrict their right to vote. It limited the granting of individual title to property for Africans, increased taxes and provided for a system of indirect representation for district councils for those living on communally owned land, who were now disqualified as a result from having the vote.[13]

The attempts to include a player of colour in a 'national' cricket side to tour overseas obviously flew in the face of the political developments taking place. Rhodes and Milton, sharing the same offices, were at one that Hendricks should not be allowed to tour. The issue could not escape the attention of the politicians who were involved in the game, many elected to official club positions. Hofmeyr led the Cape Town CC, with Sivewright his active deputy. James Rose-Innes and J.W. Sauer were the respective presidents of Mowbray and Wynberg Rovers, with the latter club also boasting Sir Henry de Villiers as its patron and Milton as a vice-president. Even a small club such as Caxton CC managed to attract three parliamentarians as vice-presidents (T.E. Fuller, A. Ohlsson and T.J. O'Reilly), a role in which Rhodes would later serve the WPCC. The high commissioner, Sir Henry Loch, was also involved in the cricket establishment, having accepted the position of president of the recently launched SACA.[14]

Hofmeyr had been instrumental in setting up Rhodes and Milton in their positions of power, and he communicated regularly with Rhodes: they were 'early risers, and it was the usual thing for the two men, often joined by Mr Sivewright, to take a ride on horseback together before the town was astir'. At a time when the composition of the team for the overseas cricket tour was receiving prominent press coverage, Rhodes conveyed his disapproval of Hendricks, using Milton as the conduit. He relayed a carefully worded message to the cricket authorities. This prevented the prime minister from being implicated in any further discussions on the subject.

William Milton was Rhodes's parliamentary secretary and could meet with the prime minister in private. He had opposed the tour, saying that South Africa was not ready to take on the English at home. He had also resigned as WPCU president shortly before because of the attempts of the clubs in the WPCU to curtail the power of the WPCC, which wished to assume the role of 'the MCC of the Cape Colony', but he was persuaded to continue as president and now moved centre stage again. Critics of the WPCU had complained it was unrepresentative and a mere extension of Milton's WPCC. He now got the WPCU to nominate him as their representative on the national selection panel and became its convener. Because Western Province had won the Currie Cup in 1892/3, the headquarters of SACA also now fell conveniently under the WPCU.[15]

In this way, cricket developments merged with Cape and South African politics at a crucial moment in the early 1890s. As Richard Parry has noted, 'It was over the role of Malay and Coloured cricketers in the broader social context that a key battle in the ongoing war over South African identity was specifically fought.'[16]

THE SPEEDSTER AND THE SECRETARY

It is almost certain that Cadwallader, as secretary of the SACA, had been looking after 'Krom' Hendricks's interests for some time. Aware of the pressure building up to exclude Hendricks from the South African team to tour England, Cadwallader now suggested, in his role as sports editor of the *Cape Times*, that the bowler could be taken as 'baggage-man': in that way 'there could be absolutely no objection to Hendricks on account of his being a Malay'.[17] Some have suggested that this was a calculated attempt by Cadwallader to bring the issue into the open. He wanted Hendricks to be given a public hearing, an assertion that is supported by a prompt, and possibly prearranged, response in the next edition of the newspaper:

> Sir – I notice in this morning's issue of your paper, under the heading of Sporting Intelligence, a wire from Johannesburg with your comment thereupon, wherein reference is made to my name as a possible candidate in the proposed cricketing team for England, and I hasten to take exception to same in the first place. I must disclaim my connection with the Malay community. My father was born of Dutch parents in Cape Town and my mother hails from St Helena – then why am I termed a Malay?

Further, I note it is taken for granted that should I be selected I would go with the team, but to the present no such application has been made to me to ascertain my views on the subject and I think this was the least the committee could have done before making my name thus public.

Then, Sir, as to your remark that I 'might be taken home as baggage-man' I would beg to state that if chosen I would not think of going in that capacity. Apologising for troubling on your space.

I am &c

H HENDRICKS[18]

The Johannesburg *Standard and Diggers News* followed up the letter by interviewing South Africa's champion batsman, A.B. Tancred, asking what he thought of Hendricks. 'Well,' replied Tancred, who was now practising as a lawyer in Pretoria,

after his impudent letter to the Association [Tancred mistakenly thought Hendricks had written to SACA], I should certainly leave him out. If he wants to go on the same footing as the others, I would not have him at any price. As baggage-man they might take him and play him in one or two of the matches when the conditions suited him. To take him as an equal would, from a South African point of view, be impolitic, not to say intolerable, and I would not have him on those terms if he were a better bowler than Lohmann.[19]

Tancred's viewpoint echoed that of a great number of white South Africans. One such was the writer of the following letter of 15 January 1894 to *The Star*:

Sir – I notice with keen regret that there is a disposition in various quarters to consider the suggestion that Hendricks, the Malay bowler, be included in the cricket team about to visit England.

I am convinced that any attempt to include a coloured player in the team will be resented by the vast majority of South Africans. I have discussed the point with numbers of cricket lovers and find that, almost without exception, the only ones who are in favour of it are those who retain certain well-intentioned but wholly impracticable views, imported with themselves quite recently, and certain others who consider that 'gate' and 'victory' cannot be too dearly bought.

I do not hold with either. I look forward to a friendly tussle between the English and South African cousins and, if we cannot do better, we can at least take a licking like white men.

We are in a country where whites are numerically out of it, and I submit that the most cursory glance into the future warns us, just as the experience of America in the past and present teaches, that we must preserve the line of demarcation intact. If distinctions of colour are to be removed, the initiative need not be taken by the whites. I do not think that those who treat the matter so lightly consider what the position of the other members of the team would be, nor yet the moral effect that will survive when the tour will be over and forgotten. The subject is a distasteful one, but, if needs must, I for one should take my stand at any time and in any place, and say that, taking in view the conditions of life in South Africa, it is imperative that the line be drawn sharp, straight, and unbroken between white and coloured.

It would belittle the intelligence of your readers to illustrate the logical results of relaxing the rule; and I need only add that those who take no heed of this aspect of the question, those who consider 'gate' and 'victory at any cost' the paramount aim, I cannot recognise as South African sportsmen, even to the extent of discussing the question with them – I am &c SCRUTATOR[20]

Tancred's disparaging remarks in the press upset Hendricks, who sought help from Cadwallader. He advised Hendricks to back down for the sake of gaining acceptance. It was a questionable and patronising approach, but Cadwallader, alone among SACA's officials, seems to have had a wider perspective and an ability to garner support for including Hendricks in the team. He sent a carefully considered letter to the *Cape Times*:

I learn from Hendricks who seems to be an unassuming man, and bears an excellent character for a number of years from his employers, that he would be pleased to go to England if required, on certain low terms for services rendered, and would not for a moment expect to be 'classed' with the rest of the team. Hearne and Mills speak of Hendricks as quite the best fast bowler in the country and Mr George Lohmann (he is an amateur with us here) says (this has reached England first from Lohmann himself): 'By all means take him Home' (for various reasons). Strong advices have come from other parts of the country in favour of this man's inclusion, but that question is, of course, a South African one for the consideration of the Final Selection Committee, and approval of guarantors.[21]

By drawing on the respected opinions of the two English professionals in South Africa, Frank Hearne and Charles Mills, as well as the support of the great English bowler George Lohmann, Cadwallader presented a strong case in favour of Hendricks.

HENDRICKS LEFT OUT: A HISTORIC OPPORTUNITY MISSED

Milton was furious that Cadwallader had placed the WPCU in an embarrassing situation, and contacted the other cricket bodies. The one province he was
wary about was the Transvaal, which had a strong, though not necessarily
united, committee, comprising Abe Bailey (chairman), Alfred Soames, E.A. Ernest
'Barberton' Halliwell, A.B. Tancred, Fred Smith and George Allsop. Although
they were restricted to nominating players from their own area, they included
Hendricks in their 'fifteen'. The *Standard and Diggers News* announced that the
selection of Hendricks was unanimous: 'The prejudice against him disappearing on the understanding that he is willing to go as baggage-man and servant.
Without a doubt the Western Province must also name him ... Hendricks is
acknowledged to be a red-hot trundler, and Halliwell, who will have to "stand
up" to him, is the gentleman who particularly insists on the inclusion of
this dusky unit.'[22]

The national selection committee met at the railway junction town of De
Aar because of its central location on Sunday, 25 February 1894. Milton was in
the chair. Among those present were Irvine Grimmer (Griqualand West), Owen
Dunell (Eastern Province), Ernest Halliwell (Transvaal), J.E. Jewell (Orange Free
State) and Harry Cadwallader, who, besides being SACA secretary, also repre-
sented Natal. The meeting lasted more than five hours.

A number of leading players were unavailable for selection, namely Milton
himself, A.B. Tancred, Irvine Grimmer, Henry Taberer, the Wimble brothers,
Charlie Vintcent, Alf Richards, Charles Fichardt and Charles Boyes. Without
such players, South Africa's hopes of making an impression in England were
adversely affected. As a result, the selectors battled to scrape together a team
and it included players whose claims to be considered South African were a little
dubious. The English professionals Frank Hearne and Charles Mills fell into this
category. Hearne was chosen because he had made his home in South Africa,
but Mills was left out because he was still playing for Surrey. Later, when Vollie
van der Bijl of Western Province dropped out of the side, Mills was drafted
into the team.

Milton dominated proceedings and had his way on virtually every issue. West-
ern Province's Herbert Castens was named as captain, and the colours of the
WPCC were chosen for the touring side. Despite the number of players unavail-
able, there was no place for 'Krom' Hendricks. It was a reprehensible decision.
Among those selected ahead of him were, for example, George Glover, who was
said to throw the ball, and Clement 'Boy' Johnson, who had been captain of
Dublin University during the previous season and had only just arrived on the
Rand. One sarcastic report asked why the Surrey star Lohmann had not been

considered because he 'has been out here longer than Johnson, and it is a sort of open secret that South Africa will be his future home'.[23]

The English magazine *Cricket Field* commented, 'It was hoped that Hendricks, the Malay fast bowler, would be included in the team. He is somewhat erratic, but most of the members of the English team who played against him admit that he was at times very difficult to play. On some of our crumbling wickets he would perhaps be highly effective. It is not unlikely that our visitors will regret before the end of the season that they were so particular as to the colour of their men.'

The former Australian captain Billy Murdoch, who had toured South Africa with Read's team, was also disappointed. 'As to Hendricks,' he said, 'I think myself he would have been of immense value to you, and in any case would have been a very great draw. I feel sure he would have knocked some of us and our pegs about on hard wickets.'[24] 'It is a case of courting a disaster for the sake of prejudice,' added the *Standard and Diggers News*.[25]

So suspicious were people of the manner in which the selection had been conducted that Milton was forced to release a copy of the minutes. They were sketchy and, if anything, prolonged the dispute. With regard to Hendricks, they simply read, 'Halliwell proposed Hendricks be added to list – not seconded.'[26]

The influential mining magnate Abe Bailey, both a member of the Transvaal team and vice-president of the Transvaal Cricket Union, would not comment on the selection until he had attended the Currie Cup tournament, which began soon after the touring side had been named. As it was held in Cape Town, it gave Bailey the opportunity to speak to Milton and to learn of Rhodes's involvement. On Bailey's return to Johannesburg, a persistent reporter from the *Standard and Diggers News* asked him whether the trip had encouraged him to change his views about Hendricks. 'That is a rather ticklish business,' he answered.

> As you know when I went down, I was strongly in favour of sending him, but I have yielded somewhat to the very good argument that, after all, our men were going to England to learn rather than with the hope of achieving any great glory. Under these circumstances, it was argued, it was not absolutely necessary to lift a coloured man up on account of the moral effect it might have on the whole coloured population ... Under these circumstances, I waived the point as I did not wish to upset things and force it. All the same, it is a great pity there is no fast bowler in the team and I wouldn't say a word against Hendricks were he to be sent after all.

The reporter then moved on to a subject that was known to irk the mining magnate, the controversial issue of team manager. 'Bailey was asked, "What about the manager ...?" A steely glance stopped the intended question.'[27]

THE PRICE OF STANDING UP TO THE SYSTEM

Together with 'Krom' Hendricks, Harry Cadwallader was jettisoned by Milton. At De Aar, Milton had requested that the appointment of manager be left over so that the guarantors might be consulted. No one was suspicious of the request; after all, Cadwallader was the only candidate and delegates had already indicated their support for him. It was a position Cadwallader dearly coveted and seemed certain to fill. But Milton postponed the appointment because he needed time to choose and promote another candidate. He strongly opposed Cadwallader and had resolved to get rid of the troublesome journalist. The other unions were not aware of this. To them, it seemed a formality that 'old Caddy' would be chosen.

Milton took the opportunity to bring in his WPCC inner circle. When the moment came to elect the manager of the touring side, the WPCU nominated current president of the South African Rugby Board, W.V. 'Billy' Simkins, to stand against Cadwallader. The national votes for the two candidates were divided equally, but Cadwallader withdrew, stating that he did not care to be considered a candidate for the management unless he received unanimous, or almost unanimous, support. In the end, Simkins was appointed manager; and Castens (who had also captained the national rugby team in 1891) became captain.

The *Cape Argus* was the first to express its surprise that 'Western Province' should treat Cadwallader so shabbily, as he had done more than anyone to put South African cricket on its feet. 'It is whispered', said the report, 'that the Western Province Cricket Union committee after having opposed the scheme at the outset, having got a majority of selections in the team, a Western Province man as skipper, and the Western Province Cricket Club colours adopted for the tour, want also to dictate about the managership and are nominating a "special" of their own fancy.'[28]

Cadwallader published an open letter in which he appealed to the guarantors of the English tour not 'to throw him overboard, after working so hard in bringing the negotiations to a successful conclusion'. He said that he was quite in the dark as to the reasons which prompted the WPCU to favour Simkins as the manager, a man who had been associated with rugby rather than cricket. His being overlooked was 'in consequence of the machinations of a clique about whose actions he could "a tale unfold"'.[29]

The controversy over Hendricks's non-selection for the 1894 tour also brought to an end Cadwallader's involvement in the administration of cricket. The man who, as first secretary of the SACA, had almost single-handedly placed the South African game on a firm footing was forced to step down without the recognition he deserved. Unfairly pushed aside as manager, he was subsequently also replaced as secretary of the SACA. The occupant of two high offices at one stage, Cadwallader next lost his position as secretary-treasurer of the South African Rugby Football Board. Particularly intriguing is the fact that when he was elected in July 1893, the self-same Simkins became president of the SARB. Cadwallader was praised for getting the 'Football Board into shape, financial and otherwise' as he had inherited 'a very muddled state' with books and records having been lost during the amalgamation of the Central and De Beers Diamond Companies'.[30] However, shortly after he left Cape Town to accompany the South African cricket side on tour as a reporter in 1894, the Board's delegates used the AGM to elect Louis Smuts as the replacement secretary-treasurer. Cadwallader was not nominated again and he effectively paid the price for instigating the 'Hendricks affair'. After losing his positions on the two national bodies, Cadwallader had to come to terms with the fact that he had virtually no support base in the Cape. He relocated to the Transvaal, where he died in 1897 in 'such grievous need' that a public fund was set up to assist his wife and children.[31]

His old rival, Charles Finlason, had once remarked, '"Old Caddy" deserves all the kudos that may be given him and it is no exaggeration to say that for the next fifty years and more the cricketers of this country will have cause to feel grateful to the first secretary of the South African Cricket Association.'[32] Yet, when M.W. Luckin – one of his successors as SACA secretary – produced the first comprehensive history of South African cricket in 1915, Cadwallader did not receive a single mention. He had been written out of history completely.[33]

It is significant that the 'clique' whose lack of fairness had sidelined Cadwallader in 1894 remained firmly in control of both cricket and rugby in Cape Town until World War I. Two of the hardline cricket leaders, Simkins and Smuts, were also the dominant influences in Western Province rugby for more than twenty years, Simkins as president from 1893 to 1905 and Smuts from 1908 to 1918.

RHODES, THE BRITISH AND RACISM IN CRICKET

Rhodes's behind-the-scenes involvement in the Hendricks affair was not made public knowledge until Pelham Warner, former England cricket captain and pillar of the establishment at Lord's, wrote about it some 50 years later. Warner recalled that in March 1895, when Rhodes and Dr Jameson had stayed at Oxford with the provost of Oriel College, he had told students, 'They wanted me to send a black fellow called Hendricks to England … but I would not have it.'[34] Warner wrote, 'the following is an almost word-for-word record of part of that conversation':

Rhodes: What are you going to do when you go down?
Warner: I am going to the Bar, and am 'eating dinners' at the Inner Temple.

Rhodes: Do you ever meet any coloured men there?
Warner: Yes, a few.
Rhodes: Do you ever sit near them?
Warner: Yes.
Rhodes: Do you like them?
Warner: Yes, I do.
Rhodes: Well, I don't. I suppose it is the instinct of self-preservation. In South Africa we have perhaps a million or two whites, and many millions more of black people.[35]

Cadwallader might well have known the full story of Rhodes's involvement in the drama. He was probably afraid to implicate the prime minister but spoke out against Milton whom, he said, had 'privately exerted influence to induce other unions for that gentleman [Simkins] against myself'.[36]

At the time of the South African tour, James Logan, cricket benefactor and member of parliament, was appalled by the fate of both Hendricks and Cadwallader. He believed that the management of the team should be in the hands of the man who had borne the brunt of the arrangements and that Hendricks should have been chosen. Logan, who enjoyed a close friendship with Lohmann and the professionals, was 'strongly in favour of the best team that South Africa can send of whatever class or colour, as most likely to ensure a successful tour'. He added that he was 'heartily sick of the whole business after the turn events have taken' and, as a result of the underhand dealings, wished to withdraw his guarantee.[37] The *Cape Times* offered its support: 'Perhaps J.D. Logan might bring his influence to bear on this point, for the Laird of Matjiesfontein tolerates colour and colour tolerates him, as witness his magnificent majority at the poll due to the coloured vote.'[38] Not long afterwards, a Reuter's telegram from Kimberley arrived, stating, 'It is the almost general opinion here that the Western Province Cricket Union has, by its high-handed action regarding various matters in connection with the team for England, muddled the whole concern.'[39]

Very little went right for the tourists in England. They had difficulties adapting to turf wickets; they were unfortunate to strike a very wet season; their matches were not given first-class status and therefore attracted poor crowds; they were not given sufficient publicity; and the tour was a financial failure, with its collapse being avoided through assistance received from steamship companies and South African businessmen in England.[40]

The South Africans had only themselves to blame. Castens was unaccountably off-hand towards the well-intentioned press, and the team paid the price. Nothing was earned at the gate for the match against Sussex, and a mere

£2 12s was taken at Leicester. The team lacked players who could draw the crowds. This fact was quickly seized upon by Cadwallader, who accompanied the side as press representative for several South African newspapers. 'Certainly everywhere we went,' he observed,

> we were asked why we didn't bring Hendricks with us. It was surprising how the general public had got to know about his reputation. We had to explain as well as we could the reason he was not brought, but the public, who are used to seeing on the cricket field coloured men like Messrs P.J.T. Henery and K.S. Ranjitsinhji playing in their universities and county elevens, could not quite understand it. They could not comprehend the difference of classes in the social, or rather sporting, kaleidoscope at this end and the Cape end.

Cadwallader felt convinced that the South Africans could have 'given all the first-class counties a "tying-up" if we only had a really good fast trundler or two'.[41]

SACA's decision not to allow Hendricks to participate in its first overseas tour in 1894 established the pattern for the future. The unfolding tragedy for the cricketer 'was a microcosm of the tragedy of thousands of black South Africans at the time. They believed the ideology; that their behaviour and attainments would allow them to pass across class lines. Cricket and Christianity were the passports to a better life on the other side of the divide.'[42] Contrary to popular perceptions today among cricket-loving English-speaking South Africans that Afrikaners and 'politics' were responsible for apartheid, it was the arch-imperialist Rhodes, his right-hand man, Milton, and the English cricket establishment – particularly in Cape Town – that supported and entrenched racial segregation in the game. It was they who were responsible for drawing a line that black cricketers could not cross.

Cecil John Rhodes, Milton and their circle made a decision that took South African cricket on a hundred-year journey into a dead-end street. Rhodes made the half-hearted excuse that Hendricks was omitted for his own good – so that he would not be subjected to indignities before the English crowds – but it was unconvincing.[43] It is a great historical irony that 120 years after this event, while the authors were busy completing this narrative, students at the University of Cape Town should deface Rhodes's statue and cause it to be removed because it symbolised dishonour.

28

The Cape Town establishment institutionalises racism in cricket

Hendricks was left out of the Colonial-born versus Home-
born fixture but created interest on the same day by taking
6 for 31 for United Services against Bishops at the College
ground. All his victims were clean bowled. He followed this
performance by returning figures of 8 for 31 against Woodstock;
7 for 6 against the Castle, and 5 for 13 against Olympics.

– Jonty Winch, 'Sir William Milton'[1]

After the 1894 overseas tour, 'Krom' Hendricks's career was frustrated, step by
mean step, over a period of nearly a decade by the Cape Town cricket establishment. Harry Cadwallader, the first secretary of the South African Cricket
Association (SACA), claimed he 'could a tale unfold' about the machinations of
the cricket authorities at the Cape who prevented Hendricks from being chosen
for the tour. These machinations continued for several years afterwards.[2] After
the tour, the men who governed the Western Province Cricket Club (WPCC)
and the Western Province Cricket Union (WPCU), with their strong links to the
Cape political elite, systematically organised Hendricks's exclusion from any
cricket at a representative level. He had to watch from the sidelines for the next
eight years, although he was universally recognised as an exceptional talent.
His persistent efforts to showcase his skills were rebuffed at every step until he
had passed his prime.

A little more than two months after the tour concluded, WPCU committee
members were called upon to make another ruling with regard to Hendricks.
He had played in the 'white' Cape Town First Cup competition during October
1894 and bowled so well that permission was sought to include him in a Colonial-Born team to play the annual match against the Home-Born. This fixture,

which demonstrated imperial sporting links, was an important cricket and social occasion. 'For some years,' writes Christopher Merrett, 'the Home-Born versus Colonial contest was the season's most significant match but it had a more far-reaching significance this time – it introduced to the game the crucial question of who was a South African, an issue that was to haunt all representative sport until the 1990s.'[3]

Castens had told *The Cricket Field* in the course of the 1894 tour that 'a reason – the most important of all – for leaving [Hendricks] out of our team, is that he never plays in any local European teams, and hardly ever against them'.[4] To an extent, this problem was rectified by Hendricks's participation in a predominantly white league in the 1894/5 season, but at the key stage that followed, the authorities wavered.

The WPCU tried to minimise the fuss over the possible inclusion of Hendricks in the Colonial-Born side by focusing on a number of Australian cricketers who also hoped to be selected. After some discussion, the constitution was revised to allow the Colonial-Born XI to include players born in 'the British colonies or in India'. Four Australians and a committee member, Indian-born Godfrey Cripps, were therefore accommodated, but the case for Hendricks was not settled.[5] E.S. Steytler told members that because Hendricks had played for the United Services Club in a competition recognised by the Union, it was difficult to exclude him from the representative match. Louis Smuts supported this viewpoint but drew attention to the fact that 'it would be very awkward if Hendricks were chosen and the opposing team refused to play'. Another member was in favour of including Hendricks, stating, 'It had always been the boast of cricket that the peer and the ploughman could meet together in the same field,' but he too equivocated, saying that the committee 'could not be blind to the fact that there was strong opposition to Hendricks in certain quarters'. Maynard Nash, the WPCU secretary and very much a Milton disciple, reminded the committee that it was 'a wider issue than the mere admittance of Hendricks'. It was therefore agreed that the problem should be deferred until a further meeting four days later. A decision could not be made without consulting Milton.

The delay increased interest in the controversy. In his newspaper column Cadwallader stressed that the matter should be debated carefully because Hendricks was, in the opinion of leading cricketers, 'one of the finest extra-fast bowlers in the world'. 'It seems to us that there are two "gates" for "coloureds" to the cricket field – the first being exceptionally good cricket, and the next exceptionally good and appropriate behaviour, and the main question is – does Hendricks fulfil these qualifications?'

The selectors did not wait for the second meeting before naming the Coloni-al-Born team. They did not include Hendricks. This annoyed Advocate H.W.S. Giddy, who represented the United Services Club, and he informed delegates when they reassembled that the question of whether Hendricks was eligible for selection should be settled 'once and for all'. Milton's opinion was keenly antic-ipated, but he was not interested in discussing the matter and moved that the meeting pass on to the next business. He pointed out that he had been in the Western Province for 17 years and did not see why a special case should be made for Hendricks, saying many good players had been overlooked in the past. Smuts immediately seconded him and the motion was carried. *The Cricket Field* stated euphemistically that Milton had 'disposed of the difficulty for the present'.[6]

The sports editor of the *Standard and Diggers News* in Johannesburg was scathing in his criticism: 'The Western Province would indeed be stultifying themselves, after their strenuous and successful objection to Hendricks' inclu-sion in the South African team to England, where race distinctions are unknown, should they include the coloured bowler in representative cricket at the Cape, where snobocracy reigns.'[7]

Although the issue took some time to die down, Milton's interventions effec-tively ended the promising career of 'Krom' Hendricks and put a stop to players of colour participating in mainstream cricket at the Cape. It was the beginning of officially segregated sport, a policy that was followed by the various centres that participated in South African cricket and, in time, by all South African sports.

Hendricks's cricket aspirations were shattered. The Woodstock bowler was not considered for the Western Province side that participated in the next Currie Cup tournament in April 1895, leading to the farcical situation in which Natal fielded the 'coloured' all-rounder Buck Llewellyn, while Hendricks was kept at home to be feted by white ladies before a sizeable crowd of white holiday-makers in a mixed women versus men's match.[8]

At Durban, Transvaal regained the Currie Cup, defeating a Western Province side that was bolstered by three professionals. This meant the administration of the SACA would transfer to the Transvaal. But Milton was determined to hold on to the reins as long as possible and worked on the assumption that a transfer of power could only take place at the next meeting of the SACA. He managed to delay the transition until the last possible opportunity – a 31 December 1895 meeting was then postponed to 31 January 1896 – and in the meantime organised the itinerary and handled contentious issues for the next cricket tour to South Africa.[9]

When Lord Hawke arranged for his side to visit South Africa during 1895/6, the question of colour was again a prominent issue. The *Cape Times* noted that 'the Indian prince with the impossible name [Ranjitsinhji]' was being considered for the team.[10] Milton reacted quickly: his efforts would probably have received sympathy from the cricket establishment in England. Brian Dobbs writes of the English overlooking Ranjitsinhji a few months later because of 'the virulence of colour prejudice at Lord's'. Sir Home Gordon, who was quoted by *Wisden* as being a friend of Ranjitsinhji and Lord Hawke, explained, 'there was so much prejudice against "a nigger showing us how to play cricket"'.[11]

Milton secured C.B. Fry as a replacement, though the details surrounding the selection did not come to light until some years later. 'Ranji would have been unwelcome in South Africa ... and therefore he took the opportunity to urge Lord Hawke to select his friend and Sussex team-mate instead.' Fry wrote of his selection in a 'particularly vivid and succinct description': 'There was the temporarily dispossessed Heir Apparent of an Indian State who had become a fantastic success as a batsman, and who with Rajput love of honour and glory desired to see Sussex champion county. There was a recent addition to the Sussex county eleven in whom the Rajput Heir Apparent saw possibilities. That is how I came to be in South Africa in the year of the Jameson Raid.'[12]

It was not so easy for Milton to keep Hendricks out of the news at the time. In November 1895 the *Cape Times* selected him in their choice of a South African team to meet the tourists. Cadwallader, who was about to depart for the Transvaal, probably had some say in a not unreasonable selection. Hendricks was left out of the Colonial-Born vs Home-Born fixture but created interest on the same day by taking six for 31 for United Services against Bishops at the college ground. All his victims were clean-bowled. He followed this performance by returning figures of eight for 31 against Woodstock; seven for 6 against the Castle; and five for 13 against Olympics.[13]

Milton, Smuts and Steytler were the selectors for all provincial and test matches to be played against Lord Hawke's team at Newlands. They were not prepared to consider Hendricks for representative selection, but Halliwell, the South African captain and chairman of the Transvaal selection committee, was keen to provide him with the opportunity he deserved. Halliwell had chaired the recent meeting of the SACA and was determined that his administration would be no pushover. A world-class wicketkeeper who had won admiration from W.G. Grace for his skills, he appeared to relish the opportunity to challenge Milton.[14]

The Transvalers resolved to invite Hendricks to the Rand for two weeks to enable the selectors 'to form an opinion as to his form' with a view to his playing for South Africa in the second test against Lord Hawke's side in 1895/6. Platnauer, a member of the committee, claimed the action of the Transvaal Cricket Union was one 'few will find fault with', but the Cape viewed the situation in a very different light.[15] Hendricks cabled his interest to Halliwell, but it was to no avail. The WPCU refused to support the selection and Hendricks was prevented from travelling to Johannesburg. The *Cape Times*, now *sans* Cadwallader, demonstrated vigorous support for the WPCU by describing the selection of Hendricks as 'a most uncalled-for insult' to Western Province cricket. The newspaper added, 'Such slights are not calculated to foster that spirit of friendliness which should exist between the two chief centres of sport in South Africa'.

Western Province cricket officials proved uncooperative in arrangements for the second test. They were determined not to lend support to Halliwell, 'who apparently thinks that every cricketer and every cricketing centre is under his regal sway'.[16] The Cape Town Cricket Club helped make life even more difficult for Halliwell by refusing James Middleton leave to play in the test, even though the WPCU had earlier expressed support for the inclusion of professionals in the South African team.[17] It resulted in the selectors frantically searching for players to represent South Africa as late as the morning of the match. This scrabbling provoked a sense of perverse satisfaction at the *Cape Times*, which reported that 'after a lot of trouble G.H. Shepstone and Fred Smith were obtained – these are by no means the best available men in the Transvaal, but they were the only players who could be got at the last moment. Thus the representative nature of the team is entirely destroyed.'[18]

In a show of solidarity, the press and clubs at the Cape had backed the WPCU to the hilt, but to the detriment of South African cricket. The *Standard and Diggers News* in contrast expressed deep disappointment at South Africa's defeat by an innings and 197 runs: 'Had Middleton and Hendricks been playing in this match, the phenomenal score [482] made by Lord Hawke's team would not have been made.'[19] The racially based selection policy of the Cape's cricket administrators had again divided the country and weakened the national side.

Such an intolerant attitude also proved an obstacle to Lord Hawke's suggestion that a Gentleman vs Players match be played that would involve composite sides being drawn from the best of both touring and local players. It was intended that the match 'should prove an immense draw as it would give cricket lovers an opportunity of watching better all-round cricket than they are likely to see again for some time to come'. The likely 'Players XI' was published in the press; it included the four touring professionals and seven professionals with South African contracts. The fact that Hendricks was one of those named meant the game would never get off the ground.[20]

By 1897 the WPCU had even banned Hendricks from playing for his club in its leagues. Prior to the 1896/7 season, Woodstock CC arranged to employ Hendricks as their professional. They hoped to make use of his services in the newly formed club 'championship' (later, the First or Premier League). The WPCU responded quickly by resorting to discriminatory legislation in order to prevent the player from making the anticipated impact. They instituted a racially discriminatory resolution which stated: 'That this union will not object to any club employing a coloured professional in matches other than championship and no coloured professional or member shall be allowed to compete in the championship.'[21] The term 'championship' came to be used more loosely than the resolution had originally implied, and, as a result, Hendricks was considered unwelcome to play in any match of consequence.

One fixture that the Union did not cater for was a non-championship inter-club encounter between the Cape Town CC and Woodstock in November 1896. The match was expected to be one-sided because Cape Town was one of the city's premier clubs while Woodstock was a struggling team with no provincial contenders. It was nevertheless billed as a match in which 'the two fastest bowlers in the Western Province' – Joseph Willoughby and Hendricks – would be on show. There was further incentive for Hendricks to shine: he had made an earlier attempt to join the Cape Town CC but had not been accepted.

Woodstock were 'powerless' against Willoughby, who captured seven for 7 in a total of 47. It placed pressure on Hendricks to perform and so he did, taking eight wickets for 32 runs. 'It was a remarkable performance,' said the *Cape Times*, 'considering the class of batsmen.' His victims included five players – Charles Prince, Howard Francis, Stanley Horwood, Frank Hearne and Willoughby – who represented South Africa at various times. The most spectacular aspect of his performance was that he hit the stumps on seven occasions, a feat that Willoughby managed twice.[22]

Cape Town's cricket followers wanted to see more of Hendricks. When Milton left the Cape to take up an appointment in Rhodesia, a brave decision was taken to give Hendricks a chance in October 1897.[23] He was chosen for an All-Comers XI to play against the WPCC. It was noted that the fast bowler 'had been creating havoc in the lower leagues' and an unusually large crowd of 1,600 surrounded the field at Milton's former club. Hendricks did not let them down. In 21.3 overs of sustained pace, he captured six for 20. His first wicket was that of Western Province batsman Allan Reid, who was bowled for six, and he followed this up by shattering the stumps of one of the country's leading batsmen, Murray Bisset, for a duck.[24] This must have pleased Hendricks; Bisset was one of the loudest voices in the choir backing his exclusion from local cricket.

Frank Robb, the white Woodstock chairman, saw it as an opportune moment for his club to confront the WPCC. His plan of action was initially to forward a letter to the *Cape Times* under the pseudonym 'Fairplay'. He argued that circumstances had altered since the colour-bar resolution had been passed. Robb's letter stated: 'The Union has by its own action put aside the objection to colour by admitting to affiliation and to competition in the championship, clubs who number among their members coloured players.'[25] He added, 'With Hendricks at one end the whole of the Woodstock bowling was improved.' Robb believed there was a 'strong feeling, rightly or wrongly, on the part of the public that Hendricks is not receiving fair treatment at the hands of the Union'. He pleaded for coloured players to be included in championship matches, noting that Simonstown and the Docks were in the same predicament.[26]

The WPCC was not sympathetic. Simkins complained that 'someone was guilty of a grave error in having selected Hendricks for the All-Comers'. He thought the Union should use all means at its disposal to ensure that the two classes 'be kept distinctly separate'. It was a powerful indication of the direction in which cricket at the Cape was moving. Smuts stated, 'It was all good and well in some countries to talk of cricket as a levelling institution but here circumstances were so very different.' Vollie van der Bijl said the selector of the composite side would, if given his way, have chosen three players of colour, but claimed that if three were chosen 'probably the other eight would not have played'. Maynard Nash, who had succeeded Cadwallader as secretary of the SACA, argued that 'rescinding the ruling would work the greatest harm to the game in the country. We must look to the future as well as the present.'[27]

The future of cricket at the Cape, it seemed, was tied to the increasing trend of racism and segregation in government and public policy. Men such as the president, John Reid, the long-serving Charles Neumann Thomas and the young Bisset were firmly in support of the lead that Simkins had provided, thereby ensuring that Robb's motion was defeated by 12 votes to 2.[28] Vivian Bickford-Smith has since viewed Robb's objection as demonstrating 'the intimate relationship between ideology and self-interest', but he was seemingly unaware that another delegate, Harry Hands, rendered support and voted with Robb. Hands was a significant voice of dissension, as he was the secretary of the WPCC during the years 1896–1913. In this role he was probably instrumental in arranging for Hendricks to play for the All-Comers XI against the club. Of interest is that Hands would some years later earn a knighthood for his services as mayor of Cape Town during World War I.[29] Three of his sons played for South Africa: two in official tests and one against Solly Joel's team, which played unofficial tests.

An important outcome of the crushing defeat that Robb suffered was that the WPCU was forced publicly to confirm its policy of exclusivity and to stand rigidly behind racial barriers in the form of its resolution. A *Cape Times* leader declared that it was not prepared to say the Union was wrong 'to exclude coloured players from Union cricket matches'. It did, however, criticise the cricket authorities for allowing multi-racial matches in the first place: 'A general free mixture of white and coloured youth in games nobody here is prepared to advocate' and it should not be followed by 'the admission to white cricket of the few coloured players good enough to be played in Union matches'. The newspaper argued that the cricket administration had only itself to blame for its predicament, but that once the problem had been created, it should 'somehow have been managed in private'. It was regretted that 'Hendricks and his friends and the coloured population' might read the report on the cricket meeting and be 'prompted to bitter and resentful impulse, nursing of grudges'.[30]

The WPCU's attitude hardened towards black players, while its policies were replicated by other sporting committees in laying the foundations for the development and entrenchment of racially divided sport. The door was locked.

But Hendricks did not give up, and kept knocking at the door. He joined the Metropolitan Cricket Club soon after it was formed in September 1898. He claimed five wickets in his first match against Cape Town 'B', but his opportunities were thereafter limited by the exclusionary resolution. To an extent he was able to supplement his playing appearances by turning out for Fernwood, a coloured team. This was a time when players of colour were being ushered towards organisations that included 'Coloured' in their titles. Those that still wished to play alongside whites were reduced to displaying their talents as bowlers in the nets.

White sport leaders approved of separate ethnic-based athletic clubs, just as there were at that time 'distinct places of residence and resort for the white, the brown and the black sections of the population'.[31] One such leader was Bisset, who, en route to becoming president of the WPCU, demonstrated his opposition to blacks playing in white leagues. Yet, as South Africa's captain, he complained bitterly to *Cricket* in 1901 that people at the Cape were losing interest in the game because there was no variety – 'the worst of it is that one always sees the same familiar faces, because we have so few clubs'.[32]

Bisset captained a South African side selected by Logan on the 1901 tour to England. Logan had been outspoken on the omission of Hendricks from the team that toured in 1894 but, given the opportunity to make amends, he failed to include any coloured players in his side in 1901. The team he chose was one 'the local newspapers attacked ... saying that it could not, or should not be, designated "the South African team"' since it was a private enterprise and that 'only six of the 14 players would have the ghost of a chance of playing for South Africa in a representative match'.[33] Such was the insensitive manner in which the side was assembled that the outstanding Henry Taberer was invited but not taken, while the selection of a player of inferior quality in Logan's son, J.D. – 'a passenger' who could only be used 'in an emergency' – was ill advised on a tour that was later granted 'South African' status.[34]

In the years which immediately followed the South African War, there were no players of colour in the Cape leagues. Hendricks wrote a long letter to the WPCU in November 1904, requesting permission to play for the Metropolitan Club. At a subsequent meeting, Simkins noted in patronising fashion that 'Hendricks was a well-conducted man' before stating it was 'important to know what was actually on the records of the Union'. He knew very well what was on the records – the resolution he had helped introduce. Hendricks's request was heard by Bisset, who later became Rhodesia's chief justice and acting governor. He had sat on the 1897 committee that refused to rescind the resolution and, seven years later, ruled that he had 'no doubt in his mind that on general principles, the application should not be acceded to'. Only W.A. Kingon, who had also attended the 1897 meeting, was of the opinion that 'a special exception be made in Hendricks' case'. As Kingon was unable to attract a seconder, Bisset's motion was carried.[35] It was the last recorded effort by Hendricks to play alongside white cricketers. 'By the early 1900s,' wrote John Nauright, 'cricket represented sporting exclusivity.'[36]

While Cadwallader was air-brushed out of the country's cricket records, cricket historians in the years that followed obligingly referred to the members of the clique that excluded him and Hendricks in glowing terms, notably Milton ('this outstanding personality was knighted'), Simkins ('loved and respected by all') and Smuts ('much respected'). A.C. Parker's *WP 100 Not Out* neatly papers over the cracks which marred the early administration and, in a brief reference to Hendricks, suggests that those alleged to be 'against the player were motivated by fear of his bowling prowess rather than colour prejudice'.[37] Milton, who spearheaded the initial campaign against Hendricks, was said to be 'the apotheosis of sporting achievement in those far-off days and what he did for the advancement of sport must never be forgotten'.[38]

The treatment meted out to Hendricks over a period of ten years reflected the determination of the WPCU to maintain a system that advantaged whites at the expense of other groups. The fact that Hendricks persevered in his attempt to secure a place within white cricket forced the WPCU to nail its colours to the mast of segregation and enforce its position in terms of rules and resolutions that limited the ability of black cricketers to compete with their white counterparts. In all this, they were perfectly in step with the march of segregation in the wider South African society. There was much sympathy for the WPCU as it strove to ward off other races wishing to play cricket within the organisation. The *Cape Times* asked, 'Where are you to draw the line?' It went on to assert that if the issue of multi-racial cricket was restricted to Hendricks, there was no problem. The concern was that whites would be overwhelmed by 'our coloured friends of all shades and of various classes in life [who] have taken to the white man's athletics with great vigour'.[39] Though there were the odd press comments to commend Hendricks for being of good character, most whites generally regarded him with suspicion as the representative of a community that posed a danger and not someone with feelings and aspirations. No effort was made to understand his plight, certainly nothing resembling the comments that Richard Parry made many years later on the disappointment Hendricks must have felt at the time of the 1894 selection controversy: 'The whole affair must have been doubly galling for Hendricks who had been required politically to swallow his pride and accept a menial status and was even then unceremoniously rejected. It is hard to imagine a more bitter cricketing blow.'[40]

Not all white South Africans of the time were blind to the wrong that was committed. We have seen that Cadwallader, Halliwell, Platnauer, Robb and Hands challenged the status quo. And the *Cape Times*, which called on South Africans to 'pursue an equal policy of mutual exclusion', was able to see that it reinforced a deeply flawed course of action. In a leading article on Hendricks, the paper referred to youngsters 'ranging from the lighter of brown looks to the darkest of black ones, going forth to various open spaces' to play sport, and asked: 'Can the English who carry their cricket and football to the uttermost parts of the earth look with disfavour on such a phenomenon?' It then turned to the good service the 'Cape-boys' had performed in quelling the recent Matabeleland Rebellion and said that coloured readers would debate 'whether he and his, though good enough to fight side by side with white men, are good enough to play side by side with them. And the answer – NO!' The newspaper accepted that it 'might be wrong to put forward these considerations, unless we are prepared to advocate the opposite answer. But we think it is just as well to show that we whites are not – many of us are not – blind to such considerations, even if we cannot in some particular matter carry them into action.'[41] Unfortunately, such fence-sitting was to become part of the problem in twentieth-century South African cricket.

The reality of the situation was that the white ruling classes and cricket establishment took a path that went against merit and promoted segregation in sport on the basis of race. As Tony Collins has demonstrated in his social history of rugby in England, the whole idea of the gentleman amateur in British sport was built on anti-competitive protocols and notions of class privilege – you belonged by not necessarily being the best but by 'playing the game', as was expected of you, and because of where you came from.[42] It is ironic, therefore, that the 'merit' argument became used so often against the official recognition of black cricketers in the post-apartheid period. While incompetent amateurs like Emile McMaster and Charles Coventry, who were no more than club cricketers, sit in *Wisden*'s sanctified account as international players, there have been hundreds of players from the unrecognised 'other' side, since Austin Ngcumbe's 11 wickets against Albert CC in 1885 and Samsodien's 50 and Hendricks's stellar bowling performance against the English professionals in 1892, who deserved to play at the highest levels.

Had Hendricks gone to England in 1894 in line with the relatively inclusive Cape Colony constitution of the time, as he should have on merit, South Africa would have preceded the route subsequently followed by West Indies cricket. Lebrun Constantine, father of the great Sir Learie Constantine, became 'the first black man allowed to play for Trinidad' in 1893, and during the first West Indies tour to England in 1900 he was one of five black players included. As Charles Lister has pointed out in his *Fire of Babylon*, one of the five, Charles Olliveirre, was persuaded to stay behind and play for Derbyshire in county cricket, starting a long tradition of West Indian stars in the English leagues and county cricket.

Seven decades before a man with a similar-sounding name as Oliveirre – Basil D'Oliveira – led an exodus of black talent from South Africa to England in the 1960s, South Africa's top five of the 1890s, in the shape of Krom and Armien Hendricks, Robert Grendon, L. Samsodien and E. Ariefdien, and the talented players who followed them, could have been sharing the same roadway as the Constantines, Olliveirre, the legendary George Headley and Sir Frank Worrell. In fact, South Africa was scheduled to meet the West Indians in England in the early 1900s, but, in an ominous portent of what the future would hold, the match never took place.

Wasted opportunity and the deliberate suppression of human potential were the biggest outcome of the decision taken by Rhodes, Milton and their jingoistic and racist allies. That meme was to become the most destructive legacy of the tragedy that was apartheid.

J.K. Glover, proprietor of Glover's Athletic Bar, where the white South African Cricket Association was established in 1890, also donated the Glover Cup for the winner of the 'Malay' Inter-Town Tournaments.

Above: His sons Charles (left) and George Glover (who played for South Africa SACA in 1894) were involved in many of the matches between white and black cricketers in Kimberley in the 1890s.

Above: Abdol Burns, a well-known community leader in Cape Town, headed the early Cape Town Cricket Union and the organising committee for the first 'Malay' Inter-Town Tournament at Newlands in January 1890, which was played in front of large crowds.

Left: The English professional Frank Hearne was one of the umpires.

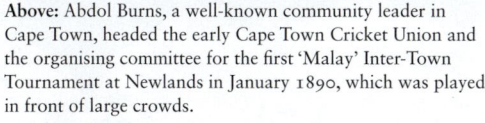

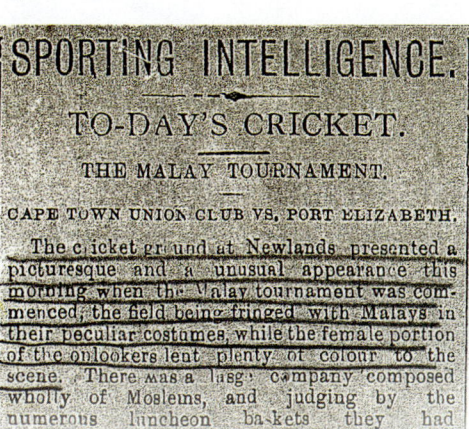

SPORTING INTELLIGENCE.

TO-DAY'S CRICKET.

THE MALAY TOURNAMENT.

CAPE TOWN UNION CLUB VS. PORT ELIZABETH.

The cricket ground at Newlands presented a picturesque and a unusual appearance this morning when the Malay tournament was commenced, the field being fringed with Malays in their peculiar costumes, while the female portion of the onlookers lent plenty of colour to the scene. There was a large company composed wholly of Moslems, and judging by the numerous luncheon baskets they had

THE MALAYS.

THE Malays of Cape Town have not made such a show for several years as they have presented for us at the Cricket Tournament at Newlands this week. However we may have lamented the spread of Asiatic influence in Cape Town, we have always had a saving clause for the Malays. They have not come here to try for their own fortunes against the European; but their fathers were brought here against their own will as slaves for the convenience and comfort of our predecessors, and they have the same right that Europeans have to regard this country as their home. Of all the people benefited by emancipation, they have proved themselves most worthy. We have had no Hayti in Cape Town by reason of the presence of Malays in our midst. As far as men of alien race can amalgamate with a European community they have become an integral part of the population of Cape Town. We fancy that old inhabitants of Cape Town, although they may occasionally say unpleasant things of the Malays and regret that Cape Town should be exposed to the reproach of being a "Malay town," would feel a little sorry if they saw no more of the familiar figures in the streets—the trustworthy Malay mason, who knows exactly what kind of work we require; the Malay laundress, whose preparation of our shirt fronts is a fine wit; the steady Malay driver, who can complacently skirt a precipice; or the invaluable "old Malay man," who knows as much as an old English factotum, and perhaps a thing or two besides.

The Malays have been subject to some changes during the last few years,

What could have been!

Had 'Krom' Hendricks been selected on merit in 1894, South Africa would have preceded the route subsequently followed by West Indies cricket.

Left: Lebrun Constantine (standing third left) became 'the first black man allowed to play' for Trinidad in 1893 and was one of five black cricketers selected for the first West Indies tour to England in 1900. His teammate, Charles Ollivierre (standing far left), remained behind to play in the English leagues and county cricket, starting a long tradition. They are pictured here on the 1906 England tour, with Harold Austin as captain (seated, second left).

Below: C.B. 'Buck' Llewellyn was the one player who escaped the colour bar and played for South Africa SACA.

What the 1891/2 English team (below) said about 'Krom' Hendricks

1. **W.W. Read**, captain: Hendricks is to my mind the Spofforth of South Africa. 2. **William Chatterton** (Derbyshire) had 'played at home against Richardson, Lockwood and Mold, and against the greatest of Australian genius, Spofforth and Turner'. Yet the very ablest bowler he had ever met he believed to be 'not Spofforth, but a South African black, Hendricks'. 'The memory of this man's pace from the pitch, his quick swing away, alternating with a fine break, stirred a cold and critical nature to enthusiasm.' 3. **Billy Murdoch**, England and former Australian captain: Hendricks 'would have been a very great draw … he would have knocked some of us and our pegs about on hard wickets.' 4. **George Hearne** (Kent): 'A Malay named Hendricks was very fast indeed … I was captain during the match and everyone began to ask me to let somebody else go in his place … The balls flew over our heads in all directions.'

Quadruplets: colonialism, cricket, racism and violence. The arch-imperialist Cecil John Rhodes, pictured here with the 7th Kimberley Regiment, was at the same time involved in the conquest of modern-day Zimbabwe, the passing of segregatory legislation as Prime Minister of the Cape colony, and the introduction of the colour bar in cricket at the same time in 1894. He said: 'They wanted to send a black fellow called Hendricks to England ... but I would not have it.' Six of South Africa SACA's first ten captains subsequently became part of Rhodesia's colonial administration after Rhodes took the land by force. They were William Milton, who became administrator of the territory, Murray Bisset (chief justice), Henry Taberer (commissioner for native affairs), Alf Richards, Percy Sherwell and H.H. Castens (secretary to Milton and acting public prosecutor).

Above: Epitome of the 19th-century gentleman officer and cricketer: Major General Robert Montagu Poore played cricket between harsh military excursions against the Ndebele and Shona, including dynamiting caves where people sought sanctuary.

Above: Star opening batsman A.B. Tancred (pictured here with a rifle on his shoulder) was one of the prominent cricketers who participated in the attempted coup d'etat in the Transvaal during the Jameson Raid. Tancred said of Hendricks: 'If he wants to go on the same footing as the others, I would not have him at any price. As baggage-man they might take him and play him in one or two of the matches when the conditions suited him. To take him as an equal would, from a South African point of view, be impolitic, not to say intolerable, and I would not have him on those terms if he were a better bowler than Lohmann.'

**Western Province XVIII vs W.W. Read's English team, 1891/2,
and what they said about 'Krom' Hendricks (see players numbered on opposite page)**

1. 'Vollie' van der Bijl: if three (like Hendricks) had been chosen, 'probably the other eight would not have played'.

2. E.S. Steytler, a WPCU selector in 1896/7, together with Milton and Smuts: they were not prepared to consider Hendricks for the representative match against Lord Hawke's English team.

3. C. Neumann Thomas was also for Hendricks's exclusion.

4. Charles Mills, WPCU, Surrey and South Africa, the first player to hit a double century on the subcontinent, was one of two players in the team who came out in favour of Hendricks: 'by far the finest fast-bowler in South Africa'.

5. The influential William Milton became administrator of the new Rhodesia and was later knighted. He led the moves to exclude Hendricks and 'did not see why a special case should be made for [him], saying many good players had been overlooked in the past'.

6. H.H. Castens, sitting next to Milton and part of his inner circle, was made SACA captain for the 1894 historic first tour to England and had to justify why 'Krom' Hendricks was excluded. Later recruited by Milton to be his secretary and acting public prosecutor in the new colony of Rhodesia, Castens secured the death sentence against the resistance leader Mbuya Nehanda. Were he and other cricketers also part of the executions at the notorious 'hanging tree' in Salisbury (Harare)? Compare the man in a white shirt and light trousers looking on in the photograph on the bottom of the next page with the ones of Castens numbered 6 (right and top of opposite page).

7. Frank Hearne (Kent and South Africa): he umpired in the 'Malay' Inter-Town tournaments, had good relations with the local black players and was another who differed from the establishment view, believing Hendricks should be selected for South Africa.

8. Murray Bisset, WPCC, WPCU and South Africa SACA captain and one of Milton's Rhodesia recruits: 'no doubt in his mind that on legal principles, the application [for Hendricks to play official cricket] should not be acceded to'.

6

Left: W.V. 'Billy' Simkin (team manager in 1894 in place of Cadwallader): the Union should use all means at its disposal to ensure that the two classes 'be kept distinctly separate'. And 'someone was guilty of a grave error in having selected Hendricks for the All-Comers'.

Middle: Louis B. Smuts (WPCU selector and made SA rugby secretary/treasurer in place of Cadwallader): 'It was all good and well in some countries to talk of cricket as a levelling institution but here circumstances were so very different.' And 'it would be very awkward if Hendricks were chosen and the opposing team refused to play'.

Right: John Reid, prominent WPCC member and later WPCU president, also supported Hendricks's exclusion.

Maynard Nash, WPCU secretary: This is 'a wider issue than the mere admittance of Hendricks. And 'rescinding the ruling would work the greatest harm to the game in the country'.

ow: There is a striking similarity between the man observing executions in this photo of the notorious 'hanging tree' in Salisbury (Harare) and SACA cricket captain H.H. Castens who, as acting public prosecutor, secured the death sentence against the resistance leader Mbuya Nehanda. his Castens (numbered 6 above and on the opposite page) standing in the centre of this photograph from *Trooper Peter Halket of Mashonaland*, ve Schreiner's famous tract against Rhodes and his methods of extending Empire and his personal fortune?

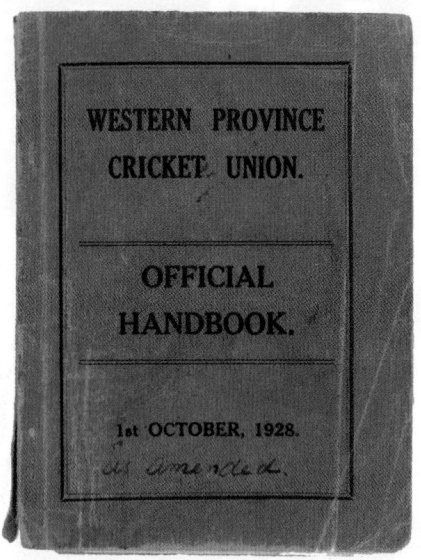

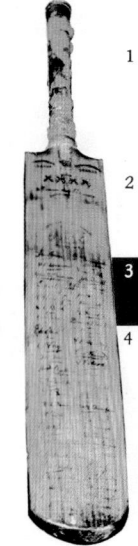

Bye=Laws.

1 GENERAL. There shall be established the several divisions hereinafter provided for, the arrangement of the fixtures for which shall, subject to the Rules and Bye-Laws of the Union, be drawn up and approved before the commencement of the Season by the Committee.

2 No match shall be played on any date other than set down in the approved list of fixtures, unless the consent of the Committee has been obtained at least three days previous to the said date.

3 No coloured professionals or members shall be allowed to compete in any matches under the jurisdiction of the Union.

4 No player who is not a permanent resident in the Western Province shall be eligible to play for a club in any match in any division unless he has been elected a bona-fide effective member of such club, and intends to reside in the Western Province for a period of 30 days immediately after the first day of the first such match in which he plays, and any club playing a member who shall fail to put in the 30 days' residence shall, in case of victory, be liable to forfeit the match.

Rhodes and Milton's legacy: the colour bar in cricket.

The military and cricket. 'Visitors to Newlands, April 3rd [1898]. Lieut-Col Spence, Lieut J.S. Rundle, Capt. C.F. Cox, Lieut F.S. Osbourne, Capt. Johnson. New South Lancers.'

10221

Native cricket match.

War and cricket, 1899–1902. Soldiers batting and bowling between duties (top and bottom). Green Point Common, the oldest cricket ground in the country (middle), was turned into a military base and prisoner-of-war camp during the South African War.

Cricket and national struggles for equal rights merge, 1909

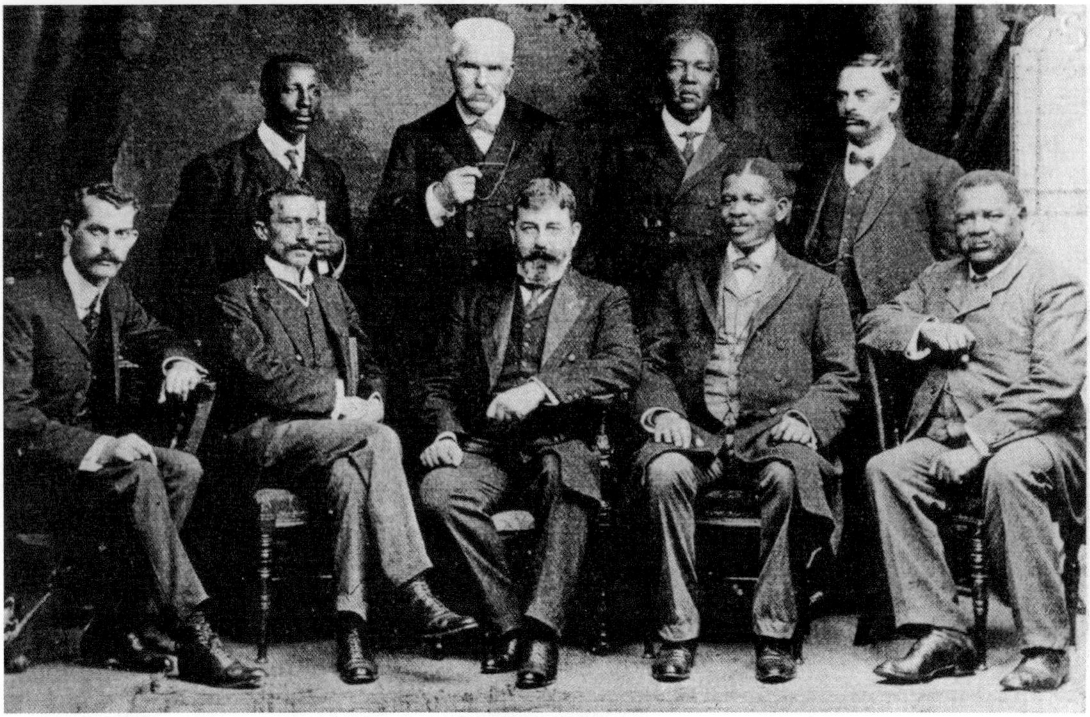

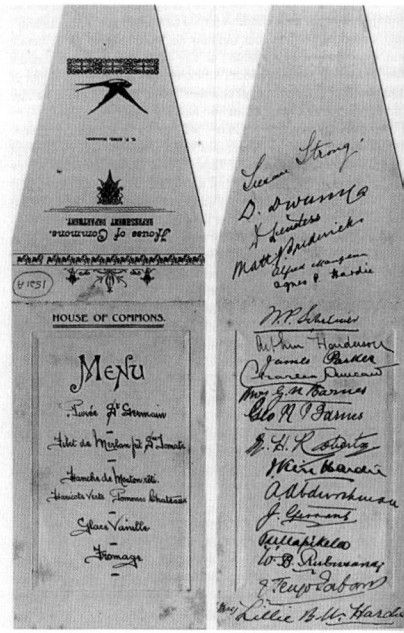

The South African War brought the whole of modern-day South Africa under British control and paved the way for the new country called the Union of South Africa in 1910. Cricket leaders who had sought equality in sport since the 1880s, opposing the hardline positions taken up by Rhodes, Milton and the white cricket establishment, were in the forefront of the protests against the colour bar in the new constitution, calling instead for equal rights. They warned that South Africa would never find peace while its black citizens were discriminated against. A specially elected South African Native and Coloured People's Delegation was sent to London in 1909 to protest before the British Parliament against the proposed discriminatory constitution for South Africa. Its composition showed how interweaved the cricket struggles and the beginnings of the national freedom movement were in South Africa.

Back row (left to right): Thomas Mtobi Mapikela, Orange River Colony Native Congress, Native Inter-Town cricketer and patron of the game in Bloemfontein; J. Gerrans, representing Bechuanaland Protectorate chiefs; Daniel Dwanya (brother-in-law of the entrepreneur, sports journalist and Native Inter-Town cricketer, Paul Xiniwe), representing Gqunukwebe chiefs; Daniel Lenders, vice-president of APO and president of the Diamond Fields Colonial Cricket Union.

Front row: Matt J. Fredericks, general secretary of APO and president of the Cape District Cricket Union; Dr Abdullah Abdurahman, president of APO and president of the Western Province Coloured Cricket Union; William P. Schreiner, MP, ex-Prime Minister of the Cape Colony, who later became president of the South African Rugby Football Board; Dr Walter Benson Rubusana, president of South African Native Congress and South African Native Convention and president of East London and Border Native Cricket Union; John Tengo Jabavu, president of Cape Native Convention, editor of *Imvo Zabantsundu*, president of the Frontier Cricket Club, and donor of the Jabavu Cup for the Inter-Town competition.

Signing on for democracy: the SA Native and Coloured delegation signatures on a menu of the House of Commons, after a function with leaders of the new Labour Party and other sympathisers.

29

The colour bar in cricket becomes fixed

*... with white cricket coat and trousers, he is great at
tea-meetings, cricket and tennis parties, but he thinks that to
do an honest day's work is far beneath his requirements.*

– Resident magistrate of Adelaide, Cape Colony, 1908[1]

In the decade before 1894, as South Africa readied itself for and then entered
test cricket, a door opened. A multi-ethnic cricket community emerged in the
Cape Colony, sharing many similarities and interacting in significant ways, and
made possible the development of an inclusive South African cricket set-up. But
Cecil John Rhodes and his influential cabals in both sport and politics, linked
to acquisitive imperialist interests and supporting hardline 'native policy', closed
the door. They made decisions and laid out policy in both politics and sport that
would set the pattern for a segregationist future.

THE REWARDS OF BEING PART OF THE SYSTEM

In cricket, the upholders of the establishment line were directly rewarded by the
system. In 1894, the same year that Hendricks was left out of the South African
team, Rhodes succeeded in passing the Glen Grey Act, one of the foundations
of apartheid legislation, which Milton had drafted. As mentioned, it was linked
to the attacks on Hendricks and the emerging black middle class – and was
meant to force Africans off their land and into the labour market.[2] Next, Rhodes
tried to take over the South African Republic through an armed coup known
as the Jameson Raid. Once again, his cricket allies were an integral part of the
plans.[3] Rhodes requested Dr Jameson, the administrator of Rhodesia, to raise a
volunteer force in Bulawayo in 1895 to support the planned uprising in the Boer
republic. Unaware of the real purpose of their existence, the Matabeleland regi-

ment of the Rhodesia Horse Volunteers participated in parades, shooting competitions and drills, which soon competed with the local cricket fixtures, prompting the *Bulawayo Chronicle* to comment, 'It is impossible to disguise the fact that the volunteer movement, whilst being an excellent innovation, has seriously threatened the high estate of our local cricket.' 'Matches all over the world are held on a Saturday, the day being so suitable above all others [for cricket] ... it seems a little rough that the volunteer authorities should always fix their manoeuvres on that day.'[4] Among the players affected were Godfrey Cripps, vice-captain of South Africa's first tour to England in 1894, and Sir Henry Mordaunt, who captained Eton at cricket, obtained his Blue at Cambridge, and played for Hampshire and Middlesex.[5] The volunteers were called away to invade the Transvaal on the weekend that Bulawayo was due to play a rare match against Salisbury, led by Henry Taberer, chief native commissioner Mashonaland, who would later captain South Africa against Australia.

On 29 December, the 'raiders' assembled and were addressed by the Hon. Charles Coventry, who had played for the English team under Monty Bowden at Newlands in 1888/9. Coventry, who had failed an army examination in Britain and chose to progress through the 'back door' with the Bechuanaland Border Police, told his men, 'We are going straight to Johannesburg. We want you all to come. It will be a short trip, everything has been arranged.'[6] But the expedition was a disaster from the outset. The wrong telegraph wires were cut by men who were allegedly drunk and, as a result, the Transvaal forces were able to monitor the movements of the raiders. Jameson and his men were arrested at Doornkop, some twenty miles from Johannesburg, on 2 January 1896. Several cricketers, including A.B. Tancred, were involved.

Three of the players on the 1895/6 English tour to South Africa – Lord Hawke,[7] Sir Timothy O'Brien[8] and Charles Wright[9] – ate and played cards in the Johannesburg Fort with the prisoners who had been captured during the Jameson Raid.[10] Hawke, in his memoirs, recorded that the team was 'telegraphed ... to go to Johannesburg to play there to turn people's minds from the raid'.[11] The England team carried with them considerable imperial ideological baggage and acted as ambassadors for Empire as South Africa moved towards another war between Britain and the Boer republics. C.B. Fry recalled that he toured with Lord Hawke's team as a replacement for the remarkable Ranjitsinhji, because the South Africans would not have approved: 'That is how I came to be in South Africa in the year of the Jameson Raid.'[12] Lord Hawke's team included ten amateurs out of 14 players and, 'with just one exception, the "gentlemen" were all Oxford or Cambridge Blues'.[13] Fry, George Lohmann, Tom Hayward, Timothy O'Brien and Sammy Woods were in a side renowned for its colourful splash of blazers, belts and hat ribbons, but who were not particularly popular 'owing to their unsportsmanlike behaviour, lack of concern for locals, their complaints about pitches, unpleasant sledging and the occasional clamouring for money'.[14]

Following Jameson's botched raid in 1896, Rhodes appointed the cricket supremo, William Milton, to succeed him as administrator of Rhodesia. It was observed that cricket was the principal qualification of his civil service appointees. No fewer than six of South Africa's first ten cricket captains subsequently departed for Rhodesia to help set up the new colonial administration. Besides Milton, they included Alfred Richards, Henry Taberer, Percy Sherwell, and H.H. Castens, the captain on the 1894 tour to England, and his deputy, Godfrey Cripps. Several of them had been part of the lobby against 'Krom' Hendricks. Castens, who scored a huge 165 in the last Inter-Town tournament, became Milton's chief secretary,[15] and was acting public prosecutor in the case of Mbuya Nehanda, the famous Shona spirit-medium and leader in the first Chimurenga (or war of resistance) in 1896–7. Castens secured a death sentence, and there was drama at Nehanda's execution, which confirmed to her followers her spiritual powers: 'Two unsuccessful attempts were made to hang her. An African prisoner present at her hanging then suggested that the hangman should remove from her belt a tobacco pouch. This was done and on the third attempt she was successfully hanged.'[16] Rejecting attempts to convert her to Christianity at the gallows, Nehanda's dying words reputedly were, 'My bones will rise again.' She became one of the inspirations in the later liberation struggle which brought independence to Zimbabwe. Other cricketers who ended up in Rhodesia were Joseph Vintcent, brother of the SACA test player Charlie, and Murray Bisset, captain of Western Province Cricket Club and of the second South African team to England in 1901, who both became chief justices of the new country.

Major General Robert Poore, the epitome of the late-nineteenth-century soldier and sportsman, who represented South Africa in 1895/6, was one of those who played cricket between military excursions against the Ndebele and Shona. Winner of the Matabeleland tennis championships and scorer of a century for the 7th Hussars in one of the many games he played during his stint in the north, Poore was in joint command of the troops that led attacks on Shona homesteads and 'forced the Shona into caves, from where they were eventually evicted with dynamite'. On one occasion, 'about 150 Matabeles were killed [and] 350 women brought in as prisoners'. In his long military career, this outstanding cricketer served under senior British commanders such as Haig, Kitchener, Roberts and Baden-Powell, and he was in charge during the controversial execution of the Australian soldier 'Breaker' Morant in the South African War.

While the traditional literature romanticises both cricket and military derring-do in the colonies, the realities on the ground do not provide a pretty picture of 'fair play' and illustrate instead how the game was spread directly through war and conquest by the British in southern Africa. The cricket establishment in South Africa became indistinguishable from the imperial venture and its accompanying violence and fundamental disrespect for African people.

The hanging tree in Salisbury was made infamous by the great novelist Olive Schreiner in her book *Trooper Peter Halket of Mashonaland*. Are there any cricketers framed in the photograph of it in her book's frontispiece which so nakedly shows the connection between European 'progress' and inhuman colonial brutality? (See photo insert.) Even if there are none, the direct link between the development of South African cricket and violent conquest in the nineteenth century was nowhere better illustrated than in the subjugation of Zimbabwe in the 1890s.

THE COLOUR BAR IN SPORT BECOMES FIXED

The discrimination that 'Krom' Hendricks was subjected to in Cape Town formed part of a pattern that became increasingly fixed in South African cricket. At the very time that the standards and enthusiasm of black cricketers were rising rapidly, the white SACA and its affiliates set about lowering the booms to keep them out permanently. A number of other cases involving black cricketers in the late nineteenth and early twentieth century underline the point.

In 1890 black cricketers were banned from playing on the Parade in Cape Town, where for decades they had enjoyed themselves on the fringes of army games.

In November 1894 cricketers from Venterstad were reportedly jailed in Bethulie in the Orange Free State for not having 'official passes'. *The Friend* newspaper described this action as 'mean'. *Imvo Zabantsundu* said the incident made the Orange Free State government 'look blacker than it really is as regards the treatment of subject races'.[17]

In 1897 a match in Stutterheim in the eastern Cape had to be suspended 'owing to the conduct of the Town Council who without assigning any feasible reason deliberately refused to allow the coloured cricketers (some of whom, by the way, are ratepayers) to play on the town commonage'. The local club, 'composed of a respectable and well-behaved section of the Native residents in the division, consisting of teachers, public servants, agriculturists, storemen etc.', protested vociferously.[18] One of the members said he could not credit 'that such treatment was practised in what is a British colony, to British subjects of a respectable standing, who through a fault, or otherwise, of Nature's design, are black'.[19]

In January 1904 'about 15 Malays ... attired in cricketing costume' entered the new Uitvlugt location in Cape Town, the predecessor of Langa, to play a game against their African counterparts. The visitors were summarily kicked out by the authorities. The local *South African News* reported: 'Our correspondent asks "Is this location a gaol or a compound?" and in the light of the alleged occurrence the question is pertinent.'[20]

In the Transvaal, blacks were not allowed to watch sports matches where whites were playing, even after the British took over after the South African War. The British high commissioner, Lord Selborne, criticised this situation in a speech in 1909:

> I will only ask the white men to consider whether they have ever calculated the cumulative effect on the Natives of what I may call the policy of pin-pricks. In some places a Native, however personally clean, or however hard he may have striven to civilise himself, is not allowed to walk on a pavement in the public streets; in others, he is not allowed to go into a public car, or to pay for the privilege of watching a game of cricket; in others he is not allowed to ride on top of a tram-car, even in specified seats set apart from him; in others he is not allowed to ride in a railway carriage, except in a sort of dog kennel; in others, he is unfeelingly and ungraciously treated by white officials.[21]

Mahatma Gandhi complained about this discrimination in sport, too. When a local newspaper suggested that a special 'enclosure should be set aside for respectable and decent Asians' at the Wanderers ground, Gandhi rejected the proposed concessions as more unacceptable than the existing outright exclusion:

> character and education distinction are not made in respect of Europeans. All that can be reasonably expected is that those who apply for admission be suitably and cleanly dressed. Nor will the suggestion that a portion of certain stands be set aside for Asiatics meet with favour. So long as prejudice is allowed to influence the deliberations of a sporting community, so long it is better that we do not have any right on entry at all, than that such right should be reorganised in a limited and niggardly spirit.[22]

In the neighbouring Orange River Colony, the inspector of locations commented in 1904 that he was not impressed by those encouraging black sport and advancement. He preferred black youngsters being forced to work rather than being given a liberal education.[23] The *Tsala ea Batho* newspaper, financed by the black land owners of Thaba Nchu, in turn commented that whites held themselves socially aloof in order to command respect from blacks, but 'the fact is no Natives respect their European neighbours as much as the Baralongs at Thaba Nchu who twice beat the whites in fair games of cricket. In other parts, where the whites will not play them the coloureds boast that the whites are afraid of them.'[24] This hostility to black middle-class advancement and leisure activities was shared by most white colonists and became part of a clear pattern of discrimination. The resident magistrate of the eastern Cape town of Adelaide recommended in 1908 that a law should be passed to force Africans to understand that 'work is no crime'. He said that the educated Africans' 'sole idea is to copy the European with white cricket coat and trousers, he is great at tea-meetings, cricket and tennis parties, but he thinks that to do an honest day's work is far beneath his requirements'.[25] The message was unambiguous: blacks should not aspire to social equality.

Attitudes and restraints such as these became the norm during the course of the twentieth century and were to frustrate the ambitions of black sportsmen. In keeping with the general practice in South African society, they were to be systematically excluded from its clubs, competitions and representative sides.

The segregated SACA decided to run cricket in the 'traditional' way, and between 1890 and 1970 it organised 45 series involving 172 test matches by all-white teams. All of these were against the 'white' countries of the Empire – England, Australia and New Zealand. Until the 1990s South Africa never played against India, West Indies, Pakistan or Sri Lanka.[26] Moreover, for more than 80 years, until 1977, no black players were allowed to participate in SACA's club leagues and the Currie Cup, its main domestic competition.

CRICKET RACISM PART OF A WIDER PROCESS

The developments in cricket at the turn of the century were part of a broader pattern and process. The war that Britain fought against the Boer republics brought the whole of South Africa under British rule for the first time, and set in motion a process of unification. This led to the birth of the Union of South Africa in 1910. The Union was founded on a constitution, drawn up by white colonial leaders in constant consultation with British administrators, that largely excluded the black population from any participation in the political life of the country.

When the terms of the constitution became known, Africans protested strongly. For the first time a national conference of black organisations from the different colonies was held in Bloemfontein in 1909. It dispatched a special delegation to London in an attempt to persuade the British government not to ratify the constitution of the new state before amendments to the colour-bar clauses were made. The so-called Coloured and Native delegation was filled with cricket personalities. Six of the nine members were cricketing as well as political leaders. One of the most prominent was Dr Walter Benson Rubusana, president of the South African Native Congress and the new South African Native Convention formed at the Bloemfontein conference to unite African opinion throughout southern Africa. This respected church minister and translator of the Bible into Xhosa was first president of the Border Native Cricket Union, and had stood as an umpire in the first match between teams from East London and King William's Town in 1883. J.T. Jabavu, the renowned editor of *Imvo*, was Rubusana's political rival but shared his love for the game. Besides publishing thousands of cricket reports in his newspaper, he donated the Jabavu Cup for the Inter-Town tournaments and was president of the Frontier CC in King William's Town. Dr Abdullah Abdurahman, leader of the African Political Organisation (APO), the mouthpiece for coloured opinion, was president of the Western Province Coloured Cricket Union. One of his APO co-delegates was D.J. Lenders, president of both the Diamond Fields Colonial Cricket Union and the South African Coloured Rugby Football Board. The other was Matt Fredericks, president of the Cape District Cricket Union. Finally, Thomas Mtobi Mapikela of the Orange River Colony Native Congress was a patron of cricket in Bloemfontein; he was probably the Mapikela who represented Queenstown (from where he came) in the Native Inter-Town Tournaments. Nothing could have shown more the convergence of the political and cricket struggles of the time. But the delegation found that Britain's economic and strategic interests far outweighed any concern it might have felt for black South Africans; it chose to go into an alliance with the recently vanquished Afrikaners instead of the colonised majority, even if it meant contradicting its own professed political ideals and legitimising institutionalised racism in South Africa. This was, after all, the logical outcome of its century-long process of conquest and colonialism. So the British parliament passed the South Africa Act, which made for Union, leaving African leaders and intellectuals feeling betrayed.

The failure of political liberalism in South Africa – symbolised by Union in 1910 – took the early black activists and leaders into a cul de sac. Instead of gaining for themselves an extended role in a non-racial political system, they were to come under increasing pressure in a system that institutionalised racial discrimination, eventually depriving them of the voting rights they had enjoyed for nearly a century. The tremendous progress black cricketers had made from the 1880s onwards would be reversed in a similar way. The influential liberal parliamentarian Saul Solomon had once declared: Will the Colony 'ever degrade itself to prevent by law any Coloured man from having the right to vote for members of the legislature or to hold an acre of land'?[27] Rhodes and the imperialists were determined to do exactly that. They simply sidelined the small Cape liberal tradition and, with it, the aspirations of black middle-class voters and cricketers.

30

'Like a rather sunburned English player'

One cricketer who bucked the system

... the best left hand bowler we ever had.

– A.D. 'Dave' Nourse, 1927[1]

[He was] dark-eyed and dark-skinned and
South Africans called him coloured.

– J.M. Kilburn, *Overthrows*[2]

'Krom' Hendricks was bullied and victimised as the heavy booms of the colour bar were lowered into place in South Africa, but one black player did slip through the net to represent 'white' South Africa in official test match cricket. He was Charles Bennett 'Buck' Llewellyn, who played for Natal from 1895 to 1898 – at the same time that 'Krom' Hendricks and others were being purged by the cricket establishment in the Cape Colony. In 1899 Llewellyn became the first South African professional player when he joined Hampshire in England, and between 1896 and 1912 he played 15 matches for South Africa. This chapter serves as the obituary of him that never appeared in the *SA Cricket Annual*.

For many years there has been a dispute about the issue of his colour, but meticulous research has finally brought clarity. Llewellyn was born in Pieter-maritzburg out of wedlock on 29 September 1876.[3] His parents were married in community of property by special licence on 15 February 1877. His father, Thomas Buck Llewellyn, who was a house painter and decorator at the time of Charles's birth, had been born in Pembroke in Wales in August 1845; so the question of Llewellyn's race rests on the origins of his mother. She was Ann Elizabeth Rich, born in 1845 in St Helena, like the mother of 'Krom' Hendricks.[4]

From 1838 onwards, hundreds of St Helenians emigrated to the Cape; some moved on to Natal, where they were regarded as being of mixed race.[5] In the 1870s another wave of people left the island for Cape Town 'owing to the great distress of traders' there because of a reduction in the British military presence and the opening of the Suez Canal, which created alternative shipping routes to Asia.[6]

Wilfred Rhodes, the Yorkshire all-rounder, described Charles Llewellyn as 'like a rather sunburned English player'; and, J.M. Kilburn, the most convincing source on the player he idolised, said of him that he was tidy-looking and of sturdy medium height but 'dark-eyed and dark-skinned and South Africans called him coloured'.[7] Nevertheless, Llewellyn participated in cricket in Natal as a white man for the seasons 1894/5 to 1897/8, during which time he played in seven Currie Cup matches and a friendly for the colony, having made a somewhat ineffective debut (24 and 0 and 1/32 and 3/39)[8] 'as a dusky eighteen year-old'[9] against Transvaal in April 1895. The following season he played for a Pietermaritzburg XV against Lord Hawke's touring England team and impressed the Hampshire batsman Major Robert Montagu Poore with match figures of seven for 150. For Natal he was prominent as a bowler with a Currie Cup record of 359 overs, 114 maidens and 50 wickets at an average of 15.36, fourteenth in the list of players from the pre-Great War period. Crowley credits him with being the first of a line of South African slow left-armers.[10] In 1897 he achieved match figures of nine for 128 against Western Province (but still ended up on the losing side by a wide margin) and 11 for 123 against Eastern Province. Remarkably, he took five wickets in an innings five times out of a theoretical maximum of 14. His batting record was less memorable, for in 15 innings, twice not out, he scored 176 runs with a highest score of 63 at an average of only 13.53. During this period he was employed by the father of the cricketer Herby Taylor in Durban as a 'coloured clerk', although there is no evidence that he ever played cricket within the community so defined.[11]

Llewellyn's lengthy, disrupted test career of 15 matches for South Africa (five against England and ten against Australia) lasted from the second test against England at Johannesburg in March 1896 (when he was 19) until the Triangular Tournament of 1912 in England.[12] His test record was a modest one by modern standards: 544 runs at 20.14 (with four half-centuries and a highest score of 90); 48 wickets at 29.60 and 7 catches. He took five wickets in an innings on four occasions and in 1902/3 he took 10/116 against Australia in the second test at the Wanderers, Johannesburg. His best bowling analysis (of 6/92) was in the first test at the same venue. Of his first appearance for South Africa, Routledge wrote: 'Although he did not succeed in getting a wicket, he bowled fairly well and deserved a little success.'[13] On the same occasion C.B. Fry mentioned him as a 'boy left-hander'.[14] In this match he scored 24 and 4 and took 0/71 as South Africa went down by an innings and 197 runs. *Wisden* notes that he was crucially missed in the Cape Town test of April 1899 when South Africa suffered their eighth consecutive defeat and lost to England by 210 runs.[15] On the 1901 tour of England he played in only one match for South Africa against London County because his commitments to Hampshire took priority. In the home series against Australia in 1902/3 he scored 113 runs (90 batting first wicket down in the first innings of the first test, including a second wicket partnership of 173 with L.J. Tancred) and took 9/216 in the first test at Johannesburg (his victims included Gregory (twice) as well as Trumper and Darling); 10/116 in the second test (also in Johannesburg); and another six, this time for 97, in the third test at Cape Town. His 25 wickets in this series were taken at 17.92 each, thus topping the South African averages. He opened the bowling in the Cape Town test, as he was later to do on the 1910/1 tour of Australia in four of the five tests.[16]

Aubrey Faulkner's magnificent batting was a high point in the 1910/1 series in which South Africa might have won the second test but failed to convert. This series came to be central to Llewellyn's identity as a South African test player. An intimation of his 'otherness' and mixed ancestry is contained in the sugges-tion that during the tour he was 'ostracized and bullied by his team mates', particularly by Jimmy Sinclair, from whom he had to hide in the toilet.[17] The story originated from Rowland Bowen's history, but its authenticity is called into question by the fact that Sinclair had seconded a suggestion by fellow player Sid Pegler that Hampshire CCC be cabled asking for confirmation of Llewellyn's availability for the tour. Indeed, Sinclair proposed a salary of £250 plus travel and hotel expenses. Opposition to Llewellyn's inclusion came, significantly, from his home province of Natal, which wrote to the South African Cricket Associa-tion (SACA) suggesting that 'he can no longer be looked upon as a South African player and the objective ... should be to encourage the younger players'. He was later referred to during the Australian tour as a 'naturalised Englishman', and a proposal was put forward that SACA should cease to consider players for South Africa after four years' absence from international competition. His selection and salary were confirmed but the expenses were amended, which caused an ongoing dispute and rejection of the idea at the end of the tour that Llewellyn should receive a bonus. A meeting chaired by Pegler on 3 October 1911 subsequently raised the question of his availability for the 1912 tour of England.[18] His bowling fell away towards the end of his career for South Africa: in the Triangular Tour-nament it was described as a 'sad failure' with 4/219 at an average of 54.75.[19] He did, however, redeem himself with two half-centuries, one each against England

and Australia, in a total of 167 runs scored at 18.55, although in his last test he made a pair.[20]

The idea that he was coloured and had been persecuted by white South African cricketers was hotly denied by his daughter in the cricket press in the mid-1970s.[21] She argued that her grandfather was born in Bootle, Lancashire, of Welsh descent and her grandmother in Essex,[22] and that neither was coloured: 'He was of white stock.' She described the claim that he was not on good terms with his fellow cricketers as 'utter nonsense' and said that when playing league cricket in later life in the Lancashire town of Accrington and in the Bradford League, he was visited by members of South African touring teams. Whether or not this is true, she had a totally erroneous picture of her grandparents, which is hard to account for unless she had been deliberately misinformed. The supposed origins of her grandparents in Lancashire and Essex are hard to fathom unless there was a deliberate attempt to confuse St Helena with the St Helens of the former county, which is only a few miles from Bootle. But if this were an attempt at dissimulation, it should have been applied to the grandmother, not the grandfather, about whose origins there has never been any question.

At the turn of the century, qualifying rules were relatively lax and Llewellyn was named in the England squad of 14 for the first test against Australia at Edgbaston in 1902, although he did not in the end play.[23] His call up by England 'would have been acceptable ... by the custom and opinion of that time'.[24] Given that his father had been born in Wales, it would also be acceptable today, although he had of course already appeared in test cricket for South Africa. However, at Birmingham in 1902 the Australian batsman Warwick Armstrong is reputed to have passed a sarcastic comment questioning whether he was playing England or South Africa.[25] By 1905 Llewellyn was being described as an 'ex-South African',[26] but in the 1909 *Wisden*, recording his benefit match in 1908 against Kent, was still writing about him as 'the South African'.[27]

In his entire first-class career from 1895 to 1912, Llewellyn scored 11,425 runs at an average of 26.75 and took 1,013 wickets at 23.41 together with 174 catches.[28] The scorer of 18 centuries, he took five wickets in an innings 82 times and ten in a match 20 times. He was thus a genuine all-rounder in a Golden Age of cricket – a left-arm orthodox slow-medium bowler with a high arm action, a forcing left-hand batsman who favoured the drive and the cut (he hit Blythe for five sixes at Dover in August 1910) and a specialist mid-off – whose talents unfortunately did not always flourish in tandem.[29] Possibly he was over-bowled by a Hampshire team lacking resources.[30] Pelham Warner called him a 'fine all-rounder' and *Wisden* described him as 'in the fullest sense of the words an all-round cricketer'.[31] The references to his batting are relatively sparse, but

Wisden commented in 1911 that he was a punishing left-hander, his 'driving power being tremendous'.[32] On the other hand, his bowling was widely praised: A.W. 'Dave' Nourse described him as 'the best left hand bowler we ever had. He turned the ball so well and kept a wonderful length' even on good wickets.[33] As one of *Wisden*'s cricketers of the year in 1911, his 'medium pace bowling' was described as 'full of life and spin'.[34] His control of length, pace and spin brings to mind a turn-of-the-century Derek Underwood: 'On the slow side of medium ... if the pitch helped him, his spin was vicious.'[35]

Altham's history of cricket names Llewellyn as the cricketer who 'until the appearance of Fleetwood-Smith, was the only left-hander known to bowl the googly', which he describes elsewhere as the Chinaman.[36] He is said to have spent several years practising this, based on advice given by Reggie Schwarz, another South African test spin bowler. Kilburn also recorded the fact that Llewellyn bowled in a cap, which is borne out by photographs.[37]

Llewellyn broke his thigh in 1960 and was crippled for the rest of his life, dying at Englefield Green in Surrey on 7 June 1964 at the age of 87, an event recorded by *Wisden* but ignored by the *South African Cricket Annual* for five years.[38] A South African obituary has yet to appear. It was an interesting reflection on Llewellyn's anonymity and the deference of the South African cricket authorities to their imperial masters. By contrast, the *SA Cricket Annual* quickly noted the death of Lady Warner in 1955.

It is instructive to compare the cricket career of an Australian Aboriginal near-contemporary of Llewellyn and 'Krom' Hendricks, the fast bowler Jack Marsh. As Bernard Whimpress has pointed out, Marsh started playing club cricket in Sydney in 1896 and the following year, amid much controversy, he was no-balled for throwing. There is a school of thought that sees Marsh victimised as an outsider for being capable of dismissing star batsmen like Victor Trumper on good wickets: 'It is possible that [the umpire] could have felt that retribution was necessary or was prevailed upon to put Marsh in his place.'[39] Marsh's opportunities to play for New South Wales were restricted and he never played for Australia. He was selected for a match between Western Districts XVIII and A.C. MacLaren's XI at Bathurst in February 1902, but the England captain demanded that Marsh be withdrawn, ostensibly as a danger to his players. The professionals in the England team were, however, prepared to play and there were strong suspicions at the time that this was a matter of racial and class prejudice. The Bathurst incident virtually ended Marsh's career, and he played his last first-class game in November 1902. He subsequently excelled in Sydney grade cricket with virtually unplayable fast-medium off-cutters that started with movement through the air. He played against the 1904 MCC touring team, who were divided in their opinion of him: some thought him the best bowler in the world; others said that he had an illegitimate action. The case for conspiracy is strong, and underlying everything was a consistent strain of racial stereotyping, with Marsh described in the press as 'dusky', a 'darkie' and a 'coon'.[40] From 1905 onwards it seems that Marsh led the life of an itinerant casual worker, compounded by the restrictions set by the 1909 Aborigines Protection Act, which codified segregation tendencies in Australian life. He found work in a circus but by 1909 was in prison in Melbourne convicted of assault. He died in May 1916 aged 42 after being beaten in a billiard-room brawl.[41]

What is to be made of Charles Bennett Llewellyn? He was an ordinary man of humble origins who, sporting ability apart, made no lasting impression upon the long march of history. With sufficient talent to become a successful, long-term cricketing journeyman, he is mentioned frequently and repetitively in the literature but left no real personal imprint. His enigmatic character will presumably never be penetrated, but the evidence suggests that his experience was emblematic of the time. Llewellyn was a professional cricketer and pressure on him must have been enormous, as he knew society could turn on him at any moment. We can, however, begin to understand him in a number of moments, such as his withdrawal from the South African team in 1898/9; his uncertainty about leaving for Hampshire; his insistence on getting the best financial deals; his reaction to hurtful graffiti on the wall at Accrington – and there are other examples.

Buck Llewellyn and his brothers were undoubtedly, in terms of Natal's social custom, considered to be of mixed blood, although his family was apparently able to pass itself off as white. In late-nineteenth-century Pietermaritzburg this would not have been difficult, as the small coloured community was to some extent integrated. Evans records the fact that many store-workers passed themselves off as Europeans. According to the same contemporary source, they were recognised as 'good citizens in every sense',[42] although they kept apart socially. St Helenians (and Mauritians) tended to be English-speaking, Roman Catholic, relatively prosperous and 'respectable'. In late-Victorian Pietermaritzburg an important distinction was made between people who were westernised and those who were not, a distinction based on appearance and dress; and cultural similarity placed St Helenians in the former category. In terms of legal standing they profited from this, retaining the franchise when people of Asian origins living in Natal lost it in 1893.

But race consciousness was deepening for a number of reasons, and social custom was beginning to be reflected in law, a process that would end in the mid-twentieth century with the enforcement of apartheid. Coloured Natalians fought in the South African War, but from 1904 separate schools were provided for their children and by the 1920s competition with Africans and Indians for jobs was becoming increasingly intense. From 1904 until 1948 coloured people in Pietermaritzburg were relatively privileged but increasingly segregated. This segment of the population in Natal was small in both absolute and proportionate terms – only 6,700 persons or 0.6 per cent of the total in 1906 – so Llewellyn's awareness of his standing in the racial hierarchy is almost certainly likely to have been suppressed most of the time. The fact that in the mid-1970s, his daughter, then an elderly woman living in Britain, vehemently refuted his origins, arguably, attests to this. The *Natal Almanac* for the last years of the nineteenth century holds a clue to the question of Llewellyn's standing in Pietermaritzburg. Population figures for Natal are given under three headings: European, Indians and Natives. But to the first heading is appended 'including St Helenians, etc.'.[43] Charles Llewellyn, in social if not official terms, was deemed 'et cetera', of another category; considered, grudgingly perhaps, a white man but marked as different on account of his mother's origins. The *Almanac* was a well-used reference tool, a compendium of annual information about the province and Pietermaritzburg, and this categorisation of the population would have been widely known. Nor was it simply notional. The Corporation, for instance, made a point not only of classifying its employees of St Helenian origin on the next rung down the ethnic ladder from whites ('coloured persons enjoying European privileges'),[44] but of discriminating against them with regard to remuneration and other matters.[45] Dickie-Clarke sums up the situation thus: 'their situation was clearly a marginal one in that there was complete cultural similarity but incomplete acceptance and participation in the White system of social relationships'. Ultimately, 'the claim of cultural similarity to equality of treatment [was] swept aside'.[46]

There was an air of considerable ambiguity about Llewellyn's nationality. Similarly, his fellow cricketers and cricket authorities showed ambivalence towards him throughout his career. First, he chose to go into virtual exile to pursue a professional career as a cricketer at a time when this was relatively rare. And, as Crowley puts it, 'Although there is no confirmed record of any strife with his contemporaries due to the colour of his skin, this fine South African player did not return to his homeland after a long professional stint but chose to remain in England.'[47] Other examples that spring to mind during Llewellyn's playing career are Frank Mitchell (Cambridge University and Yorkshire), but he was English-born, stayed in South Africa after the Hawke tour of 1898/9 and served in the South African War; and Reggie Schwarz (Middlesex and Transvaal), whose education was at St Paul's School and Cambridge University. Both of these players were amateurs. Was the absence overseas of South Africa's pioneer professional cricketer purely for financial reasons?

In spite of clear cricketing ability and the praise accorded him by authoritative judges, Llewellyn's career with Natal was extremely short and lasted only four seasons. He tried to play for Transvaal during the 1903/4 season but was debarred by the SACA on the grounds that he was a professional. Transvaal argued that in South Africa he was an amateur on the cricket field, including the matches he had participated in against Australia during the 1902/3 series. His attempts to resuscitate his South African domestic career foundered on the votes of the three Cape unions (opposed by Transvaal and Border) and the crucial abstention of Natal.[48] It is reasonable to assume that Llewellyn would have been aware of the case of 'Krom' Hendricks, who also had a parent from St Helena, but his effective emigration ensured that he would not suffer a similar fate.

There was also little consistency in his selection for South Africa, with 15 tests spread out over 16 years, unusual even by the erratic standards of the time, and of course compounded by his selection for the England squad as early as 1902. The negative attitude of officials of his home province to his selection for South Africa, despite the fact that he was good enough to earn a living from county cricket, embodies a hostility to a person who was clearly different. This attitude could have been reinforced by a disdain for professionals in an age of high amateurism.

In the second half of the twentieth century, C.B. Llewellyn came to be adopted by the anti-apartheid South African Cricket Board of Control (SACBOC) as one of 'Our Two Test Cricketers', the other being Basil D'Oliveira, who famously played for England.[49]

31

'Neither ladies nor cricketers'

Women and exclusions of another kind

A door is opened unto us, and pleasure lifts the latch;
Eleven bold Pretorians have gone to make a match.
No match that leads to Hymen, so ladies don't presume
To try a 'catch', for CRICKET takes our
'boys' to Potchefstroom.

– Albert Brodrick, 1874[1]

In much the same way that colonised people were excluded from the British imperialists' clubs (except as servants) and talented players like Robert Grendon, L. Samsodien and 'Krom' Hendricks were blocked from entering the cricket mainstream, there were deep prejudices against women playing cricket, both in England and South Africa.[2] At more or less the same time that Hendricks was being sidelined by the Western Province Cricket Club (WPCC), an attempt to allow women to become members was firmly quashed. A proposal was put to the 1893 annual general meeting of the WPCC that women be admitted. The club historian's description of the discussion describes well the tenor of the times:

Occasion, annual general meeting. Year, 1893. Attendance, twenty-six.
A timid voice: 'Mr Chairman, before we close may I propose that – er – ladies be admitted to – er – this club – er – as members? Er – of course – on payment of a small subscription'. A stunned silence. Then growls of 'Heavens … Ladies … in a CRICKET club … What's the man …?'
Chairman: 'THE PROPOSAL IS OUT OF ORDER.'[3]

That the proposal was even made indicates serious intent and some enlightened attitudes, but these did not go far in those days. The conventions in cricket about women's involvement followed the strictly defined gender roles accorded to men and women in society in the Victorian period.

The sexist notions that became rooted in cricket in the nineteenth century remain strong and continue to infect the game right up to today. Yet, contrary to the prevailing gender stereotypes, women have been part of cricket from the very beginning – and not only as social adornments, partners in socially constructed mating rituals, and makers of tea and servers of sandwiches in the kitchen. The vast literature on cricket in England has revealed women playing as early as 1745, women professionals making money and attracting bets in the 1890s, a woman inspiring the move from under-arm to round-arm bowling (when her 'full skirt' interfered with her bringing her arm through in the accepted manner), and even the influence of Martha Grace on the career of her famous son.[4] In South Africa, too, there are enough references in the historical sources to the involvement of women in what was by custom a game for men only, to show that they were part of cricket from early on.

In the early 1700s matches between village teams of women were played regularly in Surrey and Sussex in England. In the first known report of such a match in July 1745 in Guildford, 'There was of both sexes the greatest number that ever was seen on such an occasion.' And, 'The girls bowled, batted, ran and catched as well as most men could do in that game.'[5] The games of the eighteenth and early nineteenth centuries seemed to cater for the whole social spectrum, from popular contests at ale houses, which offered the chances for betting, gambling and other passions, to private matches organised by aristocrats. On one occasion, the women cricketers were sponsored by 'two amateur Noblemen of the respective counties, for five hundred guineas a side'.[6] On another, two teams of women (Married vs Single) played and earned twenty pounds and a 'hot supper' for their efforts. On yet another occasion, women cricketers apparently enjoyed themselves so much afterwards that by their 'applications to the tankard, they rendered themselves objects such as no husband, brother, parent, or lover could contemplate with any degree of satisfaction'.[7] A vivid report of a match in 1838 'in a field in the rear of the newly-erected public house near Westend' conveys the lively atmosphere that often existed:

> the novelty of the scene drew together an immense concourse of spectators, who signified their delight by repeated rounds of applause. Vehicles of almost every description were also in attendance, from the dashing phaeton and pair down to the humble donkey tandem; on the whole, there could not have been

less than 3,000 persons present ... After the two first innings, bets varying from 2 to 1 to 5 to 2 were freely offered on the married ladies and as freely taken. The fielding and batting of Miss Anne Cleaver of Bitterne, and the Misses Caroline and Patience Lee, were particularly admired; indeed, they may be safely backed against any three boys under 18 ... When the game was over they all sat down to a comfortable tea provided by the landlady, and concluded the day's sport by a dance in the evening.[8]

These contests revealed a reality different from the world of the 'lady' and 'gentleman' idealised in the literature of cricket. Women cricketers offered novel alternatives to the usual betting and gambling on games, which were so popular before sport was codified and made 'decent' by educationists, clergymen and the middle and upper classes in the second half of the nineteenth century. As the historian Keith Sandiford has concluded, 'A significant feature of the Georgian legacy [before the start of Queen Victoria's long reign] was the remarkable growth of women's cricket'. But he notes, too, that this trend of women's cricket stopped during the Victorian era. Part of the answer lies in the different cultures that surrounded the game in the two periods: 'Georgian enthusiasm gave way to Victorian earnestness.' Whereas the Georgians were (in the words of Sandiford) noted for their laxity, licentiousness and gambling, the Victorians were 'earnest, prim and evangelical' and they 'cleansed' the game and turned it into a kind of morality play. In fact, 'different notions of femininity persuaded the Victorians to abandon female cricket for about 50 years'.[9] Herein lies the answer to the eventual direction taken by women's cricket in England and in South Africa, and it is to this point that we now turn.

WOMEN AND THE BRITISH SPORTS ETHOS IN THE VICTORIAN PERIOD

During the Victorian period, the patriarchal norms that governed British society – in which men were considered the leaders and providers, and the 'fairer sex' the nurturers and procreators – were redefined and 'scientifically' rationalised. The industrial revolution and the expansion of Empire created great change, stress and fluidity in society. Under these pressures, very specific constructions of what constituted men and women, 'ladies' and 'gentlemen', emerged. Cricket became almost a metaphor for these new identities. As Kathleen McCrone has explained:

traditional Victorians summoned all the power of custom, religion and science at their disposal in defence of existing social arrangements. They insisted that God and nature had imbued women with qualities of mind and body that destined her for specific tasks, such as being man's helpmate, nurturing his children, and protecting the sanctity of his home. Their ideal woman was antithetical to sport. Passive, gentle, emotional and delicate, she had neither the strength nor the inclination to undertake strenuous exercises and competitive games.[10]

This view remained the orthodoxy for many years. Unchallenged, it 'represented a potentially fatal blow to the ambitions of women in every direction except the domestic'.

At the same time, a new definition of what constituted the British gentleman emerged. From Rugby and other public schools came the notion that exercise and sport were essential in shaping young British boys into muscular Christians and imperialists, destined to lead the world in an age of Empire and expansion. Sport toughened them up for the job. It cultivated respect for rules, a subordination of the self in service of the greater whole. It taught young boys skills and restraint and imbued them with a sense of gentlemanly 'honour'. The novel *Tom Brown's School Days* (1857), by Thomas Hughes, has often been cited as promoting and explaining the new values that sport represented:

'What a noble game it is too!'
'Isn't it? But it's more than a game. It's an institution,' said Tom.
'Yes', said Arthur, 'the birthright of British boys old and young, as habeas corpus and trial by jury are of British men.'
'The discipline and reliance on one another which it teaches is so valuable, I think', went on the master. 'It ought to be such an unselfish game. It merges the individual in the eleven; he doesn't play that he may win, but that his side may.' ...
'And then the Captain ... requiring skill and gentleness and firmness and I know not what other rare qualities.'[11]

The popularisation of these ideas coincided with the rise of modern organised sport. Cricket especially was regarded as the sport par excellence where this new masculinity could be played out. Cricket became 'the gentlemen's game', developing an ideology that reinforced gender and social distinctions. Men could not allow women to play because this would undermine them as men, even if they did so in tennis, golf and hockey.

Thus, the idea of women playing cricket was officially frowned upon during the Victorian age when cricket and other sports, such as rugby, soccer, tennis and athletics, took on their current forms. Women who played sport were regarded as almost deviant. The result was to marginalise women from the game. They were needed as supporting organisers and social adornments, but they could not play.

In polite society, girls were expected to do only the lightest exercise, such as gentle walks. A survey of private girls' schools in 1868 found that almost without exception they insisted on nothing more strenuous than crocodile walks, calisthenics, croquet and social dance, all performed according to self-conscious protocols. Some horrendous stereotypes took root about what would happen to them if they played sport. Horse riding was said to lead to 'an unnatural consolidation of the lower part of the body, ensuring a frightful impediment to future functions.' Hockey could 'disable women from breastfeeding'. Athletics was seen as 'a corrupting influence for a "properly brought up girl"' and would 'produce an unnatural race of amazons' and contribute to the 'deterioration of the human race'. Cycling was 'an indolent and indecent practice which would even transport girls to prostitution'. Sport, generally, was 'likely to do irreparable damage to the adolescent girl'. For women, 'Rude health' came to be 'considered quite vulgar'. The notion of the naturally frail women was turned into a virtuous stereotype – and an industry. So-called scientific facts about women's frailty led to an excessive belief in the benefits of spas, prescriptions and treatments. Women's conditions became medicalised and their treatment was turned into a business.[12]

Even at Oxford and Cambridge, where young women experienced greater freedom than usual, some colleges as late as the 1880s banned them from playing cricket and hockey and imposed strict rules for bicycle riding. These exclusions from the male domain of sport and vigorous exercise began to be challenged only slowly. As the women's emancipation movement grew, and the success of the boys' public school system manifested itself, women educational reformers started fighting to extend sport at girls' schools. The movement was led by first-generation Oxbridge women graduates who had come into contact with the public schools 'games' culture at university. Cheltenham Ladies College was an early pioneer in girls' sport. From the 1880s and 1890s, well-known girls' public schools such as St Leonards, St Andrew's and Roedean followed suit. They turned the old argument around and said that far from hampering girl's education, exercise enhanced their effectiveness. If they were fit, girls could 'endure, without damage, the solid strain of learning' – and of childbirth.[13] By the end of the nineteenth century, as in other spheres of life, such as university studies, the medical profession and municipal politics, British women were beginning to break through the old barriers and stifling taboos in sport.

The first games to become popular among women outside the schools were croquet, badminton and tennis. The reason was that these sports could be played genteelly in the privacy of the private gardens of the rapidly expanding middle classes, without women becoming public spectacles. In 1877 the first Wimbledon tennis championships for men were held at the All-England Croquet and

Lawn Tennis Club, with women following in 1884.[14] In the 1880s cricket started following the new pattern of organised sport for women. The first women's cricket club in England was the White Heather CC, formed in 1887. Several other clubs followed and various public schools by now also had teams. In 1890, entrepreneurs trading under the title of the English Cricket and Athletic Association Limited set up an early kind of professional women's circuit, known as 'The Original English Lady Cricketers'. They played under assumed names at county grounds, including the famous Headingley in Leeds, and drew large crowds, but the experiment folded after two years.[15]

On the whole, women's cricket in England struggled to grow. It never really spread beyond upper-class women and ex-public school girls. According to Holt, there were not many more than 50 women's clubs by the 1920s – women's cricket and football clubs 'were laughed at, scoffed out of existence'.[16] Commenting on 'The Original English Ladies Cricketers', W.G. Grace, the father-figure of the age, declared authoritatively, 'They might be original and English, but they are neither cricketers nor ladies.'[17] In a male-dominated world there was not the space to challenge the notion of cricket as a gentleman's game. Instead, hockey rather than cricket or soccer became the 'field' sport popular among middle-class girls in England, partly because men had not yet enthusiastically taken to it and invested it with gender and ideological meanings.

Despite the slow process, women had 'come out of the closet' as far as sport was concerned by the time Europe went to war in 1914. They were slowly breaking old boundaries and taboos and opening up more spaces for themselves in public life, including the professions and politics.

Whereas a little walking, croquet and gentle calisthenics was thought sufficient exercise for the young lady of the 1860s, her grand-daughter could run, bicycle, climb mountains, play tennis at Wimbledon, golf at St Andrews, hockey for England, and any number of team and individual games at college and school, and then she could read about so doing in features on 'The Sportswoman' or 'The Outdoor Girl' in respectable periodicals and newspapers. Despite prejudice, discrimination and restrictions, the lure of sport was obviously irresistible to some Victorian girls, who apparently found the rewards of participation sufficient to counter whatever social costs were involved, and sufficient to offset the stress and role conflict they must have experienced as a result of the clash between their own desire to play and social norms to the contrary.[18]

WOMEN AND EARLY CRICKET IN SOUTH AFRICA

The British sporting ethos dominated cricket in South Africa and other colonies well into the twentieth century. The participation of women in cricket and sport in general in South Africa followed the British model in many ways. From the start, women were socially involved, but active playing was frowned upon. By the late 1800s, as in England, women's participation became more socially acceptable in some quarters. Women's sport became 'less spectacles for amusement' and was regarded as having 'more decorum'.[19] But the numbers participating in cricket remained very low because of the heavily masculine ideology of the 'gentleman's game'.

As we have seen, women, black as well as white, were avid spectators of cricket from the earliest days of the game at the Cape, and remained so throughout the nineteenth century. At the first Inter-Town Tournament in Port Elizabeth in 1876, for instance, 'ample accommodation for lady visitors was ensured' in the tents and facilities set up for this South African version of Canterbury Week. Cricket events like these were great occasions in the small colonial settlements, and women played a central role.

Mission-educated Africans copied the example of the British and colonial white establishments almost exactly. When the Champion Cricket Club of King William's Town played Ngqika CC from East London at home on Boxing Day in 1883 in one of the first inter-town matches, *Imvo Zabantsundu* reported that '*langathi liphume lonke iQonce*' (it was as if the whole of King William's Town turned out). Being a hot day, we are told, the ladies and old men brought along umbrellas to shade themselves.[20] This description is typically Victorian in its self-consciousness about dress and the linking of the 'weaker sex' to old men.

Black mission-educated women deliberately emulated the British sporting ethos as well. At the mission schools they were trained for domesticity like their British counterparts. Gentility and passivity were cultivated as positive qualities, and exercise for girls was frowned upon in the same way as in England. The long Victorian skirts, bonnets, bodices and shoes depicted in the photographs of these girls were clearly not conducive to physical exercise.

In addition to all this, the mission schools generally trained black women to accept and fit 'respectably' into the discriminatory colonial order; they belonged not only to the weaker sex, but also to an inferior 'race'. (In the twentieth century, as class differences increasingly showed themselves in an industrialising society, proponents of equal rights developed the notion of the 'triple oppression' of black women in South African society.) The British curricula formed the basis of the learning at the mission stations. The Bishop of Grahamstown reported in 1885 that a Miss Lucas instructed the girls at St Matthew's College for 'fixed hours' every day 'in all the duties of domestic life, such as washing, ironing, sewing, cooking and baking'.[21]

On leaving school, educated young African women, like their male counterparts, continued to follow the Victorian norms they were taught there. The 'school people' remained a close-knit community, often intermarrying, and becoming involved in overlapping activities, such as (in the case of women) church groups, choirs, and tennis and croquet clubs. For example, in 1884, the wives and partners of the leaders of Port Elizabeth's black community set up both a croquet and a tennis club, and promptly advertised this fact in the missionary-controlled *Isigidimi samaXhosa*, printing in full an elaborate constitution in isiXhosa. The members were well known in the community. Mrs Naniwe Wauchope, the secretary of the croquet club, was the wife of the founder of Imbumba Yama Nyama, the Rev. Isaac Wauchope; and Mrs Rwexu was the wife of Peter Rwexu, the 'father' of black cricketers in Port Elizabeth. Naniwe Wauchope was present again when Kimberley first travelled to Port Elizabeth to challenge the local inter-town cricketers in January 1888. She was prominent in the welcoming ceremony and provided the bedding for the visitors. It is in events such as these that we can trace the origins of the Ladies Sections of sport clubs, which became so popular in the twentieth century.

In this way, black women began to cross boundaries through sport. A local reporter noted, 'For the first time in the history of matches in the area married men brought their wives and single men brought their partners.' He said this needed to be applauded 'as it is a symbol of change in our communities'.[22] Other evidence of the greater freedom women were starting to enjoy at this comes from the experiences of Katie Makhanya and her sister Charlotte (later Maxeke), who toured England with the African Native Choir in the early 1890s, together with the Inter-Town cricketer (and their former teacher) Paul Xiniwe. In her biography, Katie recalled how 'On Saturday afternoons [in Kimberley] before choir practice they stopped to watch a football game or cricket match and every Saturday night there was a party somewhere, sometimes to honour a visiting soccer team, more often to greet a returning traveller or to say goodbye to another'.[23]

For the Victorians, croquet and tennis were the most acceptable and genteel sports for women, so it was no coincidence that they were also the first games played by the mission-educated young women of the eastern Cape and Kimberley. Hargreaves has argued that in restricting themselves to these games and taking only supportive roles in cricket and other 'manly' games, women reinforced rather than confronted Victorian gender stereotypes. Both fashions – 'a long quilted, blue flannel dress rounded off with a tweed cap' for tennis – and protocols, such as ladies playing croquet with one hand while shielding themselves with umbrellas with the other – emphasised the point. The idea was to display 'proper demeanour, decency and modesty' and avoid 'over-exertion, bodily display and sensual pleasure'.[24] But, as Kathleen McCrone has pointed out, the mere act of women participating in sport was one of the major gains of the Victorian period: the growing freedom of the female body was part of the move towards greater political and social freedom as well.

Women's participation in sport could thus both reinforce and subtly undermine existing gender notions and power relations. This was even more so in African societies, where strict age and gender hierarchies were maintained. Any breaching of traditional social protocols undermined patriarchal values as well. It was here that African sportswomen led the way.

32

Women at the crease

The Ladies Cricket Club which included many non-members
insisted on practice facilities at extended hours (they were
ordered to leave the nets at 4.30 pm) and Mrs Kingswell
resigned from the club when it made difficulties.

– Thelma Gutsche, *Old Gold* [1]

Examples of women playing cricket in South Africa in the late nineteenth and
early twentieth centuries are rare, more so than in the other 'white' colonies such
as New Zealand and Australia, where women had greater freedom and became
enfranchised long before even England and America. All the same, accounts of
the first English tour in 1888/9 show how attached to the game the 'fairer sex'
had become and also provide the first known report of women playing the game.
In Johannesburg the England team 'did the "light fantastic" at the Globe Theatre,
honoured guests of the ladies of Johannesburg at a ball at which some 400 were
present'. Harry Cadwallader, about to become first secretary of the South African
Cricket Association (SACA), in fact commented on 'a number of the fair sex indulg-
ing in practice with the willow on the Pirates Ground [in Kimberley] and they
showed they are possessed of not inconsiderable talent. It surely will not be long
before we shall have a ladies' match at Kimberley'. However, in the typical male
idiom of the day, he rather spoilt the point he was making with the backhanded
observation, 'Who knows but we may have a match – 500 ladies of Kimberley
against Major Warton's team.'

Condescension was also evident in reports from Cape Town where a six
landing on the pavilion roof 'caused quite a flutter among the tea-sipping ladies';
from Port Elizabeth where the good humour on the pavilion was enhanced by
'the fair sex varying the monotony with their charming dresses'; from Johannesburg where the centurion Bobby Abel was carried off shoulder high before being
'deposited in the centre of the bandstand and made to bow his acknowledge-

ments to the plaudits of the ladies in the Grand Stand before he was allowed to retire blushing to the Pavilion'; and from Oudtshoorn where, at a picnic at the Cango Caves, with everyone holding a candle, the party proceeded 'into the bowels of the earth, the ladies being guided first and, of course, making the pace slow'.[2] These examples illustrate very well how, as in England, both men and women collaborated, often through the medium of fun, in drawing gender boundaries in cricket.

There are other early instances of women as players. On 7 January 1889 students from the South African College played a match against 'a team of ladies' in Sea Point. According to the *Cape Argus*, the College professors were against the match, 'fearing that the morals of the young men might be endangered'. Eighteen women took on eleven men, who all had to bat, bowl and field left-handed and use pick-handles when batting. Not surprisingly, the women won by an innings.[3]

As with the men, women in the emerging black middle class were not only spectators. The *Cape Times* of 6 January 1891 reported a similar match between Stellenbosch Ladies and Violets:

> This match played at Stellenbosch on January 1 drew a large attendance of people especially of the fair sex. Going to the wickets, the Pinkies White (so were called the ladies) ran up the good score of 125 of which Miss Langeveldt placed to her credit 32 by careful play. The bowling of Miss Florie Pool proved too fatal for the batsmen. This damsel managed to do the hat-trick taking three wickets with successive balls. The fielding was very good especially in the catching. Although the men were rather too heavily handicapped, to reach 33 in the first innings but in the second the bowling was dead on the wicket and they were disposed of for 12. The conditions against the men were that they should bat left-hand with pick-handles and bowl left-hand and in case of run-getting they had to walk from one wicket to the other, thus the females won an easy victory by an innings and 80 runs.

The Pool and Langeveldt families of Stellenbosch have produced many fine cricketers, including Charl Langeveldt, the South African bowling star of the 2000s. This account, and this source provides some of the earliest evidence in existence to show how old family linkages and cricket traditions have endured into and helped shape the present.[4]

There are regular references to games like these between women's and men's teams in which the men were handicapped in some way.[5] This tradition was carried over from England, and it underlined the point that women could not be taken seriously as cricketers. One such occasion involved 'Krom' Hendricks, barred by the cricket establishment from playing for either South Africa or his province on account of his colour. In April 1895 he was a guest celebrity in a society match played between Mr Theys's XI and Mrs Potter's XIII. The men fielded and batted left-handed and could only walk, rather than run, after the ball, but this did not prevent Hendricks from making an impression. The *Cape Times* recorded: 'Hendricks (the crack bowler) accomplished the hat-trick, taking five wickets for 8 runs.'[6] The match took place at the same time that Western Province were participating in the 1895 Currie Cup tournament in Natal. Like a circus performer, Hendricks was forced to stay at home, feted by white women before a sizeable crowd of white holiday-makers, while the real action was taking place a thousand miles away in Durban and Pietermaritzburg.

For some, even cricket as fun like this was regarded as completely unladylike. The *Lantern*, a magazine published in Cape Town, noted with disapproval that in the past 'a woman's place was in the home studying the comfort of the sterner sex ... [She] whose main duty was to be gentle, kind and pure ... now seeks to emulate man ... How fathers and husbands can allow their daughters and wives to make such public exhibitions of themselves is surprising.'

The fledgling women's game underlined not only the paternalistic and colonial culture of nineteenth-century mainstream cricket but also the recurring link between cricket and conquest. The cricket historian H.S. Altham recalled women playing cricket during the South African War: 'I remember, as a boy, seeing pictures of our nurses in South Africa playing cricket.' His observations have been confirmed by photographs in this book of military nurses dressed in the fashionable leisure wear of the time being watched by convalescing soldiers.[7] In April 1902, Mrs Dale Lace, a Johannesburg socialite, hired the Wanderers ground in Johannesburg on a Saturday afternoon for a match between 'Ladies' and 'Gentlemen' to collect funds for soldiers 'garrisoning lonely block-houses.'[8] During the Bambatha Rebellion of 1906, a Natal volunteer regiment under Colonel MacKenzie camped at Louwsberg 'on their way to arrest the Zulu King Dinuzulu'. Bertha Goudvis recalled, 'We had a gay time during the brief visit of the regiment. The ladies, captained by Mrs Bennett, the Magistrate's wife, accepted a challenge to a cricket match. The men used pick-handles instead of bats. Despite this handicap, they managed to beat us. The game became hilarious ... [and] one night we were all invited to a camp concert where we were most hospitably entertained, some of the men proving good singers and musicians.'[9]

The earliest full scorecard we have seen of such mixed matches comes from Kimberley in 1910. It shows women and men on both sides, with the women (all 'Miss') filling the top six batting positions and with men as captains. Mr Lezard's team scored 129 and Captain Bishop's team replied with 96. A Miss English top-scored with 22 and Miss Scott 'bowled exceedingly well' to take 4/20.[10] As the report of a similar match in Jamaica from 1907 shows, these games between officers, gentlemen and 'ladies' happened everywhere in colonial society at this time.[11] In *Sport and the British*, Richard Holt explains that through these leisure activities 'the young not only organised themselves for mating and for work, they asserted the identity of each generation'.[12] They allowed social interaction between the sexes in a regulated way that left the men still in charge. As we will see, this pattern of mainly single women playing would remain a distinctive feature of women's cricket into the twentieth century. Cricket was meant to be a game for playful 'misses' only, but many women would have other ideas.

THE FIRST CLUB AND SCHOOL TEAMS

Two institutional pillars provided the foundations for the development of women's cricket in southern Africa. The first was the elite clubs, especially Wanderers in Johannesburg and Ramblers in Bloemfontein. The other was elite girls' schools, like Roedean in Johannesburg and Rustenburg and Wynberg in Cape Town, which copied the English educational reform model and introduced physical education and sport for girls.

The best examples of these models come from Johannesburg. After the British had defeated the Boers and taken the city during the South African War, they began implementing almost immediately a vigorous anglicisation policy, led by Lord Milner, the new British high commissioner. He wanted the future state to be 'wholly British in language and spirit'.[13] In 1902 King Edward VII School for boys and in 1903 Roedean School for girls were established, both in close proximity to the headquarters of the British military administration. Roedean was based on the famous institution of the same name in Sussex, which was known for its pioneering role in girls sport in England. Staffed by teachers from the sister institution, the South African school immediately made sport one of its educational priorities. A highlight of the first term at the new school was a cricket match against Jeppestown High School, organised by the father of one of the pupils on 'a charming open piece of ground, with a view to the south, and a great many scented purple crocuses'. (Indicative of the educational balance and values the teachers wished to maintain, the other two high points were the production of 'the fairy part of *A Midsummer Night's Dream* as a pastoral play in the garden' and the formal opening of the school by Lady Lyttelton, 'who made a memorable speech about loyalty'.) One of the school songs at Roedean was specifically about the cricket team. It was titled 'The First Eleven' and would have made Kipling proud:

You may field, perhaps, at long-leg or at point,
Or perhaps your talent lies in fielding deep,
Or like to put your fingers out of joint
When bowling's swift – by being wicket-keep.
It doesn't matter where your place may be,
Or if batting or if bowling be your forte,
If in the Eleven you are playing;
Then of you we will be saying:
'Well stopped!' 'Well hit!' 'Well bowled!
'Well tried!' 'Well caught!'

Chorus:
Oh! The Cricket First Eleven,
We admire on every hand;
'Tis the one above all others,
'Tis the best in all the land.
May your scores be never failing,
And your bowling ever true;
Oh! Noble first eleven,
Here's the best of health to you![14]

For the next 60 years, the school magazine faithfully recorded the progress of cricket at the African Roedean, listing the school teams, publishing poems about the game and commenting critically on each player's shortcomings and strengths.[15] In 1908, when Mr McGregor and Miss Rankin laid a new pitch and nets, it was observed that 'overhand [bowling] is weak and has not been practised sufficiently', while the fielding 'is neater and more scientific, but only a few can throw long distances'.[16] In true cricket fashion, the coaches stressed the importance of a correct technique and using 'a straight bat'. Following the tradition at boys' schools, the most outstanding cricketers were awarded colours.

There was an inter-house competition for the Lorentz Cup, and the girls played regularly against the Staff, the Old Girls and the Fathers. Foundation Day on 8 March always included a cricket match. In 1908 the pupils started the day at the Auckland Park Swimming Baths, 'both swimming and boating alike', before squeezing into the school bus and coming back to play – 'some people who were tiny had to sit in the front at the driver's toes and suchlike places'. The school team started well, reaching 84/2, 'when we had to go up to the lawn at half past four for tea'. The captain, Muriel Vail, was the reporter on this occasion and she explained how a Highveld downpour brought the match to an end at that stage: 'it began to pour; so we all had to seize our cups in one hand and a plate of cake in the other and fly up to the pergola ... [our tea] being considerably the weaker on account of its having a little rain-water added to it!' Helen Acheson (34 not out), the skipper (18), Theodora Caldwell (17 not out) and Queenie van den Berg (15) were all successful in their turns at the crease. Ten of the old girls slept over after that evening's dancing and theatre and 'so, needless to say, we talked over the day's events until the small hours'.

Every season Roedean would also play 'outside' matches against the limited opponents available: the Parktown School for Boys in 1906; unnamed rivals, who were said to have gained an unfair advantage by providing 'a short pitch with a ball under regulation size' in 1907; a match against St Andrew's in 1909, which was won by an innings; and subsequently an annual match against Pretoria High School. The narrative Roedean presented was one of proper cricket, the creation of a particular camaraderie for girls, and the importance of the link with 'Home'. Both the English and the cricket orientations of the school were well reflected in the fact that by 1913 there were enough old girls living in England to challenge the second team of the sister school at Brighton to a cricket match.[17]

At the nearby Wanderers Club and fields (roughly where the Johannesburg railway station is today), the older generation started making their presence felt from 1902 onwards. According to Thelma Gutsche in her history of the club, women played the game seriously at the Wanderers in the early 1900s: 'The club had enough trouble with the lady cricketers who insisted on playing the game seriously. After Mrs Winifred Kingswell, wife of the fiery editor of the *Sunday Times* (George Kingswell), had joined in 1911, the Wanderers rang with unwonted trebles as its ladies' team under her captaincy played similar teams from [the Ramblers CC in] Bloemfontein and elsewhere, and sometimes took on the men.'[18] Gutsche drew a vivid picture of how the women continued to play as the First World War approached, amid deteriorating economic conditions and intensified class conflict: 'Johannesburg was fast approaching revolution. Sport was coming to a standstill and few people had the heart to play games. Only the Ladies Cricket Club which included many non-members insisted on practice facilities at extended hours (they were ordered to leave the nets at 4.30 pm) and Mrs Kingswell resigned from the club when it made difficulties.' Winifred Kingswell was clearly a pathbreaker in the mould of the suffragettes and the Oxbridge and girls' public school cricketers in England. She has been 'recognised as the pioneer of women's cricket' in South Africa.[19]

In Cape Town, too, girls' cricket was strong, though women were seemingly less successful in getting recognition from the premier club there. As we have seen, the WPCC turned down a proposal that women be admitted in 1893. The *Barclays World of Cricket* notes, 'In the Western Province women played cricket at the beginning of this century.'[20] A photograph of women from the two leading department stores in Cape Town, Garlicks and Stuttafords, playing against each other shows this to have been true, though there is no evidence of a women's club by the early 1900s.[21]

It was rather the elite girls' schools that provided the foundations for women's involvement in cricket in the western Cape. The Girls' Public School, later Wynberg Girls' High, was the first school in South Africa to employ a qualified physical education teacher. She was the London-educated Dolly Rees. A gymnasium was built in 1900, and physical education and sport became regular activities.[22] Inter-schools girls' cricket followed. In 1909, for example, Wynberg Girls' High beat Rustenburg. Regular inter-schools sports events began to be held in Cape Town, making more acceptable the previously taboo notion that sport was good for girls.

By the 1920s the Peninsula Schools Girls Games' Union had been formed to organise inter-schools sport, including cricket. The redoubtable Winifred Kingswell, who had in the meantime moved to Cape Town, was 'instigator and first president'. The annual Cavanagh Cup for inter-school competition was started in 1921, with the Kenilworth racecourse a popular venue. One observer noted that 'almost the whole school – children and staff included – would turn out to support the competitors'. Schools cricket started growing in this environment, and soon there was a time 'when all the girl's schools played competitive inter-schools cricket'.[23]

It was the nexus of schools and clubs, linked to the heart of the post-war English establishment, in Johannesburg, Bloemfontein and Cape Town that formed the base from which women's cricket grew in South Africa. But scattered references to cricket all over southern Africa can be found from around the turn of the century. Women and girls played some form of organised cricket in places such as Pretoria, Pietersburg (Polokwane), Barberton, Kimberley, Durban and Port Elizabeth.[24] A few photographs are the main evidence at this stage.[25] Victor Sparks, writing mainly about cricket in the country areas of the Orange Free State and Natal, noted that a 'girls' eleven ... used to function at Mount Edgecombe near Durban in the earlier part of this century'.

> They were a good team although the lads did not like to admit it. I remember particularly their two opening bowlers, Miss Gamley and a Miss Lilburn – much to my discomfiture on at least two occasions. These two ladies bowled underhand at a good pace, and they both kept a wonderful length. Then in the batting line I remember well a century made by the younger Miss Campbell, who had recently returned home from a Girls' College in England where she

had learnt cricket. Miss Campbell had all the orthodox shots. She played with a straight bat, her stroke play was good and she could drive a ball to the boundary with ease. Yes. The Mount Edgecombe team were a team to be reckoned with in those good old days – pick handle or no pick handle.[26]

It was not only white women who played cricket. The first known black women's cricket clubs were formed in Kimberley in 1909 when coloured women 'set the pace in a highly commendable way' by forming the Daisies, the Ivies and Perseverance clubs, and grouped themselves into a union under a prominent local sports administrator, Mr J.S. Lackey.[27] Reports of their activities appeared in the *APO* newspaper, the official organ of the eponymous organisation, the first large-scale political body for coloured people, which had more than a hundred branches throughout the country. The president for 40 years was Dr Abdullah Abdurahman, who was himself president of the Western Province Coloured Cricket Union. The reports in the *APO* make it clear that these cricket activities by women were an integral part of the overall life of the coloured middle class in Kimberley.

THE GROWTH OF WOMEN'S SPORT

Organised women's sport started relatively late in South Africa. The first national competition was the 'Ladies' Championship' in golf, organised in 1909, the same year as the male-controlled South African Golf Union was formed.[28] In this respect the other 'white' colonies seemed to be ahead of South Africa. The first national tennis championships for women in New Zealand were started in 1886. In Australia the first tennis competitions began in Victoria in 1884. In 1894 the first national golf tournament took place, and in that decade cricket and cycling became popular as well. The first recorded game in that country was in 1886 and in 1891 the first inter-colonial match took place.

Scholars have argued that in the colonies – where the climates were different and attitudes were sometimes less conformist than in Britain – women sometimes showed greater daring in tackling physical sports and breaking dress taboos. Swimming, frowned on in England and allowed only behind closed doors, became an Olympic sport at an early stage because of the influence of less-constrained Californian women living on the sunny west coast of America. According to one historian, 'Leisure activities in pioneering societies were spontaneous affairs in which everyone joined with great enthusiasm and informality ... On the fringe of the British empire sport may have opened fresh doors for women.'[29] In New Zealand women were permitted to vote from 1893, and in Australia radical

Model Victorians: Male and female students and staff at Lovedale College in the 1880s.

Top: Lady Loch's cricket day. Cricket players at a special event in 1893 organised by the wife of the Governor of the Cape Colony, who was also the first patron of the South African Cricket Association.

Right: Women's team from Pietersburg in 1894.

Bottom: Durban cricketers soon after the turn of the century (below).

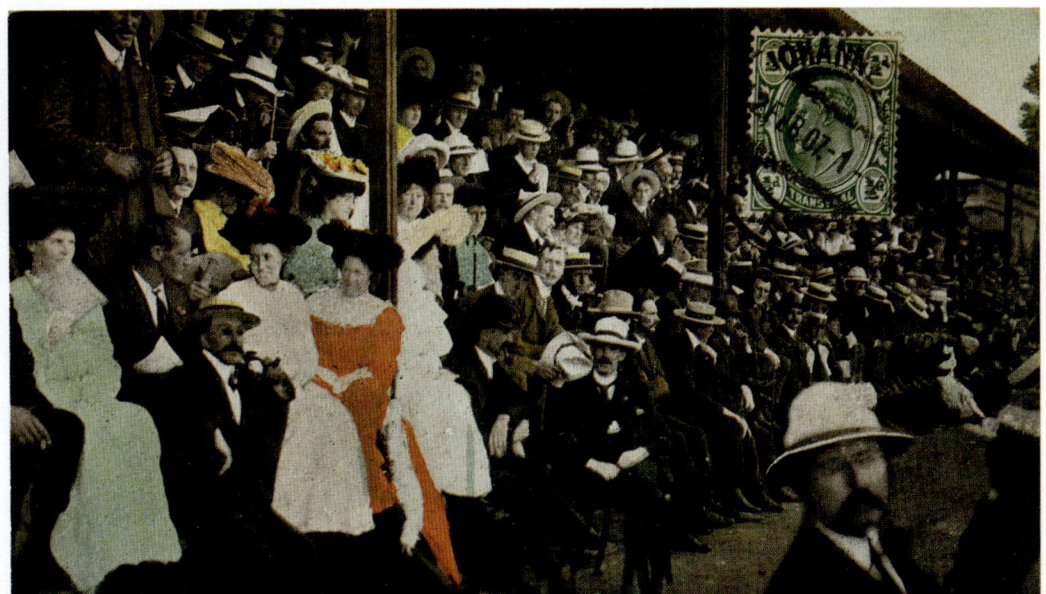

CRICKET MATCH, ENGLAND V. SOUTH AFRICA–
THE MEMBERS' STAND AT THE WANDERERS, JOHANNESBURG.
Published by HALLIS & Co., Port Elizabeth.
Museum Africa, Johannesburg. MA1956-1234A

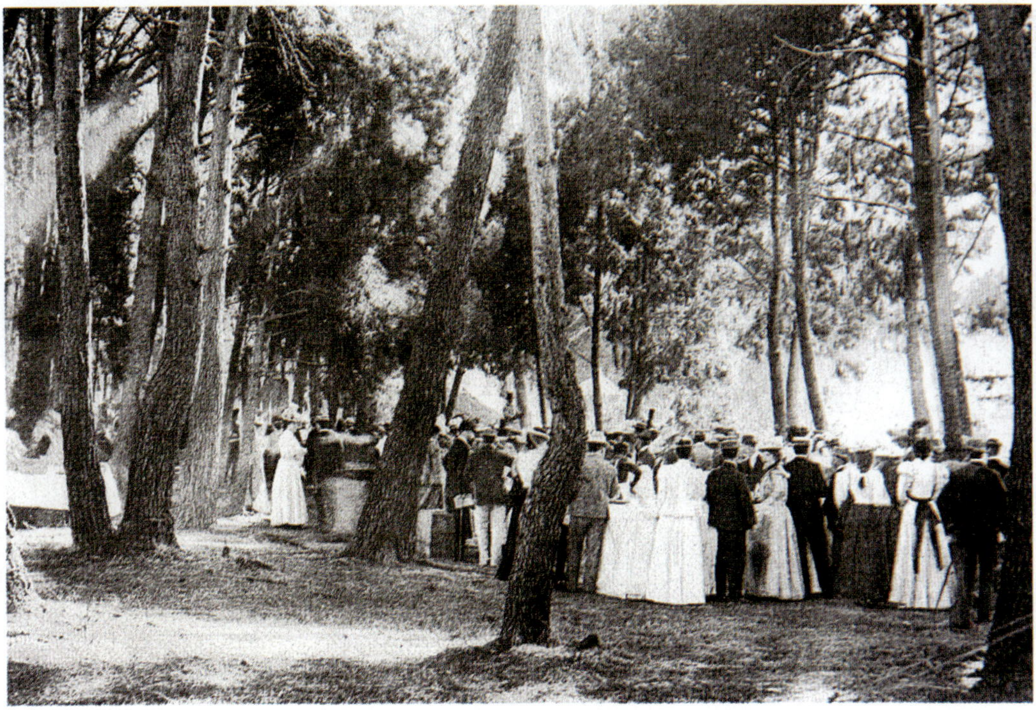

Women, cricket and high society. Test matches at the Wanderers (above) and Newlands (below) were the places to be seen in the 1890s and early 1900s.

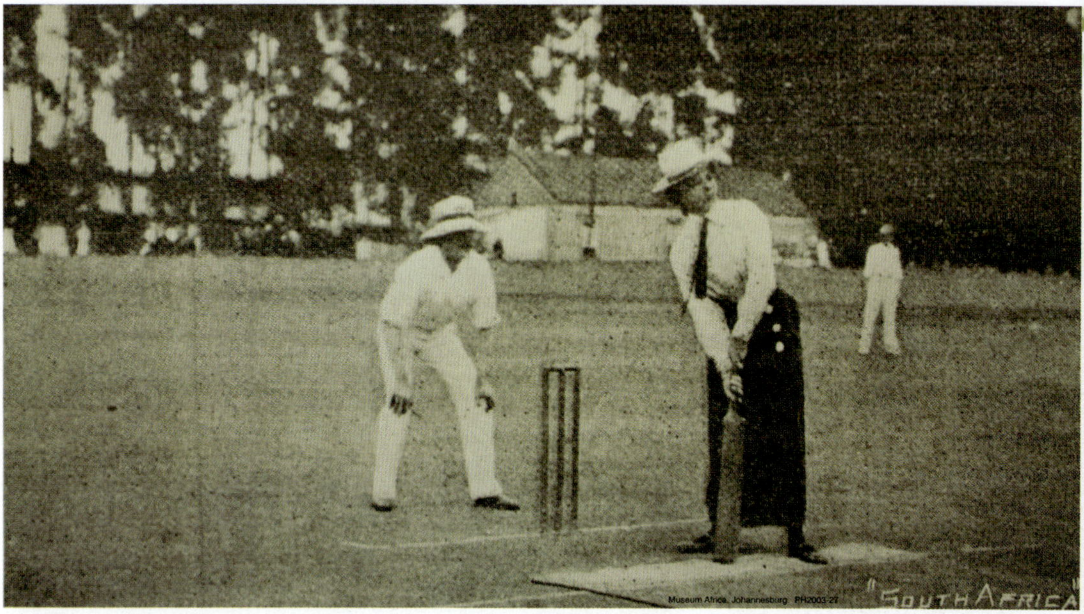

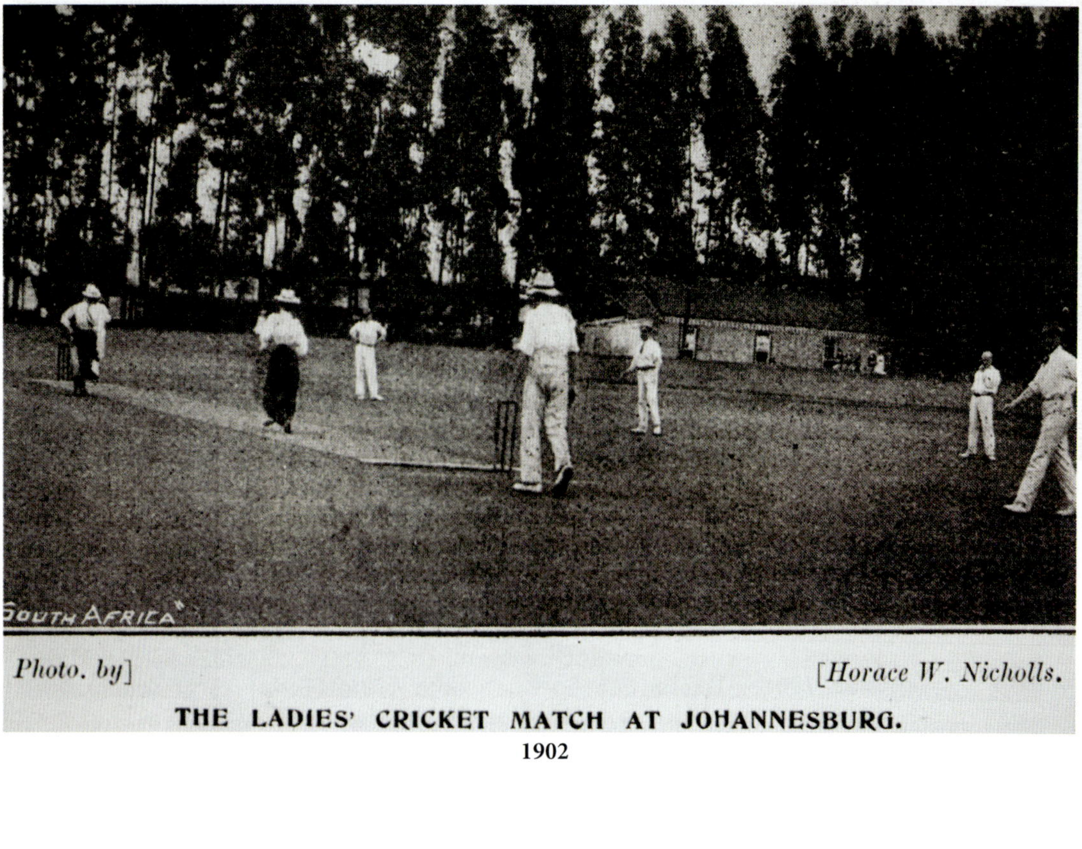

Photo. by] [*Horace W. Nicholls.*

THE LADIES' CRICKET MATCH AT JOHANNESBURG.

1902

Women and cricket in wartime South Africa. British nurses at play while convalescing soldiers look on, 1899–1902.

Above: Men and women playing together, Cape Town, c.1903.

Below: The Pioneers Cricket Club, Port Elizabeth, 1902. Back row: Misses Mona Levey, Ruby Heywood, Myrtle King, Helen André and Muriel Beauchamp. Front row: Iris Evatt, Maude Davies, Edith Sutton, Joyce Davies, Kathie Ryan and 'Myself'.

Ladies Cricket Match at Baberton
1902
Artiste I. L. R.

Mrs DuBuisson in foreground.

Ladies at Cricket: Stuttaford's Staff v. Garlick's.

Garlick's ~ batting

Above: Cricket in Cape Town. A friendly match between the women's staff of two top department stores.

Below: The Rustenburg Girls' High School XI in 1909/10.

feminists were attracted to 'more robust sports' as part of their commitment to the emancipation of women.[30]

It is arguable whether colonial white women in South Africa enjoyed the same level of freedom or participation. They received the vote only in 1930, and women's sport here does not seem to have reached the same levels as in Australia and New Zealand. The reason for this perhaps lies in the racial and sexual attitudes and anxieties of white colonials in South Africa. The large black male population in South Africa was seen as a threat to white colonial woman-hood. Several historians have written about the 'Black Peril' hysteria of the early 1900s when, during a time of increasing black unrest, the media highlighted the perceived sexual threat presented to white women. This would have acted as a restraint on any loosening of dress and exercise taboos in the context of the master–servant relationship.

A historian of West Indies women's cricket has observed in a similar vein that the women of the colonial white sugar planter aristocracy did not play cricket in the 'racialised' and 'formidable gendered' Caribbean societies. It was only when black working-class women from Jamaica became involved in the second half of the twentieth century, during a period of strong anti-colonial feeling, that women's cricket in the West Indies first got off the ground.[31]

CRICKET IN A GENDER GHETTO

Before World War I, there was very limited space for women to confront their exclusion from cricket and sport generally:

> Sport continued to be perceived as a basically masculine phenomenon in which female participation, apart from providing applause and respectability as spectators, was an anomaly. This continued as long as sport was regarded as the idealised socialisation of masculine traits that were essential to national and military leadership; as long as the ideals of femininity regarded such traits as inessential to women's success in the Victorian social world; as long as that world kept the doors to real political and economic power firmly closed to them.[32]

Those who actually played had to do so 'out of sight', in a separate world where their participation was not experienced as a direct challenge to male control of sporting space and the masculine imperial ideology of cricket. Even in the practice nets, women had to be out of sight when the men arrived after work to play, as the women members at the Wanderers found out in 1911. The idea of women playing cricket was frowned upon. The ideology of cricket did not permit men to accept women as co-participants. This was the gentleman's game, and while it was acceptable for women to play tennis, golf and hockey, they were regarded as not real women if they played cricket. Doing so would undermine all the values of manliness and muscular Christianity and the 'imperial mission' upon which the ethos of cricket was based.

The remarkable Winifred Kingswell was the most prominent of the small number of women who bucked the trend and, like the great writer Olive Schreiner, called publicly for women's rights and emancipation. Her daughter describes how her father met Winifred on a high society occasion: 'A big marquee was set up on the lawn, and [Mr] Kingswell was initiated into social cricket. He was fascinated after a sample on the leg from the lady over-arm bowler (later to be his wife) and retired, content to watch this remarkable woman – adept at cricket. Like herself, her bowling was wild: it had on one occasion knocked out some of [South African cricketer] Percy Jones's front teeth and nearly brained another player.'[33] Kingswell was also to lead attempts in the early 1930s to ensure there was sufficient coordination of women's cricket in South Africa to enable it to affiliate to the English controlling body, the Women's Cricket Association.

Where it was able to take root, women's cricket had to sustain itself in a gender ghetto throughout the twentieth century, separated from and unacknowledged by male cricket establishments. Though some clubs, such as Wanderers in Johannesburg and Ramblers in Bloemfontein, did accept women as members in the early 1900s, they could participate in men's cricket only as supporters, and only up to a certain point. They were not allowed, for example, to view the match from the same 'central point' as men, namely the members-only bars, which became features of many colonial clubs that based themselves on the model of Lord's (where women were excluded until as late as the 1990s).[34] In South Africa, women's cricket remained the preserve of a small group of white middle-class women in a strong British cultural milieu, playing very much on the margins.

PART FIVE

PROVINCIAL AND INTERNATIONAL CRICKET BECOME THE BUILDING BLOCKS OF A NATIONAL GAME, 1890–1914

33

Formation of the South African Coloured Cricket Board, 1903

> This Board does not recognise any distinction
> amongst the various sporting peoples of South Africa,
> whether by Creed, Nationality or otherwise.
>
> – Rules of the SACCB, Clause 25, 1903[1]

Black cricketers wished to be part of a unified South African cricket establishment, but the 'Krom' Hendricks saga and the general direction of South African politics made it clear to them that they would not be given a place at the table. The white South African Cricket Association (SACA), founded in Kimberley in 1890 and dominated by a chauvinistically imperialist English establishment, had decided that people of another hue could not be part of a game that represented the imperial mission.

But black sports people did not accept the subservient role set out for them by the dominant classes. Within three years of Hendricks being controversially excluded from the first South African tour to England, they decided to start their own national organisations and competitions – in both rugby and cricket. Far from having no history, as the narratives of Luckin, Wisden and other colonial recorders would have us believe, the emerging black middle class in southern Africa continued to be a global pace-setters in the game, starting provincial bodies and 'inter-colonial' (or inter-provincial) competitions similar to SACA's Currie Cup (1890), the formalised County Championship in England (1890) and the new Sheffield Shield in Australia (1892/3). This happened less than a decade after the start of these three landmark domestic competitions in world cricket.

The 'dusky' South Africans also launched one of the earliest national controlling cricket bodies in the world. The South African Coloured Cricket Board (SACCB) emerged from the decade and a half of active organising and growth already described to become only the third permanent representative national association worldwide (after the segregated SACA in 1890 and Canada in 1892). Founded in 1903, it would precede by two years the Australian Cricket Board and by a quarter of a century or more the West Indian, Indian, New Zealand and Pakistan cricket boards.

As with the founding of the white rugby and cricket boards, Kimberley was again at the centre of developments, as black sports leaders sought to emulate the example of their white counterparts. Administrators from the Griqualand West Colonial Rugby Football Union (GWCRFU) and the Griqualand West Colonial (later, Coloured) Cricket Union (GWCCU) in Kimberley took the initiative to form alternative national associations for both rugby and cricket. From the vantage point of the 'diamond city', located in the economic and geographical centre of the vast southern African region, black players and administrators watched from close up as white sportsmen set up national bodies and competitions. They too played to a high standard, enjoyed confident inter-racial interactions and had access to the patronage of powerful mining interests. The emerging black middle class in Kimberley was invigorated by the air of this 'supremely British place' and remained bullish about the future despite the reality of increasing segregation in the colony.[2] All these factors contributed to the black Kimberley administrators taking the lead. These sports people, representing the dreams of their peers for an inclusive, liberal society, were averse to any discrimination on the basis of 'colour, nationality, language and religion' in sport. However, if this non-racial vision could not be achieved in existing structures, they would form their own.

Imvo Zabantsundu reported in July 1897 that local rugby administrators persuaded Cecil John Rhodes, symbol of the town's new wealth, to present 'all the Coloured Sporting People of South Africa with a Silver Cup, valued at Fifty Guineas, for Competition amongst themselves on the same lines as the Currie Cup'.[3]

The GWCRFU sent out a notice calling on clubs and 'Unions (if any)' in 'the various towns and districts' to send delegates to a meeting at the Savona Café in Kimberley on 19 August 1897. The aim was to form a South African Coloured Rugby Football Board (SACRFB).[4] In the end, only local people attended, although Bud M'belle was requested by the Port Elizabeth Union (consisting of the Rovers and Union clubs) and African clubs from Johannesburg and King William's Town to represent them by proxy. The all-round sportsman Robert Grendon, from the Excelsior club in Beaconsfield, who had excelled for the South African Malay cricket team in 1891, was elected as the first president of the SACRFB. Bud M'belle was voted in as the SACRFB secretary and D.J. Lenders and E. Heneke were installed as auditors. The former was a foreman at a local harness and saddlery, while Heneke was a boilermaker at De Beers and secretary of the 'B' (or Coloured) Section of the South African League, a pro-British organisation formed to support Rhodes's adventures in southern Africa. Lenders later became a prominent politician and the president of the SACRFB, as well as a local cricket administrator. He was vice-president to the legendary Dr Abdullah Abdurahman in the African Political Organisation (APO) for many years. The leaders of the new rugby board were, therefore, respected community figures.[5]

At the same time as these developments were happening in rugby, Bud M'belle, on behalf of the GWCCU, persuaded Colonel (later Sir) David Harris of De Beers, and a member of the Cape parliament, to donate an expensive trophy worth 100 guineas to black cricketers. On 1 November 1897, Harris informed Bud M'belle that following his request, he had consulted with Solly Joel, and 'I have this day ordered from England a suitable silver trophy, and on its arrival I shall be glad to hand it over to the Griqualand West Colonial Cricket Union, as a Barnato Memorial Trophy'.[6] The trophy was to be in honour of mining magnate Barney Barnato, who had recently committed suicide by jumping off an ocean liner at sea. John Tengo Jabavu welcomed the news in an editorial in *Imvo*:

> The coloured sportsmen of Kimberley have had another turn of good luck. Some time back we announced that they were the fortunate recipients of a Cup from Mr Rhodes, and we then made observations on the manifest duty of millionaires to the aboriginal inhabitants, which were so appreciated by our contemporaries as to be widely commented upon. We then showed the amount of good that comparatively small gifts to Native causes were from those whom Providence has made the stewards of His bounties embodied in the mineral deposits of Africa. It is a satisfaction to us to learn that the remarks then made have come before the representatives of other millionaires ... We add our thanks ... It cannot be too strongly insisted upon that any money spent on the amelioration of the Natives is money well spent, and such as will be repaid with interest to the community in times to come. Sport is one way of increasing the wants of our people and making it obligatory to them to work to supply those wants. But as we have before said it is not the only way; and it would be well if the monied ones of the community recognised that the Missionary agencies among the raw material played no small part in rendering Natives effective citizens, and therefore a source of wealth to the country.[7]

The cricketers now had a cup, although they did not, like the rugby players, follow up by immediately forming a national board as well. At this stage, black sportsmen were prepared to cooperate with the establishment, even as it excluded them, but they remained committed to a unitary vision and were determined to show their standards and organisation could compare with the best.

The Kimberley-based officials now started planning for the first rugby and cricket tournaments. However, the unity initiatives and proactive policy of non-racialism followed by the new GWCCU were somewhat spoilt by the local underlying ethnic and religious divisions. Kimberley sports people had all initially played together, but soon after the formation of the GWCCU, three clubs – Wanderers, Universals and Progress – broke away on 8 November 1895 to form a rival Diamond Fields Colonial Cricket Union (DFCCU). Not only did the white GWCU keep itself aloof, but an anomalous situation now existed whereby Christian coloured cricketers held themselves apart from the Malays and Africans playing in the GWCCU. The divisions, described as the 'Native–Malay versus Coloured' split, became fixed and would continue to reverberate in South African cricket decades later.[8] From then on, local coloured cricketers tended to play in the DFCCU (with its own Jones Challenge Cup competition) and the African and 'Malay' cricketers for the Hassen Cup in the GWCCU.

The break-away clubs had apparently been unhappy that an African, J.S. Moss, known as Mr Interpreter Moss after his job at the local magistrate's court, was appointed as vice-president. The Union's spokesperson, Bud M'belle, condemned these attitudes. He described Moss as 'a cultured and respectable native gentleman of whom any sensible community can be proud'. Moreover, 'I could understand if the objection of the three clubs was based on the fact that a barbarous native, a street Malay, nay, even a stupid Cape Coloured man had been elected to such a post. As far as ability, education, and all other things – except an almost white colour – are concerned, Mr Moss is far superior to any of the men composing the three clubs.' Bud M'belle warned that while 'natives and Malays have always allowed Cape Coloured people to fill the official positions' in the combined bodies, this would no longer automatically be so.

The national rugby and cricket plans proceeded nevertheless. The newly formed SACRFB decided to hold the first Rhodes Cup Tournament in Kimberley in August 1898. Bud M'belle was the main organiser and worked hard, travelling to and corresponding with other areas in order to ensure that they set up provincial associations and affiliated to the new national board. When the SACRFB met again in May 1898, there were representatives from the Western Province, Eastern Province and Transvaal Coloured Unions in addition to the GWCRFU, and all had paid their registration fees. These had also been the four constituent unions of the white South African Rugby Football Board (SARFB), formed a few years earlier in the same city. The development of sport in South Africa among both black and white was clearly influenced by broader patterns in the historical development of the country as a whole.[9]

The inaugural Rhodes Cup Tournament took place from 20 to 27 August 1898. Advertisements were placed in the local *Diamond Fields Advertiser* and 'spectators rolled up in good numbers'. The mayor was in attendance to present medals to the winners and the South African rugby international, Chubb Vigne, was one of the referees. Western Province won all three of its matches to win the tournament.[10]

The success of the rugby tournament galvanised Bud M'belle and others into organising the corresponding tournament for the summer game. Early in November 1898, notices went out calling cricketers to a tournament in Grahamstown. The organisers invited seven centres, which were encouraged to form regional teams including players from surrounding towns. Invitations went out to Kimberley, Cape Town, Johannesburg and the main eastern Cape centres: Port Elizabeth, Grahamstown, Queenstown and King William's Town.[11] This was the beginning of 'colonial' (later, provincial) unions in cricket. It was also announced that during the tournament a cricket board would be elected to 'administer the Barnato Memorial Trophy'.[12] The notice pointed out that the white Currie Cup tournament would be held in Port Elizabeth over the Easter weekend, indicating the self-conscious mobilisation of the excluded black cricketers along the same lines.[13]

Not everyone bought into the strength versus strength concept, with some dissatisfaction coming from inter-town supporters in East London, Grahamstown and Uitenhage who were afraid of being left out, but it was explained that East London needed to combine with King William's Town to form 'Southern Border' and Uitenhage with Port Elizabeth to form Eastern Province.[14] *Imvo* encouraged them not to let small differences derail preparations for the tournament.[15]

The first Barnato tournament finally took place from 28 December 1898 through to 5 January 1899. Although Grahamstown was originally chosen as the venue, Port Elizabeth ended up hosting it. Western Province ended as winners, coming from behind to beat Southern Border in the decisive match. As with rugby, the composition of the teams in the first Barnato tournament reflected both the inclusive goals of the early black cricket administrators and the local specificities of the game in each area. Western Province had mainly Muslim players. Griquas were mixed, with at least two Africans, Sekile and Malunga, in the team. The three eastern Cape teams were all made up of Africans. Two things were clear from the demographics. Firstly, 'non-European' players were determined to work together. Secondly, from the first Inter-Town tournaments to Bud M'belle's initiative regarding the Barnato Cup to the organisation of the first tournament in Port Elizabeth, African administrators were at the forefront in the early moves towards cricket unity. The three regions involved had long histories of playing together and they would form a strong base for what would be called 'non-racial' cricket in the second half of the twentieth century.

Sol Plaatje reported in his *Koranta ea Becoana* newspaper that Bud M'belle had been the initiator of the tournament and that after its close 'a South African Coloured Cricket Board was formally constituted with Mr Daniel Kadi of Port Elizabeth as Honorary Secretary'.[16] Unfortunately, the South African War broke out in October 1899 before the next season got under way, putting paid to any further plans for the next three years. However, in the very month that the peace agreement was signed at Vereeniging, action was taken to formalise the founding of the new South African Coloured Cricket Board (SACCB). In May 1902, E.D. Makula, designated 'Secretary Pro Tem' of the GWCCU sent out the following notice: 'BARNATO TROPHY TOURNAMENT. I am directed to inform, through Press, all Cricket Centres that a Tournament re above Trophy will take place in Kimberley during Christmas and New Year holidays. All sportsmen interested are kindly requested to take up and communicate with the undersigned for particulars.'[17] Discussions were resumed about further tournaments on provincial lines and the formalisation of the national board.[18]

During the following season, in February 1903, S. Mtoba, apparently newly appointed as secretary of the GWCCU, based in the Malay Camp in Kimberley, sent out a notice on behalf of the Union, informing all centres interested in a tournament over the 1903/4 summer to contact Kimberley in writing so that a board could be established in time for this.[19] This time the efforts of the organisers were successful. By the end of 1903 there was a new constitution for the SACCB, and it was announced that 'the first tournament' would be held in Kimberley in April 1904. Affiliation would cost £2 2s, and the Board would be 'governed by a general body' consisting of the president, secretary (who would be resident in Kimberley) and 'two representatives from each State, Colony, or Province affiliated to the Board'.[20] The new SACCB made it clear in clause 25 of its constitution that it 'does not recognise any distinction amongst the various sporting peoples of South Africa, whether by Creed, Nationality or otherwise'. This was an obvious reference to the racial policies of the white cricket body and the governing classes in general. The SACCB also decided to 'adopt the rules of the [white] South African [Cricket] Association' in its general administration of the game, underlining its desire for unity and a best-practice approach.[21]

For every tournament, a special meeting would be called in the host city to discuss tournament arrangements and to elect a tournament secretary. It was agreed that 'in no case' would the trophy be competed for more than once in two years, and another condition was that at least three 'representative teams' from the affiliates had to participate.[22] The founding members were apparently Eastern Province, Griqualand West and Western Province, with Transvaal joining in 1904.[23] Tournaments for the Barnato Trophy, the black Currie Cup, duly followed, starting in Kimberley in 1903/4, and followed by Cape Town in 1907/8, Port Elizabeth in 1909/10 and Kimberley again in 1912/3.

This cricketing drama that unfolded at the turn of the twentieth century in South Africa represents a truly remarkable story. As cricket became organised, black players and administrators displayed an enthusiasm for the game and produced players who proved they were playing at the highest level. But after a decade of effort and various contestations, they were formally excluded from SACA and test cricket. Self-confident and undeterred, they proceeded to form their own representative cricket board with the vision of eventual unity across the colour divide. The SACCB, formed by excluded black cricketers in the first decade of the twentieth century, became the repository of a vision of unity in cricket that would only be realised in the last decade of that century.

34

The first inter-colonial and inter-provincial tournaments

SACA's Currie Cup and SACCB's Barnato Memorial Trophy

To judge by the excellent attendance on the opening day,
the gate receipts are likely to be very satisfactory.

– *Cape Times*, 25 March 1908

The different regions and territories of southern Africa were the foundations on which both the whites-only South African Cricket Association (1890) and the new South African Coloured Cricket Board (1903) rested. Each area of the subcontinent had its own peculiarities and specific history. From 1890 onwards, the different territories were consolidated into cricket 'provinces' affiliated to the national bodies, preceding by up to two decades the political creation of modern South Africa with its own provincial system. The basic geographical composition and complex of identities of modern South African cricket became fixed as a result, with each area reflecting the historical context in which the game had developed there.

Long before South Africa formally came into existence, the idea of South Africa was already in place. The fact that British literature used the term South Africa; the attempts at political federation; the 'national' sports teams selected before there was a nation, all contributed to making concrete this British imperial construct.

Once in place, the new provincial affiliates started selecting representative teams and competing against each other. The Currie Cup became the competition for the establishment white cricketers and the Barnato Memorial Trophy the competition for the excluded black players. Each grouping in each province also organised its own leagues and competitions. Remarkably, given later apartheid assumptions that cricket had always been an exclusively white game which the colonised black people were neither interested in nor temperamentally suited for, organisational developments among black cricketers closely paralleled those of the establishment associations at this top level of the sport.

In this section, an integrated narrative of the emergence of provincial organisations and their activities between 1890 and 1914 is provided for the first time. Details and scorecards of the Barnato provincial tournaments for black cricketers are also given here for the first time and should be read alongside those of the Currie Cup, about which much has been written over the years. As we have seen from the time of the early inter-town tournaments, cricket's formal organisational evolution in the nineteenth century was not only infinitely richer than what has been recorded to date, but also more integrated and closely tied together than ever thought possible until now, even though rigid segregation became the norm in the twentieth century.

SACA AND THE CURRIE CUP, 1889–1914

Major Warton's English team presented the Currie Cup to Kimberley (later Griqualand West) in 1889, immediately after the first international tour. This was a reward for being the best team to play against them. The next season the cricketers from the goldfields, centred on the new city of Johannesburg, which was then scarcely five years old, challenged their counterparts on the diamond fields to a match for the cup. Thus the first tournament – a two-team play-off – took place from 5 to 7 April 1890 in Kimberley. On the evening after Transvaal defeated the hosts, delegates representing the various regions met in the same town to establish the new South African Cricket Association (SACA). The Currie Cup was to become SACA's premier domestic trophy for the next 100 seasons. Outside international matches, winning the Currie Cup became the pinnacle of achievement for white cricketers.

Until World War I, the Currie Cup competition remained relatively undeveloped in format. The Cup was competed for only 14 times in 24 seasons and only 95 Currie Cup matches were played – an average of under four per year, or only 6.8 per season of competition. This is a sporadic record, even taking into account the South African War of 1899–1902. Over the first five tournaments organised before 1895, a mere 12 matches were played. Teams were unstable and sometimes included players who were very temporary residents but were valued because of their connections with Britain ('Home'). Rules were at first idiosyncratic: the match between Transvaal and Kimberley at Johannesburg in

April 1891, the only contest of the second Currie Cup tournament, lasted seven days and was won by the visitors by 58 runs out of an aggregate of 1,402. The holders defended the cup against a single challenger in the first two competitions. Multi-team tournaments were started in 1892/3 and for the next decade the defending champions played only in the finals while the other participating provinces fought among themselves for that honour. From 1902/3, it developed its round-robin league format. Like the earlier inter-town tournaments, Currie Cup tournaments were held at one centralised venue, except for the 1903/4 and 1904/5 seasons, when the fixtures were decentralised along the lines of the later league format. Financial and logistical challenges were still too great to standardise the later home-and-away format of play. Seasons that featured a touring side had no Currie Cup competition.

Only Transvaal competed in each of the 14 tournaments before World War I. Western Province missed two competitions and Griquas three. Natal and Eastern Province competed only nine times, Border five times, Orange Free State four times, and South Western Districts and Rhodesia once each. It was only in the third tournament of 1892/3 that Western Province joined Kimberley and Transvaal to make it more than a two-team play-off, with Natal and Eastern Province making their debuts at the fourth in 1893/4. Natal, one of the most 'British' of colonies, was subsequently missing in 1902/3 and again in 1908/9 – it played a mere 41 first-class games up to 1914.

During the quarter of a century leading up to World War I, Transvaal, Western Province and Natal all won between 70 and 76 per cent of their Currie Cup matches, starting a pattern of dominance that would continue throughout the twentieth century. The percentages for Border were 35 per cent and Eastern Province 25.9 per cent, but the remaining teams fared poorly: Griquas lost 21 of 26 matches played over nearly a quarter of a century.

The number of centuries scored was 46, a rate of 3.28 per season or roughly one every other match. The highest score was 250 not out by H.W. Taylor for Natal (vs Transvaal, 1912/3), but L.J. Tancred of Transvaal, the only player to record more than a thousand runs (1,230), scored the highest number of centuries with four. In the 1906/7 season, A.W. 'Dave' Nourse scored three centuries for Natal, including one innings of 212 (vs Griquas). Thirty seven per cent of the centuries were made against Griquas. No century was scored by any batsman for Rhodesia or South Western Districts: indeed, the highest score for the latter was 14 by the peripatetic C.H. Vintcent (vs Western Province) and his teammate G. Rogers. H.W. Taylor also possessed the best average of 50.76, but only one other player, J.E. Jewell of Orange Free State, exceeded 40, with 'Dave' Nourse averaging 38.69. Nourse recorded the best average in a specific tournament of 98.16 over seven innings in the 1906/7 season. The record wicket partnership of 283 was established by H.W. Taylor and R.H. Blake of Natal (vs Griquas, 1910/1).

In the pre-World War I era, two bowlers took over 100 wickets, J.H. Sinclair of Transvaal (165) and J.J. 'Boerjong' Kotze of Transvaal and Western Province (136), with 12 others recording 50 or more. The averages of all these 14 bowlers were under 20.00. Playing for Transvaal (vs Griquas, 1902/3), Sinclair and Kotze took 8/49 and 11/37, bowling unchanged through both innings, a feat emulated by G.A. Rowe and G.A. Lohmann for Western Province (vs Griquas, 1896/7) with 10/48 and 9/88. Another leading bowler, A.E.E. Vogler (Natal, Eastern Province and Transvaal), took 69 wickets at the best average of 10.36. For Eastern Province (vs Griquas, 1906/7) he achieved 16/38 with 10/26 off 12 overs in the second innings. Kotze managed the figures of 4.2/1/6/5 for Western Province (vs Griquas, 1906/7).

Batting standards certainly improved, but consistently heavy scorers were few: 46 centuries were spread among 38 players. Good bowling performances were also widespread, but of the 14 players exceeding 50 wickets, only five took more than 60. A significantly high proportion of outstanding performances with bat and ball were against the ubiquitous but rapidly declining Griquas side.

The story of SACA's Currie Cup has already been told in great detail from its inception to the last time it was played for exactly 101 years later. The best authorities are Brian Crowley's book *Currie Cup Story*, Luckin and Duffus's three volumes on the history of South African cricket to 1947, the 40 issues of the *South African Cricket Annual* from 1949/50 to 1990/1 and, for accurate statistics, Cricket Archive on the internet.[1] There are numerous other sources as well, including *Wisden Cricketers' Almanack*. In all of these records of cricket's development and history, there has been no mention of the inter-colonial and inter-provincial tournaments for the Barnato Memorial Trophy for cricketers excluded from the Currie Cup by SACA purely on the basis of race. So it is these parallel tournaments, copying the Currie Cup, the English County Championship and the Sheffield Shield in Australia, that we introduce in detail for the first time to the cricket literature and on which we primarily focus in this chapter.

SACCB LAUNCHES ITS OWN VERSION OF THE CURRIE CUP, THE COUNTY CHAMPIONSHIP IN ENGLAND AND THE SHEFFIELD SHIELD

Not to be outdone by the colonial cricket establishment with its whites-only Currie Cup, the cricketers excluded from it launched the parallel Barnato Memorial Trophy Tournament in Port Elizabeth from 28 December 1898 to 5 January 1899. This was eight years after the first Currie Cup match and after Surrey became first holders of the County Championship, and only six years after the introduction of the Sheffield Shield in Australia, highlighting the remarkable initiatives taken by the colonised communities in Africa. Overall, only 25 Currie Cup matches had been played before the Eastern Province pairing of W. Mtshatshisa and N. Mabelana strode out to face the bowling of Griqualand West in the corresponding Barnato tournament. The Barnato tournaments were to continue for over 60 years. From the start, they were an expression of the dogged determination of black cricketers to play first-class cricket and find a place at the top levels of the developing game in South Africa.

Newspaper reports give a good indication of the intentions and aspirations of those organising the inaugural Barnato tournament. It was played on the ground of the white Union Club in St George's Park, one of the best facilities available in Port Elizabeth. It was right next door to the Port Elizabeth CC venue in the same park where the first test match in the country had been played ten years before. Showing the transition to a higher level of representative cricket, five regions replaced the purely town teams of the past. Matches were played to a finish over four innings, and the black cricketers could boast a shiny new 100-guinea Barnato Trophy – imported from England – which cost more than the prestigious gold-leafed Currie Cup.

As with the SACA in the early 1890s, some of the regions had yet to constitute themselves into formal provincial associations, but the tournament was clearly the bridge into what is still known as provincial cricket. The participating regions in the tournament, superseding the old inter-town competitions, were the home team of Port Elizabeth/Eastern Province (newspaper reports refer to both designations), the Griqualand West Coloured Cricket Union (formed in 1895, the initiators of the trophy and the tournament), the Western Province Coloured Cricket Union, and teams drawn from *emaXhoseni* or Xhosaland and *ebaTenjini* or Thembuland in the eastern Cape heartland of African cricket. These were Southern Border (representing King William's Town and East London) and Queenstown (which in later decades became the headquarters for the black North-Eastern Districts or Midlands unions in cricket).

The GWCCU had sent out notices encouraging the main towns to constitute provincial bodies incorporating the surrounding towns in the same way as the white players had done. Southern Border and Eastern Province responded, though it is not clear if formal associations had been set up or whether (as with some of the early white provincial and international games) ad hoc committees had seen to this. Similarly, cricketers in Johannesburg formed a Transvaal board in October 1898 with the aim, most likely, of participating, although in the end they were not present. Grahamstown, originally chosen as the venue, was also keen, but Port Elizabeth ended up hosting the tournament and Grahamstown did not even participate. The cricketers in far-away Bulawayo in the new colony of Rhodesia (Zimbabwe) indicated their desire to come, but this too did not materialise. The 16 ('Native' and 'Malay') inter-town tournaments between 1884/5 and 1897/8 had provided a strong organisational platform for this next level of 'inter-colonial' cricket. Clearly, national awareness and cooperation were developing in the same way as for the white cricketers.

The tournament matches were played one game at a time at the Union Club. Only on the last day were two fixtures played. A three-day break was taken over the New Year. It was agreed that accommodation would be provided by the host town, but the visitors were expected to fend for themselves regarding meals. Gate takings would be shared after expenses had been deducted.[2]

The first match of the historic tournament was between the home team and the initiating province: Eastern Province (EP) vs Griqualand West. The hosts batted first. Eastern Province's first official side in batting order was W. Mtshatshisa, N. Mabelana (also the wicketkeeper), Nyusela, Dalaza, S. Busakwe, Fiti, D. Rune, R.Z. Haya, E. Ngcoza, Phu and T. Maloni. Continuity with the pre-provincial era was underlined by the fact that all the players, except new caps Nyusela and Fiti, had played for Port Elizabeth in the inter-town tournaments before, most of them since 1895/6. Haya was the most experienced player, having made his debut for *eBhayi* in the 1890/1 tournament.

The first match proved tough going for the batsmen. Griquas bowled EP out for 80. Dalaza scored more than half the runs with 55 to hit the first fifty in Barnato history. Limberg and one of the two Abramses (initials not given) did the damage with three wickets apiece. Griquas replied with 108. G. Abrams equalled Dalaza's newly established individual batting record of 55, and Phu took four of the first six wickets to fall. Rune was next best with three wickets. In their second turn at the crease, the home side managed 99 runs, with twenties from Fiti and the experienced bowling all-rounder Maloni. This was not enough. Griquas needed 72 to win, and they passed the score with five wickets down, Mondel steering them home with 35 after a first innings duck. Limberg was the match-winner for Griquas, complementing Abrams's batting by taking nine wickets.[3]

Imvo Zabantsundu's correspondent was scathing about the performances of the home side in the tournament. He wrote that even though they had done well in the recent inter-town Tengo Jabavu Cup, they played 'in a disgraceful manner'. Indeed, the new 'Eastern Province' fared poorly, losing all their matches, including those with Queenstown and Southern Border, who both beat them comfortably.

Western Province took on Griquas in what was described as 'the match of the tournament', winning comfortably by six wickets. Griquas collapsed to 72 all out, thanks to the Western Province slow bowling 'being unplayable'. And although they recovered somewhat with 198 in the second innings, it was never going to be enough against the 145 and 127 for four of the men from the south.

The 'Moslems' from Western Province became the first champions when they won against Southern Border in the decisive match. Going in to bat, Western Province collapsed dramatically to 27 all out in their first innings. This was due to a devastating eight wickets from opening bowler Buhlungu. Southern Border followed with a healthy first innings of 145. *EQonce*'s batting mainstay in the inter-town tournaments since 1890/1, C.N. Bopi, top-scored with an unbeaten 40 and Buhlungu this time weighed in again with 24. Western Province rallied to post 219 in the second innings. Kunene took six wickets, but the middle-order of wicketkeeper/batsman A. Hendricks (65 and three stumpings in the match) and Kenny (62) came to the rescue. Buhlungu took his match haul to ten, but was contained this time around. Thereafter, the game continued to turn against Southern Border. Needing 102 runs, they collapsed to 64 all out. The downfall of the men from Xhosaland came after the Cape Town team identified a weakness against slow bowling, so – as they had against Griquas – switched to spin. Abdol, also the opening batsman, took four wickets, ending up with nine in the match.[4]

After a remarkable decade and a half of progress by black cricketers in the Cape Colony, the first Barnato tournament had taken them to another level of playing and unity.

WAR DISRUPTIONS AND RESTARTING THE BARNATO TOURNAMENTS, 1899–1904

At the conclusion of the tournament, a South African Coloured Cricket Board (SACCB) was formally constituted.[5] It was also decided that the next contest for the Barnato Memorial Trophy would take place in Cape Town. However, the momentum of the 1890s was broken temporarily by the outbreak of the South African War in late 1899. Kimberley, headquarters of the SACCB and tournament organisers, came under siege by Boer forces for an extended period; many black cricketers signed up for active service or otherwise supported the British; the cricket sponsor and journalist John Tengo Jabavu had his newspaper closed down under martial law for remaining critically independent in his views despite being loyal to the British government; and the oldest cricket ground in South Africa, the Green Point Common in Cape Town, became a military base and prisoner-of-war camp. Nothing further happened for four seasons – the same length as the break in the Currie Cup. But within months of the bitter war ending in May 1902, efforts began to get the show back on the road. The SACCB formalised itself and, starting in the 1903/4 season in Kimberley, four more Barnato tournaments followed before World War I. The others were held in 1907/8 in Cape Town, 1909/10 in Port Elizabeth and 1912/3 in Kimberley again.

Western Province SACCB won four of the five Barnato tournaments held up to World War I (and then continued as the virtually unchallenged champions again after that), while during the same period Western Province SACA was giving way to four-time winners Transvaal and two-times champions Natal as the dominant province in the Currie Cup. The only time Western Province SACCB did not annex the trophy was in 1910, when for some reason they were absent and Griquas took the honours.

The 1904 Barnato tournament in Kimberley took place over the Easter holidays. Day one coincided with reports that Transvaal SACA had just won the SACA Currie Cup in Johannesburg. Easter from now on became the preferred end-of-season slot for the Barnato players to get together – this period was used by other sporting codes to organise national tournaments too, for example athletics, tennis and golf.[6] All of these were pioneers.

The event demonstrated again the desire of the newly established SACCB to run cricket on the same organised first-class level as that of their white counterparts in SACA's Currie Cup. Not only did the SACCB constitution mirror that of SACA, but the provincial matches were played at top facilities in the town, namely the grounds of the white Eclectics and Pirates clubs; they were scheduled for three days and were played to a finish; local white umpires were asked to officiate; full scores and reports were posted in Kimberley's main newspaper, the *Diamond Fields Advertiser*; and there were some capital performances, to use the language of the time, including the first Barnato century by G. Abrahams (123) of Eastern Province.

The first tournament century came in unusual circumstances and in a losing cause. After Western Province had dispensed with Griqualand West by 40 runs in the opening game, the hosts immediately took to the field again on day two to take on Eastern Province. Batting first, Griquas scored 239, which put them in the driving seat on the way to a win by 101 runs. When play resumed on day three, G. Abrahams (81) and his namesake L. Abrahams (47) put on a rare second-innings century partnership for the third wicket for Eastern Province. Instead of providing a base for their team to chase an unlikely target of 278, the partnership was followed by a collapse, and EP reached only 176. (J. Jabaar's match figures of 13/137 were the cause of the misery, though the start of a rich vein of form for him in Barnato cricket.) As soon as this match finished during the course of day three, the next one began, and Abrahams found himself batting for the second time on the same day against different opponents. The *Diamond Fields Advertiser* reported, 'At the conclusion of their match with Griqualand West, the

Eastern Province started their fixture with the Western Province.'[7] Opening the batting, G. Abrahams followed up his effort of 81 earlier with 123 against WP. Showing similar dominance, his runs were scored out of a total of 197.

Using seven bowlers and with yet another Abrahams (J.) opening for them, Western Province withstood the EP challenge on day four and won, thereby wrapping up the Barnato Trophy for the second successive time. The following day, 6 April 1904, the diamond barons reading the local newspaper over break- fast would have read the sports-page headline: 'THE FINAL MATCH. WEST- ERN PROVINCE WINS THE CUP.' These cricketers had become part of a broader national sports narrative in more ways than one.

HIGH SCORES AND HEAVY ISSUES AS THE BARNATO TOURNAMENTS ARE CONSOLIDATED

For the third tournament in 1907/8, the Barnato caravan stopped in Cape Town. It was the highest-scoring tournament to date and was played on a good pitch at the Cape Town CC ground in Newlands – not where the famous cricket ground now stands, but across the railway line on a field now obliterated by the concrete stands of the rugby ground and the neighbouring Sports Science Institute. The *Cape Times* reported, 'The ground of the Cape Town C.C. has been engaged for the week, and to judge by the excellent attendance on the opening day, the gate receipts are likely to be very satisfactory.'[8] This time seven scores of over 200 – and a 196 – were recorded in the six matches (all except one beating the old tournament record of 239). Two centuries were scored – by F. Nykoko and T. Hendricks, both of Griqualand West. The reigning champions, Western Province, also made it three out of three in front of big home crowds. They beat EP by an innings and 42 runs, Griqualand West by 91 runs, and Transvaal, participating for the first time, by 102 runs.

Cricket was thriving in Johannesburg. Among the Transvaal players was G.S. Rasdien, whose name would become synonymous with Transvaal cricket in the years to come – in a Transvaal SACCB team photo thirty years later, Rasdien is pictured as president of the Transvaal Coloured Cricket Union. Transvaal made an excellent start in the SACCB provincial ranks, putting 248 runs on the board in their first match against Griquas. T. Fakier scored a debut 52 with Rasdien next best on 42. (He also took three wickets, and four against Western Province.) However, if the visitors from Johannesburg rested on their laurels, it was down- hill all the way after that. Thanks to a fine 117 from Griqua vice-captain and no. three batsman F. Nykoko, who 'continued to hit out in first-class style', Griquas knocked up a new tournament record score of 329. The Griquas match-winner from 1904, J. Jabaar, continued in the same vein with a fifty and 12 wickets.[9]

In the next outing against the champions, Nykoko's teammate T. Hendricks followed up the good form with an undefeated century (101) to give Griquas a first innings lead. However, a strong second innings 262 from the home side saw them win, despite Jabaar striking again with eight wickets in the match.

Griquas were consistently the second-strongest team after Western Province in the Barnato tournaments. The long-established non-racial approach in Kimberley sport was reflected in the presence of various players with African names in the 1908 team in Cape Town. The centurion Nykoko and W. Bom were from Eccentrics CC and teammates A. Matlala and C. Ramakhutle were from the other predominantly African club in Kimberley, Duke of Wellington CC, also known as the Dukes. The captain M. Schneider, J. Jabaar and four of the other players were from Red Crescent CC (which had produced the brilliant Robert Grendon in the 1890s), while Ottomans (E. Jacobs, Jabaar's prolific bowling twin) and Good Hope CC each had one representative.[10] Because of the 'Native–Malay versus Coloured' ethno-religious split going back to 1895, there were no players in the team from the clubs, such as Wanderers, Universals and Progress, affiliated to the Diamond Fields Colonial Cricket Union (DFCCU). The GWCCU and the DFCCU did apparently play each other from time to time, but they had separate leagues for the Hassen Cup and Jones Challenge Cup respectively and DFCC-aligned players were not included in the GWCCU's Griqualand West teams for the Barnato tournaments.

The fourth Barnato tournament was held in Port Elizabeth in March–April 1910. Under the heading 'Coloured Cricket Union: Barnato Cup Tournament', the *Eastern Province Herald* ran the following notice in the build up to the event: 'The selection committee of the E.P.C.C Union once more appeals to the general public for their support in the forthcoming tournament which will commence on the 28th inst. (Easter Monday) on the Union ground, St. George's Park, when Eastern Province will meet Griqualand West. All communications to be addressed to the Hon. Secretary, Ph. Norkie, c/o J.F. Williams, Box 95.'[11]

This time the tournament scores were low – 58, 116, 119, 131, 143, 59, 117, 42 – and the quality not as strong as usual because of the unexplained absence of three-time champions Western Province. The highest score was the 178 against the hosts, who were no match for the powerful Griqualand West, going down by an innings, with the experienced opening pair of Jacobs and Jabaar taking all 20 wickets. This was the third tournament in a row in which they had excelled. Transvaal also beat Eastern Province easily by 48 runs. 'Fredricks was unplayable and had the Eastern Province beat right through,' reported the *EP Herald*. There were no fewer than five ducks in the EP second innings.[12] Griquas, by virtue of beating Transvaal, took the trophy for the first time.

The 1910 Barnato tournament was overshadowed by momentous political events. It took place just over a month before various southern African territories lost their separate identities and became one country – the Union of South Africa – on 31 May 1910. African and coloured leaders were vociferously opposed to the constitution of the new Union because it restricted the rights to the franchise that black voters in the eastern and western Cape Colony had enjoyed since 1853, and it kept black people in the Transvaal, Orange Free State and Natal completely disenfranchised. In an effort to secure equal rights in the new South Africa, a delegation representing black interest groups had the previous year gone to Britain to plead with the parliament not to accede to Union unless the colour bar was removed from the proposed constitution. This delegation included the Rev. Walter Rubusana, president of the South African Native Convention and Border Native Cricket Union; Dr Abdullah Abdurahman, president of the African Political Organisation (APO) and Western Province Coloured Cricket Union; Matt Fredericks, secretary of the APO and Cape District Cricket Union; and Daniel Lenders, vice-president of the APO and the South African Coloured Rugby Football Union. All four of them were in Port Elizabeth during the tournament for the parallel annual conference of the APO, Rubusana as a guest and the others as part of the APO's national leadership. The APO debated a motion asking that 'all coloured people observe the Union inauguration as a day of humiliation, fasting, and prayer'. In the end it took a softer line, 'regretting that it finds itself unable to recommend the coloured people to participate in the Union celebrations'. The APO and the sports people in the SACCB, who were supportive of its stand, effectively boycotted the events.[13]

The APO was the largest political organisation in the coloured communities with over a hundred branches. Abdurahman, its leader, was the grandson of freed slaves, had qualified in medicine in Edinburgh and married an Englishwoman. He handed over the Barnato Trophy at the conclusion of the tournament at 'a gathering of a large number of sportsmen and friends' at the Seamen's Institute, a building near the harbour which is today the South End Museum. Flanked by a contingent of leaders from the APO, Abdurahman 'warned the men not to give all their time to sport – and he hoped to hear that the winning team … have all joined the APO on their return to Kimberley, for a good sportsman generally makes a good politician.'[14] The black spokespeople sought greater opportunities in South African society, not the restriction of their existing rights that Union would bring. Using cricket as an analogy, one of the APO leaders explained why the Western Province cricketers, absent that year, were the strongest in the country:

The reason for that is very clear: in the Western Province the coloured people were permitted to witness the best cricket played in the Colony, and also the matches between the English and Colonial teams; whereas in the Transvaal those sources of improvement were shut to the coloured people, for no coloured man was permitted to witness a match either between the best colonial teams or the English cricketers.[15]

What was the reason the WPCCU team did not play in 1910, especially as Dr Abdurahman was also its president? There did seem to be a division among cricketers on ethno-religious grounds at the time in both Cape Town, where the Cape District Union seemed to be steering its own course, and in Kimberley, where there were now three separate pockets of cricket which sometimes overlapped: broadly, the white GWCU, the Christian coloured DFCCU, and the African–Malay GWCCU. Natal cricketer Albert Christopher, writing in the *Latest*, regarded the DFCCU's position in Kimberley as ironical since many of its members were also prominent in Dr Abdurahman's APO, which 'claims to champion the rights of all civilised coloured people'.[16]

In 1912, the APO commented that there was a move afoot to make the SACCB 'truly representative'. The newspaper added rather ambiguously: 'We regret, however, to learn that those responsible for the movement are encountering some opposition on the part of a narrow-minded section of Coloured cricketers whose grounds for objection ... is based on religion, and other absurd notions.'[17] The paper warned that a board which did not embrace 'every section of the Coloured players' would not have credibility as a national organisation.

In addition to the stresses caused by lingering ethno-religious differences in cricket, there were two other challenges facing the SACCB in the years around Union. The first was the widening gap between the SACCB's and SACA's standards arising from SACA's privileged situation in colonial society and its increasing exposure to international cricket, which led to improved standards in its own domestic competitions. Two decades on from the 'Krom' Hendricks scandal, South Africa SACA had gone on six tours abroad and received eight incoming ones, and the total of Currie Cup games had reached nearly 100 compared with less than 30 in SACCB's Barnato tournaments. The respective batting records showed the increasing gap between them. SACA relied for its revenue 'almost entirely upon' profits received from matches against 'visiting teams from overseas'. But for these profits, 'it would be running at a loss'.[18] The Currie Cup made no money and SACA's only other regular income was £18 18s from provincial subscriptions – only £3 more than the revenue of the Griqualand Coloured Cricket Board in 1912. SACCB was cut off from the economic lifeblood of tours.

Secondly, SACCB's base was also not growing adequately. While the white Transvaal and Natal were by the turn of the century becoming central to SACA's growth, winning six of the seven domestic competitions between them from 1900 to World War I, SACCB's affiliates in these two provinces took two or three decades longer to make their presence felt strongly on the national cricket scene. Reflecting the game's origins in South Africa, Cape Town, the eastern Cape and Kimberley remained the heartlands for the Barnato provincial competitions, but this would in the long term mean a narrower foundation rather than a broad, even national presence in the new country.

Another factor which would have concerned the SACCB leadership – but certainly not SACA's – was that whereas Africans formed the majority of players in the 1898 Barnato tournament, they were now in the minority. There was only one team (compared to three out of five in 1898/9) from the eastern Cape. Eastern Province, which had then been mainly, if not entirely, African, now seemed to consist mainly of coloured players. The 1913 team was M. Abrams (captain and top of the batting averages at 32.40), T. Davids (top EP score of the tournament with 127), J. Davids, Jalil, Johnson, Kafaar, Liberty, Maininka, May, Msimnka, Situnga, Solomon (best bowler with figures of 82/20/195/22) and Watson. Griquas had three Africans in F. Ntschoko, who averaged 25.30 with the bat, J. Kakozela and J. Makoti.[19]

Nevertheless, at the time of this final tournament before World War I, there was much that the SACCB and its cricketers – forced to bat on highly uneven societal playing fields – could be proud of.

LAST OUTING BEFORE YET ANOTHER WAR

For the Easter tournament in 1913, it was back to Kimberley, which served as SACCB headquarters. The hosts, GWCCU, were in a healthy state with a revenue of £15 16s 11d and a credit balance. The ubiquitous Isaiah Bud M'belle was both the GWCCU and SACCB national president. Africans and Malays were still playing together and were well integrated on the regional and national executives. In the run-up to the tournament, Eccentrics won the GWCCU premier competition for the Hassen Cup,[20] and the Duke of Wellington CC was also still a force, beating Ottomans by 145 runs. Makoti scored a century, which caused him to be 'presented with a bat and other presents by some of his admirers'.[21]

Western Province (8 points) once again participated and won. Griquas (5) assumed their usual number two position. Eastern Province, the weakest of the three founding provinces of SACCB, ended up with only 2 points. Transvaal through an unexplained administrative oversight missed the tournament. A fifth province, Natal, participated for the first time. Its team, chosen by the Durban and District Indian Cricket Union (DDICU), consisted of Indian players only and its costs came to the princely sum of £90 15s. The DDICU had six clubs playing in its top league for the Panday Shield. They were the champions Ottoman CC, Sydenham, Pirates of India, H.G. School, Greyville and Durban Railway CC.[22] The first-ever Natal team was proudly kitted out in blazers presented by the Union – 'green body with gold braid' – together with a 'hatband' from the manager. However, they came last, failing to win a match.[23]

The *Diamond Fields Advertiser* thought to carry all the cricket scores on the same page in March 1913. Directly under the Currie Cup scorecards for the Western Province vs Natal match, a report on the Barnato Cup tournament was printed with the following introduction: 'The representatives of the "coloured" cricket unions held their annual cricket tournament yesterday, on the Eclectic Ground, when Griqualand West met Natal.' Six matches were played. Each was over four innings, continuing through to a second day. As matches were played one at a time, umpiring duties were shared by senior players, nominated by each team's management, when their team had no fixture. The oppressive heat and lightning-fast outfield devoid of grass, added to the challenges. The newcomers, in particular, found the going heavy. The Natal bowlers could do little as Griquas amassed a new tournament record of 482 for six against them, including an undefeated 150 by T. Hendricks and 111 by A. Jardine. T. Davids of Eastern Province (127) also helped himself to a hundred against them.

The veteran E. Jacobs of Griqualand West, playing in his fourth tournament, was the tournament's highest wicket-taker (33 at 9.30). His haul included 12 wickets against the unbeaten Western Province (6/66 and 6/57). M. Isaacs of Western Province captured 13 wickets at a measly cost as his team thrashed Eastern Province by an innings and 213 runs. V.N. Thumbadoo of Natal also took an impressive 7/41 against Eastern Province. The best all-round performance came from G. Christian of Western Province. He finished at the top of the bowling averages with 16 wickets at 6.50 apiece and scored 159 runs at an average of 39.75 per innings.

Nellanah Sullaphen, secretary of the DDICU, attested 'to the hearty hospitality of the good people of Kimberley' in his 1913 annual report.[24] The inter-racial fellowship promoted by the tournament was reflected in the comments of the *Tsala ea Batho* newspaper, edited by Sol Plaatje, who was then campaigning abroad against racially discriminatory legislation passed by the Union parliament. It said of the all-Indian Natal team:

Social, refined, gentlemanly and scholarly, they seemed to combine these qualities in a manner which captivated all who came into contact with them, and could scarcely have had a more enthusiastic reception than was accorded these modest sons of the tea and sugar planters by Kimberley. They made so many friends as any party could wish to make, and we believe that the last thing has not been said about their visit to the Diamond Fields; and while we congratulate the Western Province on winning the trophy, we believe that in the abstract the Natal team went away with something better.[25]

This popularity was well earned. After the tournament, the Natal cricketers agreed to play in a soccer match to raise funds for the Cape Town-based black boxer Andrew Jeptha, who went abroad to fight and became the British champion, but went blind while in England. The Board also granted the blind boxer 'a season ticket gratis'; here was a sporting community with a real sense of identity looking after one of its own.

On the last day, the alpha Western Province team went through the formalities of dispensing with newcomers Natal to take the title for the fourth time out of five. The *Diamond Fields Advertiser* reported that they showed superior form throughout, their fielding being especially keen. The bowling was likewise 'deadly'.[26] The WP captain deservedly received the beautiful Barnato Trophy and memorable photographs were taken of the fifty-odd cricketers from various parts of the new South Africa for whom the SACCB had catered for a week. The pictures show clearly that the SACCB sought to be true to its constitutionally entrenched vision of not recognising 'any distinction amongst the various sporting peoples of South Africa, whether by Creed, Nationality or otherwise'. Looking at the image of the participants, one sees a profusion of different cricket identities and dress codes. It was a veritable rainbow-nation cricket community in the making – a look into a future still more than eight decades away. Today the Barnato Trophy appropriately sits in the President's Suite at Newlands cricket ground.

35

Statistics for the Currie Cup and Barnato Memorial Trophy tournaments, 1889/90 to 1912/13

> I want to suggest that in the colonial situation
> presence was the critical question, the crucial word.
> Its denial was the keynote of colonialist ideology.

> – Chinua Achebe, 1992[1]

The 1912/3 Barnato and Currie Cup tournaments were the last held for ten and eight seasons respectively. As in 1899, when both the brand-new Barnato series and the Currie Cup were temporarily halted for four seasons, war once again intervened. Just over a decade after the disruptive South African War, World War I broke out. Unprecedented in scale, it once again deeply affected South African life and sport.

The pioneering South African Cricket Association (SACA) and South African Coloured Cricket Board (SACCB) inter-colonial and inter-provincial tournaments held before World War I laid the foundations for modern domestic cricket in South Africa. Provinces remain the main basis for organising cricket in South Africa today, and the current provincial competitions clearly evolved from these two early forms of provincial cricket (whose inheritors joined at the time of cricket unity in 1991), with the addition of professional franchises now situated between the amateur and international levels of cricket.

Below we provide the first-ever statistics for the early Barnato Memorial Trophy tournaments and integrate the list of Barnato players and the abbreviated scorecards before World War I with the records of the parallel and already well-documented Currie Cup.

What is to be done with the early South African provincial statistics revealed here? Having established the influence of the pioneering non-racial SACCB on the present and demonstrated its level of organisational sophistication, as well as having traced records for the five pre-1914 Barnato Memorial Trophy provincial tournaments for the first time, we need to ask the same questions posed before about the Native and Malay Inter-Town tournaments: on what grounds can this provincial cricket not be recognised as first-class, like the concurrent Currie Cup provincial tournaments and other first-class matches of their white counterparts in SACA?

Currently, there are a number of white two-day inter-town and friendly matches from 1888/9 to 1890/1 that have been categorised as first-class. Some of these were pre-SACA and some were later given provincial status by renaming them as provincial teams, for example Eastern Province SACA and Western Province SACA. The five two-day matches played by a team from Natal in 1889/90 against Port Elizabeth, Western Province Cricket Club, a Cape Town Club XI and Kimberley were retrospectively made first-class. In the last-mentioned game, a substitute was allowed to bat as well, something that happened in three other matches in South Africa before World War I given first-class status. In another case, a match was recognised as first-class although the full bowling analysis for the only 'full innings' of one team is not available. Likewise, a two-day friendly between The Army and Sir Pelham Warner's English tourists in Pretoria in 1905/6 has been declared first-class, even though only three of the army cricketers 'played any other first-class cricket' – they essentially became first-class because a jolly good show was had by all.[2] On at least one occasion somebody was included in a match against an English touring team as a reward for his organising work rather than for any talent in cricket. Added to these examples are the cases of players, such as the aristocrat Charles Coventry and Emile McMaster (both England) and the son of the cricket sponsor James Logan (South Africa SACA), who are on the lists of international cricketers purely because of privilege rather than merit. The first two were not even of league quality. McMaster's 'test' match against South Africa was his only first-class game. Logan had never played first-class cricket and was described as a 'passenger' who could be used only 'in an emergency'.[3] Only six of the 14 players in the privately organised 1901 'South African' team – given SACA national team status and selected at a time when 'Krom' Hendricks was still in form – were regarded as even 'remotely' representative of South Africa's best.[4] It was carefully chosen to ensure 'the essential blend of socialite, gentlemen cricketers alongside more skilled players'.[5] A match between the Wanderers Club and a 'Rest of South Africa' XI was also declared first-class in 1908/9.[6] 'In view of the loose interpretation of the law on the subject of first-class status before 1947, [the above matches] have been retained as first-class,' according to the Association of Cricket Statisticians.[7]

If the current official pre-1947 records are so flexible and generous, then why not give the same first-class status to the regular, often keenly contested Barnato Trophy matches between officially selected representative teams from 1898 to 1913? The Barnato tournament matches were played to a conclusion over four innings over two days on some of the best facilities of mainstream SACA affiliates. There were official umpires and, as per the constitution of SACCB, they were run according to the general rules applying to the mainstream SACA and the MCC, except that they were of two-day rather than three-day duration. There are many two-day matches in world cricket that have first-class status. It was only from 1947 onwards that the Association of Cricket Statisticians decided to exclude these from being first-class. Yet, even so, a two-day game by North-Eastern Transvaal SACA as late as 1957/8 is today still classified as first-class.

The reality of the matter is that current first-class records for early South African cricket were decided on by three white men, who had no understanding of the SACCB or successor black cricket boards and their tournaments, and who saw the prevailing apartheid in cricket as being 'normal'. This situation the Association of Cricket Statisticians in Britain, together with the cricket media and authorities, validated and codified formally in 1981. Neither the SACCB nor any other national South African cricket association outside the whites-only SACA was considered or given a chance. *A Guide to Important Cricket Matches Played in South Africa*, published by the Association in that year, consequently covered only whites-only cricket. Thus, an official record based on apartheid and colonialism continues to reproduce itself today in a democratic South Africa and the twenty-first-century cricket world. The only relief from this so far since unity in 1991 has come from the 223 scorecards of SACBOC and SACB first-class matches compiled by Krish Reddy, which will be published in full for the first time in volume 4 of this series, on *The History of South African Cricket Retold, Statistics, 1876–2016*.

The Association of Cricket Statisticians booklet explains that N.S. Curnow was the most influential early South African statistician and that he 'apparently off his own bat and without consulting anybody' decided on what was first-class or not: 'The decisions as to which early domestic matches warranted first-class status have long been taken by general acceptance based mainly on the initiative of Curnow, rather than by conscious decision by SACA [or any other national South African cricket controlling body].' 'A happy-go-lucky outlook ... prevailed concerning the status of the late 19th century matches.' 'It seems to have [just] "happened" as to which matches came to be regarded as first-class,' according to the Association.[8]

The time has come to change this. After *Cricket and Conquest* and its three companion volumes, and given the context provided in this book, can the Association of Cricket Statisticians and Historians, Cricket Archive and the game still justify leaving these pioneering South African cricketers and their statistics out of cricket's official records?

35.1   LIST OF SOUTH AFRICAN PROVINCIAL TROPHY WINNERS, 1889/90–1912/13[9]

SEASON	CURRIE CUP (SACA)	BARNATO MEMORIAL TROPHY (SACCB)
White Inter-Town tournaments replaced by Currie Cup in 1891/92 but Native and Malay Inter-Town tournaments continue		
1889/90	Transvaal (pre-SACA)	–
1890/91	Kimberley (later GW)	–
1891/92	–	–
1892/93	Western Province	–
1893/94	Western Province	–
1894/95	Transvaal	–
1895/96	–	–
1896/97	Western Province	–
1897/98	Western Province	–
African and Malay Inter-Town tournaments superseded by Barnato Memorial Trophy tournaments from 1898/99		
1898/99	–	Western Province (pre-SACCB)
1899/1900	No competitions, South African War	
1900/01	No competitions, South African War	
1901/02	No competitions, South African War	
1902/03	Transvaal	–
1903/04	Transvaal	Western Province
1904/05	Transvaal	–
1905/06	–	–
1906/07	Transvaal	–
1907/08	–	Western Province
1908/09	Western Province	–
1909/10	–	Griqualand West
1910/11	Natal	–

| 1911/12 | – | – |
| 1912/13 | Natal | Western Province |

The First World War from 1914 to 1918 put an end to SA domestic competitions for the next eight seasons before the resumption of the Currie Cup, and for ten seasons before the resumption of the Barnato Memorial Trophy.

35.2   LIST OF SOUTH AFRICAN PROVINCIAL PLAYERS, 1889/90–1912/13

35.2.1 LIST OF SACA CURRIE CUP PLAYERS, 1890/91 to 1912/13

For the full list of SACA Currie Cup players before World War I, see the website of Cricket Archive at cricketarchive.com. The editors are Peter Griffiths and Philip Bailey. Cricket Archive claims to be the most comprehensive cricket database on the internet, including 'scorecards for all matches of first-class cricket (including Test cricket)'. There is also a list of Currie Cup players in M.W. Luckin (ed. and comp.), *The History of South African Cricket, including the full scores of all important matches since 1876* (Johannesburg, 1915), pp. 332–345, but this is not as complete as the online list at Cricket Archive.

35.2.2 LIST OF SACCB BARNATO MEMORIAL TROPHY PLAYERS, 1889/90–1912/13[10]

Following the practice of existing SACA first-class records, which include certain white Inter-Town Tournament players under provincial and first-class lists (including for the period before the launch of SACA in 1890), this list includes the players (marked unofficial) who played for the joint Cape Town and Claremont Union team from the 1889/90 Malay Inter-Town Tournament (in effect, the first Western Province provincial team), the national South African Glover Cup team of 1890/91 and 1891/92, and the Malay XVIII that played the English professionals in 1891/92. The 1898/99 pre-SACCB Barnato tournament is also included.

Player	Team(s)	Season
Abadar, A	EP	1903/04
Abardien, A	EP	1907/08
Abdol, [X]	WP	1898/99
Abrahams, G	EP	1903/04, 1907/08
Abrahams, H[11] (Cape Town XI)	WP	1889/90 unofficial, 1890/91 unofficial
Abrahams, L	EP	1903/04
Abrahams, L	GW	1909/10
Abrahams, W[12] (Cape Town XI)	WP	1889/90 unofficial
Abrams, E 'Braima' (SA Glover Cup XI)	GW	1891/92 unofficial, 1898/99
Abrams, G	GW	1898/99
Abrams, M[13]	EP	1912/13 capt
Acardien, HD	EP	1909/10

Adams, E (Cape Town XI/Malay XVIII)	WP	1889/90 unofficial, 1891/92 unofficial
Adams, I	WP	1903/04
Adams, J (SA Glover Cup XI)	EP	1890/91 unofficial
Adams, J	EP	1907/08
Adams, M (SA Glover Cup XI)	[X]	1891/92
Allie, A	WP	1912/13
Allie, [X][14]	WP	1898/99
Amerein, [X] (Malay XVIII)	WP	1891/92 unofficial
Amsterdam, C	GW	1945/46
Anthony, D	Tvl	1907/08
Apples, T	Tvl	1909/10
Ariefdien, E[15] (Cape Town XI/Malay XVIII and SA Glover Cup XI)	WP	1889/90 unofficial, 1890/91 unofficial, 1891/92 unofficial
Aysen, J	GW	1927/28
Baderoon, [X] (Malay XVIII)	WP	1891/92 unofficial
Badin, O	WP	1912/13
Bassie, FJ	S Bdr	1898/99
Bob, W[16]	Tvl	1907/08
Bom, W (Eccentric)	GW	1907/08
Bopi, CN	S Bdr	1898/99
Buckas, Hoosen S	Ntl	1912/13
Bughwan, R	Ntl	1912/13 capt
Buhlungu, B	S Bdr	1898/99
Busakwe, S	EP	1898/99
Butler, RP	Ntl	1912/13
Celloo, A (Red Crescent)	GW	1907/08
Charles, B	WP	1898/99, 1903/04, 1907/08
Christian, G	WP	1912/13
Christopher, Albert	Ntl	1912/13
Connely, F	EP	1909/10
Connoly, T	EP	1909/10
Coopman, C	Tvl	1909/10
Crutse, [X]	GW	1898/99
Dalaza, [X]	EP	1898/99
Danter, D (Cape Town XI/Malay XVIII)	WP	1889/90 unofficial, 1891/92 unofficial
Davids, A	Tvl	1907/08
Davids, J	EP	1912/13
Davids, J	GW	1909/10
Davids, L	WP	1912/13
Davids, M	EP	1909/10
Davids, T	Tvl	1907/08
Davids, T	EP	1912/13

Davies, T	EP	1909/10
Dlepu, [X]	Qtn	1898/99
Du Toit, K[17] (Cape Town XI/SA Glover Cup XI/Malay XVIII)	WP	1889/90 unofficial, 1890/91 unofficial, 1891/92 unofficial
Ellie, V	WP	1907/08
Fakie, [X]	WP	1898/99
Fakier, T	Tvl	1907/08, 1909/10
Fataar, GS	Tvl	1907/08
Fataar, J	Tvl	1909/10
Fiti, [X]	EP	1898/99
Fobe, [X]	Qtn	1898/99
Fredericks, B (Good Hope)	GW	1907/08
Fredricks, A	WP	1907/08
Fredricks, A	Tvl	1909/10
Fredricks, F	WP	1898/99
Fredricks, L	WP	1898/99
Fredricks, T	WP	1898/99, 1903/04, 1907/08
Fredricks, W	GW	1909/10, 1912/13
Fredricks, [X]	WP	1903/04
Gertzen, A	WP	1912/13 capt
Gertzen, E	WP	1907/08, 1912/13
Gertzen, G	WP	1903/04, 1912/13
Gertzen, M[18]	WP	1907/08
Ghounaree, D	Ntl	1912/13
Gihier, A (Cape Town XI)	WP	1889/90 unofficial
Gosa, [X]	S Bdr	1898/99
Grant, [X] (Malay XVIII)	WP	1891/92 unofficial
Grendon, Robert 'Bob' (SA Glover Cup XI)	GW	1890/91 unofficial, 1891/92 unofficial
Haffajee, A	Ntl	1912/13
Hardien, A	GW	1907/08
Hardien, A	Tvl	1909/10
Haya, RZ	EP	1898/99
Hendricks, A (Malay XVIII, SA Glover Cup XI)	WP	1890/91 unofficial, 1891/92 unofficial, 1898/99, 1903/04, 1907/08, 1912/13
Hendricks, A	WP	1898/99
Hendricks, A	Tvl	1909/10
Hendricks, H 'Krom' (Malay XVIII)	WP	1891/92 unofficial
Hendricks, J	GW	1898/99
Hendricks, J	EP	1907/08
Hendricks, M	EP	1903/04, 1907/08, 1909/10

THE DIAMOND FIELDS ADVERTISER, KIMBERLEY, MONDAY, MARCH 31, 1913.

Sport and Pastime.

CURRIE CUP.

EAST vs. WEST.

PENINSULA'S BIG LEAD.

...ort Elizabeth, March 29.—(Reuter).— ...e last match in the Currie Cup ...cket Tournament was commenced in George's Park this morning, when ...stern Province met Eastern Pro- ...ce under agreeable conditions. The ...tors had first knock, and encoun- ...ed disaster early in the innings, three ...uable wickets falling for ten runs, ...piled in half-an-hour. Carstens ...d Yeoman became associated, and the ...re increased steadily. Both bats- ...n, especially ... punished sev- ...ly ... ...ding ...e o... ... several ...li ... with ... ef- ...t, and 90 ... in an hour ...l 50 ... ...en were ...l together ... interval, ...en the ... ...e wickets. ...n the ... there was ...large ... ...out-out bats- ...n hit mo... runs came ...idly, but ... ...ore was at 135 ...oman was cau... at mid-on. He ...yed most pati... for his 66, ...luded five ... The part- ...rship produ... in ... hours. ...rstens was ... runs later, ...ng caught ... ...d. His inn- ...gs was ch... ...etty drives ...st point. ... batsmen ...k more li... ... R. Hands ...d Blanckenberg. The side was dis- ...ssed just before the tea interval for

...he Eastern Province commenced their ...nings after tea, and the start was ...ne too promising, two wickets falling ... the first two overs for five runs ...ter the fall of the third wicket at 20, ...useful stand was made by Glisson and ...lridge, who carried the score to 65, ...en a separation was effected by ...anckenberg, who also accounted for ...ree more wickets. The whole si... ...s dismissed before the drawing ...mps for 71.

WESTERN PROVINCE.

...mmaille, b Crouch		
... Hands, lbw, b Crouch		
...earne, c Delbridge, b Porter ...		
...oman, c Longworth, b Crouch ...		
...rstens, c Taylor, b Porter ...		
... Hands, b Walters		
...anckenberg, c Lawrence, b Porter		
... Smidt, c Bennett, b Crouch ...	0
...ort, b Crouch	0
...aylor, c Glisson, b Crouch ...	23
...dgeon, not out	0
Extras	8

GRIQUALAND WEST vs EASTERN PROVINCE.

GRIQUAS' FIRST INNINGS LEAD.

The Barnato Tournament was contin- ued on the Eclectic ground on Saturday, when Griqualand West opposed a re- presentative Eastern Province eleven.

THE TEAMS.

Griqualand West.—T. Hendricks (capt.), M. Schreuder, B. Katta, M. Jar- dine, A. Jardine, F. Ntschoko, J. Koko- zela, J. Makoti, E. Jacobs, W. Freder- icks, K. Kieviet.

Eastern Province.—G. Abrahams (capt.), T. Davids, I. Liberty, J. Wat- son, I. Msimnka, ... Solomon, A. Ka- faar, J. Davids, ... B. Situnga, K. Jalill.

B. Sigamoney (...d) ...d A. Hend- ricks (West... Pr...ce... officiated as umpires.

Griqualand ... ... toss, and sent in Jar... ... the open- ing batsm... ...lay being the first p... entrusted with the a... ...ntury was hoisted on ... ...e result of careful and ... ...ing, having taken an hour ... ...e. This was, apparently, the ... for the players to hit out, the ...ury being hoisted about 30 minut... ...r. Numerous bowling chang... ...ied, but when the score had ... Jardine was caught and b... Davids for 63, which includ... ...rs, and took the batsman ... compile. Ntschoko ... ...crease, but the fielding a... ...as keen, the batsmen finding it ... difficult to score. The total was taken to 134 when Kie- viet returned a delivery into the bowler's ha...

pl... ...to... in... sc... ... J... me... ha... however, followed the same example as

RULES

1. That the name of the Board be the **South African Coloured Cricket Board** and that it adopt the **rules of the South African Association.**

25. That this Board does **not recognise any distinction amongst the various Sporting peoples of South Africa, whether by Creed, Nationality or otherwise.**

smart fielding. The game, after lunch, lasted only 20 minutes.

Griqualand West (1st innings) 209 runs.

EASTERN PROVINCE'S VENTURE.

The Easterns opened their innings with Abrahams and Davids, to the bowling of Jacobs and Kieviet, both batsmen starting with confidence. At 16 Abrahams was run out, owing to his partner failing to answer his call. His score was 25, which included five 4's.

J. Watson was the first-wicket man, but only to see Davids place his leg before the wicket, "without increasing the score. 46—2—21.

Msimnka joined Watson, both batsmen adding 21 runs to the score between them. The former, however, was caught in the slips through mishitting a ball.

Liberty now joined his club mate, who retired with his timber yard scattered, Jacobs being the "operator." The out- going batsman had compiled 14 runs.

J. Davids, going in next, gratified his desire by hitting one from Schreuder on to the stand, Jacobs meanwhile bowling two no-balls. J. Davids skied one, which fell into the hands of Makoti, the score now reading 88—5—12.

H. May followed, only to see his vice- captain, through snicking a ball, snapped up by Katta. H. Kafaar had his timber yard scattered by the first ball. A rot now set in, the remainder of the players being unable to cope with the bowling, Schreuder and Jacobs be- ing very destructive with the ball. The last wicket, however, made a desperate stand, and saw the century hoisted amidst loud cheers, the tea interval ar- riving with the score 104 runs for nine wickets.

CONCLUDING PLAY.

...neat to leave, being run out. Jardine

GRIQUA'S POOR START

score would have been greater had the fielding not been so excellent. 200—6—46.

Schroeder was foolishly run out, ow- ing to his partner not answering the call

scores:—

Griqualand West (1st innings)	209
Eastern Province (1st innings)	126
Griqualand West (2nd innings)	56

(handwritten insert) Barnato Cup / Tournament — Mr A. Christopher read letters & telegrams in regard to the Tournament & it was unanimously resolved "That Mr Haffejee be appointed as an Delegate to a meeting of the S.A.C.C. Board at Kimberley on the Saturday, 22nd Feby 1913.

Isaiah Bud Mbelle, (back right), founding secretary of both the South African Coloured Cricket Board and South African Coloured Rugby Football Board, with his brother-in-law Sol Plaatje (back left) and other community leaders from Kimberley.

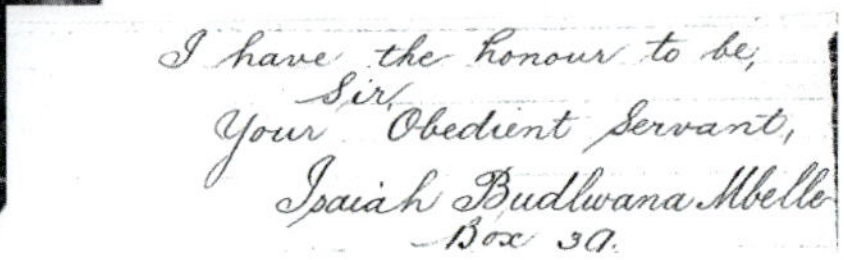

I have the honour to be,
Sir,
Your Obedient Servant,
Isaiah Budlwana Mbelle
Box 30.

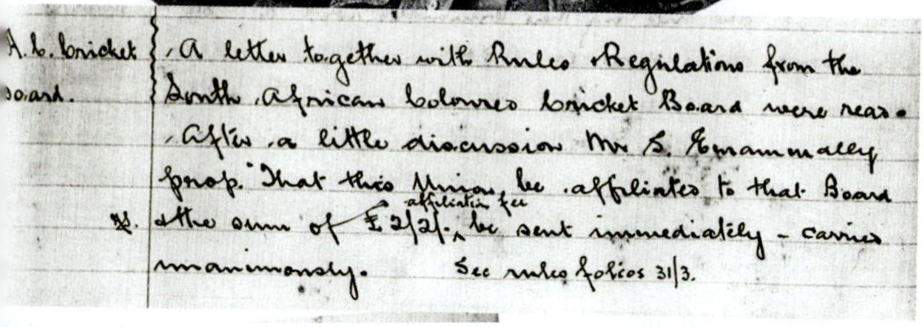

SACA's Currie Cup, 1890, and SACCB's Barnato Memorial Trophy, 1898, were, together with the County Championship, 1890, and the Sheffield Shield, 1892/3, world pioneers of domestic cricket competitions. Western Province were the strongest SACCB affiliate, winning four of the first five Barnato tournaments. Griqualand West were the other champions in Port Elizabeth in 1909/10 (below).

S.A.C. Cricket Board.

A letter together with Rules & Regulations from the South African Coloured Cricket Board were read. After a little discussion Mr S. Emammally prop. "That this Union be affiliated to that Board & the sum of £2/2/- (affiliation fee) be sent immediately – carried unanimously. See rules folios 31/3.

...ve: Transvaal and Kimberley teams that participated in the second Currie Cup tournament, ...1. Back row: G.K. Glover, F.G. Klinck, O.D. Wright, A. Soames, J. Hepburn, C.E. Finlason, ...Edington, A.E. Cooper, D. Lloyd, A.E. Ochse, J. Gyselman, E.A. Halliwell. Middle row: ...7.P. Walshe, E. Beech, D.J. Schuurman, C.S. Wimble, A.B. Tancred, F.W. Smith, G. Allsop, S. Field, ...Bailey, M.G. Williams. Front row: F. Fleischer, J.H.D. Piton, H. Tudhope, C.S.E. Rutherfoord.

...ow: Transvaal emerged as the strongest SACA province after 1900. The 1904/5 champion team, ...tained by Percy Sherwell (front centre). Jimmy Sinclair is on his right. The spin duo of Aubrey ...kner and Reggie Schwarz are standing third and fourth from the left.

CURRIE
CU
PRICE

CRICKET TOURNAMEN
FIFTH DAY, FRIDAY, APRIL 1
INTERNATIONAL
WINE & SPIRIT COMPANY
EXLEY'S BUILDINGS, SAUER STREET.
AGENTS FOR
J. H. & J. VAN RYN, CAPE TOWN.
The best House in Town for all kinds
of Cape and Foreign Liquors.
TRY OUR GOLDEN SHERRY.
W. J. BLAKE, Manager,
Printed on the Ground by the Argus Company, Limited.

The family of South African provincial cricketers: players and officials from the seven provinces at SACA's Currie Cup tournament, Durban, 1911.

The family of South African provincial cricketers: players and officials from the four provinces at SACCB's Barnato Memorial tournament, Kimberley, March 1913.

Top left: Natal captain R. Bughwan is flanked by his vice-captain D.S. Kaisval (left) and V.N. Thumbadoo, who topped the Natal team's bowling averages in the 1913 Barnato tournament in Kimberley.

Bottom left: The legendary Abdullah Abdurahman, president of the Western Province Coloured Cricket Union and the African Political Organisation (known as the APO), the first major 'coloured' political organisation, early 1900s.

Left: G.S. Rasdien, star Transvaal player in the Barnato tournament, from 1908 onwards, pictured here in later years when he was president of the Transvaal Coloured Cricket Union.

Below: Officials from the South African Coloured Cricket Board posing with the Barnato Memorial Trophy, Kimberley, March 1913. Only Natal captain R. Bhugwan (seated on the far right) and Albert Christopher (second row, fourth from left) have been identified.

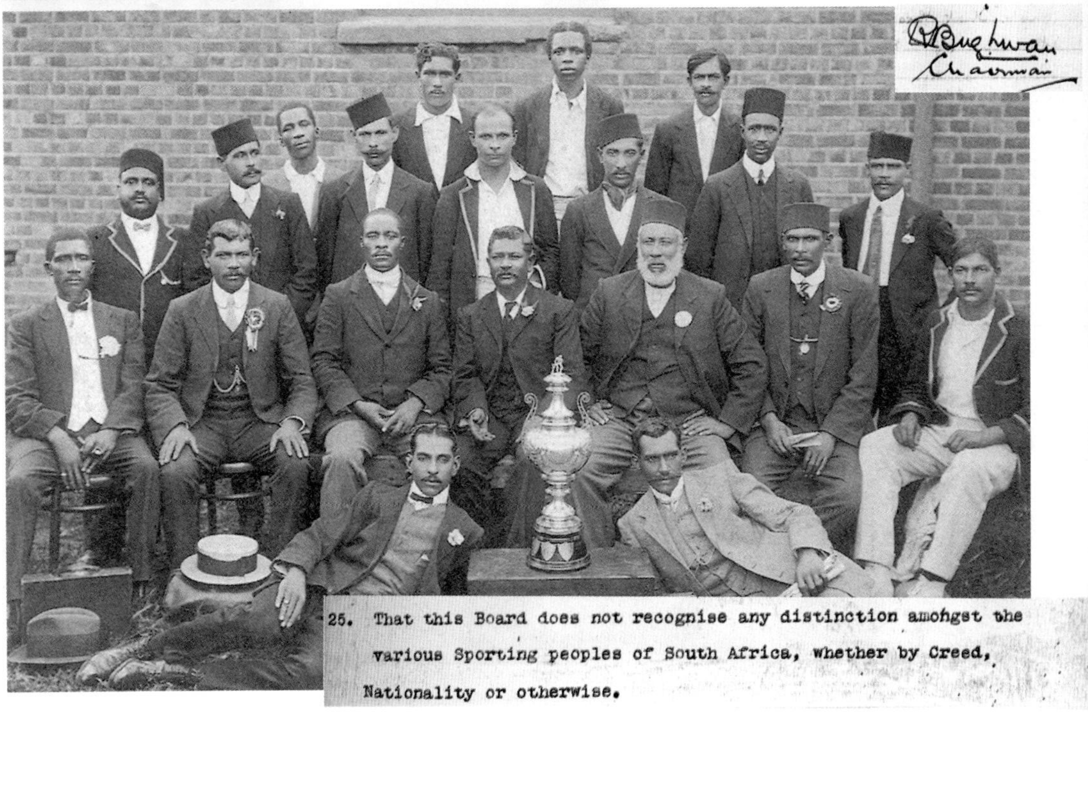

25. That this Board does not recognise any distinction amongst the various Sporting peoples of South Africa, whether by Creed, Nationality or otherwise.

Hendricks, O	WP	1912/13
Hendricks, S (Cape Town XI, Malay XVIII)	WP	1889/90 unofficial, 1891/92 unofficial
Hendricks, T (Malay XVIII)	WP	1891/92 unofficial, 1898/99
Hendricks, T (Red Crescent)	GW	1898/99, 1903/04, 1907/08, 1909/10, 1912/13 capt
Hendricks, [X]	GW	1898/99
Howell, T	Tvl	1907/08
Isaac, [X]	EP	1903/04
Isaacs, C	WP	1912/13
Isaacs, G	EP	1909/10
Isaacs, M or U[19]	EP	1903/04, 1907/08
Isaacs, M	WP	1907/08, 1912/13
Ismael, MS[20] (Cape Town XI)	WP	1889/90 unofficial
Jabaar, A	GW	1912/13
Jabaar, J[21] (Red Crescent)	GW	1903/04, 1907/08, 1909/10, 1912/13
Jacobs, D	Tvl	1907/08
Jacobs, E (Ottoman)	GW	1903/04, 1907/08, 1909/10, 1912/13
Jacobs, P	GW	1903/04
Jacobs, J (Malay XVIII)	WP	1891/92 unofficial
Jacobus, [X]	GW	1912/13
Jaffar, M[22] (Red Crescent)	GW	1907/08, 1909/10
Jalil, K	EP	1912/13
James, [X]	EP	1903/04
Jammie, I	WP	1912/13
Jappie, HG	EP	1907/08
Jardine, A[23] (Red Crescent)	GW	1907/08, 1909/10, 1912/13
Jardine, M[24] (Red Crescent)	GW	1903/04, 1907/08, 1912/13
Jocal, I[25]	EP	1909/10
Johnson, J	EP	1912/13
Johnson, J	Tvl	1907/08
Johnson, [X] (Malay XVIII)	WP	1891/92 unofficial
Joseph, [X]	WP	1898/99
Joubert, J	GW	1912/13
Kafaar, A	EP	1912/13
Kaisval, DS	Ntl	1912/13
Kasim, G	GW	1898/99
Katta, B	GW	1912/13
Kenny, A[26]	WP	1898/99, 1903/04
Kieviet, H	GW	1912/13

Kokozela, J[27]	GW	1912/13
Kriel, N	EP	1903/04
Kudoos, SA	Ntl	1912/13
Kunene, E	S Bdr	1898/99
Lachaba, [X]	EP	1909/10
Lagurdun, B	EP	1909/10
Lameke, [X]	Qtn	1898/99
Lamrah, M (Cape Town XI)	WP	1889/90 unofficial
Lazarus, Manuel B	Ntl	1912/13
Leich, C (Malay XVIII)	WP	1891/92 unofficial
Leila, [X]	EP	1903/04
Le Roux, A[28] (Cape Town XI, SA Glover Cup XI, Malay XVIII)	WP	1889/90 unofficial, 1890/91 unofficial, 1891/92 unofficial
Liberty, I	EP	1912/13
Liberty, T	EP	1903/04
Limberg, [X]	GW	1898/99
Lindeboom, S	EP	1907/08
Mabelana, N	EP	1898/99
Macumela, D	EP	1903/04
Madatt, M (SA Glover Cup XI)	[X]	1890/91 unofficial
Magied, M[29]	WP	1903/04, 1907/08
Magoda, G	Qtn	1898/99
Maininka, [X]	EP	1912/13
Majiet, A	Tvl	1909/10
Makothi, [X]	GW	1898/99
Makoti, J	GW	1912/13
Makwena (see Mokuena below)		
Maloni, T[30]	EP	1898/99
Malunga, [X]	GW	1898/99
Manga, [X]	Qtn	1898/99
Mannor, S[31] (Cape Town XI/Malay XVIII)	WP	1889/90 unofficial, 1891/92 unofficial
Martin, T (SA Glover Cup XI)	[X]	1891/92 unofficial
Matlala, A[32] (Duke of Wellington CC)	GW	1907/08, 1909/10
May, H	EP	1912/13
Mbuqe, [X]	Qtn	1898/99
Mkapa, T	S Bdr	1898/99
Mlungwana, A	Qtn	1898/99
Mohamed, S	Tvl	1907/08, 1909/10
Mokuena (or Makwena), D[33]	EP	1907/08
Mondel, [X]	GW	1898/99
Mralasi, [X]	Qtn	1898/99
Msimnka, I[34]	EP	1912/13
Mtshatshisa, W	EP	1898/99
Myburgh, F	EP	1909/10

Nackerdien, A	EP	1907/08
Neils, J	WP	1907/08
Ngcoza, [X]	EP	1898/99
Ngcweleshe, [X]	S Bdr	1898/99
Nqoro, [X]	S Bdr	1898/99
Ntshoko, F[35]	GW	1912/13
Ntshona, WB	S Bdr	1898/99
Nykoko, F[36] (Eccentric)	GW	1907/08 vice-captain
Nyusela, [X]	EP	1898/99
Palmer, J (SA Glover Cup XI)	GW	1890/91 unofficial
Phu, [X]	EP	1898/99
Ramakhutle, C[37] (Duke of Wellington CC)	GW	1907/08
Rasdien, GS	Tvl	1907/08, 1909/10
Rashe, G	S Bdr	1898/99
Regald, [X]	GW	1898/99
Ross, A	EP	1898/99
Rowan, L	EP	1909/10
Rune, D	EP	1898/99
Sahadien, [X] (Cape Town XI)	WP	1889/90 unofficial
Sakiem, E	EP	1903/04
Salayi, [X]	S Bdr	1898/99
Salie, M (SA Glover Cup XI)	GW	1890/91 unofficial
Sallie, D	GW	1909/10
Samsodien, L[38] (Cape Town XI/SA Glover Cup XI, Malay XVIII)	WP	1889/90 unofficial, 1890/91 unofficial, 1891/92 unofficial
Samsodien, R (SA Glover Cup XI)	WP	1891/92 unofficial
Schneider, M (Red Crescent)	GW	1907/08 capt
Schroeder, H	GW	1909/10
Schroeder, MC[39]	GW	1898/99, 1903/04, 1912/13
Sekile, [X]	GW	1898/99
September, I	EP	1909/10
Sheldon, A	WP	1903/04
Sigamoney, Bernard LE	Ntl	1912/13
Sinyane, P	EP	1903/04
Situnga, B[40]	EP	1912/13
Solomon, A	WP	1912/13
Solomon, AB	WP	1912/13
Solomon, S	EP	1912/13
Soobrail, M 'Tommy'	Ntl	1912/13
Souk, M (SA Glover Cup XI)	EP	1891/92 unofficial
Subban, R 'Billy'	Ntl	1912/13
Sukien, E	EP	1907/08
Taliep, [X][41]	WP	1898/99
Tape, M	WP	1907/08

Thomas, G	WP	1907/08
Thosko, F	GW	1912/13
Thumbadoo, VN	Ntl	1912/13
Toefie, T	WP	1907/08
Toefie, [X][42]	WP	1898/99
Tulwana, [X]	Qtn	1898/99
Van der Schyff, B[43] (Cape Town XI/Malay XVIII)	WP	1889/90 unofficial, 1891/92 unofficial
Vogt, J (SA Glover Cup XI)	GW	1890/91 unofficial
Watson, J	EP	1912/13
Williams, L	Tvl	1907/08

35.3 SUMMARISED SCORECARDS OF THE SACA CURRIE CUP AND SACCB BARNATO MEMORIAL TROPHY INTER-COLONIAL AND INTER-PROVINCIAL TOURNAMENTS, 1889/90–1912/13

1889/90

1st (PRE-SACA) CURRIE CUP TOURNAMENT, 5 and 7 APRIL 1890, KIMBERLEY[44]
Participating teams: Transvaal and Kimberley (later Griqualand West). A single challenge match. Kimberley were the holders of the Currie Cup after it was presented to them by the 1888/89 British touring team for being their best opponents during the tour.
Winners: Transvaal.

Transvaal beat Kimberley by six wickets
Kby 98 (AB Tancred 42; CH Vintcent 2/49, CA Smith 4/36, BS Wimble 4/8) and 235 (AB Tancred 106, CSE Rutherfoord 55; CH Vintcent 4/70, CA Smith 3/61, MP Bowden 2/7)
Tvl 117 (MP Bowden 63; GK Glover 6/50, A Rose-Innes 3/30) and 224/4 (MP Bowden 126*, CH Vintcent 60*; A Rose-Innes 2/68, IR Grimmer 2/51)

1890/91

2nd CURRIE CUP TOURNAMENT (SACA), 4–11 APRIL 1891, JOHANNESBURG
Participating teams: Kimberley and Transvaal. A single challenge match.
Winners: Kimberley.

Kimberley beat Transvaal by 58 runs
Kby 255 (J Gyselman 46, AB Tancred 89, MG Williams 30, E Beech 25; JHD Piton 7/82, AE Ochse 2/27) and 475 (J Gyselman 87, AB Tancred 62, CE Finlason 154*, AE Cooper 41; JHD Piton 6/122, FW Smith 2/73)
Tvl 313 (GE Lomas 47, AE Ochse 45, CS Wimble 62, FW Smith 36, JHD Piton 26; AB Tancred 2/47, D Lloyd 3/69, CE Finlason 3/68) and 359 (AE Ochse 99, DJ Schuurman 50, CS Wimble 46, G Allsop 33, F Fleischer 33, JHD Piton 37; D Lloyd 3/61, G Glover 3/94, AB Tancred 2/63)

Note: The fifth and final Inter-Town Tournament for the Champion Bat was also held in 1890/91 and was later officially declared first-class by SACA.

1891/92

No domestic competitions

1892/93

3rd CURRIE CUP TOURNAMENT (SACA), 15–24 NOVEMBER 1892, KIMBERLEY
Participating teams: Griqualand West, Transvaal, Western Province
Winners: Western Province.

Western Province beat Transvaal by 91 runs, 15–17 November 1892, Kimberley
WP 235 (F Hearne 102, RJ Gill 32; JH Sinclair 2/79, H Tudhope 3/65, WH Douglas 2/0) and 221 (AR Richards 47, CH Mills 31, G Cripps 27, VAW van der Bijl 61; JH Sinclair 5/90, H Tudhope 3/68)
Tvl 230 (JH Sinclair 37, TW Routledge 66, FG Klinck 33, WO Reid 33; VAW van der Bijl 2/44, CH Mills 3/49, J Middleton 3/47) and 135 (EA Halliwell 36; CH Mills 5/50, J Middleton 2/38)

Transvaal beat Griqualand West by 8 wickets, 18–21 November 1892, Kimberley
GW 154 (CSE Rutherfoord 35, AWP Walshe 32; H Tudhope 3/22, JH Sinclair 2/58, TW Routledge 2/26) and 159 (AWP Walshe 25; H Tudhope 2/70, GS Kempis 4/34)
Tvl 177 (EA Halliwell 43, TW Routledge 42, WH Douglas 50; H Graham 2/57, IR Grimmer 3/64, B Harvey 4/34) and 138/2 (TW Routledge 42*, PS Wimble 45)

Western Province beat Griqualand West by 109 runs, 21–24 November 1892, Kimberley
WP 266 (F Hearne 96, G Cripps 31, H Calder 29; GK Glover 3/82, D Lloyd 3/49) and 265 (G Cripps 102, AR Richards 27, H Calder 25, VAW van der Bijl 35*; GK Glover 5/94, IR Grimmer 2/96, B Harvey 2/28)
GW 292 (JM Powell 36, AWP Walshe 88, GK Glover 78; VAW van der Bijl 2/67, CH Mills 5/84) and 130 (CSE Rutherfoord 40, GK Glover 27; CH Mills 4/37, F Hearne 5/47)

1893/94

4th CURRIE CUP TOURNAMENT (SACA), 17–26 MARCH 1894, NEWLANDS RUGBY (NRG) AND CRICKET GROUNDS, CAPE TOWN
Participating teams: Eastern Province, Griqualand West, Natal, Transvaal, Western Province
Winners: Western Province.

Transvaal beat Eastern Province by 149 runs, 17–20 March 1894, Cape Town-NRG
Tvl 213 (CJE Smith 28, TW Routledge 33, EA Halliwell 83; E Crage 4/74, SJ Goldsmith 2/30) and 316 (JJ Slatem 34, CJE Smith 35, TW Routledge 77, FW Smith 43, CL Johnson 52; DC Parkin 3/66, RA Gleeson 2/19)
EP 241 (DC Parkin 34, RA Gleeson 67, FJ Cook 59; JH Sinclair 4/71, A Bailey 3/57) and 139 (FJ Cook 28, SJ Goldsmith 25; JH Sinclair 4/34, A Rose-Innes 2/12)

Natal beat Griqualand West by 6 wickets, 17–19 March 1894, Cape Town
GW 106 (CSE Rutherfoord 26, C Glover 31*; CFW Hime 2/46, HM Taberer 4/14, LG Robinson 3/28) and 92 (AWP Walshe 27; LG Robinson 7/50)
Ntl 123 (JC Burton 60; B Harvey 5/33, GK Glover 2/31, J Backmann 3/9) and 78/4 (CFW Hime 39; D Lloyd 2/6)

Griqualand West beat Eastern Province by 9 wickets, 20–21 March 1894, Cape Town-NRG
EP 72 (GK Glover 8/35, B Harvey 2/23) and 101 (GK Glover 7/33, B Harvey 3/56)
GW 114 (CSE Rutherfoord 34; DC Parkin 2/54, AH Britton 2/16, RA Gleeson 4/9) and 60/1 (C Glover 33*)

Natal beat Transvaal by 7 runs, 20–22 March 1894, Cape Town
Ntl 194 (CFW Hime 58, JHD Piton 36, EN Brooke 31; A Bailey 3/28, A Rose-Innes 2/9) and 127 (CFW Hime 29, CT Stuart 41; JH Sinclair 3/29, A Bailey 4/51, ID Difford 3/9)
Tvl 135 (CJE Smith 31, CL Johnson 35; JA Bell-Smyth 2/28, HM Taberer 4/41, LG Robinson 3/51) and 179 (EA Halliwell 32, MG Williams 29; CFW Hime 3/33, HM Taberer 3/72)

Western Province beat Natal by an innings and 60 runs, 24–26 March 1894, Cape Town
WP 338 (AR Richards 108, F Hearne 25, AW Seccull 43, HH Castens 61; HM Taberer 2/67, LG Robinson 5/95, BC Cooley 2/45)
Ntl 154 (HM Taberer 35, JA Bell-Smyth 28; CH Mills 4/57, GA Rowe 4/48) and 124 (LG Robinson 52; J Middleton 3/42, AW Seccull 6/48)

1894/95

5th CURRIE CUP TOURNAMENT (SACA), 13–22 APRIL, 1895, PIETERMARITZBURG/DURBAN
Participating teams: Natal, Transvaal, Western Province
Winners: Transvaal.

Transvaal beat Natal by 1 wicket, 13–16 April 1895, Pietermaritzburg
Ntl 204 (DC Davey 80; JT Hings 4/73, JH Sinclair 3/76, CJE Smith 2/28) and 236 (CFW Hime 41, CT Stuart 34, JA Bell-Smyth 55*, J Arnold 64; JT Hings 3/68, JH Sinclair 3/84, WO Reid 4/19)
Tvl 238 (JJ Slatem 25, TW Routledge 45, JT Hings 38, WO Reid 49*; HM Taberer 4/62, LG Robinson 2/48) and 203/9 (EA Halliwell 30, JJ Slatem 27, JH Sinclair 61*; HM Taberer 3/58, CB Llewellyn 3/39)

Final

Transvaal beat Western Province by 58 runs, 18–22 April 1895, Durban-Albert Park

Tvl 134 (EA Halliwell 45; GA Rowe 2/34, GA Lohmann 7/72) and 175 (AW Seccull 64, AE Ochse 41, EA Halliwell 36; GA Rowe 4/59, CH Mills 5/36)

WP 160 (CH Mills 25, H Calder 40*, J Middleton 32; JH Sinclair 3/52, JT Hings 3/47, G Beves 2/13) and 91 (C Mainon 29; JH Sinclair 7/40, JT Hings 2/36)

1895/96

No domestic competitions

1896/97

6th CURRIE CUP TOURNAMENT (SACA), 13–27 MARCH, JOHANNESBURG
Participating teams: Eastern Province, Griqualand West, Natal, Transvaal, Western Province
Winners: Western Province.

Natal beat Griqualand West by 8 wickets, 13–15 March 1897, Pirates Ground, Johannesburg

Ntl 271 (C Henwood 28, DC Davey 43, GH Whyte 58, JC Burton 25, PA Turner 47; GK Glover 4/91, AEA Eliot 4/73, FW Glover 2/36) and 41/2

GW 131 (GK Glover 46*, C Glover 32; PF Madden 5/48, CB Llewellyn 3/40) and 180 (JM Powell 26, GK Glover 76; PF Madden 2/49, CB Llewellyn 7/73)

Western Province beat Eastern Province by an innings and 7 runs, 13–15 March 1897, Johannesburg

WP 315 (CFH Prince 55, TE Etlinger 85, EL Challenor 76, JH Anderson 38; FE Tonks 3/46, H Calder 3/28)

EP 135 (RA Gleeson 27, DC Parkin 25; GA Rowe 3/71, GA Lohmann 4/49, F Kuys 2/12) and 173 (RA Gleeson 26, DJ Daly 45, FJ Cook 29*; GA Rowe 2/50, GA Lohmann 4/55, M Bisset 2/22)

Natal beat Eastern Province by 125 runs, 16–18 March 1897, Pirates Ground, Johannesburg

Ntl 90 (DC Parkin 6/29, FE Tonks 4/23) and 379 (AH Hime 34, DC Davey 57, GH Whyte 58, PA Turner 114, AW Nourse 61; DC Parkin 2/92, FE Tonks 2/81, AH Britton 3/29)

EP 91 (PF Madden 4/42, CB Llewellyn 6/43) and 253 (AH Britton 57, RA Gleeson 71, FJ Cook 25*; PF Madden 3/85, CB Llewellyn 5/80)

Western Province beat Griqualand West by an innings and 338 runs, 16–17 March 1897, Johannesburg

GW 80 (AW Powell 31; GA Rowe 5/33, GA Lohmann 4/44) and 65 (GK Glover 25; GA Rowe 5/15, GA Lohmann 5/44)

WP 483 (CFH Prince 27, AI Paine 220, TE Etlinger 111, M Bisset 58; C Glover 6/122, FW Glover 2/90)

Western Province beat Natal by 136 runs, 19–23 March 1897, Johannesburg

WP 185 (M Bisset 27, EL Challenor 46, JH Anderson 38*; PF Madden 4/60, CB Llewellyn 5/76) and 174 (F Kuys 28; PF Madden 3/58, CB Llewellyn 4/52, CFW Hime 3/28)

Ntl 94 (GA Rowe 6/43, GA Lohmann 3/42) and 129 (AH Hime 40; GA Rowe 4/60, GA Lohmann 4/26, M Bisset 2/20)

Western Province beat Transvaal by 72 runs, 24–27 March 1897, Johannesburg

WP 308 (CFH Prince 25, F Kuys 31, M Bisset 124*, JH Anderson 61; AE Cooper 8/80) and 173 (EL Challenor 34, GA Lohmann 44; AE Cooper 3/56, AW Seccull 3/46, JH Sinclair 4/66)

Tvl 311 (AB Tancred 39, JH Sinclair 78, TW Routledge 27, CJE Smith 70, LJ Tancred 40; GA Lohmann 5/96, GA Rowe 3/95, J Middleton 2/66) and 98 (G Beves 42; GA Lohmann 5/61, GA Rowe 3/12, J Middleton 2/20)

1897/98

7th CURRIE CUP TOURNAMENT (SACA), 30 MARCH – 12 APRIL 1898, CAPE TOWN
Participating teams: Border, Griqualand West, Natal, Transvaal, Western Province
Winners: Western Province.

Griqualand West beat Border by 3 wickets, 30–31 March 1898, Cape Town-NRG

Bdr 133 (SJ Snooke 29, CFH Prince 25; GK Glover 4/50, JM Powell 3/6, J Bissett 2/40) and 111 (SJH Bayly 36; GK Glover 6/49, J Bissett 4/29)

GW 95 (JM Powell 30; BE Gordon 4/35, T Riemer 4/27, SJ Snooke 2/3) and 152/7 (WA Shalders 37, JM Powell 45; BE Gordon 2/45, T Riemer 4/61)

Transvaal beat Natal by 77 runs, 30 March – 1 April 1898, Cape Town

Ntl 254 (EL Challenor 55, CB Llewellyn 63, AH Hime 51, GL Dalton 40; JH Sinclair 2/114, GH Shepstone 5/77, G Beves 2/26) and 79 (JH Sinclair 6/36, GH Shepstone 4/34)

Tvl 122 (CB Llewellyn 3/51, CP Carter 5/17, GH Whyte 2/20) and 288 (LJ Tancred 120, VM Tancred 33, GH Shepstone 37; GL Dalton 3/63, CB Llewellyn 3/67, AW Nourse 3/22)

Border beat Transvaal by 4 wickets, 1–4 April 1898, Cape Town-NRG
Tvl 223 (JH Sinclair 51, LJ Tancred 57, G Beves 33; CW King 5/41, CJ Weir 2/19) and 157 (JH Sinclair 29, VM Tancred 38, DG Cope 39; T Riemer 2/60, BE Gordon 6/60)
Bdr 220 (CFH Prince 60, SJ Snooke 31; JH Sinclair 6/63, GH Shepstone 2/49, G Beves 2/26) and 164/6 (CFH Prince 61, JC Warren 27; JH Sinclair 3/65, J McCarthy 3/41)

Griqualand West beat Natal by 7 wickets, 1–2 April 1898, Cape Town
Ntl 129 (EL Challenor 36, GC Collins 33; GK Glover 3/45, JM Powell 2/36, J Bissett 3/21, J Backmann 2/14) and 108 (DC Davey 26; JM Powell 6/42, J Bissett 2/17)
GW 205 (GK Glover 62, CJ Carroll 48; CB Llewellyn 4/75, AW Nourse 2/34, GH Whyte 3/15) and 33/3 (CP Carter 2/7)

Natal beat Border by 190 runs, 4–9 April 1898, Cape Town-NRG
Ntl 212 (GC Collins 63, BC Cooley 83; BE Gordon 6/93, CW King 2/22) and 375 (GC Collins 52, EL Challenor 54, DC Davey 78, GH Whyte 42, AW Nourse 57*; T Riemer 3/57, CW King 4/83, CJ Weir 2/20)
Bdr 183 (CFH Prince 26, CW King 55, BE Gordon 38; GL Dalton 4/27, GH Whyte 4/18) and 214 (JC Warren 45, SJ Snooke 26, T Riemer 42; CB Llewellyn 5/71, GL Dalton 2/49, GH Whyte 2/36)

Transvaal beat Griqualand West by an innings and 54 runs, 4–7 April 1898, Cape Town
Tvl 428 (JH Sinclair 73, VM Tancred 65, GH Shepstone 104, G Beves 60, J McCarthy 30; J Bissett 2/53, J Backmann 3/79, WA Shalders 3/30)
GW 138 (GK Glover 34, WA Shalders 25, H Tabuteau 37; JH Sinclair 7/58, J McCarthy 2/28) and 236 (GK Glover 26, JO Humphries 35, H Tabuteau 47, CJ Carroll 43; JH Sinclair 6/94, JJ Slatem 3/6)

Western Province beat Transvaal by 8 wickets, 9–12 April 1898, Cape Town
Tvl 68 (GA Rowe 5/29, J Middleton 5/36) and 136 (GH Shepstone 26; GA Rowe 3/46, J Middleton 7/64)
WP 83 (PS Twentyman Jones 31; JH Sinclair 8/40, GH Shepstone 2/39) and 123/2 (M Bisset 63*, HH Francis 38)

1898/99

1st (PRE-SACCB) BARNATO MEMORIAL TROPHY TOURNAMENT, 28 DECEMBER 1898 – 5 JANUARY 1899, PORT ELIZABETH[45]
Participating teams: Griqualand West, Port Elizabeth, Southern Border, Queenstown, Western Province.
Winners: Western Province.

Griqualand West beat Port Elizabeth by 5 wickets, 28 December 1898
PE 80 ([X] Dalaza 55; [X] Limberg 3/[x], [X] Abrams 3/[x], MC Schroeder 2/[x]) and 99 (T Maloni 23, [X] Fiti 22, S Busakwe 14; [X] Limberg 6/[x], MC Schroeder 2/[x])
GW 108 (G Abrams 55, [X] Hendricks 17, G Kasim 11; [X] Phu 4/[x], D Rune 3/[x], T Maloni 2/[x]) and 72/5 ([X] Mondel 35, [X] Abrams 10; T Maloni 3/[x], [X] Mtshutshisa 2/[x])

Western Province beat Southern Border by 37 runs, 29 December 1898
WP 27 ([X] Taliep 16; B Buhlungu 8/[x]) and 219 (A Hendricks 65, A Kenny 62, [X] Joseph 23; E Kunene 6/[x], B Buhlungu 2/[x])
Southern Border 145 (CN Bopi 40*, WB Ntshona 34, B Buhlungu 24; [X] Abdol 5/[x], [X] Hendricks 2/[x]) and 64 (G Rashe 20; [X] Abdol 4/[x], T Hendricks 3/[x], T Fredricks 3/[x])

Queenstown beat Port Elizabeth by 4 wickets, 30 December 1898
PE 75 (W Mtshutshisa 18, [X] Nyusela 14, D Rune 13) and 134 (W Mtshutshisa 43, N Mabelana 18, D Rune 17)
Queenstown 143 ([X] Fobe 38, [X] Mbuqe 25, A Mlungwana 22) and 69/6 ([X] Tulwana 26, A Mlungwana 20)

Western Province beat Griqualand West by 6 wickets, 2 January 1899
GW 72 and 198 ([X] Mondel 63, [X] Abrams 43)
WP 145 and 127/4

Southern Border beat Port Elizabeth by 3 wickets, 4 January 1899
PE 72 (N Mabelana 18, A Ross 16) and 81 ([X] Dalaza 23, [X] Nyusela 13, [X] Fiti 12, D Rune 12)
Southern Border 78 ([X] Nqoro 29, WB Ntshona 12) and 76/7 (FJ Bassie 42)

Griqualand West beat Queenstown by 3 wickets, 5 January 1899
Queenstown 144 ([X] Tulwana 24, [X] Dlepu 23*, [X] Mralasi 18) and 140 ([X] Mralasi 30, A Mlungwana 30, [X] Manga 24)
Griqualand West 187 ([X] Mondel 55, MC Schroeder 32, [X] Limberg 27, [X] Abrams 20) and 97/7

Western Province vs Port Elizabeth, 5 January 1899
[Details unknown]

1899/1900
No domestic competitions, South African War

1900/01
No domestic competitions, South African War

1901/02
No domestic competitions, South African War

1902/03

8th CURRIE CUP TOURNAMENT (SACA), 6–16 APRIL 1903, PORT ELIZABETH
Participating teams: Border, Eastern Province, Griqualand West, Transvaal, Western Province
Winners: Transvaal.

For the full scores of this tournament, see the website of Cricket Archive at cricketarchive.com which has 'scorecards for all matches of first-class cricket (including Test cricket)'. The Currie Cup scores also appear in M.W. Luckin (ed. and comp.), *The History of South African Cricket, including the full scores of all important matches since 1876* (Johannesburg, 1915), pp. 239–246, but these scorecards are not as complete as those online at Cricket Archive.

1903/04

9th CURRIE CUP TOURNAMENT (SACA), 24 NOVEMBER 1903 – 29 MARCH 1904, DECENTRALISED – PLAYED AT VARIOUS CENTRES
Participating teams: Border, Eastern Province, Griqualand West, Natal, Orange Free State, Transvaal, Western Province
Winners: Transvaal.

For the full scores of this tournament see the website of Cricket Archive at cricketarchive.com which has 'scorecards for all matches of first-class cricket (including Test cricket)'. The Currie Cup scores also appear in M.W. Luckin (ed. and comp.), *The History of South African Cricket, including the full scores of all important matches since 1876* (Johannesburg, 1915), pp. 239–246, but these scorecards are not as complete as those online at Cricket Archive.

* * * * *

2nd BARNATO MEMORIAL TROPHY TOURNAMENT (SACCB), 30 MARCH – 5 APRIL 1904, KIMBERLEY[46]
Participating teams: Eastern Province, Griqualand West and Western Province
Winners: Western Province.

Western Province beat Griqualand West by 23 runs, 30–31 March 1904, Eclectic CC Ground
WP 130 ([X] Magied 32, T Fredricks 23; J Jabaar 5/13, E Jacobs 5/31) and 79 (J Jabaar 9/40, E Jacobs 1/26)
GW 86 (A Sheldon 8/45, G Gertzen 2/33) and 100 (T Hendricks 41, M Schroeder 21; [X] 4/[x], [X] 4/[x])

Griqualand West beat Eastern Province by 101 runs, 31 March, 1 and 2 April 1904, Eclectic CC Ground
GW 239 and 136/9 dec (T Hendricks 44, MC Schroeder 43; [X] James 4/44, [X] Isaac 2/32, [X] Leila 2/36)
EP 98 (L Abrahams 42; J Jabaar 7/62, P Jacobs 2/17) and 176 (G Abrahams 81, L Abrahams 47; J Jabaar 6/75, M Jardine 2/6)

Western Province beat Eastern Province by [x], 2, 4 and 5 April 1904, Eclectic CC Ground
WP 139 (A Kenny 46, B Charles 22, A Hendricks 21; [X] 4/45) and [x])
EP 197 (G Abrahams 123, E Sakiem 20; A Sheldon 6/46, G Gertzen 2/37) and [x])

1904/05

10th CURRIE CUP TOURNAMENT (SACA), 25 NOVEMBER 1904 – 27 MARCH 1905, DECENTRALISED – PLAYED AT VARIOUS CENTRES
Participating teams: Eastern Province, Griqualand West, Natal, Rhodesia, South Western Districts, Transvaal, Western Province
Winners: Transvaal.

For the full scores of this tournament see the website of Cricket Archive at cricketarchive.com which has 'scorecards for all matches of first-class cricket (including Test cricket)'. The Currie Cup scores also appear in M.W. Luckin (ed. and comp.), *The History of South African Cricket, including the full scores of all important matches since 1876* (Johannesburg, 1915), pp. 239–246, but these scorecards are not as complete as those online at Cricket Archive.

1905/06

SACA or SACCB domestic competitions

1906/07

11th CURRIE CUP TOURNAMENT (SACA), 26 DECEMBER 1906 – 9 JANUARY 1907, JOHANNESBURG
Participating teams: Eastern Province, Griqualand West, Natal, Orange Free State, Transvaal, Western Province
Winners: Transvaal.

For the full scores of this tournament see the website of Cricket Archive at cricketarchive.com which has 'scorecards for all matches of first-class cricket (including Test cricket)'. The Currie Cup scores also appear in M.W. Luckin (ed. and comp.), *The History of South African Cricket, including the full scores of all important matches since 1876* (Johannesburg, 1915), pp. 239–246, but these scorecards are not as complete as those online at Cricket Archive.

1907/08

3rd BARNATO MEMORIAL TROPHY TOURNAMENT (SACCB), 23 March – 1 April 1908, CAPE TOWN CC GROUND, NEWLANDS, CAPE TOWN[47]
Participating teams: Eastern Province, Griqualand West, Transvaal, Western Province
Winners: Western Province.

Western Province beat Eastern Province by an innings and 42 runs, 23–24 March 1908[48]
WP 251 (E Gertzen 64, A Hendricks 42, G Thomas 35, M Magied 22; A Abardien 5/67, HG Jappie 2/44, J Adams 2/58)
EP 92 (M Hendricks 36, A Nackerdien 24; M Isaacs 6/26, E Gertzen 2/8, M Gertzen 2/13) and 117 (HG Jappie 35, G Abrahams 25, J Adams 14; E Gertzen 4/16, V Ellie 3/23, M Gertzen 2/23)

Griqualand West beat Transvaal by an innings and 40 runs, 24–25 March 1908[49]
Tvl 248 (T Fakier 52, GS Rasdien 42, S Mohamed 33, D Anthony 32; J Jabaar 7/[x] and 41 (A Davids 13, T Davids 10; J Jabaar 5/[x], E Jacobs 5/[x])
GW 329 (F Nykoko 117, J Jabaar 52, A Matala 32, A Jardine 26; S Mohamed 5/[x], GS Rasdien 3/[x])

Eastern Province beat Transvaal by six wickets, [x] March 1908[50]
Tvl 140 and 205 (S Mohamed 57, T Davids 45, A Davids 39; [X] Hendricks 5/[x])
EP 297 and 56/4 (M Hendricks 16, U Isaacs 14, G Abrahams 11; GS Fataar, 2/[x], S Mohamed 1/[x])

Griqualand West vs Eastern Province [details and date unknown]

Western Province beat Griqualand West by 91 runs, 28 and 30 March 1908[51]
WP 167 (M Magied 58, T Fredricks 31, M Isaacs 24; J Jabaar 5/[x], E Jacobs 4/[x]) and 262 (B Charles 71, T Toefie 51, T Fredricks 38, M Magied 36; A Jardine 4/[x], E Jacobs 3/[x], J Jabaar 3/[x])
GW 190 (T Hendricks 101*, M Jaffar 27, E Jacobs 13, J Jabaar 12; M Tape 3/[x]) and 148 (T Hendricks 38, F Nykoko 35, J Jabaar 20, M Jardine 17; M Tape 6/[x], E Gertzen 2/[x])

Western Province beat Transvaal by 102 runs, 31 March – 1 April 1908[52]
WP 196 (M Tape 42, M Magied 37, G Thomas 26, E Gertzen 23, GS Rasdien 4/[x], T Howell 3/[x]) and 203 (M Gertzen 55, M Isaacs 50, M Magied 18; GS Fataar 4/[x], T Fakier 4/[x])
Tvl 115 (A Davids 33, T Fakier 23, L Williams 11, T Davids 11; M Tape 7/11, M Isaacs 2/[x]) and 182 (GS Rasdien 53, GS Fataar 51, J Johnson 25; M Tape 4/[x], M Isaacs 2/[x])

1908/09

12th CURRIE CUP TOURNAMENT (SACA), 19–30 MARCH 1909, CAPE TOWN
Participating teams: Border, Eastern Province, Transvaal, Western Province
Winners: Western Province.

For the full scores of this tournament, see the website of Cricket Archive at cricketarchive.com which has 'scorecards for all matches of first-class cricket (including Test cricket)'. The Currie Cup scores also appear in M.W. Luckin (ed. and comp.), *The History of South African Cricket, including the full scores of all important matches since 1876* (Johannesburg, 1915), pp. 239–246, but these scorecards are not as complete as those online at Cricket Archive.

1909/10

4th BARNATO MEMORIAL TROPHY TOURNAMENT (SACCB), 28 MARCH – 2 APRIL 1910, UNION CC GROUND, ST GEORGE'S PARK, PORT ELIZABETH[53]
Participating teams: Eastern Province, Griqualand West, Transvaal – Western Province did not participate

A rest day was observed on Good Friday, 1 April 1910. At least one match started on the Thursday and was concluded on the Saturday.[54]
Winners: Griqualand West.

Griqualand West beat Eastern Province by an innings and 4 runs, 28–29 March 1910[55]
GW 178 (W Fredricks 68, J Jabaar 35, H Scroeder 21, T Hendricks 21; I Jocal 5/[x], T Davids 3/[x])
EP 58 (T Davids 12, I September 12; J Jabaar 6/[x], E Jacobs 4/[x]) and 116 (I September 43, T Davids 24, F Myburgh 21*, M Davids 10; E Jacobs 7/[x], J Jabaar 3/[x])

Transvaal beat Eastern Province by 48 runs, 30–31 March 1910
Tvl 119 (S Mohamed 36, C Coopman 14, T Apples 14; L Rowan 4/[x], F Myburgh 4/[x]) and 131 (A Majiet 29, C Coopman 28, A Hardien 16; I Jocal 3/[x], T Davids 3/[x])
EP 143 (HD Acardien 30, T Davids 29, M Davids 25, G Isaacs 20; S Mohamed 2/[x], A Fredricks 2/[x]) and 59

Griqualand West beat Transvaal, 31 March and 2 April 1910
GW 117 and 31/1
Tvl 42 and [x]

1910/11

13th CURRIE CUP TOURNAMENT (SACA), 13–28 MARCH 1911, DURBAN
Participating teams: Border, Eastern Province, Griqualand West, Orange Free State, Natal, Transvaal, Western Province
Winners: Natal.

For the full scores of this tournament see the website of Cricket Archive at cricketarchive.com which has 'scorecards for all matches of first-class cricket (including Test cricket)'. The Currie Cup scores also appear in M.W. Luckin (ed. and comp.), *The History of South African Cricket, including the full scores of all important matches since 1876* (Johannesburg, 1915), pp. 239–246, but these scorecards are not as complete as those online at Cricket Archive.

1911/12

No SACA or SACCB domestic competitions

1912/13

14th CURRIE CUP TOURNAMENT (SACA), 14 DECEMBER 1912 – 31 MARCH 1913, DECENTRALISED – PLAYED AT VARIOUS CENTRES
Participating teams: Eastern Province, Orange Free State, Natal, Transvaal, Western Province
Winners: Natal.

For the full scores of this tournament see the website of Cricket Archive at cricketarchive.com which has 'scorecards for all matches of first-class cricket (including Test cricket)'. The Currie Cup scores also appear in M.W. Luckin (ed. and comp.), *The History of South African Cricket, including the full scores of all important matches since 1876* (Johannesburg, 1915), pp. 239–246, but these scorecards are not as complete as those online at Cricket Archive.

* * * * *

5th BARNATO MEMORIAL TROPHY TOURNAMENT (SACCB), 24–28 MARCH 1913, KIMBERLEY[56]
Participating teams: Eastern Province, Griqualand West, Natal, Western Province
Winners: Western Province.

Griqualand West beat Natal by an innings and 292 runs, 24–25 March 1913
GW 482/6 dec (T Hendricks 150*, A Jardine 111, MC Schroeder 69, J Jabaar 59; A Haffajee 2/47, BLE Sigamoney 2/70, R Subban 2/118)
Ntl 96 (DS Kaisval 45; E Jacobs 6/44, J Jabaar 2/21) and 94 (R Subban 43; J Jabaar 4/27, E Jacobs 4/32, J Kokozela 2/19)

Western Province beat Eastern Province by an innings and 213 runs, 25–26 March 1913
WP 290 (G Christian 91, L Davids 73*, AB Solomon 56)
EP 33 (M Isaacs 5/[x], I Jammie 4/[x]) and 44 (M Isaacs 8/[x], I Jammie 2/[x])

Western Province beat Natal by an innings and 66 runs, 26–27 March 1913
WP 296 (M Isaacs 55, G Christian 54, A Solomon 50, I Jammie 30; SA Kudoos 4/60, DS Kaisval 2/29)
Ntl 119 (R Subban 28, R Bughwan 22; A Allie 3/16, G Christian 3/30, M Isaacs 3/33) and 111 (MB Lazarus 24, R Subban 20; G Christian 5/23, M Isaacs 3/30, O Hendricks 2/2)

Eastern Province beat Natal by 231 runs, [date unknown]
EP 129 (G Abrahams 33, I Msimnka 25*, A Kafaar 23; VN Thumbadoo 7/41, BLE Sigamoney 2/34) and 293 (T Davids 127, S Solomon 43*, G Abrahams 35, I Msimnka 25; BLE Sigamoney 3/78, DS Kaisval 2/28)
Ntl 110 (R Subban 27; S Solomon 4/33, I Msimnka 3/21, H May 2/12) and 81 (S Solomon 6/27, G Abrahams 2/16)

Griqualand West beat Eastern Province by 78 runs, [date unknown]
GW 209 (A Jardine 63, H Kieviet 49, F Ntshoko 46, T Hendricks 31*; I Msimnka 2/12, G Abrahams 2/23, H May 2/33, S Solomon 2/47) and 117 (F Ntshoko 28*, A Jardine 20; S Solomon 6/34, I Msimnka 2/28)
EP 106 (G Abrahams 25, T Davids 21; E Jacobs 5/55, MC Schroeder 4/25) and 142 (G Abrahams 45, I Msimnka 36, H May 23; E Jacobs 6/53, MC Schroeder 4/42)

Western Province beat Griqualand West by 183 runs, [date unknown]
WP 190 (L Davids 31, M Isaacs 29, AB Solomon 40*; E Jacobs 6/66, J Jabaar 4/74) and 155 (AB Solomon 74, O Hendricks 25*; E Jacobs 6/57, A Jabaar 2/52)
GW 73 (J Kokozela 22; O Badin 5/30, G Christian 3/9) and 89 (J Jabaar 30; O Badin 5/40, G Christian 5/42)

35.4 STATISTICAL OVERVIEW OF THE SACA CURRIE CUP AND SACCB BARNATO MEMORIAL TROPHY TOURNAMENT RECORDS, 1889/90 TO 1912/13

35.4.1 SACCB BARNATO MEMORIAL TROPHY, 1898/99 to 1912/13

BATTING RECORDS
Six centuries were scored in 25 games.

HIGHEST INDIVIDUAL SCORES
1. T Hendricks 150*, Griqualand West vs Natal, 1912/13*
2. T Davids 127, Eastern Province vs Natal, 1912/13
3. G Abrahams 123, Eastern Province vs Western Province, 1903/04
4. F Nykoko 117, Griqualand West vs Transvaal, 1907/08
5. A Jardine 111, Griqualand West vs Natal, 1912/13*
6. T Hendricks 101*, Griqualand West vs Western Province, 1907/08

* Note: T. Hendricks and A. Jardine batted together in recording these scores.

HIGHEST TEAM TOTALS
1. 482/6 dec, Griqualand West vs Natal, 1912/13
2. 329, Griqualand West vs Transvaal, 1907/08
3. 297, Eastern Province vs Transvaal, 1907/08
4. 293, Eastern Province vs Natal, 1912/13
5. 296, Western Province vs Natal, 1912/13

HIGHEST TOTAL BY EACH TEAM
Eastern Province 297, vs Transvaal, 1907/08
Griqualand West 482/6 dec, vs Natal, 1912/13
Natal 119, vs Western Province, 1912/13
Queenstown 144, vs Griqualand West, 1898/99
Southern Border 145, vs Western Province, 1898/99
Transvaal 248, vs Griqualand West, 1907/08
Western Province 296, vs Natal, 1912/13

LOWEST TOTAL BY EACH TEAM
Eastern Province 33, vs Western Province, 1912/13
Griqualand West 72, vs Western Province, 1898/99
Natal 81, vs Eastern Province, 1912/13
Queenstown 140, vs Griqualand West, 1898/99
Southern Border 64, vs Western Province, 1898/99
Transvaal 41, vs Griqualand West, 1907/08
Western Province 27, vs Southern Border, 1898/99

BOWLING RECORDS
10 or more wickets were taken in a match at least ten times. (Records not complete.)

BEST BOWLING IN A MATCH
1. 14/53 (5/13 and 9/40), J Jabaar, Griqualand West vs Western Province, 1903/04
2. 13/137 (7/62 and 6/75), J Jabaar, Griqualand West vs Eastern Province, 1903/04
3. 12/123 (6/66 and 6/57), E Jacobs, Griqualand West vs Western Province, 1912/13
4. 11/108 (5/55 and 6/53), E Jacobs, Griqualand West vs Eastern Province, 1912/13
5. 10/60 (4/33 and 6/27), S Solomon, Eastern Province vs Natal, 1912/13

Note:
M Isaacs took 5/[x] and 8/[x] for Western Province vs Eastern Province in totals of 33 and 44, 1912/13
J Jabaar took 7/[x] and 5/[x] for Griqualand West vs Transvaal in totals of 248 and 41, 1907/08
M Tape took 7/11 and 4/[x] for Western Province vs Transvaal in totals of 115 and 182, 1907/08
E Jacobs took 4/[x] and 7/[x] for Griqualand West vs Eastern Province in totals of 58 and 116, 1909/10
B Buhlungu took 8/[x] and 2/[x] for Southern Border vs Western Province in totals of 27 and 219, 1898/99

BEST BOWLING IN AN INNINGS
1. 9/40, J Jabaar, Griqualand West vs Western Province, 1903/04
2. 8/45, A Sheldon, Western Province vs Griqualand West, 1903/04
3. 7/11, M Tape, Western Province vs Transvaal, 1907/08
4. 7/41, VN Thumbadoo, Natal vs Eastern Province, 1912/13
5. 7/62, J Jabaar, Griqualand West vs Eastern Province, 1903/04
6. 6/26, M Isaacs, Western Province vs Eastern Province, 1907/08

Note:
B Buhlungu took 8/[x] for Southern Border vs Western Province in a total of 27, 1898/99
M Isaacs took 8/[x] for Western Province vs Eastern Province in a total of 33, 1912/13
J Jabaar took 7/[x] for Griqualand West vs Transvaal in a total of 248, 1907/08
E Jacobs took 7/[x] for Griqualand West vs Eastern Province in a total of 116, 1909/10

TEAM RECORDS

TEAM	PLAYED	WON	LOST	RESULT UNKNOWN
Eastern Province	14	2	10	2
Griqualand West	13	8	4	1
Natal	3	0	3	0
Queenstown	2	1	1	0
Southern Border	2	1	1	0
Transvaal	5	1	4	0
Western Province	11	10	0	1

35.4.2 SACA CURRIE CUP, 1889/90–1912/13

BATTING RECORDS
46 centuries were scored in 95 games.

HIGHEST INDIVIDUAL SCORES
1. HW Taylor 250*, Natal vs Transvaal, 1912/13
2. AI Paine 220, Western Province vs Griqualand West, 1896/97
3. AW Nourse 212, Natal vs Griqualand West, 1906/07
4. GPD Hartigan 176*, Border vs Eastern Province, 1910/11
5. HW Taylor 173, Natal vs Griqualand West, 1910/11

HIGHEST TEAM TOTALS
1. 509, Western Province vs Griqualand West, 1906/07
2. 503, Transvaal vs Orange Free State, 1903/04
3. 483, Western Province vs Griqualand West, 1896/97
4. 475, Kimberley vs Transvaal, 1890/91
5. 428, Transvaal vs Griqualand West, 1897/98

HIGHEST TOTAL BY EACH TEAM
Border 391/5*, vs Eastern Province, 1910/11
Eastern Province 403, vs Griqualand West, 1906/07
Griqualand West 475, vs Transvaal, 1890/91
Natal 418, vs Griqualand West, 1906/07
Orange Free State 326, vs Natal, 1910/11
Rhodesia 115, vs Transvaal, 1904/05
South Western Districts 60, vs Western Province, 1904/05
Transvaal 503, vs Orange Free State, 1903/04
Western Province 509, vs Griqualand West, 1906/07

LOWEST TOTAL BY EACH TEAM
Border 43, vs Transvaal, 1908/09
Eastern Province 40, vs Orange Free State, 1910/11
Griqualand West 31, vs Natal, 1906/07
Natal 79, vs Transvaal, 1897/98
Orange Free State 51, vs Eastern Province, 1906/07
Rhodesia 55, vs Transvaal, 1904/05
South Western Districts 45, vs Western Province, 1904/05
Transvaal 58, vs Natal, 1910/11
Western Province 83, vs Transvaal, 1897/98

BOWLING RECORDS
10 or more wickets were taken in a match 43 times.

BEST BOWLING IN A MATCH
1.   16/38 (6/12 and 10/26), AEE Vogler, Eastern Province vs Griqualand West, 1906/07
2.   15/68 (8/35 and 7/33), GK Glover, Griqualand West vs Eastern Province, 1893/94
3.   14/58 (6/34 and 8/24), AEE Vogler, Eastern Province vs Orange Free State, 1906/07
4.   13/79 (7/56 and 6/23), AT Lyons, Eastern Province vs Griqualand West, 1902/03
5.   13/85 (6/30 and 7/55), JH Sinclair, Transvaal vs Eastern Province, 1902/03

BEST BOWLING IN AN INNINGS
1.   10/26, AEE Vogler, Eastern Province vs Griqualand West, 1906/07
2.   8/12, RW Norden, Transvaal vs Rhodesia, 1904/05
3.   8/18, JJ Kotze, Transvaal vs Griqualand West, 1902/03
4.   8/20, JL Cox, Natal vs Transvaal, 1910/11
5.   8/24, AEE Vogler, Eastern Province vs Orange Free State, 1906/07

TEAM RECORDS

TEAM	PLAYED	WON	LOST	DRAWN
Border	17	6	10	1
Eastern Province	27	7	20	0
Griqualand West	26	4	21	1
Natal	27	19	8	0
Orange Free State	16	3	13	0
Rhodesia	1	0	1	0
South Western Districts	1	0	1	0
Transvaal	41	31	10	0
Western Province	34	24	10	0

36

Old wine in new vessels

The five cricket provinces in the Cape Colony

> We were agreeably surprised to observe the
> amicable relations existing between the Europeans
> and the natives who were allowed the use of the
> Pavilion and grounds for this important fixture.

> – *Izwi Labantu*, 7 January 1909

The new inter-colonial and (and from 1910) inter-provincial competitions for the Currie Cup of SACA and the Barnato Memorial Trophy of SACCB were based on established local cricket infrastructures, evolving to deal with the new reality of inter-colonial and international cricket. This chapter looks at the different geographical regions and the interlinked developments among both black and white cricketers that shaped provincial cultures.

Cape Town, Kimberley and the eastern Cape towns of King William's Town and Port Elizabeth dominated the beginnings of competitive cricket in South Africa. With the emergence of the new provincial system in the 1890s, five provinces based on these axes emerged in the Cape Colony, and provincial competitions founded on the inter-town tournaments were started. The new cricket entities for both SACA and SACCB expanded on the town-based model and became Western Province, Eastern Province, Border and Griqualand West. There was also the rural-based minnow union of South Western Districts, which played in one Currie Cup competition before 1914. It too had a strong culture of cricket in the black communities.

Bristling with confidence because of its diamond wealth, Kimberley was the launching pad for a variety of ambitious undertakings in the 1890s, not least of which was British colonial expansion into Africa. A powerful cricket team gave its administrators clout as they argued for the formation of new national sporting organisations. Kimberley formed the core of the new cricket province of Griqualand West and in administrative and political matters the town's leaders were very influential over a period of decades. The most prominent clubs in the white Griqualand West Cricket Union (GWCU) were Pirates, Eclectic and Kimberley CC. There were also various lesser known clubs such as the Wodehouse and Newtons. The non-racial GWCCU (interchangeably called the Coloured or Colonial union), formed in 1895, had its Eccentrics, Duke of Wellington, Standard, Red Crescent, Ottoman and Good Hope clubs. Copying colonial usages of Home-Born vs Colonial-Born, the GWCCU organised its own Eastern-Born vs Western-Born fixture on New Year's Day in 1896, while the senior Kimberley team participated in the Malay Inter-Town Tournament over the New Year. The two friendly teams were completely mixed racially and in religious terms, and two names that stand out are those of J. Tobin (captain of one of the teams) and Isaiah Bud M'belle, who became very well known as administrators and politicians.[1] Then there was the rival DFCCU for coloured players only, which broke away from the GWCCU soon after its formation. In 1912 this body had at least eight local clubs, as well as affiliates in Barkly West. The Kimberley clubs were Progress, Excelsior, Universals, Oddfellows, Wanderers, Empires, Thistles and Stars.[2] The GWCCU and the DFCCU did play each other from time to time, but no players of the DFCCU were included in GWCCU's Griqualand West teams for the Barnato Cup.

The period of playing dominance enjoyed by Kimberley and Griqualand West in the late 1880s and early 1890s was short-lived. Western Province took the Currie Cup away from Kimberley in 1892 and Griqualand West never won it again. The province became a whipping boy for the stronger provinces. It lost no fewer than 21 out of 26 of its matches in the Currie Cup before World War I. The playing power in SACA shifted permanently to Western Province, Transvaal and Natal.

More or less the same thing happened within the competitions of SACCB and the other black boards as cricket expanded in the twentieth century. After being the top region in the inter-town tournaments in the early 1890s and being second-best to Western Province in the pre-1914 Barnato era, Griqualand West subsequently won only one Barnato trophy in 62 years, two Sir David Harris trophies (once shared) in 31 years, and no Native Recruiting Corporation (NRC) trophies in 25 years. When Griqualand West defeated Border in the final of the Standard Bank Cup on 31 March 1999, with future Protea coach Mickey Arthur scoring 83 for the winners (and triumphant captain Kepler Wessels retiring after the match), it was the first top-flight trophy the province had won in the 52 years since a triple-tie in the Sir David Harris Trophy in 1946/7.

Griqualand West, now the Northern Cape, today plays in the lower leagues of South Africa's cricket (and other sporting competitions) but, even if Kimberley is today a modest town, its role in the early development of South African cricket can never be ignored.

EASTERN PROVINCE

The whites-only Eastern Province Cricket Union was formed in the early 1890s soon after SACA's founding, and Eastern Province competed in the Currie Cup for the first time in Cape Town in 1894, when the cup moved from being a challenge match between two teams to a centralised multi-team tournament. Eastern Province did not win the cup in the nine times it participated in the tournament before World War I. It was outside the top three provinces, winning only 7 out of its 27 matches. The best bowling figures of any Currie Cup player were Ernie Vogler's 16/38, including all ten wickets in the second innings, against Griqualand West in 1906/7. In the same match, D.S. Lumsden became the only centurion in those twenty years and Eastern Province also reached its highest total of 403. The lowest score was 40 against Orange Free State in 1910/1.

The EPCU first division in Port Elizabeth in 1915 consisted of six teams: the Port Elizabeth, Pirates, Uitenhage, Algoa and Union clubs, together with the prominent local school, the Grey Institute (later, High School). There were also three lower divisions, school teams and 'sundry mercantile and financial organisations'. Union won most of the early league competitions and the PECC, whose antecedents went back to the 1840s and 1850s, was no longer the unchallenged strong local team.

Black cricketers in Port Elizabeth and the eastern Cape maintained the progress already described as they entered the first decade of the 1900s. Port Elizabeth was host when the Barnato tournaments were launched in 1898, and African inter-town cricket remained popular. Newspaper reports mention various new cricket clubs being started: for example, Brotherly Unity CC, Wide Awake CC,[3] Gaika CC,[4] African Lion CC in the newly established New Brighton township, and the Cape of Good Hope CC in the neighbouring Korsten Township. While mixing between African and coloured cricketers continued in the provincial team and in some clubs under the Eastern Province Coloured Cricket Union (EPCCU), which emerged in the early twentieth century as the SACCB affiliate in the region, there were apparently separate leagues for the African players.

The EPCCU had seven clubs in its top league in 1912: South End United, West End, Morning Star, Empire, Rising Star, Lillywhite from Uitenhage, and Albany (Grahamstown), given in the order they were placed in the league after six matches that season.[5] Lower-league clubs included Star of the East, Break of

Day and Korsten Villagers. The senior club competition was for the Searle Cup, presented by the local member of the Cape parliament, James Searle. The African players apparently played in a separate league at the time, with Fear Not and Ethiopian CC due to play to decide 'the destination of the cup'. Neither was in the league of the EPCCU, and they were mainly clubs for Xhosa-speakers but also others, as the names Zwide, Mavavana and Rwexu (and also P. Oliver) show. Outside Port Elizabeth there was Empire B, Lillywhite, and Rose and Crown in Uitenhage, Try Again CC in Somerset East, Fear Not in Cookhouse, Royal Standard (borrowing the name of the local white club) in Cradock, Rising Star in Graaff-Reinet, and Silver Star and United in Willowmore.[6]

The achievements of the African and coloured cricketers are put into perspective by the report in Luckin's *History of South African Cricket* in 1915 about the problems within the white EPCU. According to 'Cover Point', the Port Elizabeth white league had 'not always flourished'. It had at times 'fallen into abeyance' until 1896, when it was successfully restarted with an 'average of five clubs'.[7] He also complained that Eastern Province's 'progress had been more retrogressive than progressive' since the late 1890s. One of the reasons was that although the region was large, the EPCU represented a relatively small area. The affiliates were described as 'the various Port Elizabeth clubs, the Uitenhage club, and the various Grahamstown teams'. A problem was that the country 'agricultural areas' such as Cradock, Graaff-Reinet and Bedford were not affiliated to the EPCU, although players from there were sometimes included in important Eastern Province matches. Traditional inter-town games involving these areas had also become less frequent.[8]

THE 'BORDER' BECOMES A PROVINCE AS THE FRONTIER CLOSES

The concept of 'frontier' has been employed to help explain the hundred years of 'border' wars that led to the dispossession of the Xhosa-speaking people. Some scholars argue that the frontier or border can be seen as both an 'open' and 'closed' space. In the eastern Cape, it remained 'open' for many years and this led to fluid relations in the contested spaces, allowing for alliances and cooperation and multiple forms of economic and cultural cross-pollination in addition to intense conflict. Only when the Xhosa-speaking people of the region were finally dispossessed in the 1880s did the frontier finally 'close' and the physical boundaries of the colony become fixed.

But the divisions and fluidity of past interactions continued to live on in the minds of people, in the structures that were created, and in the names they adopted. Thus, when the white settlers formed a new regional cricket union in the former territories of the Xhosa on 25 July 1896, they called it the Border

Cricket Union, although the borders of British colonial rule had by now shifted elsewhere. The imaginary line which had separated 'them' from 'us', the British from those whose land they were taking, the members of 'the club' and those who did not belong, became entrenched within the common space they now shared. Border became a province, with 'them and 'us' still a defining point.

Until 1896 the white Border cricketers had fallen under Eastern Province. When the King William's Town Cape Mounted Rifles star Stewart was selected for South Africa in March 1889, for example, it was as an Eastern Province player. Nevertheless, Xhosa–colonial wars and geographic considerations ensured that the Border developed its own character. By 1890 Border cricketers complained: 'Clubs on the Border seldom meet clubs in the western part of the Eastern Province, the distance is too great. Port Elizabeth is a long way off to be a centre for us, consequently Port Elizabeth men know little of our form, and as a matter of fact but few Border men get into Eastern Province teams.'[9]

The new whites-only Border Cricket Union participated in the Currie Cup for the first time in 1898. In the same year African cricketers in King William's Town and East London selected a provincial team to participate in the Barnato tournament. They called it Southern Border. This was soon followed by the formation of the Border Native Cricket Union (BNCU), led by Dr Walter Benson Rubusana, a church minister and one of the founders of the modern-day ANC.

From the early 1880s the separate white and black East London and King William's Town teams played against each other every year, and these matches continued through to World War I. This was a sign that East London was not only growing in importance as a port city but also catching up with King William's Town and Queenstown in cricket. In the 1890s there were regular inter-town matches and tournaments involving these three major centres and other Border towns. The country teams were not to be sneezed at. In December 1892, the white Bolotwa team lost by 17 runs to East London, and in 1893/4 Stormberg beat the coastal city eleven. Kei Road was said for many seasons to have been a 'match for any club on the Border'. Queenstown were one of the stronger teams but their cricket 'was and always has been fitful'. In 1896 and 1897 teams from Cape Town, Bloemfontein and South Western Districts toured the Border, and this helped Border SACA develop confidence as a province on its own.

In its first appearance in the Currie Cup in 1898, Border almost made the final after surprisingly beating Transvaal. But it competed in only four of the seven subsequent Currie Cup tournaments until 1913 and the BCU team won only six of the 17 matches they played. This included a satisfying best-ever score of 391/5 and a win against neighbours Eastern Province in 1910/1.

The distances and small size and scattered nature of the white population made it difficult for the establishment's Border SACA to be a strong province. In an attempt to redress this situation, a home-and-away Border Town League (involving the main towns of East London, King William's Town and Queenstown) and a Border Inter-Club League were started in the mid-1900s. The former soon fell away because of the excessive demands on the top players, but the latter flourished. King William's Town's continued predominance can be seen from the fact that the local Albert and Pirates clubs between them won the league six times after its inception in 1906/7, before Bohemians became the first East London winners in 1912/3.

The main white clubs in King William's Town and the surrounding areas in about 1890 were Albert (formed in 1878), Pirates (founded in 1888), Baker and Co., Kaffrarians, Star, Berlin, Kei Road, Ncera, Keiskamma Hoek, Stutterheim and the Garrison (which in the days of the Cape Mounted Rifles formed the backbone of King cricket and then disappeared after the South African War). In 1889 most of these clubs became part of the new King and Districts Cricket Union.[10] The main East London clubs were the Buffalo CC, Pirates, Railway, West Bank and Mechanics. The main clubs in Queenstown and the surrounding towns were Cathcart, Imvani, Bolotwa, Queenstown (formed in 1865), Willows, Golden Cross, Whittlesea, Sterkstroom, Molteno, Stormberg, Rovers, Dordrecht, Barkly East, Steynsberg and Aliwal North.[11] Schools also played in the various leagues. By 1910 Dale College had been joined by Selborne College in East London and Queen's College in Queenstown as major cricket nurseries. Two Selborne pupils, for example, played for Border against the English touring team in December 1913.

The growth of black cricket in the Border continued in the 1890s and 1900s. Fifteen fixtures were played by J.T. Jabavu's Frontier Club of King William's Town in the 1895/6 season. Frontier played local rivals Champion CC and Buffalos three times each. They also played the strong local white Albert club twice, winning once and losing once. In the other games they beat St Matthew's College, 'Junior Champ' from East London, Forward CC from Debe Nek, and Queenstown. The only other defeat was against the strong Gaika CC from East London. The final results for the season were played 15, won nine, drawn four and lost two.[12]

In 1899, shortly before the South African War, Robert Mantsayi (secretary) put out a notice informing cricketers that the Jabavu Cup Tournament that year would be held in King William's Town.[13] The Jabavu Cup Board was still functioning in 1910 with G.W. Tyamzashe as president. Like Mantsayi, he was a prominent political figure.[14] The Jabavu Cup was subsequently complemented and succeeded by other inter-town tournaments involving essentially the same major cricket centres – such as those for the T.B. Burnham King Cup from 1906 onwards and the Orpen Cup from 1918 onwards.

Inter-town tournaments for smaller centres became the vogue from the 1880s onwards, duplicating the example of the big towns. For example, *Imvo Zabant-sundu* in 1891 announced a tournament in Alice for '2nd Class Towns' – Alice, Fort Beaufort, Keiskamma Hoek (Koboqobo), Mpofu and Nyara – and in 1898 it published the full scorecards of six matches in a tournament at Gqumahashe between Alice, Fort Beaufort and two teams from Middledrift.[15] These were probably an early version of the *Macal' eGusha* (Sides of the Sheep) tournaments, dating back to that time, which are still played annually today during the Christmas and New Year holidays. Economic migrants to the cities or their now urbanised descendants return to their traditional homesteads to play enjoyable and competitive cricket in these rural areas of *emaXhoseni* or Xhosaland. The reports, notices, scorecards and correspondence of these tournaments published over the years constitute an archive waiting to be plumbed by a new generation of isiXhosa-speaking scholars, statisticians and cricket lovers.

In Queenstown, which regularly participated in the inter-town tournaments, the main clubs in the 1890s were Pioneer CC and Komani CC.[16] The Komani officials, the Rev. Samuel Mvambo (president) and Richard Nukuna (treasurer), were prominent political figures, the latter being president of the local Iliso Lomzi, or Native Vigilance Association.[17]

Southern Border, a combined team of King William's Town and East London cricketers, did well in the first black provincial tournament in 1898/9, remaining in contention for the Barnato Memorial Trophy until the final match, before losing to the 'Moslems' of the Western Province. By 1908 there were eight clubs in the East London Native Cricket Union, namely Gaika, Willows, Champion, Rising Star, Lily White, Five Great Powers, Naughty Boys and Never Despair. The president was the highly respected Dr Walter Rubusana, and 52 people attended the annual meeting that September. The report said the Union was waiting to hear from the secretaries of the Jabavu, T.B. Burnham King and Barnato trophy boards when the next tournaments would be held.[18]

Later that season, East London did indeed play against Alice, King William's Town and Queenstown for the T.B. Burnham King Cup under the auspices of the Border Native Cricket Union (whose exact founding date is unknown). The tournament was held from 26 December through to 2 January in King William's Town, and the hosts were unbeaten in their three matches, trouncing the holders Alice by an innings and 104 runs. *Izwi Labantu* noted approvingly that 'King William's Town is remarkably sportsmanlike in its friendly concessions to native cricketers and we were agreeably surprised to observe the amicable relations existing between the Europeans and the natives who were allowed the use of the Pavilion and grounds for this important fixture'. The cup, described as 'of chaste and handsome design', was presented by Dr Rubusana.[19] The following season East London were the hosts and King William's Town retained the cup.[20] This new tournament showed the increasingly organised nature of cricket in the Border region by the 1900s. There was also a 'Border Native Cricket Tournament' for the McCallum's Presentation Cup at the time; the participating teams in 1908 and 1911 were Gaika CC from East London, Border CC from Stutterheim, Try Again CC from Cathcart, and Kaffrarian CC from Queenstown.[21]

As we have seen, the black cricketers matched their white counterparts (and their inter-town and inter-club leagues) every step of the way, and it is remarkable that this deep tradition has not got the recognition it deserves. The closeness of the two experiences in the Border is also revealed in an examination of the language of white settlers and Xhosa people with regard to cricket: when the Eastern Cape farmers these days say, 'Give it horns, boet!' they mimic *yimpondo zenkomo* or 'it is the horns of a cow', the isiXhosa term for a six hit.

Cricket continued to be an integral part of the educational and social life at Lovedale and other colleges such as Healdtown and St Matthew's. Keenly contested inter-school matches between these neighbouring schools became a feature of the academic year. Lovedale had an internal league involving staff, workers and students, with the winner getting the right to use the main school field as its 'home ground' in the next season. Cricket reports came in from the unlikeliest eastern Cape villages and *dorpies*: Stutterheim, Cathcart, Tylden, Bolotwa, Whittlesea, Dordrecht, Burgersdorp, Molteno, Adelaide, Alicedale, Cookhouse, Somerset East, Richmond, Aliwal North, Herschel and many others.[22] In 1890 Aliwal North hosted a tournament of teams from Johannesburg. There were two black clubs in Burgersdorp at this stage, one of which had the grand name of Millionaire CC. You will not find any today among any section of the population here. There are hundreds of reports in *Imvo Zabantsundu* and *Izwi Labantu* in the late nineteenth and early twentieth century that show that cricket was not only the favourite sport in the African communities of the eastern Cape, but an integral part of their lifestyle and community activities.

The one area in the eastern Cape that remained relatively undeveloped in terms of cricket was the area east of the Kei, later called Transkei. By the time it was annexed in the 1880s and 1890s, the Colony was tired of the experiment of forcefully incorporating African territories, preferring instead to give them a form of indirect rule. Heavy resistance and the prohibitive cost of integrating the Transkeian population meant that while cricket was played there, it did not develop in the same way as in the other towns mentioned already in the 1880s and 1890s. The policy was to keep the Transkei as an indirectly ruled labour reservoir, and the subsequent underdevelopment and lack of transport infrastructure are still visible today. Nevertheless, both black and white cricketers battled against the odds to keep the flag flying here too. Press reports mentioned the Imfecane CC in Butterworth in 1889,[23] the Pondomise CC in Tsolo in 1896,[24] and the match between the Prince Victor CC and the Civics CC, 'i 1st XI yama Ngesi', in Mount Frere in 1900.[25]

SOUTH WESTERN DISTRICTS: MINNOW PROVINCE

An earlier chapter on the first English tour in 1889 has graphically described how the tourists made their way over the mountains from Mossel Bay to Oudtshoorn chasing ostriches and crossing a swollen river. This description highlighted two of the main factors that have influenced the development of cricket in the South Western Districts (SWD) – its relative isolation from the main cricket centres and its relatively small rural population for the game to draw from. This modern-day cricket province has for more than a century operated on the margins, playing 'country' cricket, and now and then getting an opportunity at top-class encounters, yet it remains an important nursery for the South African game.

The SACA-affiliated South Western Districts played four matches against three English touring teams before World War I, starting with a XXII who put 53 and 135 on the scoreboard in losing by an innings against the first tourists in 1888/9. Only four double-figure scores were produced by the SWD batsmen in 44 turns at the crease. H. van der Spuy did best with a 26 as the Lancashire professional Johnny Briggs cantered to 19 wickets in the match. In 1905/6 SWD took on the famous Pelham Warner's team and held out for a draw, being nine wickets down at the close. Opening bowler G. Rogers had a magnificent match analysis taking eight wickets for 79 runs off 65.5 overs, 29 of which were maidens. He and his partners Hill (3/16) and Bernhardt (2/18) bowled the English out for only 60 in the first innings. But once again the batting was weak (77 and 97/9 – top score G. Parsons 26). Then SWD got two games against J.W.H.T. Douglas's seventh team in the 1913/4 season, the first in Robertson, followed by Oudtshoorn. These were also both lost by an innings, although A. de Villiers scored 74 not out and I. Murray 49 in the first game, and E. Olivier took 4/47 in 14 overs in the second.

SWD SACA played only one first-class match before the war, when they were accepted into the Currie Cup for one season in 1904/5. They lost by an innings to Western Province, for whom the Springbok rugby player H.W. 'Paddy' Carolin scored 72. Charlie Vintcent, the brilliant youngster who had made his top-level debut in the inter-town tournaments twenty years before, was in the team but nearing the end of a glittering career. His 14 was joint top score, as the team crumbled to 60 and 45, chasing 259.

Little has been written so far about cricket at the grassroots at this time, but a 'South Western District Tournament' was organised in Mossel Bay during the New Year festivities in January 1911. Showing that a second provincial network existed in the region, the Athletic Club donated a trophy for 'competition among the Coloured cricketers in the S.-W. Districts'. After Mossel Bay easily beat Brak River and Oudtshoorn triumphed over George, the home team beat Oudtshoorn by 35 runs in the final to take the trophy.[26] There was mention in the same year of an NCC Railway Cricket Union league competition in which teams from Worcester, Robertson, Great Brak River and Mossel Bay participated.[27]

The two main clubs in Oudtshoorn were Western Hope CC and Union Star CC, which survived for many decades. Linked to the SACCB cricket network, they worked together to arrange concerts and events, using the *APO* newspaper and the St John's Café in the town to post notices. In 1912 Union Star were presented with the Olivier Cup for inter-town competition. This time the club sought possible opponents across the flat expanses of the Karoo, rather than cooperating across the mountains with George and Mossel Bay on the coast. The club appealed to Kimberley, Beaufort West, Aberdeen, Graaff-Reinet, Middleburg, Cradock, Somerset East, Uitenhage and Uniondale, among others, to participate. Were they perhaps trying to tap into the ancestral heartland of the Khoi people through old communication networks? It turned out to be a small-scale tournament of Stars. Those who accepted Union Star's challenge for the first competition at Easter 1913 were Silver Star CC from Willowmore and Rising Star CC from Graaff-Reinet.[28]

The regular president of Union Star was Mr D. Swiegelaar, grandfather of Simon Swiegelaar, who was on the first UCBSA Council in 1991 and is currently a life member of Cricket South Africa. Ever-present at the regular functions and aware of the issues at stake in the brand-new country called South Africa, which came into existence on 31 May 1910, he urged his club members to 'not only unite in sports, but also in matters political'.[29]

SWD formed part of a vast cricket playing area lying between Cape Town and Port Elizabeth, which has always had a rich history, going back to the activities in the 1860s, and which later gave rise to the Boland province as well. These country areas stretching hundreds of kilometres from Stellenbosch and Paarl to Worcester, Robertson, Oudtshoorn, Mossel Bay and elsewhere still await their own historians. A Worcester (SACA) XVIII played against the English in 1905/6 as well, and there is plenty of evidence of cricket being played around the time of Union by people who would have been loyal to the SACCB. The Paarl District

Cricket Union was formed in 1907.[30] Teams under its auspices included Good Hopes, Cavaliers and Moslem CC (all from Paarl), Tulbagh United CC, Melton CC and Pirates CC from Wellington, and Worcester Primrose CC. Over the New Year in 1910, Meltons drew with Moslems and beat Pirates and Primrose.[31] In November 1911 the nearby Drakenstein Cricket Union launched a league, which included two teams each from Union CC, Surrey CC, Avenue CC from Simondium, and Warwick CC from 'Delta'.[32] The first-mentioned two teams were traditional rivals from Pniel, originally a mission village for freed slaves. The treasurer and secretary of the new Drakenstein union were A.D. and D.S. Cyster respectively. The Cyster family has lived in Pniel for generations and Dr Peter Cyster, recently vice-president of Cricket South Africa, followed in the administrative footsteps of A.D. and D.S., the latter of whom was also the top scorer in the 1912 final.[33]

The nearby Stellenbosch Coloured Cricket Union in 1911 accommodated clubs such as 'Cup holders' Newtons CC, Victoria Swifts CC and Old Boys (The 'Babes').[34] Excelsior CC in Stellenbosch (formed in 1885) and Spes Bona in Worcester were other well-known clubs of the time whose affiliations are unclear.[35] On the white side of the line, Stellenbosch University decided in 1901 to break away from Western Province and play in the country leagues, possibly prompted by the South African War then in progress. The university's official history says that it was only in 1960 that the club was allowed back into Western Province as a 'volwaardige mededinger' (fully-fledged competitor). The university's decision in 1901 had the long-term effect of strengthening country cricket in the Boland.[36]

Community leaders and spokespeople from every part of the modern-day Boland, Karoo and SWD sent reports to the official newspaper of Dr Abdurahman's APO political organisation, which show a high level of organisation in church, education, sport and other matters. The APO, started in 1909 and read throughout South Africa, had a similar mobilising and unifying effect on cricket in this region to Jabavu's Imvo in the eastern Cape in the 1880s. The reports covered the most remote places, including Fraserburg, Carnarvon and Prince Albert with its Eastern Star CC.[37] The fixtures of the Cape Central Rugby Football Union (Coloured) under Mr W.H. Jeppe confirmed how the rural coloured middle classes were mobilising in the early years of Union. Swellendam, Heidelberg and Robertson formed the A section in 1913, and Riversdale, Ladismith and Mossel Bay comprised the B, with the finals between the winners of each section.[38] The Perseverance rugby club was started in Oudtshoorn in the same year and the first secretary was Ben Rice.[39] He lived in St John's Street, in which could also be found his cricket and tennis counterpart, Swiegelaar, and the St John's Café, where the sportsmen gathered and put up their club notices.

Even in a small province like this, we can identify, through the experiences of families like the Swiegelaars of Oudtshoorn and the Cysters of Pniel, the enduring networks upon which the non-racial struggles and cricket unification of the late twentieth century were built.

STIFF UPPER LIPS AND EASTERN AND AFRICAN INFLUENCES IN THE WESTERN PROVINCE

From countryside to metropole: Cape Town, where the game was first played in South Africa, was a key area in the development of cricketing provinces between 1890 and the outbreak of World War I in 1914. The new Western Province provincial teams won five of the 14 white Currie Cup tournaments and four of the five non-racial Barnato tournaments in that time.

The whites-only Western Province Cricket Union (WPCU) was formed on 6 September 1890 at a meeting in the Thatched Tavern on Greenmarket Square in the heart of Cape Town. This was only a winter break of six months after the formation of the South African Cricket Association (SACA) in April 1890, and the presence of the SACA secretary, Harry Cadwallader, indicated that it was part of the same process. The first point on the 'Rules' that were accepted stressed this too: 'That a local cricket union ... [be] formed with a view to being affiliated to the South African Cricket Union.'

The WPCC had organised the first English tour 'off its own bat' and was planning another when 'the other clubs [were awakened] to the necessity for the formation of some association'. Particularly resentful of the WPCC's high-handed manner was the Cape Town Cricket Club, reorganised in 1888–9 with the modern-day Newlands rugby ground as its base and the prominent head of the Afrikaner Bond, J.H. 'Onze Jan' Hofmeyr, as its president. On 28 August 1890 the Cape Town CC resolved on the necessity 'to wrest from the Western Province Cricket Club the apparent monopoly which they hold in the administration of cricketing matters in the Western Province and obtain equal representation for all first-class local clubs on a duly constituted board in whose hands the sole management should rest'.[40] At the inaugural meeting of the WPCU the following week, attended by delegates from Claremont, Cape Town and Sea Point, William Milton of the WPCC was nevertheless unanimously appointed president and P.H. de Villiers, an outstanding slow left-arm bowler, became the first secretary.

In 1893 the new WPCU started a league competition called the Senior Championship. The top teams in the 1890s and 1900s were WPCC, Claremont, Cape Town, Green Point (founded in 1893), the racially mixed Woodstock (for whom 'Krom' Hendricks played) and the Mowbray-based Alma (1895). Bishops,

357

consistently the strongest school team, and the SAC, who won in 1901, also played in the championship.[41]

At the time that the new WPCU was started there were also a large number of other white clubs, including Garrison, Wasps (later Mowbray), Cape Times, United Services, Simonstown, Letton, Barnett, Somerset, Caxton, Adderley, Wynberg Rovers, Central Telegraph, Zingari, Springfield, Reservoir, YMCA, Central, Alfred, Rosebud and Nil Desperandum. Most of these had a 'limited lifespan', according to A.C. Parker. By then there were also clubs in most of the surrounding country towns such as Stellenbosch, Paarl, Somerset West, Malmesbury, Ceres and Worcester.

Writing in the 1930s, 'Old Stager' described the 1890s as 'undoubtedly the palmy days of Western Province [SACA] cricket'.[42] Large crowds witnessed the Home-Born versus Mother Country games. English professionals had started the trend of wintering in South Africa, which remained a feature of the cricket landscape until the 1990s. Among the 1890s generation were Frank Hearne (Kent), George Davidson (Derbyshire), the accomplished Bill Lockwood (Nottinghamshire and Surrey), John Brown (Yorkshire), Len Braund (Somerset), James 'Bonnor' Middleton (who came to South Africa on army duty and stayed at the invitation of WPCC), Fred Tate (father of Maurice Tate), the great George Lohmann (Surrey), the soon-to-be-famous S.F. Barnes (Lancashire) and John Holland (Leicestershire and Lancashire). They spiced up the local club cricket, helped develop the game technically, and cemented the link with the English game.[43]

Things changed after the South African War. 'Western Province cricket was never the same afterwards'; the keenness and the quality of the pros apparently dropped and the Mother Country games 'had to be discontinued'.[44] Although these comments were perhaps as much a nostalgic reflection on a disappearing imperial ethos at the Cape as on declining standards, the statistics do bear out the fact that the early years of the century were lean ones for the province. According to Mars, a 'very large number of leading cricketers enlisted for active service' in the South African War, and although competitions continued, cricket in Cape Town was 'considerably disorganised' for several years. While Western Province produced seven players for the match against Lord Hawke's English team in 1898, they had four representatives in the 1904 South African team and three in the 1907 team. After dominating the Currie Cup with four out of five wins between 1892/3 and 1897/8, Western Province won it only once more before World War I, in 1908/9. After 1895, they did not once manage to beat English and Australian touring teams again.

The declining success experienced by the WPCU in the early twentieth century was not shared by its counterpart, the Western Province Coloured Cricket Union (WPCCU, belonging to SACCB). This Union, for those cricketers not allowed into the hallowed clubs of the colonialists, which had emerged by 1895/6 from the remarkable Glover Cup inter-town tournaments, won everything before it in the Barnato tournaments from 1898 onwards. The WPCCU was composed of different sub-unions, based on geographical and religious considerations. The Claremont and Cape Town sub-unions that were represented at the Malay Inter-Town Tournament in Cape Town in January 1890 consisted mainly of Cape Muslims, while the Cape District Cricket Union, formed in 1900, was apparently for coloured Christian clubs. Teams playing in the Cape District Union's main competition, the Bailey Shield, included Hand and Heart (champions in six of the first ten seasons), Eclectics, Oakdales, Polytechnics, Yorkshires, Riverstones and Mowbray United. The long-time president, Matt Fredericks, and treasurer and secretary, Stephen Reagon, were prominent members of the African Political Organisation.[45]

In 1911, there was also a City League, where Thistles played with Sea Point, St Augustine's and Crusaders; a Claremont and District Union, with teams like Riverstones and Albions; a Woodstock and Metropolitan Union, where St Philip's were the strongest team; and a Wednesday Union, where Rovers and West Ends dominated.[46] They were joined by the new Maitland-Parow and Districts Cricket Union (MPDCU) in 1913. Dr William Pick, a former player and professor in public health, has written a book called *One for the Chuck* on the history of the MPDCU.[47]

St Augustine's, started in 1899 and still in existence today, deserves special mention, as does Ottoman CC, formed in 1882 and also still alive and kicking. Saints went on to produce two major figures in South African cricket, Basil D'Oliveira and Paul Adams, the spinning sensation of the 1990s and youngest-ever Protea. Whereas Ottomans represented the 'Malay' tradition, Saints – and other cricket clubs like Crusaders and St Philip's, as well as rugby clubs like Temperance, Progress and Perseverance, whose names might have come straight out of John Bunyan's *Pilgrim's Progress* – were located in the coloured, Christian communities of Cape Town.[48]

Four unions – Woodstock and Metropolitan, Claremont and District, City League and Cape District – played 'for the championships of the Western Province' at the Claremont cricket ground over three weekends in December 1910 and January 1911.[49] Cape District were the first known winners of this inter-union competition in the 1911/2 season. The cup was handed over to the new president, Stephen Reagon, during a function for the touring Universals team from

Kimberley in the Masonic Hall in Cape Town. The donor, a Mr Zeeman, was there in person to do the honours. Among those sending congratulations were the former prime minister of the Cape Colony, William Schreiner, who had led the delegation to England in 1909 to protest about the discriminatory new constitution of South Africa, and Sir David Harris, an MP and leading figure in De Beers, who would sponsor an important provincial tournament in years to come.[50]

The president of the Western Province Coloured Cricket Union (WPCCU) at the time was the Edinburgh-trained Dr Abdullah Abdurahman, the first black medical doctor in South Africa, long-time president of the African Political Organisation and a City Councillor for 40 years.[51] Unlike his counterparts in the WPCU, Dr Abdurahman was a strong proponent of building unity and breaking down religious and other barriers on the sports fields. The fact that he as a Muslim worked closely with Fredericks, Reagon and Daniel Lenders and Isaiah Bud M'belle from Kimberley in the political and sports organisations – fellow leaders with Christian constituencies – underlined the point. In 1912 the WPCCU announced, 'We wish to draw attention to the fact that this Board is making a serious effort this year to bring all existing Unions in the Peninsula into one Union, and, if possible, by the beginning of next season.' Two mass meetings were called for this purpose. The one for players in the city centre was held in Buitengracht Street. The other was called for the Newlands Hall in Palmboom Road, which became a gentrified area after black families were forced out of the area under the Group Areas Act later in the twentieth century.[52]

In 1913, Dr Abdurahman was also involved in attempts to set up a general overarching sports body for coloured sporting federations in the Western Province. There had been a Western Province Amateur Athletics and Cycling Union, which 'was now defunct', and the cause, speakers said, was that 'cricket and other sports were not affiliated'. It was agreed there should be one body for all sporting clubs 'whether cycling, football and cricket'.[53]

It is not clear if Cape District and the above-mentioned sub-unions that it competed against were in the WPCCU, but Western Province nevertheless cleaned up the Barnato tournament, winning four out of the four times they played between 1898 and 1913. Small wonder, then, that the Western Cape became a stronghold of 'non-white' and non-racial cricket and rugby in the twentieth century. The sports people here were part of a long tradition. As city dwellers in relatively skilled occupations, they were relatively affluent. They took part in large numbers, and they had closer connections with white establishment sport than anywhere else in the country.

Less appreciated is the fact that Africans also played cricket from the start in Cape Town, as the path-breaking exploits of the sons of chiefs in the first

Zonnebloem College side in District Six in 1861 have demonstrated. In 1894 the racially mixed Zonnebloem team, which totalled 155 for five, beat the St Mark's Recreational Society, who managed 92 in reply.[54] In the next season, the first and second teams took on Albion CC. Names like Falati, Mbali and Moroka were involved, reminders of the College's origins as a place of training for the sons of chiefs.[55] In 1910 the mayor recalled a time when 'the College had the best cricket team in the whole Peninsula'.[56] By 1898 there were six African clubs in Cape Town. The most established was seemingly the Bantu CC under the presidency of the Rev. Elijah Mdolomba of the Wesleyan Church.[57] Mdolomba was prominent in politics and was also captain and secretary of the Wild Horse Cycling Club.

At that stage the African population in Cape Town, numbering around 10,000 out of 160,000 townspeople, lived in Cape Town proper, some in barracks at the docks in Table Bay harbour, where the famous Waterfront tourism destination now stands. The superintendent of Docks location wrote to the port captain in 1904, asking that part of the neighbouring commonage be used 'for a cricket ground, for the benefit of natives resident in this Location': 'At present the boys off duty are playing cricket in a very primitive fashion, and in a cramped space, viz the road inside Harbour Board area and outside Location Gates. A considerable amount of talent is being displayed but owing to want of space it cannot be cultivated.'[58] There was also cricket at the Uitvlugt location at Ndabeni near today's Pinelands. In 1903 the council herded Africans out of town and forcibly removed them to Uitvlugt on the pretext that they constituted a health threat. In January 1904 'about 15 Malays ... attired in cricketing costume' entered the new location to play a game against their African counterparts. Mixed matches such as these were not that unusual, as demonstrated by a contemporary newspaper report of a game in which the Ethiopian CC defeated the Rocklands CC comprising Muslim players.[59]

Black cricketers might have been good at the game, but they had to know their place. The constitution of the new South Africa promulgated in 1910 – and that of the whites-only Western Province Cricket Union – reminded them of this.

37

The new entrants

*Transvaal, Natal, Orange Free State and
Rhodesia enter representative cricket*

> Our cricketers have been looking forward for some time to
> the match and they, with the assistance of the curators of
> the recreation ground and the help of the Town Council and
> Government, have succeeded in securely fencing in the ground
> and making the cricket field as smooth and even as was
> possible ... His Honour the President arrived at 12 o'clock
> and the band struck up the Volkslied, the last strains of which
> had scarcely died away before Ferris delivered the first ball.

> – *The Friend*, 4 March 1892

The white Transvaal Cricket Union (TCU) was established on 8 October 1891 at
a meeting in the Goldfields Hotel in Johannesburg. The South African batsman
A.B. Tancred, 'the best cricketer', formerly of Kimberley, was elected chairman.
H. Eckstein was elected president and the mining magnate Abe Bailey vice-president. George Allsop, who played for Transvaal and umpired one test match, was
the secretary. The constitution, with a few minor alterations, was based on that of
the Western Province Cricket Union, formed a year earlier.

Having relieved Kimberley/Griquas of the Currie Cup in April 1890 and
being now formally organised administratively, the province was ready to take
on all-comers. There were two main items on the first agenda: tours with England
and the Currie Cup.[1] Together with Western Province and Natal, Transvaal soon
proved itself one of the top three provinces, consistently powerful in skills, numbers
and resources, due to its link with the mining industry in the rapidly growing
City of Gold.

The TCU presidents up to 1914, who included Sir George Farrar, Solly Joel, Sir Percy FitzPatrick and Sir Abe Bailey, strongly reflected the dominance of the mining industry and the British establishment. In 1897, SACA's headquarters moved to Johannesburg and stayed there permanently, explaining the province's growing importance in South African cricket and why Cricket South Africa's offices are still to be found at the Wanderers Club. Transvaal SACA had the best win rate in the Currie Cup before World War I, with 31 wins out of 41 games and ten losses, compared with next-best Western Province, with 24 wins out of 34 and ten losses. It won four successive Currie Cups after the South African War. Jimmy Sinclair of Transvaal scored the first test century for South Africa and in 1905 it was the first province to beat a touring team in a first-class match.[2]

The top clubs in Johannesburg were the Wanderers (formed in 1888) and Pirates (started in 1891). The May Consolidated CC, Langlaagte CC, Jeppe CC and the Johannesburg club were other active teams. Pretoria (still a six-hour journey by coach from Johannesburg), Potchefstroom, Krugersdorp and Barberton (which for a while had been the biggest town in the Transvaal during a short-lived gold rush) were also affiliated to the new TCU. As was becoming the custom in the bigger provinces, the Wanderers appointed the first of a string of professionals in 1892/3, and Pretoria also regularly 'used to import the very best available coaching talent'.[3]

Among the large numbers of people from throughout the world who flocked to the city of gold in search of opportunity were many mission-educated black 'school' people and artisans from the eastern Cape and Cape Town. They soon took the lead in establishing cricket in their communities. The first reports of cricket in the black communities are from as early as 1890. In the following year the Potchefstroom Native Cricket Club played against Kroonstad CC in Kroonstad, a popular venue for contests between teams from the South African Republic and Orange Free State because of its central location.[4] In October 1893, Potchefstroom played Klerksdorp, purportedly to celebrate President Paul Kruger's birthday on the 10th of that month. The day was presumably a public holiday. The Rev. Bruno Kohler of the Berlin Mission Society forbade his black parishioners from playing in case they might misbehave. Clearly the Continental missionaries in the Transvaal were not as convinced as their English counterparts in the south of the beneficial nature of the game.[5]

Many of the Indian immigrants who had landed in Durban in the preceding decades had made their way up to the Witwatersrand and in 1896, ten years after the establishment of Johannesburg, Indian cricketers started the Transvaal Indian Cricket Union. After some time it became dormant before being resuscitated again in 1930.[6]

In the same year of 1896, African players from the Morning Star CC from Johannesburg travelled down to Aliwal North for a Christmas tournament involving teams from that town, Dordrecht and Burgersdorp.[7] Over New Year in 1897/8, the Doornfontein Standard CC (DSCC) played three matches in a few days. On 27 December, DSCC took on the Bloemfontein CC at Kroonstad, winning by six wickets. On 3 January 1898, they played the Ottoman CC ('the Malays') and again emerged as winners by three wickets. The next day DSCC beat Elandsfontein Diggers CC by an innings and 59 runs.[8] It was one of the strongest clubs and the president was A. Daniel, the secretary J.W. Mguli and the captain T.G. Kwaza.[9]

In October 1898, the African clubs in Johannesburg formed a union as well. Mr E. Chake was secretary of this 'Transvaal Union'.[10] It was probably formed in view of the planned Barnato tournament, which took place in December 1898 in Port Elizabeth. Newspaper reports said that there were about ten 'native' clubs in Johannesburg in 1898, including the Johannesburg CC, Jubilee CC, Grand Zodwa CC, Progress CC, Progressive CC, Morning Star CC, Herschel CC, Five Great Powers CC, Doornfontein Standard CC, and the Elandsfontein Diggers CC from Germiston.[11] Some of these clubs had more than one team. Outside Johannesburg there were clubs like the Don't Care CC from Klerksdorp and the Wanderers CC from Potchefstroom.[12] We know of their existence because the Transvaal cricketers regularly sent reports of their activities for publication in *Imvo Zabantsundu* and later *Izwi Labantu*. New African clubs to emerge in Johannesburg in the early 1900s were Cush CC, Pioneer CC, Bra[a]mfontein CC, Try Again CC, Yinindaba CC, Fear Not CC and Head of Lion CC based at Glen Deep mine.[13] 'Bramfontein' CC came by train in November 1907 with an entourage that included white cricketers to play Cush CC at Klipspruit Location, close to where the Chris Hani Baragwanath Hospital was built when Soweto was later developed. They arrived at ten o'clock and were met by a welcoming committee of Cush CC ladies, including 'Mesdames' Sontongo and Msane, before the captains tossed at half past ten.[14] It is tantalising to wonder whether these women were related to Enoch Sontonga, composer of the national anthem 'Nkosi Sikelel' iAfrika', and the early ANC leader Saul Msane.

In December 1911, the Fear Not CC 'of the City and Suburban, Johannesburg' challenged the top Kimberley African team, Eccentrics CC. They arrived 'by the midnight train' on Christmas Eve and played on Christmas and Boxing Day. It was reported that the result of the match 'was expected with considerable interest in native sporting circles in Transvaal and Griqualand West, where they wished it to be decided at the wickets whether gold or diamonds was the toughest mineral … On reference to the score below it will be seen that the pebble came out of the affray with its reputation for sheer hardness unsullied.'[15] This was clearly a home-town report because the Johannesburg players did not do badly. In reply to the 175 all out and 199 for four of Eccentrics, Fear Not scored 124 and 123 for three. The total number of runs scored in this match was unusually high for those times.

More research needs to be done on the early Transvaal history, but it seems that the Indian and African unions formed in the 1890s went out of existence or were absorbed by other bodies by 1911. Oral testimony by one of the early cricket stars, Piet Gwele, indicates that Africans and coloured cricketers played together under the City and Suburban Union at this time. There was also a Transvaal Coloured Cricket Union based in Vrededorp by 1911. This was the predominantly Malay and coloured body affiliated to the SACCB, which participated in two of the first five Barnato tournaments before 1914. The officials elected at the annual meeting in 1909 were Mr Minnaar (president), Hadjie Gafeldien Abrahams (vice-president), G.Z. Sallie (chairman), Hadjie Abdol Samaar (treasurer) and George Manuel (secretary). Six clubs, some with as many as four teams, were affiliated, namely Progress, Fair Players, Ottoman, Border, Pirates and Brotherly United from Pretoria. They competed for the Shahabodien Cup.[16]

NATAL'S BRITISH AND ARMY INFLUENCES

The whites-only Natal Cricket Union (NCU) was formed in 1890 with its headquarters in Pietermaritzburg. It had two sub-unions, Durban and Maritzburg, later joined by Northern Districts. Natal made its debut in the Currie Cup at the first centralised five-team tournament in March 1894 along with Eastern Province. At the beginning of the next season, league cricket was started in Pietermaritzburg and Durban, with the champions of each city playing against each other for the Dunne Cup.

The colony soon made an impact, reaching the Currie Cup final at its first attempt. Natal performed well, without winning the cup, until claiming it twice in a row in 1910/1 and 1912/3. In February 1914 Natal also beat the touring MCC team. The rise of Natal SACA, after first Western Province and then Transvaal had dominated for long periods, coincided with the presence of two South African batting greats, Dave Nourse and Herby Taylor in the mid-1900s. Taylor, whose father sat in the Natal parliament, had a Currie Cup average of 50.76, and his 250 not out was the highest recorded score for the province in the Currie Cup before World War 1.

Arthur William 'Dave' Nourse arrived in South Africa as a drummer boy with the West Riding Regiment at the age of 17 in 1896, but later joined the Natal Police. He played for Natal, Transvaal and Western Province during a long career, which included 45 consecutive tests for South Africa from 1902 to 1924. The Grand Old Man of South African cricket, he worked as a soldier, policeman, railway guard, saloon keeper, commercial traveller, manager of a sports goods firm, and cricket coach. His son, Arthur Dudley, was to play 34 tests for South Africa between 1935 and 1951.

Natal SACA's cricket administration was reorganised in 1909 when the headquarters moved from Pietermaritzburg to Durban and the old NCU was replaced by the new Natal Cricket Association. The traditional inter-town match between Durban and Maritzburg, held regularly between 1888 and 1914, was a highlight of the season. Dave Nourse averaged 70.66 in these matches and held the individual batting record of 212.

After the first test match was allocated to Durban in 1910, finances improved to the extent that English professionals could be employed. By this time, the four major boys' schools in the colony – Michaelhouse, Hilton College, Maritzburg College and Durban Boys' High – were producing top-class players for the province.[17] Morrell has written about the muscular Christianity prevalent at these schools and argues that the emphasis placed on cadets and sport bred racist colonial ideas and made them training grounds for a colonial militia that had to maintain control over the numerically preponderant Zulu.[18]

With regard to the participation of black cricketers, Natal developed in a direction unique in South Africa. Those who showed the most interest in Natal were from the Indian community. Between 1860 and 1911, when further immigration was halted, just over 150,000 indentured labourers from India came to work on the sugar plantations of Natal. They were later employed on railway construction, in various unskilled labouring roles, and in service industries, particularly as barmen, or they entered self-employment as market gardeners or hawkers. Following them were 'passenger' Indians from Gujarat, who paid their own way and started shops and businesses. These traders, with whom the legendary Mohandas Gandhi was closely associated during his 20 years in South Africa, combined with the small professional class of teachers and clerks, to start the first community groups and sports clubs from 1889 onwards. In October 1894, the same year Gandhi formed the Natal Indian Congress, ten clubs met to start the Durban Indian Cricket Union.[19] In 1902 delegates from Pietermaritzburg and Durban formed a short-lived Natal Indian Cricket Union, with the Natal prime minister as patron. During the South African War of 1899–1902 there was an influx of Indian refugees from the Transvaal, who swelled the ranks of cricketers in Pietermaritzburg and Durban, but after the war cricket 'languished'. Nevertheless, by 1913 Natal Indian cricketers had a provincial team playing in the Barnato tournament hosted by Kimberley with black cricketers from other parts of the country. Selected by the Durban and District Indian Cricket Union, whose minute book attests to a high level of organisation, the team 'represented a "Who's Who" of Indian elite society in Durban', but poor batting denied them any success and there was to be no further involvement in inter-communal cricket until the 1950s.[20]

The Indian community of Natal was subjected to extreme levels of racism from most of the white population and to legislation prejudicial to its very existence. Indeed, the purpose of much of the vilification and associated laws was to encourage repatriation to India. After the grant of responsible government to Natal in 1893, a poll tax was imposed on Indians, their chances of acquiring the vote became virtually impossible, restrictions were placed on the granting of trading licences and further immigration was restricted then prohibited. At the root of much anti-Indian racism was a fear of commercial competition. In the face of freely published vituperative comments about the 'scum of Madras and Calcutta', the Indian community had to develop a high level of resilience. Perhaps the best example of communal unity was displayed in the general strike of October 1913, initiated by Gandhi, which brought together workers from the mines and sugar farms, factories and municipal and domestic service, and even hawkers. Cricket fixtures ceased and resumed in January 1914, only to be further restricted by World War I. Hundreds of Indians served in the Bearer Corps, but the Rev. Bernard Sigamoney's suggestion that a match be held at Albert Park, Durban, between European and Indian elevens to raise war funds 'fell on deaf ears'.[21]

Cricket was dependent upon the patronage of the Indian elite, often merchants, who funded schools, religious associations and sport. Indeed, a number of cricket clubs owed their existence to particular trading companies that would accommodate their workers and provide for their leisure. Although far from homogeneous and riven by differences of religion, region of origin, language, caste (although this diminished as a result of emigration), class and even colour, there was unity in diversity. Cricket club names testified to this: 'Clubs like Kismet, Bharat and Crescent had clear religious underpinnings. Schools were mainly the preserve of the emerging educated elite and Young Tailors and Railways reflected occupation'. Ottoman players were largely Urdu-speaking merchants and their Gujarati shop assistants; Greyville, bitter rivals of Ottoman, had a mixed religious membership, with a high proportion of descendants of indentured Muslims; and Pirates of India were largely from families of indentured Hindus. It would appear that some clubs were short-lived with frequent disbandments, mergers and new names, especially when cricket stagnated in the first decade of the twentieth century.[22]

The standing of patrons was considerable and the names of certain individuals recur in a multiplicity of circumstances, including sport, religious associations and politics. For example, prior to World War I, G.H. Chandabhi Miankhan, a businessman rich enough to employ a white chauffeur, donated trophies to the Durban and District Indian Cricket Union (DDICU). Yet, according to Desai et al., patronage often involved considerable ambiguity, motivated in part by a desire to emulate and gain the approval of white society. This involved a degree of mimicry that included formalism and etiquette and strict adherence to the laws of the game and the use of the English language. Congratulatory messages were sent to the white cricket authorities in recognition of various team and individual achievements. However, white approval was denied even the small educated segment of the Indian population, many of them Christians, who played a major role in the establishment of organised cricket. Discrimination forced upon a diverse community solidarity and a 'collective identity', although the material conditions of most of its members were extremely poor.[23]

High affiliation fees (three guineas per team in Durban in 1912) meant that where there was no patronage, cricket was largely confined to the elite. Playing conditions were uniformly bad and had an influence on the style of batting and bowling: lofting the ball and maintaining line and length with movement through the air were often essential to success on the field. Players had to share equipment and mark pitches and boundaries, grounds had no facilities, and mats had to be stored at and brought from the homes of officials. The failures of 1913 in Kimberley highlighted the challenges that still lay ahead for local cricketers. Pressure applied to the city councils of Pietermaritzburg and Durban for improved sports facilities were met at best by indifference: in many quarters the Indian population was still regarded as transitory. In Durban, a site set aside for Indian sport well before World War I was handed over to whites in 1921.[24]

Enforced community solidarity may explain why there was intense, and successful, hostility to the idea of coloured cricketers participating in DDICU fixtures. In October 1914 they were barred from playing and by 1919 they were also prohibited from umpiring. A small concession, one fixture per annum, was for some years extended to Malay players.[25]

Indian cricket in Pietermaritzburg and Ladysmith (Northern Districts) showed similar characteristics. The Maritzburg District Indian Cricket Union (MDICU) was established in January 1902, boosted by the influx of Transvaal refugees. A patron of Pietermaritzburg cricket was the legendary Charlie Nulliah, sugar farmer and employer of indentured labour, brick manufacturer, racehorse owner and member of the Durban and Pietermaritzburg turf clubs, and exhibitor at the Royal Agricultural Show; he was one of few Indians to transcend racial boundaries. Although a touring Teachers XI from Durban played several matches in Pietermaritzburg in January 1916, by the end of World War I 'there was little organised cricket in Maritzburg'. Indian railway workers and traders lived in

Ladysmith from the 1880s, but organised cricket was not recorded there until after World War I.[26]

While Natal was a British colony, cricket did not develop among the indigenous Zulu-speaking people in the same way as in the Xhosa-speaking communities in the Cape. The reasons were twofold. First, Christian mission efforts in that region were dominated by American, Norwegian and German missionaries from non-cricket-playing countries. Secondly, and more significantly, colonial control in Natal was based on a system of indirect rule and segregation that left old social conventions intact. Unlike the Cape, where people were forcibly integrated through conquest, most Africans in Natal were governed indirectly through the protection of the chieftaincy and customary practices.

Imvo Zabantsundu commented in 1893 that football, which had not yet been introduced to the Cape, was preferred in Natal above cricket and tennis, the popular sports in the Cape Colony.[27] Nevertheless, there are some cricket reports in the early *Inkanyiso lase Natal* (Light of Natal) and *Ilanga lase Natal* (Sun of Natal) newspapers. The influential Methodist mission at Edendale near Pietermaritzburg seemed to be the main base for cricket.[28] In December 1893, for example, Edendale played against New Scotland, an African area of Pietermaritzburg. The team list on this occasion reflected the fact that Edendale was home to one of the most affluent and influential *kholwa* (educated and Christianised) communities in Natal. It included several surnames – Msimang, Mtimkulu, Xaba, Khumalo and Gule – of people who became prominent in the politics and social life of that colony.[29] Cricket was also played at the famous Ohlange Institute, founded by the John Dube, first president-general of the ANC, although Adams College south of Durban became the main African cricket institution in the twentieth century.

ORANGE FREE STATE IN THE MIDDLE GROUND

A Free State Basutoland Cricket Union was formed on 15 November 1892 in Bloemfontein with C.G. Fichardt as president and C.J. Tate as secretary. The meeting was attended by delegates from Bloemfontein, 'Cronstadt' (Kroonstad) and nearby 'Basutoland' (Lesotho), a British Protectorate with a British administrative and military presence. There was a tradition of cricket going back to 1850 in the Orange Free State, and the game had spread by now to every part of the Republic. Bloemfontein had five teams – Church Street CC, Bloemfontein CC, Railway CC, Wanderers CC and Combined Colleges (made up of Grey College and St Andrew's College students). The following towns were listed as having teams and were invited to join: Bethlehem, Bethulie, Boshof, Clocolan, 'Cronstadt', Dewetsdorp, Fauresmith, Ficksburg, Heilbron, Hopetown, Jacobsdal,

Jagersfontein, Koffiefontein, Ladybrand, Leeu River, Parys, Reddersburg, Reitz, Rouxville, Senekal, Smithfield, Thaba Nchu, Ventersburg, Vrede, Vredefort, Wepener and Winburg.[30]

The SACA-affiliated Free State Basutoland Cricket Union was formed after the first visit of an English touring team to Bloemfontein in March 1892. Though invited to host a game on the first tour in 1888/9, the local cricketers had declined. But when the second tour came about, in 1891/2, they raised a £150 guarantee to play against W.W. Read's team and put up a good performance in what was described as 'one of the most stubbornly contested games on tour'. *The Friend* reported:

> Our cricketers have been looking forward for some time to the match and they, with the assistance of the curators of the recreation ground and the help of the Town Council and Government, have succeeded in securely fencing in the ground and making the cricket field as smooth and even as was possible ... His Honour, the President arrived at 12 o'clock and the band struck up the Volkslied, the last strains of which had scarcely died away before Ferris delivered the first ball.[31]

The completion of the railway line to Johannesburg in the early 1890s made transport easier and 'the tiresome wagon journeys for many teams were now a thing of the past'. Inter-town matches and tournaments became regular events. In Bloemfontein, the Ramblers Club was established in 1896 with its own beautiful ground and clubhouse, and during the South African War a strong British military presence in Bloemfontein stimulated the game.[32] It was said in 1915 that 'The standard of cricket displayed during the war days was probably the highest that the Free State has ever witnessed'. A Bloemfontein and Garrison Cricket Association was formed during this time. It lasted until 1909, by which time 'most of the cricketing regiments had departed'. The commander of the artillery, General R.S. Allison, and the author Conan Doyle, who worked at the hospital set up at the Ramblers during the war, were among the prominent figures in cricket. During the early 1900s, the combined Garrison team played in the seven-team Bloemfontein first league, together with Ramblers and Collegians, who had two teams each, Railway and Grey College, the latter of whom had as their professional the ex-Cambridge and Gloucestershire player A.G. Richardson. Richardson also captained Free State SACA for a number of seasons. The province played in only four of the 14 contests for the Currie Cup before World War I. Its debut was in 1903/4, when it lost its only match by an innings and 327 runs against a strong Transvaal team, which amassed 503 runs.[33]

Despite the rigid political system and discrimination in operation in this old Boer republic, black cricketers were once again involved from the start. Kroonstad played against Potchefstroom as early as 1890. In the same year, Royal CC of Rouxville travelled to Aliwal North to play in a tournament there.[34] In 1892 the Rev. Magaba, Mr Twayi, Mr Liphuku ('Lituku'), Mr Maputle, Mr Gabashane and Mr Gxasheka ('Ta-sheka') were among the enthusiasts in Bloemfontein listed in cricket reports in *The Friend*.[35] During the Easter weekend of 1894, a team from Aliwal North played against the Oriental CC in Bloemfontein.[36] In November of the same year, cricketers from Venterstad were reportedly run into jail in Bethulie for not having 'official passes', and Venterstad also features in another occasional cricket report in 1899: the Albert CC from that town travelled to Norvalspont on the banks of the Orange River to play the Orange CC.[37] Further reports mention St Peter's School in Bloemfontein playing St Patrick's in 1900 after being bought '*impahla ye bhola*' (clothes or kit) by the Rev. Rose.[38]

By 1907 there were seven black cricket clubs in Bloemfontein. Tennis, golf and football were also being played. Oriental, captained by J.B. Twayi – a leader of the O.R.C. Native Congress and captain of the first-ever football team from South Africa to tour Europe in 1899[39] – was reported to be the strongest club in the city. Matches with white teams apparently also occurred. [40] Universals, Occidentals and Orientals were the three predominantly coloured clubs.[41]

Describing social conditions in Bethulie in the southern Orange Free State in 1911, the resident magistrate wrote that 'Natives go in for tennis, football and cricket whilst nearly all the younger population attend school. Nearly all are church goers.'[42] Cricket was also being played in the Rolong enclave of Thaba Nchu, where there was a wealthy class of landowners, who also became prominent in politics and set up their own newspaper. They played against local white teams as well, and sometimes beat them.

BEYOND THE BOUNDARIES: RHODESIA AND THE SUBCONTINENT

Cricket also spread to the southern African territories bordering the modern-day South Africa during the late nineteenth century, including Basutoland (Lesotho), Bechuanaland (Botswana), Swaziland, Rhodesia (Zimbabwe) and even Portuguese-ruled Mozambique.

The mountain enclave of Basutoland, a short drive from Thaba Nchu, became a British Protectorate in 1884, when the British intervened at the request of the Sotho chief to curb the territorial expansion of the Orange Free State. A British military presence was maintained here, particularly after the so-called Basuto Rebellion in 1880. Maseru, the capital of this area, was scarcely a hundred miles from Bloemfontein and close to border towns such as

Thaba Nchu. The first recorded match in Basutoland took place at Christmas in 1881. M.W. Luckin's history records, 'upon the invitation of Colonel Bayley, Bloemfontein trekked for two days to play the Cape Mounted Rifles at Maseru. The team slept on the veldt at Thaba 'Nchu, where [the outstanding Rev C.O.] Miles contracted lumbago, and was unable to bowl. The CMR, including the Inter-Town soldier-cricketers, Lieutenants Lyndhurst Winslow and R.B. Stewart, knocked up 366, and easily defeated a good Bloemfontein team.' As we have seen, the designation of the first regional cricket body – the Free State Basutoland Cricket Union – reflected the close cooperation that occurred. The British garrison in Maseru played regularly against teams from the Orange Free State. One of the main players was Godfrey Lagden, who later became resident commissioner and was knighted for his services in 1897. His two sons – Ronald and Reginald – went on to become the first Maseru-born players to take part in first-class cricket. Ronald, a Rhodes Scholar, gained his Blue at Oxford for four successive years (1909–12), while Reginald won his Blue at Cambridge for three successive years (1912–14) and played for Surrey. It is also of interest that Ronald, who was the first Oxford student to win Blues in four sports, represented England at rugby and Reginald at hockey.

The indigenous population also started playing the game. For example, in 1906 Try Again CC from Mohalie's Hoek lost heavily to Quithing's Mangan CC, after J. Lepotane and A. Moalasi scored half-centuries.[43] In an article on Lesotho cricket for the 1996 Zone VI Cricket tournament programme, Terry Fraenkel (then president of the Lesotho Cricket Association) pointed out that cricket in the country has not been limited to white colonials. He wrote: 'Various Basotho players have been noted over the years. Some of the old familiar names are Tlale, Mohapeloa, Lebentle, Schalala and Tsotsie … There were various clubs across the country over the years and it must be noted that Matlama Cricket Club beat the white colonials on a number of occasions.'[44]

In Swaziland to the north-east, cricket became established to the extent that at a meeting of the South African Cricket Association in April 1891, *The Star* noted: 'Mr Piton then proposed and Mr Lomas seconded that Swaziland should be joined to the Transvaal for cricket purposes.' After the South African War and the introduction of British control of the Transvaal, Swaziland became a High Commission territory under British colonial administration in 1906. The arrival of administrative personnel in the country resulted in an increased interest in cricket. An article which appeared in the *Pretoria News* referred to the game being played in Swaziland in 1909; it recalled that matches arranged by J.M. Potts's XI 'sparked off the flame that was to fire enthusiasm for cricket in a wide swathe of country sweeping from Swaziland to the Limpopo'.[45]

Jumping westwards across the Highveld to modern-day Botswana, Bowen refers to cricket having been played in 'Khama's Country' as early as 1879. In April 1887, Bechuanaland played in an unofficial Champion Bat tournament at Kimberley. It was called the 'Extraneous Tournament' because it included two sides – Natal and Bechuanaland – that did not comply with the condition that the Champion Bat tournament was a competition between 'Cricketers of the Cape of Good Hope'. Bechuanaland lost all three of their matches – to Natal, Port Elizabeth and Kimberley – but were not disgraced. There were some good batting performances from Charlie Vintcent (who later represented South Africa) and his brother Joseph Vintcent (later Sir Joseph, Rhodesia's first judge and acting administrator after the Jameson Raid), while Wishart returned match figures of 9/40 against Port Elizabeth. In the early years Bechuanaland was affiliated to Griqualand West for the purpose of administering the game. However, the vast distances involved posed problems.[46]

The place outside South Africa where cricket took root in the deepest way was modern-day Zimbabwe (Rhodesia). As we have seen, the ex-England captain and Transvaal star, Monty Bowden, fresh from a century in the first Currie Cup match played in Kimberley, was one of several top-class sportsmen in Rhodes's Pioneer Column, which left Kimberley on its journey to annex Matabeleland in April 1890. The members of this expedition participated in 'the first cricket match ever played in the country' on 16 August 1890 at Masvingo (which the settlers called Fort Victoria) near the Great Zimbabwe ruins. Bowden led A Troop (Pioneers) against the B and C Troops (Pioneers). Soon cricket became 'one of the most important relaxations' in the new colony and especially in its new capital, Salisbury (now Harare). The earliest games included Police vs The World and Police vs Civilians. The latter match happened on 12 September 1891 'to celebrate Occupation Day'.

In February 1892, Bowden played in the first cricket match to be staged in the eastern province of Manicaland when the Rest of Manicaland defeated the Chartered Company in the wide main street of what was then Umtali. Bowden claimed four wickets despite struggling with fever and the after-effects of being thrown from his cart. Unfortunately, the effort proved too much for him, and after an epileptic seizure he was conveyed to the hospital – a mud hut – where he died four days later. A man with a loaded revolver sat there all night to protect the corpse from wild beasts and the next day he was buried. Owing to the scarcity of wood, the coffin was made out of whisky cases.[47]

The Ndebele were conquered, primarily by the Maxim machine gun, and Jameson's force marched into Bulawayo in November 1893. Lobengula fled northwards and a search party of 34 men sent out to capture him was cut off by the Shangani River and were attacked by the Ndebele. Three soldiers broke out and set out to call for reinforcements, but the others perished. All over England 'people thrilled to read of the little band of brave men singing "God Save the Queen" when their last round was fired, until one by one they died'.[48] Rhodes went back to Cape Town to a hero's welcome whilst the return of victorious soldiers to Salisbury was celebrated by a cricket match between those who fought in the Matabele War and the 'Stay-at-homes', as they were dubbed. It was a period when cricket contests rotated with battlefield hostilities.

Cricket grew apace with the new colony. By 1894 Bulawayo had four teams – Queens, B.A.C., the Matabeleland Mounted Police and the 7th Hussars army unit stationed nearby. In 1895 the first inter-town match between Salisbury and Bulawayo took place, necessitating a 600-mile round trip. Rhodes's former secretary, Sir William Milton, who organised the first English tour and captained South Africa in 1888/9 and 1891/2, was called to Rhodesia in 1896 to reorganise the civil service, and within four years the entire administrative establishment was unified in his hands. He was responsible for the establishment of the Salisbury (now Harare) Sports Club cricket ground, located next to President Mugabe's current residence, when the club was given free title 'ahead of other applications', and personally saw to the formation of the Rhodesia Cricket Union in 1898. Once again, cricket, conquest and colonialism were inextricably linked.[49]

In March 1899, the first English touring team, captained by Lord Hawke, visited Rhodesia and played two matches in Bulawayo. The Salisbury contingent took ten days to reach Bulawayo as the rivers were in flood, and at one stage Taberer, who could throw a cricket ball 100 yards while standing in a barrel, was called upon to hurl a ball to which a cord had been nailed across a river. James Logan, the Cape cricket patron and parliamentarian, was so impressed with the men's determination to make the game that he donated the Logan Cup, which became Rhodesia's version of the Currie Cup for competition between the provinces and which was played for the first time in 1903.

After affiliating to SACA, Rhodesia participated in the Currie Cup for the first time in 1904/5. Freddie Brooks, who later played rugby for England, struck 61 out of a total of 115 for the well-beaten Rhodesians against Transvaal.[50] This was a one-off occasion and it was only in the 1930s that Rhodesia again took part in the Currie Cup. After World War II, Rhodesia participated in this SACA domestic cricket competition on a regular basis until independence in 1980, even though the colony was never incorporated into South Africa, as had been expected in the early part of the century. Starting with Denis Tomlinson in 1935, a number of Rhodesian players were selected to play for South Africa SACA over the years.

In the 1890s, many black mission people from the eastern Cape accompanied the British colonisers as clerks, teachers and missionaries, and they soon started playing cricket as well as sending in reports to the eastern Cape newspapers. In 1898, they formed the inappropriately named Loben CC, after Lobengula, vanquished chief of the Matabele. In 1901 the Loben CC played 10 matches and won them all, according to the secretary, R.H. Sioka.[51] Asian and coloured clubs were set up as well, for example, the Ottomans, Pioneers and Californians in Bulawayo.[52] Inter-town matches were started and a framework of organisation developed which would later become knitted into cricket activities south of the border; knowing this will help us understand how M.I. Yusuf of Durban later came to score over 400 in Bulawayo and how Basil D'Oliveira led a touring team to what was then Rhodesia.

Before World War I, cricket had spread to every corner of southern Africa and had a diversity and depth which the existing cricket literature has notably failed to grasp.

38

'The bonds of Union within the Empire'

South Africa SACA in international cricket before World War I

> It has the right to be proud of its achievements, and of the
> men responsible for them. South Africa, in Vogler, gave
> the world one of its greatest bowlers. South Africa, in
> Sherwell, developed one of the finest wicket-keepers in the
> history of the game. South Africa, in Faulkner, produced a
> world's batsman. Googly bowling was not a South African
> innovation, but it took root in this country, and the fruit was
> more prolific and productive than in the country of its origin.

> – Luckin, *History of South African Cricket*, 1915[1]

Following the first English tour to South Africa in 1888/9, the formation of the
South African Cricket Association and the launch of the Currie Cup competition,
South Africa SACA joined England and Australia as the only cricket test-playing
countries in the world. There were 14 tours home and away between 1889 and the
outbreak of World War I in 1914. Half of these were English tours to South Africa,
while five were SACA tours to Britain. The only contact with Australia in the same
period was a first African tour by the Australians under Joe Darling in 1902 and a
first visit 'down under' by Percy Sherwell's SACA team – by then called the Springboks – in 1910/1. These solitary south–south exchanges took place despite the fact
that the Australians had passed by Cape Town every time they went to and from
England in the nearly four decades after the first test match in 1877.

Owing largely to the prompting of the Transvaal Cricket Union president and
cricket sponsor, Sir Abe Bailey, SACA and these countries also formed the Imperial Cricket Conference (ICC) in 1909, the precursor of today's International

Cricket Council. The formation of the ICC and the attainment of nationhood for the Union of South Africa the following year marked the growth into adulthood of South African cricket and of South Africa as a largely self-governing country or dominion within the British Empire.

South Africa SACA's first international match on 12 March 1889 at St George's Park in Port Elizabeth and the second at Newlands were the only two games of that tour in which there were 11 players on each side – most of the opponents at provincial or district level put as many as 18 or even 22 players in the field. These first two games, at first described as 'representative' matches, were to be accorded first-class status, and it was only some time later that they were recognised as official international matches.

Various writers have claimed that Major Warton's first English team was of no more than average county standard, but there were some star cricketers in it. Five of the players had represented England teams in tests against the touring Australians in 1888 – Ulyett, Abel, Briggs and Wood were in the side that beat the Aussies by an innings and 137 runs at The Oval test – Briggs taking 5/25 in the first innings and Abel making a top score of 70. England won the series 2-1. Prior to this series, Maurice Read had played in all the tests against Australia on tours there in 1886/7 and 1887/8. Smith had captained Shaw and Shrewsbury's touring side to Australia in 1887/8 and Bowden played for G.F. Vernon's party in Australia in 1887/8. Smith and Bowden also played for the W.G. Grace's Gentlemen against the Australians in 1888, while Arnold Fothergill played first-class cricket for Somerset and the MCC, and Frank Hearne from the famous cricket family was a vastly experienced player for Kent. George Lohmann was a late withdrawal.

The fact that both 'representative' matches were comfortably completed within two days is also often given as an indication of how weak South African cricket was. But if one makes wider comparisons, all three tests between Australia and England in 1888 – at Lord's, The Oval and Old Trafford – were over in two days. Australia's totals were 116, 60, 80, 100, 81 and 70, while England recorded scores of 53, 62, 317 and 172. The early standards of South African cricket perhaps need to be judged more cautiously than just taking over old 'Home' assumptions. Similarly, the way in which matches were adjudged to have been first-class or tests needs to be revisited critically to see if some of the new scorecards provided in this book for the first time should not be accorded official status as well.

The second England team that visited in 1891/2 played only one test match at Newlands (19, 21, 22 March), winning by a massive innings and 189 runs. This was regarded as the strongest of the four teams to tour South Africa in the 1880s and 1890s. (Two days after the Newlands test in late March 1892, another England team defeated Australia by an innings and 230 runs at Adelaide but lost the series 2-1.) The bowling was particularly strong, with J.J. Ferris, who had previously played for Australia, taking 13 for 91 in the solitary test match. The side also included a previous Australian captain in William 'Billy' Murdoch, and the test match produced the remarkable statistic of four members of the same family all being in action. Brothers Alec and George Hearne played for the tourists, as did their cousin John, while a third brother, Frank, made his debut for South Africa. This match also produced the first instance of a wicket-keeper scoring a test match century, with Henry 'Harry' Wood going in at no. 8 to make the match's highest score of 134 not out. It was the only century of his first-class career.

South Africa made its first tour to England in 1894, and the issue of whether 'Krom' Hendricks should be chosen caused much debate. The non-selection of Hendricks and the 18-year-old Jimmy Sinclair, and the unavailability for business reasons of A.B. Tancred, acknowledged by all to be head and shoulders above all other batsmen in South Africa at the time, weakened the team. The South Africans only received their itinerary when they arrived in England and were disappointed that it contained only half-a-dozen games against first-class counties and even more so when the counties followed what has become the modern trend of resting their senior players and giving opportunities to youngsters.

The tourists managed to win 12 out of 24 matches against seven draws and five defeats. Their memorable performance came on the first visit of a South African team to Lord's when they beat MCC and Ground by 11 runs after the W.G. Grace-led home side collapsed from 63/3 to 72 all out. The collapse was inspired by the two slow left-armers, James (better known by his nickname of Bonnor) Middleton and George Rowe, who took 6/35 and 3/37 respectively.

The South Africans had to overcome the twin difficulties of a very wet summer and the use of turf wickets. A couple of the players had county experience, but for the majority it was a new experience. This was to become the story of South African cricket, until the first home test played on turf at Newlands in 1931, of being very competitive under home conditions but struggling on their visits to England. They only possessed one bowler with any kind of pace in Clement Johnson and the burden of taking the most wickets fell to Middleton and Rowe although at a price. Johnson had learned to play his cricket in Ireland, where he represented Dublin University up to 1893 before moving to Johannesburg for health reasons.

The star batsman for the tourists was 19-year-old Cyril Sewell, who scored more than 1,000 runs at an average of 30.52. This included an innings of 170 against Somerset – the first century for South Africa – and another of 128 against Derbyshire. Unfortunately he was lost to South African cricket the following year, as he played out the remainder of his career at Gloucestershire.

Not surprisingly, the tour was a financial failure and at one stage towards the end of the itinerary the team nearly got stranded in Belfast when they were not able to pay their bills. Part of the reason for this was the South African reluctance to assist the press – Castens was under instructions following the controversy generated by the omission of 'Krom' Hendricks from the team and Harry Cadwallader's demotion for criticising this omission. Halliwell said 'a great blunder of tactics was made'.

A notable improvement was seen in some of the performances against the next touring team from England in 1895/6, who played three test matches. The series was dominated by one of England's all-time great bowlers, George Lohmann, who wreaked havoc on the matting wickets. He took 35 wickets at an average of 5.80 and was personally responsible for 12 of the record number of 23 bowled dismissals in the first match at Port Elizabeth. No other England bowler took more than five wickets in the series. Although he bowled at no more than medium pace, Lohmann swung the ball both ways and also made effective use of change of pace and angle of attack. Poor health caused him to spend English winters in South Africa, and he eventually emigrated to the dry air of the Karoo. He managed the second South African team to tour England in 1901 shortly before his death. Surrey Cricket Club members, when they follow modern England sides on tour in South Africa, make pilgrimages to his grave near the rural village of Matjiesfontein, a two-hour drive from Cape Town.

Although the South Africans were well beaten by 288 runs in the first test at Port Elizabeth and by an innings in the other two games at Johannesburg and Cape Town, the 1895/6 series did see the emergence of Jimmy Sinclair as the player who would put South African cricket well and truly on the map. He was only 19 years old and his figures for the series were not particularly impressive – 103 runs at 17.16 and eight wickets at 30.37 – but his innings of 40 in the second game was the highest for South Africa in an official international match at that stage. 'Barberton' Halliwell topped it with 41 in the second innings, but Sinclair was to regain the honour during the 1898/9 series and hold it for an unbroken seven years.

Tall and powerfully built, Sinclair liked nothing more than to hit the ball hard or bowl as fast as he could. His shining hour certainly came in the two-match series against the fourth England team in 1899, by which time he was just 22. He opened the batting in the first match at Johannesburg and was run out for 86. Surprisingly he was dropped down to no. 4 for the second match at Cape Town but responded with South Africa's first test-match century in the first innings. It was also his maiden first-class century. He had not bowled in the previous match but came on as second change in England's first innings to take 6/26 in 12 overs and become the first player to achieve this double. Thanks to Sinclair's efforts the South Africans managed to lead on the first innings for the first time in both matches, but suffered calamitous fourth-innings collapses in both matches (99 at Johannesburg and 35 in 22.4 overs at Newlands) to lose the advantage and be beaten in the end. C.B. 'Buck' Llewellyn, another gifted all-rounder, joined Sinclair in playing in both the 1895/6 and 1898/9 series. They were the advance guard of the golden generation that would beat England in both the next two home series and also put up a good fight against a full-strength Australian team in 1902/3.

But before then South Africa made its second tour to England in 1901 in highly controversial circumstances under the captaincy of Murray Bisset, who was to remain SACA's youngest captain until the end of the racial era in 1991. The tour was originally scheduled to take place in 1900, but was postponed by a year because of the outbreak of the South African War. The war was still raging in 1901 but because of a misplaced confidence that the British would soon win, the sponsor James Logan and the team, working with Lord Hawke in Britain, decided to proceed with it. SACA, which had not met since 1899, had nothing to do with the arrangements.

The war disrupted many cricketers' lives. Internationals like Jimmy Sinclair, A.B. Tancred and E.A. Halliwell became refugees in the Cape Colony rather than sign up for the Republican forces, as was required of all men living in the South African Republic. In Cape Town, a refugees team played against local clubs, which themselves were affected by call-ups, particularly after Boer commandos took the war into the Cape Colony. All sorts of war legends arose about the cricketers on the 1901 tour, including one that Sinclair very nearly did not make the tour as he had allegedly been captured by the Boers and had to escape from a POW camp and make his way to safety behind the British lines.[2] The team contained a prominent Afrikaner cricketer, the fast bowler Johannes Jacobus 'Kodgee' Kotze. However, his father had been to Bishops and he had enlisted as a loyalist member of the Cape civil service on the side of the colonial forces, so his presence on tour hardly constituted the sensation some wished it to be. Kotze was as fast as any bowler in the world, but was badly let down by his colleagues' inability to hold slip catches.[3]

The team's departure was hardly auspicious. In the first place Cape Town was in a state of war and, secondly, friends and relatives could not bid them farewell because of an outbreak of bubonic plague. When they arrived in England they were greeted by a letter from the famous Conan Doyle written to *The Spectator* to the effect that the team would have been better employed fighting in South Africa than touring England to play cricket. J.J. Kotze himself summed up the tour, which consisted of a mixture of first-class matches against counties as well as lesser opposition, as follows:

> Has the tour fulfilled expectations? Notwithstanding the lack of success against the first-class counties, I think the answer can be in the affirmative. During a run-getting season our batsmen did not do themselves justice, but then one must consider the vast difference in batting on a matting wicket and on a turf one. We in South Africa are accustomed to the ball taking an amount of spin, but generally it comes the same height. In England again at times it takes no spin and comes at all sorts of heights.[4]

The tour nevertheless produced some outstanding individual highlights. Maitland Hathorn scored 239 in five hours out of a total of 692 against Cambridge University. In another match on tour, Halliwell, whom W.G. Grace compared with the best stumpers in the world, pulled off two leg-side stumpings off successive fast yorkers and nearly completed a hat-trick of such dismissals. Hathorn, who came on tour as an unknown quantity, topped the batting averages with 1,261 runs at 35.02 while Sinclair, although not performing up to his South African form with the bat, was the pick of the attack, with 106 wickets at 16.84. C.B. Llewellyn, because of his commitments as a professional with Hampshire, only had four innings but gave a sign of things to come with an average of 38.25 and 25 wickets at 14.84. He also made a double century (216) for Hampshire against the tourists. Overall, the team played 25 matches – only 15 being first-class – for 13 wins, nine defeats, two drawn encounters and one tie.

The arrival after the war of a full-strength Australian team, captained by Joe Darling, and including such legends as Victor Trumper, Clem Hill, Monty Noble and Syd Gregory, was the most significant development since the initial visit of Sir Aubrey Smith's team. They had just beaten England 2-1 in a five-match Ashes Series and were invited to stop over in South Africa on their way home. They played three tests between October and November 1902.

In the first test in Johannesburg, the South Africans caused a sensation by compiling their highest-ever total of 454, thanks in the main to a second-wicket partnership of 173 between Llewellyn and Louis Tancred, both of whom were dismissed in the nineties by Trumper. There was good support from two new caps, Arthur 'Dave' Nourse and Hathorn. There were five new caps in this match and, of these, Nourse, Hathorn and Louis Tancred were all to contribute significantly to South Africa's success in the first decade of the twentieth century. More sensation was to follow when the South African captain, Henry Taberer, enjoyed the luxury of being able to enforce the follow-on – a privilege that no South African captain would have against Australia again until the 1949/50 series. Australia had little trouble in saving the match and could, in fact, have won had there been more time available than the three days allocated for the game.

There were extenuating circumstances as far as the visitors were concerned. They arrived in Cape Town and were immediately whisked up to Johannesburg to play the game at an altitude of 6,000 feet. They had also never played on a matting pitch before which required some adjustment. They proved themselves to be quick learners and won the second match, also at Johannesburg, by 159 runs and the third at Cape Town by ten wickets. This was in spite of Sinclair scoring centuries in both these latter matches and Llewellyn taking 25 wickets in the three-match series. Sinclair, in fact, made three centuries in only eight innings against Australia, as he got another one in a tour fixture for a Transvaal XV at Pretoria.

The 1902 Australian tour marked the start of the second phase of South African international cricket. They now advanced from being learners to competitors. The showing they put up against Australia was instrumental in the success that would follow against England. The drawn first test in 1902 was the first out of nine that South Africa had not lost, even though the first victory had eluded them. (Of interest is the fact that the third test of 1895/6 ended with stumps drawn at 5.30 pm and South Africa at 111 for nine, 'but play continued when the crowd demanded a finish'. South Africa lost by an innings and 33 runs.)[5]

According to Louis Tancred, one feature of the touring team would have a significant impact on the future strength of South African cricket. The Australian team was packed with all-rounders and, in fact, all 11 of their players bowled in the match against the Transvaal XV. It was a lesson that was quickly learned and South Africa rapidly became a team of all-rounders. In the subsequent winning series against England in 1905/6 and 1909/10, they regularly used seven bowlers in an innings with their quartet of googly bowlers supported by Sinclair, Nourse and 'Tip' Snooke. Llewellyn was not available for most of this period as he opted to play for Hampshire only, until he fell out with the county. Since then South Africa has always produced quality all-rounders, probably more so than any other country, and this remains true in the modern era.

In 1903 the South African Coloured Cricket Board (SACCB) was formed, leading to the anomalous situation that there were now two national controlling cricket bodies – the SACCB and the whites-only South African Cricket Association (SACA). Strictly speaking, therefore, the South African international team from then on should be recognised as having represented SACA – by choice (since the exclusion of 'Krom' Hendricks in 1894), only part of South African cricket and not all of 'South Africa'.

South Africa SACA's rapidly improving upward curve of performance continued when they made their third tour to England in 1904. They lost only three matches out of 26 and managed to beat an England XI convincingly at Lord's and draw with the South of England at Hastings. Once again first-class matches were arranged, as in 1901, but no test matches. All the counties put up their strongest available combinations with the exception of Lancashire and Nottinghamshire. Thus Yorkshire, against whom the tourists drew twice, fielded the likes of Wilfred Rhodes, George Hirst, F.S. Jackson, David Denton and Lord Hawke; Surrey fielded Tom Hayward and Sussex C.B. Fry and Ranjitsinhji. These were all England internationals of some note. The success of the team owed a great deal to two factors: for the first time they had a reliable opening batting combination in William Shalders and Louis Tancred, and a proper new ball attack in the form of Sinclair and Kotze.

From a cricketing point of view, the most significant advance was the development of the wrist spin attack, which was to prove so lethal under home conditions in the next two home series. Reggie Schwarz experimented with the googly before the third tour match against Cambridge University and used it for the first time in the fourth game against Oxford University, taking 5/27 in 7.2 overs. Prior to that, he had been a run-of-the-mill off-break bowler who was primarily in the team for his batting. Unusually he bowled only the googly and proved difficult to play with effective changes of pace and a packed leg-side field. His colleague Gordon White, who was also primarily in the team as a batsman, spun the ball both ways and his googly was difficult to read, according to contemporary reports, although he did not have the same control as Schwarz and thus could be expensive.

When the SACA team returned home for the 1905/6 series against England, they were joined by two other exponents of leg spin in Aubrey Faulkner, who was destined to become South Africa's top batsman, and Ernie Vogler. The 1904 side also had a much more solid look to its batting than any of its predecessors in spite of the fact that Sinclair once again failed to repeat his form in England. Hathorn and White in the middle-order had good tours while Llewellyn made a big difference when he was released by his county, averaging 56.33 from his eight innings. Of those who played regularly, Tancred topped the averages with 1,640 runs at 48.23, including an innings of 250 against Scotland, while Hathorn (1,339 runs) and the England-born and -educated captain, Frank Mitchell, also topped 1,000 runs. Schwarz, who was also England-born but who learned most of his cricket in South Africa, topped the bowling with 96 wickets at 14.81, while Kotze took 117 wickets at 19.34 and Sinclair 100 wickets at 22.85.

The 1904 tour was another financial disaster, which was not surprising given that no tests were played, although 22 out of the 26 matches were accorded first-class status. It was asking too much at this stage for a South African tour to attract as much publicity as a test series between England and Australia, which is what the local public had come to expect. However, the tour had a sponsor in Sir Abe Bailey, which meant that expenses were adequately covered. Interestingly, the touring party of 14 (not including Llewellyn) had ten players from the Transvaal and four from Western Province, which indicated that the growth of the game under SACA had become concentrated in these two main centres. Durban had at that stage not hosted a test match, while Port Elizabeth had not hosted one since 1896.

The successes in England in 1904 set the table for England's first official tour to South Africa in 1905/6 under the captaincy of Sir Pelham Warner. It was easily the strongest England team to visit South Africa up to that stage. The hosts were given a huge boost when Transvaal beat the tourists by 60 runs in the sixth match on the itinerary. Schwarz and Faulkner gave an early indication of the threat the googly quartet were to pose when they took 15 of the 20 wickets between them. Not surprisingly, eight of the Transvaal XI were included in the South African side for the test series.

The SACA selectors, it must be added, gave the team an unheard-of vote of confidence when they announced that the chosen XI would play in all five test matches, something which has happened only four times in the history of test cricket. It nevertheless came as a surprise that South Africa won the series so easily – by a 4-1 margin. After scraping home by one wicket for a historic victory in the first test, South Africa won by increasingly larger margins (nine wickets in the second match and 243 runs in the third) before there was a setback in the fourth match (defeat by four wickets). The South Africans finished the series in a blaze of victory with an innings victory in the final encounter.

Percy Sherwell, South Africa's first winning captain, commented:

Whilst one cannot say that the MCC team [all England teams toured under the banner of the MCC in those days] which visited South Africa in 1905-06 under the captain of PF Warner was thoroughly representative of All-England cricket at that time, yet it was a good side and, in the opinion of most people in this country, capable of defeating any side South Africa could put in the field. This was the first England team that participated in Test matches against

South Africa and, as a result of this tour, South African cricket was accepted by both England and Australia to be up to first-class standard.[6]

Amidst the euphoria of the triumph there was an event before the tour that could not be ignored and showed that racial attitudes had hardened since the 'Krom' Hendricks non-selection in 1894. Sinclair was one of five members of the Wanderers Club, which hosted the first three international matches, to petition the committee to allow coloured and Indian spectators to be permitted into the ground. In this they were supported by a still relatively unknown attorney, M.K. Gandhi, who went on to launch various passive resistance campaigns in the Transvaal and Natal before he returned to India and political fame. The committee first tried to postpone a decision until after the England tourists had gone home and then chose the easy way out by saying that there was no room for the additional spectators. This was not the end of the matter, as club members forced the matter to a vote, but it was lost 29-51.[7] The matter had first been raised ahead of a British rugby tour to South Africa in 1903, and it was clear that attitudes remained hardened. Gandhi made several more attempts to hire the hall at the Wanderers for functions, to no avail. SACA, as well as the country-to-be, was by now firmly on the path to an unforgiving segregation.

Returning to the historic 1905/6 series, the impact that the four South African wrist spinners had is illustrated by the fact that they took 43 wickets among them in the five matches. The South African batting had also vastly improved on what they had achieved in previous series, with White scoring 437 runs at 54.62 and Nourse 289 runs at 48.16. Both White and Hathorn scored centuries, thus bringing an end to the monopoly of Sinclair as South Africa's only centurion. White's innings of 147 in the second innings of the third test became South Africa's highest test score. The home side had also learned the lesson of the importance of having all-rounders, with all 11 batsmen reaching double figures in the first innings of the third test. Eight of the 11 players had averages in excess of 20 for the series, which was remarkable at the time.

SACA's first golden era reached its zenith during their first official test tour to England in 1907. They drew two of the three tests and went down by only 53 runs in the second match at Leeds, where they came unstuck on a sticky wicket. Despite a brilliant second innings of 54 by C.B. Fry, the South Africans might have won the match.

This was also the first tour when SACA's South African team was known as the Springboks. In 1902 SACA had decided on the rampant lion as their emblem, but it voted 16-8 in January 1907 for a name change. Henceforth, SACA's team would wear the striped green-and-gold blazer and the Springbok on the badge and cap.[8] The change emanated from the first South African rugby tour to England the previous year, when Paul Roos introduced his team as the Springbokken; instantly a new brand was created, synonymous with the gazelle-like athleticism and hardy nature of the 'bronzed colonials' brought up on the African veld. For the next 70 years, it would be SACA's highest badge of honour, though to black cricketers it would become a symbol of exclusion.[9]

Consistency of selection was again a feature of the 1907 tour to England, with the 11 players who had won the series in South Africa being retained for most of the matches and only 13 players being used in the tests. The captain, Percy Sherwell, who had batted at no. 11 when South Africa won their first-ever test match, played a brilliant innings as opening batsman in the second innings of the first match at Lord's to make the only South African century of the series and effectively save the game after England had led by 288 runs in the first innings. At the end of the series Vogler was hailed as one of the best bowlers of his type in world cricket, but the problems the batsmen had in adapting to turf pitches remained. As a result, only Sherwell and Nourse averaged 30 with the bat on tour. This was born out by comments made by Sherwell: 'Our batting, which on the matting wickets in South Africa, was so consistent, was never to be depended upon, and it was this branch of the game that failed us. I would be pleased if I could say that the good wickets produced better results, but this was by no means the case, as we failed both on good and bad wickets. Except for the first Test at Lord's, our bowling was never collared.'[10] The accuracy of Sherwell's remarks was born out when the South Africans got back on home turf for the 1909/10 series against England, when they repeated their series win of 1905/6, albeit by a narrower 3-2 margin.

The 1909/10 tour nevertheless contained the first evidence that SACA's golden era was coming to an end. The England team was not particularly strong, particularly in the bowling department. For some reason never explained, Colin Blythe, the outstanding slow left-armer who had been so effective on matting pitches, played in only two of the five test matches, taking ten wickets in England's victory in the final match at Newlands. The batting relied heavily on Jack Hobbs, who made 539 runs at 67.37. It was no coincidence that in the two matches that England won, Hobbs played a match-winning second innings of 93 not out batting at no. 5 in the third test and then set up the fifth test victory with his innings of 187 after England had won the toss. Hobbs's century enabled England to take a first-innings lead of 314, which was in stark contrast to the rest of the series, when there was virtually no first-innings advantage. Indeed, the two teams were tied on the first innings at the Lord's ground, the first test match to be played in Durban.

South Africa also had an unhealthy reliance on Faulkner for their runs. He gave signs of the excellent form that was to follow on the maiden tour to Australia, making his first test century and having an average of 60.55 from his 545 runs. Faulkner was equally brilliant with the ball, taking 29 wickets at 21.89, in partnership with the other great spinner, Vogler (36 wickets at 21.75). Hobbs rated Faulkner the best all-round cricketer in the world.

SACA's first venture 'down under' to face Australia in five test matches during the 1910/1 season had an inauspicious start when the home team rattled up 494/6 on the opening day of the series at the Sydney Cricket Ground. This remains a record for the first day of any test match. The bowling problems encountered in this series were much the same as they had been on the tours to England. Following the disappearance of Kotze from the scene, South Africa did not possess a fast bowler and the wrist spinners, who were very much the vogue in South Africa at that time, enjoyed less success than they had managed in England. Vogler only took four wickets in the entire series, while Faulkner carried such a batting load that he could not be expected to carry the bowling as well. He had a magnificent tour with the bat, scoring 732 runs at an average of 73.20, including South Africa's first-ever test double century in the second match at Melbourne. In all, he made more than 2,000 runs at an average of 69.33 for the full tour. Support for Faulkner was minimal apart from the batting of Billy Zulch, who made two centuries in only his second series. Largely through the efforts of Faulkner and Zulch, South Africa was able to lead on the first innings in both the second (when Faulkner got his double ton) and third matches. But they still lost by 89 runs at Melbourne when they needed only 170 for victory, before securing a historic victory at Adelaide by 38 runs. This latter result seemed to awaken Australia from some sort of slumber, as they won the fourth test by the record margin of 530 runs and the fifth by seven wickets.

The tour was nevertheless regarded as a success and another useful learning experience of what was required to meet the lofty standards of both Australia and England away from home. It laid the foundation of the triangular series held in England in 1912, which featured these three countries. Unfortunately, the SACA team did not measure up to the task and put up a very poor showing, being well beaten in five of their six matches and taking a first-innings lead over Australia in a match that was totally disrupted by rain. In the opening test of the tournament at Old Trafford, the Australian spinner Jimmy Matthews performed the unique feat of taking a hat-trick in each South African innings. Both instances were on the second day and these were the only wickets he took in the match. The South African wicketkeeper, Tommy Ward, was the final victim in both instances.

The sad truth is that the 1912 SACA team was outclassed. This was not altogether surprising, considering there were only a handful of survivors from the previous tour to England in 1907 and only Faulkner and Nourse could be considered to be still in their prime. A notable newcomer was Herby Taylor, who was to become the backbone of South African batting in the period immediately prior to and after World War I.

Overall, the tournament was not a success. The weather was poor and the matches that did not feature England were poorly supported. In this respect the fact that Australia were without five leading players, who declined to tour following a financial dispute, did not help. It came as no surprise that the Triangular Tournament venture was not to be repeated. The experience of the triangular series made it abundantly clear that South Africa needed some urgent rebuilding for the tour by England in 1913/4. The SACA selectors probably took it to an extreme against a very powerful England team, which included Hobbs, Rhodes, Phil Mead, Woolley and Sydney Barnes among others, and they named a total of 15 new caps for the five matches.

Taylor, Zulch and Nourse were the only notable survivors from previous successes and the former two carried the batting to the best of their ability. Taylor had the outstanding average of 50.80 from his 508 runs, while Zulch averaged almost 40 in a series in which England won four of the five matches by significant margins. South Africa did manage an even draw in the fourth game in Durban.

The series was dominated for England by Hobbs with the bat (443 runs at 63.28) and Barnes with the ball. The latter took 49 wickets in only four matches – he declined to play in the fifth test – at an average of 10.93. This is a performance that is unlikely ever to be repeated. Altogether, Barnes took 83 wickets in the seven tests he played against South Africa at an average of 9.85. This included 12 five-fers and six instances of ten wickets in a match!

An unnamed author, writing under the pseudonym of 'Free Lance' in Luckin's *History*, summed up the progress made by SACA in international cricket up to 1914 as follows:

> It has the right to be proud of its achievements, and of the men responsible for them. South Africa, in Vogler, gave the world one of its greatest bowlers. South Africa, in Sherwell, developed one of the finest wicket-keepers in the history of the game. South Africa, in Faulkner, produced a world's batsman. Googly bowling was not a South African innovation, but it took root in this country, and the fruit was more prolific and productive than in the country of its origin.[11]

This series brought to an end South Africa's participation in international cricket in the period leading up to World War I. By the time the English left for South Africa, preparations were already under way for the conflict. Lord Lionel Tennyson explained in his memoirs how he was on army manoeuvres in Buckinghamshire with his regiment when he heard that he had been selected. The War Office gave him and another 'soldier-cricketer', the wicketkeeper D.C. Robinson, leave of absence to tour. But, as he saw it, 'Germany was sharpening her sword; the Balkans were seething with hatred, intrigue, corruption and bloodshed; big trouble was brewing in Ireland; and already faint ripples of the maelstrom were touching the shores of England.'[12] There were sad events to follow, with many cricketers losing their lives in the muddy trenches of Europe.

Besides the immediate disruption to sport caused by this war, there were the first stirrings by 1914 of a longer term threat to South Africa SACA's complacent participation in the imperial old boys' club of international cricket. The voice of those bowlers and batsmen excluded from the whites-only system who wished for a seat at the table remained persistent, and it would in the long term be given muscle by the formation of a 'Native Parliament' in 1912 in the aftermath of Union; this was the South African Native National Congress (later, simply the ANC).

The president of the South African Coloured Cricket Board (SACCB), Isaiah Bud M'belle – 'a man of immense ability and wide-ranging talent' qualified to translate in six languages in the courts of the country,[13] who would soon become secretary general of the ANC as well – warned in Queenstown at the presentation of the Pelem Trophy at an inter-town tournament in 1914 that black cricketers wished to play against the MCC like everybody else.[14] The thunderous applause he received did not carry to the portals of power, but this soft reasoning would prove stronger in the long run than the racially exclusive ideas that conquering armies had brought to Africa. The succeeding three volumes of this *History of South African Cricket Retold* will tell that part of the story.

SOUTH AFRICA SACA TEST CRICKET HIGHLIGHTS, 1888/89–1913/14

BATTING RECORDS

15 centuries were scored for South Africa in 40 matches.

HIGHEST INDIVIDUAL SCORES
1. GA Faulkner 204, vs Australia, 1910/11
2. JW Zulch 150, vs Australia, 1910/11
3. GC White 147, vs England, 1905/06
4. GA Faulkner 123, vs England, 1909/10
5. GA Faulkner 122*, vs Australia, 1912
6. GC White 118, vs England, 1909/10

HIGHEST TEAM TOTALS
1. 506, vs Australia, 1910/11
2. 482, vs Australia, 1910/11
3. 454, vs Australia, 1902/03
4. 401, vs Australia, 1910/11
5. 385, vs England, 1905/06
6. 360, vs Australia, 1910/11

HIGHEST TOTAL AGAINST EACH TEAM
vs Australia 506, 1910/11
vs England 385, 1905/06

LOWEST TOTAL AGAINST EACH TEAM
vs Australia 80, 1910/11
vs England 30, 1895/96

BOWLING RECORDS

10 or more wickets were taken in a match for South Africa 3 times.

BEST BOWLING IN A MATCH
1. 12/127 (4/57 and 8/70) SJ Snooke, vs England, 1905/06
2. 12/181 (5/87 and 7/94) AEE Vogler, vs England, 1909/10
3. 10/116 (5/43 and 5/73) CB Llewellyn, vs Australia, 1902/03
4. 9/75 (6/17 and 3/58) GA Faulkner, vs England, 1907
5. 9/89 (6/26 and 3/63) JH Sinclair, vs England, 1898/99
6. 9/130 (5/64 and 4/66) J Middleton, vs England, 1895/96

BEST BOWLING IN AN INNINGS
1. 8/70 SJ Snooke, vs England, 1905/06
2. 7/65 SJ Pegler, vs England, 1912
3. 7/84 GA Faulkner, vs England, 1912
4. 7/94 AEE Vogler, vs England, 1909/10
5. 7/95 WH Ashley, vs England, 1888/89
6. 7/128 AEE Vogler, vs England, 1907

TEAM RECORDS

AGAINST	PLAYED	WON	LOST	DRAWN
Australia	11	1	8	2
England	29	7	19	3
TOTAL	40	8	27	5

EPILOGUE

IMPERIALISM, RACISM AND THE SHAPING OF A NATIONAL CRICKET ETHOS

> Cricket provided a vocabulary behind which acts of violence and brutality could be camouflaged.
>
> – D. Judd, *Empire* (1996)[1]

The Epilogue concludes the book by underlining a point that has been argued throughout the preceding pages: that cricket's quintessential imperial and military origins in South Africa have deeply shaped its character and that we need to understand how this happened if we are to create today inclusive cricket cultures that resonate with the democracy that arrived in 1994. Sir Abe Bailey described cricket as 'the Empire game';[2] and it 'became the symbol par excellence of imperial solidarity and superiority'.[3] As Birley puts it so aptly, 'The empire, like cricket, was hard to explain to outsiders, but like cricket it was a game the British played.'[4] Sissons and Stoddart go so far as to paint the metaphor in terms of 'cricket as imperial life and power'.[5] The most venerated institution in the British Empire, according to Lord Harris, was the MCC, 'the Vatican of cricket', and the game itself was 'God's playing field'.[6] Harris claimed that cricket had done more than any other single institution to consolidate the Empire, and it is highly significant that he excluded other political institutions, including the Crown, from his analysis.

Cricket was the epitome of British cultural supremacy,[7] 'a perfect system of ethics and morals which embodied all that was most noble in the Anglo-Saxon character'.[8] It was at the apogee of the nineteenth-century sports hierarchy, accompanied by extensive rhetoric about character building and self-control: as Barnett puts it, 'Cricket's influence on the upper-middle-class British mind with its sense of orthodoxy and respect for the rules and laws and the impartial authority of umpires, can hardly be exaggerated.'[9] John Astley Cooper, author of much high-flown prose about imperialism and sport, extolled the 'British conception of fair play … the attributes of which I call the British Imperial spirit of sport'. According to this ideology, the British were sporting, patriotic, healthy, chivalrous and generous, genial and good-natured, and, above all, clean in thought. Sport in general provided a set of symbols for belief and action and a system in which every white man would get his chance.[10] Mangan describes cricket's moral associations, symbolic interpretations and emotional undertones as providing the cement of imperial socialisation and bonding. He has written of the moral message carried by the 'British middle-class hero' and argues that cricket was the ideal medium for this.[11] E.W. Hornung (the creator of Raffles, the cricketing house-burglar) considered cricket a training ground for life, whose highest duty was service to Empire.[12]

Imperial sport was the propagator of moral metaphor and political symbolism, inculcating the character necessary to overcome the physical and psychological problems involved in imposing civilisation on 'lesser breeds'.[13] 'The language of games became the language of adventure and the highest endeavour, designed to sustain the young under fire, whether from fast bowlers or insurgent tribesmen.'[14] Certainly, sport encouraged the subordination of personal ambition to the needs of the team. Kirk-Greene goes so far as to say that the self-assurance engendered by sport was essential to the confidence trick involved in the domination of thousands of indigenous people by a handful of whites.[15] The more extreme writers on cricket and imperialism were of the opinion that only those of British stock or assimilation had the temperament and courage to play the game. The Germans, for example, were doomed to lose the war because they had no experience of fair play nor the 'pluck' required to play British games.[16] Cooper recalls a cricket match in West Africa and suggests that blacks were congenitally incapable of facing fast bowling.[17] Added to this vacuous racism was the glorification of war in the image of sport.

Cricket was an undeniably English invention, and gratifyingly confusing for foreigners, especially in xenophobic times. It was exported to those countries with a British culture, where it was paraded as the 'national game', an emblem of Britain, and 'the source of all light'.[18] Conveniently, it promoted ethnic unity while encouraging social distance and ascendancy, the 'cultural bond of white imperial fraternity',[19] which was characterised by a supreme self-confidence. Cricket at the turn of the century was 'heartily idealistic'.[20] The British, it was assumed, had a particular aptitude for games and this proficiency was suitably linked to a genius for government.[21] 'It was in sports above all … that the essence of Englishness, what distinguished us from the effete, inferior foreigner, was encouraged and expressed.'[22] There was but one short step from this level of rampant chauvinism to a straightforward racism, which was accepted as part of the 'natural' order. Wilkinson writes of a 'synthetic gentility' which engendered a 'mystical sense of otherness'.[23] Midwinter has identified a Victorian partiality for formalism and religious mystique whose 'twin drives converged on cricket and gave the game an apparatus of complex rules and a layer of myth and mystique'.[24] It is probable that such conventions proved a great comfort and psychological stability in a country such as South Africa in which the law and authority of a white minority were always fragile. Even in the late 1920s Theodore Cook was writing, 'For the spirit of the best of all our sport is the one instinctive factor in the English character which no foreigner will ever vanquish.'[25] Indeed, the British did not simply play cricket; they adopted a style that set them apart. As Vasili puts it in the context of the history of another very British sport, association football, '[In] the practical acquisition of (uncodified) moral values ... the goal was not the back of the net but ascendancy to a higher plane of awareness of one's individual and collective role in life.'[26] Black and Nauright argue that imperial sport, cricket in particular, 'sought to simultaneously impress and intimidate locals with its power and superiority'.[27] Perhaps the final word on the link between cricket and imperialism belongs to Midwinter: 'Cricket was the sport of the imperialists. It was evidence of the empire builder's credentials, and the badge of his Englishness.'[28]

As Birley points out, the sort of feudal Britain represented by cricket commended itself to the imperial class. Sandiford sees the origins of cricket as essentially pre-industrial and Georgian, which may in part explain why it has barely spread beyond the limits of British imperial influence. Birley maintains that cricket, like many other sports, provided a haven for reactionaries in committee rooms dominated by men operating without concession to democracy, thus fostering conformity and solidarity through traditional authority and approved values.[29] Individualism was frowned upon and team spirit extolled in the interests of group dominance. The international network of personal relationships which developed between men of like mind was to prove durable and influential well into the second half of the twentieth century and had considerable bearing upon the development of South African cricket.

The touring teams to South Africa of 1891/2 (under W.W. Read) and 1895/6 and 1898/9 (captained by Lord Hawke) had about them an air of gentlemen at leisure, but they were also characterised by imperial proselytising. The fact that a number of Australians (John Ferris,[30] Billy Murdoch,[31] Sammy Woods,[32] and Albert Trott[33]) were members meant that they might just as readily have been named 'Imperial Wanderers' as 'England'. The first visit of the South Africans to England in 1894 was considered to be worth more than that of a 'Minister or the efforts of an Agent-General'.[34] Pelham Warner,[35] captain of the 1905/6 tour to South Africa, wrote of 'fighting spirit', 'British manhood', 'fair play' and 'hearty good fellowship'. Touring teams were both promoters of the game and an imperial bonding agent, spreading cultural patterns, standards and conventions and 'raising an awareness of a shared cultural patrimony' by defining the relationship between metropolis and colony.[36] Donald Currie donated his cups to promote the 'good old English games of football [and] cricket',[37] and the name of Cecil Rhodes was often invoked in sporting circles. In the 1890s, English professionals like Charles Mills (Surrey), Johnny Briggs[38] (Lancashire) and George Davidson[39] (Derbyshire) coached in South Africa and they were followed by hundreds of 'pros' in the decades that followed.[40] Some of the amateur tourists stayed on for business reasons.[41]

Cricket tours by the MCC were indeed an integral part of the imperial social scene in South Africa. On the 1905/6 tour, Pelham Warner stayed with Godfrey Lagden, former resident commissioner of Basutoland, who was then chairing the South African Native Affairs Commission, which would pave the way for segregation and the Natives Land Act after Union in 1910, and Lord Cobham,[42] ADC to the governor-general, Lord Selborne. During the following tour of 1909/10, the MCC included in its team to meet Natal at Pietermaritzburg R. Ponsonby, secretary to ex-Governor Sir Matthew Nathan. Batting at no. ten, he scored 3 not out but appeared to do little else, his place in the side presumably owing to his social standing in colonial Natal. The 1909/10 tourists were also entertained by Lord Methuen at Government House, Pietermaritzburg, and after their win in the test at Cape Town he sent an encouraging telegram. The final England tour of South Africa before World War I, was partly overshadowed by labour troubles and 'a little unpleasantness at Bloemfontein'.[43] Lionel Tennyson wrote, 'We were regarded as ambassadors from the old country.'[44] Significantly, the team enrolled as special constables in Johannesburg, which was under martial law as a result of a transport strike called in support of the striking miners.

As noted throughout this book, military influence on the development of the game in South Africa was considerable. The details presented here reinforce, as a central thesis, the inherently violent context in which cricket as a military game took root, spread and grew in the region. It was in essence a war game seeded by a military machine in a long process of systematic conquest and violence which brought southern Africa under imperial sway. South Africa's team for the first test that played England at Port Elizabeth in 1888 included Lieutenant Robert Stewart, while Brigadier General Robert Montagu Poore, the 'imperial epitome of the sportsman and moral exemplar',[45] was another soldier who had substantial influence on the South African game. An officer in the 7th Hussars who also served in India, he was a notable shot and polo player who played cricket for Bombay Presidency in 1893 while ADC to the governor, Lord Harris, and for Natal and South Africa in 1896. A number of cricketing British soldiers stayed on in South Africa after the 1899–1902 war, including A.W. 'Dave' Nourse[46] and Frank Mitchell.[47] Matches played at the Western Province Cricket Club's ground at Newlands in the late nineteenth century were graced by military bands and the presence of the governor of the Cape and his staff.[48] One writer made a connection between cricket and military endeavour at the beginning of World War I: 'with such traditions as Natal now possesses nothing less than a German occupation of the Province will kill the spirit of cricket which prevails'.[49] Indeed, 'The sporting ethic was part of an anti-intellectual milieu in which World War One was possible because the formula did not provide any vehicle for questioning the validity of the game.'[50] Cricket was not only training for life, but also for war: 'For war by any other name is just another British game.'[51] Perhaps the most notable South African sporting casualty of the war was Major Reggie Schwartz, the googly bowler, who died in 1918. It is worth remembering that 'Cricket provided a vocabulary behind which acts of violence and brutality could be camouflaged'.[52]

South Africa was the destination for four English cricket touring teams between 1888 and 1899. None of these tours was a financial or sporting success. From 1888 to 1906, English teams were dominant in South Africa. Out of all 98 matches played, 65 were won. 'Yet, incredibly,' writes Sandiford, 'South Africa was awarded Test match status during the 1888–1889 season.' He also points out that the West Indies (1928), New Zealand (1930) and India (1932) had to wait many years for the same privilege and suggests that racism was a factor, together with Victorian concepts of hierarchy.[53] There may have been other reasons. The wealth and financial connections resulting from diamonds and gold 'bought' South African cricket international access, and transplanted 'Anglo-Saxonism' created a local nationalism among colonial societies which ironically proved a potent imperial force. There is some evidence that the January 1896 defeat of the MCC by Natal (in which Poore scored an undefeated 107) served to excite local patriotic fervour particularly among schoolboys.[54]

Early tours were heavily dependent upon Anglo-South African commerce for survival. The first touring team of 1888/9 was funded by Donald Currie and selected by Major Warton, an official at the Cape. It is said that his team was supported by black spectators: this was the setting of a trend that was to become commonplace over the next 80 years. The inaugural South African team to England (1894, referred to by *Wisden* as the 'Africans') was described as 'commonplace' and was heading for a loss of £3,000 when 'collapse was ...

avoided by the advance of money by South African friends in England', who were possibly the 'several gentlemen connected with South Africa' invited to the opening match versus Lord Sheffield's XI.[55] Cecil John Rhodes had already guaranteed £500 for this trip.[56]

Significantly, the 1901 touring side left for England before the end of the South African War although this failed to impress the English public. Indeed, a highly critical letter appeared in *The Times* on 26 March 1901:

> Sir, I observe that a team of cricketers is about to leave South Africa for this country. At a time like the present, with the call for young men to put an end to the deplorable state of affairs there, and when we ourselves are sending out the best of our manhood for that purpose, it is, to say the least of it, the most wretched of taste for these young men to leave it on a cricket tour. I trust the British public will take this view of the matter. Next year we should be delighted to see them, but today it seems quite monstrous.[57]

The cricket public seems to have boycotted the tour, which contained no test matches while 'The whole expenses of the trip were defrayed by James Logan, with whom the whole idea of the enterprise originated'.[58] Logan has been described as the 'second of the three great patrons of [South African] cricket',[59] the others being Sir Donald Currie and Sir Abe Bailey. Even after World War I, mining capital underwrote tours – the magnate Solly Joel sponsored the 1924 tour to England.[60]

In the first decade of the twentieth century, there were fears about the sufficiency of London gold reserves in view of the liabilities to be supported. These reserves were 'precariously low for much of the pre-World War I period',[61] and South Africa loomed large in British foreign policy thinking. South African gold figured prominently in the organisation of cricket from 1900 to the mid-1920s and the very idea of the Imperial Cricket Conference (ICC, originally the British Colonial Cricket Conference) came from South Africa in 1909, the year before Union of the four white colonies was achieved. In Birley's words, South Africa was the 'favoured nation'.[62] Lord Harris was 'simultaneously both Treasurer of the MCC and Chairman of Consolidated Goldfields'.[63] Significantly, figures with closer ties to Lord's than Newlands, such as H.D.G. Leveson Gower[64] and Pelham Warner, routinely represented South Africa at the ICC as late as 1921. Similarly, the idea of the Triangular Tournament of 1912 has been attributed to Bailey. *Wisden* describes it as 'The first trial of Sir Abe Bailey's ambitious scheme', which he hoped would strengthen 'the bonds of Union within the Empire'.[65] As it happened, the South African side proved conspicuously weak and the weather was atrocious. Nevertheless, Bailey had made clear the connection between South

Left: Cricket and corporate power became increasingly intermixed after diamonds and gold were discovered. Industrialist Sir Abe Bailey, who was TCU President and SACA vice-president, initiated the Imperial Cricket Conference (ICC) in 1909 and the Triangular test series in 1912.

Above: Cape Town, 1896. The writer Mark Twain (sitting fourth from right) next to cricket patron James Logan and diamond baron Barney Barnato (with cap) on his left. Abe Bailey reclines in front of them. Barnato died at sea in 1897, and the SACCB's premier tournament was named after him that year.

Below: Lord Harris (centre, in white hat) was at the same time treasurer of the MCC and chairman of Consolidated Gold Fields. Mining magnate Sir Julius Wernher, in the dark hat, is seated next to him and Aubrey Faulkner (captain of Corner House) is on Wernher's left in this team photograph of the Goldfields versus Corner House match in Johannesburg in 1904.

Right: Griqualand West.
There were three cricket unions in Kimberley in the early 1900s, namely the GWCU (Currie Cup), the GWCCU (Barnato Trophy) and the independent DFCCU. The Progress CC, 1909 holders of the Jones Cup (pictured here), belonged to the DFCCU.

Below: Border.
The *Mfundisi* and the Colonel: Dr W.B. Rubusana and Colonel R.H. Price, presidents of the BNCU and BCU respectively, and young cricketers on the field at Lovedale College in the heart of 'the black cricket belt of the Border' around the turn of the century.

Left: Eastern Province.
The EP SACA provincial team in 1903 when Port Elizabeth hosted the Currie Cup tournament. The SA star 'Bert' Vogler is seated on the far right.

Ottomans Cricket Club

Centre: Western Province.
Ottomans Cricket Club, founded in 1882, was one of the pillars of the WPCCU and is still in existence today. It had the same address in the 'Bo-Kaap' for more than 60 years.

1914

Below: Orange Free State.
The brand-new Ramblers Cricket Club with its pavilion was a centrepiece of cricket in Bloemfontein and the base of one of the strongest women's sides in South Africa at the time.

Above: Transvaal. Black citizens were not allowed to walk on the pavements or watch cricket at the Wanderers in Johannesburg, something that M.K. Gandhi (right) protested about.

Below: Natal. The descendants of indentured labourers and 'free Indians' in Natal developed deep cricket traditions in the 20th century (unknown club, early 1900s) (bottom left). Natal SACA won the last two Currie Cup tournaments before World War I (bottom right).

By the 1900s South Africa SACA was enjoying regular tours to and from England as international cricket became part of the cricket landscape.

Top: Early tours to and from England involved long boat trips.

Middle: Knees up for the 1904 SACA players on board ship to England.

Bottom: At the heart of empire. The cricketers from the colonies received hearty welcomes in England. Here the Abe Bailey-sponsored 1904 team are entertained by the British rugby teams that had visited South Africa in 1891, 1896 and 1903.

Top left: The first Australian touring team to South Africa captained by Joe Darling in 1902.

Top right: The strong 1904 South Africa SACA team to England under Frank Mitchell.

Centre: The Wanderers ground on the morning of a test match.

Below: Dave Nourse batting in Melbourne during the first South African tour to Australia in 1910/1.

A South African Boxer
IN BRITAIN

Experiences of
ANDREW JEPTHA.

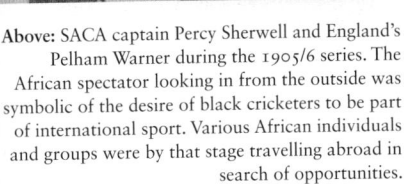

Above: SACA captain Percy Sherwell and England's
Pelham Warner during the 1905/6 series. The
African spectator looking in from the outside was
symbolic of the desire of black cricketers to be part
of international sport. Various African individuals
and groups were by that stage travelling abroad in
search of opportunities.

Top right: Andrew Jephta from Cape Town was
crowned British welterweight boxing champion in
1907. After he became blind from his injuries, the
SACCB collected funds for him during the 1912/3
Barnato tournament.

Middle left: Inter-town cricketer Paul Xiniwe
toured Britain with the African Native Choir
in 1891.

Middle right: South Africa's first Olympians. Jan
Mashiane (left) and Len Taunyane (right) ran in
the marathon in the 1904 Olympics in St Louis,
USA, while working at the World Trade Fair
in that city.

Bottom right: The first-ever SA football tour to
Britain and Europe in 1899 was by black players
from Bloemfontein. They played against teams that
are famous today, like Everton and Aston Villa.
Joseph B. Twayi, the captain (sitting centre), was
also captain of the local Oriental Cricket Club.

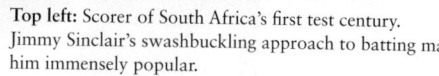

Top left: Scorer of South Africa's first test century. Jimmy Sinclair's swashbuckling approach to batting ma[de] him immensely popular.

Top middle: One of the game's great all-rounders, Aubrey Faulkner bowled high-quality googlies, hit South Africa SACA's first double century and was the first man [to] score more than 700 runs in a series, against Australia.

Top right: 'Barberton' Halliwell was famous for standin[g] up to the fastest bowlers. He impressed W.G. Grace with his brilliant wicketkeeping and was known to protect hi[s] hands with steak in his gloves.

Far Left: Many international players thought 'Bert' Vogle[r] the best bowler in the world in 1907. Together with Faulkner, Reggie Schwarz (left, above) and Gordon Whit[e] (left, below), Vogler was part of South Africa's formidabl[e] Googly Quartet after 1904.

Bottom left: 'The fastest bowler in the world': J.J. 'Boerjong' Kotze was fast and tireless, capturing mor[e] than 300 wickets in his first-class career.

Right: Three jolly captains for the Triangular Tournament held in England in 1912: Frank Mitchell (South Africa), C.B. Fry (England) and Syd Gregory (Australia). Mitchell was born in Yorkshire, played rugby for England and worked for Abe Bailey. C.B. Fry also played football for England, equalled the world long jump record, wrote several books and stood for Parliament.

African cricket and his imperial ambitions, which were accentuated by antipodean antagonism in view of the threat they posed to the primacy of Australia's sporting relations with England. The founding of the ICC cemented South Africa's position in the international fixture list, giving it the confidence to request at the outset of World War I that the schedule be advanced by one year to allow the Australians to tour in 1915/6. This was turned down by Australia pending 'the wishes of the M.C.C.', but the suggestion became of course academic.[66]

Before World War I there were many references to 'Home' in South African cricket literature: 'cricketing teams from all parts of the Empire look to Lord's as the home, and to the M.C.C. as the head of the game'. Lord Hawke's 1895/6 team to South Africa was described as the 'men from the Homeland'. Conversely, a book of biographical sketches of England players on the 1909/10 tour of South Africa describes them as arriving at the 'short end of the Dark Continent'.[67] Lord Harris wrote about a forthcoming tour as 'a strand in the elastic cord which unites the colonies and the Mother Country'. South Africa's cricket, cricketers and spectators were regularly referred to as 'colonial' and, by implication, as of a lesser standard than those of the 'Mother Country'. Even Ranjitsinhji contributed to the image with a particularly apposite South African example: 'No doubt when people play the game on a rough jumble of veldt-grass and mine-tailings in the outskirts of Johannesburg ... the feel of a bat and its sound against the ball bring back memories of the green turf and cool breezes of England.'[68] Predictably, Pelham Warner had something to say: 'wherever British men and women are gathered together there will the stumps be pitched'[69] (although horse races and golf courses seem to have made earlier appearances in many colonial settings).[70] Lord Hawke spoke in a similar vein: 'The greatest game in the world is played wherever the Union Jack is unfurled ... cementing the ties that bind together every part of the Empire.'[71] Indeed, 'The early success of the Rhodes Scholarship scheme, despite initial misgivings, was due as much to the prowess of the Australians in cricket, rowing and rugby football as to the fact that several of the scholars obtained First Class degrees.'[72] In South Africa, the governor-general remained the president of the South African Cricket Association (SACA) until South Africa left the Commonwealth in 1961, and even as late as the 1950s the literature of cricket was redolent of imperialism and the 'Home' connection. SACA's annual report of 1955 even noted the death of Lady Warner, widow of Sir Pelham.

'Australian and South African cricketers were expected to be rough-hewn, and they often were. They were additionally expected to lose, and often did.'[73] The image created was that of parent and child ('the Mother Country and her sturdy Australian and South African sons')[74] although by 1905 it was being written that '[South Africa's] education was almost complete'.[75] This proved prophetic because in 1906 South Africa won its first-ever test against England. Even this was turned to imperial advantage, as it displayed 'that grit and courage which we are so proud of saying are inherent in the British race'.[76] Local identity and imperial pride were thus conjoined, although this created ambiguous feelings about the nature of being South African and amounted to what might well be termed deferential nationalism.[77] Warner comfortingly attributed the improvement in South Africa's fortunes to visits by English teams and coaches. Historians of Australian sport have noted that matches against English touring sides resulted in 'mutual self-congratulation',[78] placing British achievement on a pedestal. Perkin puts forward the interesting idea that beating England, the Mother Country, was a rite of passage for settler communities, an indicator perhaps of eventual fitness for dominion status.[79] Meanwhile, the rules continued to be written and tours organised by the MCC in London, where most of the cricketing manuals and books were published.[80] A historian of West Indian cricket records a parallel phenomenon: 'white West Indian colonials seeking approval and recognition of their achievements from their "motherland" in this cultural arena … frantic … in the quest for approval from the MCC'.[81] Sport proved a suitably elastic bond, durable but allowing leeway for pupil to beat master and thus providing a safety valve for local aspirations. This system worked well as long as England maintained the overall sporting ascendancy. But it failed to persuade the MCC to send a full-strength England team to South Africa over ten tours until 1938/9. Before World War I, England played many matches against odds with provincial teams of more than XI.

In a very real sense, cricket was an activity that helped to define British space in a context in which 'there was little of substance to bind together geographically divided and quite distinctive colonial locales'.[82] One quarter of the globe's landmass might be coloured red on the maps, but psychological security required the regularising of local conditions and the familiarity of established customs. As Spufford comments, the red portions were no longer 'abroad' to all intents and purposes: exotic and far-flung parts of the world were 'ultimately gathered in a British hand'. He writes about 'geographic assurance' as part of the Edwardian era,[83] and there is every reason to consider the game of cricket as part of that spatial confidence. Baucom describes 'contagiously English places scattered throughout the British Empire' making up 'England's authentic and auratic architectures of belonging'.[84] One may even go so far as to emphasise the territoriality of the individual cricket field, the importance of the boundary, and the psychological impact of the safe zone behind the popping crease. Certainly, the club was a 'comforting enclave of Englishness' for people who were often, if subconsciously, ill at ease with their surroundings.[85] Anywhere in the world a cricket ground might be interpreted as a distinctive space of unquestionable, socially engineered

British origin.[86] As Barnett puts it, the playing field was 'a powerful instrument for inculcating common responses, common values and outlook'.[87] But in so far as it engendered feelings of security and togetherness and an 'accentuated Englishness',[88] it demanded social conformity and racial exclusivity. Bose notes similar tendencies in India: 'the British saw cricket as a way of keeping their own community together with little or no place there for the Indians'.[89] The imperial atmosphere, as Katz points out, was a mixture of insecurity and aggression,[90] desiring comforting symbols and space. These induced complacency and created 'protected markets of the mind' such that 'the values and beliefs of the imperial world settled like a sediment in the consciousness of the British people'.[91] For the British colonial settler, the game of cricket – and everything associated with it – was one of the storehouses of national memory.

Lowerson argues that sport perpetuated social distance in Edwardian England while effective geographical distance shrank. Thus 'middle-class bodies established a spatial hegemony, increasing significantly the number of places from which the non-select were excluded'. Hobsbawm believes that middle-class identity is essentially diffuse but that sport has been one of its defining factors and a means of acquiring and entrenching social distance.[92] Cape liberalism, with its assimilationist, paternalist approach, gave way in South Africa, in the face of fear of black competition, to a segregationist policy in which exclusive social institutions played a key role. Blacks were increasingly denied the franchise, land ownership and commercial opportunity, and their removal from middle-class sport was a natural accompaniment. Hutchinson points out that in England cricket was not a democratic game, but it did 'accommodate class differences during the contest itself', after which the participants returned to their appointed station and space.[93] Not even this was permitted in South Africa: 'attachment to cultural exclusivity remained more powerful in South Africa than elsewhere in the settler Empire'.[94] 'Social distances', argues Stoddart, 'were considered an important and integral part of maintaining order.'[95] In the context of the West Indies, Marina Warner makes an observation that applies equally well to South Africa: 'the lime demarcation lines in the turf that divided Englishmen from foreigners and natives could be rubbed out in the climate of the islands all too easily by passing feet'.[96] Jarvie's point that 'sport must not be understood abstractly or simply in the context of ideas about racial prejudice, but rather in the context of the ensemble of social relations characterizing the South African social formation' is highly apposite.[97]

C.L.R. James was able to argue, before the globalisation of the game, that cricket reflected local society.[98] While the constitution of SACA declared that its 'object ... shall be to foster and develop cricket throughout South Africa',[99] this applied solely to the white community. While ignoring South Africa's black cricketers, SACA originally included a union for Portuguese East Africa, and the 1886/7 Extraneous Inter-Town tournament involved a white team from Bechuanaland. Rhodesia was admitted to the Currie Cup competition in 1904/5, but played only one match and did not appear again until 1930.[100] The Currie Cup was instituted in 1889 as the prize for racially exclusive white cricket.[101] Apart from a few aberrations, cricket was thus thoroughly segregated and, although South Africa was to participate in 172 test matches in 41 series between 1888 and 1970, these were played only against England, Australia and New Zealand. A proposed tour to Philadelphia was called off in 1907, but in 1912/3 a Transvaal team visited Rhodesia and Portuguese East Africa.[102]

South African cricket reflected the customs and traditions of English-speaking whites and the roots of their attitudes may be found in the racism of mid-Victorian England. This involved the acceptance of race-based stereotypes and, ironically for Victorian society, the denial of individualism and self-improvement. People were thus condemned in determinist fashion to rigid, unequal groups from birth in what has been described by Lorimer as 'a new pessimism about human nature'.[103] This was justified by a paternalist attitude and linked to a class–colour dichotomy. Thus, 'among the articulate, influential wealthy middle class the cult of gentility encouraged a greater social exclusiveness and arrogance'.[104]

White attitudes towards Indians in Natal at the turn of the century are indicative of hardening attitudes to race, and they have a major bearing on the issue of sport and recreation. The reaction of a self-perceived beleaguered minority was to emphasise its homogeneity while exaggerating, by gross stereotyping, the otherness of communities that were not white. The perceived threat posed by urbanised, free immigrants from the Indian subcontinent (colloquially known as Arabs) led to virulent racism. As early as 1880, Indians had to have a pass to be on the streets after nine o'clock in the evening.[105] Racist laws were passed concerning immigration (the 'Natal formula'), the franchise and licensing to counter the 'Asiatic curse'. The trading and finance skills of the newcomers 'aroused the petty bourgeois establishment', which was unimpressed that they failed to 'wait patiently, hat in hand, outside the shrine of Victorian Anglo-Saxonism'.[106] Sir Abe Bailey, the great cricket benefactor, believed that Indians should have no rights in Natal and the Transvaal, and by 1922 he was arguing for their repatriation. Legislation against Indians was enacted in all provinces except the Cape to reinforce a segregation process assumed by white South Africans to be 'natural'. The effect of such legislation, however imperfectly enforced, was to encourage the idea that the Indian fraction of the South African population was not permanent; citizenship was given to people of Asian origin only in 1961.

Africans were regarded as minors and treated by whites intended to preserve a subordinate status.[107] Native policy at the turn of the twentieth century was a matter of limited welfare and growing control in which subject people, it was anticipated, would be civilised by a self-governing European community of higher intellect.[108] The heated debate which took place in Pietermaritzburg in 1904 and 1905 about the use of pavements is an interesting example of the dynamics of the race–space struggle. As the local paper put it, 'The majority of persons are agreed in condemning the practice of allowing natives and coloured persons generally to walk on the pavements of the City' and went on to describe the 'impertinent obstruction of superiors' and the insanitary repercussions of 'brushing shoulders' with Africans. There were now enough whites, it was argued, to ban blacks from the pavements 'to effectively prevent ladies and white men being impertinently jostled by offensive blacks'.[109] Black prison warders walking three abreast in Church Street, Pietermaritzburg, were ordered off the pavement even though they were obstructing no one. When they refused, they were arrested and charged.[110] Soon after the black cricketers of King William's Town beat a local white cricket team, Africans were barred from the pavilion.[111]

As ethnic identification and racism developed in Cape Town in the last quarter of the nineteenth century, so parallel white and black sporting bodies emerged. The *Cape Argus* argued: 'The races are best socially apart, each good in their way, but a terribly bad mixture.'[112] Newlands was made available for the Malay tournament in the 1889/90 season, but, as we have seen, segregation in cricket became institutionalised in the mid-1890s and, in spite of his excellent performances, the outstanding H. 'Krom' Hendricks was systematically excluded from the South African team, Western Province team and eventually club cricket, by the Western Province Cricket Union.[113] There was strong feeling that tests between South Africa and England could only be played by 'civilised' white men; and, as demonstrated in earlier chapters, the malign influence of Cecil Rhodes was involved. When a British army officer included his servant in a team, he was told that this was not customary; while British soldiers commented on sports segregation during the South African War. In the Transvaal, black spectators were banned from cricket, a decision deplored in 1909 by Lord Selborne, the British high commissioner. In short, the remnants of social equality were suppressed, and blacks were banished to their assigned role as a labouring class. Black middle-class aspirations and sports like cricket were marginalised.[114]

By 1900, argues Shula Marks, 'White attitudes towards Africans ... were a curious blend of paternalism, fear and contempt.' The context of these attitudes was one of racial hierarchy, solidarity and networking. White supremacy was based on supreme self-confidence and unwritten codes of conduct that determined the inclusion or exclusion of certain people, reinforced if necessary by violence. Inculcated at school level, these values and attitudes were then extended into adulthood by clubs and societies.[115] Indeed, racism and segregation in cricket owed a great deal to the schools system from which many of the influential white players emerged. The English social historian G.M. Trevelyan wrote that the muscular Christianity and games ethic which became a hallmark of English public school education in the second half of the nineteenth century encouraged a certain kind of closed conformism. He argued, 'The leisure and initiative of the individual boy was increasingly sacrificed to meet the demands of the athletic time-table, with the organised mass opinion of the boys and often of the masters to enforce obedience of a stereotyped ideal of games and good form.'[116] Robert Morrell goes further, making the point that elite white boys' schools in colonial South Africa were built on structural violence. The actions of staff and prefects were often brutal and, matched by pupil bravado, created a culture of violent masculinity. Some of the powerful people at white schools were severely damaged characters and, more commonly, simply jingoistic racists, he concludes. It was accepted that the route to male adulthood was marked by bullying, beatings and humiliation. At the same time, conventional masculine values concerning physical and mental toughness were articulated through team sport and reinforced by the cadet corps, which prepared colonial white men for the wars they were often called out to fight in. Those who did not subscribe to this ethos, the non-sportsmen for example, were openly disparaged and stigmatised even in the school magazine.[117] Sexism also became deeply inculcated into the culture of sport in these environments.

Cricket and rugby became icons of white virility. As Hattersley put it, 'In South Africa the popularity and reputation of a school tends to be judged largely by its achievements on the sports field.'[118] The first headmaster of Hilton College, the Rev. W.O. Newnham, 'was a strong supporter of [cricket] which taught a boy to play with a straight bat ... and to respect the rules of the game'. His successor, H.V. Ellis, 'welcomed organised games on account of the moral qualities which they were held to inspire'.[119] In his view, they helped to bind whites together and train them to rule over barbaric, heathen Africans and unclean Indians, 'in spite of the enervating influence of a semi-tropic sun'.[120]

Victorian-rooted mentalities and ideas about the role of sport at the boys' schools have proved remarkably resilient and account for the fact that 20 boys' schools – led by Durban High School, Diocesan College (Bishops), King Edward VII School and Grey High School – provided 212 or 65 per cent of the 326 South Africa test players between 1889 and 2016.[121] A.M. Barrett, the historian of Michaelhouse, noted the views in the school magazine in 1951 that rugby provided 'a training in courage and self-control and the best sort of toughness' – and, more importantly, a school's sporting prowess being 'a more or less accurate indication of the tone of the school'.[122] Writing thirty years later in his classic *Little England on the veld*, Peter Randall commented that 'it is probably enough to acknowledge that – despite the constant references to religion and morality – the 'tone' of the private schools is judged in public most commonly by external factors like sports results and examination and scholarship successes'. These comments about private schools would also apply to South African state schools that operate on the English public school model. Sport and 'tone' and 'standards' went together, Randall observed, but when asked to describe tone, school leaders become incoherent. A headmaster of St John's talked of 'that indefinable quality', while a headmistress of St Andrew's preferred 'that indefinable spirit'.[123]

The domination of the traditional boys' sports schools has diminished since unity in 1991 as the national players' pool in all formats has broadened, but Grey College, King Edward and Durban High School remain top of the list. The top 25 boys' schools, which continue to meet regularly under the Conference of South African Boys' Schools, mostly still have sport and 'tradition' as a core part of their value system and marketing. They pride themselves on their cricket 'cultures'. School teachers and players alike still often emerge here unquestioning about the roots of these cultures of masculinity and play that are given such prominence. And the system continues happily to perpetuate itself, inter alia, through a focus on bursaries for talented black children and the creation of elites across the colour line amid poor standards and underperformance in the general post-democracy school system. Educational psychologists have warned that the 'particular history' of local boys' schools has left them with explicit challenges in the democratic dispensation: how to honour their pasts, preserve their culture and celebrate masculinity without reproducing unhealthy practices, power relations and exclusions.[124]

Racism and sexism are still deeply embedded in modern cricket mentalities. *Cricket and Conquest* will hopefully give educationists and young cricketers something to think about regarding the construction of masculinities and the ideas that have for a long time gone with this in South Africa, as they seek to transform in changing twenty-first-century environments. By extension, this re-examination of culture and tradition should apply to the graduates of these schools, who still play disproportionately prominent roles in current sports administration, as well as the allied sports media and business which play such an important role in the corporatised world of modern-day sport.

A long, long journey

Writing and statistics require a certain discipline. Constructing an innings behind the computer or rescuing a scorecard from a 130-year-old archival haystack is a little like Tayfield bowling to Compton and Cowdrey at Newlands in 1956/7. The poetic Alan Ross described how:

> Tayfield bowled fifteen overs at a stretch for 16 runs, no one square or at mid-wicket or behind the bowler, and Compton was content, or at any rate prepared, to push him gently back. Cowdrey was mellifluous and controlled as Flagstad singing Isolde, but he was not willing to sacrifice grace to force, with the result that he took twenty minutes to score, took an hour over 6 and remained on 10 for three-quarters of an hour. At last Compton swept and connected at Tayfield, and then Cowdrey hooked Adcock, who bowled fairly fast after tea, twice to the Oaks. Compton reached 50 out of 150, and he then relaxed to the extent of 6 runs in forty-five minutes.[1]

Concentration. Discipline. Slow, hard work. Satisfying, with now and then a flash of inspiration that makes one see into infinity. Cricket and writing are similar in that way.

This book, *Cricket and Conquest*, as well as the broader research accompanying it, is part of a labour of love in a rich four-decade-long journey through the South African cricket landscape. André Odendaal, Krish Reddy and Christopher Merrett decided in May 2001 to pool their resources to write a history of South African cricket, but the story is rooted in their specific cricket experiences and the non-racial cricket struggles of SACBOC and SACB in the 1970s and 1980s. The struggle for freedom on and off the field has been our inspiration since we set out 40 years ago, each in our own way, to retell the story.

Krish Reddy grew up in the SACBOC tradition and became a collector of cricket memorabilia, which led to a passion for collecting statistics and the publication of his first compilation on the history of the Natal Cricket Board in 1986. The bibliophile Christopher Merrett stood as an umpire in windy fields next to the highway in Pietermaritzburg in the 1970s, gaining the experience with Aurora CC that would set him on the path of activism and writing knowledgeably about sport and segregation in South Africa, starting with his first article for the *Black Sash* magazine in 1983. Meanwhile, a thousand miles away, André Odendaal, an undergraduate at Stellenbosch University playing in the same team as Eddie Barlow, set out in the mid-1970s to write a book calling, within his limited understanding, for an end to apartheid in cricket.

The genesis of *The History of South African Cricket Retold* goes back to that time. Hungry to find out more about the backgrounds of black cricketers, some of whom he now met for the first time on a social level, Odendaal opened files with subject names that now constitute chapter headings in this quartet of books. Three slim almanacks, unobtainable in bookshops in this university town inspired him to start conceptualising this history. They were the 1953/4 and 1954/5 versions of the *South African Non-European Cricket Almanack* and the successor *South African Cricket Almanack*, which came out in 1969. All three were edited by Syd J. Reddy and Damodar 'Bennie' Bansda, a barman from Cape Town. These almanacks and various other related brochures and publications were in effect the inside histories of black and non-racial cricket told from the perspective of those who were marginalised.

For a quarter of a century, until the 1990s, the few systematic attempts at writing about the history of black cricketers were based largely on Reddy and Bansda's work. It provided a structure of sorts for approaching black cricket history and helped indicate what was known and what was not.

The Stellenbosch student set off in search of Syd. The soft-spoken man, in the sunset of his life, ended up leaving André his valuable collection of brochures, clippings, minutes, reports and writing. A fire was lit and André set out to do justice to a lovingly preserved story. After finishing *Cricket in Isolation* (1977), he started research for his Master's and PhD dissertations on the beginnings of black protest politics. For the second time he came across a gold mine. He was amazed, from 1979 onwards, to discover voluminous cricket reports in English and isiX-hosa in the newspaper *Imvo Zabantsundu* about Africans playing as far back as the 1880s. This started a decades-long love affair with the alternative media in South Africa, which widened his vista on the past. Starting with contributions to the *South African Cricketer* (1983), *The Barclays World of Cricket* (1985) and a chapter on 'South Africa's black Victorians' in a collection on British culture and sport at home and abroad (1988), he began writing up this wholly new (and hitherto deliberately ignored) picture of cricket. This was around the time when Krish Reddy and Christopher Merrett were beginning to publish as well, with their debut contributions in 1986 and 1983 respectively. Merrett's journey led him to becoming a first-class cricket umpire and an anti-apartheid activist in the Pietermaritzburg Detainees Support Committee, opposing rebel cricket tours and supporting the Black Sash and other community groups. Odendaal, a SACU provincial cricketer, similarly joined the non-racial SACB/SACOS and became involved in anti-apartheid activism through sport, the campus, his UDF Area Committee and the NECC. Joining the struggle meant accepting a whole new paradigm.

By the time cricket unity and political democracy arrived in the early 1990s, the three authors of this book were poised from within the perspective of non-racial sport to help redress imbalances and validate lived cricket experiences that had been shamefully neglected in the past. Each from their own vantage points in work and cricket – including positions on newly united provincial executive committees – continued their writing in that decade. With the old mainstream caught offside by the swirl of history, Reddy found his niche as the acknowledged statistician of the black experience after being requested by Ali Bacher, first CEO of the UCBSA, to start contributing on a regular basis to the *SA Cricket Annual* from 1996 onwards.

The immediate trigger for writing *The History of South African Cricket Retold* was the UCB's National Vision Conference held in Johannesburg in November 1998. There, South African cricket adopted the Transformation Charter, which had ten main 'thrusts' for the future, including 'Recording the full history of South African cricket'. The stated aim was 'to acknowledge, record and appreciate Black cricket during the past century in order to establish a rich and comprehensive history of South African cricket, recognizing our diversity as a source of strength'. André, then director of Robben Island Museum, was appointed chairperson of the UCB's Transformation Committee (TMC). He discussed with Krish the possibility of working together on history tasks. The TMC took the lead and a steady flow of activity followed. It drew up a three-year action plan and supported various history projects, including newspaper articles, recognition ceremonies and the award-winning four-part film documentary, *Iqakamba* (Hard Ball).

In 1999 Krish Reddy launched *The Other Side: A miscellany of black cricket in Natal* and André Odendaal started writing *The Story of an African Game*. As part of the new initiatives, André contacted Christopher Merrett in May 2001 about possible collaboration on a broader history. Christopher had completed a manuscript, 'Batting on a sticky wicket: A cultural, political and social history of cricket', for which he was unable to find a publisher. This provided the missing link of original work that could enable Reddy and Odendaal's niche research to be broadened into a solid general history of South African cricket. André drafted an outline for a 23-chapter book of 80,000 words on the history of South African cricket, 'which will be complemented by a second statistical companion volume by Krish Reddy [which] will provide the full scorecards of the 223 three-day games played by black cricketers [from 1972 to 1991], thus finally enabling these records to be integrated into official South African and international first-class records'.

The project was now on the road. The 2001 UCB National Transformation Review Conference, held at KwaMaritane Bush Lodge, Pilanesberg, accepted the proposal and it was formally endorsed by the UCB. The rewriting impetus gathered strength in 2002 with the publication by Krish Reddy and three outstanding activist academics, Dr Ashwin Desai, Dr Goolam Vahed and Professor Vishnu Padayachee, of *Blacks in Whites: A century of cricket struggles in KwaZulu-Natal cricket* through Natal University Press. In July of the same year, the UCB General Council decided that the Transformation Monitoring Committee, which had been driving the 'Recording Our History' thrust, would be disbanded but that Professor Odendaal 'has been charged now with recording the full history of South African cricket'. In July 2003 *The Story of an African Game* was published, bringing to the fore, in a richly illustrated way, the remarkable history of black African cricketers in South Africa from the 1850s onwards. An official UCB publication jointly brought out by David Philip Publishers and the HSRC, it was shortlisted for the Cricket Society's Book of the Year award in Britain. This ongoing work was in the meantime supported by a number of complementary projects and publications, such as Mogamad Allie's *More Than a Game* on the history of the non-racial Western Province Cricket Board (2001) and Aslam Khota's edited volume *Across the Great Divide* on black cricketers in the old Transvaal (2003).

With the momentum of critical rewriting gathering pace, André went on sabbatical to the University of Missouri-St Louis in the United States in January 2004 to write full-time on the planned history, with a launch date of the year-end in mind. His research led to the fleshing out of whole new sections – on women's cricket, the earliest African inter-town tournaments and the deeper pre-1950s histories of the old racially based boards. The possibility of creating narratives, scorecards and stats for each cricket community going back to the very beginning now became a goal, and the project escalated to a new level.

However, in August 2004 André took up employment as CEO of WPCA and WCC. His period of full-time writing came to an end, and the whole pace and context of the project changed. The plan for the books became a long- rather than short-term one. Nevertheless, the goal remained to complete a critical, well-researched and socially relevant series which could help reposition and 'decolonise' South African cricket history. The three authors persevered on their own with the research and writing of the manuscript through seven drafts, meeting from time to time to review progress and goals. The book was also kept on the agenda of CSA.

Meanwhile, the authors made various writing detours of their own. In 2004 Christopher Merrett brought out *Caught Behind: Race and politics in Springbok cricket* with Bruce Murray, drawing partly on his 2001 manuscript. This was followed by Christopher's doctoral degree, published in 2009 as *Sport, Space and Segregation: Politics and society in Pietermaritzburg*. Krish's historical knowledge also remained in demand, and in 2007 the UK-based Association of Cricket Statisticians and Historians chose him as their Statistician of the Year. André initiated various legacy projects at Newlands and in 2011 he spent a sabbatical at the University of Kentucky in Lexington, and was able to work on the manuscript again, as well as finalise a detour book on the statistical history of Western Province cricket. The research material generated by the broader project provided the foundation for *The Blue Book: A history of Western Province cricket, 1890–2011*, for which Reddy and Andrew Samson, the official CSA statistician, were co-authors. It covered all 11 Western Province boards that had existed and showed it was possible for provinces to do their own inclusive histories in ways not thought achievable before, including the tracing back of common roots statistically and in narrative ways to the very earliest years of cricket in every region.

The CSA Board again resolved to support the project, but for the next two years CSA was engulfed by a leadership crisis and the history plans slipped off the agenda once more. However, the whole process was dynamically reactivated after the major CSA Transformation Indaba held at Fourways near Johannesburg in September 2013. The Indaba approved the fundamental transformation of the existing operational model for South African cricket under the new CEO, Haroon Lorgat. Odendaal was asked to give one of the conference addresses, on 'History and legacy'. Important recommendations for the future of CSA emerged. 'History', and the need to acknowledge the past properly, featured as one of the main categories in these decisions. Six resolutions were passed, including: 'CSA to ensure completion of the commissioned history of CSA cricket and, off this platform, produce portable exhibition starter packs and seek support from sponsors and TV to do a full-scale TV series (as big as rugby's Springbok Saga).'

Following the Indaba, CSA started again to promote actively a range of cricket legacy initiatives, as had happened in the post-Charter period going into the new millennium. These included a budget for the preparation and finalisation of the history, the award of CSA Heritage Blazers to pre-1991 national players, the acquisition of the Krish Reddy Collection for a new museum at the KZNCU headquarters at Kingsmead, a commemoration event in Kimberley where the 'Gatting Gate' from the rebel tour protest era was memorialised, an initiative to translate the laws of cricket into isiXhosa, and support for two local cricket histories, *The Level Playing Field*, on the path-breaking Aurora CC by Mike Hickson and Judge Chris Nicholson, and Professor William Pick's *One for the Chuck*, on the history of the Maitland-Parow and District Cricket Union from 1912 to 1976. This process was driven by the CEO, the CSA Transformation

Committee and the Transformation director, Max Jordaan. André Odendaal helped as a co-ordinator and consultant.

On 31 January 2015 André stepped down after a decade as CEO at WPCA/Cobras and started writing full-time again with the specific aim of finishing a project that had grown in focus and content to four volumes, going back to day one in 1795 following the first British invasion. In December, the authors met in Durban to assess progress, discuss the development of the history, and decide on an action plan for getting it published. It was agreed that Jonty Winch should be invited to become a co-author of volume 1, in recognition of his path-breaking recent work. His book on Monty Bowden (2003), followed by his doctoral study of William Milton (2013), fundamentally extended the boundaries in important areas of South African cricket history. He accepted. This meant that the general history would be grounded even more in original research and knowledge, particularly with regard to the internal dynamics and imperialist mindsets of the nineteenth-century British cricket establishment in southern Africa. Moreover, the authors decided to ask the experienced Michael Owen-Smith to write the chapter on SACA in test cricket up to 1914 as a guest contributor, as this was not among their core areas of expertise. Michael was cricket writer on the *Cape Times* for many years and he is the son of a former SACA Springbok, 'Tuppy' Owen-Smith, and godson of Louis Duffus, who covered more than 100 of the 172 tests played by South Africa SACA before isolation.

As a result of the renewed activation of the CSA legacy projects and of Odendaal's return to writing full-time again, a big jump forward took place and the first volume of the history was completed in mid-2016. The HSRC Press agreed to publish it by year-end, followed by the remaining three books in the series.

This book did not emerge from an academic exercise, but from something deep inside, a desire, a dream, a vision.[2] It has been a long, long journey. At times the authors wondered whether such an ambitious project could ever get off the ground. But the gravity of the challenge and the magnitude of the task meant that it was always going to be a daunting job. We dedicate this book to the generations before us who opened the way for the future by holding onto an unflinching vision of human dignity and equality for both cricket and society in South Africa, despite the institutionalised violence and indignities they endured under colonialism and its stepchild, apartheid.

Endnotes

Note to the Acknowledgements

1 For some of the work produced by these writers, see A. Odendaal, 'Sport and liberation: The unfinished business of the past' in C. Thomas (ed.), *Sport and Liberation in South Africa: Reflections and suggestions* (Sport and Recreation South Africa and University of Fort Hare, 2006).

Notes to the Introduction

1 For an earlier version of this argument, see A. Odendaal, 'Foreword' in B. Murray and G. Vahed (eds.), *Empire and Cricket: The South African experience 1884–1914* (Unisa Press, Pretoria, 2009), pp. xv–xvi.
2 See Murray and Vahed, *Empire and Cricket*, p. 3.
3 D. Brailsford, *Sport, Time and Society: The British at play* (Routledge, London, 1991), p. 45.
4 B. Stoddart, 'Other cultures' in B. Stoddart and K.A.P Sandiford (eds.), *The Imperial Game: Cricket, culture and society* (Manchester University Press, Manchester, 1998), p. 148.
5 H.M. Wesso, 'The colonization of geographic thought: The South African experience' in A. Godlewska and N. Smith (eds.), *Geography and Empire* (Blackwell, Oxford, 1994), p. 332.
6 J. Bale, *Landscapes of Modern Sport* (Leicester University Press, Leicester, 1994), p. 27; M. Marqusee, *Anyone but England: Cricket and the national malaise* (Verso, London, 1994), p. 38.
7 P. Bailey, *Leisure and Class in Victorian England: Rational recreation and the context for control, 1850–1885* (London, 1978), p. 170.
8 Bailey, *Leisure and Class in Victorian England*, p. 72.
9 O. Patterson, 'The cricket ritual in the West Indies', *New Society*, 26 June 1969, p. 989.
10 KZNCU Archives: Krish Reddy Collection, Durban District Indian Cricket Union report/meetings, 1912/13, SA Coloured Cricket Board – rules etc.
11 See, for example, *Diamond Fields Advertiser*, 26 and 28 March 1913.
12 C. Bundy, 'Remaking the past: New perspectives in South African history' (UCT, Department of Adult Education and Extra-Mural Studies, 1986), p. 69.
13 T. McGirk, 'Neither ladies nor cricketers' in L. Frewin (ed.), *The Boundary Book: Second innings* (Spring Books, London, 1986), p. 196.
14 On this see, for example, R. Gupta, 'Bowled out of the game: Nationalism and gender equality in Indian cricket', *Berkeley Journal of Entertainment and Sports Law*, 2, 1, November 2013.
15 The SAICCB later became the South African Coloured Cricket Association and, more than 50 years after its founding, the pioneering SACCB was pressured into changing its name to the South African Malay Cricket Board, for reasons that will be explained in volume 2.
16 https://en.wikipedia.org/wiki/Robert_Emmet#Capture_and_trial.

Notes to Chapter 1, Cricket comes by boat to Africa

1 H.G. Nahuys van Burgst, *Adventures at the Cape of Good Hope in 1806*, translated and edited by M.A. Bax-Botha (Friends of the South African Library, Cape Town, 1993), p. 78. This is the first known reference to a cricket match at the Cape and the first researchers to find it were L. Moult and P. Hartman, *Playing the Game: The story of the Cape Town Cricket Club* (Cape Town Cricket Club in association with the Western Province Cricket Association, Cape Town, 2012), p. 13.
2 T. Couzens, *South African Battles* (Jonathan Ball, Johannesburg and Cape Town, 2014), pp. 41–2.
3 N. Worden, E. van Heyningen and V. Bickford-Smith, *Cape Town: The making of a city – An illustrated social history* (David Philip Publishers, Cape Town, 1998), p. 86.
4 N. Mostert, *Frontiers: The epic of South Africa's creation and the tragedy of the Xhosa people* (Pimlico, London, 1993), pp. 95–101. The quote is on p. 96.
5 T. Lewis, *Double century* (Hodder & Stoughton, London, 1987), p. 23.
6 https://www.cricketarchive.co.uk/Archive/Players/79/79356.html; https://en.wikipedia.org/wiki/Charles_Anguish; https://en.wikipedia.org/wiki/List_of_English_cricketers; N.S. Curnow, 'The origins and early development of cricket in South Africa' (unpublished article, n.d.), p. 1.

7   Lewis, *Double century*, p. 10.
8   J. Winch, *England's Youngest Captain: The life and times of Monty Bowden and two South African journalists* (Windsor Publishers, Windsor, 2003), p. 53; on suicide, see J. Winch, *Cricket in Southern Africa: Two hundred years of achievement and records* (Windsor, Rosettenville, 1997), p. 16.
9   A. Barnard, edited by H.J. Anderson, *South Africa a Century Ago, 1797–1801* (Maskew Miller, Cape Town, n.d.), pp. 21–2.
10 Obituary in the *Gentleman's Magazine*, 82, July–December 1797, p. 889. See also http://landedfamilies.blogspot.co.uk/2014/10/144-anguish-of-great-melton-hall-and.html.
11 R. Bowen, *Cricket: A history of its growth and development throughout the world* (Eyre and Spottiswoode, London, 1970), p. 267.
12 T. Couzens, *Battles of South Africa*, found at www. battle.blaauwberg.net.
13 Couzens, *South African Battles*, p. 54. See also pp. 50–60.
14 D. Oakes (ed.), *Reader's Digest Illustrated History of South Africa: The real story* (Reader's Digest, Cape Town, 1988), p. 94.
15 For his biography, see https://nl.wikipedia.org/wiki/Huibert_Gerard_Nahuys_van_Burgst.
16 Nahuys van Burgst, *Adventures at the Cape of Good Hope*, pp. 1, 78 and Moult and Hartman, *Playing the Game*, p. 13.
17 Bowen, *Cricket*, p. 85.
18 *Cape Town Gazette and African Advertiser*, 2 January 1808.
19 www.geni.com/people/Brig-Gen-Henry-Clavering; https://en.wikipedia.org/wiki.Douglas_Clavering. Britain banned trading in slaves in 1807 but only banned slavery as an institution across the Empire in 1834. South African slaves had to endure another four years of 'apprenticeship' before they were finally, properly, liberated in 1838.
20 'Lieutenant T. Austin – 1810' in C. James, 'A collection of the charges, opinions and sentences of general courts-martial (1820)', http://books.Google.co.za/books?id=4kdfAAAAcA; https://www.napoleon-series.org/militaryorganisation. Thomas's name was spelt both Austen and Austin.
21 'Lieutenant T. Austin – 1810'.
22 Curnow, 'The origins and early development of cricket in South Africa', p. 1.
23 H.A. Wyndham, *The Early History of the Thoroughbred Horse in South Africa* (Oxford University Press, London, 1924), p. 16.
24 The quotes are from Wyndham, *The Early History of the Thoroughbred Horse*, pp. 17, 20–1.
25 *Cape Town Gazette* and *African Advertiser*, 15 October 1814.
26 Winch, *England's Youngest Captain*, p. 53; J. Winch, 'Sir William Milton: A leading figure in public school games, colonial politics and imperial expansion, 1877–1914' (PhD dissertation, University of Stellenbosch, 2013), p. 7.
27 Quoted in P. Alegi, *African Soccerscapes: How a continent changed the world's game* (C. Hurst, London, 2010), pp. 1–2.
28 Barnard, *South Africa a Century Ago*, pp. 21–2.

Notes to Chapter 2, First port of call

1   'An old peripatetic', 'Cape Town and cricket', *Cape Monthly*, VI, 1873, pp. 162–3.
2   B. Maclennan, *A Proper Degree of Terror: John Graham and the Cape's eastern frontier* (Ravan Press, Johannesburg, 1986), p. 2.
3   Maclennan, *A Proper Degree of Terror*, p. 5.
4   R. Guha, *A Corner of a Foreign Field: The Indian history of a British sport* (Picador, London, 2003), p. 3.
5   M. Bose, *A History of Indian Cricket* (André Deutsch, London, 2002), p. 20.
6   N.S. Curnow, 'The origins and early development of cricket in South Africa' (unpublished article, n.d.), p. 1. My thanks to Robin Isherwood for providing me with a copy of this article by one of South Africa's first official statisticians.
7   Curnow, 'The origins and early development of cricket in South Africa', p. 1.
8   N. Worden, E. van Heyningen and V. Bickford-Smith, *Cape Town: The making of a city – An illustrated social history* (David Philip Publishers, Cape Town, 1998), pp. xx.
9   Worden et al., *Cape Town*, pp. 132–3, 153, 156.
10 Worden et al., *Cape Town*, pp. 88 (quote) and 86–92, 96–7.

11   My thanks to John Young for going in search of the exact location of this field in today's Cape Town landscape. He concludes that the field was bounded on the west by Main Road, Plumstead, on the east by what is now Exeter Road, on the north by Waterbury Road and on the south by Hemyock Road. A red-roofed house (with what could be original trees) stands on the one corner on Main Road. J. Young, pers. comm., 3 March 2016.

12   Curnow, 'The origins and early development of cricket in South Africa', p. 2.

13   R. Bowen, *Cricket: A history of its growth and development throughout the world* (Eyre and Spottiswoode, London, 1970), p. 277.

14   M.W. Luckin, *The History of South African Cricket, including the scores of all important matches since 1878* (W.I. Horton, Johannesburg, 1915), p. 791.

15   L. Moult and P. Hartman, *Playing the Game: The story of the Cape Town Cricket Club* (Cape Town Cricket Club in association with the Western Province Cricket Association, Cape Town, 2012), pp. 19-20.

16   D. McIntyre, *The Diocesan College, Rondebosch, South Africa: A history of Bishops* (Juta, Cape Town, 1950), p. 20; A. Parker, *The Springboks, 1891-1970* (Cassell, London, 1970), p. 2.

17   J. Hodgson, 'A history of Zonnebloem College, 1858-1870: A study in church and society (MA, UCT, 1979), p. 453.

18   See A. Odendaal, *The Story of an African Game: Black cricketers and the unmasking of one of cricket's greatest myths, South Africa, 1850-2003* (David Philip in association with the Human Sciences Research Council and the United Cricket Board of South Africa, Cape Town, 2003), p. 358.

19   Worden et al., *Cape Town*, p. 198.

20   R. Archer and A. Boullion, *The South African Game: Sport and racism* (Zed Press, London, 1982), p. 82.

21   W.H. Mars, 'The history of cricket in the Western Province' in Luckin, *The History of South African Cricket*, p. 135.

22   Worden et al., *Cape Town*, p. 239.

23   Mars, 'The history of cricket in the Western Province' and F. Reid, 'The Western Province Cricket Club' in Luckin, *History of South African Cricket*, pp. 139, 363.

24   Moult and Hartman, *Playing the Game*, p. 12.

25   Moult and Hartman, *Playing the Game*, p. 363.

26   S.E.L. West and W.J. Luker (eds.), *Century at Newlands, 1864-1964: A history of the Western Province Cricket Club* (WPCC, Cape Town, 1965), p. 12.

27   *Cape Argus*, 6 April 1872.

28   F. Reid, 'The Western Province Cricket Club', p. 361.

29   For example, Worden et al., *Cape Town*, pp. 153, 157-9.

30   'Rugby notes' in *Merchiston Castle School Register, 1833-1903*.

31   *Cape Times*, 14 August 1878.

32   'An old peripatetic', 'Cape Town and cricket', pp. 161-2.

33   N. Hendriksz, *The History of the Van der Stel Club*, http://www.vanderstel.co.za, accessed 27 January 2010.

34   *Cape Times*, 21 April 1876.

35   'An old peripatetic', 'Cape Town and cricket', pp. 162-3.

36   *Cape Times*, 29 January 1884.

37   Bose, *A History of Indian Cricket*, p. 20.

38   *Cape Mercury*, 20 January 1876.

39   Mars, 'The history of cricket in the Western Province' and Reid, 'The Western Province Cricket Club', pp. 135, 361-4.

Notes to Chapter 3, Second port of call

1   Quoted in N. Mostert, *Frontiers: The epic of South Africa's creation and the tragedy of the Xhosa people* (Pimlico, London, 1993), p. 389.

2   D. Oakes (ed.), *Reader's Digest Illustrated History of South Africa: The real story* (Reader's Digest, Cape Town, 1988), p. 103 and map on p. 68.

3   Oakes, *Reader's Digest Illustrated History of South Africa*, p. 95 and map on p. 104.

4   For a full discussion of the concept of the opening and closing frontier, see R. Elphick and H. Giliomee (eds.), *The Shaping of South African Society, 1652–1820* (Maskew Miller Longman, Cape Town, 1989), pp. 296–316.

5   Mostert, *Frontiers*, p. 390.

6   Oakes, *Reader's Digest Illustrated History of South Africa*, p. 98.

7   Oakes, *Reader's Digest Illustrated History of South Africa*, p. 95.

8   *Grahamstown Journal*, 4 May 1843, quoted in http://stgeorgespark.upe.ac.za. Sidbury CC has built a new ground and clubhouse on the banks of the Bushmans River as the old village now falls within a game farm. Having suffered something of a playing slump, the club recovered to such an extent that they recently won the Port Alfred and Bathurst Cricket Tournament, popularly known as the Pineapple Tournament. In 2015 the tournament was held for the 109th time. (Ian Suttie, conversation with John Young, 31 January 2016.)

9   *Cape Frontier Times*, 18 January 1844, quoted in http://stgeorgespark.upe.ac.za.

10   *Cape Frontier Times*, 1 February 1844, quoted in http://stgeorgespark.upe.ac.za.

11   Souvenir of the Commemoration of the Centenary of the 1820 Settlers of Albany, printed by the East London *Daily Dispatch*, 1920, p. 13.

12   Souvenir of the Commemoration of the Centenary of the 1820 Settlers, pp. 14–15.

13   Mostert, *Frontiers*, p. 657.

14   R Godlonton, *Memorials of the British Settlers of South Africa*, p. 121 quoted in G. Butler (ed.), *The 1820 Settlers: An illustrated commentary* (Human and Rousseau, Cape Town, 1974), pp. 329–30. My thanks to John Young for this material and the sources. In 1994 a celebration game was played at Salem, to commemorate that game 150 years before. Some students found in the ash heaps of the old settler homes a bottle with a picture of a cricketer on it. (Source: Young's interviews with members of the Long and Emslie families, 1994.)

15   'Izingata ngezingata', *Imvo Zabantsundu*, 10 June 1897.

16   André Odendaal Collection: S.J. Reddy Papers, 'South End United Cricket Club', Typescript on the club's history written in 1950.

17   http://aridareas.co.za/roses-s-roundup/cricket-in-graaff-reinet-1854/. © Rose's Roundup, September 2010 (2, 84).

18   G.K.C. Fuller, 'History of Border cricket' in Luckin, *History of South African Cricket*, p. 18.

19   'The outline of Queenstown's history, sport and other entertainment', *Daily Representative*, Queenstown Centenary Issue, September 1953.

20   Bishop Henry Cotterill, *Journal of the Bishop of Grahamstown in a Visitation of the Kaffrarian Missions in September and October 1860* (London, 1861), 27 September 1860. I am grateful to Michael Berning for this reference.

21   A.F. Hattersley (ed.), *John Sheddon Dobie, South African Journal, 1862–6* (Van Riebeeck Society, Cape Town, 1945), p. 46.

22   G. Williams (ed.), *One Hundred Years of Border Cricket*, Border Cricket Board, 1896–1996, Centenary Brochure, p. 10.

23   P.M. Nongogo, 'Origins and development of black rugby in East London since the late nineteenth century and its response to South African sports unification: A study of selected clubs' (MA dissertation, Rhodes University, 2004), p. 2.

24   Fuller, 'History of Border cricket', p. 20.

25   Quoted in R. Guha (ed.), *The Picador Book of Cricket* (Picador, London, 2001), p. 3.

Notes to Chapter 4, The beginnings of a unique African cricket tradition

1   Quoted by J. Schoots, 'The sociological imagination of S.E.K. Mqhayi' (Master's dissertation, UCT, 2014), p. 39.

2   Bishop Henry Cotterill, *Journal of the Bishop of Grahamstown in a Visitation of the Kaffrarian Missions in September and October 1860* (London, 1861). The date of the entry is 27 September 1860.

3   The narratives about early African cricket in chapter 3, this chapter and chapters 11 and 12 below are drawn mainly from A. Odendaal, *The Story of an African Game: Black cricketers and the unmasking of one of cricket's greatest myths, South Africa, 1850–2003* (David Philip in

association with the Human Sciences Research Council and the United Cricket Board of South Africa, Cape Town, 2003), Part 1.

4   A. Odendaal, 'African political mobilisation in the eastern Cape, 1880–1910' (PhD dissertation, University of Cambridge, 1983), p. 14.

5   H. Calderwod, *Caffres and Caffre Missions*, pp. 210–11, quoted in D. Williams, *Umfundisi: A biography of Tiyo Soga, 1829–1971* (Lovedale Press, Lovedale, 1978), p. 82.

6   R.H.W. Shepherd, *Lovedale South Africa: The story of a century 1841–1941* (Lovedale Press, Lovedale, 1940), p. 508.

7   *The Kaffir Express*, 1 December 1870, p. 4.

8   Cape Archives, NA 467, Ecclesiastical 1875–1890, J. Buchanan to C. Brownlee, 21 June 1877.

9   'Grand cricket match', *Queenstown Free Press*, 4 November 1870. My thanks to Janet Hodgson for giving me this reference in 1981.

10   *Queenstown Free Press*, 4 November 1870.

11   *Queenstown Free Press*, 4 November 1870.

12   *Queenstown Free Press*, 4 November 1870. See also *Queenstown Free Press*, 8 March 1875, for a match between St Mark's and the Bolotwa mission.

13   'Grand cricket match', *Queenstown Free Press*, 4 November 1870.

14   R. Guha, *A Corner of a Foreign Field: The Indian history of a British sport* (Picador, London, 2003), pp. 18–19.

15   'Cricket, St Mark's vs Queenstown', *The Queenstown Representative*, 17 February 1871.

16   M.W. Luckin, *The History of South African Cricket, including the scores of all important matches since 1878* (W.I. Horton, Johannesburg, 1915), p. 92.

17   P.W.H. Kettlewell, 'Cricket at St Andrew's College, Grahamstown' in Luckin, *History of South African Cricket*, p. 800.

18   N. Mostert, *Frontiers: The epic of South Africa's creation and the tragedy of the Xhosa people* (Pimlico, London, 1993), p. 1259.

19   A. Odendaal, 'African political mobilisation in the eastern Cape, 1880–1910' (PhD dissertation, University of Cambridge, 1983), ch. 2.

20   J.M. Coetzee, *Stranger Shores: Essays 1986–1999* (Secker and Warburg, London, 2001), p. 340

21   Quoted in R. Christiansen, *The Visitors: Culture shock in nineteenth-century Britain* (Chatto and Windus, London, 2000), p. 179. I am grateful to John Young for this reference.

22   On this see B. Willan, 'An African in Kimberley: Sol T. Plaatje, 1894–8' in S. Marks and R. Rathbone (eds.), *Industrialisation and Social Change in South Africa: African class formation, culture and consciousness, 1870–1930* (Longman, London, 1982), pp. 250–2 and A. Odendaal, 'South Africa's black Victorians: Sport and society in South Africa in the 19th century' in J.A. Mangan (ed.), *Pleasure, Profit and Proselytism: British culture and sport at home and abroad, 1700–1914* (Frank Cass Publishers, London, 1988), chapter 11.

Notes to Chapter 5, Berthing in Port Natal, 1840s onwards

1   *Natal Witness*, 24 March 1848, quoted by J.T. Henderson, 'Early cricket in Natal' in M.W. Luckin, *The History of South African Cricket, including the scores of all important matches since 1878* (W.I. Horton, Johannesburg, 1915), p. 85.

2   *Natal Witness*, 24 March 1848.

3   *Natal Witness*, 8 September 1848.

4   See Henderson, 'Early cricket in Natal', pp. 85–8.

5   A. Desai, V. Padayachee, K. Reddy and G. Vahed, *Blacks in Whites: A century of cricket struggles in KwaZulu-Natal* (University of Natal Press, Pietermaritzburg, 2002), p. 126.

6   A. Odendaal, 'Some forgotten South African cricket history', *South African Cricketer*, Winter 1983, p. 29.

7   Desai et al., *Blacks in Whites*, p. 125.

8   Quoted in 'Cypher', 'The history of cricket in Natal' in Luckin, *History of South African Cricket*, pp. 63–5.

9   Quoted in Henderson, 'Early cricket in Natal', p. 89. This overview of early cricket in Natal is taken almost exclusively from the two chapters in Luckin's history used here.

10 This account of the war is drawn from J. Laband, *Zulu Warriors: The battle for the South African frontier* (Yale University Press, New Haven, 2014), chapters 16–21, see especially pp. 198–200, 205, 228–34.

11 S. Davids, *Zulu: The heroism and tragedy of the Zulu war*, quoted in https://books.google.co.za/books?isbn=0141901438. The number of weapons given here is also taken from Davids; Laband gave the number as 800.

12 Laband, *Zulu Warriors*, pp. 235–9 and ch. 20.

13 Another reference that still needs verification has a soldier, Poterhill, losing his life in 'the Berg during the Bushman's River Pass expedition' shortly after a match near Ulundi in August 1873, 'involving officers of the Karkloof Volunteers'. It also claims that 'two of Cetshwayo's brothers had been playing cricket for years by that time, but not in Zululand'. Was this true? If so, did the brothers play at Zonnebloem College in Cape Town where Nathaniel Umhalla had done so well? See www.rorkesdrift.com/forum/viewtopic.php?t=2500&sid=64c50fd74e1e547fa728a8cf9ecod491.

14 Quoted in 'Cypher', 'The history of cricket in Natal' in Luckin, *History of South African Cricket*, p. 68.

Notes to Chapter 6, Cricket reaches the interior Highveld

1 Quoted in M.W. Luckin, *The History of South African Cricket, including the scores of all important matches since 1878* (W.I. Horton, Johannesburg, 1915), p. 811.

2 J.T. Henderson, 'Early cricket in Natal' in Luckin, *The History of South African Cricket*, p. 85.

3 T.R.H. Davenport, *South Africa: A modern history* (Macmillan, Johannesburg, 1977), pp. 61–4.

4 Luckin, *History of South African Cricket*, p. 55.

5 Luckin, *History of South African Cricket*, p. 55.

6 Luckin, *History of South African Cricket*, pp. 55–7.

7 From J. Jeppe, 'Early days of cricket in the Transvaal' in Luckin, *History of South African Cricket*, pp. 807–15.

Notes to Chapter 7, The New Rush

1 G. Tyamzashe, 'Life at the Diamond Fields', August 1874, in F. Wilson and D. Perrot (eds.), *Outlook on a Century, 1870–1970* (Lovedale Press, Lovedale, 1973), pp. 19–20.

2 R. Parry, 'Diamonds, cricket and William Ling', *Cricket Lore*, 3, 4, p. 41.

3 D. Oakes (ed.), *Reader's Digest Illustrated History of South Africa: The real story* (Reader's Digest, Cape Town, 1988), p. 166.

4 Oakes (ed.), *Reader's Digest Illustrated History of South Africa*, p. 167.

5 G. Tyamzashe, 'Life at the Diamond Fields', August 1874.

6 Parry, 'Diamonds, cricket and William Ling'.

7 Parry, 'Diamonds, cricket and William Ling'.

8 Parry, 'Diamonds, cricket and William Ling'.

9 Luckin, *History of South African Cricket*, p. 35.

10 Luckin, *History of South African Cricket*, p. 37.

11 Luckin, *History of South African Cricket*, p. 37.

12 Luckin, *History of South African Cricket*, p. 37.

13 G. Tyamzashe, 'Life at the Diamond Fields', August 1874.

14 Parry, 'Diamonds, cricket and William Ling', p. 42.

15 M. Rall, *Peaceable Warrior: The life and times of Sol Plaatje* (Sol Plaatje Educational Trust, Kimberley, 2003). p. 35.

16 For a detailed discussion of the social life and activities of the black elite in Kimberley, see B. Willan, 'An African in Kimberley' in S. Marks and R. Rathbone (eds.), *Industrialisation and Social Change in South Africa: African class formation, culture and consciousness, 1870–1930* (Longman, London, 1982), ch. 9 and B. Willan, *Sol Plaatje: A biography* (Ravan Press, Johannesburg, 1984), ch. 2. We have relied heavily on Willan and Parry in developing our understandings of early Kimberley.

17 D.B. Coplan, *In Township Tonight! South Africa's black city music and theatre* (Ravan Press, Johannesburg, 1985), p. 40.

Notes to Chapter 8, Southern Africa and the spread of cricket across the world

1   J.A. Mangan, 'Imperial origins: Christian manliness, moral imperatives and pre-Sri Lankan playing field – Beginnings', *International Journal of Sports History*, 19, 2–3, June–September 2003, pp. 11–29.

2   G.B. Kirsch, *The Creation of American Team Sports: Baseball and cricket, 1838–1872* (University of Illinois Press, Urbana, 1989), chs. 2, 9.

3   See, for example, D. Cooper, 'Canadians declare "It isn't cricket": A century of rejection of the British imperial game, 1860–1960', *Journal of Sports History*, 26, 1, Spring 1999. See also G. Gillespie, 'Wickets in the west: Cricket, culture and constructed images of nineteenth-century Canada', *Journal of Sports History*, 27, 1, Spring 2000.

4   R. Bowen, *Cricket: A history of its growth and development throughout the world* (Eyre and Spottiswoode, London, 1970).

5   This summary of early West Indian cricket comes from H.M. Beckles and B. Stoddart (eds.), *Liberation Cricket: West Indies cricket and culture* (Manchester University Press, Manchester, 1995), especially pp. 36–40, 44–7.

6   M. Bose, *A History of Indian Cricket* (André Deutsch, London, 2002), p. 20.

7   R. Guha, *A Corner of a Foreign Field: The Indian history of a British sport* (Picador, London, 2003), pp. 14–15.

8   R. Cashman, 'The phenomenon of Indian cricket' in R. Cashman and M. McKernan (eds.), *Sport in History: The making of modern sporting history* (University of Queensland Press, St Lucia, 1979), pp. 183–5, 195–7.

9   Mangan, 'Imperial origins', pp. 11–29.

10 W. Vamplew, Katharine Moore, John O'Hara, Richard Cashman and Ian Jobling (eds.), *The Oxford Companion to Australian Sport* (Oxford University Press, Melbourne, 1992), p. 100.

11 J. Arlott (ed.), *The Oxford Companion to Sports and Games* (Oxford University Press, London, 1975), p. 211.

Notes to Chapter 9, Cricket, war and change

1   N. Mostert, *Frontiers: The epic of South Africa's creation and the tragedy of the Xhosa people* (Pimlico, London, 1993), p. 1245.

2   See W. Vamplew, 'Sport and industrialisation: An economic interpretation of the changes in popular sport in nineteenth-century England' in J.A. Mangan (ed.), *Pleasure, Profit and Proselytism: British culture and sport at home and abroad, 1700–1914* (Frank Cass Publishers, London, 1988), pp. 7–17.

3   Vamplew, 'Sport and industrialisation', pp. 7–17. The quote is on p. 13.

4   K. Beavon, *Johannesburg: The making and shaping of the city* (University of South Africa Press, Pretoria, 2004), pp. 8–9.

5   R. Parry, 'Diamonds, cricket and William Ling', *Cricket Lore*, 3, 4.

6   T.R.H. Davenport, *South Africa: A modern history* (Macmillan, Johannesburg, 1977), p. 99.

7   See C. Saunders, 'Through an African's eyes: The diary of Nathaniel Umhalla', *Quarterly Bulletin of the South African Library*, 34, 1, 1979; J. Laband, *Zulu Warriors: The battle for the South African frontier* (Yale University Press, New Haven, 2014), p. 146.

8   https://en.wikipedia.org/wiki/list_of_cricketers_who_were_killed_during_military_service, p 2/121.

9   B. Murray and G. Vahed (eds.), *Empire and Cricket: The South African experience 1884–1914* (Unisa Press, Pretoria, 2009).

10 W.G. Schulze, 'The Boer prisoners of war in Ceylon and the "Great and Grand Only Manly Game" of cricket' in Murray and Vahed, *Empire and Cricket*, p. 181.

11 https://en.wikipedia.org/wiki/list_of_cricketers_who_were_killed_during_military_service, pp. 4–8/121.

12 Schulze, 'The Boer prisoners of war', pp. 182–5.

13 For detailed descriptions of the subjection of the various African chiefdoms between 1868 and 1906, see M. Wilson and L. M. Thompson (eds.), *The Oxford History of South Africa, vol. 2* (Oxford University Press, Oxford, 1971), ch. 5; D. Oakes (ed.), *Reader's Digest Illustrated History of South Africa: The real story* (Reader's Digest, Cape Town, 1988), pp. 176–92.

14 W.D. Hammond-Tooke, *Command or Consensus: The development of Transkeian local government* (Oxford University Press, Cape Town, 1975), pp. 23–4.

15 Quoted in A. Odendaal, 'Liberalism and the African National Congress' (Paper presented at Conference on Liberalism in South Africa, Houw Hoek Inn, 30 June – 3 July 1986).

16 Odendaal, 'Liberalism and the African National Congress'.

17 D. Olusoga and C.W. Erichsen, *The Kaiser's Holocaust: Germany's forgotten genocide and the colonial roots of Nazism* (Faber and Faber, London, 2010), pp. 41–4.

18 B.M. Magubane, *The Political Economy of Race and Class in South Africa* (Monthly Review Press, New York, 1979), pp. 193–4; M. Hardt and A. Negri, *Empire* (Harvard University Press, Cambridge, Mass., 2000), p. xii. My thanks to James Early for this reference.

19 H. Beckles, *Liberation Cricket: West Indies cricket culture* (Manchester University Press, Manchester, 1995), p. 33.

Notes to Chapter 10, Champion Bat ushers in new era

1 https:/en.wikipedia.org/wiki/Canterbury_Cricket_Week.

2 'The cricket tournament', *Eastern Province Herald*, 7 January 1876, p. 5.

3 'The cricket matches', *Eastern Province Herald*, 18 January 1876.

4 M.W. Luckin, *The History of South African Cricket, including the scores of all important matches since 1878* (W.I. Horton, Johannesburg, 1915), pp. 19, 168.

5 A. Trollope, *South Africa* (A.A. Balkema, Cape Town, 1973), pp. 156–8, 161–2. My thanks to John Young for this source.

6 For more details, see B. Maclennan, *A Proper Degree of Terror: John Graham and the Cape's eastern frontier* (Ravan Press, Johannesburg, 1986), p. 233.

7 'The cricket matches', *Eastern Province Herald*, 18 January 1876, p. 2.

8 R. Parry, 'Diamonds, cricket and William Ling', *Cricket Lore*, 3, 4, pp. 41–2.

9 J. Laband, *Zulu Warriors: The battle for the South African frontier* (Yale University Press, New Haven, 2014), pp. 138–40.

10 N. Mostert, *Frontiers: The epic of South Africa's creation and the tragedy of the Xhosa people* (Pimlico, London, 1993), p. 1255.

11 T. Couzens, *South African Battles* (Jonathan Ball, Johannesburg and Cape Town, 2014).

12 R. Packham et al. (eds.), *A Pictorial History of Sussex County Cricket Club* (Sussex Cricket Museum and Educational Trust, Hove, 2014), pp. 65, 67, 61.

13 'Alphabetical list of the British settlers of 1820' in Souvenir of the commemoration of the centenary of the 1820 settlers of Albany, printed by the *East London Daily Dispatch*, 1920, pp. 95–116.

14 Mostert, *Frontiers*, pp. 777, 987.

15 Mostert, *Frontiers*, p. 656.

16 Mostert, *Frontiers*, p. 824.

17 M. Legassick, *The Struggle for the Eastern Cape, 1800–1854* (KMM Review, Johannesburg, 2010), p. 72.

Notes to Chapter 11, 'Native' champions

1 The title Native Inter-Town Tournament has been maintained here because this was the designation given to it by its African organisers and in a literal sense the word aptly describes the pioneering nature and African roots of one of the oldest and most distinctive cricket traditions in South Africa.

2 *The Cricketing Record of Major Warton's Tour 1888–9: A detailed account of the first English tour to South Africa*, with a new introduction by David R. Allen (J.W. McKenzie, Cambridge, 1987), p. 136.

3 'Eze bola', *Isigidimi samaXhosa*, 15 August 1884.

4 'Kubadlali bola', *Isigidimi samaXhosa*, 1 November 1884.

5 Editorial notes, *Isigidimi samaXhosa*, 15 October 1883.

6 For a fuller description of the newspaper's establishment, see A. Odendaal, 'African political mobilization in the eastern Cape, 1880–1910' (PhD dissertation, Cambridge University, 1983), pp. 103–15.

7   'Editorial notes', *Imvo Zabantsundu*, 3 November 1884.
8   'Ezababaleli', *Imvo Zabantsundu*, 3 November 1884.
9   'Editorial notes', *Imvo Zabantsundu*, 3 November 1884.
10   'Ibala le cricket', *Imvo Zabantsundu*, 19 January 1885.
11   'Ibala le cricket', *Imvo Zabantsundu*, 19 January 1885.
12   'Native cricket matches', *Cape Mercury*, 15 January 1885.
13   'Native cricket matches', *Cape Mercury*, 15 January 1885.
14   'Imidlalo yeholide', *Imvo Zabantsundu*, 19 January 1885.
15   See reports in *Imvo Zabantsundu*, 21 January 1885.
16   See match reports, *Imvo Zabantsundu*, 21 and 26 January 1887.
17   See match reports, *Imvo Zabantsundu*, 21 January 1885.
18   'Champion club versus Try Again club', *Cape Mercury*, 31 December 1884.
19   'Umdlala we bhola', *Isigidimi samaXhosa*, 16 February 1884.
20   'Champion club versus Try Again club', *Cape Mercury*, 31 December 1884.
21   A. Odendaal, *The Founders: The origins of the ANC and the struggle for democracy in South Africa* (Jacana, Auckland Park, 2012), p. 68.
22   'An Anglo-African team', *Imvo Zabantsundu*, 25 October 1888.
23   M.W. Luckin, *The History of South African Cricket, including the scores of all important matches since 1878* (W.I. Horton, Johannesburg, 1915), pp. 15–19.
24   Luckin, *History of South African Cricket*, p. 19; 'Cricket tournament', *Cape Mercury*, 3 January 1885. The four teams participating were Port Elizabeth, King William's Town, Kimberley and Cape Town.
25   I.D. Difford, *The History of South African Rugby Football, 1875–1932* (The Specialty Press, Wynberg, 1933), p. 14. The same four centres as in cricket participated.
26   R. Archer and A. Boullion, *The South African Game: Sport and racism* (Zed Press, London, 1982), p. 103.
27   Paper read by Rev. Elijah Makiwane to the United Missionary Conference, *Imvo Zabantsundu*, 19 July 1888; 'Izimiselo ze Kroki', *Isigidimi sama Xhosa*, 16 June 1884.
28   en.wikipedia.org/wiki/James_Lillywhite_(cricketer,_born_1825), accessed 2 February 2016.
29   For example, *Imvo Zabantsundu*, 10 September 1896. His vice-presidents at one stage were Rev. P. Kawa, Paul Xiniwe and W.D. Soga.
30   See examples given by Archer and Boullion, *The South African Game*, pp. 8–9. The Springbok rugby captain, Dawie de Villiers reflected these attitudes when he said around 1980, 'Don't forget that the Blacks have really known Western sports [only] for the last ten years'.

Notes to Chapter 12, *Abantu namaNgesi*

1   B. Willan, 'An African in Kimberley: Sol T. Plaatje, 1894–8' in S. Marks and R. Rathbone (eds.), *Industrialisation and Social Change in South Africa: African class formation, culture and consciousness, 1870–1930* (Longman, London, 1982), p. 242.
2   See, for example, 'Ibali laba dlali', *Imvo Zabantsundu*, 23 November 1887.
3   'Ixesha le bhola, 1889', *Imvo Zabantsundu*, 17 October 1889.
4   M.W. Luckin, *The History of South African Cricket, including the scores of all important matches since 1878* (W.I. Horton, Johannesburg, 1915), p. 19.
5   'Cricket – Native Champion vs Alberts', *Cape Mercury*, 3 March 1885.
6   A. Odendaal, 'African political mobilization in the eastern Cape, 1880–1910' (PhD dissertation, Cambridge University, 1983), pp. 100, 138
7   On collaboration and resistance at this time, see for example, J. Peires, Draft manuscript on Richard Kawa (2011). For Umhalla's diary during this period, see C. Saunders, 'Through an African's eyes: The diary of Nathaniel Umhalla', *Quarterly Bulletin of the South African Library*, 34, 1, 1979.
8   Editorial notes, *Imvo Zabantsundu*, 9 March 1885.
9   Quoted in *Imvo Zabantsundu*, 9 March 1885.
10   'Notes', *Cape Mercury*, 3 March 1885.
11   'Cricket', *Cape Mercury*, 24 March 1885; 'Amangesi nabantsundu', *Imvo Zabantsundu*, 23 March 1885.

12 'Cricket', *Cape Mercury*, 24 March 1885.
13 'Editorial notes', *Imvo Zabantsundu*, 2 March 1885.
14 'Natives and cricket', *Imvo Zabantsundu*, 9 March 1885.
15 'Notes', *Imvo Zabantsundu*, 23 March 1885.
16 'Amangesi nabantsundu', *Imvo Zabantsundu*, 30 March 1885.
17 'Editorial notes', *Imvo Zabantsundu*, 30 March 1885.
18 *Imvo Zabantsundu*, 30 March 1885.
19 See match reports, *Imvo Zabantsundu*, 21 January 1885.
20 See match report, *Imvo Zabantsundu*, 27 January 1887.
21 'Ibala laba dlali', *Imvo Zabantsundu*, 21 December 1887.
22 Luckin, *History of South African Cricket*, p. 18.
23 'Editorial notes', *Imvo Zabantsundu*, 16 February 1885; 'Ibola e komani', *Imvo Zabantsundu*, 9 December 1885; 'Blacks vs whites', *Imvo Zabantsundu*, 18 October 1888.
24 'Ibala labadlali', *Imvo Zabantsundu*, 15 December 1892.
25 M. Bose, *A History of Indian Cricket* (André Deutsch, London, 2002), p. 28.

Notes to Chapter 13, The MCC of the Cape Colony

1 A. Trollope, *South Africa* (A.A. Balkema, Cape Town, 1973), p. 175.
2 *Cape Times*, 6 September 1886.
3 J. Winch, 'Sir William Milton: A leading figure in public school games, colonial politics and imperial expansion, 1877–1914' (PhD, University of Stellenbosch, 2013), p. 5.
4 V. Bickford-Smith, *Ethnic Pride and Racial Prejudice in Victorian Cape Town: Group identity and social practice 1875–1902* (Cambridge University Press, Cambridge, 1995), pp. 48–9.
5 *Cape Argus*, 27 September 1884.
6 *Cape Argus*, 22 August 1884.
7 *Cape Argus*, 4 September 1884.
8 Derek Birley, *The Willow Wand: Some cricket myths explored* (Aurum Press, London, 2000), pp. 89–90.
9 Brian Stoddart, 'Sport, cultural imperialism and the colonial response to the British Empire', *Comparative Studies in Society and History*, 30, 4, 1988, p. 662.
10 J. Morris, *The Spectacle of Empire: Style, effect and the Pax Britannica* (Faber, London, 1982), ch. 8.
11 R. Guha, *A Corner of a Foreign Field: The Indian history of a British sport* (Picador, London, 2003), p. 6.
12 J. Williams, *Cricket and Race South Africa* (Berg, Oxford, 2001), p. 175.
13 Winch, 'Sir William Milton', p. 8.
14 M.W. Luckin, *The History of South African Cricket, including the scores of all important matches since 1878* (W.I. Horton, Johannesburg, 1915), p. 365.
15 *Cape Times*, 8 January 1880.
16 *Cape Times Weekly*, 4 April 1887.
17 'Mother Country v Colonial Born, Opening of "The Newlands Ground"', *Cape Times*, 3 January 1888.
18 *Daily Independent*, 19 April 1888.
19 Letter from 'Old Cricketer', *Daily Independent*, 25 April 1888.
20 Guha, *A Corner of a Foreign Field*, p. 18.
21 *The Lantern*, 23 April 1888.
22 *Daily Independent*, 25 April 1888.
23 On discrimination against Jews at the Cape around the turn of the twentieth century, see M. Shain, 'Jewish community's long fight against discrimination', *Cape Times*, 7 September 2016. This article deals interestingly with a delegation to the Cape Attorney General, Thomas Lynedoch Graham, who was a member of the WPCC and one of the organisers with Milton of the first international tour.

Notes to Chapter 14, The balance shifts from the military to the money

1   M.W. Luckin, *The History of South African Cricket, including the scores of all important matches since 1878* (W.I. Horton, Johannesburg, 1915), p. 45.
2   R. Parry, 'Diamonds, cricket and Major Warton', *Cricket Lore*, 3, 6, p. 38.
3   Parry, 'Diamonds, cricket and Major Warton', p. 38.
4   *Cape Times*, 25 October 1886.
5   Luckin, *The History of South African Cricket*, p. 46.
6   After the tour, Finlason paid tribute to his people: 'No town in the Colony supports sport in the liberal way that Kimberley does. At Cape Town they have wretched grounds and not a single pavilion … Kimberley has two magnificent grounds and it will soon have three. The three pavilions which have been subscribed for by the public are monuments of Kimberley's generosity' (*Cape Town Weekly*, 30 March 1887).
7   Reproduced in *Daily Independent*, 25 January 1888.
8   'Ibala labadlali', *Imvo Zabantsundu*, [x] January 1888. Date not legible.
9   'Ibala labadlali', *Imvo Zabantsundu*, [x] January 1888. Date not legible.
10   'Ibala labadlali', *Imvo Zabantsundu*, [x] January 1888. Date not legible.
11   B. Willan, 'An African in Kimberley: Sol T. Plaatje, 1894–8' in S. Marks and R. Rathbone (eds.), *Industrialisation and Social Change in South Africa: African class formation, culture and consciousness, 1870–1930* (Longman, London, 1982), pp. 251–2.
12   R. Parry, Black cricketers, white politicians and the origins of segregation at the Cape to 1894, p. 32; Parry, 'Diamonds, cricket and Major Warton', p. 40.
13   Willan, 'An African in Kimberley', p. 238.

Notes to Chapter 15, Subjugated memories

1   Quoted in address by the President of South Africa, Mr Thabo Mbeki, at the occasion of the launch of Freedom Park, Pretoria, 16 June 2002.
2   *A Guide to Important Cricket Matches Played in South Africa*, compiled by the Association of Cricket Statisticians (Association of Cricket Statisticians, Derby, 1981), p. 7.
3   'Malays or Afrikanders', Letter from 'A Coloured Cricketer' to *Diamond Fields Advertiser*, 13 January 1894.
4   André Odendaal compiled these first-ever consolidated statistics for the 'Native' and 'Malay' Inter-Town tournaments in this chapter, including the trophy winners, list of players and abbreviated scorecards. It is the result of research between 1979 and 2016 in colonial newspapers. Thanks to John Young, Carol van Vuuren and Ameena Smith for the assistance and patience over the years in helping to create a coherent record of this early cricket. John helped me to find valuable last-minute details. The librarians at the South African Museum during my initial research many years ago provided generous back-up that enabled me in the first place to find out about these remarkable competitions. Robin Isherwood spent many hours helping me to standardise and double-check these statistics. Original sources for each of these tournaments are indicated so that future statisticians can take forward the work of verifying, correcting and finalising this rare but still incomplete record.
5   Adderjance, H and Aderjance, [X] of Claremont 1889/90 have similar spellings (at a time when spellings were often confused but they are definitely two players in the same team).
6   Ariedien, also Affridien and Arifdien in scorecards.
7   Also initial B for Bob.
8   Also initial S in same scorecard, for bowling, and Kerindien, G in another.
9   Also Leech.
10   Also Manoor and Marnoor.
11   Also initial H.
12   For full scorecards, see W.M. Luckin, *The History of South African Cricket, including the scores of all important matches since 1878* (W.I. Horton, Johannesburg, 1915), pp. 164–8.
13   For full scorecards, see Luckin, *History of South African Cricket*, pp. 172–5.
14   For full scorecards, see Luckin, *History of South African Cricket*, pp. 176–80.
15   For original source material on the 1884/85 Native Inter-Town Tournament, see *Imvo Zabantsundu*, 19 January 1885. (Researched and compiled by André Odendaal.)

16 For the report and two full scorecards of the 1885/86 Native Inter-Town Tournament, see *Imvo Zabantsundu*, 10 February 1886. (Researched and compiled by André Odendaal.)

17 For full scorecards of the 1886/87 Native Inter-Town Tournament, see *Imvo Zabantsundu*, 21 and 26 January 1887. (Researched and compiled by André Odendaal.)

18 For full scorecards, see Luckin, *History of South African Cricket*, pp. 191–4.

19 For full scorecards, see Luckin, *History of South African Cricket*, pp. 181–4.

20 For original source material on the 1890/91 Malay Inter-Town Tournament, see 'Sporting intelligence', *Cape Argus*, 13 January 1890; 'Today's cricket. The Malay tournament', *Cape Argus*, 14 January 1890; 'Sporting Intelligence. The Malay tournament', *Cape Times*, 14 January 1890; 'Cricket. The Malay tournament', *Cape Times*, 15 January 1890; 'Sporting Intelligence', *Cape Times*, 21 January 1890; 'Cricket. The Malay tournament', *Cape Times*, 22 January 1890; 'Sporting Intelligence', *Cape Times*, 23 January 1890; 'Sporting Intelligence', *Cape Times*, 28 January 1890; 'Sporting Intelligence', *Cape Times*, 30 January 1890. (Researched and compiled by André Odendaal.)

21 For full scorecards, see Luckin, *History of South African Cricket*, pp. 189–90.

22 For original source material on the 1890/91 Native Inter-Town Tournament, see 'Native Tournament', *Port Elizabeth Telegraph*, 8 January 1891; *Imvo Zabantsundu*, 12 March 1891 and 5 February 1981. (Researched and compiled by André Odendaal.)

23 For original source material on this first of the two Malay Inter-Town tournaments in the 1890/91 season, see 'Sport and Pastime: Cricket. Malay tournament', *Diamond Fields Advertiser*, 29 December 1891; *Port Elizabeth Telegraph*, 5, 6, 7 and 8 January, 1890; 'The Malay Tournament', *Eastern Province Herald*, 5, 7, and 9 January 1891; *Diamond Fields Advertiser*, 17 January 1891 and 'Malay Tournament'. Letter from H. Kimmie, secretary of Star of the East CC to the Editor, *Eastern Province Herald*, 14 January 1891. (Researched and compiled by André Odendaal and John Young.) Note Kimmie's claims that Cape Town were declared winners of the tournament after a dispute in which Kimberley refused to continue with the game.

24 For full scorecards for all nine games in the second of the two Malay Inter-Town tournaments in the 1890/91 season, see 'Sport and pastime', *Diamond Fields Advertiser*, 27 March 1891; 31 March 1891; and 3, 4, and 6 April 1891. (Researched and compiled by André Odendaal.)

25 For original source material on the 1891/92 Inter-Town Tournament for the Glover Cup, see *Diamond Fields Advertiser*, 29, 30 and 31 December 1891, pages 3, 3 and 7 respectively. (Researched and compiled by André Odendaal and John Young.)

26 For full scorecards of the 1892/93 Native Inter-Town Tournament, see *Imvo Zabantsundu*, 5 and 19 January 1893. (Researched and compiled by André Odendaal.)

27 For original source material on the 1892/93 Inter-Town Tournament for the Glover Cup, see *Cape Times*, 6, 9, 10 January 1893, all p. 3.

28 For original source material on the 1892/93 Extraneous Malay Inter-Town Tournament, see *Cape Times*, 6, 9, 10 January 1893, all p. 3. (Researched and compiled by John Young.)

29 For original source material on the 1895/96 Inter-Town Tournament for the Glover Cup, see 'Sporting Intelligence', *Cape Times*, 6 January 1896, p. 6; 'Cricket: Coloured tournament', *Cape Times*, 11 January 1896; 'Sporting Intelligence', *Cape Times*, 11 January 1896, p. 7. (Compiled by André Odendaal, Jonty Winch and John Young.)

30 For original sources on the Extraneous 1895/96 Native Inter-Town Tournament, see *Imvo Zabantsundu*, 4 April 1896. (Researched and compiled by André Odendaal.)

31 For original source material on the Extraneous 1896/97 Native Inter-Town Tournament, see 'Amanqanku', *Imvo Zabantsundu*, 14 January 1897; 'Ibala labadlali', *Imvo Zabantsundu*, 12 January and 25 February 1897. (Researched and compiled by André Odendaal.)

32 For the full scorecards of the 1897/98 Native Inter-Town Tournament (the first for the Jabavu Cup), see *Imvo Zabantsundu*, 30 December 1897 and 6 January 1898. (Researched and compiled by André Odendaal.)

33 For original source material on the 1897/98 Inter-Town Tournament for the Glover Cup, see '"Glover Cup" tournament', *Diamond Fields Advertiser*, 29 December 1897, p. 6; 'Glover Cup contest', *Diamond Fields Advertiser*, 5 January 1898, p. 8. (Sourced and compiled by André Odendaal and John Young.)

Notes to Chapter 16, 'Time for South Africa to send Home something besides gold, diamonds and millionaires'

1   *Daily Independent*, 14 January 1889.
2   *Cape Times*, 13 September 1880.
3   *Cape Argus*, 26 May 1881 and 4 July 1881.
4   Editorial notes, *Imvo Zabantsundu*, 3 November 1884.
5   'Eze bola', *Imvo Zabantsundu*, 15 August 1884.
6   A.A. Thompson, 'Bat, ball and boomerang' in R. Guha (ed.), *The Picador Book of Cricket* (Picador, London, 2001), pp. 229–37.
7   R. Christiansen, *The Victorian Visitors: Culture shock in nineteenth-century Britain* (Chatto and Windus, London, 2000), p. 170. See his description of the tour in ch. 5.
8   *Diamond Fields Advertiser*, 29 October 1888.
9   A letter dated 4 July 1881, published in the *Cape Argus* the following day.
10 Report in *Whitehall Review* published in *Cape Times*, 25 December 1886.
11 *Cape Argus*, 1 November 1886; *Cape Town Weekly*, 23 February 1887.
12 Rowland Hill letter, *Cape Times*, 27 August 1888.
13 *Daily Independent*, 12 April 1888.
14 Report in *Empire* published in *Daily Independent*, 30 March 1888.
15 Report in *Lantern* published in *Daily Independent*, 14 June 1888.
16 *The Lantern*, 12 June 1888.
17 *Daily Independent*, 14 June 1888 and 25 June 1888.
18 *Daily Independent*, 25 June 1888.
19 Peter Wynne-Thomas, *The Complete History of Cricket Tours at Home and Abroad* (Hamlyn, London, 1989), p. 219.
20 *Cape Times*, 23 August 1888.
21 *Cape Times*, 28 August 1888.
22 *Cape Times*, 28 August 1888.

Notes to Chapter 17, First international team arrives in Africa

1   *Daily Independent*, 13 February 1889.
2   *Cricket: A Weekly Record of the Game*, 24 January 1889, p. 2.
3   *Daily Independent*, 20 December 1888; *Cricket*, 24 January 1889, p. 2.
4   *Daily Independent*, 27 December 1888.
5   *Daily Independent*, 20 December 1888.
6   *Cricket*, 24 January 1889, p. 3
7   Ulyett did not arrive until early February 1889.
8   D.M. Harding, *Cricket Indulgence: An anthology of the cricket writings of Chris Harte* (PB Enterprises, n.p., 1991), pp. 42–3.
9   *Diamond Fields Advertiser*, 15 January 1889.
10 *Cricket*, 24 January 1889, p. 2.
11 *Daily Independent*, 13 February 1889.
12 *Cricket*, 24 January 1889, p. 3.
13 *Daily Independent*, 14 March 1889.
14 D.R. Allen, *Sir Aubrey: A biography of C. Aubrey Smith* (Elm Tree Books, London, 1982), p. 67.
15 J. Winch, *England's Youngest Captain: The life and times of Monty Bowden and two South African journalists* (Windsor Publishers, Windsor, 2003), p. 75.
16 Winch, *England's Youngest Captain*, p. 75.
17 Winch, *England's Youngest Captain*, pp. 76–8.
18 *Cricket*, 24 January 1889, p. 4.
19 *Daily Independent*, 20 December 1888.

Notes to Chapter 18, Journey that inscribed Empire and cricket onto the landscape of a subcontinent

1   *Diamond Fields Advertiser*, 4 October 1888.
2   Charles W. Alcock (ed.), *Lillywhite's Cricketers' Annual* (London, 1889).
3   *Cape Times*, 8 March 1930.
4   The details of the team's epic journey across southern Africa in this chapter are taken from J. Winch, *England's Youngest Captain: The life and times of Monty Bowden and two South African journalists* (Windsor Publishers, Windsor, 2003).
5   *The Friend* said of Barratt: 'He elicits a smile from those who know the financial condition of the club. The requisite amount of money (say £300) could be raised in town with comparatively little difficulty.'
6   *Cape Times Weekly*, 2 January 1889.
7   *Port Elizabeth Telegraph*, 3 January 1889.
8   *Cricket: A Weekly Record of the Game*, 21 February 1889, pp. 22–3.
9   *Cricket: A Weekly Record of the Game*, 21 February 1889, pp. 23, 27.
10 *Cricket: A Weekly Record of the Game*, 21 March 1889, p. 43.
11 *Daily Independent*, 2 February 1889.
12 See Winch, *England's Youngest Captain*, ch. 10, on the visit to Johannesburg.
13 *Cricket: A Weekly Record of the Game*, 18 April 1889, p. 52.
14 C. Alcock report and chart in *Lillywhite's Cricketers' Annual*, 1889.

Notes to Chapter 19, The first South African team and test matches

1   *Diamond Fields Advertiser*, 21 January 1889.
2   G. Allsop, 'Reminiscences of cricket' in M.W. Luckin, *The History of South African Cricket, including the scores of all important matches since 1878* (W.I. Horton, Johannesburg, 1915), pp. 123–6.
3   J. Winch, *England's Youngest Captain: The life and times of Monty Bowden and two South African journalists* (Windsor Publishers, Windsor, 2003), p. 74.
4   *Daily Independent*, 27 December 1888.
5   *Diamond Fields Advertiser*, 14 January 1889.
6   *Daily Independent*, 1 March 1889.
7   Correspondence with Robin Isherwood, 26 October 2008.
8   *Daily Independent*, 2 March 1889.
9   Luckin, *History of South African Cricket*, p. 69.
10 For more on this, see J. Winch, 'Sir William Milton: A leading figure in public school games, colonial politics and imperial expansion, 1877–1914' (PhD, Stellenbosch University, 2013).
11 *Daily Independent*, 23 March 1889.
12 *Daily Independent*, 23 March 1889.
13 *Daily Independent*, 23 March 1889.
14 *Daily Independent*, 20 March 1889.
15 C. Finlason in *Daily Independent*, 23 March 1889.
16 *Diamond Fields Advertiser*, 23 March 1889.
17 *Daily Independent*, 23 March 1889.
18 Winch, *England's Youngest Captain*, pp. 155–8.
19 C. Cox, *The Cricketing Record of Major Warton's Tour 1888–89* (Advertiser Office, Port Elizabeth, 1889), p. 203.
20 Cox, *The Cricketing Record*, p. 203.
21 C. Finlason, *A Nobody in Mashonaland* (Books of Rhodesia, Bulawayo, 1970), p. 72.

Notes to Chapter 20, 'Home', 'new chums' and the assertion of South African cricket identities

1   *Diamond Fields Advertiser*, 29 October 1888.
2   R. Holt, *Sport and the British: A modern history* (Oxford University Press, Oxford, 1992), p. 229.

3   *Daily Independent*, 30 January 1889.
4   J. Winch, *England's Youngest Captain: The life and times of Monty Bowden and two South African journalists* (Windsor Publishers, Windsor, 2003), pp. 98–106.
5   *Daily Independent*, 30 January 1889.
6   See Professor J. Honey, *Tom Brown in South Africa* (Rhodes University, Grahamstown, 1971), p. 18.
7   C.E. Finlason, *A Nobody in Mashonaland* (Vickers, London, 1895), p. 72.
8   *Daily Independent*, 1 May 1890.
9   *Daily Independent*, 18 January 1889.
10 Winch, *England's Youngest Captain*, p. 102.
11 *Daily Independent*, 1 May 1890.
12 *Daily Independent*, 18 January 1889.
13 *Daily Independent*, 18 January 1889.
14 *Daily Independent*, 28 January 1889.
15 *Diamond Field's Advertiser*, 13 February 1889.
16 'Notes on current events', *Imvo Zabantsundu*, 4 October 1888.
17 *Daily Independent*, 2 February 1889; *Diamond Field's Advertiser*, 21 January 1889.
18 B. Hall, R. Parry and J. Winch, 'More than a game' in B. Murray and G. Vahed (eds.), *Empire and Cricket: The South African experience 1884–1914* (Unisa Press, Pretoria, 2009), p. 6.

Notes to Chapter 21, 'Gentlemen, we beg you to reconsider your decision'

1   'Notes on current events', *Imvo Zabantsundu*, 4 October 1888.
2   On this, see R. Christiansen, *The Visitors: Culture shock in nineteenth century Britain* (Chatto & Windus, London, 2000); R. Holmes, *The Hottentot Venus: The life and death of Saartjie Baartman* (Johannesburg, 2007); A.A. Thompson, 'Bat, ball and boomerang' in R. Guha, *The Picador Book of Cricket* (Picador, London, 2002), pp. 229–37.
3   'Notes on current events', *Imvo Zabantsundu*, 4 October 1888.
4   R. Guha, *A Corner of a Foreign Field: The Indian history of a British sport* (Picador, London, 2002), pp. 14, 32.
5   *Cricket*, 6 September 1888, p. 392; *Imvo Zabatsundu*, 4 October 1888; articles and letters appeared regularly until the end of December 1888. The Parsis won one match out of 28 on their 1866 tour of England and eight out of 31 in 1888.
6   *Diamond Fields Advertiser*, 29 October 1888; *Cricket*, 27 December 1888, p. 473.
7   *Cricket*, 29 November 1888.
8   *Cricket*, 24 January 1889, p. 13.
9   *Potchefstroom Budget*, 25 January 1889.
10 Editorial notes, *Imvo Zabatsundu*, 28 February 1889.
11 *Port Elizabeth Telegraph*, 3 January 1889.
12 *Cricket*, 21 March 1889, p. 43.
13 *Cricket*, 21 February 1889, pp. 22–3.
14 *Imvo Zabantsundu*, 30 March 1889.
15 M. McCord, *The Calling of Katie Makanya* (David Philip, Cape Town, 2000), p. 34.
16 McCord, *The Calling of Katie Makanya*, pp. 54–5.
17 McCord, *The Calling of Katie Makanya*, p. 37.
18 D.B. Coplan, *In township tonight!*, p. 54. See also pp. 55–7.
19 Cape Archives, 3/KWT 2/1/1/10/9, Bennie Tele, secretary to Town Clerk, King William's Town, 27 September 1892.
20 Cape Archives, 3/KWT, 2/1/2/62, P. Xiniwe to Mayor and Councillors, King William's Town, 15 November 1892, and other letters.
21 See tournament report, *Imvo Zabantsundu*, 5 January 1893.
22 Phyllis Martin quoted in A. Odendaal to M. Kornbluh, 11 September 2007: 'Evaluation: Dr Peter Alegi'.

Notes to Chapter 22, 'The most gorgeous of Eastern spectacles'

1   'The Malays', *Cape Times*, 15 January 1890.

2   A. Davids, 'The revolt of the Malays: A study of the reactions of the Cape Muslims to the smallpox epidemics of nineteenth century Cape Town' in C. Saunders et al. (eds.), *Studies in the History of Cape Town* (Centre for African Studies, UCT, 1984), vol. 5, p. 50.

3   G. Lewis, *Between the Wire and the Wall: A history of South African 'Coloured' politics* (David Philip, Cape Town, 1985), p. 21.

4   We are grateful to the late Achmat Davids for these insights.

5   M. Galant, 'A history of Western Province cricket' (People's History Project, UWC, 1987), p. 2.

6   'Our history' (based on an article by A. Adams, *Muslim News*, 11 December 1981) in Ottomans Cricket Club souvenir brochure, 115th anniversary, 1882–1997, Ghatam-al Quran, 14 December 1997, Jamiah Mosque, Cape Town.

7   R. Parry, 'Black cricketers, white politicians and the origins of segregation at the Cape to 1894' in B. Murray and G. Vahed (eds.), *Empire and Cricket: The South African experience 1884–1914* (Unisa Press, Pretoria, 2009), p. 31.

8   Parry, 'Black cricketers, white politicians', p. 31.

9   Parry, 'Black cricketers, white politicians', p. 13.

10   For details see, 'Sporting Intelligence, *Cape Argus*, 13 January 1890; 'Today's cricket. The Malay tournament', *Cape Argus*, 14 January 1890; 'Sporting Intelligence. The Malay tournament', *Cape Times*, 14 January 1890; 'Cricket. The Malay tournament', *Cape Times*, 15 January 1890; 'Sporting Intelligence', *Cape Times*, 21 January 1890; 'Cricket. The Malay tournament', *Cape Times*, 22 January 1890; 'Sporting Intelligence', *Cape Times*, 23 January 1890; 'Sporting Intelligence', *Cape Times*, 28 January 1890; 'Sporting Intelligence', *Cape Times*, 30 January 1890.

11   Parry, 'Black cricketers, white politicians', p. 33.

12   'Sporting Intelligence. The Malay tournament', *Cape Times*, 14 January1890.

13   'Sport and pastime', *Diamond Fields Advertiser*, 27 March 1891; 31 March 1891; 3, 4 and 6 April 1891.

14   V. Bickford-Smith, E. van Heyningen and N. Worden, *Cape Town: The making of a city* (David Philip, Cape Town, 1989), pp. 210–11. See also A. Hartley, 'Bo-Kaap marches in steps of SA's first protesters', *Cape Times*, 18 January 2010.

15   A. Davids, 'Politics and the Muslims of Cape Town: A historical survey' in C. Saunders et al. (eds.), *Studies in the History of Cape Town* (Centre for African Studies, UCT, 1984), vol. 4, p. 190.

16   'The Malays', *Cape Times*, 15 January 1890.

Notes to Chapter 23, The formation of the South African Cricket Association, April 1890

1   Reported in the *Diamond Fields Advertiser*, 23 November 1888.

2   *Daily Independent*, 23 November 1888.

3   *Diamond Fields Advertiser*, 23 November 1888.

4   *Diamond Fields Advertiser*, 9 February 1890.

5   *Diamond Fields Advertiser*, 9 February 1890.

6   T. Partridge and F. Heydenrych (eds.), *The 1990 Protea Cricket Annual of South Africa* (Published in association with the South African Cricket Union, Cape Town, 1990), p. 32.

7   *Diamond Fields Advertiser*, 10 April 1890.

8   *Diamond Fields Advertiser*, 10 April 1890.

9   *Diamond Fields Advertiser*, 11 April 1890.

Notes to Chapter 24, Cricket and the Imperial mission

1   *Diggers News*, 6 April 1889.

2   *Cricket*, 5 September 1889, p. 881.

3   *Daily Independent*, 28 October 1890.

4   J. Winch, *England's Youngest Captain: The life and times of Monty Bowden and two South African journalists* (Windsor Publishers, Windsor, 2003), p. 166.

5   L.E. Neame, *City Built on Gold* (Central News Agency, Parow, 1969), p. 41.

6   *Graaff-Reinet Advertiser*, 16 October 1889.

7 T. Gutsche, *Old Gold: The history of the Wanderers Club* (Howard Timmins, Cape Town, 1966), p. 42.

8 Mosenthal's wealthy cousin Harry, friend of C.J. Rhodes and a director of De Beers, famously imported Angora goats into South Africa and raised money for the cricket pavilion for Grey High School in Port Elizabeth from the Beit Bequest and the will of Sir Julius Wernher, wealthy Randlords both. J. Young, *The Spirit of the Tower: The Grey 1856–2006* (The Grey Schools, Port Elizabeth, 2006), p. 39.

9 *Cricket Field*, May 1895.

10 Anna de Brémont, *The Gentleman Digger: A study of Johannesburg life* (Sampson Low, Marston, London, 1889), p. 90.

11 See G. Allsop, 'Reminiscences of cricket' in M.W. Luckin, *The History of South African Cricket, including the scores of all important matches since 1878* (W.I. Horton, Johannesburg, 1915), pp. 127–8.

12 Finlason complained of spending 'six dreary months' at the Palace Hotel in Klerksdorp, but had in the rural environment taken 55 wickets at a cost of 6.41 runs each.

13 *Diamond Fields Advertiser*, 7 April 1890.

14 *Diamond Fields Advertiser*, 8 April 1890.

15 *Diamond Fields Advertiser*, 11 April 1890.

16 R. Cary, *The Pioneer Corps* (Galaxie Press, Salisbury, 1975), p. 20.

17 *Cape Argus*, 24 November 1889.

18 *Daily Independent*, 23 May 1891.

19 *Daily Independent*, 28 October 1890.

20 *Daily Independent*, 3 May 1890.

21 *Natal Mercury*, 9 May 1890.

22 I.D. Difford, *The History of South African Rugby Football (1875–1932)* (Speciality Press, Wynberg, 1933), pp. 27–8; A.C. Parker, *The Springboks, 1891–1970* (Cassell, London, 1970), pp. 7–8.

23 *Rhodesia Herald*, 18 September 1914.

Notes to Chapter 25, 'What man's accomplish'd ye can do'

1 *Ilanga lase Natal*, 11 December 1903 in T. Couzens, 'Robert Grendon: Irish traders, cricket scores and Paul Kruger's dreams', *English in Africa*, 15, 2, October 1988, p. 49.

2 For the tournament match reports and scorecards, see *Diamond Fields Advertiser*, 3 April 1891.

3 R. Parry, 'Black cricketers, white politicians and the origins of segregation at the Cape to 1894' in B. Murray and G. Vahed (eds.), *Empire and Cricket: The South African experience 1884–1914* (Unisa Press, Pretoria, 2009), p. 36.

4 For the match report and scorecard, see *Diamond Fields Advertiser*, 6 April 1891.

5 J.A. Noble, 'Early days of Kimberley cricket' in M.W. Luckin, *The History of South African Cricket, including the scores of all important matches since 1878* (W.I. Horton, Johannesburg, 1915), pp. 41, 46.

6 Kimberley tourism office website, http://kimberleytourism.co.za.

7 *Cape Times*, 29 December 1891.

8 See, for example, Couzens, 'Robert Grendon'.

Notes to Chapter 26, Demon Spofforth of Africa

1 R. Parry, 'Black cricketers, white politicians and the origins of segregation at the Cape to 1894' in B. Murray and G. Vahed (eds.), *Empire and Cricket: The South African experience 1884–1914* (Unisa Press, Pretoria, 2009), p. 37.

2 B. Willan, 'An African in Kimberley: Sol T. Plaatje, 1894–8' in S. Marks and R. Rathbone (eds.), *Industrialisation and Social Change in South Africa: African class formation, culture and consciousness, 1870–1930* (Longman, London, 1982), pp. 257.

3 Willan, 'An African in Kimberley', pp. 251–2.

4 Parry, 'Black cricketers, white politicians', p. 36.

5 'Ibala labadlali', *Imvo Zabantsundu*, 26 August 1897.

6   J. Comaroff and B. Willan, with S. Molema and A. Reed (eds.), *The Mafeking Diary of Sol T. Plaatje* (David Philip, Cape Town, 1999), p. 11.

7   Willan, 'An African in Kimberley', p. 244; and T. Karis and G.M. Gerhart (eds.), *From Protest to Challenge: A documentary history of African politics in South Africa* (Stanford, 1977), vol. 4, p. 12.

8   A. Grundlingh, A. Odendaal and B. Spies, *Beyond the Tryline* (Ravan Press, Johannesburg, 1995), pp. 37–8.

9   Willan, 'An African in Kimberley', p. 252.

10 *Cape Times* report in B. Bassano and R. Smith, *The Visit of Mr W.W. Read's 1891–92 English Cricket Team to South Africa* (Ewell J. McKenzie, n.p., 2007), pp. 173–5; 'The "D'Oliveira" incident of the 1890s', undated *Cape Times* article by E. Rosenthal in the André Odendaal Collection.

11 The spelling for the scorer of this historic fifty is given as Samoodien in the above sources, but we have used Samsodien on the basis of other newspaper reports and ensuing discussions.

12 A.E. Knight, 'The complete cricketer' (1906) in John Bright-Holmes, *The Joy of Cricket* (Martin Secker & Warburg, London, 1984), p. 241.

13 *Cape Times*, 11 January 1894.

14 See R. Barker, 'The Demon against England' in R. Guha (ed.), *The Picador Book of Cricket* (Picador, London, 2001), pp. 301–17.

15 *Cape Times*, 2 February 1894.

16 E. Rosenthal, 'The D'Oliveira incident of the 1890s', undated *Cape Times* article in the André Odendaal Collection.

17 Rosenthal, 'The D'Oliveira incident of the 1890s'.

Notes to Chapter 27, Fateful decision

1   *Standard and Diggers News*, 14 February 1894.

2   J. Winch, 'Sir William Milton: A leading figure in public school games, colonial politics and imperial expansion, 1877–1914' (PhD, University of Stellenbosch, 2013), pp. 117–18.

3   Winch, 'Sir William Milton, p. 118.

4   *Cape Times*, 11 January 1894.

5   *Cape Times*, 11 January 1894.

6   Cape Times, 9 February 1894.

7   R. Parry, 'The real Mr Hendricks', *Cricket Lore*, 2, 4, p. 17.

8   Parry, 'The real Mr Hendricks', p. 17.

9   Parry, 'The real Mr Hendricks', p. 17.

10 *Cape Times*, 9 December 1891, described it as the 'finest bit of diplomatic work in South Africa in recent years'.

11 R.I. Rotberg, *The Founder: Cecil Rhodes and the pursuit of power* (Oxford University Press, Oxford, 1988), p. 372.

12 Rotberg, *The Founder*, p. 458

13 A. Odendaal, *The Founders: The origins of the ANC and the struggle for democracy in South Africa* (Jacana, Johannesburg, 2012), ch. 14; http://www.sahistory.org.za/topic/natives-land-act-1913.

14 Winch, 'Sir William Milton', p. 119.

15 Winch, 'Sir William Milton', p. 11.

16 R. Parry, 'Black cricketers, white politicians and the origins of segregation' in B. Murray and G. Vahed (eds.), *Empire and Cricket: The South African experience 1884–1914* (Unisa Press, Pretoria, 2009), pp. 40–1.

17 *Cape Times*, 11 January 1894.

18 *Cape Times*, 12 January 1894.

19 *Standard and Diggers News*, 14 February 1894.

20 *The Star*, 16 January 1894.

21 *Cape Times*, 21 February 1894.

22 *Standard and Diggers News*, 17 February 1894.

23 *Cape Times*, 27 February 1894.

24 *Standard and Diggers News*, 2 October 1894.
25 *Standard and Diggers News*, 2 March 1894.
26 *Cape Times*, 5 March 1894.
27 *Standard and Diggers News*, 29 March 1894.
28 *Cape Argus*, 27 February 1894.
29 *Cape Times*, 5 March 1894.
30 I.D. Difford, *The History of South African Rugby Football, 1875–1932* (Speciality Press, Wynberg, 1933), p. 29.
31 E. Hayden in the 'Licensed Victuallers' Gazette' reported in *Standard and Diggers News*, 26 May 1897.
32 *Daily Independent*, 16 May 1890.
33 M.W. Luckin, *The History of South African Cricket, including the scores of all important matches since 1878* (W.I. Horton, Johannesburg, 1915), Preface.
34 P.F. Warner, *Lord's 1787–1945* (Sportsman's Book Club, London, 1951), p. 60.
35 P.F. Warner, *Long Innings* (George G. Harrap, London, 1951), p. 60.
36 *Cape Times*, 5 March 1894.
37 *Cape Times*, 6 March 1894.
38 *Cape Times*, 6 March 1894.
39 *Cape Times*, 12 March 1894.
40 W.V. Simkins told *Cricket: A Weekly Record of the Game*, 13 September 1894, p. 389: 'Financially, it has been as complete a failure as it could be. The total gate did not reach £500. The guarantors in the Colony will have to pay twenty shillings in the pound.'
41 *Standard and Diggers News*, 2 October 1894.
42 Parry, 'The real Mr Hendricks', p. 17.
43 See Warner, *Lord's 1787–1945*, p. 60; J. Winch, 'I Could a Tale Unfold' in B. Murray and G. Vahed (eds.), *Empire and Cricket: The South African experience 1884–1914* (Unisa Press, Pretoria, 2009), p. 66.

Notes to Chapter 28, The Cape Town establishment institutionalises racism in cricket

1   J. Winch, 'Sir William Milton: A leading public figure in public school games, colonial politics and imperial expansion, 1877–1914' (PhD dissertation, University of Stellenbosch, 2013), p. 140.
2   *Cape Times*, 5 March 1894.
3   Bruce Murray and Christopher Merrett, *Caught Behind: Race and politics in Springbok cricket* (Pietermaritzburg, Wits and KwaZulu-Natal UP, 2004), p. 12.
4   *The Cricket Field*, 4 August 1894, p. 348.
5   The Australians selected were C.D'O. Mainon ('an Australian of repute' – *Cricket*, 15 March 1913), A. Goldman, T. Tunnicliffe and C. Drake.
6   References to the meetings appear in the *Cape Times* and *Cape Argus*, 21–28 October 1894.
7   *Standard and Diggers News*, 2 November 1894.
8   *Cape Times*, 19 April 1894.
9   There had been no meeting of the South African Cricket Association since March 1894; the new secretary, G.A. Parker, was informed that he would have to obtain the general accounts/ records from Maynard Nash in Cape Town.
10 *Cape Times*, 18 September 1895.
11 B. Dobbs, *Edwardians at Play* (Pelham, London, 1973), p. 140; B. Green (ed.), *The Wisden Book of Cricketers' Lives: Obituaries from Wisden Cricketers' Almanack* (Queen Anne Press, London, 1988), p. 316. Lord Harris, president of the MCC and, six years previously, governor of Bombay, stated that he was not in favour of playing 'birds of passage': A. Ross, *Ranji: Prince of cricketers* (Collins, London, 1983), pp. 62 and 207.
12 I. Wilton, *C.B. Fry: King of sport* (London, Metro, 2002), p. 78.
13 Matches reported in *Cape Times*, 30 November – 20 December 1895.
14 M.W. Luckin, *The History of South African Cricket, including the scores of all important matches since 1878* (W.I. Horton, Johannesburg, 1915), p. 645.
15 *Standard and Diggers News*, 25 January 1896.

16   *Cape Times*, 20 February 1894.
17   *Cricket*, 9 April 1896, p. 54, reported: 'Middleton was ordered to Cape Town to take part in a club match and his recall by the executive of this club gave rise to a great deal of unpleasantness.'
18   *Cricket*, 4 March 1896.
19   *Standard and Diggers News*, 7 March 1896.
20   *Cape Times*, 11 February 1895.
21   The wording of the resolution is outlined in *Cape Times*, 6 November 1897.
22   *Cape Times*, 23 November 1896.
23   Milton's initial task was to overhaul Rhodesia's civil service.
24   *Cape Times*, 1 November 1897.
25   V. Bickford-Smith, *Ethnic Pride and Racial Prejudice in Victorian Cape Town* (Witwatersrand University Press, Johannesburg, 1995), p. 150.
26   *Cape Times*, 5 November 1897.
27   *Cape Times*, 6 November 1897.
28   Robb then asked if a special ruling could be made to allow Hendricks to play, but it was defeated 11-3.
29   H. Schulze, *South Africa's Cricketing Lawyers* (Interdoc Consultants, Halfway House, 1989), p. 106.
30   *Cape Times*, 13 November 1897.
31   *Cape Times*, 13 November 1897.
32   *Cricket*, 1 August 1901, p. 305.
33   P. Wynne-Thomas, *The Complete History of Cricket Tours at Home and Abroad* (Hamlyn, London, 1989), p. 231. See also *Cape Times*, 15 April 1901.
34   *Rhodesia Herald*, 3 April 1901; Taberer captained South Africa in their next test against Australia at Johannesburg in October 1902.
35   *Cape Times*, 17 November 1904.
36   J. Nauright, *Sport Cultures and Identities in South Africa* (David Philip, Cape Town, 1995), p. 28.
37   A.C. Parker, *W.P. Cricket: 100 not out* (WPCU, Cape Town, 1990), pp. 17, 20 and 21; Difford, *The History of South African Rugby Football*, p. 701.
38   *Rhodesia Herald*, 26 July 1929; the comment was made by Sir Clarkson Tredgold.
39   *Cape Times*, 13 November 1897.
40   R. Parry, 'The real Mr Hendricks', *Cricket Lore*, 2, 4, p. 18.
41   *Cape Times*, 13 November 1897.
42   T. Collins, *A Social History of English Rugby Union* (Routledge, London, 2009), especially chs. 2 and 5.

Notes to Chapter 29, The colour bar in cricket becomes fixed

1   G.19-1909, Blue Book on Native Affairs 1908, p. 25.
2   http://www.sahistory.org.za/topic/natives-land-act-1913.
3   See A. Odendaal, *The Founders: The origins of the ANC and the struggle for democracy in South Africa* (Jacana, Johannesburg, 2012), p. xx; http://www.sahistory.org.za/topic/natives-land-act-1913.
4   *Bulawayo Chronicle*, 9 October 1895.
5   B. Green (ed.), *The Wisden Book of Cricketers' Lives: Obituaries from Wisden Cricketers' Almanack* (London, 1986), p. 634. Mordaunt scored 127 in the 1889 University match.
6   Jameson's officers included Monty Bowden's brother, Frank, and were not particularly experienced or, for that matter, possessed of 'military genius'. Willoughby was no help, being of similar adventurous spirit. Captain Cyril Foley of Eton, Cambridge, Worcestershire and Middlesex cricketing fame, irritated Jameson and was reprimanded because, 'Not intentionally but idiotically he has been talking too much'.
7   Martin Bladen, 7th Lord Hawke (1860–1938), was for 28 years captain of Yorkshire and its president for 40, 'remembered far and wide as the leader of those amateur teams which he organised to visit various parts of the Empire' (*Wisden* obituary).
8   Timothy Carew O'Brien, 3rd Bart. (1861–1948).
9   Charles William Wright (1864–1932).

10 C.B. Fry, *Life Worth Living: Some phases of an Englishman* (Pavilion, London, 1986), p. 111. Charles Burgess Fry (1872–1956) was the epitome of the amateur sportsman. He played cricket (as captain) and soccer for England and held the world long-jump record for 21 years. He was a notable public figure, journalist and aspirant Liberal politician who was once apparently offered the throne of Albania.

11 M.B. Hawke, *Recollections and Reminiscences* (Williams and Norgate, London, 1924), p. 151; Fry, *Life Worth Living*, p. 109. The England team was held up at Vereeniging by an armed group of Transvalers who, according to legend, were given two cricket bats as a peace offering.

12 Iain Wilton, *C.B. Fry: King of sport* (London, Metro, 2002), p. 78.

13 Derek Birley, A Social History of English Cricket (London, 1999), p. 165.

14 Wilton, *C.B. Fry*, pp. 84–5.

15 R. Blake, *A History of Rhodesia* (Eyre Methuen, London, 1977), p. 152; G.H. Tanser, *A Scantling of Time: The story of Salisbury, 1890–1900* (Stuart Manning, Salisbury, 1965), p. 179. Milton described himself as a 'servant to Rhodes' (*Rhodesia Herald*, 30 October 1913) but in matters of cricket he was powerful and feared. 'On a match day,' recalled Castens, 'when anything goes wrong, he puts on a very big pipe and sits quite still, looking very solemn. At such time we don't, as a rule, think it appropriate to address him on frivolous subjects' (*Cricket Field*, 4 August 1894, p. 348).

16 See Wikipedia article on Nehanda Nyakasikana.

17 'Imprisoning cricketers', *Imvo Zabantsundu*, 28 November 1894.

18 R. Magengelele, secretary, Native Cricket Club, Stutterheim, to Mayor and Councillors, 18 October 1897 and R. McN. Plaatjes, treasurer, to Mayor and Councillors, 2 November 1897, quoted in *Imvo Zabantsundu*, 25 November 1897.

19 'A Native Farmer', Upper Kabousie, Stutterheim, to the editor, 12 November 1897, quoted in *Imvo Zabantsundu*, 25 November 1897.

20 For details, see Cape Archives NA 636, File number 2207: Memorandum by J. Jones, 'Re cricketers ejected from the native location Uitvlugt', 9 January 1904, and attached correspondence.

21 *Indian Opinion*, 6 March 1909, p. 104.

22 *Indian Opinion*, 4 May 1912, quoted in A. Desai, V. Padayachee, K. Reddy and G. Vahed, *Blacks in Whites: A century of cricket struggles in KwaZulu-Natal* (University of Natal Press, Pietermaritzburg, 2002), p. 6. See also *Imvo Zabantsundu*, 2 August 1910.

23 South African Native Affairs Commission, Evidence of J.W. Hancock (Inspector of Locations), ORC, 22 September 1904, p. 393.

24 'Colour and sports', *Tsala ea Batho*, 19 August 1911.

25 G.19-1909, Blue Book on Native Affairs 1908, p. 25.

26 C. Merrett, 'A political and cultural history of South African cricket' (Unpublished MS, 2000), p. 7.

27 N. Mostert, *Frontiers: The epic of South Africa's creation and the tragedy of the Xhosa people* (Pimlico, London, 1992), p. 1247.

Notes to Chapter 30, 'Like a rather sunburned English player'

1 A.D. Nourse, 'A peep into the past' in M.W. Luckin, *South African Cricket, 1919–1927* (The Author, Johannesburg, 1927), p. 48.

2 J.M. Kilburn, *Overthrows: A book of cricket* (Stanley Paul, London, 1975), pp. 11, 13.

3 General sources of information on Llewellyn are S.H.P., 'Charles Bennett Llewellyn' in 'Five Cricketers of the Year', *Wisden* 1911, pp. 172–3 and *Wisden* 1964, p. 968 (obituary). Llewellyn was known by a number of names. The cricket literature lists his initials consistently as G.C.B. but this is now known to have resulted from a careless compilation of a team list early in his career. The name Buck is also attributed to him, presumably after his father. However, in a letter written to his mother dated 8 January 1915 about a Bible left to him in his father's will and sent from 218 Burnley Road, Accrington, he signed himself Charlie (Deceased estate, Office of the Master of the Supreme Court, Pietermaritzburg, vol. 53/239).

4 Deceased estate 5108 at the Natal Archives Depot, Pietermaritzburg, contains a death notice dated 7 April 1920 which shows (clearly typed) her birthplace as St Helena. Her marriage declaration in

CSO 2286 (also Natal Archives Depot) has a handwritten entry for place of birth which is given as James Town, St Helena. Anne Elizabeth Llewellyn died intestate, left £1,000 and was buried in the Wesleyan Cemetery. No trace of the Rich family has been found by the writer, but at the turn of the century a J. Rich was active on St Helena in the Poor Society and the Ancient Order of Foresters (E.L. Jackson, *St. Helena: The historic island from its discovery to the present date* (Ward Lock, London, 1903), pp. 102–3).

5   *Natal Almanac and Register 1876*, p. 164.
6   Jackson, *St. Helena*, pp. 88–9.
7   Kilburn, *Overthrows*, pp. 11, 13.
8   M.W. Luckin, *The History of South African Cricket, including the scores of all important matches since 1878* (W.I. Horton, Johannesburg, 1915), p. 71.
9   B. Crowley, *Currie Cup Story* (Nelson, Cape Town, 1973), p. 32.
10 Crowley, *Currie Cup Story*, pp. 74, 85.
11 A. Odendaal, *Cricket in Isolation: The politics of race and cricket in South Africa* (The Author, Cape Town, 1977), p. 326.
12 B. Bassano, *South Africa in International Cricket, 1888–1970* (Chameleon, East London, 1979), pp. 30, 46, 51; *South African Cricket Annual*, 1, 1951–2.
13 T. Routledge, 'The third English team in South Africa, 1895–6' in Luckin, *The History of South African Cricket*, p. 521.
14 C.B. Fry, *Life Worth Living: Some phases of an Englishman* (Pavilion, London, 1986), p. 117.
15 *Wisden 1911*, p. 172.
16 E.W. Swanton, G. Plumptre and J. Woodcock (eds.), *The Barclays World of Cricket; The game from A to Z* (Collins, London, 1980), p. 234.
17 R. Archer and A. Bouillon, *The South African Game: Sport and racism* (Zed, London, 1982), p. 90; R. Bowen, *Cricket: A history of its growth and development throughout the world* (Eyre and Spottiswoode, London, 1970), p. 150.
18 South African Cricket Association minutes dated 19 August 1910; letter from Natal Cricket Association (NCA) to SACA dated 28 August 1910 included in minutes dated 19 September 1910; minutes dated 23 September 1910, 6 January 1911, 27 June 1911 and 3 October 1911.
19 *Wisden 1913*.
20 C. Martin-Jenkins, *The Complete Who's Who of Test Cricketers* (Stanton, Johannesburg, 1980), p. 265.
21 A. Anderton, C.B. Llewellyn [letter], *Cricketer*, 57, 3, March 1976, p. 29.
22 This error has entered the literature; see D. Hayes, *Famous Cricketers of Hampshire* (Spellmount, Tunbridge Wells, 1993), p. 100.
23 Bassano, *South Africa in International Cricket*, p. 30; S.H.P., 'Charles Bennett Llewellyn', pp. 172–3. Tom Hayward and J.R. Mason were also left out. The Edgbaston test was drawn and England used only four bowlers. In Australia's first innings of 36, Hirst and Rhodes bowled 22 of a total 23 overs. The batting line-up is regarded as probably the strongest ever to start a test for England and Llewellyn's presence is testimony to the high regard in which he was held. The team comprised A.C. McLaren, C.B. Fry, K.S. Ranjitsinhji, F.S. Jackson, J.T. Tyldesley, A.F.A. Lilley, G.H. Hirst, G.L. Jessop (batting at 8), L.C. Braund, W.H. Lockwood and W. Rhodes.
24 Kilburn, *Overthrows*, p. 10.
25 I. Tennant, 'Henry's breakthrough recalls mystery of C.B. Llewellyn', *Sunday Times* (London), 18 January 1987.
26 *South African Cricketers Annual 1905–6*, p. 89.
27 *Wisden 1909*, p. 157.
28 Martin-Jenkins, *The Complete Who's Who*, p. 265.
29 P. Allen, 'C.B. Llewellyn: An early D'Oliveira', *The Cricketer*, 57, 2, February 1976, p. 21.
30 S.H.P., 'Charles Bennett Llewellyn', p. 173.
31 P. Warner, *Long Innings: The autobiography* (Harrap, London, 1951), pp. 50–1; S.H.P., 'Charles Bennett Llewellyn', p. 173.
32 *Wisden 1911*, p. 173.
33 Nourse, 'A peep into the past', p. 48.
34 *Wisden 1911*, p. 173.

35   H.S. Altham et al., *Hampshire County Cricket: The official history* (Phoenix, London, 1957), p. 54.
36   H.S. Altham, *A History of Cricket* (Allen and Unwin, London, 1962), vol. 1, p. 268.
37   Kilburn, *Overthrows*, p. 13. The Chinaman, in British parlance, is the left-arm wrist spinner's googly, in effect a leg break, which would in any case have been Llewellyn's stock delivery using his natural finger spin action. He would presumably have possessed an arm ball (M. Rundle, *The Dictionary of Cricket* (Oxford University Press, Oxford, 1995), p. 37). He was not the only test cricketer to bowl in a cap. 'Dave' Nourse also did so, as shown by a picture from Old Trafford in the South Africa vs Australia test of the 1912 Triangular Series (D. Frith, *The Golden Age of Cricket, 1890–1914* (Omega, London, 1983), p. 153).
38   *South African Cricket Annual*, 16, 1969.
39   B. Whimpress, *Passport to Nowhere: Aborigines in Australian cricket 1850–1939* (Walla Walla, Sydney, 1999), p. 171.
40   Whimpress, *Passport to Nowhere*, p. 188.
41   Whimpress, *Passport to Nowhere*, pp. 164–200; C. Tatz, *Obstacle Race: Aborigines in sport* (University of New South Wales Press, Sydney, 1995), pp. 72–5.
42   M.S. Evans, *Black and White in South East Africa: A study in sociology.* (Longmans, Green, London, 1916), p. 298.
43   *Natal Almanac, Directory and Yearly Register*, 1896, p. 607.
44   *Corporation Yearbook* 1912, p. 42.
45   Pietermaritzburg, City Council Minutes, 14 August 1916 and 10 September 1918; *Corporation Yearbook* 1917, p. 10.
46   H.F. Dickie-Clarke, *The Marginal Situation: A sociological study of a coloured group* (Routledge and Kegan Paul, London, 1966), pp. 56 and 74.
47   Crowley, *Currie Cup Story*, p. 33.
48   Hayes, *Famous Cricketers of Hampshire*, p. 101; Minutes of an Ordinary Meeting of the South African Cricket Association at the EP Cricket Union, Port Elizabeth, 10 April 1903.
49   André Odendaal Collection, 'Our two test cricketers', Undescribed fragment from SACBOC brochure edited by S.J. Reddy.

Notes to Chapter 31, 'Neither ladies nor cricketers'

1   J. Jeppe, 'Early days of cricket in the Transvaal' in M.W. Luckin, *The History of South African Cricket, including the scores of all important matches since 1878* (W.I. Horton, Johannesburg, 1915), p. 809.
2   This is the first attempt to write women's contributions into a general history of South African cricket in any detail. It is based on André Odendaal's work-in-progress since 2004, particularly '"Neither cricketers nor ladies": Towards a history of women and cricket in South Africa, 1860s–2000s' in S. Cornelissen and A. Grundlingh (eds.), *Sport Past and Present in South Africa: (Trans)forming the nation* (Routledge, London, 2012), pp. 114–35, which was first presented as a paper at the Sports History Conference at the University of Stellenbosch on 30 June 2008 and also appeared in the *International Journal of the History of Sport*, 28, 1, January 2011. See also '"Neither cricketers nor ladies": A short history of women's cricket in South Africa, 1850–2005' in *Women's Cricket World Cup 2005 South Africa* (Brochure published by the IWCC and UCBSA, 2005), pp. 6–9; articles in WPCA annual reports from 2005 to 2014, especially 'A women's place is out in the middle' in *Western Province Cricket Association Annual Report 2008/09*, pp. 19–21 (Cape Town, 2009); Eighth Annual New Year's Address at Sahara Park Newlands by André Odendaal, 3 January 2012; A. Odendaal, K. Reddy and A. Samson, *The Blue Book: A history of Western Province cricket, 1890–2011* (Fanele, Cape Town, 2012), introduction and chs. 7, 11; and 'Girls and boys: Looking back at cricket's strange history', Brochure for CSA Girls U19 Cricket Week, Western Province, 4–9 December 2013, pp. 7–12.
3   Quoted in J. Winch, *Cricket in Southern Africa: Two hundred years of achievement and records* (Windsor, Rosettenville, 1997), p. 270.
4   B. Frindall, 'Unveiling the ladies' in L. Frewin (ed.), *The Boundary Book: Second innings* (Spring Books, London, 1986), pp. 214–15.
5   Frindall, 'Unveiling the ladies', p. 214.

6   K.A.P. Sandiford, *Cricket and the Victorians* (Scolar Press, Aldershot, 1994), p. 29.
7   Frewin, *The Boundary Book*, pp. 214–15.
8   T. Lewis, *Double century* (Hodder and Stoughton, London, 1987), pp. 22–3.
9   Sandiford, *Cricket and the Victorians*, pp. 1–2, 29.
10   K.E. McCrone, 'Play up! Play up! And play the game! Sport at the late Victorian public school' in J.A. Mangan and R.J. Park (eds.), *From 'Fair Sex' to Feminism* (Frank Cass Publishers, London, 1987), p. 99.
11   Quoted in R. Christiansen, *The Victorian Visitors: Culture shock in nineteenth-century Britain* (Chatto and Windus, London, 2000), p. 179.
12   See J. Hargreaves, 'Victorian familism and the formative years of female sport' in Mangan and Park, *From 'Fair Sex' to Feminism*, pp. 134–5, 137, 141.
13   On the educational reformers and schools sport, see McCrone, 'Play up! Play up!'
14   R. Holt, *Sport and the British: A modern history* (Oxford University Press, Oxford, 1992), p. 125.
15   Frindall, 'Unveiling the ladies', p. 217.
16   Holt, *Sport and the British*, p. 128.
17   T. McGirck, 'Neither cricketers nor ladies' in Frewin, *The Boundary Book*, p. 196.
18   McCrone, 'Play up! Play up!, pp. 119–20.
19   H. King, 'The sexual politics of sport' in R. Cashman and M. McKernan (eds.), *Sport in History: The making of modern sporting history* (University of Queensland Press, St Lucia, 1979), p. 76.
20   'King William's Town NCC vs East London NCC', *Isigidimi samaXhosa*, 16 January 1884.
21   *St Matthew's SPG Mission, Keiskamma Hoek, Visit of the Lord Bishop of Grahamstown and a Short Account of the Mission*, May 1884, p. 10.
22   'Ibala labadlali – ibhola eBhayi', *Imvo Zabantsundu*, 18 Januray 1888.
23   Margaret McCord, *The Calling of Katie Makanya* (David Philip, Cape Town, 2000), p. 27.
24   Hargreaves, 'Victorian familism and the formative years of female sport', pp. 136–7.

Notes to Chapter 32, Women at the crease

1   T. Gutsche, *Old Gold: The history of the Wanderers Club* (Howard Timmins, Cape Town, 1966), quoted in J. Winch, *Cricket in Southern Africa: Two hundred years of achievement and records* (Windsor, Rosettenville, 1997), p. 270.
2   All these examples and quotes are from J. Winch, *England's Youngest Captain: The life and times of Monty Bowden and two South African journalists* (Windsor Publishers, Windsor, 2003), pp. 64, 71, 76, 80, 85, 117–18, 125.
3   Quoted in J. Winch, *Cricket in Southern Africa*, p. 270.
4   See A. Odendaal (comp. and ed.), *Cricket and Community in Stellenbosch* (Stellenbosch Cricket, Stellenbosch Academy of Sport and Masikhulisane Cricket Academy, 2016), especially pp. 11, 18, 27, 29.
5   Winch, *Cricket in Southern Africa*, p. 270.
6   *Cape Times*, 19 April 1895.
7   Winch, *Cricket in Southern Africa*, p. 270.
8   Winch, *Cricket in Southern Africa*, p. 270.
9   B. Goudvis and M. Leveson (ed.), *South African Odyssey: The autobiography of Bertha Goudvis* (Picador Africa, Johannesburg, 2011), p. 127.
10   *Diamond Fields Advertiser*, 16 April 1910, p. 7.
11   D. Ravern Allen, 'Crumpet cricket', *Wisden Cricket Monthly*, September 1979, p. 37.
12   R. Holt, *Sport and the British: A modern history* (Oxford University Press, Oxford, 1992), p. 16.
13   N. Mostert, *Frontiers: The epic of South Africa's creation and the tragedy of the Xhosa people* (Pimlico, London, 1993), p. 1264.
14   My thanks to Jean and Rosemary Wilke and the Roedean archivist, Diana McGurk, for 'The First Eleven' song, photographs and annual reports on cricket from the school magazines between 1907 and 1966.
15   See, for example, H. Colleton, 'Sonnet on the Mistresses v. Girls cricket match', *The African Roedean*, April 1911, p. 14.
16   'Cricket', *The African Roedean*, May 1910, p. 23.
17   N.P. Acheson, 'Cricket match', *The African Roedean*, December 1913, pp. 18–20.

18 This quote is from Winch, *Cricket in Southern Africa*, pp. 270–1, which was the most comprehensive account of early women's cricket in South Africa before this one.

19 R. Heyhoe Flint and N. Rheinberg, *Fair Play: The story of women's cricket* (Angus and Robertson, London, 1976), p. 102. The title of the schools' body used in the text is from Jonty Winch; the above authors give it as the Peninsula Girls' School Cricket Union.

20 20 'South Africa' in E.W. Swanton, G. Plumptre and J. Woodcock (eds.), *The Barclays World of Cricket: The game from A to Z* (Collins, London, 1980), p. 349.

21 Quoted in Winch, *Cricket in Southern Africa*, p. 270.

22 http://en.wikipedia.org/wiki/Wynberg_Girls'_High_School.

23 A. Odendaal, '"Neither cricketers nor ladies": Towards a history of women and cricket in South Africa, 1860s–2000s' in S. Cornelissen and A. Grundlingh (eds.), *Sport Past and Present in South Africa: (Trans)forming the nation* (Routledge, London, 2012), pp. 121–2; André Odendaal Collection, Winifred Jeffrey Papers, Handwritten notes by W. Jeffrey, n.d.

24 L. Vorster to A. Odendaal, with article on 'St George's Park, Port Elizabeth, South Africa, Women's cricket', 5 February 2009 (from the Wynberg Girls' High website).

25 André Odendaal Collection: Mounted photographs of 'Ladies cricket at Barberton 1902', artist I.L.R. My thanks to Bob Edgar and Leteane Monatsi for this gift. 'Mrs Du Buisson' is prominent here. For Durban, see André Odendaal Collection, Oenone Gradwell scrapbook. My thanks to Colleen Roberts for this valuable source of information. For Port Elizabeth, see http://stgeorgespark.upe.ac.za/content/pecc/displayarticle.asp?artid_001.

26 V.G. Sparks, *The Cricketer's Compendium or Cricket from a Country Angle, being a complete history of cricket and other items on the good old game – How to play successfully etc* (Durban, n.d.), p. 117.

27 *APO*, 24 May 1909.

28 R. Archer and A. Boullion, *The South African Game: Sport and racism* (Zed Press, London, 1982), p. 104.

29 S.A.G.M. Crawford, 'Pioneering women: Recreation and sporting opportunities in a remote colonial setting' in Mangan and Park, *From 'Fair Sex' to Feminism*, pp. 170–1, 174–6.

30 H. King, 'The sexual politics of sport' in R. Cashman and M. McKernan (eds.), *Sport in History: The making of modern sporting history* (University of Queensland Press, St Lucia, 1979), p. 77.

31 H. Beckles, 'A purely natural extension: Women's cricket in West Indian culture' in H. Beckles, and B. Stoddart, *Liberation Cricket: West Indies cricket culture* (Manchester University Press, Manchester, 1995), pp. 224–6.

32 K.E. McCrone, 'Play up! Play up! And play the game! Sport at the late Victorian public school' in Mangan and Park, *From 'Fair Sex' to Feminism*, p. 117.

33 Winch, *Cricket in Southern Africa*, p. 271.

34 King, 'The sexual politics of sport', p. 79.

Notes to Chapter 33, Formation of the South African Coloured Cricket Board, 1903

1 KZNCU Archives, Krish Reddy Collection: *South African Coloured Cricket Board Rules*, n.d.

2 B. Willan, 'An African in Kimberley: Sol T. Plaatje, 1894–8' in S. Marks and R. Rathbone (eds.), *Industrialisation and Social Change in South Africa: African class formation, culture and consciousness, 1870–1930* (Longman, London, 1982), pp. 239–58; A. Odendaal, *The Founders: The origins of the ANC and the struggle for democracy in South Africa* (Jacana, Johannesburg, 2012, ch. 19.

3 'A Rhodes Cup', *Imvo Zabantsundu*, 29 July 1897.

4 'Ibala labadlali', *Imvo Zabantsundu*, 26 August 1897.

5 A. Grundlingh, A. Odendaal and B. Spies, *Beyond the Tryline* (Ravan Press, Johannesburg, 1995), p. 38–9. (For a profile of D.J. Lenders, see *APO*, 13 January 1912.)

6 D. Harris to I. Bud M'belle, 1 November 1897, reproduced in *Imvo Zabantsundu*, 2 December 1897.

7 'A Barnato Trophy', *Imvo Zabantsundu*, 2 December 1897.

8 'The colonial cricket split', *Diamond Fields Advertiser*, 14 November 1895 and *Diamond Fields Advertiser*, 12 November 1895, p. 6.

9 Grundlingh, Odendaal and Spies, *Beyond the Tryline*, p. 39.

10   Grundlingh, Odendaal and Spies, *Beyond the Tryline*, pp. 41–2.
11   'Itumente e Rini', *Imvo Zabantsundu*, 7 November 1898.
12   *Imvo Zabantsundu*, 7 November 1898.
13   *Imvo Zabantsundu*, 7 November 1898.
14   W.W. Mjokozeli to the Sports Editor, 8 November 1898 and 'Makaya Akude' to the Editor, 9 November 1898, *Imvo Zabantsundu*, 14 November 1898.
15   'Ukuzigcobisa', *Imvo Zabantsundu*, 14 November 1898.
16   *Koranta ea Becoana*, 29 November 1902.
17   See notice in *Izwi Labantu*, 21 October 1902.
18   See 'Iqakamba', *Imvo Zabantsundu*, 18 November, 1902 and 'Barnato Trophy tournament', *Imvo Zabantsundu*, 4 December, 1902.
19   'Barnato Board', *Imvo Zabantsundu*, 11 March 1903.
20   *South African Coloured Cricket Board Rules*, n.d., in the Krish Reddy Collection.
21   *South African Coloured Cricket Board Rules*, n.d., in the Krish Reddy Collection.
22   *South African Coloured Cricket Board Rules*, n.d., in the Krish Reddy Collection.
23   A.E. Docrat, 'A new era in South African cricket', *South African Non-European Cricket Almanack 1952/53*, p. 83.

Notes to Chapter 34, The first inter-colonial and inter-provincial tournaments

1   B. Crowley, *Currie Cup Story* (Don Nelson, Cape Town, 1973).
2   'Itumente e Rini', *Imvo Zabantsundu*, 7 November 1898.
3   'Ukuzigcobisa' and 'Imvo special wires, Native tournament. Barnato Trophy', *Imvo Zabantsundu*, 12 January 1899.
4   'Ukuzigcobisa' and 'Imvo special wires, Native tournament. Barnato Trophy', *Imvo Zabantsundu*, 12 January 1899.
5   *Koranta ea Becoana*, 29 November 1902.
6   See, for example, *Diamond Fields Advertiser*, 30 March 1904 for the cricket Currie Cup; 'SA tennis champs preparations', *Diamond Fields Advertiser*, 25 February 1908, p. 8; report on the SA golf tournament, *Diamond Fields Advertiser*, 26 February 1908; and 'SA Amateur Athletics and Cycling Association', *Diamond Fields Advertiser*, 21 April 1908.
7   *Diamond Fields Advertiser*, 4 April 1904.
8   *Cape Times*, 25 March 1908, p. 8.
9   *Cape Times*, 26 March 1908, p. 7.
10   'GWCCU. Barnato tournament', *Diamond Fields Advertiser*, xxxx 1908.
11   *EP Herald*, 25 March 1910, p. 8.
12   *EP Herald*, 1 April 1910, p. 5.
13   *Diamond Fields Advertiser*, 1 April 1910, p. 8.
14   Presentation of Barnato Cup, *APO*, 23 April 1910.
15   *APO*, 23 April 1910.
16   *Latest*, 3 May 1913, quoted in A. Desai, V. Padayachee, K. Reddy and G. Vahed, *Blacks in Whites: A century of cricket struggles in KwaZulu-Natal* (University of Natal Press, Pietermaritzburg, 2002), p. 44; *APO*, 19 April 1913.
17   *APO*, 10 August 1912, p. 11.
18   M.W. Luckin, *The History of South African Cricket, including the scores of all important matches since 1878* (W.I. Horton, Johannesburg, 1915), p. 818.
19   *APO*, 19 April 1913.
20   'GWCCU, Kimberley', *APO*, 5 October 1912.
21   'Griqualand West CC Union', *APO*, 14 December 1912.
22   KZNCU Archives: Krish Reddy Collection, Annual report by N. Sullaphen, secretary and treasurer, Durban District Indian Cricket Union, 1912/13 season.
23   KZNCU Archives: Krish Reddy Collection, Durban District Indian Cricket Union report/meetings, 1912/13, SA Coloured Cricket Board – rules etc.
24   Durban and District Indian Cricket Union, Secretary's report, 9 August 1913.
25   Comments in *Tsala ea Batho*, 12 April 1913.
26   *Diamond Fields Advertiser*, 27 March 1913, p. 6.

Notes to Chapter 35, Statistics for the Currie Cup and Barnato Memorial Trophy tournaments, 1889/90 to 1912/13

1   C. Achebe, 'African literature as celebration', *Dissent*, Summer 1992, p. 346.
2   About this match, Pelham Warner wrote, 'This was one of the most enjoyable games of the whole tour, and one may not unreasonably hope that future English teams going to South Africa will always play the Army ... Wherever there was a military station we were always entertained right royally by the soldiers.' See P.F. Warner, *The MCC in South Africa* (Juta, Cape Town, 1906), p. 89.
3   *Rhodesia Herald*, 3 April 1904.
4   P. Wynne-Thomas, *The Complete History of Cricket Tours at Home and Abroad* (Hamlyn, London, 1989), p. 231; *Cape Times*, 15 April 1901; J. Winch, 'Sir William Milton: A leading figure in public school games, colonial politics and imperial expansion, 1877–1914' (PhD, University of Stellenbosch, 2013), pp. 182–3.
5   D. Allen, *Empire, War and Cricket: Logan of Matjiesfontein* (Penguin, Cape Town, 2015), p. 243; D. Allen, 'Cricket's "Laird": James Logan' in B. Murray and G. Vahed (eds.), *Empire and Cricket: The South African experience 1884–1914* (Unisa Press, Pretoria, 2009), p. 154.
6   See *A Guide to Important Cricket Matches Played in South Africa*, compiled by the Association of Cricket Statisticians (Association of Cricket Statisticians, Derby, 1981), pp. 6–9.
7   *A Guide to Important Cricket Matches Played in South Africa*, p. 6.
8   *A Guide to Important Cricket Matches Played in South Africa*, p. 6.
9   André Odendaal compiled these first-ever consolidated statistics for the early Barnato Memorial Trophy tournaments in this chapter, including the trophy winners, list of players and abbreviated scorecards. Thank you to John Young, Carol van Vuuren and Ameena Smith for the assistance and patience over the years in helping to create a coherent record of the early years. Robin Isherwood also spent many hours helping to standardise and double-check these statistics. André found Barnato scorecards that had eluded him for decades at the last minute in the Africana Library in Kimberley, thanks to Bernice Nagel and Annelize Rowan; to find these in the yellow-stained pages of the old *Diamond Field Advertiser* they carried out from the stacks brought a completeness to this research and a sense of satisfaction which is difficult to describe. Original sources for each of these tournaments are indicated so that future statisticians can take forward the work of verifying, correcting and finalising this rare but still incomplete record.
10 The list of SACCB provincial players was drawn up from the following sources:
    1889/90: 'Sporting intelligence. The Malay tournament. Cape Town and Claremont vs Port Elizabeth and Johannesburg', *Cape Times*, 28 January 1890.
    1890/91: Sport and pastime', *Diamond Fields Advertiser*, 27 March 1891; 31 March 1891; 3, 4, and 6 April 1891.
    1891/92: M.W. Luckin, *The History of South African Cricket, including the scores of all important matches since 1878* (W.I. Horton, Johannesburg, 1915), pp. 517–18.
    Plus those sources indicated in the relevant footnotes below for each of the five Barnato tournaments to 1913.
11 Also spelt Abraham and Abrams in reports.
12 Also spelt Abraham in reports.
13 Also spelt Abrahmse, Abrams.
14 Spelt Ellie in *Imvo Zabantsundu*.
15 Also spelt Affridien in reports.
16 Also spelt Bol in another scorecard.
17 Also spelt Detoie in reports.
18 Also spelt Gertze in 1907/08 reports.
19 Both initials are given in scorecards though it appears to be the same top-order batsman.
20 Also spelt Esmael in reports.
21 I. and J. Jabaar are mentioned in often-feint scorecards and we have concluded because of the outstanding figures of both over several tournaments that this was the same cricketer. See especially 'GWCCU. Barnato Trophy', *Diamond Fields Advertiser*, xx.xx. 1908, which seems to be an official team announcement.
22 Also spelt Jaffaar in scorecard.

23 Also spelt Jardien, but Jardine became the accepted spelling of this well-known cricket family of later years.
24 Also spelt Jardien, but Jardine became the accepted spelling of this well-known cricket family of later years.
25 Also spelt Joel.
26 Also spelt Kennie in 1907/08 reports.
27 Also spelt Kokazela and initials J. and G. are used in reports, but they refer to the same person. *Diamond Fields Advertiser* team list, which seemed official, used for the 1912/13 tournament.
28 Spelt Laroe in reports.
29 Also spelt Maged in 1903/04 and Majied in 1907/08 reports.
30 Also given as M. Maloni or Maloney in scorecards.
31 Also spelt Manor and Manoor in reports.
32 Also spelt Matala in scorecard.
33 The first spelling is the seSotho version and the second the isiXhosa version.
34 Also spelt Msimuka.
35 Also spelt Ntschoko.
36 Also spelt Nykoka and Mtyoko in reports.
37 Also spelt Ramohkutte in scorecard.
38 Standard spelling used here – Samoodien and Samsoedien are also used in sources.
39 Also spelt Schroeder.
40 Also spelt Situngu.
41 Spelt Tallip in *Imvo Zabantsundu*.
42 Spelt Toffie in *Imvo Zabantsundu*.
43 Also spelt Van der Schyf in reports.
44 Our thanks to Andrew Samson for providing the scorecards used in this book for pre-1914 Currie Cup and South Africa SACA matches.
45 For sources on the 1898/99 Barnato tournament, see 'Ukuzigcobisa' and 'Imvo special wires, Native tournament. Barnato Trophy', *Imvo Zabantsundu*, 12 January 1899. (Researched and compiled by André Odendaal.)
46 For sources on the 1903/04 Barnato tournament, see *Diamond Fields Advertiser*, 31 March 1904, p. 8; 1 April 1904, p. 7; 2 April 1904, p. 3; 4 April, 1904, p. 7; 5 April, p. 7; 6 April 1904, p. 7; 11 April 1904; 13 April 1904, p. 11; and 16 April 1904, p. 7. (Researched and compiled by André Odendaal.)
47 For sources on the 1907/08 Barnato tournament, see *Diamond Fields Advertiser*, 13 March 1908; *Cape Times*, 24 March 1908, p. [x], 25 March 1908, p. 8; 26 March 1908, p. 7; 30 March, p. 8; 1 April 1908, p. 9; 2 April 1908, p. 6. (Researched and compiled by André Odendaal, assisted by John Young.)
48 'Cricket. tournament', *Cape Times*, 25 March 1910, p. 8.
49 'Cricket. tournament for Barnato Cup', *Cape Times*, 25 March 1908, p. 8; 'The Barnato Cup. Griqualand's big score', *Cape Times*, 26 March 1908, p. 7.
50 'Barnato Cup. Eastern Province v. Transvaal', *Cape Times*, 30 March 1908, p. 8.
51 'Barnato Cup. Griqualand West v. Western Province', *Cape Times*, 30 March 1908, p. 8 and 31 March 1908, p. 3.
52 *Cape Times*, 1 and 2 April 1908, p. 6.
53 For sources of the 1909/10 Barnato tournament, see *Diamond Fields Advertiser*, 23 March 1910, p. 7; *Eastern Province Herald*, 19 March 1910, p. 6; 25 March 1910, p. 8; 29 March 1910, p. 5; 30 March 1910, p. 7; 31 March 1910, p. 8; 1 April 1910, p. 5; *APO*, 1 April 1910, p. 8; 'Sport. Cricket. Presentation of Barnato Cup', *APO*, 23 April 1910. (Researched and compiled by André Odendaal, assisted by John Young.)
54 *EP Herald*, 1 April 1910, p. 5.
55 'Coloured Cricket Union. Barnato Cup tourney', *EP Herald*, 30 March 1910, p. 7.
56 For sources on the 1912/13 Barnato tournament, see *Diamond Fields Advertiser*, 23 March 1913, p. 8; 'Barnato Cup tournament', *Diamond Fields Advertiser*, 23 March 1913, p. 3; 'Cricket. Currie Cup and Barnato Cup tournament', *Diamond Fields Advertiser*, 25 March 1913, p. 8; 'Cricket. The Barnato tournament', *Diamond Fields Advertiser*, 26 March 1913, p. 8; 'Cricket. Currie Cup tournament and the Barnato tournament', *Diamond Fields Advertiser*, 27 March 1913, p. 6, 'Sport

in Mail Week', *Diamond Fields Advertiser*, 28 March 1913, p. 6; 'Sport and Pastime. Cricket. Barnato Cup', *Diamond Fields Advertiser*, 29 March 1913, p. 7; 'Sport and Pastime. Cricket', *Diamond Fields Advertiser*, 31 March 1913, p. 6; 'Sport and Pastime. Cricket', *Diamond Fields Advertiser*, 1 April 1913, p. 8; 'Sport and Pastime. Cricket. Griquas record victory', *Diamond Fields Advertiser*, 2 April 1913, p. 3; 'Cricket. Barnato tournament', *Diamond Fields Advertiser*, 4 April 1913, p. 6; 'Cricket. Westerns the winners', *Diamond Fields Advertiser*, 7 April 1913, p. 7; 'Barnato Cup tournament', *APO*, 5 April 1913, 19 April 1913. (Researched and compiled by André Odendaal.) See also KZNCU Archives: Krish Reddy Collection, 'Batting and bowling averages of all the participants in the Barnato Cup Tournament 1913. Compiled by Mr E.J. Choonoo, who acted as the official scorer for Natal'. Supplied by Krish Reddy. There are some discrepancies in the reports and in the spellings in the different newspapers sources, and we have generally preferred the *Diamond Fields Advertiser* and *APO* versions because of their awareness of Afrikaans name spellings and their record of reporting on the Barnato tradition in cricket.

Notes to Chapter 36, Old wine in new vessels

1   'Sport and pastime. G.W. Colonial Cricket Union', *Diamond Fields Advertiser*, 31 December 1895, p. 7.
2   'Sport', *APO*, 12 March 1910; 'DFCC Union, Kimberley', *APO*, 14 December 1912.
3   *Izwi Labantu*, 12 November 1901.
4   *Izwi Labantu*, 15 September 1908.
5   *APO*, 9 March 1912.
6   'Sport. Cricket', *APO*, 29 January 1910; 'Sport. Cricket', *APO*, 6 December 1912.
7   Luckin, *History of South African Cricket*, p. 31.
8   'Cover Point', 'Eastern Province cricket' in Luckin, *History of South African Cricket*, pp. 27-33.
9   Circular by H.P. Warren, secretary, Kei Road Cricket Club, 18 April 1894, quoted in G. Williams (ed.), *One Hundred Years of Border Cricket: Border Cricket Board, 1896-1996* (Centenary Brochure), p. 9.
10 Williams, *One Hundred Years of Border Cricket*, pp. 9, 21.
11 For the early history of the white Border CU cricket, see in Luckin, *History of South African Cricket*, pp. 15-25 and Border Cricket Union, *Diamond Jubilee Souvenir Brochure, 1896/97-1956/57*.
12 'Ibala labadlali', *Imvo Zabantsundu*, 2 July 1896.
13 Notice, *Imvo Zabantsundu*, 8 February 1899.
14 For further details, see *Imvo Zabantsundu*, 19 July 1910.
15 'Ibala labadlali', *Imvo Zabantsundu*, 17 December 1891; 'Ibala labadlali', *Imvo Zabantsundu*, 14 January 1897.
16 'Ibala labadlali', *Imvo Zabantsundu*, 24 October 1894.
17 *Imvo Zabantsundu*, 10 December 1891, p. 3.
18 See report in *Izwi Labantu*, 22 September 1908.
19 'Native cricket tourney', *Izwi Labantu*, 7 January 1909; 'Unyadala we qakamba', *Izwi Labantu*, 14 January 2003.
20 See reports in *Izwi Labantu*, 16 January 1910.
21 'I tumente e Cumakala', *Izwi Labantu*, 14 January 1909; 'Notice', *Imvo Zabantsundu*, 26 December 1911.
22 See, for example, *Imvo Zabantsundu*, 7 January 1901; *Izwi Labantu*, 6 March 1906.
23 'Ibala labadlali', *Imvo Zabantsundu*, 11 April 1889.
24 'Ibala labadlali', *Imvo Zabantsundu*, 28 May 1896.
25 See report in *Imvo Zabantsundu*, 22 January 1900.
26 'Sport. Cricket', *APO*, 28 January 1911.
27 *APO*, 7 October 1911, p. 11.
28 'Cricket. Oudtshoorn', *APO*, 8 March 1913.
29 'Oudtshoorn', *APO*, 26 February 1910; 'Oudtshoorn', *APO*, 18 November 1911; 'Oudtshoorn. The Oliviers Cup', *APO*, 13 July 1912.
30 'One of the Meltons' to the Editor, *APO*, 26 March 1910, p. 10.

31 *APO*, 15 January 1910, p. 5; 'Paarl-Wellington Cricket Union', *APO*, 22 February 1913; 'Sport, Cricket. Paarl and Wellington C. Union', *APO*, 8 February 1913.
32 'Drakenstein Cricket Union', *APO*, 22 February 1913.
33 'Sport, Cricket. Groot Drakenstein – a new cricket league', *APO*, 18 November 1911; 'Drakenstein cup final', *APO*, 24 February 1912.
34 *APO*, 13 January 1912, p. 11. See also the reports in *APO*, 23 and 30 December 1911.
35 'Sport. Cricket', *APO*, 22 March 1913.
36 For Stellenbosch cricket, see A. Odendaal (comp. and ed.), *Community and Cricket in Stellenbosch* (Stellenbosch CC, Stellenbosch Academy of Sport and Masikhulisane Academy, 2016); H.B. Thom, *Stellenbosch 1866–1966: Honderd jaar hoër onderwys* (Nasionale Boekhandel, Cape Town, 1966), pp. 408–9. Prof. Floris van der Merwe has also written on the university's cricket background.
37 *APO*, 9 April 1910, p. 11.
38 'Cape Central Rugby Football Union (Coloured)', *APO*, 20 April 1913.
39 'Oudtshoorn', *APO*, 20 April 1913, p. 11.
40 A.C. Parker, *W.P. Cricket: 100 not out* (WPCU, Cape Town, 1990), p. 11.
41 W.H. Mars, 'History of cricket in the Western Province' in Luckin, *History of South African Cricket*, pp. 142–53.
42 'Palmy days of province cricket', *Cape Times*, 10 April 1935.
43 Luckin, *History of South African Cricket*, p. 145.
44 'Palmy days of province cricket', *Cape Times*, 10 April 1935.
45 'Cape District Cricket Union', *APO*, 26 February 1910, 9 April 1910 and 16 November 1912.
46 'Concerning clubs in the Peninsula', *APO*, 11 February 1911.
47 W. Pick, *One for the Chuck: Glimpses into the history of the Maitland-Parow and Districts Cricket Union, 1912–1976* (Western Province Cricket Association in association with Cricket South Africa, Cape Town, 2015).
48 The history of St Augustine's is currently being written by Dr F.J. Cleophas of Stellenbosch University.
49 'Sport. Board matters', *APO*, 19 November 1910.
50 'Sport. Cricket', *APO*, 20 April 1912.
51 See J.H. Raynard, *Dr A. Abdurahman*, ed. M. Adhikari (Friends of the South African Library in association with the District Six Museum, Cape Town, 2002).
52 'W.P. Cricket Board', *APO*, 16 November 1912.
53 'Western Province (Coloured) C. and A. Union', *APO*, 19 April 1913.
54 'Ibala labadlali', *Imvo Zabantsundu*, 19 December 1894.
55 'Ibala labadlali', *Imvo Zabantsundu*, 27 December 1895.
56 'Zonnebloem College', *APO*, 24 September 1910.
57 'E Kapa', *Imvo Zabantsundu*, 5 December 1898 and 'E Kapa', *Imvo Zabantsundu*, 8 February 1899.
58 Cape Archives, NA 428: H. Adams Lowe to Port Captain and Dock Superintendent, Table Bay Harbour Board, 3 August 1904, plus attached correspondence.
59 'Umnyadala we qakamba, e-Kapa', *Imvo Zabantsundu*, 14 January 1908.

Notes to Chapter 37, The new entrants

1 C. Bryden (ed.), *The First Century, 1890–1990: The Transvaal centenary book* (Transvaal Cricket Council, 1990), p. 2.
2 Bryden (ed.), *The First Century*, pp. 2, 152.
3 Bryden (ed.), *The First Century*, p. 149.
4 H. Kidson, *The History of Transvaal Cricket* (Transvaal Cricket Board, Johannesburg, 1995), p. 214.
5 *Berliner Missionsberichte*, 1894, p. 291. My thanks to Dr Werner van der Merwe for this reference.
6 A. Odendaal, *Cricket in Isolation: The politics of race and cricket in South Africa* (Cape Town, 1977), p. 307.
7 'Ibala labadlali', *Imvo Zabantsundu*, 7 January 1897.
8 'Ibala labadlali', *Imvo Zabantsundu*, 7 January 1897.
9 'Ibala labadlali', *Imvo Zabantsundu*, 13 January 1898.

10 'E Transvaal', *Imvo Zabantsundu*, 31 October 1898.
11 'Ibala labadlali', *Imvo Zabantsundu*, 13 January 1898.
12 'Ukuziugcobisa', *Imvo Zabantsundu*, 15 March 1899.
13 See, for example, the detailed scorecards in 'Iqakamba', *Izwi Labantu*, 3 December 1907, 11 July 1907 and 14 January 1908.
14 'Klipspruit location (Johannesburg)', *Izwi Labantu*, undated cutting from André Odendaal Collection.
15 *Tsala ea Becoana*, 30 December 1911, p. 2.
16 'Transvaal Coloured Cricket Union', *APO*, 20 November 1911.
17 For the history of white cricketers in Natal, see M.W. Luckin, *The History of South African Cricket, including the scores of all important matches since 1878* (W.I. Horton, Johannesburg, 1915), pp. 63–97.
18 See, R. Morrell, *From Boys to Gentlemen: Settler masculinity in colonial Natal 1880–1920* (Unisa Press, Pretoria, 2001), pp. 60–1, 65, 79, 85, 88, 95, 96, 101–3, 121, 129.
19 The clubs were Eastern Stars, Western Stars, Union Jacks, Yorkshire, Greyville, Evening Stars, Rainbow, Railways, NGR Morning Stars and Point Road School. The imperial influence is clear. See A. Desai, V. Padayachee, K. Reddy and G. Vahed, *Blacks in Whites: A century of cricket struggles in KwaZulu-Natal* (University of Natal Press, Pietermaritzburg, 2002), p. 40.
20 Desai et al., *Blacks in Whites*, pp. 44–8.
21 Desai et al., *Blacks in Whites*, pp. 34–5, 49.
22 Desai et al., *Blacks in Whites*, pp. 6, 62, 63, 69.
23 Desai et al., *Blacks in Whites*, pp. 7, 31, 35, 54–5, 56.
24 Desai et al., *Blacks in Whites*, pp. 13, 43, 47, 51–3.
25 Desai et al., *Blacks in Whites*, pp. 69–70.
26 Desai et al., *Blacks in Whites*, pp. 73–6, 79.
27 *Imvo Zabantsundu*, 5 April 1893, p. 2.
28 Desai et al., *Blacks in Whites*, p. 126.
29 Match report, *Inkanyiso Yase Natal*, 5 January 1894.
30 Details from a speech by John Blair during the centenary of the Free State Cricket Union, 1992. My thanks to him for these references. See also R. van Rensburg (ed.), *100 Years of OFS Cricket* (n.p., 1993)
31 *The Friend*, 4 March 1892.
32 http://www.sahistory.org.za/bloemfontein/afrikaans-community-1820-1899.
33 See G.F. Floyd, 'The history of cricket in the Orange Free State' in Luckin, *History of South African Cricket*, pp. 58–62.
34 See report in *Imvo Zabantsundu*, 6 February 1890.
35 From a speech by John Blair during the centenary of the Free State Cricket Union, 1992.
36 'Ibala labadlali', *Imvo Zabantsundu*, 25 April 1894.
37 'Ikrikiti', *Imvo Zabantsundu*, 19 April 1899.
38 'Ukuzigcobisa', *Imvo Zabantsundu*, 10 December 1900.
39 C. Bolsmann, 'The 1899 Orange Free State football team tour of Europe: 'Race', imperial loyalty and sporting contest, *The International Journal of the History of Sport*, vol. 28, no. 1, January 2011, pp. 81–97.
40 'Imidlalo', *Izwi Labantu*, 22 October 1907.
41 'Sport', *APO*, 9 April 1910.
42 National Archives, Pretoria, 1/33 N.A. 765, Correspondence files F130 1907-1911: Resident Magistrate Bethulie, OFS, to Acting Secretary for Native Affairs, 16 February 1911.
43 See report, *Izwi Labantu*, 6 February 1906.
44 J. Winch, *Cricket in Southern Africa: Two hundred years of achievement and records* (Windsor, Rosettenville, 1997), pp. 335–6.
45 Winch, *Cricket in Southern Africa*, pp. 334–5.
46 Winch, *Cricket in Southern Africa*, pp. 333–4.
47 R. Blennerhassett and L. Sleeman, *Adventures in Mashonaland* (Books of Rhodesia, Bulawayo, 1969), pp. 226–7.
48 *Sunday Mail*, 12 September 1965.

49   See J. Winch, *Cricket's Rich Heritage: A history of Rhodesian and Zimbabwean cricket, 1890–1982* (Books of Zimbabwe, Bulawayo, 1983) and SACA minutes, 29 August 1898.
50   *Rand Daily Mail*, 16 March 1905.
51   See, for example, 'KwaMzilikazi', *Imvo Zabantsundu*, 4 September 1899 and 2 July 1901.
52   'Sport. Cricket. Bulawayo', *APO*, 16 December 1911.

Notes to Chapter 38, 'The bonds of Union within the Empire'

1   M.W. Luckin, *The History of South African Cricket, including the scores of all important matches since 1878* (W.I. Horton, Johannesburg, 1915), p. 623.
2   C. Martin-Jenkins, *The Complete Who's Who of Test Cricketers* (Stanton, Johannesburg, 1980), p. 282.
3   D. Allen, *Empire, War and Cricket: Logan of Matjiesfontein* (Penguin, Cape Town, 2015), pp. 239–48.
4   Luckin, *History of South African Cricket*, p. 668.
5   B. Frindall, *The Wisden Book of Test Cricket, vol. I, 1877–1977* (Macdonald Queen Anne Press, London, 1990), p. 61.
6   Luckin, *History of South African Cricket*, p. 547.
7   Thelma Gutsche, *Old Gold: The history of the Wanderers Club* (Howard Timmins, Cape Town, 1966), pp. 118–19, 128.
8   B. Murray and C. Merrett, *Caught Behind: Race and politics in Springbok cricket* (Wits University Press and University of KwaZulu-Natal Press, Johannesburg, 2004), p. 7.
9   On the history of the Springbok as a sporting emblem, see A. Odendaal, 'The hundred years' war: Brown balls, bronzed colonials and the persistence of colonial biases in twenty-first century rugby cultures', Plenary address to the Conference on Afrikaners, Anglos and Springboks, 1906–2006, organised by the Museum of Rugby, Twickenham, the Centre for the Study of Britain and its Empire, University of Southampton, and the International Centre for Sports History, De Montford University, 19 September 2006.
10   Luckin, *History of South African Cricket*, p. 716.
11   Luckin, *History of South African Cricket*, p. 623.
12   L. Tennyson, *Sticky Wickets* (Christopher Johnson, London, 1950), p. 72.
13   J. Comaroff and B. Willan, with S. Molema and A. Reed (eds.) *The Mafeking Diary of Sol T. Plaatje* (David Philip, Cape Town, 1998), p. 11.
14   *Imvo Zabantsundu*, 27 January 1914.

Notes to the Epilogue

1   D. Judd, *Empire: The British imperial experience from 1765 to the present* (HarperCollins, London, 1996), p. 301.
2   A. Bailey, 'South Africa' in P.F. Warner, *Imperial Cricket* (London and Counties Press Association, London, 1912), p. 315; C. Bolt, *Victorian Attitudes to Race* (Routledge & Kegan Paul, London, 1971), p. 208.
3   J.A. Mangan (ed.), *The Cultural Bond: Sport, empire and society* (Frank Cass Publishers, London, 1992), p. 2.
4   D. Birley, *Playing the Game: Sport and British society, 1910–45* (Manchester University Press, Manchester, 1995), p. 126.
5   R. Sissons, and B. Stoddart, *Cricket and Empire: The 1932–33 bodyline tour of Australia* (Allen and Unwin, London, 1984), p. 35.
6   J. Bradley, 'MCC, society and empire' in J.A. Mangan, *The Cultural Bond*, p. 27; D. Birley, *Sport and the Making of Britain* (Manchester University Press, Manchester, 1993), p. 334.
7   V. Packenham, *The Noonday Sun: Edwardians in the tropics* (Methuen, London, 1985), pp. 172, 174.
8   K. Sandiford, *Cricket and the Victorians* (Scolar Press, Aldershot, 1994), p. 1.
9   C. Barnett, *The Collapse of British Power* (Eyre Methuen, London, 1972), p. 35.
10   J.A. Cooper, 'The British imperial spirit of sport and the war' in *United Empire*, 7, 9, 1916, pp. 581, 593; J.A. Mangan, 'Play up and play the game: Victorian and Edwardian public school vocabularies of motive', *British Journal of Educational Studies*, 23, 3, 1975, p. 333.

11 J.A. Mangan, '"Muscular, militaristic and manly": the British middle-class hero as moral messenger', *International Journal of the History of Sport*, 13, 1, 1996, pp. 28–47.

12 M.A. Tozer, 'A sacred trinity' in Mangan, *The Cultural Bond*, p. 17.

13 A. Guttmann, *Games and Empires: Modern sports and cultural imperialism* (Columbia University Press, New York, 1994), p. 64.

14 P. Bailey, *Leisure and Class in Victorian England: Rational recreation and the context for control, 1850–1885* (Routledge and Kegan Paul, London, 1978), p. 127.

15 A. Kirk-Greene, 'Imperial administration and the athletic imperative: the case of the district officer in Africa' in W.J. Baker, and J.A. Mangan, (eds.), *Sport in Africa: Essays in social history* (Africana, New York, 1987), p. 107.

16 As in the poem by Will Whittam: 'Because they haven't got the pluck to stand before the wicket, sir.'

17 Cooper, 'The British imperial spirit of sport and the war', pp. 583–4.

18 C.L.R. James, *Beyond a Boundary* (Pantheon, New York, 1984), p. 39.

19 Mangan, *The Cultural Bond*, p. 6; J.A. Mangan, *The Games Ethic and Imperialism: Aspects of the diffusion of an ideal* (Viking, London, 1986), p. 110.

20 J. Arlott, 'Sport' in S. Nowell-Smith (ed.), *Edwardian England, 1901–1914* (Oxford University Press, London, 1964), p. 486.

21 R. Holt, *Sport and the British: A modern history* (Oxford University Press, Oxford, 1990), p. 351.

22 J. Hargreaves, *Sport, Power and Culture: A social and historical analysis of popular sports in Britain* (Polity, Cambridge, 1986), p. 34.

23 D. Birley, *Sport and the Making of Britain* (Manchester University Press, Manchester, 1993), p. 334; R.H. Wilkinson, 'The gentleman ideal and the maintenance of a political elite: Two case studies', *Sociology of Education*, 37, 1, 1963, pp. 10.

24 E. Midwinter, *Fair Game: Myth and reality in sport* (Allen and Unwin, London, 1986), p. 36.

25 T. Cook, *Character and Sportsmanship* (Williams and Norgate, London, 1927), p. 321.

26 P. Vasili, *The First Black Footballer: Arthur Wharton 1865–1930: an absence of memory* (Frank Cass Publishers, London, 1998), p. 78.

27 D.R. Black, and J. Nauright, *Rugby and the South African Nation: Sport, culture and the new South Africa* (Manchester University Press, Manchester, 1998), p. 26.

28 Midwinter, *Fair Game*, p. 67.

29 Birley, *Playing the Game*, pp. 16, 258, 271; Sandiford, *Cricket and the Victorians*, p. 31; T. Mason, 'Football on the maidan' in Mangan, *The Cultural Bond*, p. 142; Hargreaves, *Sport, Power and Culture*, p. 44.

30 Ferris died in Durban on 17 November 1900 at the age of 33 while serving in the Imperial Light Horse.

31 William Lloyd Murdoch (1854–1911) was the dominant Australian batsman of the early 1880s.

32 Samuel Woods (1867–1931) was a high-class Australian all-rounder and one of the great fast bowlers of all time who played most of his cricket for Somerset.

33 Albert Trott committed suicide in 1914 at the age of 41. As an all-rounder for Australia, he was at his peak in the mid-1890s and played for Middlesex from 1898 to 1910.

34 'Sport as a connecting link', *Cape Illustrated Magazine*, 4, 10, 1894, p. 370.

35 Pelham Francis Warner (1873–1963) epitomised the MCC establishment. He served on the committee from 1904 and was president in 1950.

36 J. Bradley, 'MCC, society and empire', pp. 38–9; R. Sissons and B. Stoddart, *Cricket and Empire*, p. 33; G.T. Vincent, 'Practical imperialism: The Anglo-Welsh rugby tour of New Zealand, 1908', *International Journal of the History of Sport*, 15, 1, 1998, p. 124; R. Cashman, 'Australia' in B. Stoddart and K.A.P. Sandiford, *The Imperial Game: Cricket, culture and society* (Manchester University Press, Manchester, 1998), p. 39.

37 G.A. Parker, *South African Sports: An official handbook* (Sampson, Low, Marston, London, 1897), p. 3. Donald Currie (1825–1909) was a shipowner and philanthropist.

38 John Briggs (1862–1902), the Lancashire slow left-arm bowler and all-rounder, died of epilepsy at the age of 39.

39 George Davidson (1866–1899), the Derbyshire all-rounder, died of pneumonia.

40 Sandiford, *Cricket and the Victorians*, p. 102.

41 R. Knowles, *South Africa versus England: A test cricket history* (New Holland, London, 1995), p. 17.

42   John Cavendish Lyttelton, 9th Viscount Cobham (d. 1949) was ADC to the high commissioner from 1905 to 1908 and MCC president in 1935.

43   P.F. Warner, *Long Innings: The autobiography* (Harrap, London, 1951), p. 71; and *Wisden 1912*, pp. 477, 491; H. Leveson Gower, *Off and on the Field* (Stanley Paul, London, 1953), pp. 159–64.

44   L. Tennyson, *Sticky Wickets* (Christopher Johnson, London, 1950), p. 73.

45   B. Stoddart, 'Sport, cultural imperialism and colonial response in the British Empire', *Comparative Studies in Society and History*, 30, 4, 1988, p. 665. Poore (1866–1938) reputedly learned about cricket from a textbook while at Government House, Bombay. He was very much a cricketing free spirit. After playing for Natal, he tried to enrol with Lord Hawke's team but permission was refused by the Army (M.B. Hawke, *Recollections and Reminiscences*, p. 152). He played county cricket for Hampshire from 1898 until 1906 as a prolific batsman: in 1899 he scored 1,499 runs at an average of 107.07 including three consecutive centuries. These were scored within the same two weeks that he won a fencing title at the Royal Tournament and was a member of the winning team in an inter-regimental polo tournament.

46   Arthur William 'Dave' Nourse (1879–1948) arrived in South Africa as a drummer boy with the West Riding Regiment in 1896 but later joined the Natal Police. He played for Natal, Transvaal and Western Province during a long career which included 45 consecutive tests for South Africa from 1902 to 1924. The Grand Old Man of South African cricket, he worked as a soldier, policeman, railway guard, billiard marker, saloon keeper, commercial traveller, manager of a sports goods firm – and cricket coach. His son, Arthur Dudley (1910–1981), played 34 tests for South Africa between 1935 and 1951. Father and son played in provincial cricket against each other.

47   Frank Mitchell (1872–1935) was a Cambridge triple blue in cricket, rugby and athletics. He played both cricket and rugby for England; and cricket for South Africa, which he captained in 1904 and on the Triangular Test tour. He arrived in South Africa in 1900 with the Yorkshire Dragoons and later became secretary to Sir Abe Bailey.

48   H.S. Altham, *A History of Cricket*, vol. 1 (Allen and Unwin, London, 1962), p. 294.

49   Cypher [E.H. Holmes], 'History of Natal cricket' in M.W. Luckin, *The History of South African Cricket, including the scores of all important matches since 1878* (W.I. Horton, Johannesburg, 1915), p. 81.

50   M.C.C. Adams, *The Great Adventure: Male desire and the coming of World War* (Indiana University Press, Bloomington, 1990), p. 42.

51   A 1914 song quoted in Adams, *The Great Adventure*, p. 45.

52   D. Judd, *Empire: The British imperial experience from 1765 to the present* (HarperCollins, London, 1996), p. 301.

53   Sandiford, *Cricket and the Victorians*, p. 153.

54   A.F. Hattersley, *Hilton Portrait: South African public school, 1872–1945* (Shuter and Shooter, Pietermaritzburg, 1945), p. 53.

55   H.S. Altham, and E.W. Swanton, *A History of Cricket* (Allen and Unwin, London, 4th edn, 1948), p. 311; Parker, *South African Sports*, p. 3; *Wisden 1895*, pp. 333 and 336.

56   Knowles, *South Africa versus England*, p. 24.

57   Letter written by Mr G. Lacy to *The Times* on 26 March 1901, reproduced in M. Williams, *The Way to Lord's: Cricketing letters to The Times* (Willow, London, 1983), p. 71.

58   D. Allen, *Empire, War and Cricket: Logan of Matjiesfontein* (Penguin, Cape Town, 2015), ch. 7; Altham and Swanton, *A History of Cricket*, p. 295.

59   Altham and Swanton, *A History of Cricket*, p. 311. Logan had been financially involved in the second of Lord Hawke's tours, 1898/9.

60   D. Birley, *Land of Sport and Glory: Sport and British society 1887–1910* (Manchester University Press, Manchester, 1995), p. 266; W.T. Stead, 'Mr Abe Bailey: On South Africa and its problems', *Review of Reviews*, December 1904, p. 589; L.E. Neame, *Some South African Politicians* (Maskew Miller, Cape Town, 1929), p. 167; *Dictionary of South African Biography*, vol. 2, p. 20.

61   R. Ally, *Gold and Empire: The Bank of England and South Africa's gold producers, 1886–1926* (Witwatersrand University Press, Johannesburg, 1994), p. 19; M. De Cecco, *Money and Empire: The international gold standard, 1890–1914* (Blackwell, Oxford, 1974), p. 69.

62   Birley, *Playing the Game*, p. 25.

63   B. Murray and G. Vahed (eds.), *Empire and Cricket: The South African experience 1884–1914* (Unisa Press, Pretoria, 2009), p. xvi.

64 Henry Dudley Gresham Leveson Gower (1873–1954) was on the MCC tours to South Africa in 1905/6 and 1909/10 (as captain).

65 H.W. Taylor, 'South African cricket, 1910–1924' in *Cape Times, Sports and Sportsmen: South Africa* (Atkinson, Cape Town, 1925), p. 125; *Wisden* 1913, p. 230; Bailey, 'South Africa', p. 324.

66 *Wisden* 1915, p. 208.

67 H.D.G. Leveson Gower, *The MCC's South African Tour, 1909–1910* (Metropolitan Advertising, Cape Town, 1909).

68 *South African Cricketers Annual* 1905–6, p. 5; Ranjitsinhji in *The Jubilee Book of Cricket* quoted in Sissons and, *Cricket and Empire*, p. 29; H.V. Dorey, *The Triangular Tests, 1878–1912* (Cricket and Sports Publishers, London, 1912), p. 187; T. Routledge, 'The third English Team in South Africa, 1895–6' in Luckin, *The History of South African Cricket*, p. 521.

69 Warner, *Imperial Cricket*, p. ix.

70 R. Hyam, *Britain's Imperial Century, 1815–1914: A study of empire and expansion* (Batsford, London, 1976), p. 151.

71 Hyam, *Britain's Imperial Century*, p. 1.

72 R. Symonds, *Oxford and Empire: The last lost cause* (Macmillan, Basingstoke, 1986), p. 22.

73 D. Frith, *The Golden Age of Cricket, 1890–1914* (Omega, London, 1983), p. 16.

74 Warner, *Imperial Cricket*, p. ix.

75 H.P. Swaffer (ed.), *South African Sport, 1914* (Transvaal Leader, Johannesburg, 1914), p. 31.

76 P.F. Warner, *The MCC in South Africa* (Chapman and Hall, London, 1906), p. 68.

77 W.F. Mandle, 'Cricket and Australian nationalism in the nineteenth century', *Journal of the Royal Australian Historical Society*, 59, 4, 1973, p. 233; R. Cashman, 'Australia' in Stoddart and Sandiford, *The Imperial Game*, pp. 46–7.

78 D. Adair and W. Vamplew, *Sport in Australian History* (Oxford University Press, Melbourne, 1997), p. 11.

79 H. Perkin, 'Teaching the nations how to play' in Mangan, *The Cultural Bond*, p. 217.

80 Stoddart, 'Sport, cultural imperialism and colonial response in the British Empire', p. 659.

81 H. McD. Beckles, 'The making of the first "West Indian" teams, 1886–1906' in H. Beckles, and B. Stoddart, *Liberation Cricket: West Indies cricket culture* (Manchester University Press, Manchester, 1995), p. 195.

82 M. Adas, *'High' Imperialism and the 'New' History* (American Historical Association, Washington, D.C., 1993), p. 15.

83 F. Spufford, *I May Be Some Time: Ice and the English imagination* (Faber, London, 1996), pp. 249–50.

84 I. Baucom, *Out of Place: Englishness, Empire and the location of identity* (Princeton University Press, Princeton, N.J., 1999), pp. 17–18. Baucom argues that a sense of place was particularly important to the British as a 'mongrel race' (p. 17).

85 J. Morris, *Pax Britannica: The climax of an empire* (Faber, London, 1968), pp. 290, 301.

86 J. Bale, *Landscapes of Modern Sport* (Leicester University Press, Leicester, 1994), pp. 72–3, 124, 153–5.

87 Barnett, *The Collapse of British Power*, p. 35.

88 W.R. Katz, *Rider Haggard and the Fiction of Empire: A critical study of British imperial fiction* (Cambridge University Press, Cambridge, 1987), p. 82.

89 M. Bose, *A History of Indian Cricket* (André Deutsch, London, 1990), p. 19.

90 Katz, *Rider Haggard and the Fiction of Empire*, p. 59.

91 J.M. Mackenzie, *Propaganda and Empire: The manipulation of British public opinion, 1880–1960* (Manchester University Press, Manchester, 1984), pp. 257, 258.

92 J. Lowerson, *Sport and the English Middle Classes, 1870–1914* (Manchester University Press, Manchester, 1993), pp. 11, 16; T. Mason, *Sport in Britain: A social history* (Cambridge University Press, Cambridge, 1989), p. 346.

93 R. Hutchinson, *Empire Games: The British invention of twentieth-century sport* (Mainstream, Edinburgh, 1996), p. 164.

94 D.R. Black and J. Nauright, *Rugby and the South African Nation*, p. 35.

95 Stoddart, 'Sport, cultural imperialism and colonial response in the British Empire', p. 662.

96 M. Warner, 'Between the colonist and the creole: Family bonds, family boundaries' in S. Chew and A. Rutherford (eds.), *Unbecoming Daughters of the Empire* (Dangaroo, Sydney, 1993), p. 199. Marina Warner is the granddaughter of Sir Pelham.

97 G. Jarvie, *Sport, Racism and Ethnicity* (Falmer, London, 1991), p. 182.

98 K. Surin, 'C.L.R. James' materialist aesthetic of cricket' in Beckles and Stoddart, *Liberation Cricket*, p. 326.

99 Parker, *South African Sports*, p. 47.

100 L. Duffus, *Play Abandoned* (Timmins, Cape Town, 1969), p. 28.

101 Donald Currie, a diamond and gold magnate, owned Castle Mail Packets Ltd, which provided the sea link between South Africa and England. He presented three other cups for white, inter-provincial sport (rugby, soccer and swimming) but cricket was the first, and the most famous.

102 R. Bowen, *Cricket: A history of its growth and development throughout the world* (Eyre and Spottiswoode, London, 1970), pp. 317, 325.

103 D.A. Lorimer, *Colour, Class and the Victorians: English attitudes to the Negro in the mid-nineteenth century* (Leicester University Press, Leicester, 1978), p. 202.

104 Lorimer, *Colour, Class and the Victorians*, p. 210.

105 C.J. Ferguson-Davie, *The Early History of Indians in Natal* (South African Institute of Race Relations, Johannesburg, 1977), p. 18.

106 R.A. Huttenback, *Racism and Empire: White settlers and colored immigrants in the British self-governing colonies, 1830–1910* (Cornell University Press, Ithaca, 1976), pp. 197, 198.

107 S. Marks, *Reluctant Rebellion: The 1906–8 disturbances in Natal* (Clarendon, Oxford, 1970), pp. 11.

108 M. Legassick, 'British hegemony and the origins of segregation in South Africa, 1901–14' in W. Beinart and S. Dubow, *Segregation and Apartheid in Twentieth-century South Africa* (Routledge, London, 1995), pp. 46–52.

109 'Preserving the pavements', *Natal Witness*, 24 August 1904, p. 5; 'For whites only', *Natal Witness*, 26 August 1904, p. 5.

110 'Blacks on sidewalks', *Natal Witness*, 14 November 1904, p. 6.

111 A. Odendaal, 'South Africa's black Victorians: Sport and society in South Africa in the nineteenth century' in J.A. Mangan (ed.), *Pleasure, Profit, Proselytism: British culture and sport at home and abroad, 1700–1914* (Frank Cass Publishers, London, 1988), p. 204.

112 V. Bickford-Smith, *Ethnic Pride and Racial Prejudice in Victorian Cape Town* (Cambridge University Press, Cambridge, 1995), p. 149, quoting the *Cape Argus* of 30 March 1894.

113 Swanton and Woodcock, *Barclays World of Cricket: The game from A to Z* (Collins, London, 2nd edn, 1980), p. 108; B. Bassano, *South Africa in International Cricket, 1888–1970* (Chameleon, East London, 1979), p. 17; Bowen, *Cricket*, p. 149; Bickford-Smith, *Ethnic Pride*, p. 149; *Cape Times*, 6 and 13 November 1897.

114 Odendaal, 'South Africa's black Victorians', pp. 204, 206.

115 Marks, *Reluctant Rebellion*, p. 11; R. Morrell, *From Boys to Gentlemen: Settler masculinity in colonial Natal 1880–1920* (Unisa Press, Pretoria, 2001), pp. 88, 121, 129.

116 Quoted in D. Marquard, 'Sport the old and the new' in R.M. de Villiers (ed.), *Better Than They Knew* (Purnell, Cape Town, 1972), p. 224.

117 Morrell, *From Boys to Gentlemen*, pp. 60–1, 65, 79, 85, 95, 96, 101–3.

118 A.F. Hattersley, *Merchiston: A South African school, 1892–1953* (Balkema, Cape Town, 1953), p. 54.

119 Hattersley, *Hilton Portrait*, pp. 36 and 51. Newnham was headmaster from 1872 to 1877 and Ellis from 1877 to 1904.

120 *Hiltonian*, 3, 1902, p. 13.

121 J. Young to A. Odendaal, 17 March 2016. Our thanks to John Young and Andrew Samson for these statistics.

122 Quoted in P. Randall, *Little England on the Veld* (Ravan Press, Johannesburg, 1982), p. 122.

123 Randall, *Little England on the Veld*, p. 121.

124 J. Bantjies, 'Boys' schools examined afresh', *Cape Times*, 8 July 2015.

Notes to A long, long journey

1 A. Ross, *Cape Summer and the Australians in England* (Hamish Hamilton, London, 1957), p. 169.

2 Taken from a quote by Muhammad Ali, who died on the day these final lines were written.

Select bibliography

Adair, D. and W. Vamplew, *Sport in Australian History* (Oxford University Press, Melbourne, 1997)

Allen, D., *Empire, War and Cricket: Logan of Matjiesfontein* (Penguin, Cape Town, 2015)

Allen, D.A., Introduction to *The Cricketing Record of Major Warton's Tour 1888–9: A detailed account of the first English tour to South Africa* (J.W. McKenzie, Cambridge, 1987)

Altham, H.S., *A History of Cricket* (Allen and Unwin, London, 1962)

Archer, R. and A. Boullion, *The South African Game: Sport and racism* (Zed Press, London, 1982)

Arlott, J., 'Sport' in S. Nowell-Smith (ed.), *Edwardian England, 1901–1914* (Oxford University Press, London, 1964)

Arlott, J. (ed.), *The Oxford Companion to Sports and Games* (Oxford University Press, London, 1975)

Association of Cricket Statisticians (Compiler and Publisher), *A Guide to Important Cricket Matches Played in South Africa* (Derby, 1981)

Bailey, P., *Leisure and Class in Victorian England: Rational recreation and the context for control, 1850–1885* (Routledge and Kegan Paul, London, 1978)

Bassano, B., *South Africa in International Cricket, 1888–1970* (Chameleon, East London, 1979)

Baucom, I., *Out of Place: Englishness, Empire and the location of identity* (Princeton University Press, Princeton, 1999)

Beckles, H. McD., 'The making of the first "West Indian" teams, 1886–1906' in H. Beckles and B. Stoddart (eds), *Liberation Cricket: West Indies cricket culture* (Manchester University Press, Manchester, 1995)

Bickford-Smith, V., *Ethnic Pride and Racial Prejudice in Victorian Cape Town* (Cambridge University Press, Cambridge, 1995)

Birley, D., *A Social History of English Cricket* (Aurum Press, London, 1999)

Birley, D., *Land of Sport and Glory: Sport and British society 1887–1910* (Manchester University Press, Manchester, 1995)

Birley, D., *Sport and the Making of Britain* (Manchester University Press, Manchester, 1993)

Birley, D., *The Willow Wand: Some cricket myths explored* (Aurum Press, London, 2000)

Bose, M., *A History of Indian Cricket* (André Deutsch, London, 1990)

Bowen, R., *Cricket: A history of its growth and development throughout the world* (Eyre and Spottiswoode, London, 1970)

Bryden, C. (ed.), *The First Century, 100, 1890–1990: The Transvaal centenary book* (Transvaal Cricket Council, 1990)

Cashman, R. and M. McKernan (eds), *Sport in History: The making of modern sporting history* (University of Queensland Press, St Lucia, 1979)

Christiansen, R., *The Victorian Visitors: Culture shock in nineteenth-century Britain* (Chatto and Windus, London, 2000)

Comaroff, J. and B. Willan, with S. Molema and A. Reed (eds.), *The Mafeking Diary of Sol T. Plaatje* (David Philip, Cape Town, 1999)

Cooper, D., 'Canadians declare "It isn't cricket": A century of rejection of the British imperial game, 1860–1960', *Journal of Sports History*, 26, 1, Spring 1999

Couzens, T., 'Robert Grendon: Irish traders, cricket scores and Paul Kruger's dreams', *English in Africa*, 15, 2, October 1988

Cox, C., *The Cricketing Record of Major Warton's Tour 1888–89* (Advertiser Office, Port Elizabeth, 1889)

Crowley, B., *Currie Cup Story* (Nelson, Cape Town, 1973)

Davenport, T.R.H., *South Africa: A modern history* (Macmillan, Johannesburg, 1977)

Davids, A., 'Politics and the Muslims of Cape Town: A historical survey' in C. Saunders et al. (eds.), *Studies in the History of Cape Town* (Centre for African Studies, UCT), vol. 4, 1984

Desai, A., V. Padayachee, K. Reddy and G. Vahed, *Blacks in Whites: A century of cricket struggles in KwaZulu-Natal* (University of Natal Press, Pietermaritzburg, 2002)

Dobbs, B., *Edwardians at Play* (Pelham, London, 1973)

Dorey, H.V., *The Triangular Tests, 1878–1912* (Cricket and Sports Publishers, London, 1912)

Frindall, B., *The Wisden Book of Test Cricket, Vol. I, 1877–1977* (Macdonald Queen Anne Press, London, 1990)

Frith, D., *The Golden Age of Cricket, 1890–1914* (Omega, London, 1983)

Fry, C.B., *Life Worth Living: Some phases of an Englishman* (Pavilion, London, 1986)

Gillespie, G., 'Wickets in the west: Cricket, culture and constructed images of nineteenth-century Canada', *Journal of Sports History*, 27, 1, Spring 2000

Green, B. (ed.), *The Wisden Book of Cricketers' Lives: Obituaries from Wisden Cricketers' Almanack* (Queen Anne Press, London, 1986)

Grundlingh, A., A. Odendaal and B. Spies, *Beyond the Tryline* (Ravan Press, Johannesburg, 1995)

Guha, R., *A Corner of a Foreign Field: The Indian history of a British sport* (Picador, London, 2003)

Gutsche, T., *Old Gold: The history of the Wanderers Club* (Howard Timmins, Cape Town, 1966)

Guttmann, A., *Games and Empires: Modern sports and cultural imperialism* (Columbia University Press, New York, 1994)

Hargreaves, J., *Sport, Power and Culture: A social and historical analysis of popular sports in Britain* (Polity, Cambridge, 1986)

Hawke, M.B., *Recollections and Reminiscences* (Williams and Norgate, London, 1924)

Heyhoe Flint, R. and N. Rheinberg, *Fair Play: The story of women's cricket* (Angus and Robertson, London, 1976)

Holt, R., *Sport and the British: A modern history* (Oxford University Press, Oxford, 1992)

Hutchinson, R., *Empire Games: The British invention of twentieth-century sport* (Mainstream, Edinburgh, 1996)

James, C.L.R., *Beyond a Boundary* (Pantheon, New York, 1984)

Jarvie, G., *Sport, Racism and Ethnicity* (Falmer, London, 1991)

Judd, D., *Empire: The British imperial experience from 1765 to the present* (HarperCollins, London, 1996)

Knowles, R., *South Africa versus England: A test cricket history* (New Holland, London, 1995)

Legassick, M., 'British hegemony and the origins of segregation in South Africa, 1901–14' in W. Beinart and S. Dubow (eds.), *Segregation and Apartheid in Twentieth-century South Africa* (Routledge, London, 1995)

Leveson Gower, H.D.G., *The MCC's South African Tour, 1909–1910* (Metropolitan Advertising, Cape Town, 1909)

Lowerson, J., *Sport and the English Middle Classes, 1870–1914* (Manchester University Press, Manchester, 1993)

Luckin, M.W., *The History of South African Cricket, including the scores of all important matches since 1878* (W.I. Horton, Johannesburg, 1915)

Mackenzie, J.M., *Propaganda and Empire: The manipulation of British public opinion, 1880–1960* (Manchester University Press, Manchester, 1984)

Mandle, W.F., 'Cricket and Australian nationalism in the nineteenth century', *Journal of the Royal Australian Historical Society*, 59, 4, 1973

Mangan, J.A. (ed.), *The Cultural Bond: Sport, empire and society* (Frank Cass Publishers, London, 1992)

Mangan, J.A., 'Imperial origins: Christian manliness, moral imperatives and pre-Sri Lankan playing field – Beginnings', *International Journal of Sports History*, 19, 2–3, June–September 2003

Mangan, J.A. (ed.), *Pleasure, Profit and Proselytism: British culture and sport at home and abroad, 1700–1914* (Frank Cass Publishers, London, 1988)

Mangan, J.A., *The Games Ethic and Imperialism: Aspects of the diffusion of an ideal* (Viking, London, 1986)

McCord, M., *The Calling of Katie Makanya* (David Philip, Cape Town, 2000)

McCrone, K.E., 'Play up! Play up! And play the game! Sport at the late Victorian public school' in J.A. Mangan and R.J. Park (eds.), From 'Fair Sex' to Feminism: Sport and the socialization of women in the industrial and post-industrial eras (*Gender and Society*, 4, 1, March 1990)

Merrett, C., 'A political and cultural history of South African cricket' (Unpublished MS, 2000)

Midwinter, E., *Fair Game: Myth and reality in sport* (Allen and Unwin, London, 1986)

Morrell, R., *From Boys to Gentlemen: Settler masculinity in colonial Natal 1880–1920* (Unisa Press, Pretoria, 2001)

Morris, J., *Pax Britannica: The climax of an empire* (Faber, London, 1968)

Mostert, N., *Frontiers: The epic of South Africa's creation and the tragedy of the Xhosa people* (Pimlico, London, 1993)

Moult, L. and P. Hartman, *Playing the Game: The story of the Cape Town Cricket Club* (Cape Town Cricket Club in association with the Western Province Cricket Association, Cape Town, 2012)

Murray, B. and C. Merrett, *Caught Behind: Race and politics in Springbok cricket* (Wits and KwaZulu-Natal UP, Johannesburg and Pietermaritzburg, 2004)

Murray, B. and G. Vahed (eds.), *Empire and Cricket: The South African experience 1884–1914* (Unisa Press, Pretoria, 2009)

Nauright, J., *Sport, Cultures and Identities in South Africa* (David Philip, Cape Town, 1997)

Oakes, D. (ed.), *Reader's Digest Illustrated History of South Africa: The real story* (Reader's Digest, Cape Town, 1988)

Odendaal, A., 'African political mobilisation in the eastern Cape, 1880–1910' (PhD dissertation, University of Cambridge, 1983)

Odendaal, A. (comp. and ed.), *Cricket and Community in Stellenbosch* (Stellenbosch Cricket, Stellenbosch Academy of Sport and Masikhulisane Cricket Academy, 2016)

Odendaal, A., *Cricket in Isolation: The politics of race and cricket in South Africa* (Cape Town, 1977)

Odendaal, A., '"Neither cricketers nor ladies": Towards a history of women and cricket in South Africa, 1860s–2000s' in S. Cornelissen and A. Grundlingh (eds.), *Sport Past and Present in South Africa: (Trans)forming the nation* (Routledge, London, 2012)

Odendaal, A., 'South Africa's black Victorians: Sport and society in South Africa in the 19th century' in J.A. Mangan (ed.), *Pleasure, Profit and Proselytism: British culture and sport at home and abroad, 1700–1914* (Frank Cass Publishers, London, 1988)

Odendaal, A., *The Founders: The origins of the ANC and the struggle for democracy in South Africa* (Jacana, Johannesburg, 2012)

Odendaal, A., *The Story of an African Game: Black cricketers and the unmasking of one of cricket's greatest myths, South Africa, 1850–2003* (David Philip in association with the Human Sciences Research Council and the United Cricket Board of South Africa, Cape Town, 2003)

Odendaal, A., K. Reddy and A. Samson, *The Blue Book: A history of Western Province cricket, 1890–2011* (Fanele, Cape Town, 2012)

Ottomans Cricket Club souvenir brochure, 115th anniversary, 1882–1997 (Jamiah Mosque, Cape Town)

Parker, A.C., *W.P. Cricket: 100 not out* (WPCU, Cape Town, 1990)

Parker, G.A., *South African Sports: An official handbook* (Sampson, Low, Marston, London, 1897)

Ross, A., *Ranji: Prince of Cricketers* (Collins, London, 1983)

Sandiford, K., *Cricket and the Victorians* (Scolar Press, Aldershot, 1994)

Schulze, H., *South Africa's Cricketing Lawyers* (Interdoc Consultants, Halfway House, 1989)

Schulze, W.G., 'The Boer prisoners of war in Ceylon and the "Great and Grand Only Manly Game" of cricket' in B. Murray and G. Vahed (eds.), *Empire and Cricket: The South African experience 1884–1914* (Unisa Press, Pretoria, 2009)

Sparks, V.G., *The Cricketer's Compendium or Cricket from a Country Angle, being a complete history of cricket and other items on the good old game – How to play successfully etc* (Durban, n.d.)

Stoddart, B., 'Sport, cultural imperialism and the colonial response to the British Empire', *Comparative Studies in Society and History*, 30, 4

Stoddart, B. and K. Sandiford (eds.), *The Imperial Game: Cricket, culture and society* (Manchester University Press, Manchester, 1998)

Swaffer, H.F. (ed.), *South African Sport, 1914* (Transvaal Leader, Johannesburg, 1914)

Swanton, E.W., G. Plumptre and J. Woodcock (eds.), *The Barclays World of Cricket; The game from A to Z* (Collins, London, 1980)

Tennyson, L., *Sticky Wickets* (Christopher Johnson, London, 1950)

Vamplew, W. et al. (eds.), *The Oxford Companion to Australian Sport* (Oxford University Press, Melbourne, 1992)

Warner, M., 'Between the colonist and the creole: Family bonds, family boundaries' in S. Chew and A. Rutherford (eds.), *Unbecoming Daughters of the Empire* (Dangaroo, Sydney, 1993)

Warner, P.F., *Imperial Cricket* (London Counties Press Association, London, 1912)

Warner, P.F., *Long Innings: The autobiography* (Harrap, London, 1951)

Warner, P.F., *The MCC in South Africa* (Chapman and Hall, London, 1906)

West, S.E.L. and W.J. Luker (eds.), *Century at Newlands, 1864–1964: A history of the Western Province Cricket Club* (Western Province Cricket Club, Cape Town, Newlands, 1965)

Whimpress, B., *Passport to Nowhere: Aborigines in Australian cricket 1850–1939* (Walla Walla, Sydney, 1999)

Willan, B., *Sol Plaatje: A biography* (Ravan Press, Johannesburg, 1984)

Williams, G. (ed.), *One Hundred Years of Border Cricket: Border Cricket Board, 1896–1996* (Centenary Brochure)

Winch, J., *Cricket in Southern Africa: Two hundred years of achievement and records* (Windsor, Rosettenville, 1997)

Winch, J., *Cricket's Rich Heritage: A history of Rhodesian and Zimbabwean cricket, 1890–1982* (Books of Zimbabwe, Bulawayo, 1983)

Winch, J., *England's Youngest Captain: The life and times of Monty Bowden and two South African journalists* (Windsor Publishers, Windsor, 2003)

Winch, J., 'Sir William Milton: A leading figure in public school games, colonial politics and imperial expansion, 1877–1914' (PhD, University of Stellenbosch, 2013)

Worden, N., E. van Heyningen and V. Bickford-Smith, *Cape Town: The making of a city – An illustrated social history* (David Philip Publishers, Cape Town, 1998)

Wynne-Thomas, P., *The Complete History of Cricket Tours at Home and Abroad* (Hamlyn, London, 1989)

Index

This index is arranged alphabetically, letter by letter. CC indicates Cricket Club; BFN Bloemfontein, CT Cape Town, DBN Durban, EL East London, EP Eastern Province, GTN Grahamstown, JHB Johannesburg, KBY, Kimberley, KWT King William's Town, PE Port Elizabeth, PMB Pietermaritzburg and WP Western Province.